Boatowner's Mechanical and Electrical Manual

How to Maintain, Repair and Improve Your Boat's Essential Systems

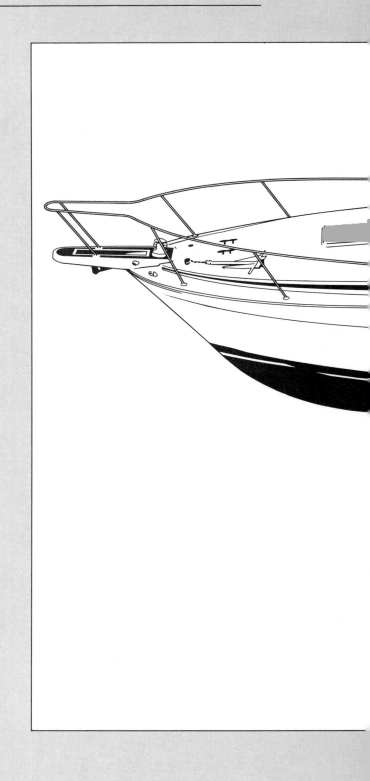

Boatowner's Mechanical and Electrical Manual

Nigel Calder

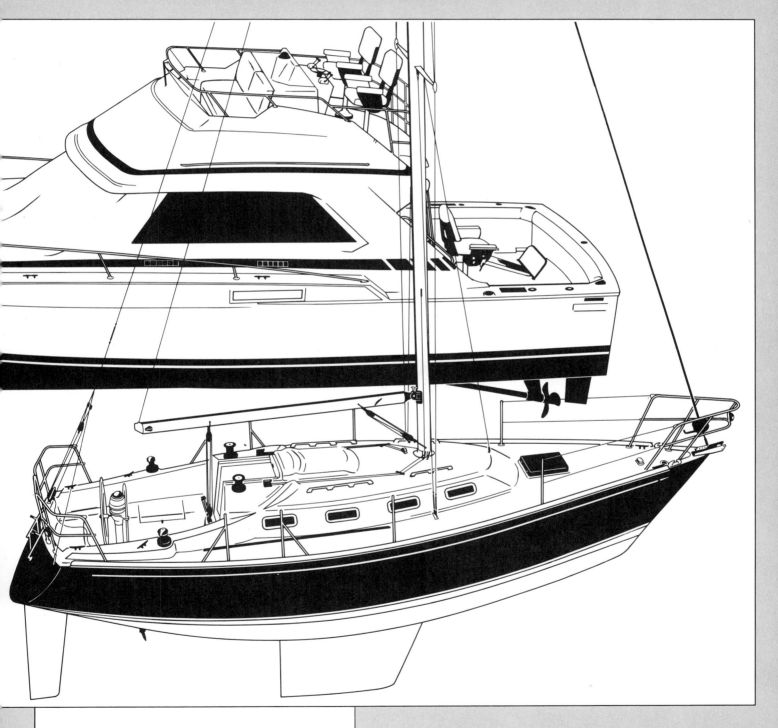

International Marine
Camden, Maine

Other Books by Nigel Calder

Marine Diesel Engines
Refrigeration for Pleasure Boats
Repairs at Sea
The Cruising Guide to the Northwest Caribbean

Published by International Marine

10 9 8 7 6 5

Library of Congress Cataloging-in-Publication Data
Calder, Nigel.
    Boatowner's mechanical and electrical manual : how to maintain,
  repair, and improve your boat's essential systems / Nigel Calder.
    p. cm.
      Includes index.
      ISBN 0-87742-982-0
      1. Boats and boating—Maintenance and repair—Handbooks, manuals,
  etc. 2. Boats and boating—Electric equipment—Maintenance and
  repair—Handbooks, manuals, etc. I. Title.
  VM322.C35 1989
  623.8'223'0288—dc20   89-35213
                                     CIP

Questions regarding the content of this book should be addressed to:

International Marine
P.O. Box 220
Camden, ME 04843

Typeset by Graphic Composition, Athens, Georgia
Printed and bound by Alpine Press, Stoughton, Massachusetts
Design by Edith Allard, Somerville, Maine
Production by Molly Mulhern
Edited by Jonathan Eaton, James Babb, Heidi Brugger

DEDICATION

To Liz Calder, Mrs. Calder, Laura Gary, and Terrie;

and for Pippin and Paul; may this book hasten the day when they take over the maintenance of the boat.

Contents

CHAPTER 15. ## Spars and Standing Rigging

CHAPTER 16. ## Running Rigging, Deck Hardware, and Roller Reefing

List of Troubleshooting Charts

Acknowledgments

I have set out to provide a comprehensive maintenance, troubleshooting, and repair manual for pleasure boat owners. This is a tremendously ambitious project. To be successful it must be rooted in detailed personal experience. Although I have been involved with the practical side of boats for many years, no one person could ever hope to accumulate sufficient hands-on knowledge for such a book. I have thus drawn deeply on the experience of numerous boaters we have met in our travels. To all of them my grateful thanks.

I have also corresponded with, and received help from, literally dozens of boat and equipment manufacturers. Some have devoted considerable amounts of time and resources to reviewing and correcting draft chapters; others have shown me their plant and equipment or helped in other ways. The following have provided information and support: ABI, AC/Delco, Adler Barbour, Allcraft Corporation, Allison Marine Transmissions, American Boat and Yacht Council (ABYC), American Insulated Wire Corp., Ampair, Ample Power Co., Aquadrive, Arco, Atlantic/Trident Solar Products, Autohelm, Automate, Balmar, Barient, Barlow, Battery Council International, Beckson Marine, Bertram Yacht, Blake and Sons, Borg Warner Corporation, Brookes and Gatehouse, C. H. Corporation, Camper and Nicholson, Carol Cable Co., Caterpillar, Cetrek/Navstar, Climate Control Inc., CPT Inc., Cruising Equipment Co., Danforth, Danfoss, Dart Union Co., Delco Remy, Detroit Diesel, Dole Refrigeration Co., Don Allen Co., Edson International, Force 10, Forespar, Four Seasons, Frigoboat, Furino, Furlex, Garrett Automotive Products Co., Givens Buoy, Gougeon Brothers, Groco, Grunert Refrigeration, Guest, Halyard Marine Ltd., Hamilton Ferris, Harken, Hart Systems Inc., Heart Interface, Henderson Pumps, Holset Engineering Co., Hood Yacht Systems, Hurth, Hydrovane Yacht Equipment Ltd., Interstate Batteries, ITT/Jabsco, Kemp Masts, Kenyon Marine, Kohler Corporation, L. Q. Moffit, Lasdrop Shaft Seal, Leeward Rigging, Lewmar Marine, Lirakis Safety Harness Inc., Loos and Co., Lucas Marine, Lucas/CAV Parts and Service, Lunaire Marine, Mansfield Sanitary, Marine Power Ltd., Marine Vane Gear Ltd., Marinetics Corporation, Marlec, Mars Electronics, Martec, MaxProp, MDC, Mercantile Manufacturing, Merriman Yacht Specialties, Metalmast Marine, Micrologic, Morse Controls, Munster Simms Engineering Ltd., Navico, Navstar, Navtec, NewMar, Nicro Fico, NMEA, Norseman/Gibb, Onan, Parker Hannifin Corporation, Parker Industrial, PDC Labs International, Perkins Engines Ltd., Plastimo, ProFurl, PYI, Raritan, Raytheon Marine Co., Rolls and Rae, RVG, S and F Tool Co., Sailomat, Sailtec, Sanden International, Schaefer, Sea Frost, Sea Inc., Sealand Technology, Shaft Lok Inc., Shakespeare, Shipmate Stove Division, Signet Marine, Simpson Lawrence, Solar Power Corporation, Southwire Company, SpaCreek Inc., Sta-Lok, Stowe, Stream Stay, Surrette Storage Battery Co., Tartan Marine Co., Taylor's Para-Fin, Tecumseh, Tracor Instruments, Universal Enterprises, VDO Marine, Vernay Products, Wagner Marine, Walker and Sons, Wallas Marin, Westerbeke Generators, Whale, Whitlock Marine, Wilcox-Crittenden, Wolter Systems, and York.

With two babies, living aboard and writing has become increasingly difficult. This book, in particular, became an impossible project. The mountains of manuals alone weighed hundreds of pounds and swallowed every inch of spare space on the boat and then some. My brother Chris Calder and his wife provided us with a home *and an office* (what a luxury!) for three months in England; my sister-in-law Laura Gary, her husband, Ron, and his parents, Art and Ruth, did the same for us in Montana.

My wife Terrie set aside her own artwork and put in many long hours babysitting while I worked on this book 12 hours a day, seven days a week. Amy Peters did an outstanding job interpreting my scribblings when she typed the second draft. James Babb, Heidi Brugger, and Jon Eaton, my editors at International Marine, were as helpful as ever. Jim Sollers, illustrator extraordinaire, did an astounding job interpreting my rough sketches. Molly Mulhern, the International Marine production director, showed great patience with the rest of us and somehow kept the manuscript and illustrations organized and on schedule. Technical advisers, such as Richard Thiel of *Power and Motoryacht* and Keith Lawrence of *Better Boat* and *Boatbuilder,* provided invaluable guidance. Without all this unseen, and unsung, backup, I would never have finished on time, perhaps not at all.

So you see, although it is my name on

the dust jacket this book is really a collective effort, and I would like to keep it that way. A book such as this has the potential to grow into future editions. Should any readers find parts of it wrong, misleading, inapplicable to their situation, or just hard to understand, please let me know. And if you have any special tricks to solving specific problems, I would love to hear from you (this holds true for my previous books, *Marine Diesel Engines,* and *Repairs at Sea*).

Write to me care of International Marine Publishing Co., PO Box 220, Camden, Maine 04843. I cannot promise to answer all letters received, but I *will* try.

In a work as wide in scope and as specific in detail as this, there must inevitably be some errors. These are mine!

Nigel Calder
Montana, August 1989

Introduction

In the past two or three decades boat equipment has taken a quantum leap in complexity. The next few years will see not a slowing down, but an acceleration of this process. Soon the first fully automated boats will be available, with a central microprocessor controlling sophisticated hydraulic and electronic systems that run the boat. The technology and equipment is already available to pre-program a boat's course and set it on its way across an ocean (including, for sailboats, all necessary tacking, reefing, and sail-handling). Theoretically, the owner could then fly across and meet his waiting yacht on the other side!

It is no longer possible to keep things operating with a monkey wrench, hammer, and grease gun. More and more equipment needs specialized servicing, and the cost of professional help is going through the roof. In such areas as the Virgin Islands, labor rates are already up to $50 an hour. In other cruising areas help is not available at *any price*. More and more boaters are going farther and farther afield, and must increasingly fall back on their own resources. Every year there are two or three organized crossings of the North Atlantic from Europe to the West Indies and back, each one involving *hundreds* of boats.

This raises another point. Many production boatbuilders set standards applicable for weekend and coastal cruising, but their boats are being taken around the world! Equipment is being used for longer periods and pushed harder than ever before.

While the public may think that boatowners are rich, in reality most are middle-income salary earners who strain their budgets to support their boating habit. The boatowner of today with limited funds needs:

- a good working knowledge of all systems aboard
- the ability to keep up with all maintenance
- the means to troubleshoot and repair a broad range of breakdowns

This book is intended to make attaining these three objectives a realistic possibility for the basic equipment found on most modern, mid-sized boats—power or sail.

Using the premise that "a little knowledge is a dangerous thing," the biggest problem I have had is in deciding where to draw the line between what a talented amateur in a jam can reasonably be encouraged to undertake, and leading people into trouble. Since I have a high regard for most people's capabilities, I have gone well beyond the information currently available in a number of quite technical areas, such as generators and refrigeration systems.

I have taken great pains to ensure the accuracy of this book. All information is given in good faith. Nevertheless, I must caution the reader: *If you doubt what you are doing, leave things alone.* I cannot accept liability for any damage or injuries arising from the reader's attempts to follow the procedures in this book. If you wreck a piece of equipment, sink the boat, or hurt yourself, the responsibility has to be yours.

Now that I've got that off my chest, a word on how to use this book. There are four distinct levels at which it can be useful:

- Many maintenance problems and equipment failures are the result of inadequate or improper installations. A quick skimming of the book, skipping over the detailed sections on equipment repair, may well highlight a number of potential difficulties on your boat and enable you to take corrective action *before* something goes wrong. This is especially relevant for anyone buying a new boat. Proper liaison with the boatbuilder can eliminate *most* "built-in" problems at a fraction of the cost of a later cure (and frequently more effectively. See the section on noise suppression in Chapter 7, for example).
- When buying new equipment, a review of the pertinent section(s) will give you an idea of what can go wrong. Although I don't recommend one brand name over another, I can arm you with appropriate questions to ask about *any* brand. This may save a lot of grief later.
- Routine maintenance is covered in some detail in each chapter. Of prime importance is the annual haulout (winterizing) summary in Appendix A.
- When equipment does malfunction or break down, the table of contents and index will point you to the relevant sections on troubleshooting and repair.

After reading this book, boatowners may think that maintenance and repair is a full-time job in itself. Sometimes it does seem like that. In one week recently our kerosene stove went completely kaput, we broke the main shaft on the anchor windlass, and we wrecked the outboard motor's lower unit on a reef! You may be inclined to throw up your hands in horror and just let things slide until something breaks. That is the one sure way to remove all the fun from your boating, and guarantee that maintenance *does* become a full-time job.

In reality, most routine maintenance procedures take little time. The key is to be methodical and organized. And keep in mind that boat equipment *likes to be used frequently*. In the marine environment, more things seize up from lack of use than from *being* used. Your boat will be least troublesome if you get the maintenance done, then go out on the water as often as possible.

Happy Boating!

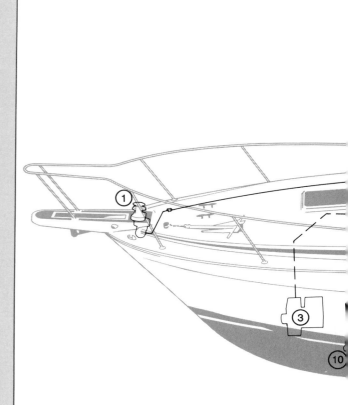

CHAPTER 1

Figure 1-1. These two representative boats illustrate just how complicated the electrical system of an average modern pleasure boat has become.

(1) anchor windlass
(2) macerator pump
(3) air conditioner
(4) engine instruments, radios, navigation instruments
(5) engine starter switch
(6) distribution panel
(7) battery isolation switch
(8) 120-VAC shoreside receptacle
(9) bilge pump
(10) sump pump
(11) batteries
(12) air conditioning compressor
(13) blower
(14) starter motor
(15) refrigerator
(16) water heater
(17) head pump
(18) cabin lights
(19) navigation lights
(20) pressure water pump

———————— 12 VDC

------------ 12 V ground (return)

— — — — 120 VAC

············ bonding strap jumper

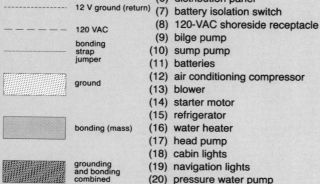

ground

bonding (mass)

grounding and bonding combined

Understanding Your Battery-Powered Electrical System

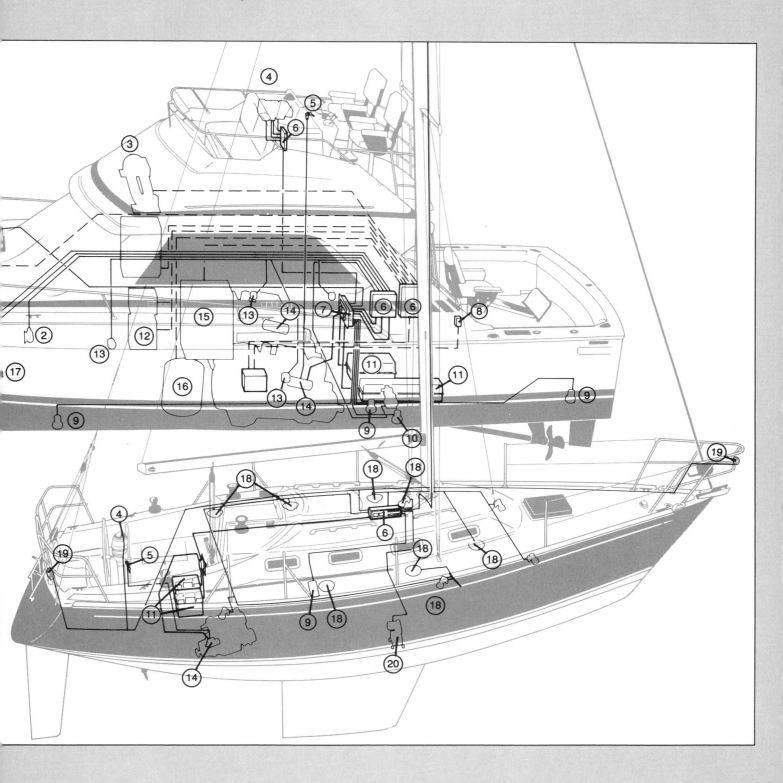

System Overview

Today's pleasureboats have become increasingly dependent on electricity. Most engines can't be started without it; many boat owners can't navigate without it; a growing number of toilets can't even be *flushed* without it! While the explosive growth of electrical and electronic equipment over the past decade or two has brought about a revolution in comfort and ease of boat handling, electrical equipment malfunctions have become the most common maintenance problem aboard boats, especially those with aging, hodge-podge, or jury-rigged electrical circuits.

The marine environment is a terrible place for electricity. To be trouble free, electrical circuits must be installed with great care and to the highest standards—topics which are dealt with in Chapter 3. But no matter how carefully an electrical installation is carried out, the entire system must be properly balanced in the first place or it will soon become a source of endless problems and a constant drain on the pocketbook.

Because of improperly set-up systems, many boat owners repeatedly find themselves with dead batteries, outright battery failures, and lengthy charging times. Fixing immediate problems does nothing to resolve the overall imbalance in the system, guaranteeing that the next difficulty is just around the corner. A large number of boats come straight off the production line with these potential problems built in. Thus the first requirement for electrical problem solving and repair is to understand the peculiar needs of a boat's 12-volt electrical system, and to make sure that the overall system is in balance. This chapter takes a look at these general considerations; Chapter 2 deals with detailed maintenance, troubleshooting, and repair procedures for specific pieces of 12-volt electrical equipment. Although we focus on 12-volt systems, all information is equally applicable to 24 or 32 volts.

A Balanced System

Consider first an automobile. A 12-volt battery provides the energy to crank a starter motor, normally for just a second or two, after which the engine fires up and the alternator cuts in. The alternator subsequently supplies all the car's electrical needs, plus an extra margin to replace the juice the starter motor drew from the battery. *The car's electrical system runs on the energy supplied by the alternator, not that supplied by the battery.* Although starter motors use a tremendous amount of energy, they do so for a very brief time, and thus pull next to nothing from a battery. For example, a 400-amp starter motor would consume 400 amperes of current in one hour, but cranking it for 15 seconds drains the battery by only $400 \div (4 \times 60) = 1.66$ amps. This is replenished by the alternator in just a few minutes. In normal usage a car battery is almost always fully charged, and the batteries do very little work. This holds true for all cars, regardless of size, electrical complexity, or use. The only variable from one car to another is the capacity of the alternator—cars with high electrical loads need bigger alternators.

Contrast this with a sailboat. The "average" boat spends most of its time in a slip. Periodically the owner cranks the engine, motors out of the slip, shuts the engine down, and goes sailing. Apart from the time spent motoring, the boat's electrical system runs directly off the battery. The battery will be discharged more deeply than an automobile battery; the engine will be run far less than an automobile engine, and the charging time will be minimal. Now consider the "average" powerboat. The engine will be run for longer periods of time than a sailboat's, with usage patterns similar to those of an automobile. But most powerboats, especially cruising boats, still will have extended periods when the engine is shut down and the boat's electrical system is running off the batteries. Even many boat owners with on-board AC generators and substantial power requirements are discovering that with a good quality DC/AC inverter (see Chapter 5), they can shut down their generators for most of the day, enjoying peace and quiet while on the hook and saving money at the same time! In this case, battery use closely resembles that of cruising sailboats. From this a couple of things are evident: Compared with cars, the majority of boats need both bigger batteries to withstand the extra electrical drain, and bigger alternators to replenish the juice more quickly during the reduced engine running times.

But of course there really are no "average" sail or power boats. Some have shoreside power and battery chargers in their slip; others go cruising, often anchoring out for months with little or no engine run time; some have auxiliary generators running 24 hours a day, keeping the boat's batteries constantly topped up; others have solar panels and wind and water generators. No two boats—even identical production boats—experience the same usage or have the same electrical needs. It is not possible to deal in generalities, as one can do with cars: Every boat must be treated as a separate entity and its electrical system evaluated in relation to its particular usage. This is the first priority in coming to terms with electrical problems.

There are four steps to take in evaluating a boat's DC electrical system:

• determine the power requirements of the boat

• provide the necessary electrical storage capacity
• provide adequate charging capabilities
• establish correct voltage regulation levels to maintain system harmony

All four interact, but for clarity they are treated separately here. The following sections focus broadly on the needs of a mid-sized cruising boat—sail or power—which has a moderate electrical load and relies on its batteries to supply power for extended periods of time. The needs of a boat with different parameters can readily be extrapolated.

How to Determine Your Power Requirements

Overall power needs are normally calculated on a 24-hour (daily) basis. For some boats, this may not be a suitable unit of time, but it is easily adjusted: for example, divide by 24 to find hourly use; multiply by three to find needs for three days.

All electrical appliance loads are rated in either *watts* or *amps*—a 100-watt light bulb, a 3-amp electric motor. The magnitude of the current flowing through an appliance is measured in amps (short for amperes); the work done by that current is measured in watts. The rating will be in the manufacturer's installation bulletin or on a label attached to the equipment. When adding up loads on an electrical system, it does not matter if you use watts or amps, just as long as you stick to one or the other (although it is generally easier to use amps). In any case, watts and amps are easily interchangeable, since watts = volts × amps, and amps = watts ÷ volts.

Most boats have 12-volt systems, but some do not. All the following examples can readily be converted to 24 or 32 volts by substituting the appropriate voltage.

Let's say we have a 25-watt light bulb on a 12-volt system, and we want to know our load in amps. How many amps is this?

Amps = 25 watts ÷ 12 volts = 2.08 amps.

Perhaps our DC refrigeration unit has a 7-amp, 12-volt motor. How many watts does it draw?

Watts = 12 volts × 7 amps = 84 watts

The first step, then, in calculating our daily load is to list all the onboard electrical equipment and convert the power needs into either watts or amps (see Table 1-1). The next step is to estimate the normal daily usage, in hours, for each piece of equipment. The load for each piece is then multiplied by the number of hours of use and the whole lot added up to give a total daily load, expressed in *watt-hours* or *amp-hours*. (For a more detailed discussion of amp hours, see page 12.)

Table 1-1. Typical Power Consumption of Electrical Loads (12 volts).

Anchor light	1.0 amp
Anchor windlass	80–300 amp
Autopilot	1–30 amp
Bilge blower	2.5 amp
Bilge pump	5.0 amp
Cabin fan	1.0 amp
Cabin light (incandescent)	1.5–3.5 amp
Depth sounder	0.1–0.5 amp
Fluorescent light	0.7–1.8 amp
Freshwater pump	5.0 amp
Spotlight	10.0 amp
Knotmeter	0.1 amp
Loran	1.0–1.5 amp
Masthead light	1.0–1.7 amp
Radar	4.0–8.0 amp
Refrigeration (typical)	5.0–7.0 amp
Running lights (port, starboard, and stern)	3.0 amp
SatNav	0.2–0.8 amp
Spreader lights	8.0 amp
SSB (receive)	1.5–2.0 amp
(transmit)	25–35 amp
Strobe light	0.7 amp
Stereo/tape deck	1.0 amp
VHF (receive)	0.7–1.5 amp
(transmit)	5.0–6.0 amp
Wind speed indicator	0.1 amp

We have answered the first question: How much power does our boat demand each day? The sample system in Table 1-2 has a daily load of 100 amp-hours (abbreviated to 100 Ah). The next question we must resolve is how much battery storage capacity we need to meet this demand.

Batteries: How They Work

The required capacity of a battery is intimately related to the intervals between charges. A boat such as our sample in Table 1-2, which uses an engine-driven alternator as its principal means of battery charging and restricts engine usage to once a day, must be capable of storing and delivering the desired 100 Ah between charges. This is a typical usage pattern for a cruising boat—sail or power—that spends much of its time at anchor. A boat with onboard power sources equal to demand, however, such as a boat that uses the main engine continuously, or runs a battery charger off a constantly operating auxiliary generator, or has large banks of solar panels or a wind- or water-driven generator, is in a position similar to an automobile: The battery is primarily for engine starting. The main engine, auxiliary generator, solar panels, or wind generator supply the boat's electrical needs and keep the battery topped up.

As solar panels and wind generators become more popular and widespread, most boats fall somewhere between these two extremes. But it must always be remembered that auxiliary generators break down, the sun may not shine for days, and the wind may fade away. At other times these charging sources may not meet all the electrical demands, and the battery will become a power source. When determining battery capacities, in order to ensure an adequate margin for all eventualities it is best to omit such charging methods from the calculations.

So how much battery capacity do we need to deliver our 100 Ah a day? This question opens a can of worms, but it is one which boat owners must address, and which many have ignored at considerable cost.

First, we need to know a little bit about how batteries are built and how they work. A battery cell contains alternating negative and positive plates, between which are plate separators. All the negative plates are connected, as are all the positive plates. Each plate has a grid configuration, and within the grid is bonded the plate's active material.

When fully charged, the active material in the negative plates is pure "sponge" lead; in the positive plates, it is lead dioxide. The plates are immersed in a solution of sulfuric acid (the *electrolyte*). As a battery discharges, the acid from the electrolyte combines with the active material in the battery plates, forming lead sulfate and weakening the acid solution. When a battery is recharged, acid is returned to the solution, increasing the strength of the electrolyte; the used portion of the plate material that formed the lead sulfate is reconverted to active material.

If a heavy load is placed on a battery, the acid in immediate contact with the surface of the plates is the first to react, releasing electrons. If the battery is to continue producing electricity, the acid must diffuse through the active material to the more inaccessible parts of the plates, a process

Table 1-2. Daily Power Requirements (12 Volts) of a Hypothetical Cruising Boat Anchored Off a Bahamian Beach.

Equipment	Rating	Hours of Use (in 24 hours)	Total Load (in 24 hours)
6 lights	1.5 amps each	2 hours each = 12	18 amp-hours
1 refrigeration compressor	5 amps	10 hours	50 amp-hours
Masthead navigation lights	1.5 amps	8 hours	12 amp-hours
2 fans	1 amp each	5 hours each = 10	10 amp-hours
VHF radio, tape deck, etc.	2 amps total	5 hours total	10 amp-hours
		TOTAL	100 amp-hours

Notes:
1. Power consumption will vary enormously according to the boat's intended cruising area; refrigeration and fan usage in northern climates will be a fraction of that in the tropics.
2. Large items of occasional and short-term use, such as an electric anchor windlass, can in most instances be ignored, since they have little impact on the overall picture. On the rare occasions where sustained use is required, as when breaking out a deeply embedded anchor, the engine can be run during operation to provide a charging backup.

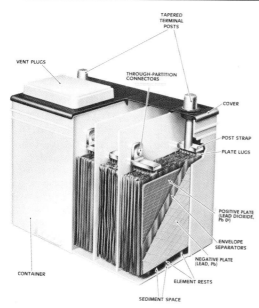

Figure 1-2. **Typical automobile-type battery construction.** There are six cells; within each is a series of alternating negative and positive plates, each one isolated from its neighbors by intervening insulators called separators. The plates are immersed in a sulfuric acid solution. On discharge, the lead atoms of the negative plates give up electrons and form lead ions, which combine with the sulfuric acid to form lead sulfate. The lead dioxide in the positive plates consumes electrons, yielding lead ions which again react with the acid to form lead sulfate. The negative plates are connected with each other and with the anode or negative terminal; the positive plates are collectively connected with the cathode or positive terminal.

which takes time. This is why, if a car is cranked until the battery dies and then left for a short period of time, the battery will frequently recover and crank again; the acid has diffused to unused portions of the plates, providing a fresh burst of energy.

The chemical process in the positive plates—converting lead dioxide to lead sulfate and back again—tends to weaken the bond between the active material and the plate grid. The more deeply discharged a battery, the greater the stresses generated. Every time a battery is discharged deeply some of this active material is loosened and "shed," falling to the bottom of the battery case and reducing the overall capacity of the battery. If enough material is shed it can fill the base of the battery until it reaches the level of the plates and shorts them out. The battery will then be stone dead.

The lead sulfate formed during discharges is initially soft and relatively easy to reconvert into active material through battery charging. If a battery is left in a discharged state, however, the sulfate hardens into crystals that prove increasingly difficult to reconvert, effectively reducing battery capacity and slowly killing the battery. This is an acute problem with batteries that are deeply discharged regularly or never recharged fully, a common occurrence on boats and the number one cause of battery failures.

At the other end of the scale, periods of overcharging or prolonged trickle charging (such as when connected to a battery charger in the slip), lead to *gassing*, a process in which excess charging current breaks down water in the electrolyte into its component parts, hydrogen and oxygen, which then boil off; this is why batteries need "topping up" with water from time to time. Of more concern is the fact that galvanic activity within the battery itself attacks the positive plate grids, causing them to deteriorate. This constitutes the second major cause of battery failures.

Automotive (cranking) vs. deep-cycle batteries. Automotive batteries are designed for engine starting, which requires the rapid release of a tremendous burst of energy. These batteries have many thin plates, maximizing the plate surface area and minimizing the diffusion time of the acid. The active material has a low density to accelerate acid diffusion.

Thin plates and low-density active material cannot handle repeated deep discharges. This is of little concern in automotive (cranking) use since the batteries are rarely discharged more than a few percent. But in marine use, where repeated deep discharges are common, automotive batteries can quickly disintegrate internally, a process accelerated by any pounding at sea. At the other end of the spectrum, the flimsy plate grids in automotive batteries cannot tolerate much overcharging during charging cycles without disintegrating.

Deep-cycle batteries have much thicker plates, stronger grids, denser active material, heavier plate separators, and generally tougher construction. There is still some shedding of material from the plates at every discharge cycle, but nowhere near the same amount as that from thin-plate batteries. *Deep-cycle batteries will tolerate repeated discharges in a way no automotive (cranking) battery can.* The heavier grids also will withstand considerable abuse during battery charging.

Not all deep-cycle batteries are created equal. There are *deep-cycle* batteries, and there are "deep-cycle" batteries. Many of those advertised for marine and RV (recreational vehicle) use are *not* particularly suitable for marine use, especially a number of "no-maintenance" (sealed, gel-type) batteries. Let us first look at conventional "wet" (liquid electrolyte) batteries.

Figure 1-3A. Deep-cycle battery anatomy. Compare this battery's sturdy construction with the automotive-type battery in Figure 1-2.

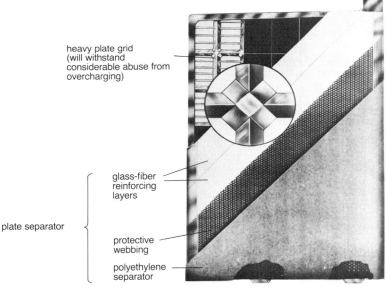

heavy plate grid (will withstand considerable abuse from overcharging)

plate separator

glass-fiber reinforcing layers

protective webbing

polyethylene separator

Figure 1-3B. A cutaway view of a positive plate from a top-of-the-line deep-cycle battery; the lead dioxide has been removed to show the heavy grid. Note the complexity of these multilayer plate separators compared with the thin separators in Figure 1-4.

Conventional wet batteries. Since the differences between automotive and deep-cycle batteries are matters of degree (the latter having thicker plates, stronger grids, heavier separators, tougher case, etc.) rather than fundamental design changes, there is no clear dividing line between them. Some high-quality automotive batteries are just as well built as some cheap deep-cycle batteries. It is not possible simply to rely on a manufacturer's description of a battery as "deep-cycle." The key in judging one battery against another is *life cycles:* the number of times that a battery can be pulled down to a certain state of discharge, and then recharged, before it fails.

It is important to make sure that we're comparing the same things. Some manufacturers may estimate life cycles by using a 50-percent discharge and recharge cycle. Others might use 80- or even 100-percent discharge. In general, the greater the degree of discharge, the fewer the number of life cycles (i.e., the shorter the life expectancy of the battery). If one battery has the same number of life cycles at 80-percent discharge as another has at 50-percent discharge, then the former is superior; it will have far more life cycles at 50-percent discharge than the latter. For our purposes, the number of life cycles at the 50-percent discharge level is the key criterion in assessing battery suitability. When buying any deep-cycle battery, ask the battery supplier for this information. If it is not available, the battery is almost certainly not suitable for marine deep-cycle applications.

No-maintenance batteries. Some no-maintenance batteries are no more than conventional "wet" batteries with excess electrolyte contained in partially sealed cases. During service the excess electrolyte is slowly used up. Because there is no way to top up the batteries, once the plates begin to uncover they are doomed. These batteries have no place in the harsh marine environment.

Gel-type batteries are a different story. The electrolyte is in gel form, which means the plates must be kept thin to achieve adequate diffusion of the gel around them. Since the batteries are sealed, the gel cannot be topped up; thus, the batteries must not be permitted to *gas* during charging. The plate grids of conventional batteries are strengthened by adding antimony to the lead, but this adds to gassing problems and contributes to a high rate of internal self-discharge when the battery is standing idle. In gel-type batteries the antimony is replaced with calcium, which reduces gassing and therefore electrolyte loss. Some gel-type batteries have oversized negative plates, which in normal use are never fully charged and therefore do not gas.

Understanding Your Battery-Powered Electrical System

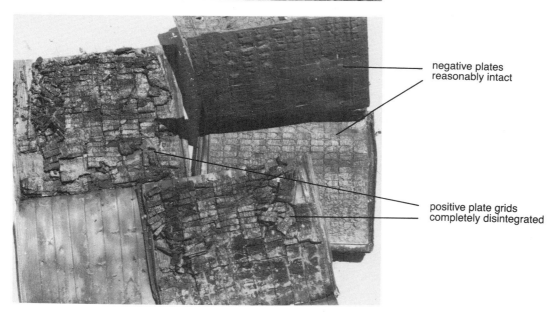

thin plastic bags
used as plate separators

negative plates
reasonably intact

positive plate grids
completely disintegrated

Figure 1-4A. **Battery autopsy. This automotive battery came from a tractor with a defective alternator and was deeply discharged and then overcharged repeatedly.**

A number of gel-type batteries are now widely advertised as being suitable for "deep-cycle" use. Promoters claim that they have a faster rate of charge than conventional deep-cycle batteries. But this is because they have a large number of thin plates, typical of *automotive* (cranking) batteries.

The use of gel-type batteries in deep-cycle applications flies in the face of experience. The thin plates necessary for proper acid diffusion are prone to fall apart, a tendency exacerbated by the fact that lead/calcium grids are not as strong as lead/antimony grids. Extended overcharging of gel-type batteries still will cause gassing (although not as much as with wet batteries), leading to a loss of electrolyte. Since the batteries cannot be topped up, they will dry out and fail. Moreover, the fragile, thin-plate grids are more vulnerable to extended periods of *mild* overcharging (such as occurs with dockside battery chargers that are left on permanently, regulated to the normal 13.8 volts) than the grids in conventional batteries.

Gel-type batteries are especially prone to failure when left partially charged for long periods, a common condition on many boats. Under similar conditions, conventional wet batteries can generally be restored to partial service (see page 27), but

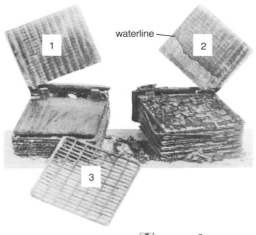

Figure 1-4B. Effects of overcharging on battery plates. The group of plates marked **1** is from a deep-cycle battery; those marked **2** are from an automotive battery. The topmost negative plates are folded up to expose the positive plates below. The deep-cycle plate (**3**) has had all its plate material removed to show that the grid is still intact. The positive plate grid of the automotive battery has disintegrated. This battery was shorted out and using a lot of water; hence the low waterline mark on plate **2**. Plate **4** shows a conventional battery plate grid, and plate **5** shows a sturdy deep-cycle grid.

Figure 1-4C. The effects of cycling on battery plates. This series of positive plates, each containing a different density of lead dioxide, has been subjected to 136 discharge-charge cycles. Number 1 is typical of lightweight automotive batteries; number 6 is found in top-of-the-line deep-cycle batteries. Note the almost total loss of plate material in the former; the latter is virtually intact. The densities of lead dioxide (grams per cubic inch) in each one are as follows: #1—50; #2—55; #3—60; #4—65; #5—70; #6—75.

gel-type batteries often fail completely. Finally, it should be noted that few gel-type batteries ever achieve their claimed amp-hour ratings.

Since gel-type deep-cycle batteries are typically half again as expensive as equivalent-capacity wet batteries and have far fewer life cycles, there seems to be little justification for using them. Should they be used, it is important to exercise precise voltage regulation during charging, particularly in relation to overcharging and *float charging* (trickle charging over extended periods to keep a battery fully charged—see page 49). They tolerate far less of the abuse typically found in marine service than do conventional batteries.

Understanding Your Battery-Powered Electrical System

Battery Facts: Capacity, Discharge Rate, and Life Cycles

Figure 1-5A shows the relation between the rate of battery discharge and the capacity it will provide. Note the following:

- Batteries in the USA are rated by their ability to sustain a given rate of discharge for 20 hours. In other words, a battery discharging 5 amps for 20 hours is rated as a 100-Ah battery.

- An increase in the discharge rate to 8.4 amps reduces the battery capacity of a nominal 100-Ah battery to 84 Ah (84 percent). It is dead in 10 hours. Seen another way, 84 Ah is the maximum 10-hour output for a battery rated at 100 Ah in the USA.

- Since 10 hours is the standard UK rating period, a battery rated 100 Ah in the UK will deliver its rated capacity in 10 hours, and will deliver more than that at a slower discharge rate. A battery rated 100 Ah in the UK thus has more capacity than a U.S.-manufactured battery of similar rating.

- An increase in the discharge rate to 14 amps reduces the capacity of a U.S.-rated 100 Ah-battery to 70 Ah (70 percent). An increase in the discharge rate to 27 amps reduces capacity to 54 Ah. An increase to 44 amps reduces capacity to 44 Ah. Imagine what a 400-amp starter motor does to battery capacity!

Figure 1-5B shows how temperature and initial state of charge affect rated battery capacity. Initial state of charge can be ascertained by measuring the specific gravity of the electrolyte as described in Chapter 2. Note that even a fully charged battery at 0°F can deliver only 40 percent of its capacity at 80°F.

From Figure 1-5C it is clear that routine deep discharging of a battery will drastically shorten its useful life. Assuming one 50-percent discharge per day, the battery tested in Figure 1-5C will yield 2,600 life cycles or 7.1 years of daily service.

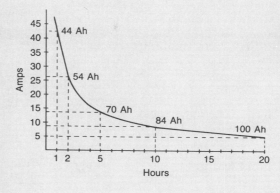

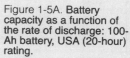

Figure 1-5A. Battery capacity as a function of the rate of discharge: 100-Ah battery, USA (20-hour) rating.

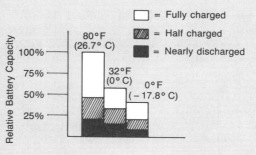

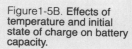

Figure1-5B. Effects of temperature and initial state of charge on battery capacity.

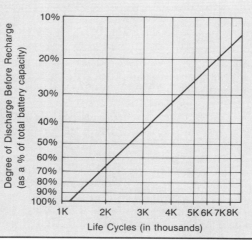

Figure 1-5C. Life cycles under laboratory conditions of a top-of-the-line deep-cycle battery.

Nickel-cadmium batteries. Nickel-cadmium batteries are virtually indestructible, with a life span of up to 25 years. They can be discharged completely, left shorted out indefinitely, and still be recharged without damage! When left idle, they have an extremely low rate of self-discharge. Amp for amp they are much bulkier and far more costly than conventional batteries, and for these reasons are rarely used in boats. Should you plan to keep your boat for the life span of the batteries, they will pay for themselves handsomely. Over a number of years the electrolyte will deteriorate and need replacing; consult the manufacturer.

Conclusions. Almost all boats—power or sail—periodically "deep-cycle" their batteries; many cruising boats do this on a daily basis. Conventional cranking batteries will not last long under these conditions; some kind of purpose-built, deep-cycle battery is needed.

For marine use the best batteries money can buy are nickel-cadmium batteries. If your budget will not stretch this far, conventional wet (liquid electrolyte) batteries are preferable to sealed, gel types. Although it is not the purpose of this book to make judgments between competing manufacturers, in this instance I propose to make an exception. The preeminent deep-cycle battery manufacturer in the USA is Surrette, of Tilton, NH. Given the importance of batteries aboard boats, it seems sensible to go only for the best. Properly cared for, top-quality deep-cycle batteries have a life expectancy of 5 years on up—some have been in service for 20 years!

How Much Battery Capacity Do You Need?

How deeply should a battery be discharged? This is extremely important. Assuming a 100-Ah daily consumption, a 100-Ah battery will meet our immediate needs (but will leave no reserve for engine starting) if we plan to discharge our batteries 100 percent at each cycle. *However, no battery should ever be fully discharged.* This applies to deep-cycle batteries just as much as automotive batteries. Repeated 100-percent discharge of any battery will shorten its life drastically (see the accompanying sidebar).

But if we do not fully discharge a battery, we cannot utilize its full capacity. If we need 100 Ah, and we only intend to discharge a battery to the 50-percent level, we will need a 200-Ah battery. Bigger batteries last longer, but they cost more, weigh more, and take up more space. Somewhere we must make a trade-off between battery size and the degree of discharge in daily use (i.e., battery life). With deep-cycle batteries this is normally done at around 50-percent discharge. We try to set up our total electrical system so that the battery is not discharged beyond 50 percent of its capacity in normal use. Occasional discharge to 80 percent or so then can be taken in stride.

We are close to determining the necessary battery capacity, but there are two more factors to consider:

- A discharged battery can be recharged rapidly to around 70 to 80 percent of the fully charged level. Thereafter, the rate of charge must be tapered off sharply or battery damage will result. (This is covered in more detail later in this chapter.) Since charging time is at a premium on most boats, it makes sense to bring batteries back merely to the 80-percent level

(with certain caveats: see Chapter 2, "Sulfation and Equalization: Is There Life after Death?") As we are only discharging to the 50-percent level, our regular, usable storage capacity is reduced to just 30 percent of overall battery capacity.
- No battery operates at 100 percent over its full life. To take this into account, we need to make an allowance—a fudge factor—of, say, 20 percent.

Where does this leave us? For our hypothetical boat's 100-Ah daily consumption, taking a conservative approach utilizing only 30 percent of battery capacity, we need 333 Ah. Add in the 20-percent fudge factor, and we need 400 Ah of battery capacity. This is close to the capacity of two size "8D" deep-cycle batteries, which in point of fact is an excellent combination for most of today's electrically loaded mid-size boats. (The designation "8D" refers *only* to the external dimensions of the battery; it says nothing about its all-important internal construction.) If we are a little less conservative and are using top-of-the-line deep-cycle batteries, which can be discharged consistently to 30 percent of capacity before recharging, we would only need a battery capacity of 250 Ah to meet a 100-Ah daily demand. However, this is an *absolute minimum*, leaves almost nothing in reserve, and will virtually halve anticipated battery life compared with a battery discharged only to 50 percent of capacity (see Figure 1-5C).

Series and parallel. When more than one battery is included in an electrical system, they can be treated as separate entities and hooked into the boat's circuit independently via a suitable battery isolation switch, or they can be hooked together to boost output.

When in series, the total amp-hour (Ah) capacity of the two batteries together remains the same as the Ah rating of either one, but the output voltage is doubled. In our example, with two 200-Ah 12-volt batteries, series connection still would give us only 200-Ah capacity, *but at 24 volts. Never connect 12-volt batteries in series on a 12-volt electrical system: The high voltage will seriously damage equipment.*

Paralleling batteries leaves the system voltage unchanged, but doubles its Ah capacity. Two 200-Ah 12-volt batteries in parallel still will produce only 12 volts, but will have a 400-Ah capacity. *Connecting addi-*

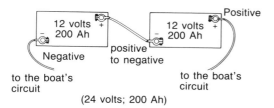

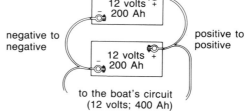

Figure 1-6A. Series connection. Capacity is unchanged from the single-battery capacity, but output voltage is doubled. Never connect 12-volt batteries in series on a 12-volt electrical system. The high voltage will seriously damage equipment.

Figure 1-6B. Parallel connection. Output voltage is unchanged from that of a single battery, but capacity is doubled.

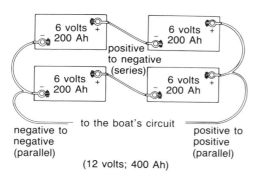

Figure 1-6C. Series/parallel connection. In this example each pair of 6-volt batteries connected in series delivers 12 volts, and connecting the pairs in parallel doubles system capacity. Thus this array achieves the same effect as two 12-volt batteries in parallel, but permits the use of high-capacity 6-volt batteries, which are individually less bulky than high-capacity 12-volt batteries.

Figure 1-6D. Four 8-volt batteries connected in series, for a system output power of 32 volts.

tional batteries in parallel increases system capacity. Use the total Ah capacity of all the paralleled batteries to calculate the system's total capacity.

Both series and parallel connections are often made where a large storage capacity is needed but single batteries would be too cumbersome to handle. Typically in a 12-volt system, two 6-volt batteries are placed in series to give 12 volts, and then another two 6-volt batteries, also in series, are connected in parallel with the first two to double capacity while maintaining 12 volts.

Note, however, that when batteries are paralleled, one dead cell in one battery can pull down all the batteries, potentially killing them. Additionally, small circulating currents between the batteries increase their rate of self-discharge (see Chapter 2, "Self-Discharge"). Where large-capacity battery banks are needed, it is preferable to use two high-capacity 6-volt batteries *in series* rather than two smaller-capacity 12-volt batteries *in parallel.* For very large-capacity systems, six high-capacity 2-volt cells can be connected in series.

Batteries for engine starting. Starter motors draw very high amperages for short periods of time. During operation considerable heat is generated in the starter motor's windings. When voltage falls off, the motor compensates by pulling more amps, thus generating more heat. Not only will cranking be sluggish, but there is a risk of burning up the starter motor. Thus, it is essential to maintain an adequately sized, fully charged battery that is reserved solely for engine cranking.

Many people erroneously believe that deep-cycle batteries are unsuited for cranking applications. In fact, they can be used, but because the thicker plates in deep-cycle batteries retard the rate of acid diffusion compared with thin-plate (cranking) batteries, and therefore retard the rate at which energy can be released, a larger capacity deep-cycle battery is required to produce the same *cranking* capability as a thin-plate battery. (See the accompanying sidebar.)

How much larger? If a deep-cycle battery is to be used for engine cranking it is

Battery Capacity

Battery capacity is defined in three different ways: amp-hours; reserve capacity; and cold-cranking amps.

Amp-hours defines a battery's overall capacity, telling us how many amps we can pull from the battery at a relatively slow rate of discharge before the battery is "dead" (its voltage falls below a threshold level). For definition purposes, in the USA the discharge period is 20 hours; in the UK 10 hours. This means that a battery rated at 200 Ah is capable of delivering 10 amps per hour for 20 hours (USA), or 20 amps per hour for 10 hours (UK).

Because of problems with acid diffusion through the plates, the faster a battery is discharged the less power can be pulled from it before its voltage falls to the "dead" level (i.e., a battery has a lower Ah capacity at higher rates of discharge; see Figure 1-5A). Thus, a 200-Ah battery rated in the USA will have a lower capacity when rated in the UK due to the higher rate of discharge used for definition purposes. In other words, a 200-Ah UK battery has a larger capacity than a 200-Ah USA battery. This relationship between battery capacity and rate of discharge becomes very important when considering high-load DC items such as DC/AC inverters (see Chapter 5). Amp-hours are the best criterion for comparing battery *capacity* in slow discharge situations (most deep-cycle uses), although they tell us nothing about the *type* of battery, or how well it is built.

Reserve capacity is an automobile industry rating. If a car's alternator dies the whole electrical load will be thrown on the battery. The reserve capacity tells us how long (in minutes) that battery will support a 25-amp load, such as the car's ignition system, lights, etc., before the battery dies.

Cold-cranking amps are the real yardstick of starting battery performance. As temperatures decrease it takes more energy to crank an engine while at the same time batteries have far less power. The cold-cranking rating assumes a cold day (0°F) and a recalcitrant

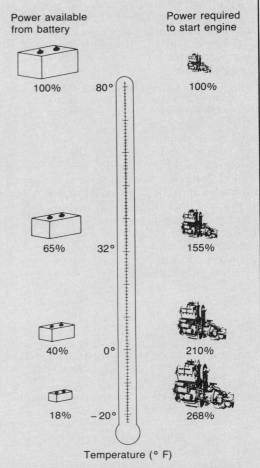

Power available from battery

Power required to start engine

100%	80°	100%
65%	32°	155%
40%	0°	210%
18%	−20°	268%

Temperature (° F)

Figure 1-7. As the temperature drops, your battery's starting power (cold-cranking amps) also drops, while your engine's starting power requirement increases. (See also Figure 1-5B.) The obvious implications must be considered when designing a battery system.

engine that needs to be cranked for 30 seconds, and tells us how many amps the battery can deliver to the starter motor for those 30 seconds.

---

necessary to make sure that it has sufficient *cold-cranking amps* to start the boat's engine. This should be given in the engine specifications; if not, the battery should have at least as many cold-cranking amps as the cranking battery it is replacing. (This information can be obtained from any battery supplier.)

We now have two options for engine cranking:

1. Reserve a separate, good-quality *cranking* battery solely for engine starts. This battery must be maintained permanently in a state of full or nearly full charge. The rest of the boat's system can be run from a bank of deep-cycle batteries (the "house" batteries; see Figure 1-8A).

2. Have two banks of deep-cycle batteries, each with at least the necessary cold-

cranking amps to start the engine (in practice, any good-sized bank of deep-cycle batteries will have the necessary cold-cranking amps). These two banks then can be alternated for "house" use (Figure 1-8B). This provides greater overall capacity and versatility, but at a higher cost.

Whatever is done, there should be a means of *paralleling* both battery banks for difficult engine starts. This is normally done via a dual-purpose battery isolation and selector switch having the following functions: OFF, BAT 1; BAT 2; and BOTH batteries. See Chapter 2 for more information on battery isolation switches.

Where a boat has an onboard generator with its own cranking battery, it is also advisable to have the means to parallel this with the main engine batteries to aid difficult starts on either the generator or the main engine. This can be done with another battery selector switch or, quite simply, with a set of heavy-duty jumper cables.

Properly set up, with one bank of batteries in a state of full charge for engine cranking and a bank of deep-cycle batteries serving the boat, any boat, sail or power, can enjoy the maximum possible time of peace and quiet at anchor without damaging its batteries, yet still be confident that the engine will start on demand.

Here are some examples. Aboard our ketch we have very modest 12-volt demands: a couple of fans, lights, stereo, and the VHF. We rarely use more than 50 to 60 amps in any 24-hour period. One deep-cycle "8D" battery (approximately 220-Ah capacity) provides a 4:1 margin of capacity over demand and meets our house needs, while a second deep-cycle "8D" is kept in reserve for engine starts. A half-hour or so of daily engine running both recharges the house battery and cools down our holding plate refrigeration system (see Chapter 10). We switch batteries daily. In 18 months of anchoring out in the Bahamas and Caribbean, we have enjoyed the unspoiled beauty of many a secluded bay, in peace and quiet, and never had a moment's anxiety about our ability to crank the engine.

Friends with 12-volt refrigeration (including a freezer) have higher 12-volt demands, typically over 100 Ah per day in the tropics. They have two banks of deep-cycle batteries, each with a capacity of 262 Ah, provided by placing two 262-Ah 6-volt

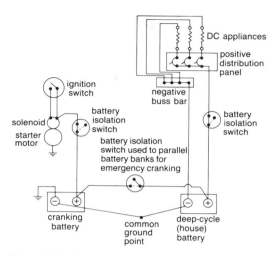

Figure 1-8A. **One way to satisfy engine-cranking as well as "house" power requirements. Here a cranking battery is reserved for engine starting.**

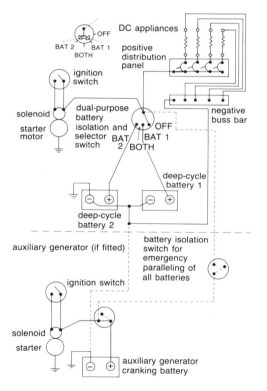

1–8B. **In this alternative to Figure 1-8A there are two deep-cycle battery banks.**

batteries in series in each bank. With a battery capacity-to-demand ratio of only 2.5:1, they are close to the lower limits of what is acceptable. However, they have a powerful wind generator; in the trade wind breezes of the Virgin Islands, they can go for days on end and never need to crank the engine. In periods of calm, running the engine less than one hour each day recharges their batteries.

Finally, we have met powerboaters who have found that an adequate bank of deep-cycle batteries coupled with a DC/AC inverter (see Chapter 5) enables them to use almost all their AC appliances, sans the air conditioning, without running the generator. In all but the hottest, most airless conditions the loss of the air conditioner is more than compensated by the fuel savings and tranquility that follow when the generator is shut down.

Meeting Your Power Requirements

What Factors Affect Battery Charging?

I recently worked on a sailboat, used extensively for cruising, that had seen minimal engine running and therefore minimal battery charging time. Its frugal electrical system worked well for years; then it changed hands. The new owner installed a small, poorly insulated 12-volt refrigeration unit. The batteries died. The owner concluded that he had insufficient battery capacity and added another battery. This died also. He added two more, and these died! I removed five miscellaneous batteries from the boat, scattered around in different lockers.

Regardless of how much battery capacity a boat has, if the various charging devices are not putting back what is being taken out, the batteries eventually must go dead. The solution to this boat's problem was not more batteries, but a more efficient refrigerator and *more charging capability,* in the guise of longer engine running time, a high-output alternator, or a solar panel or wind generator. We eventually used a combination of all these.

The primary source of battery charging for almost all boats is still an engine-driven alternator. Where engine running time must be kept to a minimum, the charging system must be designed to get the job done as quickly as possible without damaging the battery. This is in contrast to automotive applications, where the function of the alternator is to handle the car's electrical load and merely top off the battery, which typically is discharged no more than 5 percent.

The rate of charge of a battery is a complex function of a number of variables, including the degree of battery discharge, its temperature, the power of the alternator (its *amperage*), and the output *voltage* of the alternator (see "Regulating Voltage," later in this chapter).

Degree of battery discharge. A large battery, fully discharged, will readily accept just about anything that most alternators can throw at it. But as it starts to come up to charge, internal resistance increases; if the alternator continues to pump in a heavy amperage, the battery begins to gas and heat up. This point is generally reached at around 70 to 80 percent of full charge. A conventional voltage regulator starts to taper off the charge well before this (around 50 to 60 percent of full charge) to protect the battery.

Temperature. The warmer a battery, the more readily it will accept a charge; the heat enhances the chemical reactions. But beyond a certain point, high temperatures lead to internal self-destruction; the plates warp and buckle, thus shorting out. The maximum safe temperature for a battery is 125°F (52°C). This is an internal temperature.

Lacking temperature-sensing equipment, any time a battery case becomes warm to the touch you should suspect that the internal temperature is becoming dangerously high. (Battery temperature can be determined more accurately by using a digital thermometer on the battery post, or withdrawing a sample of electrolyte, using a hydrometer with a built-in temperature gauge. See Chapter 2, "Testing Your Battery.") *Again, the maximum battery temperature is 125°F (52°C). In practice, temperatures should be kept below 110°F (43°C) if at all possible.* Battery charging can be accelerated only until this point is reached; the rate of charge then must be tapered off to ensure no further rise in temperature. When this point will occur is unpredictable. For example, the ambient temperature may vary from subzero in the arctic to well over

100°F (38°C) in an engine room in the tropics.

Alternator amperage. Alternators are rated in amps—anywhere from 35 amps for a compact automobile to 200 amps or more for large trucks and marine alternators. This rating refers to the maximum output in one hour at a certain temperature and speed of rotation. At higher temperatures rated output will be a little lower; at lower temperatures, a little higher. This amperage rating can be misleading, however. A typical alternator in automotive use puts out at full load for just a few minutes after engine cranking and then tapers off. Many automotive alternators cannot be run continuously at full load in high ambient temperatures (such as are found in engine rooms on boats in the tropics) without burning up. But this is precisely what we want our alternator to do when we try to bring a large-capacity, deeply discharged battery back up to full charge in the shortest possible time.

Therefore, to provide a safety margin, an alternator for marine use needs to be rated at full continuous load in *temperatures up to 200°F (93°C)*.

Sizing an Alternator

There are a couple of rules of thumb to follow. It takes around 120 percent of the energy drawn from a battery to bring it back to full charge. To replace 100 Ah drawn from two 8D's, we would need to put back 120 amps. The maximum rate of charge that a deep-cycle battery will accept without internal self-destruction is around 25 percent of its rated capacity; for example, a well-discharged 400-Ah battery or two 200-Ah batteries connected *in parallel* can be charged at up to 100 amps. This rate of charge can be maintained only as long as battery temperatures remain below 125°F (52°C), and assumes the charge is tapered off rapidly as the battery comes up to near 75 percent of full charge.

For long life, even continuously rated marine alternators are best run at less than 100 percent of full output. A fudge factor of at least 25 percent should be built in: A 133-amp alternator will be ideal for a 100-amp output. We must remember to add in the boat's total load at the time of charging, since this also will be coming from the alternator. This may include heavy electrical equipment that is only switched on when the engine is running, such as

holding-plate DC refrigeration. We may well need a 200-amp alternator.

Such an oversize alternator has an important side benefit. Battery charging frequently is done at anchor, with the engine idling and the alternator operating below its rated speed and output. With the correct pulley sizes, a 200-amp alternator will easily reach 100 amps at a little above engine idle speed, but still will not overspeed at full throttle.

Speed of alternator rotation. The pulleys supplied with most alternators are not suitable for marine use. Most automobile engines cruise at 3,500 to 4,000 r.p.m. Many boat engines spend much of their time refrigerating or battery charging at idle speeds between 700 and 1,000 r.p.m. But boats and usage patterns differ, and alternator pulley sizes must be geared to individual use. Follow this procedure to size your alternator pulleys:

1. Determine the maximum *required* alternator output as described earlier. Note that this is *not* the maximum *alternator* output, and in general should not exceed 75 percent of maximum output in order to guard against overloading and overheating.

2. Find out the maximum safe operating speed for the alternator (usually 10,000 r.p.m.).

3. Determine the *minimum* engine running speed in normal use (or normal battery charging and refrigerating speed if this is the predominant use, such as on a cruising boat spending much of its time at anchor).

4. Set up the alternator pulley ratio to achieve the maximum *required* output at this *minimum* engine speed, and then check to make sure that the alternator will not overspeed at maximum engine revolutions. If the alternator will overspeed, its pulleys will have to be powered down to the point at which it reaches maximum speed only at maximum engine revolutions.

For example:

- We have a 130-amp alternator and a maximum required output of 100 amps (77 percent of rated output). The alternator reaches 100 amps at 3,000 r.p.m.
- The maximum safe operating speed is 10,000 r.p.m.

- The boat spends much of its time at anchor, running its engine at 1,000 r.p.m. to drive the mechanical refrigeration unit.
- We need a pulley ratio of 3:1 to achieve an alternator speed of 3,000 r.p.m. Maximum engine speed is also 3,000 r.p.m., giving a maximum alternator speed of 9,000 r.p.m., which is within safe operating limits.

Horsepower requirements of alternators. An alternator's output is about 14 volts. At 100 amps an alternator is therefore producing: 14v × 100a = 1,400 watts. There are 746 watts in 1 horsepower; therefore this alternator will require 1400 ÷ 746 = 1.88 horsepower.

There are various energy losses involved, however, such as drive belt and pulley friction. To take these into account, a 100-percent fudge factor should be made. This gives us a power requirement of 3.76 horsepower at 100 amps. Obviously, at reduced loads the alternator will need less power. It should be noted that friction is a major source of energy loss. Great improvements have been made in belt design over the past few years; quality belts reduce friction and extend belt life.

Regulating Voltage

The "brain" of a charging system is the voltage regulator. Its function is to match alternator output with the load and the battery's state of charge. Simply put, the voltage regulator maintains system voltage at a certain level. When a battery is discharged or a load is placed on the system, voltage drops. The regulator responds by increasing output (amperage) until voltage levels are restored, and then it tapers off output to a level just sufficient to maintain this voltage.

When charging a battery, charging voltage always must be higher than battery voltage or no current will flow. The greater the differential, the greater the flow (up to 100 percent of the capacity of the charging device). A fully charged battery has an open-circuit voltage of 12.6 to 12.8 volts (see page 22), so voltage regulators are always set a little higher than this to get the battery up to this level. In marine use the difficulty is in deciding how much higher. See Figure 1-9.

For any given battery terminal voltage (which can be loosely translated into the

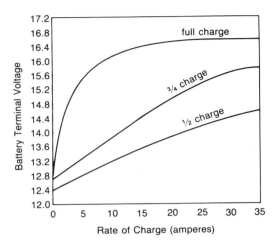

Figure 1-9. Charge acceptance rates of a 100-Ah "wet"-type battery as a function of voltage level and state of charge. Since it is wise to avoid routine discharges of greater than 50 percent (failure to do so will shorten battery life), this chart covers the charge states of greatest interest. Battery terminal voltage can be loosely translated as voltage regulator setting. The implications of the chart are discussed in the accompanying text.

voltage regulator setting), find the voltage on the left of the chart, trace across horizontally until you meet a curve, and then move vertically to read off the charge acceptance rate at that voltage for a battery in that state of charge. For example, with a regulator set to 13.6 volts, a fully charged 100-Ah battery will accept approximately 1 amp, a three-quarter charged battery 7½ amps, and a half-charged battery 17 amps. If regulator voltage is raised to 14.4 volts, the figures become 2 amps, 14 amps, and 30 amps respectively. (For a 200-Ah battery these figures can be approximately doubled.) An increase of only 0.8 volt on the battery voltage (read regulator setting) almost doubles the charge acceptance (and therefore the charging rate) throughout the critical 50-percent-of-charge-to-full-charge range that we are interested in; this cuts charging times in half.

If we turn these figures around we can see another interesting relationship. At 13.6 volts, a half-charged battery will take 17 amps; a three-quarter-charged battery, 7½ amps; and a fully charged battery, 1 amp. *The charge is tapering off rapidly.* To go from three-quarter charge to full charge will take a very long time, as the charge rate winds down toward 1 amp. Even at 14.4 volts the charge rate from three-quarter charge to full charge winds down from 14 amps to 2 amps. On a boat where charging is intermittent and engine run-time restricted, it will be nearly impossible to bring batteries up to full charge, even with an elevated voltage regulator setting.

Now assume a battery is at full charge. A voltage regulator setting of 13.6 volts, producing a charge rate of around 1 amp, will only minimally overcharge a battery. In practice, other losses—both internal and external to the battery—will probably prevent overcharging. But a regulator setting of 14.4 volts, producing a charge rate of 2 amps, will create excessive battery gassing over an extended period, with a consequent loss of electrolyte and potential damage to the battery plate grids.

High versus low regulator settings. The dilemma is clear. In many pleasure boat situations, batteries are deeply discharged periodically (to at least the 50-percent level), but charging times are restricted. Thus, fast charges are required, which call for higher voltage regulator settings; otherwise the batteries will suffer from undercharging, sulfation, and a permanent loss of capacity. With higher voltage regulator settings, periods of extended engine running time likely will result in overcharging, excessive gassing, and plate damage.

Voltage regulator settings must be tailored to individual boat usage in such a way as to maximize battery charge levels while causing minimal battery damage. Lower settings are needed where batteries are normally only slightly discharged, higher settings where they are deeply discharged routinely. In the latter case, limited battery damage may result from overcharging during extended periods of engine running, but this is a small price to pay to avoid more extensive battery damage due to persistent undercharging if lower voltage regulator settings are used. Some very sophisticated (and expensive!) marine voltage regulators can eliminate this contradiction, as will the use of certain voltage regulator bypasses. These are all covered in Chapter 2.

Automotive regulators. The source of al-most all marine charging equipment is the automotive industry. Since automobile batteries are rarely discharged more than 5 percent and the alternator is running almost all the time electrical equipment is on, regulator settings tend to be fairly low (below 14.0 volts). This avoids the problem of overcharging batteries—although the tendency in recent years has been to increase settings to deal with greater electrical loads. Most regulators are not adjustable. This makes the majority of automobile alternators and regulators unsuitable for most marine uses!

However, certain specialized automotive regulators are set considerably higher than normal, for uses approximating a "typical" situation on a boat. For instance, the police load their cars with extra electrical equipment such as radios, spotlights, and radar, which they expect to use even with the engine shut down. Some automotive alternators are regulated as high as 14.3 volts (Lucas/CAV) to cope with these situations; many Bosch alternators are regulated to 14.1 volts. Other regulators are field-adjustable and can be set to an appropriate level for any particular use by turning a small screw, by lifting up and rotating a cap (some Delco Remy alternators; see Figure 1-10), or by selecting a different connection on the regulator. Some Lucas/CAV alternators have a high-, medium-, and low-voltage regulator connection.

Conclusion. Voltage regulation on boats can be determined only in relation to specific patterns of use.

Where minimal engine running time is of paramount importance (as on many cruising boats), a regulator setting as high as 14.4 volts may be called for. Where extended engine running is the norm, a more typical automotive setting as low as 13.8 volts may be appropriate.

All boats are best served by external, field-adjustable voltage regulators to facilitate adjustment. See Chapter 2 for adjustment procedures.

Figure 1-10. Voltage regulator adjustment on some Delco Remy alternators. In this enlarged view the adjustment cap is in the "low" position.

Summary: A Balanced System

There is hardly a boat around that does not at some time shut down its engine and run off its batteries, deeply discharging them. Even the best automotive batteries cannot be deep-cycled more than 30 to 40 times before failing. *Unless a boat has a permanent charging capability equal to demand, it should be fitted with deep-cycle batteries.* The

Table 1-3. Designing Your Boat's 12-Volt Electrical System.

Question	Answer
1. Do you regularly or even periodically draw power from your battery or batteries, other than to start the engine, when you aren't charging them (i.e., when the engine isn't running)? Note: Do not consider auxiliary charging devices such as solar panels and wind generators in your answer, since their output is not wholly predictable and your system should be able to function adequately without them.	If your answer is "No," one or more automotive (cranking) batteries will suffice. Go to Question 8, then 10. If your answer is yes (the great majority of cases), you need deep-cycle batteries. Go to Question 2.
2. Does your boat have an engine?	If no, go to Questions 3 through 6, then study Chapter 5 to ascertain how you can provide sufficient charging capability for your battery bank. If yes, go to Question 3.
3. How long (in days or in a fraction of a day) between charging intervals? (See page 3. Note that engine running time must be long enough during each charging cycle to bring the battery to a reasonable state of charge. Variables include degree of discharge and voltage regulator setting. See discussions of voltage regulation in Chapters 1 and 2.)	_____ day(s)
4. What is your boat's total 12-volt electrical demand per day? (See Tables 1-1 and 1-2.)	_____ amp-hours
5. What is the anticipated battery drain between charges? (Multiply Answer 3 by Answer 4.)	_____ amp-hours
6. What is the necessary battery capacity? (Multiply Answer 5 by at least 2½, and preferably by 4.)	_____ amp-hours
7. Will you carry a separate automotive (cranking) battery for engine starts, or will you have two banks of deep-cycle batteries to be alternated for "house" use and engine starts? Put a checkmark next to your choice. Note: When two deep-cycle battery banks are installed, *each one* should have the capacity computed in Answer 6.	_____ Option #1 Cranking battery (go to Question 8, then 10) _____ Option #2 Second deep-cycle battery bank (proceed with Question 8)
8. How many cold-cranking amps does your engine need to start in the coldest weather you can imagine? (See page 12.)	_____ amps
9. If you intend to use your deep-cycle banks for engine starting, does their capacity exceed the foreseen demand in Answer 8? Note: If you plan to install two deep-cycle battery banks, each alone should have the necessary capacity for engine starts. In practice, the capacity computed in Answer 6 is almost certain to suffice. Banks can be paralleled via the battery selector switch for difficult starts (see page 13).	_____ yes _____ no
10. What is your maximum required alternator output? Note: Unless your answer to Question 1 was "No," the output should be one-third the capacity of one battery bank *plus* the additional load imposed by the boat's operating systems during charging (see Tables 1-1 and 1-2). This may include refrigeration and other large loads that are turned on only when the engine is running. If your answer to Question 1 was "No," maximum alternator output should equal the boat's load while the engine is running plus a 33-percent margin to prevent alternator overheating.	_____ amps
11. What should your alternator pulley ratio be? Note: This is the ratio of the engine output-pulley diameter to the alternator drive-pulley diameter. Adjust the ratio to achieve the output called for in Answer 10 at the minimum projected engine running speed. Make sure the alternator will not exceed its maximum safe operating speed (usually 10,000 r.p.m.) at maximum engine r.p.m. See page 15.	_____ : _____
12. What voltage regulator setting should you maintain? Note: A high setting, perhaps as high as 14.4 volts, promotes faster charging when engine time is limited, but may overcharge the battery during extended engine running. If your answer to Question 1 was "No," an automotive regulator setting of 13.8 to 14.0 volts will be ideal, but automotive regulators are otherwise inappropriate. Regulator bypass devices (see Chapter 2) are available. See also the discussion on pages 16–17 in this chapter.	_____ volts
13. Through your answers to the preceding questions you have designed a sensible 12-volt system for your boat. You may well be curious about the effects on this equation of power inputs from other sources—DC/AC inverters, wind and water generators, solar panels, and diesel generators. These are the subjects of Chapter 5 and 6. Return to Chapter 1 for more specifics of battery bank configuration to attain the capacity called for by Answer 6.	

lone exception is a marine cranking battery reserved for engine starting. Remember the following:

- Auxiliary charging devices such as solar panels, wind generators, and battery chargers powered by onboard generators should be left out of the equation. All may fail to produce at some time or be inadequate to meet total demands, in which case the batteries will be steadily discharged.
- Deep-cycle batteries vary enormously in quality of construction and suitability for marine use. The key criterion in most boating applications is the number of life cycles at the 50-percent discharge level. Top-of-the-line deep-cycle batteries will have a thousand or more life cycles and will last up to 20 years.
- Battery capacity, as a rule of thumb, should be *four times* the anticipated demand between charging periods. Charging capability should be around one-third of battery capacity *plus* any additional boat loads during the charging period. Most of today's mid-sized cruising boats, charging batteries on a daily basis, will use 100 Ah between charges, requiring 400 Ah of total battery capacity and an alternator of between 133 and 200 amps output (depending on additional boat loads during charging).
- Voltage regulation can be determined only by specific usage patterns. Marine use requires an adjustable, external voltage regulator.

This simple statement of a balanced electrical system reveals the woeful inadequacy of the electrical systems on most boats. Problems start on the production line. Boatbuilders are constantly pressured to keep down costs; good-quality deep-cycle batteries and large-capacity alternators with external voltage regulators are expensive and rarely fitted. Much electrical equipment is "extra"; builders frequently install batteries and an alternator barely adequate to handle the standard items; additional equipment rapidly overwhelms the system.

Year by year, the electrical loads increase even on small boats. Powered windlasses, winches, and sail-reefing devices are some of today's hot items; all of them pull very high amperages. High amperages require heavy cables, connectors, and so on (see Chapter 3). Although this chapter has focused on 12-volt systems, it makes more sense to go to 24 or 32 volts, and prospective boat buyers should be pushing for this with builders. The argument that high-voltage equipment is unavailable just does not hold water; commercial fishermen and high-quality boatbuilders in the USA have used 32 volts for years; 24-volt equipment is readily available in the UK and Europe.

Finally, the electronics revolution is hitting the boat market with a vengeance. Increasingly, central microprocessors complement Satnavs, Lorans, Deccas, and a host of other electronic equipment; all can be completely disabled by electrical interference. *The primary sources of electrical interference aboard boats are alternators and voltage regulators.* When present, interference can be at least partially screened by various techniques detailed in Chapter 7, but the process is likely to be time-consuming, expensive, and not always effective. It makes far more sense to remove interference at its source. If taking delivery of a new boat or upgrading an old one, insist on a fully shielded alternator and voltage regulator (see Chapter 7). The cost will be about double that of a conventional alternator and regulator, but the investment will be worthwhile.

So much for general considerations; let's get into more specific details of maintenance and overhaul.

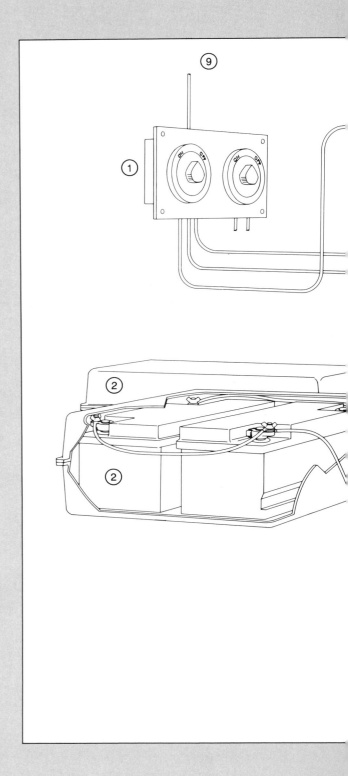

CHAPTER 2

Figure 2-1. **Keeping your batteries and charging system trouble free should be the first systems maintenance priority of any boater.**

(1) battery isolation switch
(2) batteries
(3) starter
(4) to starter
(5) alternator
(6) to positive terminal of battery
(7) common ground point
(8) diode
(9) to distribution panel

Maintaining and Troubleshooting Your Battery-Powered Electrical System

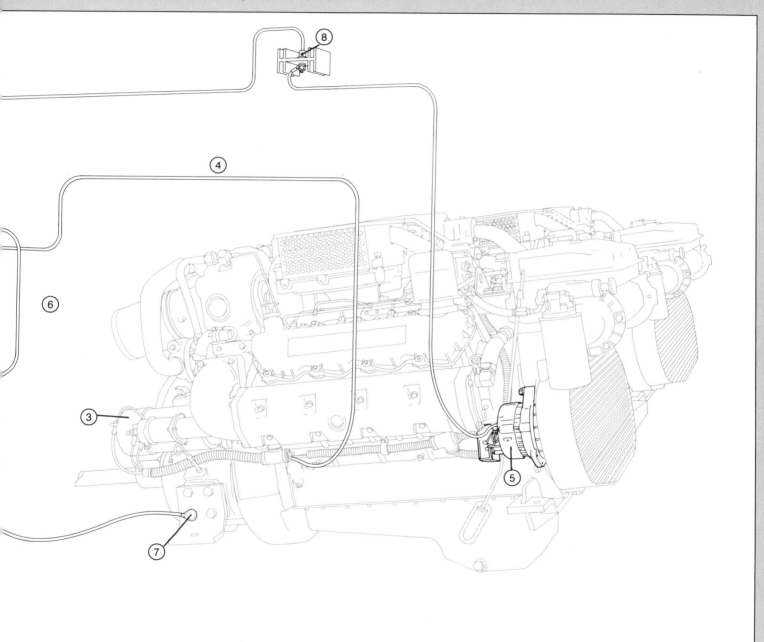

Batteries

Safety

Batteries constitute an underestimated danger aboard boats. A fully charged battery contains a tremendous amount of stored energy—more than enough to melt in half a wrench placed carelessly across its terminals. A battery's electrolyte—a solution of sulfuric acid—will eat through clothing and cause severe burns. *Take great care with battery acid.* Any splashes should be immediately and liberally doused with water, then neutralized with an antacid solution such as baking powder or soda, household ammonia, or antacid medicines.

The battery compartment should be well ventilated. When being charged or rapidly discharged, batteries emit explosive, lighter-than-air gases—hydrogen and oxygen. Never generate sparks around a charging battery, or one that is being rapidly discharged, such as during prolonged engine cranking. Batteries can explode, spraying acid in all directions. The Hydrocap Corporation makes catalytic battery caps that replace the standard filler caps. These convert most of the oxygen and hydrogen back into water, which then is returned to the battery cells.

Batteries also emit corrosive fumes. Never install electronic equipment near a battery compartment. The equipment will likely suffer irreparable damage.

Batteries should be kept in well-built, acidproof (plastic, fiberglass, or epoxy-saturated wood) boxes with secure, vented lids (Figure 2-2). Ventilation is important not just to remove explosive gases, but to dissipate heat generated during rapid charging. Because of this, the degree of ventilation may well have a significant impact on charging times. It also will prolong battery life by keeping batteries cool. As long as the batteries don't freeze, the cooler the temperature the longer the battery life.

Routine Maintenance

- Keep batteries topped up with distilled or clean fresh water. The battery's internal plates are irreparably damaged by exposure to air. Maintain fluid levels one-quarter to one-half inch above the plates, but no higher: Overfilling will lead to spewing of electrolyte from the filler caps during charging.

- Keep the tops of batteries clean. A small amount of dirt, water, or acid will provide a path for electrical leaks that will drain the battery over time. Wiping with a rag dipped in a solution of baking powder, soda, or household ammonia will neutralize any acid, but never sprinkle baking soda directly on a battery case—if any were to enter a cell through a vent hole, it could destroy the cell.

- Periodically remove the battery cables (negative first) and clean the terminal posts and clamps. When removing the clamps, do not lever them up with a screwdriver. This is likely to damage the battery plates and may tear a terminal post loose, destroying the battery. Loosen the clamp bolt and ease the clamp jaws open; work the clamp *gently* from side to side and then lift it off. A pair of battery terminal pullers is a cheap and excellent investment for the tool box. Why wreck a $400 battery for lack of a $10 tool? After replacing the cable clamps, coat them liberally with grease or petroleum jelly to inhibit corrosion.

Testing Your Battery

There are three ways to test a battery: by measuring its *open-circuit voltage;* by measuring the *specific gravity* of its electrolyte; and by using a *load tester.*

Reading open-circuit voltage. A battery is open-circuited when no load is being drawn from it and no charge is being fed to it. The simplest way to open-circuit a battery is to switch off the battery isolation switch. Never do this with the engine running, however—it can blow out the alternator. There may be some equipment, such as a VHF radio or a solar panel, hooked directly to the battery; such equipment must be switched off or disconnected to achieve meaningful test results. The battery then must be allowed to sit for at least 10 minutes; an hour or two would be better; overnight would be best (gel-type batteries may take 48 hours to stabilize). Battery voltage is then measured with a digital volt-ohm meter (VOM; see Chapter 3), or a meter with an expanded scale (such as those fitted in Marinetics electrical panels), which generally covers only the

Battery Installation

The battery box illustrated in Figure 2-2A represents the ideal. The vent (which leads outside, and *not* to interior boat spaces) is at the top of the compartment, since the explosive hydrogen gas given off during charging is lighter than air. The removable lid permits ready access for servicing. Batteries are well secured so that even in a capsize they will not break loose. Air is introduced at the base of the compartment to encourage thorough ventilation. The optional fan further increases ventilation, which also increases the efficiency of battery charging. (If a fan is used, it *must* be sparkproof.) The box is constructed of acidproof material such as plastic, fiberglass, or epoxy-saturated wood.

In practice, many boats have no battery box at all, or something that falls far short of this ideal. The owner of any boat venturing offshore would be well advised to fit a decent box if one is not present. Good-quality batteries weigh around three-quarters of a pound per amp-hour of capacity (at 12 volts); a 200-Ah battery thus weighs about 150 pounds, a 400-Ah battery, 300 pounds. This is a highly concentrated weight, coupled with gallons of highly corrosive sulfuric acid (about 1¾ gallons per 100 Ah of capacity at 12 volts). Batteries that come loose in a seaway constitute a major safety threat. Containing the batteries and battery acid in an acidproof container is a matter of common sense.

Building a simple battery box.
Begin with a 4- by 8-foot sheet of 1/2-inch exterior-grade plywood. Mark it out in panels to form a box ¼ inch longer and wider on its *inside* than the battery or batteries it is to hold, and ½ inch higher than the battery depth (including terminal posts), as in Figure 2-2B. Before cutting out the panels, place a layer of fiberglass cloth (just about any weight will do) over the plywood (Figure 2-2C) and thoroughly wet it out with catalyzed polyester resin or epoxy resin, the latter being preferable for this purpose. Add resin until the weave of the cloth is filled; the cloth will turn transparent, allowing the pencil marks for the panel cuts to show through.

When the resin has cured, cut out the panels and then saturate all the sawn edges with resin.

Glue and nail the box together with the fiberglass on the inside, making sure all the seams are completely filled with glue. Use an epoxy paste (or epoxy resin with appropriate filler) to seal the seams, even if you used polyester resin for the sheathing; polyester resin is brittle and has no gap-filling ability.

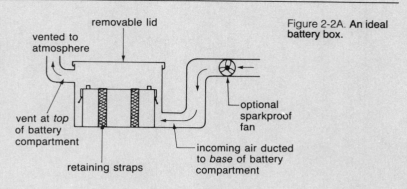

Figure 2-2A. **An ideal battery box.**

vented to atmosphere — removable lid — optional sparkproof fan — incoming air ducted to *base* of battery compartment — retaining straps — vent at *top* of battery compartment

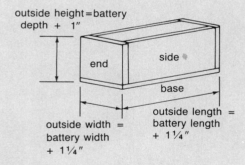

Figure 2-2B. **Dimensions for a do-it-yourself box of 1/2-inch plywood.**

outside height = battery depth + 1″ — end — side — base — outside width = battery width + 1¼″ — outside length = battery length + 1¼″

Figure 2-2C. The "ingredients": plywood, fiberglass cloth (which will give a smoother, more finished appearance than woven roving), epoxy resin and hardener, a roller and brush, acetone for cleaning tools, and a mason jar for saving used acetone.

(cont.)

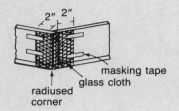

Figure 2-2D. Sealing and reinforcing the outside corners of the box.

2″ 2″

masking tape
glass cloth
radiused corner

Figure 2-2E. The finished box.

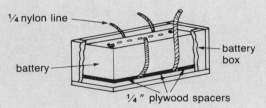

Figure 2-2F. Two lengths of 1/4-inch line provide a means of lifting the battery out of the box when necessary. Make sure the line is nylon, which is acid-resistant.

¼ nylon line

battery box

battery

¼″ plywood spacers

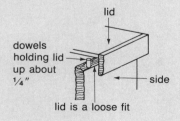

Figure 2-2G. Fitting a lid.

lid

dowels holding lid up about ¼″

lid is a loose fit

side

Radius (round off) the outside corners and bottom edges of the box. Now use masking tape to temporarily affix strips of fiberglass cloth around each corner and edge, overlapping on each side of the seam by 2 inches (Figure 2-2D). Wet out the cloth with resin and, progressing from the corner to the edges, work out the wrinkles and air bubbles to achieve a firm bond.

Lay a second strip of cloth over the first, overlapping its edges by one inch, and repeat. Radius the inside corners with fillets of epoxy paste (Figure 2-2E).

The box will need to be fastened in place, a task that may involve some imagination as well as an appreciation for the forces that could come to bear in a seaway. Any fasteners through the sides or bottom will need liberal bedding, preferably with a polyurethane adhesive such as 3M 5200. If the batteries have no handles, place three spacers of 1/4-inch ply in the bottom of the box to separate two lengths of 1/4-inch nylon line, the ends of which will emerge above the box sides (Figure 2-2F). With this arrangement the battery can be removed without having to destroy the box!

There remains only the task of fitting a lid. The lid can simply rest on and overlap the box sides, as shown in Figure 2-2G, provided some short dowels or nails are set into the box sides and ends to stick out ¼ inch or so. This holds the lid slightly above the box, permitting adequate ventilation. Alternatively, fit a vent in the lid (a screened hole will suffice).

Strap the lid down with straps sturdy enough to restrain the batteries in the event of a capsize.

range from 8 to 16 volts. With the battery temperature between 60°F and 100°F (15.5°C and 38°C), the following approximate correlation applies:

Open-circuit volts	Percent of full charge
12.6 or greater	100%
12.4 to 12.6	75% to 100%
12.2 to 12.4	50% to 75%
12.0 to 12.2	25% to 50%
11.7 to 12.0	0% to 25%
11.7 or less	0%

Note that the difference between a fully charged battery and a half-charged battery is only 0.4 volt! From full charge to full discharge is just 0.9 volt. A dial-and-needle (analog) volt-ohm meter is quite useless in these circumstances; a meter with an expanded scale is questionable; only a digital VOM will give an accurate assessment of the state of charge—and even this may be unreliable.

Specific gravity. The liquid electrolyte in a battery is a solution of sulfuric acid, which is denser than water. As a battery discharges, this acid progressively weakens, becoming less dense. Samples of the electrolyte can be withdrawn from each battery cell using a *hydrometer* (Figure 2-3A). The hydrometer contains a floating indicator that comes to rest at a specific

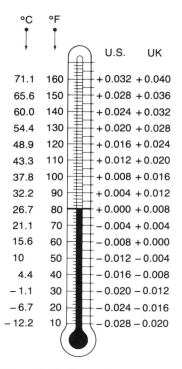

°C	°F	U.S.	UK
71.1	160	+0.032	+0.040
65.6	150	+0.028	+0.036
60.0	140	+0.024	+0.032
54.4	130	+0.020	+0.028
48.9	120	+0.016	+0.024
43.3	110	+0.012	+0.020
37.8	100	+0.008	+0.016
32.2	90	+0.004	+0.012
26.7	80	+0.000	+0.008
21.1	70	-0.004	+0.004
15.6	60	-0.008	+0.000
10	50	-0.012	-0.004
4.4	40	-0.016	-0.008
-1.1	30	-0.020	-0.012
-6.7	20	-0.024	-0.016
-12.2	10	-0.028	-0.020

Figure 2-3B. Temperature corrections for hydrometer readings in the United States and in the United Kingdom. Baseline temperature is taken as 80°F (26.7°C) in the U.S., and 60°F (15.6°C) in the UK. Given a hydrometer reading of 1.250 and an electrolyte temperature of 20°F, for example, in the U.S. you would subtract .024 for a corrected specific gravity of 1.226. Comparing this with the specific gravity of 1.265 for a fully charged battery (Table 2-1), we see that the battery in question is about 25 percent discharged. In the UK, the correction factor for an electrolyte temperature of 20°F (-6.7°C) is -0.016, yielding a corrected specific gravity of 1.234. Turning again to Table 2-1, we see that the reference value for a fully charged battery in the UK is 1.273, and the table once more indicates that our battery is 25 percent discharged.

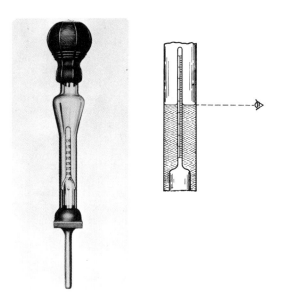

Figure 2-3A. A battery-testing hydrometer. The correct method of reading it is shown on the right. Your eye should be level with the liquid surface. Disregard curvature of the liquid against the glass parts.

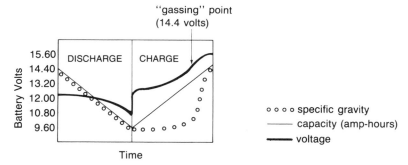

Figure 2-3C. Voltage and specific gravity during constant rate discharge and charge. During discharge there is direct correlation of the specific-gravity decrease with the loss of capacity. During recharge, however, the specific gravity lags behind the actual state of charge until gassing mixes the electrolyte, at which point specific gravity climbs steeply. Because voltage rises rapidly during initial charging, it is necessary to maintain a high voltage regulator setting for fast charges.

Table 2-1. Battery Electrolyte Specific Gravity as a Function of Temperature and State of Charge.

Specific gravity:	(80°F; 26.7°C)	(60°F; 15°C)	Percent charge
	1.265	1.273	100%
	1.225	1.233	75%
	1.190	1.198	50%
	1.155	1.163	25%
	1.120	1.128	0%

level in pure water, this level being calibrated for a specific gravity of 1.000. The denser acid solution floats the indicator higher, giving a higher specific gravity reading, but as the solution weakens, the indicator sinks. The indicated specific gravity can be correlated accurately with the battery's state of charge. Because specific gravity varies with temperature, better hydrometers incorporate a thermometer. In the USA, 80°F (26.7°C) is taken as normal; in the UK, normal is understood to be 60°F (15.6°C). Your battery's state of charge can be determined accurately using Table 2-1. For other temperatures consult the conversion charts in Figure 2-3B (USA and UK).

These figures in Table 2-1 are for industry-standard batteries. The specific gravity of fully charged batteries, however, varies considerably—from 1.230 to 1.300. The lower figure may be found on some deep-cycle batteries sold in the tropics, where the higher prevailing temperatures promote more efficient battery operation, requiring a less concentrated acid solution. (This can lead to longer battery life.) The higher figure may be found on cranking batteries sold in cold climates, where more concentrated acid solutions are needed to boost output. After a new battery is installed, it should be fully charged and then tested to establish its actual specific gravity (be sure to note the temperature of the electrolyte); the figures should be logged for future reference. Note that a full charge may be assumed when further charging over a 3-hour period fails to produce any further increase in specific gravity.

When a discharged battery is recharged, some of the heavier acid created by the charging process sinks to the base of the battery, where it cannot be reached by the hydrometer. Because of this, hydrometer readings taken from the fluid at the top of a battery lag behind the actual state of charge. When the battery is almost fully charged it begins to *gas* (boil), emitting hydrogen and oxygen, and the bubbles mix the solution, producing a uniform density.

A hydrometer is an accurate way to assess a battery's state of charge in normal circumstances, and one should be found on every maintenance-conscious boat. Be sure to get one designed for *battery* testing; some are for antifreeze, others for winemaking! Each is purpose-built to cover an appropriate range of specific gravities. Note that to check a battery's condition thoroughly, each cell must be tested individually, which is easily done by withdrawing a sample of electrolyte from each in turn.

Testing under load. A battery can show a full or nearly full charge on both an open-circuit voltage test and a specific gravity test, yet still fail to operate correctly due to sulfation of the plates (discussed later in this chapter). In these circumstances, it really can be checked only with a *load tester* (high-rate discharge tester)—a device, connected either across each cell in turn or across the battery terminals, that artificially creates an extremely high load on the battery while measuring voltage. A cell or battery in good condition will maintain a steady voltage for up to 10 seconds; a weak cell or battery will begin to fall off rapidly. If battery voltage falls below 9.5 volts after 15 seconds the battery is in sorry shape. High-load testers are specialized pieces of equipment and rarely found on boats.

The effect of a high-load tester can be simulated by cranking a diesel engine for 15 seconds. You can close the throttle or open the decompression levers (if fitted) to keep the engine from starting, but some diesels have an automatic starting advance that is difficult to outfox; on these you must shut off the fuel supply to the engine. *Do not crank for more than 30 seconds;* the starter will overheat. This test takes very little out of the battery. Even if the starter motor is pulling 400 amps, at 15 seconds this amounts to a total of only $400 \div (4 \times 60) = 1.66$ amps. The battery voltage should remain constant during the test—probably around 10.5 volts. This will vary according to load, battery size and type, and temperature.

Testing individual cells. Some larger batteries have individual, external cell connections, enabling the individual cells to be tested for open-circuit volts or load tested. The volt-ohm meter or load tester is connected across the lead straps on either side of each filler cap. Individual measurements should be one-sixth of overall battery measurements. Most batteries, however, have internal cell connections and, using a VOM, only the battery as a whole can be tested. The overall open-circuit voltage might show an almost-charged battery, although one cell may be seriously deficient—the deficiency being masked by all the others. In actual use (under load) the battery is only as good as its weakest link. Overall voltage tests provide incomplete information. We need to know the state of individual cells, which is why every boat should carry a hydrometer.

Signs of Trouble

Dead batteries may be the result of prolonged power drain. Check for:

- a piece of equipment left on (especially navigation lights);
- any leaks to ground in the boat's wiring (see Chapter 3, "Troubleshooting Techniques");
- dirt and moisture on top of the battery;
- and the possibility that the battery is not receiving a proper charge (see the relevant discussions under "Alternators" and "Voltage Regulators" later in this chapter).

A battery that shows nearly full voltage with no load, but a falling voltage when a load is added, needs to be charged. On the other hand, a discharged battery whose voltage comes up rapidly on charging is sulfated (see below). It will go dead rapidly in use, since only a small fraction of its plate area is still active. An isolated and unused battery whose voltage shows an appreciable drop over two to three weeks has an internal short. A drop from full charge to 75 percent or less should certainly be considered appreciable.

Finally, a battery may simply be old and dying. It may have an accumulation of problems: sulfation, shorts, shedding of active material, etc. Like everything else, even well-maintained batteries wear out.

When testing cells with a hydrometer, write down all the specific gravities. If all the cells are uniformly low, the battery needs recharging, and if it cannot be brought up to full charge (as measured by its specific gravity), it is dying. If the difference between the highest and lowest cell readings is more than 0.050, then the low cell is probably dying. And if after recharging the difference remains over 0.050, this cell almost certainly is dying.

If a battery never needs topping up with water, it is being undercharged. This is certain to lead to sulfation and premature death.

If a battery needs frequent topping with water, it is being overcharged. Overcharging occurs when more amps are pumped in than the battery can accept. It responds by overheating and gassing. In extreme cases it will spew electrolyte from the filler caps, giving off an acrid acid smell; *it may even blow up.* If overcharging is allowed to continue, permanent damage will result. Water loss should amount to no more than two ounces of water per cell (12 ounces per battery) in 30 to 50 hours of battery charging time.

If just one cell is using excessive water, it is probably shorted.

Sulfation and Equalization: Is There Life after Death?

During repeated charges and discharges a coating of lead sulfate builds up throughout battery plates. This is called *sulfation,* and it inhibits the battery's ability either to accept a charge or to discharge. Initially the sulfate is relatively soft and porous, and the battery continues to operate, although not at peak efficiency. Over time, however, the sulfate hardens and battery performance declines steadily.

Sulfation is a particularly acute problem with deep-cycle batteries that are deeply discharged repeatedly and never brought back up to a 100 percent charge—*precisely the operating conditions of many boat batteries.* What happens is that the more accessible areas of the battery plates are recharged at each cycle, while the less accessible interior parts of the plates remain discharged; the sulfate slowly hardens. If, after charging, all cells test low with a hydrometer, sulfation is a likely problem. While the process of sulfation is inevitable, certain steps can be taken to contain the damage done.

Sulfation needs to be dealt with before it hardens. *Never leave batteries in a discharged state: The sulfate formed will harden and ruin the battery.*

Soft sulfates can be reconverted into active plate material or dislodged from plate surfaces by slowly bringing the battery back up to full charge over an extended period of time. This is known as *equalization* or "conditioning," and should be carried out on all conventional (wet) boat batteries at least once a month (more frequently in hot climates)—*especially with deep-cycle batteries.* (Gel-type batteries should *not* be equalized.) The long, slow charge allows the acid to diffuse through all the interior plate areas.

Unfortunately, there is a catch. The process of sulfation increases internal battery resistance. The battery voltage rises as accessible plate surfaces are charged, but before less accessible areas are fully charged. This fools most voltage regulators into thinking that a battery is fully charged when it is not. The regulator then shuts down the charging output and, regardless of engine running time, equalization fails to occur.

To equalize a sulfated battery, it is necessary to boost charging output voltages—sometimes as high as 16 volts. At this voltage an alternator with a standard automotive regulator would pump out too much amperage and cook the battery, with potentially explosive results. Some form of current (amperage) limiting ability is needed to hold the charging amperage under 5 percent of the total amp-hour rating of the batteries being equalized (3 to 4 percent would be better; for methods of doing this, see pages 46 to 50). The voltage regulator generally must be set to limit amperage to 3 to 5 amps, although two 8D-size batteries in parallel (400 + Ah) could probably take up to 20 amps. If the battery voltage rises rapidly, the amperage is too high. The battery temperature will need constant monitoring to make sure it does not go above 125°F (52°C). Quite a bit of gassing will occur, and the battery will need topping up with water when equalization is complete.

Remember, the gases being given off are hydrogen and oxygen, a potentially explosive mix. Be sure to vent the battery compartment adequately and ensure that nothing creates a spark. The only sure way to test for proper equalization is with a hydrometer, testing all cells repeatedly until all are up to full charge. Specific gravity then will be around 1.265 for most batteries, but will vary from battery to battery (see "Testing Your Battery" in this chapter). The battery will accept no more charge when the specific gravity readings remain unchanged for three hours. This testing is a tedious business, especially if the battery is hard to reach. Once you've done it a few times, however, the weakest cell in the battery (slowest to come to a full

charge) will become apparent, and this then is the only cell that needs to be monitored. Experience will show at what rate (amperage) the battery can be charged without overheating or excessive gassing.

To repeat, equalization cannot be carried out with standard automobile voltage regulators. It requires a purpose-built marine voltage regulator, a voltage regulator bypass device (discussed later in this chapter), or a battery charger with an adjustable output. A large-array solar panel (3 amps or more) without voltage regulation and hooked directly to the battery will work also, as will an unregulated wind generator (see Chapter 5), as long as careful attention is paid to battery voltage and temperature and the solar panel or wind generator is disconnected when equalization has occurred.

Important note: Most sensitive electronic equipment has a rated input voltage from around 11 volts DC to 16 volts DC. *Equalization voltages of 16 volts may damage such equipment.* Whenever equalizing batteries at voltages above 14.5 volts, always isolate the battery in question; at the very least, be absolutely certain all electronic equipment hooked to the battery is turned off.

Sulfated material dislodged from battery plates occasionally accumulates in the base of the battery until it partially or completely shorts out one or more cells, preventing them from coming up to charge. If slow charging at higher voltages fails to cure the problem, more drastic steps may restore at least some life to the battery. All the electrolyte (acid) must be drained (be careful!) and stored in a glass or plastic container, such as a plastic milk jug. The battery should be filled repeatedly with water, gently sloshed around and bumped, then drained. (This water will still contain some acid, so watch what you do with it.) With any luck the water will dislodge the offending debris. The electrolyte should then be strained (a pair of pantyhose works well) and put back in the battery. Top up the cells with water as necessary, then put the battery on an equalization charge and test the cells again. If one or more still will not accept a charge, the battery is useless.

Dead Gel-Type Batteries

Gel-type batteries that will not accept or hold a charge can sometimes be brought back into service with the following brutal treatment:

- Place a load on the battery (10 amps would be fine) and drag it all the way down until it shows a voltage of 1.0 volt or so. Use equipment that will not burn up as the voltage falls, such as incandescent lights.
- When the battery is completely down, finish it off by shorting out its two terminals with a length of heavy-gauge, *insulated* wire—12 gauge or larger (jumper cables work well). If the wire gets really hot the battery is not down enough; put the load back on. Leave it shorted for several hours.
- Recharge the battery. It will not recover to full capacity, but after several normal discharge-and-recharge cycles it may come back nearly to full capacity.

Self-Discharge

All batteries will discharge slowly when standing idle. The rate of discharge depends to a great extent on temperature and on certain features of internal construction. A wet lead/antimony battery will run down faster than a gel-type battery with no antimony in the plate grids. Lead/antimony batteries lose approximately 1 percent of their charge per day at 80°F (27°C), rising to 2 percent per day at 100°F (38°C) (see Figure 2-4A).

If a battery is left uncharged for two to three months, especially over the summer months, self-discharge will lead to sulfation, the sulfate will harden, and the battery will be damaged permanently. During any extended lay-up, be sure to put batteries on charge at least once a month. A small array solar panel will keep a battery topped up and prevent sulfation (see Chapter 5).

Note also that some capacity loss will occur at elevated temperatures whether the battery is in use or not. This loss is irreversible and is part of a battery's aging process (Figure 2-4B). Batteries in storage should be kept as cool as possible without freezing (Figure 2-4C).

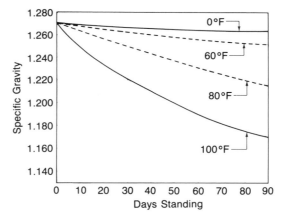

Figure 2-4A. Self-discharge rates for conventional batteries.

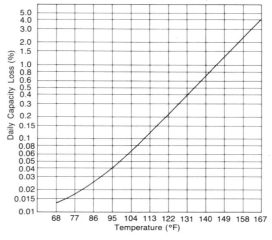

Figure 2-4B. Loss of battery capacity at high temperatures.

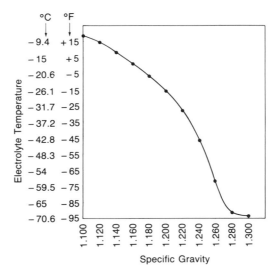

Figure 2-4C. Battery freezing points at different states of charge.

Alternators

How They Work

A magnet (the *rotor*) is spun inside a series of coils (the *stator*), as shown in Figure 2-6A. As the north and south poles of the rotor pass the coils in the stator, an electrical pulse is generated—positive for the north pole, negative for the south pole. This is alternating current (AC), so called because the direction of current flow alternates from positive to negative and back. Two alternations make a *cycle,* which can occur from a few to several million times per second. The number of cycles per second is the *frequency,* expressed as *Hertz* (Hz). Household current (AC) is commonly 60 cycles per second in the USA (50 cycles per second in the UK); its frequency is 60 Hz. The voltage and amperage generated in the alternator are determined by the strength of the magnetic field in the rotor, the number of turns of wire in the stator coils, and the speed of rotation.

In place of permanent magnets in the rotor, a soft-iron core is wrapped in a coil of wire (the *field winding*). When *direct current* (DC), which flows in only one direction, passes through the coil, the iron core is magnetized. The stronger the current, the greater the degree of magnetism. Alternator output is controlled (*regulated*) by varying the current (the *field current*) fed to the field winding.

Current is fed to the field winding via two slip rings—smooth, round, insulated discs mounted on the rotor shaft—each connected to one end of the field winding and each contacted by a spring-loaded carbon brush contained in a brush holder fixed to the alternator housing.

A refinement of the system is attained by compounding the rotor in multiple inter-

Figure 2-5. **Alternator.**

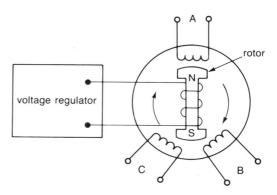

Figure 2-6A. Alternator operating principles. The rotor contains the field winding. The voltage regulator varies the direct current passing through the field winding and thus the strength of the resultant magnetic field. Three sets of windings (A, B, and C) are built into the stator, each producing AC output.

Figure 2-6B. Alternator construction. The labeled parts are: (1) multifingered rotor with field winding inside; (2) slip rings on rotor shaft; (3), (4) rotor shaft bearings; (5), (6) end housings; (7) stator housing; (8) stator windings; (9) stator laminations (serving as core for stator windings); (10) brushes (which contact slip rings when unit is assembled).

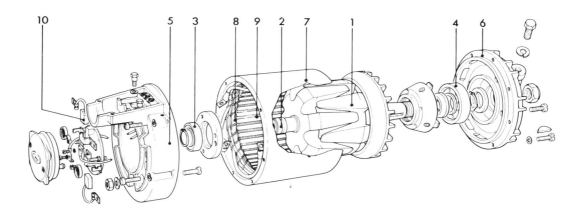

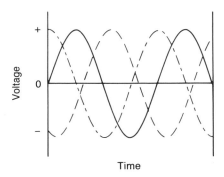

Figure 2-7. **Three-phase alternator output.**

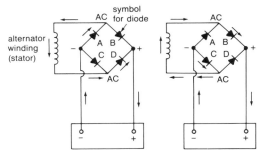

Figure 2-8A. Operation of a single-phase bridge rectifier. In the symbol for a diode, the arrow indicates the direction in which it will pass electricity. In the left-hand schematic, current is flowing in one direction from the stator winding, through diode D to the battery's positive terminal. Diodes C and B block the flow in the other direction. The return path from the battery's negative terminal to the winding (necessary to complete the circuit) is through diode A. In the schematic on the right, the AC current flow from the stator winding has reversed, passing through diode B to the positive terminal. The return path is through diode C. *The generated current has reversed direction but still flows in the same direction into the battery.*

locking fingers. This has the effect of producing multiple north and south magnetic poles when the field winding is energized.

As noted, as these north and south poles spin inside the coils of the stator, alternating current is generated in the coils. Regardless of the number of coils or windings (this varies among alternators), they are hooked up in such a way as to produce just three effective coils, the resulting power output being known as *three phase* (Figure 2-7).

Despite the multiple phases, the current from each phase is still alternating. To be of any use in charging a battery it must be *rectified* to direct current. This is done with *silicone diodes.* A diode is an electronic switch or check valve that allows electricity to flow in only one direction.

Imagine first a single-phase alternator. Each end of the stator winding is connected to two diodes. The first diode is so placed to pass only positive impulses, and is connected to the battery's positive terminal. The second diode is oriented to pass only negative impulses, and provides a return path from the negative terminal to the winding. The complete diode setup is known as a *bridge rectifier* (Figure 2-8A). Despite a constantly reversing current flow in the stator, current flows in only one direction to the battery. In a three-phase alternator the configuration is a bit more elaborate. Three positive diodes are tied together to form the alternator's positive terminal, which is connected to the positive terminal of the battery. Three more diodes are generally grounded to the alternator frame and connected to the battery via the engine block and battery ground strap. Another three auxiliary diodes (for an overall total of nine diodes) frequently are installed on the positive side of the three phases, feeding positive current to the voltage regulator and rotor field winding (via the brushes and slip

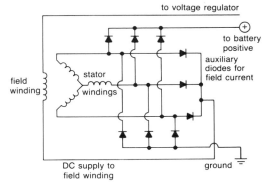

"Star"—connected nine-diode bridge

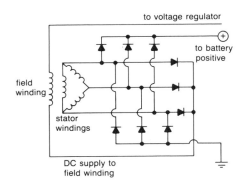

"Delta"—connected nine-diode bridge

Figure 2-8B. Schematics of two common three-phase bridge rectifiers. The only difference between the two is in the manner in which the stator windings are connected. This is not a distinction we need be concerned with. (See Appendix E for a table of electrical symbols.)

rings) to energize and control the alternator (Figure 2-8B). Sometimes there is only one auxiliary diode; occasionally none.

Since an alternator's brushes carry only the small amount of current needed to energize the field winding in the rotor they are subject to very little load and wear and rarely require maintenance. The full alternator output is taken directly from the stator.

Alternator Problems: Initial Testing

Persistent undercharging from an otherwise functioning alternator.

- The alternator may be just fine. *First check the batteries.* As discussed earlier in this chapter, dead and dying batteries will not accept a charge.
- Check the belt tension. It should not be possible to depress the longest stretch of belt with moderate finger pressure more than 3/8 to 1/2 inch. If the output has been fluctuating wildly—especially on initial start-up—perhaps accompanied by belt squeal each time the output rises, the belt is loose.
- Check that the alternator is adequately sized for the demands being made on it and that its speed of rotation is not too slow (see Chapter 1, "Sizing an Alternator")
- Check for voltage drop between the output terminal on the alternator and the positive battery post. (Voltage drop is covered in detail in Chapter 3, "What Is Electricity?") With the engine off, momentarily turn on a few loads (lights, etc.) to discharge the battery. Now start the engine and immediately, while the alternator is still at full output, test between the alternator output terminal and the battery positive post with a volt-ohm meter (VOM) set to the 10 volts DC scale. (The meter's positive lead goes to the alternator output terminal. Stay clear of the alternator drive belt!) If the meter shows no deflection, or only a slight deflection, switch to a lower scale (2.5 volts DC; see Figure 2-9A). If you're not sure how to use a VOM, see Chapter 3, "Multimeters: The Essential Tool."

In a system with split-charging diodes (discussed later in this chapter) the meter should show no more than 1.0 volt at full alternator output; without diodes, no more than 0.5 volt (Figure 2-9). *Any reading above this indicates excessive voltage drop;* the wiring is inadequate or there is unwanted resistance in the circuit, possibly caused by loose, dirty, or corroded terminals (see Chapter 3, "Troubleshooting Techniques").

Troubleshooting Alternators
(see also Charts 2-1, 2-2, and 2-3)

Undercharging

- Check the batteries.
- Check the belt tension.
- Check that the alternator capacity and speed of rotation are adequate.
- Check for voltage drop between the alternator output terminal and the battery positive post *at full alternator output.*
- If voltage drop is present check all wiring, connections, and switches. Where split-charging diodes are fitted, check that voltage regulation has been compensated to match.
- Check all wiring and connections to external regulators; check the voltage regulator setting.
- Check the alternator: brushes, brush springs, diodes, and stator.

Overcharging

- Check the batteries and their temperature
- Check any voltage regulator bypass or unregulated wind charger, solar panel, etc.
- Check the voltage regulator sensing line for breaks or poor connections, and the voltage regulator for shorts.
- Adjust the voltage regulator.

No Output

- Check for a loose or broken drive belt.
- Check all external wiring and connections.
- Determine P or N type and provide field current via a test lamp where possible.
- *If output:* Check the voltage regulation and field circuit for lack of excitation; an open circuit in the voltage regulator or its wiring; brushes worn or out of contact with slip rings; a shorted or open-circuited rotor.
- *If no output:* Check for a shorted or open-circuited stator or diode.

Troubleshooting Chart 2-1.

Battery/Alternator/Regulator Problems: Undercharging.
Symptom: Battery never seems to regain full charge.

Is the battery dead, dying, sulfated, or shorted? (*Sulfated:* charges rapidly but won't hold charge in use. *Shorted:* loses charge rapidly while standing idle. *Dying:* Cannot be brought up to full charge. *Dead:* Will not accept charge; may gas and lose electrolyte during attempts to recharge.) **TEST:** Check specific gravity, measure open-circuit voltage, or use load tester (page 26).	**YES → FIX:** A sulfated battery will sometimes recover with equalization (page 27). External shorts may be caused by dirt and moisture on battery top; clean carefully (page 22). Look for leaks to ground in boat's wiring (Chapter 3) or equipment inadvertently left on. Dead, dying, and internally shorted batteries must be resurrected (rarely possible) or replaced.
Is belt tension inadequate? (Belt squeals, output fluctuates wildly.) **NO → TEST:** Look for slipping belt; check tension. Belt should depress no more than ½ inch in response to moderate finger pressure.	**YES → FIX:** Increase belt tension.
Is circuit between alternator and battery incomplete, inadequate, or dirty? **NO → TEST:** With volt-ohm meter (VOM) check for voltage drop between alternator output terminal and battery positive post at full alternator output (page 32). Voltage drop with split-charging diodes should be no more than 1.0 volt; without diodes, no more than 0.5 volt.	**YES → FIX:** Clean and tighten loose, dirty, or corroded connectors and terminals; replace faulty or undersize wiring.
Is alternator too small or its speed of rotation too slow? Is charging time inadequate? **NO → TEST:** Compare demands on alternator with its size and speed of rotation as outlined in Chapter 1. Try charging the battery for at least 3 hours, measuring battery voltage frequently.	**YES → FIX:** Match alternator with demands (see Chapter 1). Increase routine charging time.
Are one or more connections in any external voltage regulator field circuit (page 46) dirty or loose? **NO → TEST:** Check external wiring and connectors.	**YES → FIX:** Clean and tighten.
Is the voltage regulator functioning improperly or at a setting that is too low? **NO → TEST:** With the batteries at or near full charge, the alternator running, and all loads turned off, measure voltage between battery positive and negative posts. Should be no less than 14.0–14.4 volts.	**YES → FIX:** See "Voltage Regulators" section in this chapter.
Is alternator broken? **TEST:** Check diodes, stator windings for open circuits; check for worn brushes, brush springs, or improper contact with slip rings. Check for shorted rotor.	**YES → FIX:** Clean, repair, or replace as necessary (pages 38–43).

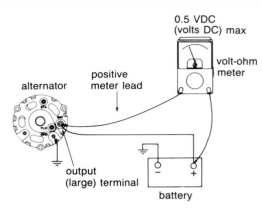

Figure 2-9A. Measuring the voltage drop between an alternator and a battery: no split-charging diodes. First draw down the battery slightly by turning on cabin lights, freshwater tap, etc., with the engine off. Then start the engine and immediately hook up the volt-ohm meter as shown, being careful to avoid the alternator drive belt. You should detect no more than a 0.5-volt drop.

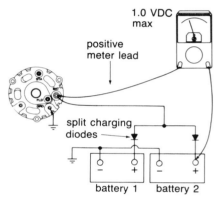

Figure 2-9B. Measuring the voltage drop between an alternator and batteries: with split-charging diodes. You should detect no more than a 1.0-volt drop.

• With the batteries *at or near full charge, the alternator running,* and *all loads turned off,* check the battery voltage from the positive to the negative post. It should read at least 14.0 volts —on many marine systems, as high as 14.4 volts. If the measured voltage is less than this refer to "Voltage Regulators," later in this chapter.

• Check all the connections in any external field circuit (see below, page 46) to make sure they are clean and tight.

• Only if none of the preceding tests reveals the problem should you suspect the alternator. One or more diodes or stator windings may be open-circuited (page 39), or the brushes may be worn or not

making good contact with their slip rings—in which case output is likely to be erratic (page 40).

Persistent overcharging. This is a problem with the batteries or voltage regulation. Refer to the relevant sections in this chapter and in Chapter 1.

No output. If an alternator appears not to be charging at all (the ignition warning light stays on, the battery remains discharged, etc.), the first task is to confirm that it is really the alternator that is at fault.

• With the engine shut down, all auxiliary charging devices (wind generator, solar panels) turned off, the battery switched into the starting circuit (the relevant battery isolation switch "ON"), and the engine ignition switch "ON" (but without the engine running), check the battery voltage across the battery terminals with a voltmeter. The voltage should be around 12.5. Now check the voltage between the output, or positive, terminal (the big one) on the alternator and a good ground, or negative, such as a clean spot on the engine block, unless the alternator has an insulated return (see page 65), in which case the ground or negative connection must be made at the negative terminal on the alternator or battery.

• In a single-battery installation without isolating diodes, the voltage at the alternator output should be the same as battery voltage (Figure 2-10A). In a dual battery installation, there may well be isolating diodes between the alternator and batteries to provide independent split charging of the batteries, in which case the voltage at the alternator output (with the engine shut down) will read zero (Figure 2-10B). *If the voltage is neither battery voltage nor zero, there is a problem in the circuit between the alternator and battery.*

• If the circuit seems OK, start the engine, speed it up, and recheck the voltage at the alternator output. *Whatever the system it should read a volt or more above the original battery voltage.* If it does not, there is a problem with the alternator or its voltage regulator; the next task is to decide which.

P-and N-type alternators. Some alternators have internal regulators, and in this

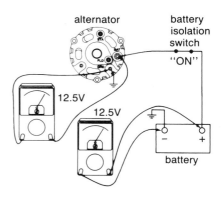

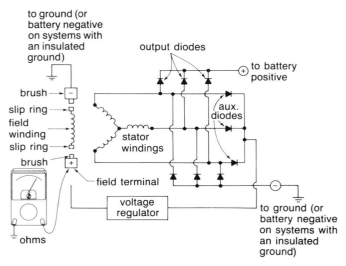

Figure 2-10A. Measuring voltage at the battery and at the alternator output terminal: no split-charging diodes. The battery isolation switch and the ignition switch are on, but the engine is *not* running. There should be a 12.5-volt reading across the battery terminals, and the voltage reading between the alternator output terminal and ground should also be 12.5.

Figure 2-11A. P-type alternator schematic. See accompanying text for test procedure.

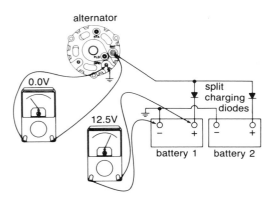

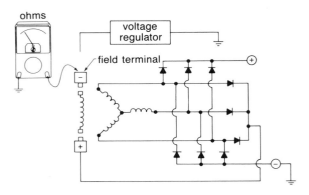

Figure 2-10B. Measuring voltage at the battery and at the alternator output terminal: with split-charging diodes. Preparations are as outlined in Figure 2-10A. Voltage reading across the battery terminals should be 12.5; voltage reading between the alternator output terminal and ground should be zero.

Figure 2-11B. N-type alternator. Like the P type except that the voltage regulator is on the negative side of the field winding. See accompanying text for test procedure.

case there is little to be done when a problem is traced to the alternator or regulator except fit a new alternator. (The section on voltage regulators later in this chapter has a few more suggestions.) Many alternators, however, have external regulators controlling the current to the alternator field winding via a terminal on the back of the alternator marked "F," "DF," or "FIELD." Most external regulators are connected on the positive side of the field winding (these are P-type alternators), but a few are connected between the negative side of the field winding and ground (N-type alternators). More on this in the section on voltage regulators, later in this chapter. The first task is to decide whether you have a P- or N-type alternator (see Figure 2-11).

Shut down the engine, *turn off the ignition and battery isolation switches*, and disconnect the field wire from the alternator. Using a volt-ohm meter on its lowest ohms scale (R × 1), test between the field terminal on the alternator and ground. P types will give a reading near zero ohms; N types give a high reading (Figure 2-11).

Voltage regulator or alternator? Now we need to bypass the voltage regulator and supply current directly to the alternator field winding. If this causes the alternator to work, it tells us that the voltage regulator is bad. If the alternator still fails to work, it tells us the alternator itself is at fault. To bypass the voltage regulator we

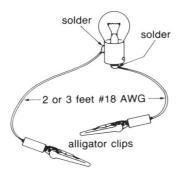

Figure 2-12A. **Test light.**

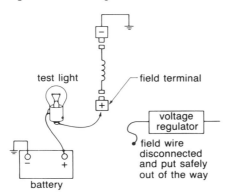

Figure 2-12B. **Bypassing the voltage regulator on a P-type alternator.** Connect the test light as shown, start the engine, and measure the alternator output voltage as in Figure 2-10. If it is now normal (a volt or more above original battery voltage), the regulator is defective; if it is not, the alternator is defective.

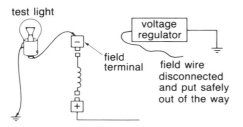

Figure 2-12C. **Bypassing the voltage regulator on an N-type alternator.** Test as in Figure 2-12B.

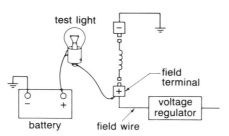

Figure 2-12D. **"Flashing the field" on a P-type** alternator. If the test in Figure 2-12B showed normal output, shut down the engine, then reconnect the field wire from the voltage regulator. Start the engine. With the engine running, connect the test light momentarily between the battery and field terminal. If alternator output is restored (test as in Figure 12-10), the excitation circuit has failed.

need to make up a test light as shown (Figure 2-12A), with a minimum 12-watt (1-amp) light bulb. Disconnect the wire at the field terminal ("F," "DF," or "FIELD") on the alternator and put it safely out of the way, where it cannot short out.

If the alternator is a P type, connect the test light between the positive terminal on the battery and the field terminal (Figure 2-12B).

If the alternator is an N type, connect the test light between the field terminal and a good ground (Figure 2-12C).

Start the engine. If the alternator is putting out now it means that it is OK, but its voltage regulator is defective. The current flowing through the test light is energizing the field winding and so bypassing the voltage regulator, which is why we now have output. If the alternator still does not produce output, the alternator itself is defective.

If a VOM is not available, or if there is any doubt as to whether the alternator is a P or N type, with the engine running try connecting the test light from the field terminal, first to the battery positive and then to ground. If there is no output on either test, the alternator is bad.

Excitation tests. The last test: If the test light from the battery to the field terminal produced output from a P-type alternator, *reconnect the field wire from the voltage regulator* and crank the engine. Connect the test light *momentarily* between the battery and field terminal *with the engine still running.* This is known as *flashing the field* (Figure 2-12D). If the test light restores output and the alternator continues to work after the light is disconnected, we have nothing more than a failure of the excitation circuit—a simple problem to fix (see page 50).

N-type excitation is a little more complicated. If an N-type excitation circuit has failed, none of the tests to date will have produced any output.

N-type alternators with external regulators generally have either an auxiliary output terminal (sometimes marked "AUX") or an external excitation wire supplying current to the field winding (sometimes both; see Voltage Regulators, page 46). Connecting the test light momentarily between the battery positive and either the auxiliary or excitation terminal will restore lost excitation.

Last resort. With a really dead battery many alternators just will not start produc-

Maintaining and Troubleshooting Your Battery-Powered Electrical System

ing output, and none of the above tests is possible. However, a 6-volt battery or half a dozen flashlight (torch) batteries connected in series will provide enough current to get things moving. Connect the battery ground (negative) to the alternator case or a good ground on the engine and the positive as described in the previous excitation tests. In the case of an alternator with an insulated ground, connect the battery ground to the boat battery's negative terminal or the alternator's negative terminal.

Troubleshooting voltage regulators is dealt with in more detail later. The following sections deal with alternator repairs.

Alternator Problems: What May Be Wrong

Mechanical problems. The more obvious mechanical failures include: a slipping or broken drive belt; a stripped pulley key, so that the pulley turns on its shaft; worn bearings, normally at the pulley end of the shaft (these make a distinctive, medium-pitched rumble). If the drive belt is removed it should not be possible to move a pulley from side to side; it will move only fractionally in and out.

Note that the tachometer on many engines works by measuring the frequency of the alternator's AC output (before rectification), which varies directly with engine speed. Any time a tachometer reading is low or erratic, suspect a slipping alternator drive belt. Belts are especially prone to slip immediately after engine start-up, when alternator loads are at their highest. A slipping belt will frequently give off a high-pitched, often cyclical squeal.

Burnout. Marine alternators are subjected to prolonged periods of high loading in hot engine compartments, and thus are far more likely to burn out than in the comparatively benign automotive environment. Factors contributing to their early demise are the need to recharge deeply discharged large-capacity batteries and, in order to speed up charge rates, the use of higher voltage regulator settings, often coupled with devices that bypass or override voltage regulators altogether.

Prolonged high loading will overheat bearings, diodes, and voltage regulators, and cause any of these to fail. It also will melt the thin, lacquered insulation on coils. This could result in a short circuit or

---

Troubleshooting Chart 2-2.
Battery/Alternator/Regulator Problems: Overcharging.
Symptoms: Battery overheats, "boils," requires frequent topping up with water, and gives off an acrid smell.

Is battery dead, dying or sulfated? (If so, it may behave as if overcharged, but will not come to or hold a full charge.) **NO** **TEST:** Check specific gravity, measure open-circuit voltage, or use load tester (page 26).	**YES** **FIX:** Equalization (page 27) may restore battery to service. If not, replace.
Is battery in a location that is too hot? **NO** **TEST:** Measure temperature of battery compartment. If excessively hot, should be remedied.	**YES** **FIX:** Increase ventilation to compartment, or move battery.
Is the voltage regulator set slightly high for faster charge rates? **NO** **TEST:** Monitor the battery voltage during charging. As the battery comes up to full charge, its voltage should not go above 14.4 volts.	**YES** **FIX:** It may be wise *not* to "fix" this. Occasional mild overcharging is often the price to be paid for realistically fast charge rates. See text.
Is a voltage regulator bypass device being used incorrectly? **NO** **TEST:** Monitor the battery voltage and battery temperature during charging. Voltage should not go above 14.4 volts (except during equalization, page 27) and battery temperature should not go much above 110°F (43.3°C).	**YES** **FIX:** Adjust manual rheostat on bypass device to reduce alternator output. Switch off manual bypass when battery is fully charged.
Is an unregulated wind generator or solar panel overcharging the battery? **NO** **TEST:** As above. See Chapter 5 to estimate probable inputs from these sources.	**YES** **FIX:** See Chapter 5.
Is the voltage regulator's battery-sensing wire disconnected or broken? Has a diode been installed backwards in the sensing wire? Both will lead to violent overcharging, causing vigorous boiling and rapid water loss. **NO** **TEST:** Visual inspection. Corroded sensing-wire terminals will have a similar though less dramatic effect.	**YES** **FIX:** Replace sensing wire. Clean terminals. Put the diode in correctly (see page 52).
Is the voltage regulator short-circuited? This will lead to violent overcharging. **TEST:** Fit a spare and see whether problem disappears.	**YES** **FIX:** Replace voltage regulator.

could burn through the coil wire like a fuse, breaking the circuit. Burned coils have a distinctive smell—once encountered, easily remembered!

Brush wear. In time, brushes wear down, spring pressure decreases, and the brushes fail to seat properly on their slip rings. Brush failure will lead to improper energizing (*excitation*) of the field winding and erratic or failed alternator output.

Corrosion. With a few honorable exceptions (Lucas Marine alternators for one), alternators are not built of marine-grade materials. Exposure to salt spray, or just to the marine atmosphere, will lead to corrosion of parts and electrical terminals. Moving parts tend to freeze with intermittent use; brush springs are particularly prone to failure. A periodic shot of WD 40 or electrical cleaner in and around alternator housings goes a long way toward keeping things moving and reducing corrosion on terminals.

Marine-grade alternators should have the following characteristics: an insulated ground (earth) return that does not use the alternator frame (see page 65); brass brush holders; plated brush springs and other metal parts (the springs are especially important); impregnated windings to maintain insulation levels; and effective electrical noise (interference) suppression (see page 188). Marine alternators will cost twice as much as automotive alternators with the same output, but will last five times longer.

Dirt. The cooling fans on alternators located in dirty, greasy, smoky engine rooms pick up the oily mist and blow it all through the alternator. In time a greasy buildup of dirt coats and *insulates* coils, diodes, etc., causing the alternator to run hot, making burnout more likely.

Open-circuit and reverse polarity. Anytime an alternator is electrically disconnected (such as by turning off the battery isolation switch) *while still running,* the residual energy in the stator and field windings momentarily produces continued output with no place to go. This voltage can easily peak at several hundred volts or more, blowing out all the diodes and the voltage regulator. *This can happen in a fraction of a second! Never disconnect a running alternator!* The diodes will be blown out even more certainly by connecting a battery with reverse polarity—connecting the

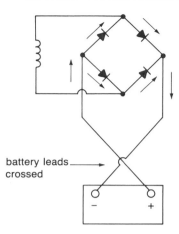

Figure 2-13. **The effect of reverse polarity on diodes.** The result is a direct electrical path from positive to negative terminal—a dead short. Full battery current will flow, burning out the diodes instantly.

positive lead to the negative terminal and vice versa (Figure 2-13). *When reconnecting batteries be absolutely sure to get the cables the right way around!* Be especially careful when installing new batteries; the position of the terminals may be reversed from one model to another.

It is possible to fit *snubbers* (reverse-avalanche silicon diodes)—otherwise known as surge-protection devices—between an alternator output terminal and ground. These special diodes are set to open well above alternator output voltage, but well below the destruction voltage of the alternator diodes. Anytime an alternator is open-circuited, the snubber senses the rising voltage and dumps the alternator output to ground, deenergizing the field winding, stopping any further output, and so saving the diodes. Snubbers have a limited load-carrying capability; larger alternators would need to have two or more fitted in parallel.

It is also possible to fit special "fast fuses," which will protect against accidental reverse polarity. Lucas makes three sizes suitable for alternators up to 120 amps output.

Maintaining and Repairing Alternators

Alternators are virtually maintenance-free. After prolonged use the brushes may need replacing (see page 39), but some alternators are brushless. Should an alternator fail altogether the most likely culprit is blown diodes or a defective voltage regulator. To determine which see "Alternator

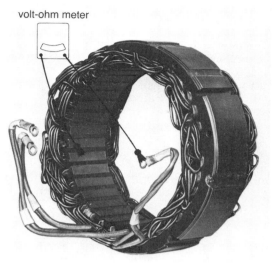

volt-ohm meter

Figure 2-14. Checking a stator for shorts to ground.

Problems: Initial Testing," earlier in this chapter. If the alternator itself is at fault, it is usually possible to determine whether the problem is in the rotor assembly or the stator and diodes (see page 40), but this is generally academic since repair parts are unlikely to be on board! If the problem is in the stator and diodes, the diodes are almost certainly to blame; but confirming this is a fairly involved procedure requiring a certain amount of alternator disassembly. Those adventurous souls wishing to get heavily into alternator repairs should obtain a copy of *The 12-Volt Doctor's Alternator Book,* by Edgar J. Beyn. The rest of us should always carry a spare alternator. Have the deceased rejuvenated by a professional alternator rebuilder; it then becomes the spare.

Replacing brushes. Unfortunately there are not just dozens but hundreds of different alternators. Some have external brush holders; some brush holders are internal; others are incorporated in externally attached voltage-regulator housings. If the brush holders are not self-evident, but the alternator has an externally attached regulator—often a fairly compact, box-like unit, normally held on with two screws—unscrew this and the brushes usually will be found inside.

Independently mounted external brush holders generally consist of a small plastic housing held with one or two screws, within which are one or two spade terminals. The housing is withdrawn from the alternator and the spade terminals released by pressing down their retaining tags with a small screwdriver and pushing

Troubleshooting Chart 2-3.
Battery/Alternator/Regulator Problems: No Alternator Output.
Symptoms: Ignition warning light stays on, battery remains discharged.

Is the drive belt loose or broken? **NO TEST:** The belt should respond to finger pressure with no more than ½ inch give at its midpoint.	**YES FIX:** Tighten or replace.
Is the circuit between the alternator and battery at fault? **NO TEST:** Shut down engine, isolate or shut down auxiliary chargers (solar panels, wind generator, etc.), turn on battery isolation switch, turn on engine ignition switch (but without starting engine) and check voltage (1) across the battery terminals and (2) between alternator output and ground. Voltage across the battery terminals should be about 12.5. If voltage at alternator output terminal is neither about the same as battery voltage (no isolating diodes) or zero (isolating diodes, dual battery installation), the circuit between alternator and battery is faulty.	**YES FIX:** Check all wiring and connections. Clean and replace as necessary.
Does the alternator have an internal voltage regulator? **NO TEST:** Look for absence of alternator field terminal, field wire, and external regulator.	**YES FIX:** If a lack-of-output problem has been traced this far and the regulator is internal, there is little option but to install a new alternator.
If the voltage regulator is external, is it a P-type or an N-type? **TEST:** Shut down engine, turn off ignition and battery isolation switches, and disconnect field wire from alternator. Measure resistance between field terminal and ground. P-type = reading near zero ohms; N-type = high reading.	►**P-type FIX:** Proceed with Steps 1–3 below. ►**N-type FIX:** Proceed with Steps 4–6 below.
(1) Does the alternator fail to work when the P-type voltage regulator is bypassed? **NO TEST:** Connect a test lamp between alternator field terminal and battery positive terminal. Start the engine. Look for alternator output in excess of battery voltage.	**YES FIX:** Alternator is broken. Check for shorted or open-circuited stator or diode. See pages 38–43 for possible repair procedure.
(2) If the alternator worked in Step 1, the voltage regulator is defective. Is it merely a failure of the excitation circuit? **NO TEST:** Shut down the engine. Reconnect the alternator field wire. Restart the engine. Connect the test lamp momentarily between the field terminal and the battery positive terminal. If alternator output is restored and continues after the light is disconnected, the excitation circuit is at fault.	**YES FIX:** Repair is comparatively simple (page 50).

(Chart 2-3 continued)

(3) If Step 2 failed to restore continuous output, the regulator needs to be replaced.

(4) Does the alternator work when the N-type voltage regulator is bypassed? **NO** **TEST:** Connect a test lamp between alternator field terminal and a good ground. Start the engine. Look for alternator output in excess of battery voltage.	**YES** **FIX:** Voltage regulator is defective and needs to be replaced.
(5) Is the voltage regulator's excitation circuit defective? **NO** **TEST:** Shut down the engine. Reconnect the alternator field wire. Restart the engine. Connect the test lamp momentarily between the battery positive terminal and the alternator auxiliary or excitation terminal. See whether alternator output voltage comes up and stays up.	**YES** **FIX:** Repair is comparatively simple (page 50).

(6) If Step 5 failed to restore output, the alternator is defective. Check for shorted or open-circuited stator or diode. See pages 38–43 for possible repair procedures.

them inward; this will free the brushes. The housing needs cleaning before new brushes are fitted. When being fitted, some brushes must be held in place in their housings with a small screwdriver or a toothpick inserted through a small hole in the body of the alternator.

Internal brushes are trickier. The whole rear end of the alternator—generally held on with four screws—must be removed. Be careful not to damage or break any wire as the rear end comes loose. Make a note of the position of any wiring you may need to disconnect. The brush holders will be self-evident. Disconnect any wires to the brushes (note their position once again); the holders then can be unscrewed and the brushes replaced.

Testing rotors. *Isolate the alternator* (switch off the battery isolation and ignition switches). This is essential to avoid damaging your volt-ohm meter during the following tests.

On alternators with external regulators, disconnect the field wire coming from the voltage regulator; disconnect the alternator output lead; set a VOM (volt-ohm meter) to the R × 1 scale, and test between the field terminal and the alternator case.

With P-type alternators (the alternator type was determined earlier during the initial testing; see page 34), the meter should give a very low reading—close to zero ohms. A very high reading indicates an open circuit in the field winding (it is burned out) or the brushes are not in contact with their slip rings. Check the brushes and springs before writing off the rotor. With a low reading the field winding may be OK, but then again it may be shorted to ground; most meters are insufficiently sensitive to tell. To test for a short, connect a line containing a low-amperage fuse (5 to 10 amps maximum—the fuse is *very important*) from the positive terminal of the battery to the field terminal of the alternator. If the fuse blows, the rotor is shorted.

With N-type alternators, a volt-ohm meter (R × 100 scale) connected between the field terminal and ground (with the field wire disconnected) should show an open circuit (a very high reading). A low reading indicates a short to ground. The high reading may also be due to an open circuit in the rotor itself, but there is no easy way to check this.

Rotors on alternators with internal or attached regulators (i.e., with no external field terminal) can be tested if access can

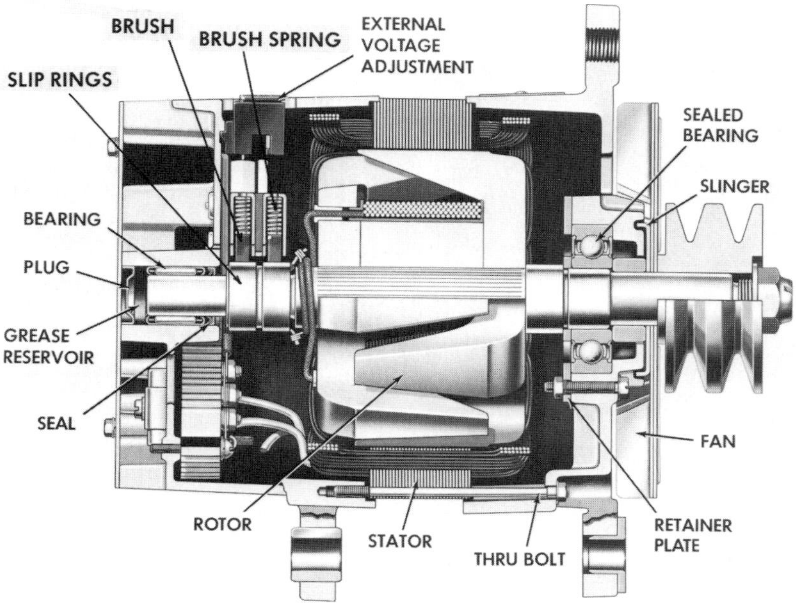

BRUSH
BRUSH SPRING
SLIP RINGS
EXTERNAL VOLTAGE ADJUSTMENT
SEALED BEARING
SLINGER
BEARING
PLUG
GREASE RESERVOIR
SEAL
ROTOR
STATOR
THRU BOLT
RETAINER PLATE
FAN

Figure 2-15A. Internally regulated alternator.

Figure 2-15B. Alternator and regulator connections: two variations.

tachometer connection
field terminal
ground connections
diode
alternator output
rectifying diodes
regulator voltage sensing wire

externally attached voltage regulator
regulator ground wire
ground wire (to engine block)
field (battery) excitation connection (goes to the ignition switch)
alternator output

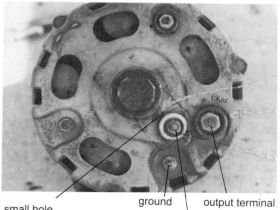

small hole used to hold back brushes during reassembly
ground terminal
field terminal
output terminal (to battery)
field terminal

Figure 2-16A. (**Left**) Brush location and replacement on an alternator with external voltage regulator but internal brushes. This is a back view of the alternator.

Figure 2-16B. (**Right**) A toothpick in the hole holds back the brushes. (The nut and insulating washer on the field terminal have been removed.)

Figure 2-16C. Internal views of the same alternator.

Figure 2-16D. Close-up of the brush holder with brushes in place. The two alternator halves must be separated and the rotor removed in order to gain access to the brushes. In this alternator the brush holder does not have to be unscrewed to change the brushes; the brushes pop out of the holders under their spring pressure when the rotor is removed. The new brushes are pushed in against their springs and held with the toothpick until the rotor is replaced.

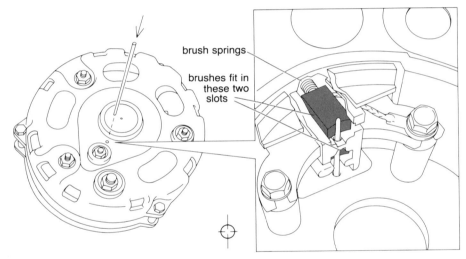

brush springs

brushes fit in these two slots

Figure 2-17A. (**Left**) Rotor testing, P-type alternator, external regulator. BAT is the output terminal (leading to the battery's positive terminal); FLD is the field terminal.

Figure 2-17B. (**Right**) Rotor testing, N-type alternator, external regulator.

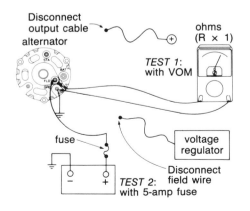

Disconnect output cable
alternator

ohms (R × 1)

TEST 1: with VOM

voltage regulator

fuse

TEST 2: with 5-amp fuse

Disconnect field wire

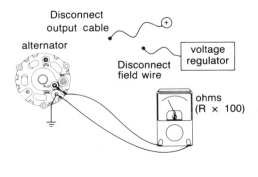

Disconnect output cable
alternator

voltage regulator

Disconnect field wire

ohms (R × 100)

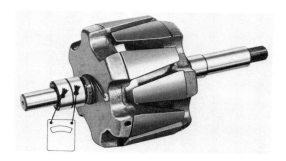

Figure 2-18. Alternator rotor testing with a VOM. Touching the leads to the two slip rings as shown should yield a low ohm reading. A high reading indicates an open circuit in the rotor. Check also from each slip ring to the rotor shaft (R × 100 scale); there should be no continuity (i.e., the reading should be infinity).

be gained to the brushes or slip rings. The VOM leads are touched to the two slip rings for the ohms test. Both P and N types should give a low reading. A high reading (infinity) indicates an open circuit in the rotor. The fuse test is made by connecting the wire from the battery to the positive brush or slip ring. If in doubt, try both brushes. With P-type alternators, only the negative brush should blow the fuse; with N types *neither* brush should blow the fuse. If both brushes blow the fuse, regardless of alternator type, the rotor is shorted.

Voltage Regulators

In Chapter 1 we identified *undercharging* as the number one cause of battery death (via sulfation), and *overcharging* as the number two cause (via erosion of the positive plate grid). We also noted that in cases of intermittent battery charging—and that describes the situation on most boats—voltage regulator settings high enough to minimize damage from undercharging are almost certain to cause occasional damage from overcharging. In this chapter, we have seen the need to equalize batteries from time to time, something that cannot be done with conventional voltage regulators.

This section looks at voltage regulators and some ways to deal with these problems.

How They Work

A voltage regulator controls the output of an alternator by varying the current supplied to the field winding (see page 30). A change of only 1 amp in the field current will alter alternator output by up to 50 amps. Formerly, voltage regulation was a mechanical affair; now it is almost always done with solid-state electronics. Whatever the method, the process is essentially the same, and is most easily understood by referring to mechanical regulators.

Mechanical regulators. These normally are found with generators (dynamos) and

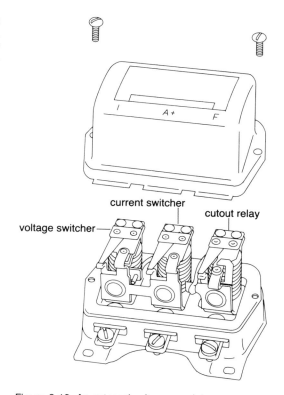

Figure 2-19. **An external voltage regulator.**

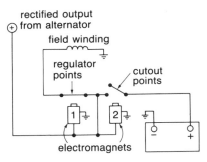

rectified output
from alternator

field winding

regulator
points

cutout
points

electromagnets

Figure 2-20A. Operating principles of a P-type mechanical voltage regulator. The engine is at rest. The cutout points are open; the regulator points, closed. The field winding is isolated from the battery.

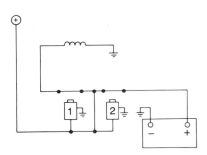

Figure 2-20B. Initial generator output. Electromagnets are energized. Electromagnet 2 closes the cutout points, allowing charging current to reach the battery. But generator output is insufficient for electromagnet 1 to open the regulator points against spring pressure. The generator also feeds the field winding.

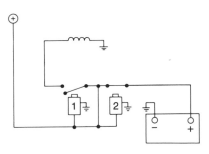

Figure 2-20C. As generator output increases, the cutout points are held closed while increasing magnetism on electromagnet 1 opens the regulator points against spring pressure. This cuts the field current, causing generator output to decline. Electromagnet 1 loses magnetism until the regulator points close once again, restoring the field current and causing output to build back up. This cycle is repeated hundreds of times per minute.

invariably are mounted as a separate unit from the generator. The regulators have spring-loaded switches (*points*). One set of points (the *cutout points*) is held open when the generator is not producing current; the other set (the *regulator points*) is held closed. The open cutout points isolate the generator so that no current drains from the battery into the field winding when the unit is not running (Figure 2-20A).

When the generator is running it feeds current into an electromagnet on the cutout points, energizing it, which closes the cutout points and completes the circuit back to the battery. When the engine stops the generator stops generating current, the electromagnet deenergizes, the spring opens the cutout points, and the circuit is broken once again (Figure 2-20B).

Actually regulating the voltage is the function of the regulator points. When the generator starts to generate, current to the field winding passes through them, and through the points' electromagnet, energizing it and pulling open the points against a spring. This open-circuits the field winding, its magnetism declines, and the output of the generator falls off, in turn reducing the current to the electromagnet holding open the regulator points; the electromagnet loses magnetism, and the spring closes the regulator points once again, restoring current flow to the field winding and restarting the process. Typically the regulator points open and close hundreds of times a minute. By altering the spring pressure on the points, it is possible to regulate the voltage at which they open, and thus regulate the output of the generator (Figure 2-20C).

There may well be a third set of points, operating in much the same fashion, to limit the maximum output (amperage) of the generator and so protect it from overloading and burning up. These will be connected in series with the regulator points (Figure 2-19).

Solid-state regulators. Alternators are almost universally equipped with solid-state regulators. The principles of operation are the same as with mechanical regulators, except that the mechanical contact points are replaced with transistors. These are set to open at a certain voltage, cutting the current to the field winding (rotor). When output voltage has fallen to a preset level, the transistors close. This cycle happens *hundreds of times a second* (as opposed to hundreds of times a minute in a mechanical regulator), making for extremely precise voltage regulation, but at the cost of often severe radio interference (see page 185).

Since the rectifying diodes in an alternator prevent the flow of current from a battery back into the field winding (rotor) when the unit is at rest (see page 31), solid-state regulators require no cutout circuit. However, should a battery be hooked up backward (negative and positive leads crossed over), reverse current will flow through the diodes, which will overheat and blow out immediately. You'll need a new alternator. I'll risk being redundant: *Hook your battery up correctly—negative to negative, positive to positive.*

Ignition circuits and excitation. The observant reader will have noticed that the generator or alternator output is used to supply current to the field winding. However, when a generator or alternator is first started, there is no output. Without output there is no field current. Without field current there can be no output. Some initial *excitation* of the field winding is needed to break this vicious circle. Two approaches are used:

• The field winding in the rotor is designed to retain a certain amount of residual magnetism when the generator or alternator is shut down. This is sufficient to produce a low output when the generator or alternator rotor begins to spin. This output feeds back to the field winding, builds up its magnetism, and restores full output.

• A separate feed from the battery to the field winding provides initial excitation. Since the field winding would drain the battery through this line when the generator or alternator is shut down, a switch is incorporated in the circuit. This is normally an ignition switch, but sometimes an oil pressure or fuel pressure switch (or both) is used. With a pressure switch the engine must build up pressure to close the switch before the generator or alternator will kick in. (If problems are experienced with excitation, try jumping out the switches; Figure 2-21.)

An ignition warning light included in an excitation circuit will glow as long as current flows from the battery through the field winding to ground. Once the generator or alternator starts to put out, it supplies current to the winding. There is now the same, or nearly the same, voltage at both ends of the excitation circuit: generator or alternator output at one end; battery voltage at the other. Without a voltage differential no current will flow (see Chapter 3) and the warning light goes out.

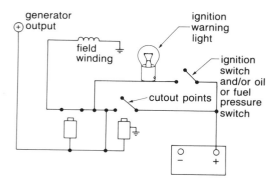

Figure 2-21. Mechanical voltage regulator (P type) with excitation circuit. Closing the switch provides initial field current. The battery discharges through the ignition light into the field winding, lighting up the lamp. When generator output builds, the cutout points close. There is now equal voltage on both sides of the ignition warning light, and the light goes out.

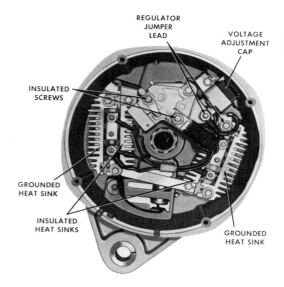

Figure 2-22. An N-type regulator, just one of hundreds of available internal regulators.

Different Regulators: Internal, External; P and N

There are hundreds of different regulators in common use. Many are completely internal; others are classified as internal but are attached to the alternator's outside casing, which makes them and their wiring more accessible. Some alternators—especially high-output alternators—have separate, external regulators mounted as an independent unit. These are preferred in boat use as they make troubleshooting and emergency repairs so much easier.

Regulators fall into two broad types: P and N. As we have seen, all regulators function by repeatedly making and breaking the current to the field winding. It is irrelevant whether this is done on the supply side (P—positive) of the winding or the return side (N—negative, or ground): the end result is the same (see Figures 2–11A and 2–11B). Almost all external regulators are P type; most internal regulators, especially on smaller alternators (up to 55 amps), are N type.

"Alternator Problems: Initial Testing" (earlier in this chapter), outlined a procedure for testing external regulators and determining their type. Some attached regulators can be unscrewed and their wires disconnected without removing the brush holders. These can be tested the same way, by connecting the test light to the field wire brush (see below). If the alternator has a wire to only one brush, it is probably a P type (the other brush is grounded). If wires run to both brushes, it is probably an N type. To double-check, turn off the ignition and battery isolation switches, disconnect the voltage regulator leads from the brushes, and test in turn between each brush and ground with a volt-ohm meter set to its lowest scale (R × 1). P types will read near zero ohms on both brushes; N types will give high readings.

The field wire. Alternators with external regulators have a terminal on the back to receive the field wire. This terminal will be labelled "F," "DF," or "FIELD." Externally attached internal regulators must be unscrewed from the back of the alternator to expose the field wire or wires. Some externally sensed units have two field wires: one connected to the battery excitation line, the other to the voltage regulator. This is the main field wire. The field wire normally is connected by a spade terminal (marked "F" or "DF") to one of the two brushes. In the absence of internal identification, or in the case of completely internal regulators, determining the field wire becomes rather involved and is beyond the scope of this book.

The excitation wire. If fitted, the battery excitation wire will come from the alternator (internal regulator) or regulator (externally attached and external regulators) to a pressure switch mounted on the engine block and/or to the ignition switch, generally via an ignition warning light.

Battery sensing (voltage regulation) wire. The battery sensing wire, which determines voltage regulation, may come from the battery itself (*battery sensed*) but is more likely to be taken from the alternator (*machine sensed*), either from an auxiliary terminal (sometimes labeled "AUX") on the back of the alternator (external and attached regulators) or from inside the alternator itself. Where fitted, an auxiliary terminal will have an *insulated* stud and will have *no connections to ground*. Normally it will be smaller than the main output terminal.

Common alternators. The most commonly found alternators in the USA are made by Motorola and Delco Remy. In the UK, Lucas/CAV and Bosch are most common. The wiring on those with external regulators should be clear enough.

Many Motorola alternators with attached regulators have the following wiring: A white wire with its own separate spade terminal is the excitation line; the black wire goes to ground; and the red wire goes to an auxiliary terminal post on the back of the alternator. This is the battery-sensing (voltage regulation) line. The field wire(s) is (are) under the regulator.

Delco Remy alternators with internal regulators have two spade lugs on the back. The lug numbered "1" is the excitation connection; number "2" is the battery-sensing (voltage regulation) terminal.

Voltage regulator adjustments. Regulator adjustments should be made only on fully charged batteries in good condition. Make any alterations in regulated voltage a little at a time (even a 0.5 volt change can have a major impact on charging rates) and then *give the system plenty of time to stabilize at the new level* before considering further adjustments. Mechanical regulators are adjusted by altering spring tension; some solid-state regulators use a potentiometer screw; some Delco Remys have a four-position cap; some Lucas/CAVs have high-, medium-, and low-output wires. Many regulators are not adjustable.

Voltage Regulator Bypass Devices

As a battery comes up to charge its internal voltage rises. The regulator senses this rising voltage and cuts back output. Because battery voltage rises faster than the state of charge (refer back to Figure 2-3C), the charge rate starts to taper off around the 50- to 60-percent-charged level, approaching zero near the fully charged level (Figure 2-23A).

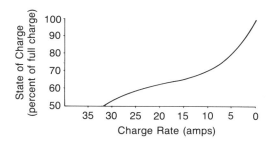

Figure 2-23A. Conventional voltage regulator output to a 100-Ah battery. Note that since battery voltage rises faster than its state of charge (see also Figure 2-3C), the charging current is cut back early in the charging process.

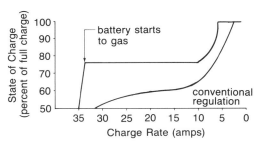

Figure 2-23B. Maximum charge rates that can be accepted by a 100-Ah battery. Note that a high rate of charge (35 amps) is possible until the battery nears 80 percent of full charge, at which point it begins to gas and heat up. The charge current should then be cut back so that the battery voltage at no time goes above 14.4 volts (or terminated altogether on the tried-and-true assumption that an 80-percent-charged battery of ample capacity is good enough for most purposes). An equalization charge (at monthly or longer intervals) begins like a conventional charge until battery voltage reaches 14.4 volts and vigorous gassing occurs. At this point the voltage is held at 14.4 volts by progressively cutting back the charge rate until it is no more than 5 amps. Charging is then continued at this rate until battery voltage stabilizes at 15 to 16 volts. This may take several hours.

However, most batteries in good condition will accept a high rate of charge all the way up to 70 to 80 percent of full charge, at which point the battery will start to gas vigorously and heat up internally (Figure 2-23B). The rate of charge then must be cut back sharply to avoid permanent battery damage—*especially with thick-plate, deep-cycle batteries*. The slower rate of charge allows the acid to diffuse into the interior of the plates, which is necessary to produce a completely charged battery.

Charging at a maximum practical rate all the way to the 80-percent level will reduce battery-charging times considerably. To this end, a number of devices on the market effectively bypass the voltage regulator altogether, allowing a *constant current* to be pumped into the batteries. Some are manually operated; others have a preset "trip" point whereby they turn themselves off and return the system to its voltage regulator when the battery reaches a preset voltage level. The best known are the *Auto-Mac* and *T-Mac* units manufactured by SpaCreek Inc. (Figure 2-24). These can really shorten charging times, but with the attendant risk of cooking alternators, voltage regulators, and batteries due to equipment malfunction or operator error.

In general a well-discharged battery will safely accept a charge of 25 percent of its Ah rating up to around the 80-percent-charged level. At this point the battery will be gassing and its voltage will be around 14.4 volts—a charge sufficient for most sit-

Figure 2-24. Voltage regulator bypass devices for alternators up to 75 amps (left) and above 75 amps (right).

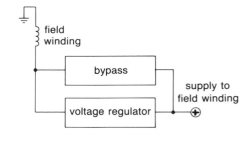

Figure 2-25A. **Voltage regulator bypass device for a P-type regulator.**

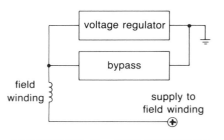

Figure 2-25B. **Voltage regulator bypass device for an N-type regulator.**

uations. The engine then can be shut down or the alternator returned to normal regulation.

To bring the batteries up to a 100-percent charge, such as when equalizing (see page 27), once the battery starts gassing and voltage has reached around 14.4 volts *cut back the charge rate to no more than 10 percent of the battery's Ah rating. Watch the voltage.* When the voltage goes above 14.4 volts or the battery gasses freely, cut back the charge rate progressively to keep within the 14.4 volt level. When the charge rate at 14.4 volts declines to 5 percent of the battery's Ah rating continue with a constant current at the 4-to 5-percent level until the battery voltage stabilizes at its highest natural level—around 15.0 to 16.0 volts. This most likely will take three or four hours; the specific gravity readings will remain unchanged over a period of three hours.

Note that all figures are for conventional, wet-type batteries at an internal temperature of 77°F (25°C). At higher temperatures the charge rates should be cut back sooner. Gassing is the real key as to when to ease up. At 100°F (38°C) vigorous gassing will start at 14.35 volts. Likewise, if voltage rises rapidly in the final stages, the charge rate is too high.

To prevent equipment damage when equalizing at these high voltages, *be sure to first disconnect all equipment from the batteries.*

Voltage regulator bypass devices leave all existing wiring and regulators in place. They are connected to the existing alternator field terminal *in parallel* with the voltage regulator. On P-type alternators,

the bypass is connected between the field terminal and the battery positive terminal; on N-type alternators, between the field terminal and ground (Figure 2-25). A manual rheostat controls current to the alternator field winding, thus controlling alternator output. Bypass units *must* incorporate an ammeter and voltmeter in the charging circuit to monitor alternator output and battery voltage (see below).

As noted, a deeply discharged battery can be charged at a rate of up to 25 percent of its amp-hour rating; an alternator can put out continuously at up to 75 percent of its rating. The rheostat is turned until the ammeter shows a rate of charge equal to the *lesser* of these two figures. For example, assume a 200-Ah battery with a 60-amp alternator. The battery can take up to 50 amps, but 75 percent of the alternator rating is 45 amps; therefore output should be increased only to this level. With a 90-amp alternator, 75 percent of its rating would be 68 amps; in this case the limiting factor would be the battery charge acceptance at 50 amps.

In practice, things are not quite this simple. The boat's own DC load may be 20 amps while the engine is running. In this case the *net* charge (what is actually going into the battery) of the 60-amp alternator operating at 75 percent of its full rating would be $45 - 20 = 25$ amps, and of the 90-amp alternator, $68 - 20 = 48$ amps—neither figure coming up to the maximum battery-charge acceptance rate. The alternators are the limiting factor in this situation.

This brings up another point. The usual practice is to install ammeters in such a way as to measure net charge to the batteries. *But we cannot tell from this what the alternator is really doing.* With voltage regulator bypass devices *a second ammeter that measures gross alternator output should be fitted.* Otherwise there is a risk of overloading and burning up the alternator, especially on electrically "loaded" boats (Figure 2-26).

It is essential to monitor continuously alternator and battery temperatures the first few times the bypass device is used. If the alternator becomes much too hot to touch or the battery starts to rise above 110°F (43°C), the charge rate is too high. When the battery voltage rises and the battery begins to gas noticeably, it is time to reduce the charge rate or switch back to the voltage regulator.

Many bypass units incorporate a voltage sensing circuit that turns the unit off when battery voltage rises to a preset level (normally around 14.2 volts), and returns control of the alternator to its voltage regulator. I have had reports of factory cutout point settings ranging from 13.8 volts—virtually useless—to 14.8 volts, which will fry the batteries. Check the cutout point carefully the first time you use the unit and reset it as necessary with the potentiometer (variable resistor), which should be located somewhere in the unit. Note that if the unit's automatic shutdown circuit fails, the batteries will surely fry. Automatic or not, it is still important to keep an eye on battery voltage. Units with automatic voltage trips should have a manual override to make periodic battery equalization possible.

Other units are strictly manual. The battery voltage must be monitored and the unit turned off when the voltage comes up. *Failure to do so just once will result in battery damage—even explosion.* If the voltage rises high enough, electronic equipment hooked to the battery will be damaged. Some manual units incorporate a timer to switch off the unit after a preset period of operation.

All these devices provide a constant field current to the alternator (determined by the rheostat setting). If engine speed is increased, alternator output also will increase even though the field current is unchanged. The field current must be cut back to compensate for speed increases or alternator and battery damage are likely.

Once a battery has been fully charged using a regulator bypass, it requires only a minimal charge rate (a *float charge*) to keep it there. In most situations a voltage regulator setting of 13.2 volts is adequate—certainly no more than 13.6 volts. This is below all normal voltage regulator settings, which means a mild degree of overcharging is inevitable with continued engine running. If regulator settings have been elevated (e.g., to 14.4 volts), more serious overcharging is likely. This can be avoided by placing a switch in the alternator field circuit and disabling the alternator when the batteries are fully charged.

Voltage-regulator bypasses must be used with circumspection, with a full understanding of what is being done, and with a recognition of the limits of what is possible without equipment damage or risk of battery damage or explosion. It also should be noted that most are not made with heat-protected components. With a powerful alternator it is quite possible to overload many units, with a consequent fire risk. A

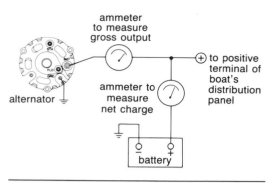

ammeter to measure gross output

alternator

ammeter to measure net charge

to positive terminal of boat's distribution panel

battery

Figure 2-26. **Net charging current versus gross alternator output readings.**

boosted alternator output may also overload the capacity of existing circuits. All wiring will need to be checked to ensure it has sufficient current-carrying capacity (see Chapter 3).

Marine Voltage Regulators

Used wisely a voltage regulator bypass will overcome most of the inadequacies of automotive regulators in marine use. Depending on the degree of "automation," however, these devices need close monitoring. A lapse of attention on just one occasion can do irreparable harm to batteries and cause a potentially dangerous situation.

Certain very sophisticated—and expensive—purpose-built marine voltage regulators, which obviate the need for regulator bypass devices and take care of *all* these problems, are coming onto the market. Ample Power Co., and Cruising Equipment Co., both of Seattle, are two suppliers of such devices. These maintain a high constant-current charge rate to around the 14.4 battery-terminal voltage level, at which point they trip to a conventional voltage regulator setting, holding 14.4 volts while the charge rate tapers off as the battery comes up to full charge. When the battery charge acceptance rate at this voltage level has tapered off to below 5 percent of the battery's Ah rating, the battery is at least 90-percent charged. The regulator then trips to a float charge of from 13.2 to 13.6 volts. Periodically the regulator can be set for a constant current of 5 percent of the batteries' Ah rating in order to achieve equalization. Such a regulator coupled to a high-output alternator makes a very powerful charging system. A word of caution is in order, however. These devices are very new to the marketplace and it remains to be seen whether they will stand the test of time in the rugged marine environment. The popularity

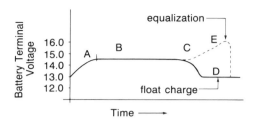

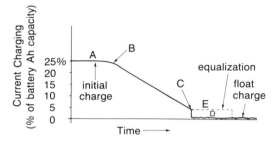

Figure 2-27. Desirable characteristics of a marine voltage regulator for wet-type deep-cycle batteries. In region A of the graph, the charging current is regulated at a constant 25 percent of the battery's Ah rating. At point B, when the battery terminal voltage reaches 14.4 (around 80 percent of full charge), the regulator trips to a conventional setting, holding 14.4 volts while the charge rate trickles off as the battery approaches full charge. (At temperatures above 80°F or 26.7°C, the trip point should be 14.3 volts.) At point C, where the charge rate falls to less than 5 percent of the battery's Ah rating, the regulator trips to a float voltage of 13.2, yielding curve D. Periodically (curve E), the regulator is set to maintain a constant charge current of 5 percent of the battery's Ah rating, until specific gravity readings stabilize at their highest levels (at about 16.0 volts).

of the voltage-regulator bypasses and purpose-built marine voltage regulators finally has caught the eye of corporate America. It is my understanding that Motorola soon will produce an inexpensive marine regulator that will perform most of these functions at a fraction of the cost of existing devices.

Troubleshooting Voltage Regulators

No alternator output at all. "Alternator Problems: Initial Testing" (page 33), outlined a procedure for *external* regulators to determine if the alternator or regulator is at fault (see Figure 2-12). Some attached regulators can be removed without disturbing the brushes and treated in a similar fashion. If the voltage regulator is malfunctioning, we have an open circuit (no current) to the field winding. This may be the result of a defective switch circuit on battery-excited alternators, a broken or shorted wire, blown diodes or transistors on solid-state regulators, or open points on a mechanical regulator.

Battery-excited alternators. Always suspect the switches first. The excitation line may run to an oil pressure or fuel pressure switch mounted on the engine block, to the ignition switch, or to both (see Figure 2-21). Rig a jumper wire incorporating a minimum 12-watt test light from the battery positive terminal, crank the engine, and touch the jumper for just a second or two to the battery excitation terminal on the voltage regulator. If the alternator now works we know this circuit is faulty. The alternator may continue to work after the jumper is disconnected, but when the engine is shut down and then restarted the alternator field winding will need reexciting to get things going again.

Self-exciting alternators. These are designed so that the iron core of the field winding retains sufficient residual magnetism when the unit is shut down to get things moving again when it is put back in operation. Sometimes, however, this residual magnetism will decline to the point below which it will not bring the alternator back to life. Revving up the engine may bring the alternator back into commission. If not, give the field winding its initial excitation with a small positive current to the field or auxiliary terminal on the alternator. The easiest way to do this is to connect a minimum 12-watt test light from the battery positive terminal to the field or auxiliary terminal (see Figure 2-21).

Continuity tests. With the ignition off, *and the battery isolation switch off*, use a VOM on its lowest ohms scale (R × 1) to test the regulator wiring for continuity. We should get a reading of zero ohms (needle all the way to the right) when the meter probes are touched to both ends of an individual wire. Infinite ohms indicate a break in the wiring. It may prove necessary to push the probe tip through the insulation at the voltage regulator end of the wires as the connections are inaccessible on many regulators.

If earlier tests showed the regulator is at fault, but all its wiring and external circuits are OK, the regulator needs replacing. If no spare is on board, an emergency regulator can sometimes be rigged up as detailed on page 53.

Mechanical regulators. These are easier to troubleshoot since all wiring, connections, and points are accessible. If the internal wiring has burned, the ends will be visible—just like a blown fuse. Emergency repairs can be made with copper wire of approximately the same diameter. Contact points should be cleaned with 400-or 600-grit wet-and-dry sandpaper. To make a crude test of the regulator, run up the engine and gently hold the regulator points open and shut. The generator or alternator should not put out at all with the points open (or at a very low level if externally excited), and then put out at full blast with the points closed. Don't keep the points closed for any length of time, or something is likely to burn up!

Persistent undercharging of the battery. The alternator may just be too small for the demands being placed on the system, its speed of rotation too slow (wrong pulleys; see page 15), its belt slipping, or its charging time inadequate. Given a correctly sized alternator and pulleys and sufficient charging time, however, persistent undercharging must be the result of incorrect voltage regulation for the system in question.

• First, it is necessary to bring the battery(s) to full charge by one means or another. (This is important; test with a hydrometer.) Set the engine to its normal charging speed and check the *battery* voltage. This will show the regulated voltage from the alternator that is actually reaching the battery. Depending on the design parameters of the system, this should be anywhere from 13.8 to 14.4 volts. Most boats will want to be somewhere between 14.0 and 14.4 volts for reasonably rapid battery charging without risk of excessive overcharging. An exception to this is if the boat is fitted with one of the marine regulators previously mentioned. In this case, if the battery is *fully charged*, the regulator may have "tripped" to a setting between 13.2 and 13.6 volts.

• If voltage levels are down, no amount of engine running time will bring the battery(s) to full charge. In this case, check the voltage *at the output terminal on the alternator*. With the engine running, test between the terminal and a good ground. On alternators with an insulated ground, test between the output terminal and the ground terminal. Voltage may well be a volt or more higher than the battery voltage already measured.

• Voltage drop from the alternator to the

batteries can be caused by inadequate wiring and poor connections (see Chapter 3) but is more likely to occur as a result of fail-safe and split charging (isolation) diodes fitted to allow two or more batteries to be charged from the same alternator. The diodes allow current to flow *from* the alternator to each battery, but not *back*. When the alternator is shut down, current cannot flow from one battery to another via the charging circuit.

• All diodes, regardless of size, create a voltage drop of from 0.6 to 1.0 volt (Figure 2-28A). Many voltage regulators sense battery voltage for regulation purposes at the alternator end of the charging circuit (Figure 2-28B). This means that the voltage regulator is sensing system voltage from 0.6 to 1.0 volt above what is actually going into the battery (i.e., if the regulator senses 14.2 volts the battery actually is receiving 13.2 to 13.6 volts, depending on the voltage drop across the diode). *Unless the voltage regulator is set high enough to compensate for any diodes that may be present, the batteries will be permanently undercharged.* Since the difference between the open-circuit voltage of a half-charged and a fully charged battery is only 0.4 volt, even a 0.6-volt diode drop will play havoc with battery charging.

• If an alternator is undercharging because of diode-induced voltage drops, one of the following methods will correct the situation:

Adjustable regulators: Raise the voltage setting. On mechanical regulators this is done by a screw that increases the spring pressure on the regulator points. Some solid-state regulators have a potentiometer with a screwdriver slot in its end. Some Delco Remy alternators have a four-position rotating cap to vary regulator settings (Figure 1-10). Some Lucas alternators have low-, medium-, and high-output terminals on the regulators. All adjustments should be made only *with a fully charged battery,* and in small increments, allowing the system to stabilize before making further changes.

Nonadjustable regulators: Take the regulator sensing wire directly to the battery positive terminal, thus bypassing any diodes (Figure 2-28C); or fit a diode with the same voltage drop as the battery isolation diodes into the sensing wire (Figure 2-28D). Either way the regulator is now sensing the same voltage that the battery is receiving.

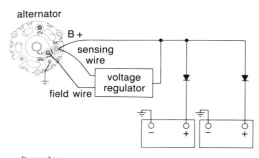

Figure 2-28A. Correct voltages on systems with split-charging diodes when the batteries are fully charged. Voltage drop can be measured directly between the alternator output terminal and the battery's positive post as shown. Set the meter to the 2.5 volts DC scale.

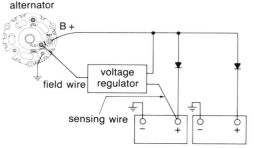

Figure 2-28B. Machine- (**opposite**) and battery-sensed (**below**) voltage regulators. B+ is the alternator output terminal. FLD is the field terminal.

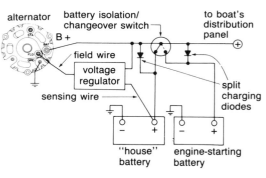

Figure 2-28C. Battery sensing wire connected to a "house" battery.

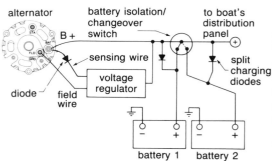

Figure 2-28D. Fitting a diode in a sensing wire to compensate for voltage drop from split-charging diodes.

1. Battery-sensing wire connected to house battery. If the sensing wire is moved to the battery make sure it does not pass through any switches that may be opened while the engine is running. If this happens the regulator will sense no voltage and will respond by increasing field current to its maximum. The sensing wire can go to only one battery; otherwise the batteries would be paralleled via the sensing wire, defeating the purpose of the diodes. If the sensed battery is fully charged and the other battery low, the alternator output will shut down and the second battery will be inadequately charged. Normal practice is to connect the sensing wire to the battery on the boat's house circuit (as opposed to engine cranking), as this battery is generally in the lowest state of charge. Should the engine-starting battery be lower, the batteries should be paralleled manually during charging by turning the battery isolation/changeover switch to the "BOTH" position (Figure 2-28C).

2. If a diode is fitted into the sensing line its arrow must point *toward the voltage regulator.* If it is fitted in reverse it will block the sensing line altogether; the regulator will respond with maximum field current at all times, and the batteries will be overcharged (if nothing burns up first).

• If *none* of the tests to date reveals a problem, shut the engine down, turn on some equipment, and drain the battery for a few minutes. Now crank the engine once again and immediately test for a voltage drop between the alternator output terminal and the battery positive terminal. The battery drain will cause the alternator to put out at full output for at least a few minutes. If a voltage drop is now present where none showed on the earlier tests (which were made with a fully charged battery and therefore low alternator output) the output wiring is inadequate and needs upgrading.

Persistent overcharging of the battery.
The battery or batteries overheat, "boil" or gas, use excess water, and give off an acrid, acid smell. Regardless of the size of the alternator, in normal circumstances *overcharging cannot occur with correct voltage regulation.*

• First, check the batteries. Dead and dying batteries will frequently gas and lose electrolyte as if they were overcharged. Note that *excessively hot batteries will automatically overcharge;* there may be no fault in the system itself. The batteries will need to be moved to a cooler location.

- Next, check for improper use of a voltage regulator bypass (page 46), unregulated wind generator (page 133), or unregulated solar panel (page 141). Since regulators in marine use frequently are set to achieve faster charge rates through higher voltage settings than in automotive use, extended engine running generally will result in mild overcharging and moderate water loss; this is to be expected.
- Serious overcharging—battery voltage above 14.4 volts, vigorous gassing, substantial water loss—will occur if an external or externally attached voltage regulator's battery-sensing wire is disconnected or broken. The regulator senses low battery voltage (actually no voltage), and responds by increasing field current to its maximum. Especially check *battery-sensed* regulators that have a long wire running to the batteries rather than a short one to the alternator (*machine-sensed*). Any voltage drop *in the sensing wire,* such as would result from corroded terminals, will have a similar, though less dramatic, effect.
- Finally, a short circuit on the voltage regulator will result in permanent maximum output since the regulator supplies maximum field current at all times, a situation similar to the loss of the sensing wire. This, however, is not repairable. Carry a spare.

Emergency Voltage Regulation

The excitation current for almost all alternators ranges up to a maximum of around 5 amps at full output, although some high-output alternators may go as high as 7 to 8 amps. Any external source can be used to supply this current if the voltage regulator is first removed or disconnected. A test wire connected to a 12- or 15-watt DC lamp (Figure 2-12) will feed approximately 1 amp to the field winding (12-volt system). The lamp acts as a fixed resistance, preventing excessive amperage from reaching the field winding. The higher the lamp wattage, the more amperage it will pass. Divide the wattage by the system voltage to find out how many amps. For example, a 15-watt bulb on a 12-volt system will pass 1.25 amps; a 40-watt bulb, 3.33 amps.

With P-type alternators, the lamp must be connected between the battery's positive terminal and the alternator's field terminal. With N-type alternators, it is connected between the field terminal and ground (Figure 2-12).

Alternator output and battery voltage must be monitored closely to guard against overheating and overcharging. If output is too high, the lamp wattage should be decreased, or two lamps should be wired *in series;* if output is lower than desired, lamp wattage can be increased, or two lamps can be wired *in parallel.* When the battery is fully charged this field current must be switched off or disconnected; likewise when the engine is shut down. If it is left hooked up, it will drain the batteries through the field winding.

Battery Isolation Switches; Split Charging Diodes and Relays

Charging More Than One Battery: Three Approaches

If two batteries are to be charged from the same alternator, it is desirable to isolate them electrically. Then, when charging is complete and the engine is shut down, one battery can be used on the boat's house (i.e., non-engine cranking) circuit without pulling the other battery down. Three approaches are possible.

Battery isolation/changeover switch. The alternator output is fed to a battery changeover (isolation) switch and from there directed manually (by turning the switch) to whichever battery is to be charged. This is subject to operator error. If the operator forgets to switch the batteries over, one battery is likely to go dead. If the switch is turned to "OFF" with the engine running, it is likely to open-circuit the alternator and blow it out, unless it also breaks the alternator field circuit (see page 55).

Split charging diodes in combination with a battery isolation changeover switch. The alternator output is fed to two diodes—electrical check valves—that al-

Figure 2-29. Battery isolation/changeover switch. Many such switches have a fourth position, usually labeled "BOTH," which brings both batteries on line (in parallel) for difficult engine starts.

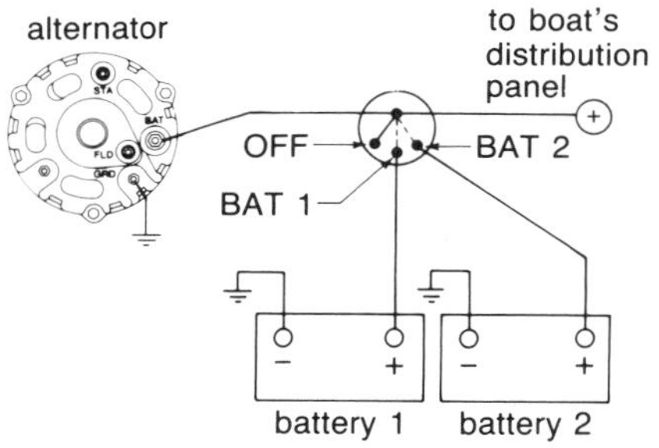

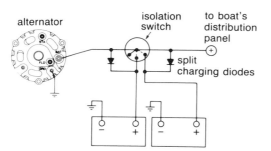

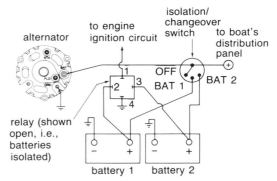

Figure 2-31. Split-charging relay. Turning on the engine ignition circuit energizes an electromagnet in the relay via terminal 1. The magnet is grounded via terminal 4 to complete the circuit. The magnet closes a set of points between terminals 2 and 3, thus paralleling the batteries. When the ignition is turned off the magnet deenergizes, the points open, and the batteries are isolated. Even with the relay closed and the batteries paralleled, if the isolation/changeover switch is in the "OFF" position the alternator will be open-circuited. Although the relay parallels the batteries, the charging circuit still goes through the switch.

Figure 2-30. Split-charging diodes in combination with a battery isolation/changeover switch. Note that even if the isolation/changeover switch is inadvertently turned off while the engine is running, the alternator is not open-circuited.

low current to flow from the alternator to the batteries but not back. The alternator first charges the lowest battery; when its voltage equalizes with the second battery, both are charged. When the alternator is shut down the batteries are isolated from one another. Where diodes are fitted problems may arise with voltage regulation; the regulator may need to be battery sensed (see page 52). Diodes frequently are used in combination with an isolation/changeover switch, the diodes bypassing the switch for automatic split charging, while the switch allows either battery to be selected for boat use.

Split charging relay. The alternator output is fed to a split charging relay—a kind of electrically operated switch. The alternator is machine sensed. Any time the engine is cranked the relay closes and both batteries are charged in parallel. When the engine is stopped the relay opens and isolates the two batteries from the charging circuit. Once again the relay is used in combination with an isolation/ changeover switch, the switch being used to select the battery for boat use. The system is independent of the user and introduces no extra voltage drops in the charging line.

Battery Isolation Switches

Battery isolation switches should do exactly what their name implies: *Isolate the batteries*. Apart from the cables from the batteries to the switch, *there should be no connections to the switch nor to batteries on the battery side of the switch*. In practice there are almost always a few exceptions to this rule: certain pieces of electronic equipment that need to be hooked directly to a battery to operate properly; automatic bilge pumps, so that the boat can be left with the batteries isolated but the pumps operational; and battery-charging devices that are to operate when the boat is unattended.

All equipment that bypasses an isolation switch must be wired to the highest standards and properly fused. This includes even small-capacity solar panels (which are rarely fused in practice). Any short in wiring hooked to the battery will carry *full battery current*. I know of one boat that burned up when the unfused wires from a small solar panel shorted. The fuses need to be as close to the battery as possible to reduce the length of unprotected wiring to a minimum.

Note that charging circuits with split charging (isolation) diodes almost invariably bypass the isolation switch, so that all batteries can be charged even though only one is switched into the boat's circuit. Although the diodes prevent battery drain back into the charging circuit, fuses still should be installed at the batteries. If the fuses blow while the alternator is running, however, it will potentially open-circuit the alternator and blow out its diodes (all the fuses would have to blow, and the isolation switch would have to be "OFF"). For added peace of mind the alternator can be protected with a *snubber* (page 38).

Battery isolation switches carry the full starting current of an engine and must be rated to carry this load—at least 300 amps in most situations. The cables to the switch and back to the starter must be adequate to the task, as voltage drop can be very damaging to starter motors. On longer cable runs, size 1/0 stranded copper welding cable works well.

On those charging circuits that pass through the switch, turning off the switch with the engine running can blow out all the alternator diodes. To guard against this, isolation switches need to:

• Have either a clearly printed label, "STOP ENGINE BEFORE SWITCHING TO 'OFF' POSITION," or better still, be of the type that disconnects the field circuit to the alternator momentarily before the battery circuit is broken. This effectively disables the alternator and prevents diode loss even if the engine is still running.

• Be of the type that "makes before it breaks." In other words, when switching from one battery to another the switch makes the circuit to the second (so both are now "ON") before breaking the circuit to the first. In this way there is no interruption of the alternator output to the batteries.

Diodes

How they work. Diodes are essentially switches that allow electricity to flow in one direction, while preventing its flow in the opposite direction. Earlier in electronics history, diodes were vacuum tubes. Now, all diodes are semiconductors—materials whose conductivity falls midway between that of good conductors, such as copper, and insulators, such as bakelite. Diodes are most commonly made of silicon, although germanium diodes are often found in electronics work.

Various other materials, such as gallium, indium, and other jawbreakers, are added to the silicon base to produce either an excess of electrons, producing P-type material, or a deficiency of electrons, producing N-type material. Diodes are produced by bonding N- and P- type materials together in such a way as to encourage the flow of electrons in one direction, while preventing its flow in the opposite direction. This produces a switch, or one-way valve, which

Diode Identification

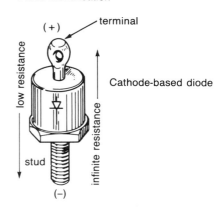

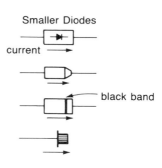

Figure 2-32. **Diode identification. Diodes are rated by** (1) their current-carrying capacity when conducting (e.g., 50 amps), and (2) the voltage they are capable of blocking in the other direction, known as peak inverted voltage or PIV (e.g., 50 PIV). The bottommost of the smaller diodes is frequently used in alternators and pressed into a heat sink, in which instance the diode case is electrically in common with the heat sink, and usually grounded (or negative).

fortunately is all we need to know about the workings of diodes.

Identification. Diodes are imprinted with an arrowhead-like symbol with its tip crossed by a perpendicular line. The arrow points in the direction of conduction; the perpendicular line symbolizes the resistance to conduction in the opposite direction.

One connection is made to the terminal on the diode's top, the other to the threaded stud on its base. If the arrow points from the terminal to the stud, conduction is from the terminal to the stud. This is a *cathode-based* diode. If the arrow points from the stud to the terminal, conduction is from the stud to the terminal. This is an *anode-based* diode.

Heat sinks. Current passing through a diode heats it up. More current produces

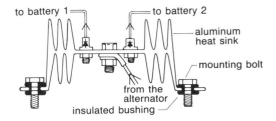

Figure 2-33A. Anode-based diodes mounted on shared heat sink for battery isolation. Note that the heat sink is live during alternator operation.

to battery 1   to battery 2

aluminum heat sink

mounting bolt

from the alternator

insulated bushing

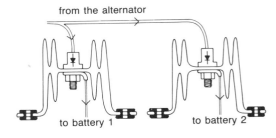

Figure 2-33B. Cathode-based diodes must be mounted on independent, electrically isolated heat sinks to avoid paralleling the batteries. These heat sinks are connected to the two battery positive terminals and are always live.

from the alternator

to battery 1   to battery 2

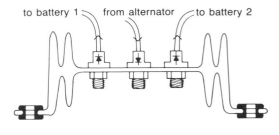

Figure 2-34. Three-diode split-charging setup. Note that the voltage drop is doubled relative to that of a two-diode configuration. The heat sink is still live during alternator output.

to battery 1   from alternator   to battery 2

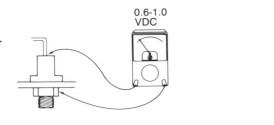

Figure 2-35. Testing for voltage drop across a diode. The positive meter lead goes on the alternator side of the circuit.

0.6-1.0 VDC

more heat. To dissipate this heat, diodes are mounted on finned aluminum plates called *heat sinks.*

Since one side of a diode is connected electrically to its heat sink via the mounting stud, *heat sinks are live.* With cathode-based isolating diodes the heat sink is connected to the battery positive terminal. *Shorting out the heat sink to ground is much the same as shorting out the battery terminals.* With anode-based isolating diodes the *heat sink is connected to the alternator and is hot (live) whenever the engine is running* (Figure 2-33).

Since the heat sink on a cathode-based diode is common with the battery positive terminal it is not possible to mount two diodes on the same heat sink; this will parallel the batteries through the heat sink and defeat the purpose of the diodes. Be-

cause the heat sink on an anode-based diode is common with the alternator output, any number of diodes can be mounted on the same heat sink without affecting the batteries.

Some battery isolation units use three diodes: The alternator feeds into a cathode-based diode, then two anode-based diodes feed out to the batteries. Note that the voltage drop to the batteries (see below) is doubled (Figure 2-34). The diodes are sometimes mounted in an insulated block fitted to the heat sink. In this case the heat sink is electrically isolated from its diodes permanently.

Capacity. Diodes come in different sizes to fit different needs. Since the full charging output of an alternator passes through the isolation diodes they must be rated to accept this high amperage. If you are upgrading to a high-output alternator, any existing isolating diodes will most likely also need upgrading. This can be done by fitting additional diodes in parallel with the original ones.

Testing. All diodes create a voltage drop, normally around 0.6 volt, but sometimes as high as 1.0 volt. To find out how much, check with a volt-ohm meter (VOM) across the two diode terminals, *while the alternator is running,* with the voltmeter set to the 2.5-volt scale. The positive meter lead goes to the alternator side of the circuit (Figure 2-35).

To test a diode's operation, shut down the alternator and turn off the ignition and battery isolation switches. Check with a VOM (or test light) from the battery side of the diode to ground. It will show battery voltage (or light). Now test from the generator side to a good ground. It should show no or very little voltage (there may be a small leakage current). If there is battery voltage on the alternator side (if the test lamp lights), the diode is shorted, another diode in the charging circuit has been installed backward, or some equipment has been wired incorrectly in such a way as to bypass the diodes. If the diode is shorted, the battery still will receive a charge, but will not be isolated from the other battery (although the other battery will still be isolated from this one via *its* isolating diode). If one of the diodes is in backward the relevant battery will receive no charge when the alternator is running and will soon go dead.

Diodes also can be tested with an ohmmeter, *but only after disconnecting the batteries* (otherwise you will blow out the ohmmeter). The meter is set to its lowest ohms scale (R × 1) and the probes touched to the two diode terminals. The probes are then reversed. If the diode is functional it will show continuity in one direction (zero or near zero ohms) and an open circuit in the other (infinite or very high ohms). Where there is continuity the direction of flow is from the negative probe to the positive probe.

A shorted diode will show continuity in both directions. An open-circuited diode will show infinity in both directions.

Soldering and connections. Excessive heat will damage a diode. Do not solder to the top terminal with the diode mounted on its heat sink; the heat sink will draw the heat down into the diode. Use a large enough soldering iron to get the job done as quickly as possible and so avoid the need to hold the iron to the terminal for prolonged periods. A ring terminal is used to make the connection to the diode stud and is held in place with the same washer and nut used to lock the diode to its heat sink. When soldering small diodes with attached wires, clamp a pair of small Vise Grips or pliers around the wire between the solder joint and the diode. This will act as a heat sink and protect the diode (Figure 2-36). Alternatively, wrap a strip of aluminum cut from a soft drink can around the wire. For more information on soldering, see Chapter 3.

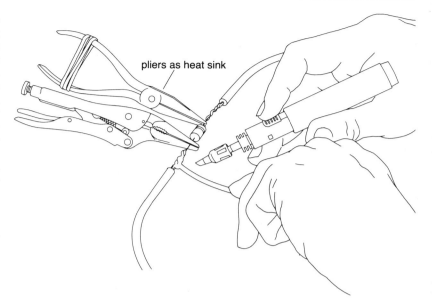

pliers as heat sink

Figure 2-36. **Soldering small diodes.**

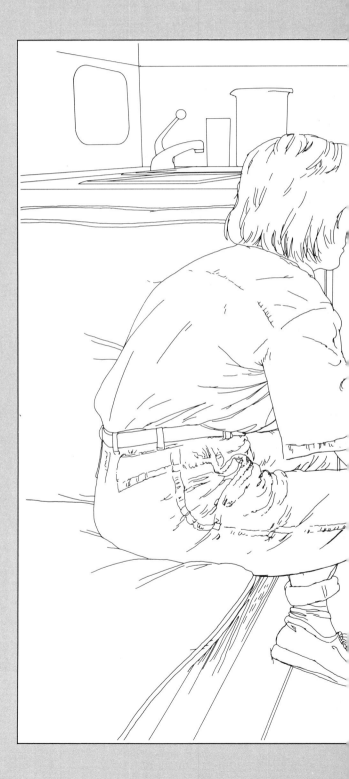

Figure 3-1. Effective troubleshooting of recalcitrant electrical circuits begins and ends with a thorough understanding of the dynamics involved.

Understanding and Troubleshooting Electrical Circuits

What is Electricity?

The basic problem with electricity is that you can't see it. This makes its movement something of a mystery. As you may remember from science classes, electrical circulation is directly analogous to the circulation of water in a pressurized water system. Most people have little trouble understanding water flow; thus there should be few obstacles to understanding electrical circuits.

In a pressurized water system the *rate of flow* through any given pipe is governed by the *pressure of the water* and the *size of the pipe*. The higher the pressure the greater the flow; the larger the pipe the greater the flow, up to the capacity of the system's pump.

In an electrical circuit the rate of flow (*amperage*) through any given wire is governed by the pressure in the wire (*voltage*) and the size of the wire. The higher the pressure (voltage) the greater the flow (amperage). The larger the wire, the greater the flow, up to the capacity of the system's generator or battery.

With a pipe of a given size, the longer the pipe the more the cumulative resistance and therefore the less the flow. Moreover, pressure will decline steadily along the length of the pipe, but the *flow rate* will be the same at all points. If four gallons per minute comes out at the far end, four gallons per minute must go in at the beginning, and four gallons per minute will flow through the pipe at all points.

With a wire of any given size, the longer the wire the more the cumulative resistance (*ohms*) and therefore the less the flow (amps). Moreover, pressure (voltage) will decline steadily along the length of the wire (this is called *voltage drop,* and is very significant in boat electrics as we shall see), but the rate of flow (amps) will remain constant at all points.

Consider an open tank of water with a pump on its outlet feeding a pipe with a valve. The outlet from the valve runs through a second pipe onto the ground. The pump is running but the valve is closed, creating, in effect, infinite resistance to flow. In other words, there is no flow through the pipes. The pump will build system pressure upstream from the valve.

A *switch* is the electrical equivalent of a closed valve; it offers infinite resistance to electrical flow. In other words, it stops all flow (amperage) through the system. System pressure (voltage) will build upstream from the switch.

Water is used if the valve is opened and water allowed to flow. If the valve is barely cracked (Figure 3–2) it offers a very high resistance to flow and allows only a small amount of water to pass. The pump is more than capable of maintaining system pressure upstream from the valve while water flows through the valve out onto the ground. In other words, the pressure drop from one side of the valve to the other is equal to system pressure.

Electricity is used when a switch is closed and electricity allowed to flow. Current flowing through a high resistance, such as a light bulb, is the electrical equivalent of a barely cracked valve; it allows only a small amount of current (amps) to flow. Downstream from the resistance the circuit runs to ground—either the negative terminal on a battery or the white neutral (*grounded*) wire on an AC system. Voltage falls to zero (*ground potential*). The voltage drop from one side of the resistance to the other will equal system voltage (see "Understanding AC Circuits," later in this chapter).

The more the water valve is opened the lower the resistance to flow and the more water will pass through it. At some point, if the pipe and valve are large enough, the rate of flow will exceed the ability of the pump to maintain system pressure, and pressure will begin to decline upstream from the valve.

The lower the resistance in a circuit the more current (amperage) will flow. At some point, if the wire is large enough and the resistance low enough—a starter motor is a good example—the rate of flow will exceed the ability of the generator or battery to maintain system pressure (voltage). This is why battery voltage falls—generally to around 10.5 volts—when cranking an engine.

As long as the pipes leading to and from the valve are large enough to accommodate the flow without resistance, and as long as the rate of flow does not exceed the capability of the pump to maintain system pressure, the water pressure will always be at pump pressure above the valve and drop to zero downstream from the valve. In other words, the pressure drop across the valve will be equal to the pressure on the system. At very high rates of flow, however, the pipes themselves may begin to of-

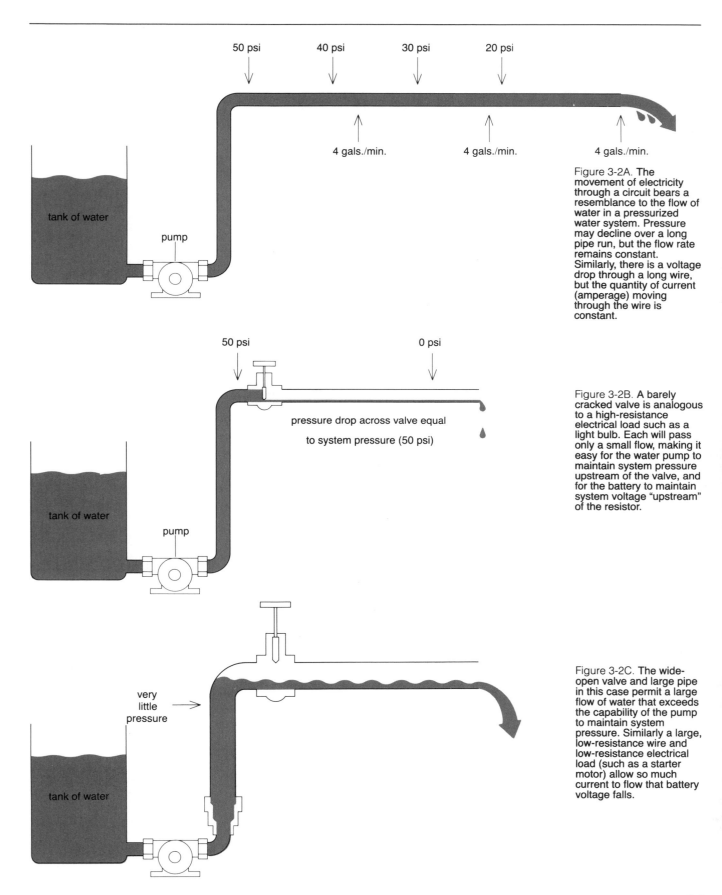

50 psi 40 psi 30 psi 20 psi

4 gals./min. 4 gals./min. 4 gals./min.

tank of water

pump

Figure 3-2A. The movement of electricity through a circuit bears a resemblance to the flow of water in a pressurized water system. Pressure may decline over a long pipe run, but the flow rate remains constant. Similarly, there is a voltage drop through a long wire, but the quantity of current (amperage) moving through the wire is constant.

50 psi 0 psi

pressure drop across valve equal to system pressure (50 psi)

tank of water

pump

Figure 3-2B. A barely cracked valve is analogous to a high-resistance electrical load such as a light bulb. Each will pass only a small flow, making it easy for the water pump to maintain system pressure upstream of the valve, and for the battery to maintain system voltage "upstream" of the resistor.

very little pressure

tank of water

Figure 3-2C. The wide-open valve and large pipe in this case permit a large flow of water that exceeds the capability of the pump to maintain system pressure. Similarly a large, low-resistance wire and low-resistance electrical load (such as a starter motor) allow so much current to flow that battery voltage falls.

What is Electricity? 61

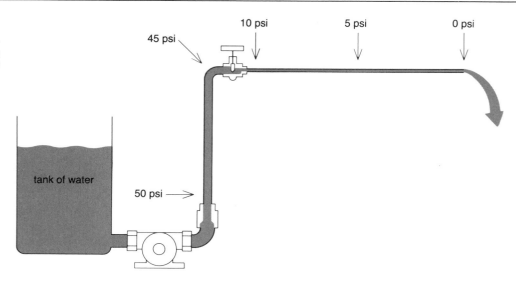

Figure 3-2D. At high flow rates, a narrow pipe or inadequately sized wire (or faulty connections) creates its own pressure or voltage drop. Pressure (voltage) drop across the valve (or electrical load) no longer equals system pressure or voltage.

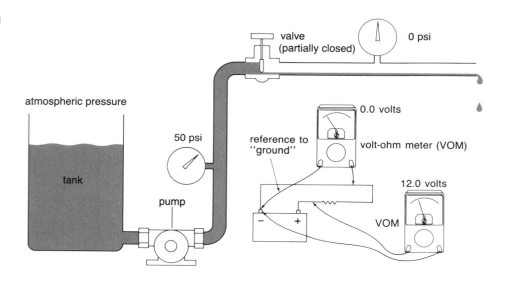

Figure 3-3. **Pressure and voltage measurements.**

fer resistance. There now will be a pressure drop along the length of the pipes, followed by a drop of less than system pressure across the valve. The *total* pressure drop will equal the pressure on the system.

As long as the wires leading to and from a resistance (*load*) are large enough to accommodate the flow (amperage) and free of extra resistance, such as loose or corroded connections, and as long as the rate of flow (amperage) does not exceed the capability of the generator or battery to maintain system pressure (voltage), the pressure (voltage) will always be at system pressure (voltage), above the resistance (load) and drop to zero downstream from the resistance. In other words, the pressure drop (voltage drop) across the resistance will be equal to the pressure (voltage) on the system. At very high rates of flow (amperages), the wires and/or their connections may begin to offer their own resistance to flow: they will heat up. There now will be a pressure (voltage) drop along the length of the wires, followed by a drop of less than the system pressure (voltage) across the resistance. The *total* pressure (voltage) drop will equal the voltage on the system.

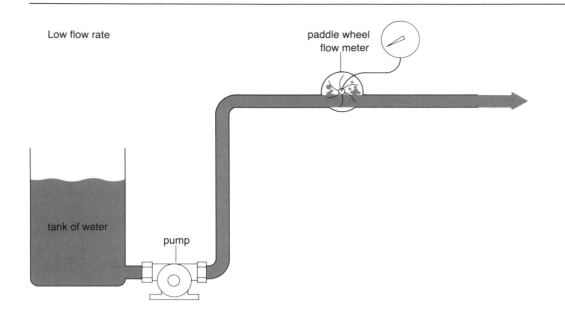

Low flow rate

paddle wheel
flow meter

tank of water

pump

Figure 3-4. **Water and current flow measurements.**

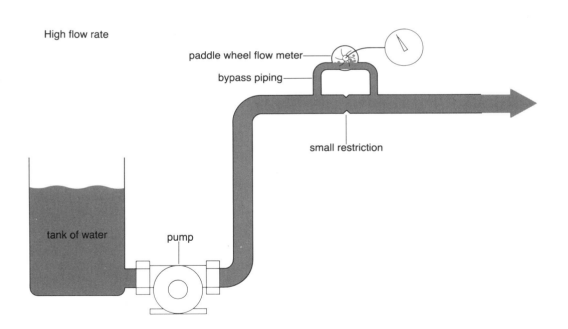

High flow rate

paddle wheel flow meter

bypass piping

small restriction

tank of water

pump

Measuring Electricity

In a pressurized water system we can insert gauges at any point to measure the pressure and rate of flow. So too with electrical circuits. We can even go one better and measure resistance to flow (ohms) quite easily; this must be deduced in the water system.

Measuring pressure (voltage). Water pressure is measured by teeing in a small line and leading it to a pressure gauge. Voltage is measured the same way, with one difference: Water pressure gauges are calibrated with reference to atmospheric pressure. Since atmospheric pressure is all around us, this reference point can be built into the meter quite simply by leaving one side open to atmosphere; only one

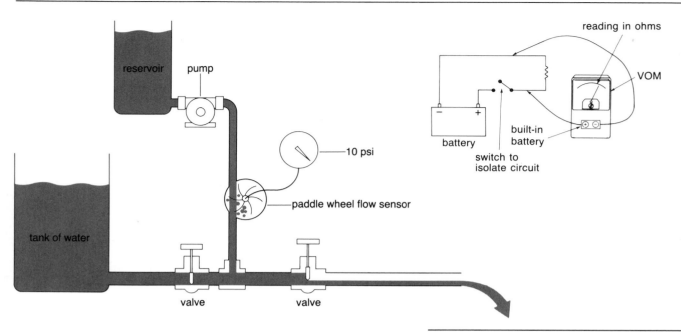

Figure 3-5. Measuring resistance. In either instance current is metered at a carefully measured pressure (or voltage). Resultant flow through the pipe or circuit is measured, and the resistance of the system is either inferred (in the water example) or displayed on the meter reading (as ohms, by the VOM).

connection is needed to the water pipe. What we are measuring is the pressure *differential* between the system pressure and atmospheric pressure.

Voltage is measured with reference to *ground* (or "ground potential"). A volt-ohm meter cannot measure without being connected to this reference point in some way; a hole in the side of the meter will not work! Therefore *two* connections are needed to measure voltage: one to the pressure point in the circuit and one to its ground. This ground connection performs the reference function of the open side of the water pressure gauge; we are measuring the pressure *differential* between the system and its ground potential.

Measuring flow (amperage). In a water system, rate of flow is measured by installing a paddle wheel *in the pipe* and seeing how fast it spins. Amperage is measured in the same way by installing an *ammeter*—the electrical equivalent of a paddle wheel—in the electrical circuit.

With larger volumes of water it is impractical to measure the whole flow rate—the meter would have to be huge. A small restriction is made in the main pipe to

cause a slight pressure drop. A smaller pipe bypasses this restriction. The slight pressure drop in the main pipe causes water to flow through the bypass pipe and a paddle wheel in this pipe measures the rate of flow. This is multiplied by a suitable factor to determine the rate of flow in the main pipe.

High amperage is measured the same way. A specially calibrated, low-resistance *shunt* is installed in the main wire (*cable*). A small circuit containing an *ammeter* is connected across the terminals of the shunt, bypassing it. The ammeter measures the flow in the bypass, which then is multiplied by a suitable factor to give the overall rate of flow.

Measuring resistance (ohms). If we pump water through a pipe at a carefully regulated pressure and measure the rate of flow we can deduce resistance. The greater the flow, the less the resistance.

In electrical work, this is the function of an *ohmmeter* (or, in most toolboxes, *one* of the functions of a volt-ohm meter). It contains its own power source (a battery) that is the electrical equivalent of a pump and reservoir of water. The meter supplies current (amperage) at a carefully regulated pressure (voltage) to the circuit to be tested—the same as a pump pushing water through a pipe at regulated pressure. The meter measures the rate of flow (amperage); the less the flow the greater the resistance (ohms). Instead of displaying this rate of flow (amperage), the meter dial is simply reconfigured to display ohms of resistance.

Ohm's Law. As we have seen, pressure (voltage), rate of flow (amperage), and resistance to flow (ohms) are all interrelated. This relationship is summed up in a simple formula known as Ohm's Law (named for Georg Simon Ohm [1787–1854], a German physicist):

$I = E \div R$ where I = amperage; E = voltage; and R = resistance (ohms).

The formula can be rearranged to find either voltage or resistance:

$E = I \times R$ or $R = E \div I$

With this formula, if we can measure any two of voltage, amperage, or resistance, we can easily calculate the third.

Understanding DC Circuits

What is Direct Current?

Direct current is easy to understand. The flow of electrons—the fundamental unit of electricity—is all in one direction, making a DC system directly analogous to the flow of water in a pressurized water system. When a battery powers a circuit, the electrons flow around in one direction; when the battery is recharged the flow is reversed. All batteries and solar panels produce direct current (DC).

Ground Return; Insulated Return

The type of DC circuit that people are most familiar with is the *ground ("earth") return circuit* found on automobiles. This utilizes the car's frame as the ground (negative) side of the system. *Hot* (positive) wires carry current through switches to all lights, instruments, etc.; these are then *grounded* (earthed) to the car frame, which forms the return path to the battery's negative terminal. The negative terminal is connected by a heavy cable to the engine block, which in turn is connected to the car's frame via its mounts to complete the circuit. The big advantage of such a system is that only one (hot) wire need be run to electrical equipment.

Almost all marine engine installations use a ground-return circuit. That is to say, electrical equipment on the engine, such as the starter motor or alternator, is grounded to the engine block, which in turn is connected to the battery's negative terminal with a heavy cable.

Although it is commonly used, this is not a recommended procedure for boats. Imagine a poor (resistive) connection between the battery ground strap and the engine block.

The battery's negative post usually will be tied into the boat's *common ground point,* which in turn likely will have the bonding strap connected to it (more on this later). All the through-hull fittings will be connected to the bonding strap. Rather than take the electrical return path through the resistive battery ground strap, equipment grounded to the engine block may find a path back to the battery via the propeller shaft and propeller, through the water, into a through hull, up the bonding strap, through the common ground point, and so back to the battery. Stray current corrosion will follow (more on this later).

Engine-mounted electrical equipment should be of the *insulated-return* type. This requires purpose-built alternators and starter motors, or equipment mounts that electrically isolate the equipment from the engine block. A second ground conductor is installed to form an insulated return path to the battery. *The engine block is never part of the circuit.*

All good purpose-built marine alternators and starter motors have insulated grounds. Existing ground-return alternators can be converted to insulated-ground types by drilling out all mounting holes and installing nylon bushings and washers so as to completely insulate the alternator from the engine block. Then a separate ground wire must be run from the alternator case to the battery's negative post (or, preferably, the boat's common ground point). This wire must be at least as heavy as the main output wire from the alternator, since it will be a full current-carrying conductor.

If you decide not to convert an existing alternator to an insulated-ground one, a

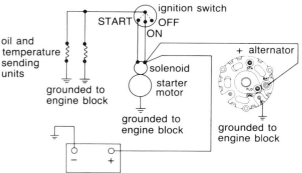

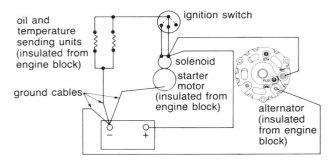

Figure 3-6A. **Ground-return circuit schematic.**

Figure 3-6B. **Insulated-ground circuit.**

heavy ground wire always should be connected from the alternator case to the engine block, since the alternator mounting brackets frequently form a poor ground connection and are electrically "noisy," causing interference.

Uninsulated starter motors are harder to insulate than alternators, but since they only operate for a second or two, the duration of any leakage currents will be strictly limited.

The electronic sending units that are mounted on most modern engines and that monitor oil pressure and water temperature are generally grounded through the block, as is other electrically operated equipment such as solenoid-type fuel shutdown valves. Anytime the ignition is on, small currents flow to ground through these units. The only way to stop this is to replace the sending units (and other devices) with purpose-built insulated-ground units. These will have a separate ground wire, carried back to the battery's negative terminal. VDO, among others, makes insulated-ground sending devices.

Whether or not engine installations use a ground-return circuit or have an insulated ground, *the rest of the DC system never should use a ground-return circuit, even if possible,* such as on steel boats or a fiberglass boat with a copper bonding strap running the length of the boat. In a steel boat using the hull as a ground circuit, or a fiberglass boat using the bonding strap, different parts of the hull and underwater fittings will have slightly different voltages; corrosion will be rampant.

All DC equipment on boats must have a separate insulated-ground cable that runs back to the ground (negative) side of the distribution panel. The panel ground *buss bar* is in turn connected to the battery's negative terminal. At no point is the hull or any fittings or fixtures used as an electrical path. To do so is to invite corrosion.

The normal practice is to install fuses and single-pole breakers in the hot wires leading to equipment, leaving the ground side connected permanently to the battery's negative terminal (Figure 3–7). Occasionally, however, both hot and ground wires are fused and fitted with two-pole breakers and switches. Anytime the breakers are tripped or switches turned off, the individual circuits are *totally* isolated, which helps to reduce the risk of any ground (earth) leaks (see page 83).

Standard wiring practice is to use red or orange cable for the hot or positive side of DC appliances, and black or white cable for the ground, or negative, side. It is preferable to use duplex wire—wire with two separate insulated conductors included in a common jacket—rather than individual cables. Where separate cables are used, several circuits often end up sharing the same ground wire, which becomes overloaded, resulting in excessive voltage drop (see page 80). This is unlikely to happen with duplex cables.

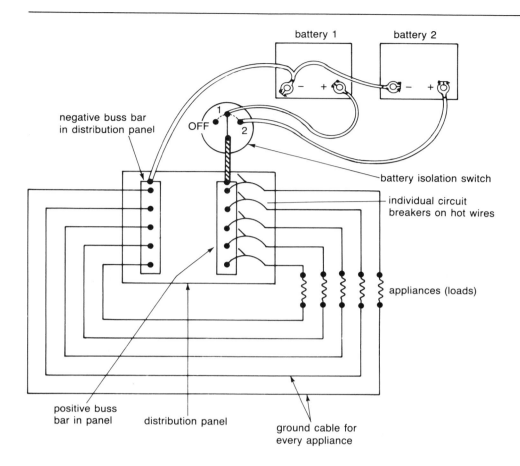

Figure 3-7. **Typical 12-volt circuit aboard a boat.**

battery 1

battery 2

negative buss bar
in distribution panel

OFF

battery isolation switch

individual circuit
breakers on hot wires

appliances (loads)

positive buss
bar in panel

distribution panel

ground cable for
every appliance

Understanding AC Circuits

AC power on board is broadly the same as in a household, with one or two subtle but important differences dictated by the more hazardous marine environment and the need to prevent stray-current (*electrolytic*) corrosion.

What is Alternating Current?

Alternating current theory is a bit harder to grasp than direct current. Unlike DC, which is conveniently analogous to water flow, the flow of electrons in AC circuits constantly reverses direction. Consider an ore-carrying train in a quarry. It moves in and out, coming out loaded and going back empty; it never really goes anywhere, but does a lot of work.

As we saw in Chapter 2 ("Alternators: How They Work"), electricity is generated either by spinning a magnet inside a set of coils or by spinning a set of coils around a magnet. As the positive and negative poles of the magnet pass a coil, positive and negative pulses are generated in the coil, causing the electrical output to oscillate continuously from the positive to negative *polarity* and back, rather than flowing in one direction. From a positive voltage peak to a negative voltage peak and back to a positive peak is a *cycle*. The number of cycles in one second (hertz, or Hz) is the *frequency*. In the USA, all alternating current cycles from positive to negative and back 60 times per second; it therefore has a frequency of 60 Hz. In the UK and Continental Europe, frequency is 50 Hz. A graph of voltage against time forms a series of sine waves (Figure 3-8).

The normal system voltage—115 volts, 230 volts, etc.—is in fact an average known as *root mean square,* or RMS. The voltage at the peak of the sine waves—both positive and negative—is actually considerably higher than the nominal (RMS) voltage of

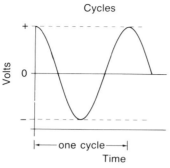

Cycles

Root mean square (RMS) voltage

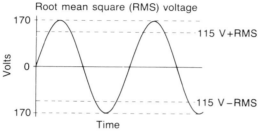

Figure 3-8. Characteristics of AC power. The current cycles back and forth from positive to negative polarity, reaching voltage peaks that are considerably greater than its effective or root mean square (RMS) voltage.

the system. Find peak voltage by dividing the RMS voltage by 0.707. A 110-volt (RMS) circuit actually has a peak voltage of 110 ÷ 0.707 = 155.59 volts; a 115-volt (RMS) circuit has a peak voltage 162.66 volts, and a 240-volt (RMS) circuit, a peak voltage of 399.46 volts.

Why use such an odd divisor as 0.707? Because from any given peak voltage *this gives us an RMS voltage that will do the equivalent amount of work as the same DC voltage:* 155.59 peak volts of AC will do the same work as 110 volts of DC (110 ÷ 0.707 = 155.59). In any event, you needn't remember these figures! The sole reason for mentioning them is that the sine wave nature of AC power is relevant to DC/AC inverters, covered in Chapter 5.

The earth—meaning the planet, globe, world—is the common reference point for electrical circuits (with the exception of isolated circuits; see below). The earth has its own *ground potential* or voltage. Alternating current of 115 volts surges first to 162.66 volts positive and then to 162.66 volts negative for an *RMS* value of 115 volts with respect to this common reference point.

The earth is made this common reference point by "tying" the return side of AC circuits to it. This is done quite literally by connecting a conductor between a generator and a large metal plate buried in the earth; hence the ground-connection circuit is often referred to as *earth.* A basic AC circuit thus comprises a hot (positive) wire from the generator to an appliance and a

return (neutral, or negative) wire back to the generator to complete the circuit, which is maintained at the earth's ground potential through its connection to the earth. Any conductor between a hot wire and earth's ground will become live, conducting current to ground (*shorted* to ground; Figure 3-9A).

A person who becomes part of a circuit between a hot wire and ground receives a shock; the current flows through the person to earth (Figure 3-9B).

Typical AC Circuits: Afloat and Ashore

In the USA, a 115-volt circuit (actual range 110 to 120 volts, depending on regional power grids and the voltage drop in the shore-power cable) uses three wires: a green (or bare) *ground* wire; a white *neutral* wire; and a black *hot* wire.

A 230-volt circuit in the USA (not the UK) uses four wires: a green (or bare) *ground* wire; a white *neutral* wire; a black *hot* wire; and a red *hot* wire. A 240-volt circuit in the UK (*NOT* the USA) uses three wires but with different color codes. By the old UK code: a green or bare *ground* (earth) wire; a black *neutral* (negative) wire; and a red *hot* (positive) wire. The new European standard code uses: green and yellow for *earth;* light blue for *neutral;* and brown for *positive* (hot). *IN WHAT FOLLOWS ALL COLORS REFER TO USA COLOR CODES.*

The white (neutral) and black (hot) wires (plus the red on a USA 230-volt circuit) are the two current-carrying conductors: the black (and red) supply current to an appliance; the white forms the return line to the power source. The black (and red) wires are *never* connected to the ground—this would create a direct short. The white wire is *always* connected to ground eventually to keep the system tied to the earth's ground potential (except with Type-A isolation transformers, as discussed later in this chapter).

In household installations the ground connection on the white (neutral) wire is reinforced by running all the white wires in the household circuits into a neutral *buss bar*—a metal terminal strip with cable-retaining screws—which in turn is connected to both the incoming white wire from the electric company and also to the household ground, which is generally a buried metal plate or pipe (see Figure 3-10A).

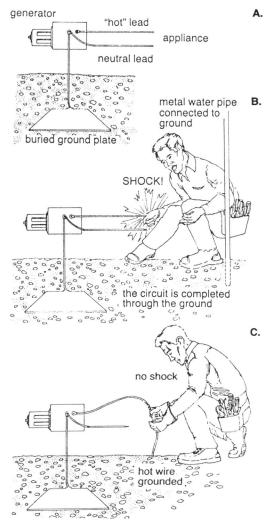

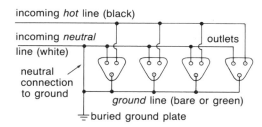

A.

incoming *hot* line (black)

incoming *neutral* line (white)

neutral connection to ground

outlets

ground line (bare or green)

buried ground plate

Figure 3-10A. Household electrical circuits. (USA color codes are shown.) The neutral and ground circuits are tied together.

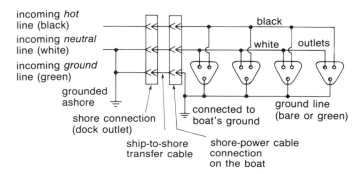

incoming *hot* line (black)

incoming *neutral* line (white)

incoming *ground* line (green)

grounded ashore

shore connection (dock outlet)

ship-to-shore transfer cable

black

white   outlets

connected to boat's ground

ground line (bare or green)

shore-power cable connection on the boat

Figure 3-10B. Shipboard AC circuits. The neutral and ground circuits are not tied together on the boat—only on shore. The ground line can be connected to the boat's ground as shown, but minor onboard electrical leaks or stray currents brought aboard through the shore-to-ship ground line may then corrode underwater hardware. If the connection to boat's ground is eliminated, as some authorities recommend, a corroded terminal or other discontinuity in the shoreside ground connection could pose a severe shock hazard.

Figure 3-9. Basic AC circuits and safety. Note that a hot wire grounded as in **C** could be handled safely but would short-circuit the generator. In practice the only sensible thing to do is to stay away from the hot wire of a live circuit.

On boats (see Figure 3-10B), the white (neutral) wires are *never* grounded to *any* point on the boat (except where "Type-B" isolation transformers are used; see below). The ground is provided via the shoreside hook-up cable or onboard generator frame. The explanation for this is simple enough:

- For many reasons the boat's ground is not always at exactly the same potential (voltage) as the earth. If the white wire is grounded *within the boat* and the boat ground and earth are at different voltages, *current will flow through underwater fittings to ground.* This can lead to devastating stray-current corrosion, which in extreme cases can destroy fittings *in days* (see page 102).

- Should a boat with a grounded neutral system be hooked up with *reverse polarity* (the hot and neutral wires crossed)—a common enough occurrence from improper wiring or the use of two-prong plugs—the incoming hot line will be shorted directly to ground via the neutral ground connection and the boat's underwater fittings. Very high currents will flow.

To repeat: except for a few isolation transformers (and onboard generators, which have the neutral grounded at their frame), no current-carrying AC wire is ever grounded on a boat!

Since the hot (black, or red where fitted) wire(s) are ungrounded at any point in the circuit—either on the boat or on land—they present a severe shock hazard. Any person or conductive object touching un-insulated portions of these wires creates *a path to ground and current will flow*. However, since the white wire is grounded (ashore or at the onboard generator frame), even though it is a full current-carrying conductor, touching it generally will not cause a shock. The current will continue to flow via the wire rather than the person or object touching it. Should the white wire's path to ground be broken, however, such as through a disconnected or corroded terminal, touching the wire on the hot side of the break presents the same shock hazard as touching a hot wire. Similarly, touching any hot wire and any neutral wire *at the same time* will cause severe shock.

The most fundamental safety requirement in working with electrical circuits is effective earthing; this prevents a person becoming part of a hot path.

The green (or bare) ground (earth) wire is a safety wire and *is never a current-carrying conductor in normal use*. In household use, it is connected to the buried ground and to the external (metal) cabinets of appliances, the metal framework of motors, and so on. If a short develops in any appliance so that its exterior becomes "hot" and presents a shock hazard, this ground wire conducts the current safely to ground. *The only time a ground wire should carry current is when there is a short in wiring or in an appliance.*

On a boat the equipment grounding wire is normally connected to both the shoreside hook-up and the boat's common ground point. If a short develops such that the exterior of an appliance becomes hot and presents a shock hazard, this ground wire conducts the current to earth via either the shoreside hook-up ground or underwater hardware connected to the boat's ground. (Note that this may present a shock hazard to nearby swimmers!) The problem with this system is that any current flowing to ground (earth) through underwater hardware poses the threat of stray current corrosion. Major shorts will likely trip a circuit breaker and so draw attention to themselves, but minor leaks—common enough in the damp marine environment—are likely to go undetected and damage underwater hardware.

To try and eliminate the threat of stray current corrosion to underwater hardware, the United States Power Squadron recommends a "floating AC system." This uses the shoreside ground connection, only omitting the connection to the boat's ground. In theory the boat is protected against AC-generated stray currents, since the underwater hardware is no part of any AC ground circuit; in practice, however, an accidental connection to the boat's ground is often made via onboard generators (the frames of which are almost invariably connected to the boat's ground) or via bonding straps (more on this later). If such a connection is made we are back with the first grounding system and the threat of stray current corrosion. If, on the other hand, no such connection is made, the floating AC system increases the shock hazard to those on board, since any break or resistance in the shoreside ground connection—such as frequently arises from a corroded terminal in a ship-to-shore cable—leaves ground-fault current with no place to safely go.

Other equipment grounding systems have been developed to reduce the threat of stray current corrosion without increasing the risk of shock. The most notable are those using *isolation transformers* and *isolators*. These are covered later in this chapter.

In both households and boats, *switches are never installed in any ground wire. This would defeat its purpose:* to provide a redundant path to earth in the event of electrical system failure. On a 115-volt circuit (USA) and 240-volt circuit (UK), the ground connection to an appliance is made via the third pin of a three-prong plug. Two-prong outlets (receptacles) and plugs have no ground connection and lack this important safety feature. *Two-prong outlets and plugs are not suitable for use in the damp marine environment.* In the USA, 115-volt receptacles are wired with the black (hot) lead to the black or brass screw and the white (neutral) lead to the silver screw. Switching these will lead to reverse polarity.

As noted, 230-volt circuits (*in the USA only*) incorporate a second hot, 115-volt wire, which is color-coded red. The incoming breaker box will have two hot buss bars, one connected to the black wire and one connected to the red; it also will have the neutral buss bar and ground connection. All 115-volt appliances are connected to either the black or the red buss bar, together with the normal neutral and ground connections. Usually an attempt is made to spread the load of 115-volt appliances equally between both hot buss bars. All 230-volt appliances are connected to *both* the black and red bus bars, omitting

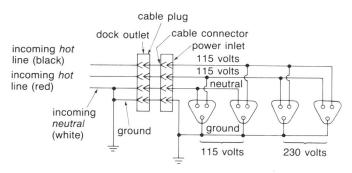

Figure 3-11. A 230-volt AC circuit (USA wiring practices). As in Figure 3-10B, the neutral line is not grounded on board. The 115-volt appliances are spread equally between the two hot buss bars in order to balance the electrical load. The 230-volt appliances have two hot terminals and no neutral.

the neutral connection (the red wire takes its place) but retaining the green (or bare) safety wire to ground (Figure 3-11).

Onboard AC Power: Specific Components

Polarity testers. Most AC panels sold for marine use now incorporate a polarity testing light (Figure 3-12). If it glows green, polarity is correct. If it fails to light, or on some units if it glows red, polarity is reversed. On units with red lights, no light indicates correct polarity. (See page 103 for important considerations on polarity light installations and stray-current corrosion.) In the absence of a testing light, polarity is easily checked. Connect a volt-ohm meter or test light (115-volt in the USA; 240-volt in the UK) between the *incoming* AC hot wire(s)—*before* an isolation transformer if fitted—and a good ground, such as a through-hull fitting that is below the waterline. The meter should show system voltage or the light should glow. Next connect the meter or light between the incoming neutral line and ground. The meter should read no volts or the light should remain unlit. If there is voltage or the lamp lights between neutral and ground, but nothing between the hot side and ground, polarity is reversed. If there is nothing on either side, the shore power is not hooked up or switched on, or the test light is grounded improperly.

Two-pole circuit breakers. Household circuits use single-pole circuit breakers in the hot lines to appliances. In a reverse-polarity situation, the breaker operates on the neutral side of the circuit. It still will work effectively as a switch (no current will flow) but the appliance and wiring all the

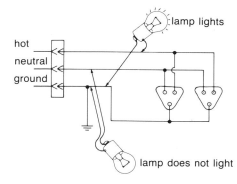

Figure 3-12. Polarity testing. A test lamp should light when placed between the hot wire and ground; if it does not light, either the polarity is reversed or the circuit is dead. The lamp should fail to light when placed between neutral and ground. If it lights, the circuit polarity is reversed. Polarity lights built into electrical panels should have momentary-type switches that will shut off when released. Otherwise the light will contribute to stray-current corrosion.

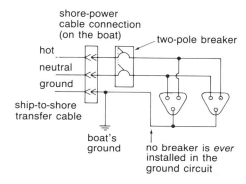

Figure 3-13. When a two-pole breaker trips, it stops current flow to the entire circuit regardless of whether polarity is normal or reversed.

way through to the breaker are now hot. This creates a potentially hazardous situation in the damp marine atmosphere.

Two-pole breakers cut both the hot and neutral lines simultaneously, rendering the circuit safe *irrespective of polarity*. At the very least *the main incoming AC breaker on a boat should be of the two-pole type*. Better yet, two-pole breakers also should be used on all branch circuits.

Remember: No breaker or fuse ever should be included in the green (or bare) ground (earth) line (Figure 3-13).

Ship-to-shore transfer switch. Boats with both shoreside hookups and onboard AC generating capability use the same AC circuit. If ever the two power sources are switched into the AC circuit at the same time, the generator is likely to suffer extensive damage. Therefore a proper two-pole, ship-to-shore transfer switch is needed; this switch will break both current-carrying conductors from one power source before making the connec-

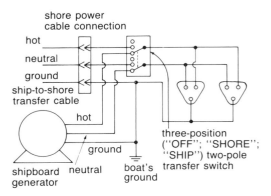

Figure 3-14. Ship-to-shore transfer switch. Power must never be admitted to an AC circuit from more than one source at a time.

shore power cable connection

hot

neutral

ground

ship-to-shore transfer cable

hot

ground

neutral

boat's ground

shipboard generator

three-position ("OFF"; "SHORE"; "SHIP") two-pole transfer switch

tion to the other power source (Figure 3-14). Where a DC/AC inverter is used the same considerations apply. *It must never be possible to switch two AC power sources into the same circuit at the same time.*

Volt and frequency meters. Boats venturing abroad will find a variety of different voltages and frequencies. Even "at-home" voltages in many marinas may be low because of voltage drop in inadequate wiring (see later in this chapter). Appliances with resistive loads, such as light bulbs, heaters, toasters, or ovens, will tolerate fairly wide variations in voltage and frequency. Most appliances that use induction motors, such as refrigerators, freezers, washing machines, tape decks, and sewing machines, will not. Because we need to know the voltage and frequency of AC power, all AC circuits should have a voltmeter and frequency meter connected at the main breaker.

The most commonly encountered problem is stepping up from 115 to 240 volts (USA to UK), or down from 240 to 115 volts (UK to USA) with a concomitant change in frequency from 60 Hz to 50 Hz (USA to UK) or 50 Hz to 60 Hz (UK to USA). The voltage change is easy enough: It merely requires an appropriate transformer. A frequency change is a little trickier.

A 115-volt motor designed to operate on 60 cycles will overheat and ultimately fail if fed 115 volts and 50 cycles. Changes in frequency also will affect the speed at which motors turn. This is immaterial with most appliances but obviously critical for tape decks and record players. The only effective way to compensate for speed changes is by altering internal pulley ratios—an involved procedure.

Ground fault interruptors (GFIs). A ground fault interruptor (GFI), also known as a residual current circuit breaker, is a device that senses the current flow through both a hot and a neutral wire in a circuit. Any short to ground, such as someone receiving a shock, creates an imbalance (less current flows through the neutral wire than the hot) and the GFI trips the circuit. GFIs are incredibly sensitive and fast acting, and provide a large measure of safety from shock.

The very effectiveness of GFIs is sometimes a drawback, however. In the marine environment, there are invariably minute current leakages in AC systems. The accumulation of these over half a dozen individual branch circuits on a boat often will be enough to trip a central GFI even when no real (or curable) problem exists. For this reason, it is preferable to install individual GFIs on each branch circuit rather than have one central unit. Note: *GFIs provide no protection against touching both hot and neutral wires at the same time,* since the current flow through both is affected equally and the GFI senses no imbalance.

Isolation transformers. The concept of an isolation transformer is simple. Shore power is fed into one side of a transformer and transferred *magnetically* to the other side. *There is no direct electrical connection.* The transformer itself is insulated from the boat, and its case is grounded (earthed) *back to shore* via the green (bare) equipment grounding wire. (Where a 115/230-volt system [USA] is installed, i.e., two hot wires, shoreside neutral is not brought aboard the boat. See Figure 3-15C.)

This provides onboard AC power—via hot and neutral lines from the boat side of the transformer—that has *no electrical connection to the earth's ground.* The earth forms no part of the boat's AC circuit. This means that even if you touch a live wire on board, the current will not run to ground—you will not get shocked—because the earth is not part of the circuit. The only way to get shocked is to insert yourself into the *boat's* circuit by touching hot and neutral leads simultaneously. I will call this isolation circuit a "Type-A" circuit.

A circuit with an isolation transformer is inherently safer not just for people but also for boats. Because the earth's ground is not part of the circuit, stray currents will not flow to ground via underwater fittings. Properly installed, isolation transformers can eliminate all AC-generated stray cur-

Understanding and Troubleshooting Electrical Circuits

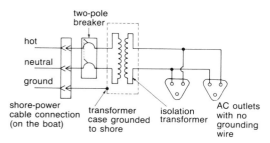

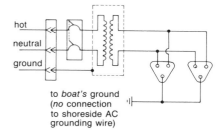

Figure 3-15A. Schematic of a "Type-A" isolation transformer circuit, in which the onboard grounding line is eliminated. This is advocated by some writers but is considered unacceptable by the ABYC due to potential shock hazard (see text).

Figure 3-15B. Here the shipboard grounding circuit is retained and connected to the boat's central ground point. This elaboration serves no obvious purpose, since the earth's ground is unrelated to the shipboard circuit, and electrical shorts will not follow this path to ground. It does not increase protection against potential shock hazards.

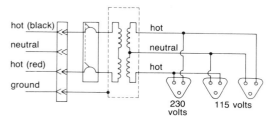

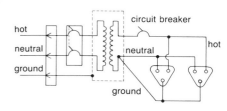

Figure 3-15C. Isolation transformer schematic for a 115/230 volts AC (USA) system. Note that, as in Figure 3-11, 230-volt appliances are wired to both hot wires but not the neutral, and 115-volt appliances are spread equally between the two hot wires. The circuit may be grounded as in Figure 3-15D or E. Note that the shore-power neutral line is not brought aboard the boat.

Figure 3-15D. Isolation circuit with an onboard grounding line. A short to ground will find its way back into the neutral line, completing the circuit while bypassing the resistance; a large amount of current will flow, tripping the breaker.

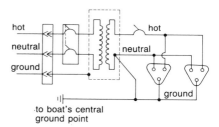

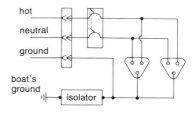

Figure 3-15E. Type-B isolation circuit: In this ABYC-recommended elaboration of the ground return shown in Figure 3-15D, the shipboard AC ground is tied via the boat's central ground point to earth's ground.

Figure 3-15F. This AC circuit has no isolation transformer but does incorporate an isolated ground. It is otherwise similar to the circuits shown in Figures 3-10B and 3-13.

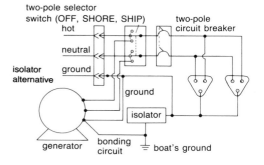

Figure 3-15G. A bonding circuit bypassing and thereby negating a ground isolator. Note that if the isolator were moved to the alternative placement shown, this inadvertent bypass could not occur.

rents between boat and water. For this reason they are especially recommended for boats with corrosion-susceptible steel and aluminum hulls.

Opinions differ as to the mechanics of Type A isolation transformer installation. Because the earth's ground is in no way related to the onboard circuit, one school of thought is to eliminate the green (or bare) grounding wire altogether (Figure 3-15A); the other is to retain it and tie it in to the boat's central ground point (see page 113 and Figure 3-15B). The rationale for this is a little hard to grasp. Since the earth's ground is of no relevance to the isolated circuit, electrical shorts cannot follow this path to ground; so it is difficult to see what protection it provides.

Now enter the ABYC. The ABYC assumes that in the real world faults will occur from the hot side of an isolation circuit to ground. A short circuit in an appliance would be one example. An improper wiring project would be another. Since earth's ground forms no part of the onboard circuit, no current will flow through such a fault and *the main circuit breaker will not trip* (it takes a current flow greater than the circuit breaker's rating to make it trip). There is now a potential shock hazard—against which the circuit breaker can offer no protection—to anyone who completes the circuit between the grounded hot side of the isolation circuit and the neutral side. The ABYC feels a ground system is needed to eliminate this shock hazard.

This ground system is provided by running a green (or bare) equipment grounding wire to all receptacles and external metal cases of AC appliances, *and then tying the white (neutral) side of the boat's AC circuit to this grounding circuit,* just as the neutral buss bar in a household circuit is tied to ground. The boat now has its *own* ground circuit, to which all appliances are grounded. Any equipment that shorts to this ground will cause high currents to flow and will trip the main circuit breaker (Figure 3-15D).

Note that this ground is still not tied to the earth's ground and, in fact, may "float" at a different potential. The ABYC, however, specifically ties it to the boat's central ground point, which, in turn, is tied to the earth's ground via various pieces of underwater hardware in the boat's bonding circuit and also via the engine and propeller shaft and the radio grounds connected to the DC ground system (Figure 3-15E). The net effect is to hold the grounding circuit and the neutral side of the AC circuit

at the earth's potential. I will call this a "Type B" isolation transformer.

Since a Type B isolation circuit includes no direct electrical connection between the shoreside ground (which terminates at the transformer case) and the boat's grounding circuit, leakage currents in the shoreside ground cannot find a path into the boat's ground circuit. On the boat side of the transformer, despite the neutral connection to the boat's ground, any leaks in the AC system will not run to earth via underwater hardware, since the earth is not a part of the isolation circuit; the ground-fault circuit is completely contained in the boat's AC wiring.

Testing an isolation transformer: Type A (no connection to earth's ground)—Connect a volt-ohm meter or a test light between each of the two current-carrying wires of the boat's AC system and a well-grounded connection to earth, such as a through hull below water level; if the meter shows voltage or the light glows on either wire, there is leakage to ground within the transformer. Type B (onboard neutral side grounded to boat's ground)—Disconnect the *onboard* neutral wire from the grounding circuit and test as for Type A above.

Isolators. I have mentioned stray-current corrosion before and will deal with it in more detail later; it's an important subject. Stray-current corrosion is often caused by minute differences in ground potential between a boat and the earth that cause small currents to flow through underwater fittings. We have seen how in a typical AC system such a leakage current may find a path to ground via underwater hardware. Leakage may originate from within the boat *or from other boats and dockside,* in which case *it is brought on board via the green, or bare, equipment grounding wire.*

Leakage from the AC grounding system can be prevented by using an *isolator* between the AC grounding circuit and the boat's common ground point (Figure 3-15F). An isolator is a device that blocks small voltages (generally up to 1.5 volts) but conducts readily when hit by large voltages. As a result, it effectively isolates the AC grounding circuit from the earth's ground in normal circumstances. A short in the AC system closes the circuit and conducts the short safely to ground.

There is a snag, however. To work properly, every part of the AC grounding circuit must be electrically independent of any bonding circuit or DC ground circuit, since these are also tied to the common ground point. If any single piece of AC equipment is grounded both to the AC grounding circuit and to the bonding circuit or the DC ground circuit, this will effectively bypass the isolator *for the whole AC grounding circuit* (Figure 3-15G). Since many boats often do have some equipment (such as onboard generators) included in both bonding and/or DC ground circuits, and AC grounding circuits, careful planning is required for an isolator to work.

This problem can be overcome with a slight loss of protection for underwater hardware by installing the isolator on the *incoming shore-power ground connection.* It will still effectively block the path of any leakage current emanating from ashore or from other boats, but it will not prevent leakage currents arising within the boat from finding a path to ground via underwater hardware; in fact, where small leaks are concerned, the resistance of the isolator will actually encourage them to run to earth via the boat's ground.

Multimeter: The Essential Tool

A multimeter—also called a VOM (volt-ohm meter) or AVO (amps-volts-ohms meter)—is the essential electrical trouble-shooting tool. They sell for $15 and up; *no boat should be without one.* Meters vary from one brand to another, but most incorporate the following scales:

- AC voltage scales from 10 to as much as 10,000 volts.
- DC voltage scales from 2.5 to as much as 1,000 volts.
- DC amperage scales from 0 to 250 mA (milliamps: thousandths of an amp).
- Ohms scales of "R × 1," "R × 10," and "R × 100."

Better meters incorporate more sensitive measurements and greater ranges. Boat owners should look for meters with the following refinements:

- A DC voltage scale of 0 to 15 volts. The more commonly found 0-to-10 volt and 0-to-50-volt scales are too low and too high respectively for accurate measurements on a 12-volt system.
- A DC-amp capacity of up to 10 amps. The milliamps scales are useful only for troubleshooting ground leaks and electronics, and the latter are best left alone by the average boatowner.
- An expanded ohms scale in low range. Most cheap ohmmeters have a scale calibrated from 0 to 1 K (1,000) ohms, with fairly even spacing up to 100 ohms and then a compressed scale to 1K ohms. This scale makes accurate readings at the lower end of the scale impossible; the numbers are just too close together. What is needed is an expanded scale to around 30 ohms—from 0 to 30 ohms should take up half the scale—with a more compressed scale up to 1K ohms. It should be noted that cheap meters are, in any case, highly inaccurate on the low ohms scales.

Digital multimeters are now commonly available. Like a digital watch, these reduce the possibility of error when reading scales. Although more expensive (about $50.00 on up) than most standard multimeters, one would be a good investment for the serious troubleshooter.

A meter's different functions and scales are accessed by plugging jacks into different holes or by turning a multiposition switch (preferable). The meter will have two output leads: one red, one black. Red is hot ("+" or "POS"); black is ground ("−" or "COMMON"). Switch-type meters sometimes have a different plug-in point for AC and DC measurements; the meter will be clearly marked. Resistance readings are made using the DC output terminals.

When taking AC voltage readings it is immaterial which way you place the leads, but for reading DC voltages and amperages the red (+) lead must go to the positive side of the circuit and the black (−) to the negative side, or the meter will read backwards. On most resistance tests the leads can be either way around unless the circuit contains a diode (see Chapter 2, "Diodes").

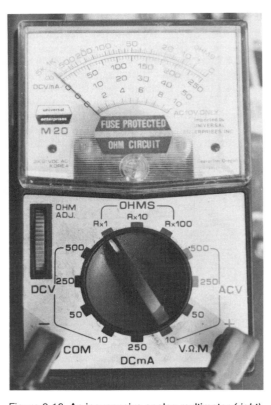

Figure 3-16. An inexpensive analog multimeter (right) and a more expensive but more useful digital meter (left). The selector switch on the analog meter points to the R × 1 scale, indicating that the operator will be measuring resistance and will not need to multiply his reading in ohms by 10 or 100 to obtain the correct measurement. The following abbreviations are common: ACV (or VAC), volts AC; DCV, volts DC; DCmA, milliamps DC. When measuring voltages of unknown magnitude, start with the selector on a high scale, to be safe, and change to lower scales as necessary for sensitivity. There are two test leads. The red is hot and should be plugged into the + jack; the black is ground and should be plugged into the − jack. When you are testing DC voltages and amperages the red lead must go to the positive side of the circuit; this distinction is not important when you are testing AC voltages. The meter may have different jacks for AC and DC measurements; these will be clearly marked. The needle should point to zero volts when the leads are removed; adjust as necessary with the null adjustment screw. Use the ohms adjustment knob to "zero out" the resistance scale before each ohms measurement; to do this, hold the probes together, then turn the knob as necessary. Alligator probes are handy for most tests; needle probes sometimes reach places that alligator probes cannot.

Using a Multimeter

AC circuits can kill! If you doubt what you are doing, don't go poking around AC circuits!

AC and DC circuits frequently share the same distribution panel. Be sure to *disconnect the AC power cord* and turn off any DC/AC inverters before opening such panels. Merely switching off the incoming breaker will *not* do since it will leave hot wires on the supply side in the panel.

Any voltage (AC or DC) can blow out a meter (and possibly injure the operator) when the meter is in the resistance or amps mode. *When measuring ohms be absolutely certain to electrically isolate the relevant circuit. When measuring amps be careful not to bridge the power leads with the meter probe.*

Recently I tested a piece of equipment using the DC amps mode, and immediately afterward tested an AC circuit for voltage. I turned the selector switch to the correct AC position, but on this meter—which I was using for the first time—it is also necessary to reposition the leads in different jack sockets, which of course I forgot to do. *The instant I bridged the AC power lines the meter leads exploded in my hands* with a loud bang and a big cloud of smoke! Luckily I was unhurt, though I was left dazed and mumbling: "What the hell did I do?"

Moral: *Always check and recheck meter lead and switch positions before making a reading.*

In order to avoid draining its battery, a meter must be turned off when not in use, or turned to the highest AC volts scale if it has no "OFF" position.

Reading voltage. Always begin by selecting the highest potential voltage scale on the meter. For example, if the boat has 230- and 115-volt AC circuits set the meter to the 250 VAC scale initially, even when checking 115-volt circuits. If you tap a 230-volt line inadvertently, the meter will not be damaged. Switch down to a more appropriate scale, such as 150 volts, only after you're sure your meter probes are positioned properly.

The meter is more accurate and easier to read the closer the measured voltage is to the limit of the scale being used; 115 volts will be displayed more accurately on a 150-volt scale than a 250-volt scale.

Voltage can be read at any point in a circuit by connecting the meter between a ground and an uninsulated terminal or section of wire. Most meter probes have

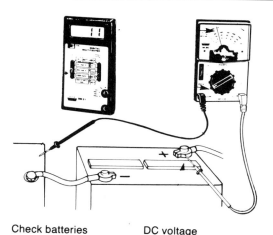

Check batteries   DC voltage

Figure 3-17. **Using multimeters.**

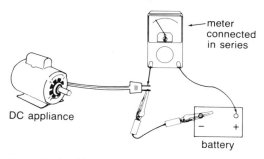

Figure 3-18A. **Measuring current draw (in amps) of a DC appliance.**

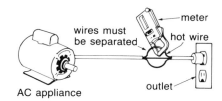

Figure 3-18B. **Measuring amperage draw of an AC appliance.** This purpose-built meter (Amprobe is one brand) clips around individual hot wires to measure their magnetism, which is directly related to the current they carry. A simple device known as a line splitter can be inserted between the plug and outlet to obviate the need for separating the wires in the cable as shown here.

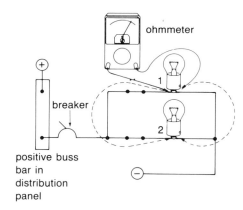

Figure 3-18C. **Testing a circuit with an ohmmeter.** In this example two lights are installed with common DC supply and ground wires. Because the breaker is open you might think you are testing light bulb 1 for resistance, when in fact you may instead be testing the circuit all the way around through light bulb 2 (dashed line). To avoid ambiguity, always isolate specific pieces of equipment or parts of a circuit.

sharp points; if necessary the probe can be forced into contact with a conductor through the wire's insulation, although this should not be done unless it is absolutely necessary. The wound in the wire can be covered with a dab of silicone sealant.

Reading amperage. DC and AC amperages are read in different ways; few multimeters have an AC amperage capability, although many can be adapted with a special fitting.

DC amps can only be read by connecting a meter (or a shunt and meter) *in series* with the conductor (Figure 3-18A). This means that the circuit must be broken and the meter inserted in it. It also means that *the circuit's full current (amperage) will flow through the meter.* Since most meters cannot handle more than 250 mA (thousandths of an amp) and very few appliances draw less than half an amp, the amperage scales are generally of little use except for troubleshooting electronics and ground faults (*earth leaks;* see below).

DC stereos, fans, and pumps generally draw from 0.5 amp to a maximum of 6 or 7 amps. For these, a meter with a capability of 10 amps DC is very useful. Electric winches, windlasses, and sail-furling systems have power-greedy motors, well beyond this range; measuring their amps requires expensive specialized equipment. At the very top end of the scale are starter motors, drawing several hundred amps.

Measuring AC amps is much easier. Alternating current sets up a magnetic field within its wires. The more the amperage, the greater the magnetism. Specially designed meters measure the flow (amps) when clipped around the hot wire(s) in AC circuits. The circuit needn't be broken, but the meter must be clipped around individual hot wire(s) only; if there is more than one hot wire, it must be clipped around each in turn (Figure 3-18B). Each hot wire must be separated from the neutral and ground wires and from any other hot wire. Special "line-splitters" can be bought to separate leads in a common housing without having to cut into the insulating sheath.

In general, amperage is far lower in AC circuits than in DC circuits. This is easy to understand. Since watts = volts × amps, amps = watts ÷ volts. Therefore, a 100-watt appliance will draw only 0.87 amps (110 ÷ 115) on a 115-volt system, whereas the same appliance will draw 8.3 amps (110 ÷ 12) on a 12-volt system.

Reading resistance. An ohmmeter is a delicate instrument. If it is hooked into a circuit under pressure, such as a circuit connected to a power source, the existing pressure will blow out the meter. An ohmmeter can be used only on disconnected circuits—i.e., those that have been isolated from voltage input. When isolating circuits, solar panels are frequently overlooked, but even the limited output of a small solar panel will blow an ohmmeter fuse.

Remember: Use an ohmmeter *only on isolated circuits*.

Ohms scales are displayed opposite to voltage and amperage scales. That is, zero ohms reads all the way to the right; infinite ohms reads all the way to the left. Most meters have three ohms scales: R × 1; R × 10; and R × 100. On R × 10 and R × 100, the displayed meter reading must be multiplied by 10 and 100 respectively.

Since the internal power source, and therefore the reference point, for an ohmmeter comes from a battery whose state of charge declines over time, the meter must be recalibrated to the existing state of charge of the battery before every use. This is done by touching the meter probes *firmly* together and turning a knob until the meter reads zero ohms.

Every time a meter is reused or the ohms scale changed (e.g., from R × 1 to R × 100), the meter needs recalibrating.

If the needle does not move when the probes are touched together—i.e., it stays all the way to the left on infinity—the probe wires are broken, the fuse is blown, the battery is dead or missing (or its terminals corroded and not making electrical contact), or the meter is defective.

When the meter probes are touched to two points in a circuit, the resistance is measured between these points (e.g., on either side of a switch). However, if the circuit has not been properly isolated you may think you are measuring resistance between the probes when, in fact, you are measuring it around the rest of the circuit! In order to avoid confusion, always disconnect the specific pieces of equipment—wires, switches, and so on—that are being tested for resistance (Figure 3-18C).

Troubleshooting Techniques

Testing DC Circuits

Reading voltage. The following tests all refer to a volt-ohm meter. A test light (see Figure 2-12) would be used in exactly the same way. Where the meter shows 12 volts, the test light will light; no volts, no light; low volts, dim light (or the test light barely glows). Remember: To test for voltage, a meter or test light must be connected between a "hot" line and ground, or at least a part of the circuit at a voltage closer to ground potential. The meter is measuring difference between system voltage and ground (or the lower voltage) at that point.

Basic circuit test. The most basic circuit test is simply to connect the meter between the positive and negative terminals on a 12-volt battery to read battery voltage—i.e., directly from "hot" to ground.

Load on circuit. Now let us make a circuit from the positive terminal to the negative terminal and put a piece of electronic gear in it (i.e., a resistance). We are placing a load on the circuit.

The line all the way to the resistance is "hot" and all the way back from it is at the battery "ground potential". A meter connected anywhere from the hot side to the ground side, right up to the two terminals on the equipment, will show 12 volts, but a meter with both probes on one side of the equipment or the other will give no reading (the meter is not bridging any voltage differential).

Circuit with switch. Now let's put in a battery isolation switch. When the switch is closed we have exactly the same situation as in the test above and the same procedures apply. A meter placed across the

Test Lights

In the absence of a multimeter, many useful tests can be made with a test light. On occasion a test light may give even better results than a multimeter.

For example: The points on a switch are badly corroded. The switch is closed, but there is no load (i.e., amperage flow) on the circuit. Because of its high sensitivity and low current draw, the voltmeter may show 12 volts downstream of the switch, whereas the test light will impose a small load on the circuit, which will reveal the resistance in the switch (the light will glow dimly).

To understand this, think of a pressurized water pipe with a severe restriction in it and a closed valve farther down the line. (The closed valve is the equivalent of no load, therefore no flow, on the electrical circuit.) Pressure will equalize on both sides of the restriction all the way to the closed valve, and a pressure gauge will not reveal the restriction. However, if we open the valve a little and let some water flow, pressure will drop downstream of the restriction and thus reveal its presence. The drain caused by a test light is the equivalent of opening the valve a little.

We can draw a useful conclusion from this analogy. When possible, circuits should be tested under normal load rather than in a no-load situation. This will reveal weaknesses that otherwise may be hard to find.

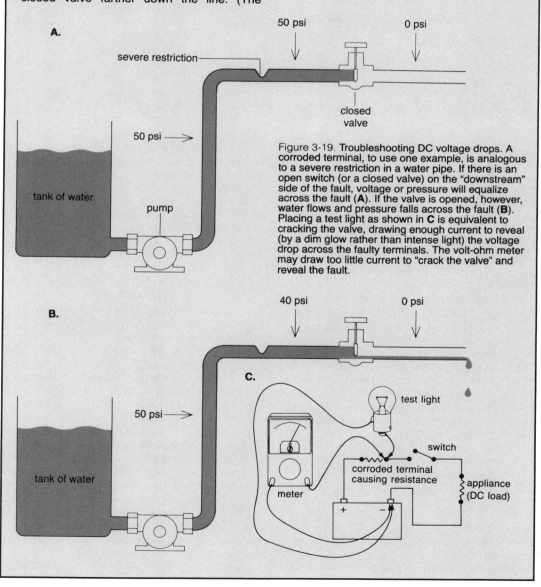

Figure 3-19. Troubleshooting DC voltage drops. A corroded terminal, to use one example, is analogous to a severe restriction in a water pipe. If there is an open switch (or a closed valve) on the "downstream" side of the fault, voltage or pressure will equalize across the fault (**A**). If the valve is opened, however, water flows and pressure falls across the fault (**B**). Placing a test light as shown in **C** is equivalent to cracking the valve, drawing enough current to reveal (by a dim glow rather than intense light) the voltage drop across the faulty terminals. The volt-ohm meter may draw too little current to "crack the valve" and reveal the fault.

Figure 3-20.
Troubleshooting DC
voltage drops. In a healthy
circuit meter 1 will show no
voltage reading, meter 2
will read the system
voltage, and meter 3 will
again show no voltage
drop.

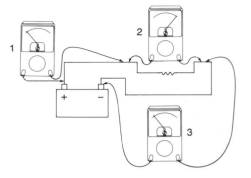

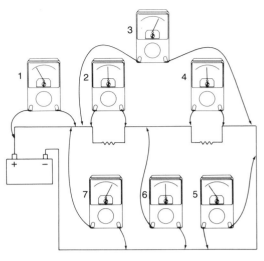

Figure 3-21.
Troubleshooting DC
voltage drops. Meters 1
and 4 should both show
the full system voltage
drop. Meters 2 and 3
should read 0 volts.

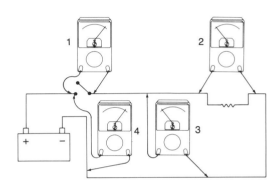

Figure 3-22. Troubleshooting DC voltage drops. We
now have two resistance loads in series, each of
which (meters 2 and 4) will show a voltage drop of
less than the total system voltage. Meter 3 will show
the system voltage, as should meter 7. Meter 6 should
give the same reading as meter 4, and meters 1 and 5
should read 0 volts. One of the two resistances is
unwanted (a faulty switch, for example), and these
tests will find it.

switch will not read anything. However, when the switch is open only the cable from the battery positive terminal to the switch is hot, and the whole of the rest of the circuit is "bled down" to ground. A meter placed across the switch will read system voltage, but if placed across the resistance (the piece of equipment) will read nothing.

Consider the analogy with a pressurized water system. If a valve is placed in the line before a restriction (resistance) as long as the valve is open the pressure (i.e., voltage) will be constant all the way to the restriction (resistance) and will then drop on the other side of the restriction (resistance). But if the valve is closed the pressure will bleed off the whole system downstream of the valve and the only pressure differential will be across the valve.

Unwanted resistance. Now let's put some wear and tear on our switch so that the points are dirty and pitted and the switch causes a resistance. When the switch is open, the situation is the same as when it is open in the test above. When the switch is closed, it is electrically the same as placing a second load in the circuit in series with the equipment load. In effect we have the situation shown in Figure 3-22.

There will be a voltage drop across both resistances. What is more, the voltage drop across each resistance will be proportional to the amount of its resistance as a percentage of the total resistance in the circuit. What does this mean in practice?

On a closed circuit, if a voltage test across the input and output terminals of any switch, terminal block, or length of wiring reveals *any voltage*, there is unwanted resistance in the switch, terminal block, or wire. If the voltage is less than 10 volts, switch to a lower scale on the meter for a more accurate reading.

The unwanted resistance is proportional to the voltage shown. For example, a reading of 6 volts on a 12-volt circuit indicates that the resistance is half the total resistance in the circuit. In other words, it is equal to the resistance of the equipment in the circuit, and the equipment will receive only half of its rated amperage. A reading of 3 volts indicates a resistance of 25 percent of the total resistance in the circuit; the equipment will receive only 75 percent of its rated amps.

Put another way, if a voltage test across the input and output terminals of a piece of equipment reveals less than battery voltage, we have unwanted resistance in the circuit due to inadequate wiring or poor connections and switches. The unwanted resistance is proportional to the extent of

Understanding and Troubleshooting Electrical Circuits

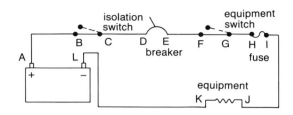

Figure 3-23.
Troubleshooting DC voltage drops: a comprehensive procedure.

Test sequence (left to right)

Readings	A to L	A to B	B to C	C to L	C to D	D to E	E to L	E to F	F to G	G to L	G to H	H to I	I to L	I to J	J to K	K to L
Battery check; should read about 12.6 volts																
Should be no reading. To be certain, switch down progressively to the lowest voltage scale on the meter. Low reading indicates unwanted resistance; 12.6 volts, a break in the line.		•			•			•			•			•		•
Should be no reading. To check, switch down to the meter's lowest scale again. Low reading indicates dirty or corroded switch terminals or points, or too small a switch; 12.6 volts, an open switch or, in H to I, a blown fuse.			•			•			•			•				
Should be 12.6 volts. No reading indicates an open switch; or in I to L, a blown fuse. Less than 12.6 volts in C to L, a voltage drop between A and C. Less than 12.6 volts in J to K indicates unwanted voltage drop somewhere in the circuit.				•			•			•			•		•	

the voltage drop at the equipment. It may be on either the hot side or the ground side of the equipment.

Many pieces of equipment (e.g., lights) will run perfectly well with a 10 percent voltage drop. (Assuming a fully charged battery with an open-circuit voltage of 12.6 the voltage across the input and output leads to the equipment *when it is switched on* would read 11.3 volts, given a 10 percent voltage drop elsewhere.) But other equipment is sensitive to voltage drop—especially some electric motors, which tend to overheat when run on low voltage. Boat circuits should be designed to limit voltage drop to a maximum of 3 percent at the equipment (i.e., a voltage reading of 12.2 volts given a fully charged battery at 12.6 volts). The major causes of unwanted voltage drop are poor connections and inadequate wiring (see below).

Circuit with multiple switches and a fuse. Now let us extend our circuit one more time and add a distribution panel with a breaker, another switch for the piece of equipment, and a fuse.

There is really nothing new here, just an elaboration of the previous situation. To make a circuit all switches must be closed and the fuse operative. Any voltage drop across a closed switch or a fuse indicates unwanted resistance; the higher the voltage the more the resistance. Anything less than system voltage across the terminals of the equipment likewise reveals unwanted resistance in the circuit, on either the hot or ground side.

If there is no voltage or reduced voltage at the equipment, a comprehensive and logical procedure to test every part of the circuit would be to close all switches, check the fuse, and then test for voltage following the 16 tests in Figure 3-23.

Naturally, no one wants to go through this whole procedure! The trick is to narrow down the problem area with as few steps as possible. For example, after finding the battery is OK (12.6 volts) an initial test across J and K might show 10 volts, which indicates a severe voltage deficit at the equipment. A test from K to L shows no voltage, so the ground line is OK. This means the voltage drop is in the "hot" side of the circuit. A test from E to L (or K, since K to L indicates no voltage drop) shows 12.6 volts—again no voltage drop). *Therefore the problem must lie between E and J*—probably the switch or its terminals, or the fuse terminals.

Open circuits and short circuits. An open circuit occurs anytime there is a break in an electrical path for any reason (an open switch; a disconnected or broken wire; etc.). Even when there is no physical break, excessive corrosion on terminals and switch points can create an open circuit.

A short circuit occurs when a direct path to ground is found, bypassing the resistance caused by the equipment installed in the circuit. Without this resistance, large amounts of current (amperage) will flow, blowing fuses and tripping circuit breakers. Without this circuit protection—or if oversized fuses and breakers have been fitted—current flow will be limited only by the most resistive section of the new (short) circuit—generally the smallest-diameter section of the wiring in the circuit. The high amperage will heat up the wiring, melting insulation and starting fires, until something burns through and so breaks the circuit, much like a fuse. Note that burned wires and melted insulation probably are *not* the source of the original short—just the result of it. Replacing the wires does not necessarily fix the short.

A system with an open circuit cannot carry a load (nothing will flow), nor can one with a short circuit (something will burn up); in either instance, then, a voltmeter has a limited application. This is where an ohmmeter really comes into its own. But remember, *before using an ohmmeter always electrically isolate the circuit in question or the meter may be damaged.*

In searching for an open circuit we are looking for breaks (infinite resistance) where an electrical path (*continuity*) should exist; a short has continuity where *none* should exist. An ohmmeter displays a short (continuity) as zero ohms (needle all the way to the right); an open circuit, as infinite ohms (needle all the way to the left).

Open circuits. To find an open circuit test for continuity at all those places where

it *should* exist, using the least sensitive scale on the meter (usually R × 100). In Figure 3-23, first *disconnect the circuit from the battery,* close all switches and circuit breakers, and then test from A to J—which should read zero ohms. Infinite ohms indicates a break in the hot supply to the equipment. In this case, test from A to C—you should have zero ohms. Infinite ohms indicates the break is between A and C. If A to C is OK, test from C to E—which should read zero ohms. Infinite ohms indicates the break is in this section. And so on. Test the most accessible terminals first, until the problem area is narrowed down, concentrating on switches, terminal blocks, and connections; broken wiring is the least likely culprit.

If the first test (A to J) showed continuity, we would test from K to L to check the ground side of the circuit—which, once again, should read zero ohms. Infinity indicates a break.

If there is continuity both to and from the equipment, disconnect the equipment to isolate it from the rest of the circuit and then test across its input and output leads. All electrical equipment creates resistance, so there may be some reading on the ohmmeter (perhaps not on the R × 100 scale). Very high or infinite ohms indicate an open circuit in the equipment itself (brushes are worn out; it is burned up; etc.)

Short circuits. To find a short, look for continuity where it should *not* exist. *Disconnect the circuit from the battery and disconnect the equipment from the circuit.* There now should be no path from the hot side of the circuit to the ground side. Close all switches and circuit breakers and, using the most sensitive ohms scale (R × 1), test from any part of the hot side to any part of the ground side. (The terminals where the equipment was disconnected are generally the most accessible place.) The meter should show infinite ohms: Any other reading indicates a short; zero ohms a serious ("dead") short (Figure 3-24A).

If there is a short, leave the ohmmeter connected across the terminals where the equipment was disconnected and switch off the nearest switch in the circuit (or pull a fuse). If the meter stays on zero ohms, the short is on the equipment side of the switch (or fuse). If the meter jumps to infinity, the short is on the other side (Figure 3-24B). In the latter case, close the switch (or put back the fuse) and open the next switch back in the circuit. If the meter stays on zero ohms, the short is between the two

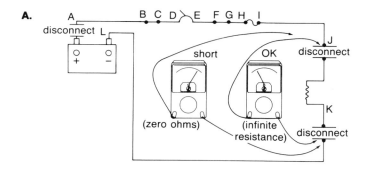

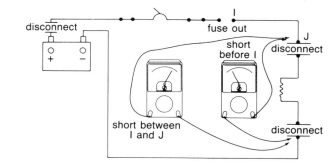

Figure 3-24. **Using an ohmmeter to test for a short in a DC circuit. Disconnect the circuit from the battery and the appliance from the circuit, then make a series of measurements as illustrated here.**

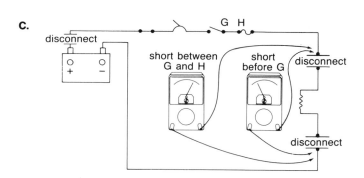

switches; if it jumps to infinity, it is on the far side of the second switch (Figure 3-24C). Continue this testing procedure.

Where no switches exist, connections can be undone at junction boxes and distribution panels. When a short is isolated, check more than just the offending section of cable, switch, or whatever: *Find out what it is shorted to!* (It may well have burned through insulation on wires in a bundle.)

If the original test (across the terminals the equipment connects to) showed no short, then the equipment itself may be shorted. Test across the equipment leads themselves (with the equipment still disconnected). You should expect to find some resistance—how much depends on the nature of the equipment. The higher its rated amperage, the lower the resistance. Very heavy-draw items (starter motors, electric anchor windlasses) will show almost no resistance; lighter-draw items (fans, stereos, lights), anything from a few ohms to 30 ohms. A reading of zero ohms indicates a short in the equipment itself.

With most cheap meters, heavy-amperage 12-volt DC equipment presents a problem: The meter most likely will not be sensitive enough to distinguish between a short and normal internal resistance. If the equipment has separate hot and ground leads, switch back to the R × 100 scale and test between the hot lead or terminal and the equipment case. Be sure to make a good connection—scratch through any paint if necessary. A reading of zero ohms definitely indicates a short. (If the equipment has only a hot lead and is grounded through its case—e.g., most starter motors—this test will show a near-short even when none exists.)

Note that for equivalent wattages, resistances of 115-volt AC equipment will be approximately 100 times higher than those of 12-volt DC equipment. This is easy to understand, since watts = volts × amps, and amps = watts ÷ volts. As mentioned earlier, a 100-watt lightbulb will draw 0.87 amp at 115 volts, and 8.3 amps at 12 volts.

Resistance (ohms) = volts ÷ amps. Therefore the respective resistances of the 100-watt lightbulb will be 132 ohms at 115 volts and 1.4 ohms at 12 volts.

Ground Faults ("Earth" Leaks)

One of the more insidious problems on board is leakage of very small amounts of current through poor wiring, switches, connections, and equipment insulation to ground. Such leaks slowly drain batteries

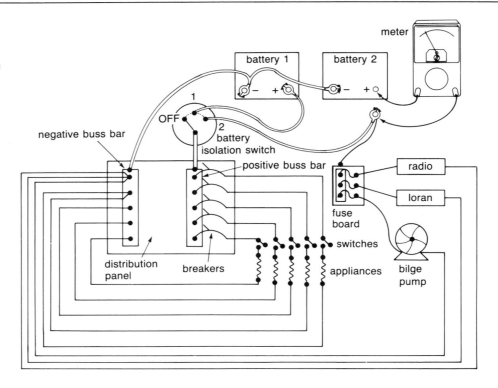

Figure 3-25. **Using the DC volts scale of a volt-ohm meter to test for current leaks to ground: preliminary test.** A meter in the position shown should read 0 volts if all equipment is turned off and the battery isolation switch is in the OFF position. If it reads 12 volts, there is either a live circuit or a ground leak between the battery and the isolation switch.

and also can contribute to devastating stray-current corrosion (more on this later). Leaks to ground are an ever-present possibility in the damp marine environment, especially from bilge pumps and other equipment or wiring located in damp areas of the boat or actually in water.

To locate ground faults, look for current flow to ground that bypasses normal circuits but is not normally great enough to show up as a short circuit. Depending on where in a circuit the leak is, it may occur only when equipment is switched on or all the time.

Preliminary test. Switch off absolutely all equipment and the battery isolation switch. Disconnect the positive cable from the battery and connect a multimeter on an appropriate scale for 12 volts DC between the battery post and the cable. *The voltmeter should give no reading.* If it reads 12 volts one of two things is happening:

1. One or more circuits connected between the battery and the isolation switch (e.g., radios, bilge pumps) is still on, providing a path to ground. Double-check all circuits.
2. There is a ground leak of 1 mA (one milliamp) or more between the battery and the isolation switch, or in circuits

connected directly to the battery at the clamp. (It takes about 1mA to make a meter register.)

The meter shows a leak. Switch to the highest DC amps range on the meter (probably 250 mA). Note that *if any equipment has been left on inadvertently, its current now will be flowing through the meter and may damage the meter if it is not rated for the load.* If there is no measurable deflection on the 250 mA scale, switch to a lower scale. Continue to switch down until the meter gives a good reading; this is the leak. Clean up the battery and isolation switch terminals, wipe up any moisture, and disconnect the individual circuits to the battery terminal clamp one at a time until the leak disappears (pull the fuses). This will determine where the leak is. Of course, there may be more than one leak, in which case disconnecting just one circuit will not drop the meter all the way to zero.

A similar test can be made using the ohms scale of the meter. This time connect the meter (R × 1 scale) between the disconnected positive battery cable clamp and the negative battery terminal post. A reading of less than 10 ohms indicates a piece of equipment left on; 10 to 1,000 ohms is a serious ground leak. If the reading is more than 1,000 ohms, switch to the R ×

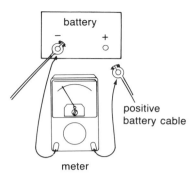

Figure 3-26. Pinpointing a ground leak with the ohms scale of a multimeter. Disconnect the cable clamp from the positive terminal, and connect the meter between the negative terminal and the positive cable clamp. Readings may be interpreted as follows: less than 10 ohms = equipment left on; 10 to 1,000 ohms = serious ground leak; 1,000 to 10,000 ohms = minor ground leak; greater than 10,000 ohms = little or no leak.

100 scale. A reading of 1,000 to 10,000 ohms (10 to 100 ohms on the meter since we are now on the R × 100 scale) indicates a minor leak; anything over 10,000 ohms, an insignificant leak.

Testing the boat's circuits. If there are no leaks between the battery and the isolation switch, return the meter to the DC volts scale and switch the battery into the boat's distribution panel (i.e., turn on the battery isolation switch). With the meter between the positive battery post and its disconnected terminal, the reading should be zero volts. If the reading is 12 volts, one or more of the boat's circuits is turned on, providing a path to ground (recheck all switches), or there is a ground leak.

Switch to the highest DC amps range and work down until the meter gives a good reading. On many older boats, individual circuits have fuses (but no breakers) in the distribution panel and the specific pieces of equipment are switched at the equipment. Newer boats usually have breakers in the distribution panel for most circuits; even so, some circuits will not be on a breaker. An example is the hot cable from the battery selector switch to the starter motor solenoid, which, in turn, likely feeds into the engine ignition circuit.

Begin disconnecting the hot wires from any circuits that are not on a breaker until the leak disappears. Start with the most likely circuits (e.g., low in the boat and in damp locations). If disconnecting a circuit makes no difference in the meter reading, reconnect it before going to the next. Any circuits left disconnected need to be la-beled. If disconnecting a faulty circuit causes only a partial drop in the meter reading, there may be more than one ground leak.

If a leak still exists after all un-breakered circuits have been broken loose and checked, one of the panel breakers must be leaking, or there is a leak in the panel itself and its wiring. Test the breakers with an ohmmeter on the R × 1 scale, placing the probes on the two breaker terminals. With the breaker OFF, the meter should show infinite ohms; with the breaker ON, zero ohms.

Further tests. All leaks as far as the circuit breakers in the distribution panel and on circuits not switched at the panel probably are cleaned up. However, if the majority of the circuits are switched at the panel, the greater part of the boat's circuits still will be untested. To test these, return the meter to its original position (between the battery's positive post and the disconnected positive cable clamp) and set it back on the highest DC amps scale.

To test individual circuits, disconnect the ground (return) leads from the individual pieces of equipment at the negative buss bar in the distribution panel and put the leads safely out of the way. Where several items share a common breaker or switch, *all grounds must be disconnected.* This will break the individual paths to ground. Now turn on the breaker and/or switches for this circuit. Any current flow (amps) indicates a leak. Be sure to return the multimeter to its highest scale before starting each new test, and reconnect or label any disconnected wires before breaking more loose.

Bonding. Most boats today are bonded. That is to say, all the major metal items (through hulls, engine, rudderpost, equipment casings, etc.) are connected to a copper strap and this, in turn, is connected to a common ground point (more on bonding later). Ground leaks into the bonding system are potentially a major source of stray-current corrosion. To check, disconnect the bonding wire from bonded electrical equipment and connect the meter (on DC amps) between the bonding wire and the equipment both with the equipment turned on and off. There should be absolutely no current flow. Now:

1. Disconnect all bonding wires from underwater through hulls and then test for current flow between the bonding

USA household receptacle and plug
rated for 125 volts and 15 amps

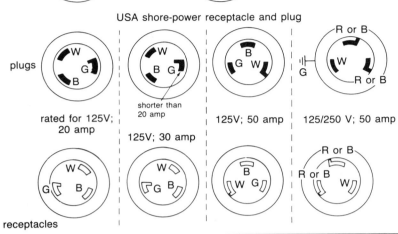

plugs

rated for 125V;
20 amp

125V; 30 amp

125V; 50 amp   125/250 V; 50 amp

receptacles

Figure 3-27A. Receptacle and plug configurations. W = neutral (white); R or B = hot (red or black); G = ground (green or bare).

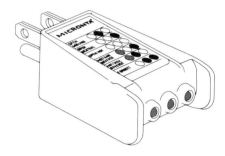

Figure 3-27B. Ground-fault tester.

wires and through-hull fixtures. Switch down to the lowest DC amps scale. Any reading indicates a leak, which may be either inside or outside the boat. Turn off all DC circuits, isolate the batteries, disconnect the shore-power cable and test again. If the leak persists it is external to the boat; if it ceases, it is internal. Recheck all the circuits.

2. Make up a couple of very long leads and test between isolated (i.e., un-bonded) underwater through hulls at both ends of the boat and from side to side on the DC milliamps scale. Reverse the meter or meter leads at each test. Any reading indicates stray currents in the water.

3. If you have access to a DC millivolt meter (reading in thousandths of a volt), fit two extra-long leads to it and dangle them in the water at both ends of the boat and at different points around it. Switch the negative and positive leads at each test. Any voltage readings reveal the presence of potentially damaging stray currents in the water.

If stray currents *external* to your boat are present, refer to Chapter 4, "Stray-Current Corrosion."

Testing AC Circuits

Remember, AC voltage can kill! *If in any doubt about what you are doing, don't do it.* Be-

Switch down to the lowest voltage scale: *any reading indicates a serious leak.*

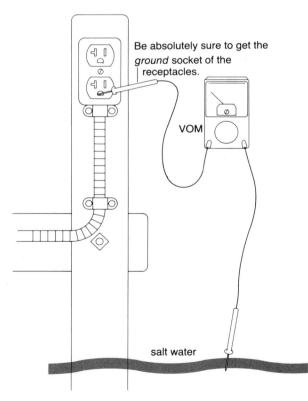

Be absolutely sure to get the *ground* socket of the receptacles.

VOM

salt water

Figure 3-27C. Using a multimeter to test a shore-power receptacle for leaks. Be sure to place the probe in the ground socket of the receptacle (see Figure 3-27A), and start with a high AC voltage scale, switching to lower scales as necessary to increase sensitivity. Any reading indicates a serious leak.

fore working on AC circuits always disconnect the shoreside cable, or turn off the generator or DC/AC inverter.

Dockside. AC troubleshooting generally starts dockside. Things to look for are correct voltage, correct polarity, and ground faults.

1. Correct voltage: Test with the volt-ohm meter on the 250 volts AC scale. There will be three sockets in a dockside receptacle. A 115-volt system (USA) should give the following results:

Hot to ground	115 volts
Hot to neutral	115 volts
Neutral to ground	0 volts

   A 230-volt system (USA) should give the following results:

Hot 1 to neutral	115 volts
Hot 2 to neutral	115 volts
Hot 1 to hot 2	230 volts
Hot 1 to ground	115 volts
Hot 2 to ground	115 volt
Neutral to ground	0 volts

   A 240-volt system (UK) should give 240 volts for hot-to-ground and hot-to neutral tests and no reading (0 volts) for the neutral-to-ground test.

2. Correct polarity: The hot and neutral sockets are as shown (Figure 3-27A). If the meter shows them to be reversed, the receptacle is wired with reverse polarity. *Do not use it—to do so is to invite the risk of corrosion* (see Chapter 4, "Stray-Current Corrosion").

3. Ground faults: *The ground (green or bare wire) side of an AC circuit is never a current-carrying conductor in normal use.* It is advisable to carry a portable ground-fault indicator on board (see Figure 3-27B). If you have this device, always plug it in and test the dockside receptacle before making a hook-up. The shore-power cord should not be plugged in if the indicator shows any leaks to ground whatsoever; you risk stray-current corrosion unless your boat has an isolation transformer or properly functioning AC ground isolator.

   In the absence of a ground-fault indicator, test 115-volt receptacles (240 volts in the UK) by putting one probe of the voltmeter in the ground (green or bare wire) socket of the receptacle (*be absolutely sure to get the right socket*) and dangling the other probe in the water. On 230-volt receptacles (USA), touch the first probe to the metal shell of the

receptacle. Progressively switch down to the lowest AC volts scale. If there is any indication of voltage, there is a serious ground leak (Figure 3-27C).

Onboard circuit testing. A 115-volt circuit (240 volts in the UK) is essentially the same as a 12-volt circuit with one hot (black in the USA; red or brown in the UK) wire to the equipment, and one wire—the neutral (white in the USA; black or blue in the UK)—back. The third wire (green or bare in both the USA and UK, with green and yellow in newer UK installations), although called a ground wire, is not part of the circuit in normal circumstances. If in any doubt about this read the section on page 68. The same voltage tests can be made between the hot and neutral sides of the circuit (using an appropriate AC scale) as between the hot and ground sides of a DC circuit, keeping in mind *the lethal nature of AC voltage.*

With shore power connected—unless the system has a Type-A isolation transformer, which is not grounded on board—any test from a hot wire to the safety ground wire should yield 115 volts (240 volts in the UK), and from the neutral wire to the ground wire, zero volts. If these are reversed, so is polarity. If the dockside receptacle did not show reverse polarity, the wires are crossed on board and need sorting out.

A 230-volt circuit (USA) is a little different since it has two hot wires and no neutral wire. Again, the third (green or bare) wire is not part of the circuit in normal circumstances—and may not even be present where isolation transformers are fitted. Any test across the two hot wires should yield 230 volts; any test from either wire to the green or bare ground wire should yield 115 volts unless a Type-A isolation transformer is fitted.

Open-circuit and short-circuit testing is done on all circuits using an ohmmeter, just as with DC circuits, *but only after disconnecting the shoreside cable.* The following additional tests can be made for ground leaks and short circuits.

With the shoreside cable disconnected, the AC selector switch turned to SHORE, and all equipment unplugged or switched off, set the meter on the R × 1 scale and test first between the hot wire(s) and the ground wire (green or bare), and then between the neutral wire and the ground wire. This is most easily done by poking the ohmmeter probes into an AC recep-

Figure 3-28. **Testing AC circuits.** These resistance tests are carried out with the shore power disconnected and all appliances unplugged or switched off. Meters 1 and 2 should show no continuity; any reading less than infinity indicates a leak to ground. Meter 3 also should show no continuity unless the circuit incorporates an isolation transformer and the main breaker has not been tripped.

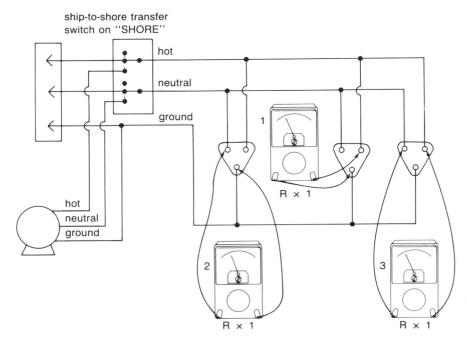

tacle socket. There should be no continuity at any time—i.e., the meter reading should stay on infinity (Figure 3-28). The sole exception is when a Type-B isolation transformer (one leg grounded on the boat) is fitted. In this case, break this leg loose from the ground and proceed with the rest of the tests.

Any continuity indicates a leak to ground in the wiring circuits. If the neutral wire is at fault, it may have been incorrectly wired into the boat's ground point. If so, disconnect it. While both the ground and neutral wires are grounded ashore, the neutral is *never* grounded on board except with Type-B isolation transformers (and inside onboard generators). Now, *with the shoreside power still disconnected,* plug in and switch on all equipment, one piece at a time. Any continuity between a hot or neutral wire and the green or bare wire shows a short or leak to ground in that piece of equipment. *The equipment is dangerous and needs repairing.*

The ohmmeter can be used for another test. Once again, *with the shoreside cable disconnected,* the AC selector switch turned to SHORE, and all equipment unplugged or switched off, set the meter on the R × 1 scale and test between the hot and neutral wires (USA, 115 volts; UK, 240 volts), or the two hot wires (USA, 230 volts). Boats with standard AC systems should show infinite ohms—anything less indicates a leak

between the wires or some equipment plugged in and left on. (Note: A frequency meter in the circuit will give a high ohms reading.) Boats with isolation transformers will show a low reading (near zero ohms), since the meter now in effect is connected across the coil in the transformer. With such circuits, the next step is to trip the main breaker—the meter should jump to infinity, since the transformer has been taken out of the circuit. Any reading other than infinity now indicates a leak, assuming the meter is connected on the downstream side of the breaker.

Finally, test between the green or bare wire and the boat's common ground point. Boats with standard AC systems and isolation transformers grounded on board (Type B) should show continuity (the AC equipment safety ground should be wired to the common ground point). Even some Type-A isolation transformers that are *not* grounded on board have a green (or bare) equipment grounding wire which is tied into the boat's common ground point. Note, however, that if an isolator is fitted between the AC grounding system and the boat's common ground point, an ohmmeter should indicate infinity—anything less means the isolator is not doing its job or (more likely) some bonding or DC ground circuit has bypassed the isolator, rendering it useless (see Figure 3-15G).

Proper Electrical Installation Practices

The marine environment is naturally damp and corrosive. Sooner or later all boats receive their share of salt water and salt spray down below. In these conditions only the most carefully fitted circuits will remain trouble free year after year. Special attention must be paid to three areas: wire type and size; connections; and fastening cables.

Sizes and Types of Wire

Wire has to be selected to minimize voltage drop, prevent ground leaks, and have enough strength to resist the vibration and pounding experienced in boats.

Voltage drop. Voltage drop is a function of resistance. Resistance is inherent in all wire; the smaller the wire and the longer its run, the greater the resistance. Some metals are less resistive (i.e., more conductive) than others. At the top of the scale (least resistive, most conductive) is silver, then copper. Somewhere farther down is aluminum. Silver wiring is impractical, but copper is readily available and should always be used. *Aluminum wire has no place on boats.*

The conductivity of copper wire and its resistance to corrosion can be improved during the manufacturing stage by drawing it through a "bath" of tin, coating the wire (and impregnating its strands) with the solder. This tinned wire is preferable to straight copper wire, but it generally has to be specially ordered through marine electrical supply houses.

DC circuits carry much higher amperages than AC circuits for the same power output (wattage). This is because of the low voltages involved. As a result, *DC wiring has to be correspondingly heavier* to keep resistance—and therefore voltage drop—within acceptable levels. It is a common practice, which gives rise to all kinds of problems later, to use undersized wiring.

Tables 3–1 and 3–2 give correct wire sizes for different loads at different levels of voltage drop. When these tables are used, the length of wire must include the ground (return) wire from the equipment—in other words, the length of wire is *twice* the distance from the equipment to the distribution panel, junction box, or whatever. Table 3-3 gives conversion factors from USA wire gauge (AWG) to European standards. Note that columns 2 and 4, when converted, do not correlate exactly; this is because column 2 gives *minimum* areas, and column 4 *average* areas.

While many appliances (particularly lights) will function adequately with a 10 percent voltage drop, many others (particularly some electric motors) will not. Table 3-2 also allows no margin for other resistances that may creep in (poor connections; corroded switches). The 3-percent voltage drop tables (Table 3-1) should always be used when calculating wire sizes. Larger wire sizes than even these can never do any harm and will only enhance the performance of electrical circuits.

Ground leaks. Preventing leaks to ground from wires themselves (connections are dealt with below) is largely a matter of using the correct insulation and keeping the wire dry. Insulating materials have different properties: Moisture resistance, heat resistance, oil and diesel resistance, and the ultraviolet resistance of external wiring are the four with which we are concerned.

The two most common insulating materials are polyvinylchloride (PVC) and polyethylene (PE). PVC is the cheapest and, therefore, the most common. It has good insulating properties and is reasonably moisture resistant but is susceptible to attack from other chemicals. PE has even better insulating properties, is tougher and more resistant to chemicals, but is stiffer and more expensive. Another less common insulating material (because of its higher price), which is recommended in some of Lloyds of London's specifications, is butyl rubber; it has excellent insulating properties and moisture resistance.

Once a wire is given its basic insulation, it frequently is sheathed or jacketed—given a thin outer sleeve of some other material to enhance its resistance to abrasion, chemicals, or ultraviolet degradation. The most common sheathing materials are PVC, nylon, and neoprene (also known as polychloroprene or PCP). All are reasonably oil, diesel, and gasoline resistant. Nylon is highly abrasion resistant. Neoprene (recommended by Lloyds in many specifications) is resistant to weathering (ultraviolet).

The most commonly available wire in the USA that is suitable for general purpose marine wiring is classified as THWN (thermoplastic, heat resistant, for wet locations, and with a nylon jacket), or

Table 3-1. Conductor Sizes for 3 Percent Drop in Voltage.

(Total current on circuit in amps.) — (Length of conductor from source of current to device and back to source—feet)

Amps	10	15	20	25	30	40	50	60	70	80	90	100	110	120	130	140	150	160	170
12 volts																			
5	18	16	14	12	12	10	10	10	8	8	8	6	6	6	6	6	6	6	6
10	14	12	10	10	10	8	6	6	6	6	4	4	4	4	2	2	2	2	2
15	12	10	10	8	8	6	6	6	4	4	2	2	2	2	2	1	1	1	1
20	10	10	8	6	6	6	4	4	2	2	2	2	1	1	1	0	0	0	2/0
25	10	8	6	6	6	4	4	2	2	2	1	1	0	0	0	2/0	2/0	2/0	3/0
30	10	8	6	6	4	4	2	2	1	1	0	0	0	2/0	2/0	3/0	3/0	3/0	3/0
40	8	6	6	4	4	2	2	1	0	2/0	2/0	2/0	3/0	3/0	3/0	4/0	4/0	4/0	4/0
50	6	6	4	4	2	2	1	0	2/0	2/0	3/0	3/0	4/0	4/0	4/0				
60	6	4	4	2	2	1	0	2/0	3/0	3/0	4/0	4/0	4/0						
70	6	4	2	2	1	0	2/0	3/0	3/0	4/0	4/0								
80	6	4	2	2	1	0	3/0	3/0	4/0	4/0									
90	4	2	2	1	0	2/0	3/0	4/0	4/0										
100	4	2	2	1	0	2/0	3/0	4/0											
24 volts																			
5	18	18	18	16	16	14	12	12	12	10	10	10	10	10	8	8	8	8	8
10	18	16	14	12	12	10	10	10	8	8	8	6	6	6	6	6	6	6	6
15	16	14	12	12	10	10	8	8	6	6	6	6	6	4	4	4	4	4	2
20	14	12	10	10	10	8	6	6	6	6	4	4	4	4	2	2	2	2	2
25	12	12	10	10	8	6	6	6	4	4	4	4	2	2	2	2	2	2	1
30	12	10	10	8	8	6	6	4	4	4	2	2	2	2	1	1	1	1	1
40	10	10	8	6	6	6	4	4	2	2	2	2	1	1	1	0	0	0	2/0
50	10	8	6	6	6	4	4	2	2	2	1	1	0	0	0	2/0	2/0	2/0	3/0
60	10	8	6	6	4	4	2	2	1	1	0	0	0	2/0	2/0	3/0	3/0	3/0	3/0
70	8	6	6	4	4	2	2	1	0	0	2/0	2/0	3/0	3/0	3/0	3/0	3/0	4/0	4/0
80	8	6	6	4	4	2	2	1	0	0	2/0	2/0	3/0	3/0	3/0	4/0	4/0	4/0	4/0
90	8	6	4	4	2	2	1	0	0	2/0	2/0	3/0	3/0	4/0	4/0	4/0	4/0		
100	6	6	4	4	2	2	1	0	2/0	2/0	3/0	3/0	4/0	4/0	4/0				
32 volts																			
5	18	18	18	18	16	16	14	14	12	12	12	12	10	10	10	10	10	10	8
10	18	16	16	14	14	12	12	10	10	10	8	8	8	8	8	6	6	6	6
15	16	14	14	12	12	10	10	8	8	8	6	6	6	6	6	6	6	4	4
20	16	14	12	12	10	10	8	8	6	6	6	6	6	4	4	4	4	4	2
25	14	12	12	10	10	8	8	6	6	6	6	4	4	4	2	2	2	2	2
30	14	12	10	10	8	8	6	6	6	4	4	4	4	2	2	2	1	1	1
40	12	10	10	8	8	6	6	4	4	4	2	2	2	2	1	1	1	1	1
50	12	10	8	8	6	6	4	4	2	2	2	2	1	1	0	0	0	0	0
60	10	8	8	6	6	4	4	2	2	2	2	1	1	0	0	0	2/0	2/0	2/0
70	10	8	6	6	6	4	2	2	2	1	1	0	0	0	2/0	2/0	2/0	3/0	3/0
80	10	8	6	6	4	4	2	2	1	1	0	0	0	2/0	2/0	3/0	3/0	3/0	3/0
90	8	6	6	6	4	2	2	2	1	0	0	2/0	2/0	2/0	3/0	3/0	3/0	4/0	4/0
100	8	6	6	4	4	2	2	1	0	0	2/0	2/0	2/0	3/0	3/0	3/0	4/0	4/0	4/0

(Wire sizes in AWG)

XHHW (cross-linked polyethylene, high-heat resistant, for wet locations). Other suitable grades are MTW (machine tool wire)—which is rated for wet locations and is oil, gasoline, and diesel resistant—and AWM (appliance wiring material)—similar to MTW but with a higher heat rating (up to 221°F or 105°C), which makes it suitable for engine rooms. MTW is always stranded.

Wire insulation will frequently carry more than one designation, for example: THHN-THWN. In this instance the insulation has a higher heat (HH) rating in dry locations (up to 194°F or 90°C) than it does in wet locations (up to 167°F or 75°C). Table 3-4 outlines the principal types of wire commonly available.

No normal insulation is suitable for prolonged immersion in water. Sooner or later current leaks will develop. Cables should never be run through perpetually damp or wet areas of the boat. If they must be, special waterproof, oil-resistant insulation is required, and naturally this is more expensive.

Strength. Wire comes as solid core or multistranded cable. Solid core is in almost universal use for household AC circuits and often is found on boats; however, *it is not suitable for marine use.* Over time, minute flexing and vibration of electric cables causes the copper to work-harden and finally to break. Such breaks are frequently not easy to find or repair, since the wiring

Understanding and Troubleshooting Electrical Circuits

Table 3-2. Conductor Sizes for 10 Percent Drop in Voltage.

(Total current on circuit in amps)	(Length of conductor from source of current to device and back to source—feet)																		
	10	15	20	25	30	40	50	60	70	80	90	100	110	120	130	140	150	160	170
12 volts																			
5	18	18	18	18	18	16	16	14	14	14	12	12	12	12	12	10	10	10	10
10	18	18	16	16	14	14	12	12	10	10	10	10	8	8	8	8	8	8	6
15	18	16	14	14	12	12	10	10	8	8	8	8	8	6	6	6	6	6	6
20	16	14	14	12	12	10	10	8	8	8	6	6	6	6	6	6	4	4	4
25	16	14	12	12	10	10	8	8	6	6	6	6	6	4	4	4	4	4	2
30	14	12	12	10	10	8	8	6	6	6	6	4	4	4	4	2	2	2	2
40	14	12	10	10	8	8	6	6	6	4	4	4	2	2	2	2	2	2	2
50	12	10	10	8	8	6	6	4	4	4	2	2	2	2	2	1	1	1	1
60	12	10	8	8	6	6	4	4	2	2	2	2	2	1	1	1	0	0	0
70	10	8	8	6	6	6	4	2	2	2	2	1	1	1	0	0	0	2/0	2/0
80	10	8	8	6	6	4	4	2	2	2	1	1	0	0	0	2/0	2/0	2/0	2/0
90	10	8	6	6	6	4	2	2	2	1	1	0	0	0	2/0	2/0	2/0	3/0	3/0
100	10	8	6	6	4	4	2	2	1	1	0	0	0	2/0	2/0	2/0	3/0	3/0	3/0
24 volts																			
5	18	18	18	18	18	18	18	18	16	16	16	16	14	14	14	14	14	14	12
10	18	18	18	18	18	16	16	14	14	14	12	12	12	12	12	10	10	10	10
15	18	18	18	16	16	14	14	12	12	12	10	10	10	10	10	8	8	8	8
20	18	18	16	16	14	14	12	12	10	10	10	10	8	8	8	8	8	8	6
25	18	16	16	14	14	12	12	10	10	10	8	8	8	8	8	6	6	6	6
30	18	16	14	14	12	12	10	10	8	8	8	8	8	6	6	6	6	6	6
40	16	14	14	12	12	10	10	8	8	8	6	6	6	6	6	6	4	4	4
50	16	14	12	12	10	10	8	8	6	6	6	6	4	4	4	4	4	4	2
60	14	12	12	10	10	8	8	6	6	6	6	4	4	4	4	2	2	2	2
70	14	12	10	10	8	8	6	6	6	6	4	4	4	2	2	2	2	2	2
80	14	12	10	10	8	8	6	6	6	4	4	4	2	2	2	2	2	2	2
90	12	10	10	8	8	6	6	6	4	4	4	2	2	2	2	2	1	1	1
100	12	10	10	8	8	6	6	4	4	4	2	2	2	2	2	1	1	1	1
32 volts																			
5	18	18	18	18	18	18	18	18	18	18	18	16	16	16	16	14	14	14	14
10	18	18	18	18	18	18	16	16	14	14	14	14	12	12	12	12	12	12	12
15	18	18	18	18	18	16	14	14	14	12	12	12	12	10	10	10	10	10	10
20	18	18	18	16	16	14	14	12	12	12	10	10	10	10	8	8	8	8	8
25	18	18	16	16	14	14	12	12	10	10	10	10	8	8	8	8	8	8	8
30	18	18	16	14	14	12	12	10	10	10	10	8	8	8	8	6	6	6	6
40	18	16	14	14	12	12	10	10	8	8	8	8	8	6	6	6	6	6	6
50	16	14	14	12	12	10	10	8	8	8	6	6	6	6	6	6	4	4	4
60	16	14	12	12	10	10	8	8	8	6	6	6	6	6	6	4	4	4	4
70	14	14	12	10	10	8	8	6	6	6	6	6	4	4	4	4	2	2	2
80	14	12	12	10	10	8	8	6	6	6	6	4	4	4	4	2	2	2	2
90	14	12	10	10	10	8	6	6	6	6	4	4	4	4	2	2	2	2	2
100	14	12	10	10	8	8	6	6	6	4	4	4	4	2	2	2	2	2	2

(Wire sizes in AWG)

is likely to be bundled in a harness, to be inaccessible, or both. Multistranded copper cable should always be used in boat installations, both in AC and DC circuits.

Making Connections

Poor connections are the bane of many an otherwise excellent electrical installation. Three factors have to be considered: mechanical strength, electrical conductivity, and insulation.

Mechanical strength. Excellent mechanical strength is provided by twisting wires together; by crimped-on terminals; and by wires wrapped under screwheads or in-serted into terminal blocks and held with screws (Figure 3-29). In all instances it is important to cut back insulation with care to expose bare wire for the connection and the wire end should be tinned with solder (see below). Nicking the strands in the cable will not only reduce mechanical strength, but will also reduce current-carrying capability (i.e., increase voltage drop).

Crimped-on terminals, retaining screw heads, and terminal blocks must all be matched to the wire size. No matter how tightly crimped, an oversize terminal will not grip properly, and the wire will be prone to pull out. Undersized retaining screwheads will grip only a portion of the wire, and oversized holes in terminal

Table 3-3. Conversion of American Wire Gauge (AWG) to European Standards.

Conductor Size (AWG)	Minimum Acceptable Circular Mil (CM) Area (ABYC specs)[1]	Conductor Diameter (mm)	Conductor Cross-sectional Area (mm²)
25		0.455	0.163
24		0.511	0.205
23		0.573	0.259
22		0.644	0.325
21		0.723	0.412
20		0.812	0.519
19		0.992	0.653
18	1537	1.024	0.823
17		1.15	1.04
16	2336	1.29	1.31
15		1.45	1.65
14	3702	1.63	2.08
13		1.83	2.63
12	5833	2.05	3.31
11		2.30	4.15
10	9343	2.59	5.27
9		2.91	6.62
8	14810	3.26	8.35
7		3.67	10.6
6	25910	4.11	13.3
5		4.62	16.8
4	37360	5.19	21.2
3		5.83	26.7
2	62450	6.54	33.6
1	77790	7.35	42.4
0 (1/0)	98980	8.25	53.4
00 (2/0)	125100	9.27	67.5
000 (3/0)	158600	10.40	85.0
0000 (4/0)	205500	11.68	107.2
00000 (5/0)	250000	13.12	135.1
000000 (6/0)	300000	14.73	170.3

1. 1 circular mil (CM) = 0.0005067 mm²

blocks will allow wire strands to work loose up the sides of the retaining screw.

Excessive force when crimping or tightening screws is certain to break wire strands and lead to premature failure. Crimped-on terminals, in particular, must be put on with a wire or cable crimper and not attempted with pliers, hammer, or whatever comes to hand. Ring type and captive fork (spade) crimped terminals are preferred over flat-fork (spade) terminals, since even if the retaining screw loosens the terminal will not come adrift.

The source of most crimped-on terminals is the automotive industry. These are often *steel* terminals, which are *not* suitable for marine use. Use only tin-plated copper terminals, which are available from marine electric supply houses.

Electrical conductivity. The ends of stranded copper wire sooner or later become tarnished in the marine environment. This tarnish slowly wicks its way back up the cable under the insulation. This surface corrosion increases electrical resistance, particularly in connections. The only sure way to make an electrically perfect connection that will hold up over time is to solder all joints (see below). The

Understanding and Troubleshooting Electrical Circuits

time to do this is when first making the connections, not some years down the road when problems start developing.

Once tarnish has a foothold, solder will not take without the use of aggressive acid fluxes, and these are strictly taboo since they create all kinds of other corrosion problems. To solder already-tarnished wire, cut back the insulation and wire until clean, shiny copper is exposed.

All connections, terminals, and terminal blocks *must be kept dry.* There almost certainly will be several dissimilar metals—copper crimped terminals, stainless steel screws, etc.—which when augmented by salt water and electric current create the perfect mix for corrosion. After assembling terminals, cover them with Teflon-based grease or petroleum jelly, or paint them with varnish or something similar to inhibit moisture ingress.

Insulating Connections

Insulating tape does not work well in the marine environment. Sooner or later it tends to unravel and become obnoxiously sticky. Even at its best, it does not provide an adequate moisture barrier. Far better to use one of the available heat-shrink products.

Heat-shrink (or self-amalgamating) insulation materials come in the form of long tubes of different sizes (similar to drinking straws, they are sometimes known as "spaghetti") or rolls of tape. The tubes are slid up over a wire before adding a crimped terminal or making a splice. When soldering is complete, the tube is slid back down to the terminal, or over the splice, and gently heated (a hair dryer works well; a cigarette lighter will do). The tube shrinks tightly around the wire, providing quite effective insulation. Tubing should be cut 50 percent longer than the wire to be insulated and matched as closely as possible to the wire size.

Heat-shrink tape is wrapped around a joint, overlapping each layer by 50 percent, and then heated as above. The layers partially melt and fuse into one another, forming a much better seal than regular insulation tape.

Some joints that need insulating are an awkward shape with protruding corners and screws. In these instances, electricians' putty comes in handy. It is a pliable substance, similar to plasticene, which is molded around the connection to fair it so that it can be wrapped smoothly with heat-

Table 3-4. Common Electric Cables and Their Designations (USA).

TW: *T*hermoplastic[1] Insulation (usually PVC), suitable for *W*et locations (60°C/140°F heat-resistance rating)

THW: *T*hermoplastic Insulation (usually PVC), *H*eat Resistant (75°C/167°F rating), suitable for *W*et locations.

THWN: Same as for THW except *N*ylon jacket over reduced insulation thickness. Also rated THHN.

THHN: *T*hermoplastic Insulation (usually PVC), *H*igh *H*eat Resistant (90°C/194°F rating), dry locations only, *N*ylon jacket. Also rated THWN.

TFFN: *T*hermoplastic Insulation (usually PVC), Flexible *F*ixture wire, *N*ylon jacket. Also rated MTW and AWM

XHHW: Crosslinked Synthetic Polymer[2] Insulation, *H*igh *H*eat Resistant (90°C/194°F rating) for dry locations only, suitable for *W*et locations but de-rated to 75°C/167°F.

RHH: *R*ubber Insulation (commonly crosslinked polyethylene because it qualifies for rubber), *H*igh *H*eat Resistant (90°C/194°F rating) for dry locations only.

RHW: *R*ubber Insulation (commonly crosslinked polyethylene, as in RHH), *H*eat Resistant (75°C/167°F rating), suitable for *W*et locations.

USE: *U*nderground *S*ervice *E*ntrance. Most utilize crosslinked polyethylene insulation rated for 75°C/167°F in direct burial applications. Product is usually triple-rated RHH-RHW-USE.

MTW: *M*achine *T*ool *W*ire. Usually thermoplastic insulation (PVC) or thermoplastic insulation with nylon jacket. Moisture, Heat, and Oil Resistant. Most MTW is rated 60°C/140°F. Much stranded copper type THHN is also rated MTW (see AWM).

AWM: *A*ppliance *W*iring *M*aterial. Usually thermoplastic insulation (PVC) or thermoplastic insulation with nylon jacket. Thermosetting[3]. Much stranded copper type THHN in AWG sizes 14 through 6 is also rated AWM. As AWM, the product carries a 105°C/221°F rating.

Key: W = moisture resistant
   H = heat resistant, 75°C/167°F
  HH = high-heat resistant, 90°C/194°F
   M = oil resistant
   T = thermoplastic

1. A plastic that can be softened by heating.
2. A plastic formulation in which polymers are linked chemically by polymerization.
3. A plastic that is heat-cured into an insoluble and infusible end product.

shrink tape. The putty itself has a high insulating value but is too soft to be left uncovered.

Wire nuts (Figure 3-29) frequently are used to insulate connections in household circuits in the USA, though not in the UK. They are not very suitable for marine use since the threaded metal insert is made of steel and will rust; what is more, the lower

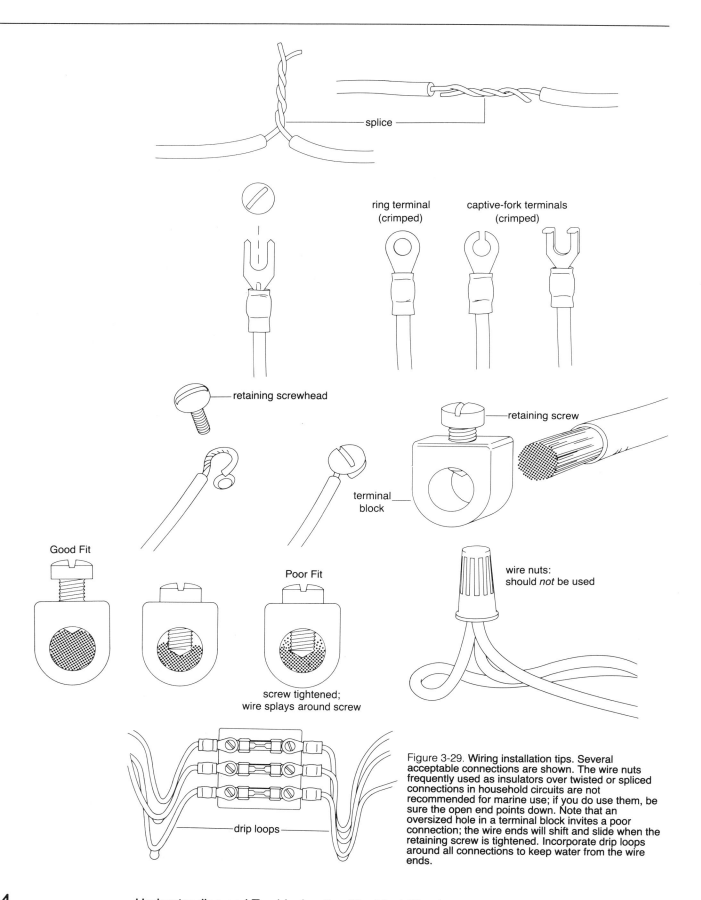

splice

ring terminal
(crimped)

captive-fork terminals
(crimped)

retaining screwhead

retaining screw

terminal
block

Good Fit

Poor Fit

wire nuts:
should *not* be used

screw tightened;
wire splays around screw

drip loops

Figure 3-29. Wiring installation tips. Several acceptable connections are shown. The wire nuts frequently used as insulators over twisted or spliced connections in household circuits are not recommended for marine use; if you do use them, be sure the open end points down. Note that an oversized hole in a terminal block invites a poor connection; the wire ends will shift and slide when the retaining screw is tightened. Incorporate drip loops around all connections to keep water from the wire ends.

Table 3-5. U.S. Wiring Color Codes for Marine Engine Installations.

Color	Application
Purple	Ignition switch controlled
Black	Grounds
Red*	Unprotected battery wires
Red/purple	Overcurrent protected battery wires
Yellow	Alternator AC output and alternator field
Green	Bonding
Brown and brown/stripe	Alternator starter to ignition module
Orange	Alternator DC output and accessory feeds
Light blue	Oil pressure
Tan	Water temperature
Grey	Tachometer
Green/white	Engine trim in and/or tilt down
Green/orange	Engine independent trim down
Blue/white	Engine trim out and/or tilt up
Blue/orange	Engine independent tilt up
White	Must not be used in under 50v wiring
Yellow/red	Starting circuit
Yellow/black	Choke
Black/yellow	Ignition stop
Brown/white	Trim position sender
Manufacturer's discretion	Ignition triggering and color/stripe for functions not designated

*Red/purple may be used for overcurrent protected wires.

end of the nut is open to the atmosphere. If used, wire nuts always should be installed with the open end down so that the nut does not become a water trap. It is a good practice then to seal the nut with silicon caulking or epoxy (this holds true for just about any terminal). Wires should enter junction boxes *from the bottom* whenever possible to reduce the ingress of water. All wiring at any type of connection should include drip loops (Figure 3-29).

Installing Cables

The sheer amount of cable in a modern boat is quite remarkable, and so is the size of some of the wiring bundles. (Our 40-foot ketch has around 1800 feet of electrical circuits!) It is essential to label both ends of every wire for future identification and to keep some account of which wire numbers go with what piece of equipment and to what switches and breakers—otherwise troubleshooting circuits can become a real headache.

The best way to label wires is with "wire markers," available from all good electrical stores. They come in "books" and consist of adhesive-backed numbers and letters, which peel off a backing page and are wrapped around the wire to be labeled. Markers should be placed close to a wire terminal, and will be easier to read if they are wrapped around once and the two ends pressed together and left sticking out (rather than wrapping the marker around and around the wire).

Cables must obviously be run in the driest, highest, and most protected (i.e., not through lockers) areas possible. Under the deck is generally the best place.

All cables must be securely fastened against vibration either in conduit (plastic pipe works well) or with suitable cable ties at least every 18 inches; Ny-Lok and Ty-Wrap are two widely available brands of cable ties. Staples, which are commonly used ashore, are not suitable for securing cables. Plastic ties come with or without a screw lug, or mounting head. Those with a screw lug can be mounted to a batten or deck beam and pulled up tight around a bundle of cables; those without are only suitable for holding cables to each other or to an existing pipe or something similar. It

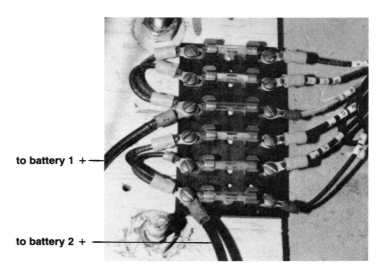

to battery 1 +

to battery 2 +

Figure 3-30. The correct way to install any equipment connected directly to a battery (bypassing the distribution panel and battery isolation switch). This particular setup is for a two-battery system. The positive cable to battery 1 exits left at the top; battery 2, left bottom. The three incoming lines on the right are (top to bottom): wind generator (battery 1), battery charger (battery 1), solar panel (battery 1); the three incoming circuits below are the same, but for battery 2.

is best to use black ties, especially in areas exposed to direct sunlight, since the clear ones degrade in ultraviolet.

Any DC wires running within three feet of a compass need to have the hot and ground wires to each piece of equipment twisted around each other in a continuous spiral. This twisting helps eliminate the magnetism that flowing current induces in the two wires.

Soldering

Most soldering aboard can be done with a 50- to 100-watt soldering iron; a few large jobs (e.g., battery cable terminals) are best done with a propane torch. Soldering irons can be bought for use with 12-volt systems but are electrically greedy (a 50-watt iron will draw close to 5 amps). Since the iron is used intermittently and for short periods, this is not a great problem. Also available now are small, pocket-sized temperature-controllable butane soldering torches.

Solder is always used with a *flux*—an agent that helps to keep the metal surfaces clean while being soldered. Fluxes are either acid based or rosin based. Only rosin-based fluxes can be used in electrical work—acid fluxes will corrode copper wire.

There are numerous grades of solder, rated by its percentage of tin, lead, or silver. The best all-around solder for electrical work is 60/40 (60 percent tin; 40 percent lead). Avoid cheap solders with higher percentages of lead. Solder comes in rolls of either solid or rosin-cored wire, the latter having a hollow center with flux already in it whereas solid solder requires an external application of flux. The rosin-cored solder is suitable for most marine uses and is much more convenient.

The keys to successful soldering are a well-tinned soldering iron and the tinning of the individual pieces to be bonded *before* the joint is made. To tin the iron, clean its tip down to bare metal with a file, heat it up, and then touch rosin-cored solder to it. The solder should flow over the whole tip to form a clean, shiny surface. If it will not adhere to areas of the tip, there are impurities. Sometimes scratching around with a knife and the solder (to lay on more rosin) will clean these areas, but it may be necessary to go back and start again with the file. During soldering the tip of the hot iron should be wiped periodically with a damp rag to remove burnt flux and old solder.

To tin wire ends and terminals, clean them down to bare, shiny metal and then hold the iron to the part to heat it. Touch the solder *to the part,* not to the iron. When the part is hot enough, the solder will flow over and into it. Then the iron is withdrawn, and the tinning is complete. Once again, if the solder will not adhere to certain areas, they are not clean enough. To speed the heating of the part, place a drop

Understanding and Troubleshooting Electrical Circuits

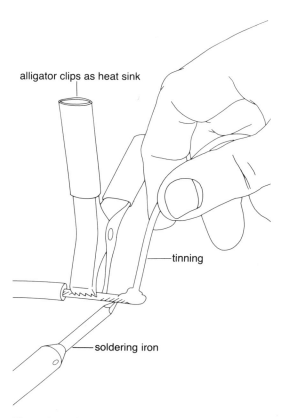

alligator clips as heat sink

tinning

soldering iron

Figure 3-31. Soldering practices. Note that an alligator clip or a strip of aluminum used as a heat sink protects the insulation from melting. When tinning (applying solder to the wire), touch the solder to the wire, not the iron. As a preparatory step, sandpaper or file the tip of the iron to a pyramid-shaped point of bright metal; then heat the iron, file it bright again, and, working fast, run on a little solder. Try to achieve a good coating of solder over the entire point and a half-inch or so down the tip. Before making a joint, scrape the wire clean and bright. Place the parts to be soldered into firm contact. Use enough heat, but don't overheat. Pull the iron away as soon as the solder flows. Keep the joint and wire immobile while the solder cools.

you always risk overheating the insulation at the wire and melting it, especially if your soldering techniques are clumsy. An effective heat sink can be made by cutting a strip of metal from an aluminum soft drink can and wrapping this around the end of the insulation. Alternatively, clamp an alligator clip, Vise Grips, or pliers on the wire.

of solder on the iron itself where it is in contact with the part; the actual tinning should always be done by applying the solder as above.

Where both halves of a joint are tinned—e.g., two wires to be twisted together—the joint is made and then heated until the solder from both halves flows together. Generally no more solder is needed. Where only the wire end has been tinned, a terminal is crimped on or the wire screwed up, then the joint is heated, and more solder flowed in. If the terminal rather than the tinned wire is heated, when the solder in the tinned wire begins to melt the terminal must be hot enough for solder to "take." When soldering wires,

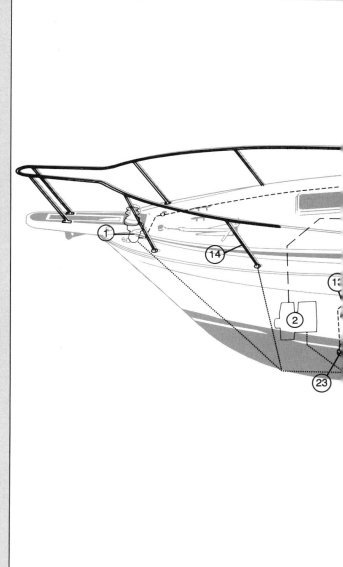

Figure 4-1. Effective bonding and grounding techniques will head off problems with corrosion and electrical interference, not to mention prevent damage from lightning strikes.

(1) windlass
(2) air conditioner
(3) bonding strap
(4) freezer
(5) air conditioner compressor
(6) refrigerator
(7) water heater
(8) radio and instruments
(9) steering and engine controls
(10) batteries
(11) battery isolation switch
(12) fuel tanks
(13) through hull
(14) stanchions
(15) metal keel
(16) chainplates
(17) deck fills
(18) stem fitting
(19) metal rudder
(20) distribution panel
(21) generator
(22) struts
(23) pump
(24) blower
(25) lights
(26) lightning rod

———————— 12 VDC

- - - - - - - - 12 V ground
(return)

— — — — — 120 VAC

············· bonding
strap
jumper

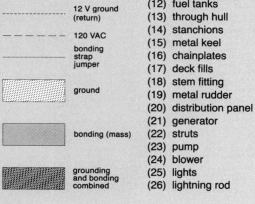

ground

bonding (mass)

grounding
and bonding
combined

Corrosion, Bonding, Lightning Protection, and Grounding

A Hostile Environment

The subjects dealt with in this chapter are of vital interest to all boatowners. Unfortunately, they are fraught with problems and ambiguities for the nontechnical layperson about which even the experts cannot agree. As I write I have before me the following two opinions:

"A husky, low-resistance bonding system is a *must* on inboard powered, nonmetallic boats." (Conrad Miller: *Your Boat's Electrical System,* page 88)

"There is a common marine practice called bonding. From where the procedure has arisen I know not, but it has for some reason become a marine tradition and cure-all. Bonding as a tradition arose before knowledge of metal chemistry or it wouldn't have arisen." (Robert L. Kocher, *National Fisherman,* September 1979: "Corrosion process shows why bonded fittings are a bad idea")

The marine environment is so diverse, and the metals, other materials, and conditions with which boats operate are so variable, that it is almost impossible to lay down blanket edicts whether to bond or not to bond. For example, our boat, flying in the face of conventional practice in the USA (bonding is nowhere near as common in the UK), has been in tropical seawater for five years completely unbonded and without a single sacrificial zinc anode. The only trace of corrosion is between the bronze propeller and the stainless steel propeller shaft, where it slides in and out of our variable-pitch propeller unit. I do make regular inspections and have sacrificial zincs on hand to protect specific items of hardware at the first sign of trouble.

Galvanic Corrosion

Almost any metal placed in seawater will corrode. Although metal looks inert and the seawater may be perfectly still, constant movement, collisions, and interactions within their atomic structures will lead to the displacement of electrons within the metal, manifested as surface corrosion and oxidation. Almost all metals (gold excepted) take on a slightly negative voltage with respect to the surrounding water.

Each metal behaves differently and has its own *voltage potential.* Table 4-1 lists metals and their voltage potentials relative to a standard. Every metal immersed in seawater has a voltage potential, and they are all different.

Seawater is not a particularly good conductor of electricity at low voltages. Although metals have negative voltages with respect to the surrounding seawater, without other disturbing influences they tend to stabilize at their innate voltage potential rather than equalize with ground through the seawater's poor conductivity. Thus a balance is reached and corrosion slows almost to a halt. (But note: This is in static seawater. For various reasons moving water provides more opportunity for the movement of electrons.)

We disrupt this equilibrium, however, if we connect a wire between two dissimilar metals that have stabilized at different voltages. Electrons will flow between them along the wire. We have, in effect, created a battery, and an ammeter in the wire would register a tiny current. Note that the flow of electrons along the wire does not damage the metals involved: Electric cables carry current year after year without harm.

The flow of electrons will raise the voltage potential of the *anode* (the metal with the most negative, or least *noble,* voltage) to more nearly equal the voltage of the *cathode* (the metal with the *less* negative, or most noble, voltage), and the anode will once again interact with the surrounding seawater in an attempt to stabilize at its own voltage potential. This is where the damage is done. This interaction is not just a straight movement of electrons, but a chemical process that eats up the surface of the metal: *galvanic corrosion* (Figure 4-2).

The farther apart the voltage potential of two metals, the greater will be the voltage differential between them, and the more likely will be galvanic corrosion. If the metals are electrically connected and immersed in seawater, anytime this difference exceeds 0.25 volt corrosion is pretty well certain. The metal being pulled *above* its voltage potential (the *anode*) will be eaten away, while any metal being pulled *below* its voltage potential (the *cathode*) will not corrode.

De-Zincification and Crevice Corrosion

So far we have considered two different and dissimilar metal objects. But most metals in marine use are *alloys*—mixtures of

Table 4-1. Galvanic Series of Metals in Seawater.[1]

Metals and Alloys	Corrosion-Potential Range in Volts[2]	
Magnesium and Magnesium Alloys	−1.60	to −1.63
Zinc	−0.98	to −1.03
Galvanized Steel or Galvanized Wrought Iron	NA	
Aluminum Alloys	−0.76	to −1.00
Cadmium	−0.70	to −0.73
Mild Steel	−0.60	to −0.71
Wrought Iron	−0.60	to −0.71
Cast Iron	−0.60	to −0.71
13% Chromium Stainless Steel, Type 410 (active in still water)	−0.46	to −0.58
18/8 Stainless Steel, Type 304 (active in still water)	−0.46	to −0.58
Ni-Resist	−0.46	to −0.58
18.8, 3% Mo Stainless Steel, Type 316 (active in still water)	−0.43	to −0.54
Inconel (78% Ni, 14.5% Cr, 6% Fe) (active in still water)	−0.35	to −0.46
Aluminum Bronze (92% Cu, 8% Al)	−0.31	to −0.42
Naval Brass (60% Cu, 39% Zn)	−0.30	to −0.40
Yellow Brass (65% Cu, 35% Zn)	−0.30	to −0.40
Red Brass (85% Cu, 15% Zn)	−0.30	to −0.40
Muntz Metal (60% Cu, 40% Zn)	−0.30	to −0.40
Tin	−0.31	to −0.33
Copper	−0.30	to −0.57
50-50 Lead − Tin Solder	−0.28	to −0.37
Admiralty Brass (71% Cu, 28% Zn, 1% Sn)	−0.28	to −0.36
Aluminum Brass (76% Cu, 22% Zn, 2% Al)	−0.28	to −0.36
Manganese Bronze (58.5% Cu, 39% Zn, 1% Sn, 1% Fe, 0.3% MN)	−0.27	to −0.34
Silicone Bronze (96% Cu max, 0.80% Fe, 1.50% Zn, 2.00% Si, 0.75% MN, 1.60% Sn)	−0.26	to −0.29
Bronze, Composition G (88% Cu, 2% Zn, 10% Sn)	−0.24	to −0.31
Bronze, Comp. M (88% Cu, 3% Zn, 6.5% Sn, 1.5% Pb)	−0.24	to −0.31
13% Chromium Stainless Steel, Type 401 (passive)	−0.26	to −0.35
90% Cu − 10% Ni	−0.21	to −0.28
75% Cu − 20% Ni − 5% Zn	−0.19	to −0.25
Lead	−0.19	to −0.25
70% Cu − 30% Ni	−0.18	to −0.23
Inconel (78% Ni, 13.5% Cr, 6% Fe) (passive)	−0.14	to −0.17
Nickel 200	−0.10	to −0.20
18/8 Stainless Steel, Type 304 (passive)	−0.05	to −0.10
70% Ni − 30% Cu Monel 400, K-500	−0.04	to −0.14
18.8, 3% Mo Stainless Steel, Type 316 (passive)	−0.0	to −0.10
Titanium	−0.05	to +0.06
Hastelloy C	−0.03	to +0.08
Platinum	+0.19	to +0.25
Graphite	+0.20	to +0.30

anodic / least noble ↑ (cathodic ↕ anodic) most noble / cathodic ↓

1. Each metal has a unique voltage potential.
2. Half-cell reference electrode, silver-silver chloride.

more than one metal. Even "pure" metals contain impurities. Add a little salt water and many can generate internal galvanic corrosion—a notorious example being screws made of brass, an alloy of copper and zinc. These two metals, being widely separated on the galvanic scale, can become highly interactive, eating up all the zinc in the alloy and leaving a soft, porous, and worthless fastener.

Stainless steel is a special case. There are a number of different alloys in widespread marine use, 304 (18/8 or 18 percent chromium and 8 percent nickel) and 316 (includes 2 percent molybdenum) being the most common. Chromium in stainless steel oxidizes (reacts with oxygen in the atmosphere) to form an inert skin that protects the metal from corrosion. Stainless steel oxidized in this fashion is called *passivated,* and is one of the more corrosion resistant metals available for marine use (see Table 4-1).

Take away the oxygen and that surface layer of oxidized chromium, however, and stainless steel becomes *active,* offering little better corrosion resistance than its principal component, iron. Active areas of stainless steel frequently evidence themselves by rust stains. Since oxygen is readily available in the atmosphere and in seawater, there is little risk of corrosion in most circumstances. But if stainless steel is used in an area where stagnant water can collect, sooner or later its passivity will break down, and it will become active (normally in isolated pinholes and crevices) and will begin to "feed" on itself (Figure 4-2B), just

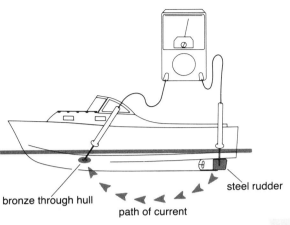

steel rudder

bronze through hull

path of current

Figure 4-2A. Galvanic corrosion. The bronze through hull acts as a cathode. It is pulled *below* its stabilized voltage potential and will not corrode. The steel rudder, pulled *above* its voltage potential, becomes an anode, and will corrode.

as the copper in a brass screw feeds on the zinc.

Areas notorious for pinhole and crevice corrosion of stainless steel are:

- Between a propeller shaft and propeller, in the threads under the propeller nut, around the keyway, in the cutless bearing, and under barnacles.
- *Inside* the lower terminals of swaged-on rigging fittings, which tend to collect water, and inside barrel-type turnbuckles. In both instances the corrosion is invisible and the first sign of trouble is likely to be a rigging failure.
- Inside centerboard trunks—particularly around hinge pins—where the water is stagnant and oxygen levels depleted.
- Within the spreader sockets, in cases where the spreaders are held with clevis pins through the spreader. This is especially true of wooden spreaders, which tend to hold water.

Stray-Current Corrosion

Galvanic corrosion can set up currents between fittings measured in milliamps and millivolts—a *thousandth* of an amp or volt. Faulty electrical circuits can establish currents *hundreds* of times stronger. Such "stray currents" can originate from within a boat, from shoreside fittings and ship-to-shore cables, or from neighboring boats. In all cases a leak from a hot wire allows current to find a path to ground through bilge water, damp areas of the boat, and

Figure 4-2B. Crevice corrosion on a stainless steel propeller shaft caused by stagnant water of low oxygen content in the stern tube.

the seawater rather than through proper channels.

Any electrical currents that lead to a flow of electrons in and out of fittings in contact with water will corrode the piece of metal feeding the current into the water. Galvanic corrosion is by its nature a relatively slow process (the metals themselves have to generate the flow of electrons) but stray-current corrosion, which carries the potential for greatly accelerated electron flow, can be devastating. In worst-case scenarios, stray currents can wipe out hardware in a matter of hours.

Some of the more common sources of stray electric currents are:

- Faulty insulation and poor connections in damp areas of the boat.
- Inadequate wiring, leading to voltage drop. Different parts of the ground circuits will then be at different voltages, encouraging current to find other paths to ground.
- Leaks within equipment from the hot side to the equipment case, and thence

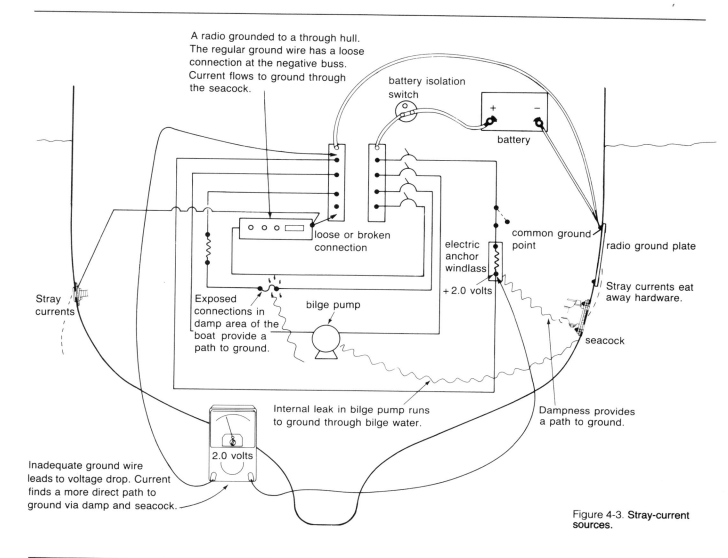

A radio grounded to a through hull. The regular ground wire has a loose connection at the negative buss. Current flows to ground through the seacock.

battery isolation switch

battery

loose or broken connection

electric anchor windlass

+2.0 volts

common ground point

radio ground plate

Stray currents eat away hardware.

seacock

Stray currents

Exposed connections in damp area of the boat provide a path to ground.

bilge pump

Internal leak in bilge pump runs to ground through bilge water.

Dampness provides a path to ground.

2.0 volts

Inadequate ground wire leads to voltage drop. Current finds a more direct path to ground via damp and seacock.

Figure 4-3. **Stray-current sources.**

through bilge water or damp areas of the boat to ground.

- Voltage drop in radios with external (immersed) ground plates. The voltage on the plate will differ from the negative battery terminal voltage, generating currents between the plate and any underwater metal grounded to the battery, such as the engine and propeller shaft (Figure 4-3).

- Any grounding system that haphazardly grounds different circuits and pieces of equipment to through hulls, etc. All equipment should have an insulated ground that leads back to a central ground buss bar in the main distribution panel, which in turn leads to a *common ground point* (see below), and from there back to the battery negative terminal.

- Battery chargers without isolation transformers. The neutral wires on both sides of the transformer are in common with the DC ground side (see page 119). In a reverse polarity situation these chargers will create strong stray currents.

- Tying the neutral side of an AC system into the boat's ground system. Combined with reverse polarity this will generate strong stray currents unless a Type-B isolation transformer is in use. The neutral side is only grounded ashore, never on board, except with Type-B isolation transformers (see Chapter 3).

- Reverse polarity lamps themselves, since these function by making a direct connection between the hot or neutral wire and ground. Reverse polarity lamps should have a spring-loaded (normally off) switch that is held on momentarily to check polarity and remains off the rest of the time, isolating the polarity indicator.

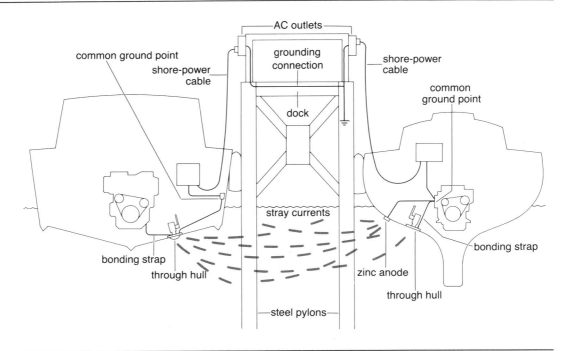

Figure 4-4. Stray-current mischief at a marina: a common scenario.

• Defective shore-power wiring that allows leaks from marina and dockside wiring to ground—particularly reverse polarity in any dockside receptacles and long cable runs that, together with overloading, result in voltage drop. Voltage differentials in the ground circuits encourage current to find other paths to ground. Note that ABYC recommendations call for a boat's AC system to be grounded to the boat's common ground point. Two or more boats connected to shoreside power will be electrically connected to the dock and to each other via the green (or bare) grounding wire, while their underwater hardware will be hooked into the same circuit via any bonding straps, which will also terminate in the common ground points. *Any voltage differences between a boat and the dock or another boat will lead to stray currents* unless a properly fitted isolator or isolation transformer is installed. Normally the boat with the most zincs will lose zinc to the dock and other boats (Figure 4-4).

The first priority in eliminating stray-current corrosion is to eliminate all ground leaks. The sections on pages 83–88 outline a number of detailed steps to track down and isolate ground leaks in both AC and DC circuits. These should be followed, and all leaks cleaned up where possible. (It may not be possible to deal with leaks external to your boat.)

From this point on, opinions diverge as to how to provide further protection to a boat, the principal debate being over whether to "bond" the boat.

To Bond Or Not To Bond

Bonding is the practice of electrically tying together all major metal objects on the boat: rigging and chainplates, engine and propeller shaft, stove, metal water tanks, metal cases on electrical equipment, etc. A substantial copper strap is installed through the length of the boat, to which the individual pieces of equipment are connected by *jumper wires.* The bonding strap terminates at the boat's common ground point—generally a substantial bolt on the engine block. This is not the best place, however, especially if the engine has an insulated-ground alternator and starter motor. Far better to use a keel bolt to an *external* keel, or the lug on an *external* ground plate.

A bonding system is entirely separate from any AC or DC ground system, although all terminate at the common ground point (except for some AC systems with a Type-A isolation transformer). The bonding system is not a current-carrying conductor except during lightning strikes (see below).

At this point we run into trouble. Where two dissimilar pieces of metal with different voltage potentials are immersed in seawater, such as a stainless steel propeller shaft and a bronze through-hull fitting, *bonding the two may make precisely the circuit needed to promote galvanic corrosion!*

If the bonding system is connected to a piece of zinc immersed in seawater, however, the zinc, being lower on the galvanic table than any boatbuilding metal, will be the one to corrode, providing protection to all the metals "above" it. When the zinc is gone, the next lowest metal on the table will start to corrode.

This is the logic behind sacrificial zinc anodes. All the boat's metal fittings are bonded, and the bonding system is connected to one or more well-placed zincs; the zincs must be in reasonable proximity to the metal fittings they are protecting. The zincs are eaten up, and thus protect the hardware. In technical parlance, the zincs drive the rest of the hardware cathodic. As long as the zincs supply enough current, corrosion will be held at bay. Clearly it is vital to renew the zincs from time to time to provide fresh sacrificial material.

The problem with such a system is that it provides protection to a lot of items—such as bronze through-hull fittings if included in the system—that are high enough on the galvanic scale not to need protecting under normal circumstances. The bronze hardware will steadily consume the zincs—no big deal since zincs are relatively cheap—but this robs more needy items, such as iron engine blocks, of protection. Moreover, the extra electrochemical activity encouraged by tying the zincs to bronze through hulls generates alkaline peroxides and hydroxides around the through hulls that attack organic materials—read *wood*.

"Wood around bonded through-hull fittings becomes severely softened and deteriorated, often producing a dangerously weakened condition over a period of years." (Kocher, op. cit.)

This would seem to be a problem exclusive to wooden boats, but not necessarily so. Almost all quality through-hull installations on fiberglass boats utilize a wooden backing block. If the through hull is in a damp area, as it often is, the backing block may well succumb to alkali attack. Next time you check your through hulls, take a close look at those backing blocks.

Kocher's conclusion is that "the unnecessary bonding of bronze, copper, or monel fittings to zinc and to the electrical system is a destructive and dangerous practice." He is in favor of unbonding through-hull fittings in nonmetallic hulls,

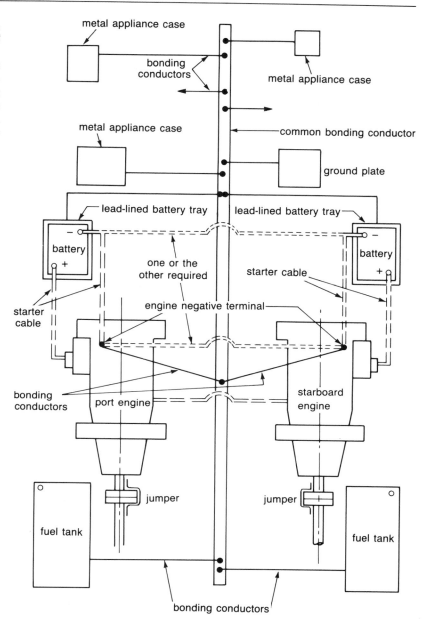

Figure 4-5. **Bonding system.**

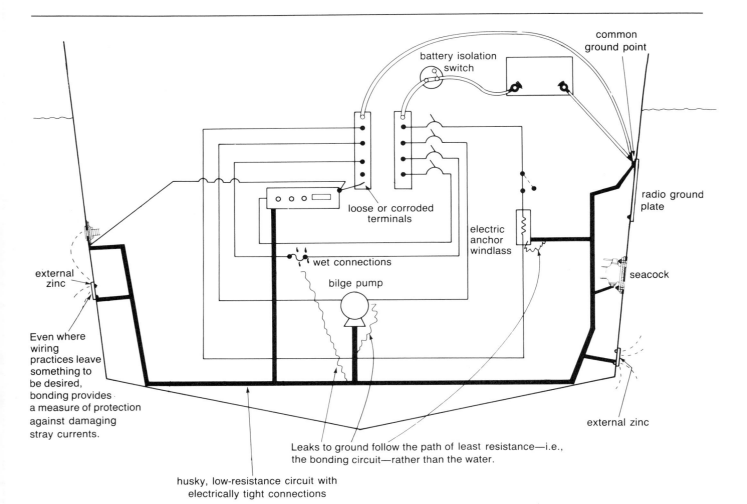

battery isolation switch

common ground point

loose or corroded terminals

electric anchor windlass

radio ground plate

wet connections

seacock

bilge pump

external zinc

external zinc

Even where wiring practices leave something to be desired, bonding provides a measure of protection against damaging stray currents.

Leaks to ground follow the path of least resistance—i.e., the bonding circuit—rather than the water.

husky, low-resistance circuit with electrically tight connections

Figure 4-6. **Bonding and ground leaks.**

and reserving the sacrificial zinc protection for the boat's iron, such as the engine.

This flies in the face of most current boatbuilding practice in the USA, as well as the standards advocated by the American Boat and Yacht Council (ABYC)—the industry-wide voluntary standards-setting body. However, the ABYC does state: "Electrically isolated through-hull fittings need not be connected to the bonding system."

It is also debatable whether bonding may accelerate corrosion in other circumstances. For example, assume an electrical leak, perhaps from a poorly grounded shoreside hook-up, running to ground through the water surrounding the boat. Since seawater is not a very good conductor at low voltages, different parts of the water will take on slightly different potentials, in which case any bonding strap connected to through hulls will form the path of least resistance for the stray currents in the water, which then will flow in one

through hull, down the bonding strap, and out another. One through hull will be anodic with respect to this current and will corrode; the other will be cathodic and will be protected.

In the above example the only result may be faster than normal consumption of the sacrificial zincs, protecting both the through hulls. What is clear is that *it is absolutely critical to maintain zinc anodes in good condition on bonded boats.* If the zinc is too remote, or the stray current strong enough to overwhelm the current produced by the zinc, corrosion will follow.

This latter point is important. Bonding and zincs are in no sense a substitute for solving stray-current leaks. Any leakage current, either from inside or outside the boat, that is strong enough to overwhelm the protective current from zinc anodes will generate corrosion, sometimes at a devastating rate.

So where does this leave us?

Preventing Corrosion

Certain general steps can be taken to reduce underwater galvanic corrosion. First and foremost, as far as possible, never mix underwater metals. This will minimize differences between the voltage potentials of the various metals involved, and minimize the potential for corrosion.

All hardware should be attached with fastenings at least as noble (high on the galvanic scale) as the fittings, preferably slightly more noble. The small fastener will then become cathodic with respect to the large fitting, which will be anodic. The small amount of galvanic corrosion produced in the fitting is unlikely to be harmful, but a large cathodic fixture soon would devour a small anodic fastener. The fixture and fastener should not be too far apart on the galvanic table, however. Passivated stainless steel fasteners, for example, frequently do considerable damage to aluminum fittings when exposed to salt-water spray or immersion.

Non-metallic paints (vinyls and epoxies) can be used to put a protective (insulating) skin on underwater hardware. But in the presence of stray currents any pinholes or scratches can produce quite serious localized corrosion. At the other end of the scale, many metallic-based paints (e.g., most antifouling paints) may interact galvanically with underwater hardware. This is why it is important to match the paint to the fittings where possible. For instance, copper-based paints are galvanically close to bronze, but can be quite destructive if used on aluminum.

There are then two broad schools of thought on corrosion prevention:

Unbond and Isolate

One philosophy is to unbond all underwater fittings, isolate them electrically, and allow them to reach equilibrium at their own voltage potentials. For this to work it is necessary to have all top-quality underwater fittings (e.g., bronze); if they are in close physical proximity they should be of a similar metal; and they must be insulated from all electrical circuits. In practice, since most through hulls on fiberglass boats are connected to rubber or plastic hoses, they are already electrically isolated unless connected by a bonding circuit. On metal boats, through hulls generally are mounted on insulated blocks to reduce galvanic interaction between the hull and fittings.

An unbonded hull will need electrical systems of the insulated-return type (which should be mandatory in boats in any case, with the possible exception of engine circuits). In addition, the AC system should have an isolation transformer. Failing that, the AC grounding circuit will need an isolator (page 74). A close watch will have to be kept for external sources of stray currents when in marinas and around other boats. Part of our success with an unbonded hull is undoubtedly due to the fact that we spend most of our time anchored out, where external stray currents are not possible. In addition our internal circuits are wired to high standards throughout with very heavy wire, and we have no external radio grounds or other potential sources of stray current. Our radio is grounded to an internal ground plane; see Chapter 7.

Unbonded boats still will need sacrificial zinc anodes at specific spots, such as a zinc collar where a stainless steel propeller shaft interacts with a bronze propeller or zincs in the raw-water engine cooling circuits.

Whenever there is the potential for external stray currents, such as in marinas, an unbonded boat should get extra insurance by suspending one or two *guppies* (zinc anodes designed to hang over the sides) in the water at strategic locations around the boat. These should be fastened to electric cables and clipped to vulnerable hardware, such as a rudderstock or propeller shaft.

Unbonded boats may have problems providing adequate lightning protection and adequate grounding systems for SSB radio and Lorans. More about this later in this chapter and in Chapter 7.

Bonding

The conventional wisdom is to bond absolutely everything possible and to tie in sacrificial zincs. The key to successful bonding is to have a conductor large enough to ensure absolutely no voltage differences between fittings, and to have electrically perfect connections.

The main bonding strap needs to be at least #8 AWG copper wire, or 3/4-inch (22 mm) or 1-inch (28 mm) copper tubing squashed flat. All jumper wires to individual fittings and pieces of equipment need to be at least #8 AWG wire. *All joints should be soldered, without exception.*

Propeller shafts need special attention. The connection between the propeller shaft coupling and the engine is not adequate for bonding purposes (especially with flexible couplings). A jumper wire should be connected across the coupling and a spring-loaded bronze brush set up against the shaft and tied into the bonding strap (see Figure 7-9).

The fastening of zincs also must be electrically perfect. *They will not work if they are not tied electrically to the metal they are protecting.* Direct fastening (e.g., to a metal rudder) is best. With remotely fastened zincs on wood and fiberglass hulls, putting a stainless steel bolt through the zinc and connecting a bonding wire to that *will not do.* The zinc soon will corrode where it contacts the stainless steel, and the connection will deteriorate. Zincs should have cast-in plates and fasteners to maintain a good electrical contact throughout the life of the zinc.

Connections from the anode to the bonding system once again must be soldered where possible. Always remember what small currents and voltages (hopefully!) we are dealing with and how little resistance it takes to defeat the purpose of the circuit.

Zincs must never be painted, and need replacing *before* they wear out. As surface area diminishes and corrosive residues build up, protection declines. Any zinc that is 80 percent used up is overdue for renewal. Some people advocate renewal after only 20 percent is used up!

Finally, no matter how carefully your boat is bonded and protected, if it is connected to shore power it is vulnerable to stray currents from the dock and other boats. *Even on bonded boats, the AC ground should be effectively isolated from the boat's common ground point,* either via an isolation transformer or an isolator (see pages 73–75).

Impressed-Current Systems

Zinc anodes work by generating a small current that makes the boat's underwater fixtures cathodic with respect to the zinc. The same effect can be produced by passing controlled amounts of current through fittings (and hull, if metallic). This is the basis for impressed-current cathodic protection systems.

A *reference electrode* senses voltage potential in the water. A control unit then uses the boat's batteries to send current to one or more anodes projecting through the hull (and attached to it electrically in the case of metal boats). The anodes are made of a very noble metal and therefore do not corrode. The battery power raises the anodes above their voltage potential, causing them to release an electrical current into the water. This current drives the underwater hardware cathodic (just as with the current generated by a zinc anode) and so prevents corrosion.

Such systems are principally used on large steel vessels and find little application in pleasureboats (for one thing, they put a constant drain on the battery). They must be set up by professionals and monitored carefully. Excess impressed current, particularly on aluminum hulls, can do as much damage as inadequate cathodic protection.

Lightning Protection

In some parts of the world lightning is a rarity, but in others it can be quite common. Parts of the eastern seaboard of the United States are notorious for electrical storms. Lightning tends to strike the highest object around; at sea this will be *any* boat in the vicinity! While the consequences of a strike are unpredictable—ranging from negligible to the sinking of boats and loss of life—it makes no sense to take chances. You and your boat are a target; you should be protected.

Lightning protection should be a relatively simple affair. After all, lightning rods connected by a heavy wire to ground have been doing yeoman's duty on barns since Faraday. But as usual, opinions differ on how to protect a boat; the basic problem is that many of the measures that increase protection from lightning strikes may at the same time increase the potential for electrolytic corrosion.

The Zone of Security

A well-grounded lightning rod is generally considered to provide a "zone of security" for an area around its base equal to the height of the rod (Figure 4-7). "Zone of security" is an ambiguous term. Although it

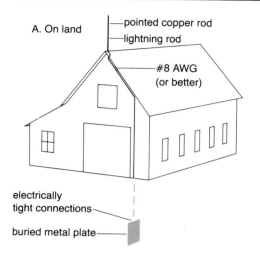

A. On land

pointed copper rod

lightning rod

#8 AWG
(or better)

electrically
tight connections

buried metal plate

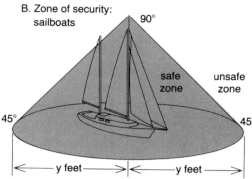

B. Zone of security:
sailboats

90°

safe
zone

unsafe
zone

45°   45°

y feet   y feet

Figure 4-7. Lightning protection. Note that, particularly on power boats, it may prove impossible to include all deck areas in the zone of security. If so, stay clear of unprotected areas during lightning storms. A grounded metal spike higher than any mast-mounted antenna will provide additional protection.

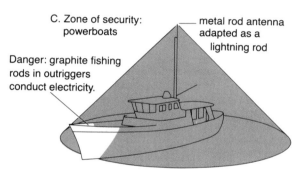

C. Zone of security:
powerboats

metal rod antenna
adapted as a
lightning rod

Danger: graphite fishing
rods in outriggers
conduct electricity.

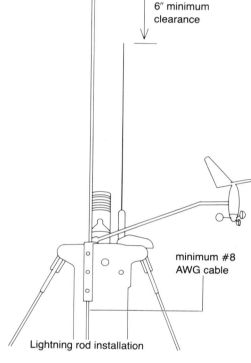

6″ minimum
clearance

minimum #8
AWG cable

Lightning rod installation

will provide a fair measure of protection to people, in the event of a lightning strike, all onboard electronics may be barbecued and a hole blown in the boat. Some security!

Given the height of a sailboat mast, if it is used as a lightning conductor the whole boat is bound to fall within its zone of security, which is why we rarely, if ever, hear of people on sailboats being injured by lightning strikes. Powerboats, on the other hand, will need some form of elevated lightning rod, high enough to provide the necessary security zone. Certain antennas—and sometimes an outrigger—can serve in this capacity (see below). Otherwise a separate lightning rod is required.

Whatever is used as a lightning rod, its tip must be at least six inches (150 mm) above anything else on the boat, and its performance will be enhanced if it terminates in a sharp point.

The Path to Ground

The basic philosophy behind lightning protection is to conduct the strike to ground as cleanly as possible. The key to success is to keep the lightning moving on the most direct path (i.e., straight down) to as large an immersed ground plate as possible.

An aluminum mast is an excellent conductor, especially if capped with a pointed lightning rod higher than any radio antennas. A wooden mast needs a conductor (#8 AWG copper wire or larger) run straight down the mast. The sail track will serve if it has no electrical discontinuities and is suitably connected to a lightning rod.

Powerboats can use *metal rod* radio antennas (fiberglass antennas are generally not suitable) as long as:

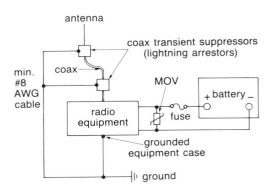

Figure 4-8. Protecting electronics from lightning strikes. Transient voltage suppressors and MOVs (metal oxide varistors) are discussed in the accompanying text.

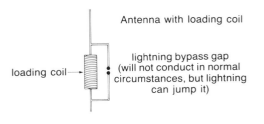

1. The antenna is high enough to provide the necessary zone of security.

2. The antenna is adequately grounded via a lightning arrestor (see below) and #8 AWG cable (or larger).

3. Any loading coil (a cylinder at the base of the antenna) has a lightning bypass (see below).

The direct path to ground must be maintained from the base of a mast or radio antenna all the way to the external ground plate. Lightning does not like to make tight curves. If forced to do so it is likely to jump unpredictably (*side flashes*) to other metallic fixtures, generating dangerous sparks and heat and perhaps starting fires.

Seawater is not a particularly good conductor. In order to dissipate a strike rapidly, *a minimum ground plate area of one square foot (900 square centimeters) is recommended* (ABYC). Fresh water is even less conductive than salt and *as much as 10 times the contact area may be needed.*

Metal boats have no problem. The whole hull can serve as a ground plate. Wood and fiberglass sailboats can use *external* ballast keels, metal centerboards, or metal rudders. Where these are not available, and on wood and fiberglass powerboats, an adequate ground plate area must be provided. Many radio ground plates are considered sufficient. Sailboats with two masts should have a direct path to ground *from each mast.*

Without adequate ground plate area the ground-plate-to-seawater interface will become a bottleneck. The lightning is likely to seek other paths, generating side flashes and potentially blowing seacocks and other through hulls clean out of the boat!

Bonded boats and lightning. In practice, very few nonmetallic boats have a lightning ground plate below the mast. Since most are bonded (which will have tied together aluminum masts, the engine and propeller shaft, and through hulls), the totality of the bonded underwater fixtures is considered adequate to dissipate a strike (though this clearly involves a lot of bends!). The key, once again, is good-sized conductors (minimum #8 AWG copper wire) and electrically tight connections.

The ABYC also calls for all chainplates to be tied into the bonding circuit, as well as all other fixed external metal masses such as lifelines, winches, davits, stovepipes, etc., and any internal metal objects within six feet (two meters) of a lightning conductor (to reduce the risk of side flashes). It is particularly important to bond internal chainplates. Otherwise a strike is likely to run down the shrouds and then jump through the hull to the surrounding water, blowing a hole in the hull in the process.

Protecting Onboard Systems

We recently met a sailor with extensive electronic equipment who had it all (baring one VHF radio) fried twice in one year by electrical storms off the east coast of the USA. What, if anything, can be done about this?

Lightning generates tremendous electromagnetic forces over a fairly wide range of frequencies. Amperages in a strike will range from 10,000 all the way up to 175,000 amps. Temperatures may run as high as 60,000°F. The effects can be felt hundreds of feet away.

Any conductor within range of a strike will act as a radio antenna, tending to pick up some of this energy. If the conductor has the bad luck to be the same length as the particular frequency generated by the lightning strike, it will pick up even more energy. If conductors form a loop they will attract yet *more* of the electromagnetic energy. Antennas in particular *are designed to be efficient collectors of electromagnetic energy,* but only at specific frequencies. If the strike falls within this frequency, high voltages and amperages will be picked up, potentially damaging much onboard equipment. Lorans and SSBs fall within the normal frequency range of lightning; VHF radios are above it.

Electronic equipment. A couple of general points are immediately apparent:

1. Keep all leads (power leads, ground connections, antennas) as short as possible.
2. Avoid any loops in wiring circuits, particularly the boat's ground (earth) circuits. This is one of the reasons why it is important to have one central ground point and not have equipment grounded (earthed) indiscriminately around the boat.

The next thing is to isolate sensitive equipment from any energy radiated into its circuits. The most protection during electrical storms will be provided by *disconnecting all external wiring*—power leads, antenna, and microphone—combined with keeping the equipment within *a well-grounded metal case.* This will save most equipment in most strikes but still will not save particularly sensitive equipment (especially microprocessors) in a major strike. Given the forces involved, nothing will.

Circuit breakers. Because their response time is too slow, circuit breakers do not provide protection from lightning strikes. By the time a breaker opens, the damage is done. Even if opened manually before a storm, they do not provide adequate protection—lightning can bridge the circuit breaker terminals. It is far better to *physically disconnect equipment and put the leads well out of the way.*

Transient voltage suppressors. Almost the same degree of protection gained by disconnecting equipment is available by fitting *transient voltage suppressors* to power lines and antennas. Most of these devices are constructed around metal oxide varistors (MOVs). Varistors are solid-state devices, which under normal voltage conditions have an open circuit (i.e., are nonconductive) but become conductive when hit by large transient voltages (voltage *spikes*).

A varistor installed between the positive and negative power leads on DC equipment is normally nonconductive. When hit by lightning-induced high voltages, it becomes conductive, shorting the voltage to

ground and protecting the equipment (Figure 4-8). Clearly, to be effective the varistor must react with incredible rapidity.

Different transient voltage suppressors are used on DC lines, antennas, and AC power lines.

1. *DC power lines:* After considerable testing of lightning protection devices, the Amateur Radio Relay League (ARRL) determined that the best value was a GE MOV V36ZA80 Metal Oxide Varistor. It can be bought in any good radio parts store, and is connected across the incoming power leads.
2. *AC power lines:* The problem with AC power lines on shore or when connected to the dockside is that the long cable runs tend to pick up much energy. In various tests, however, the short cable runs to standby generators were found to be safe, and the small generators themselves came through the lightning strikes unscathed. Thus it would seem protection is required only on AC lines when connected to shoreside power. In this case the ARRL recommended a T11 Model 428 Plug-In Powerline Protector (radio parts stores).
3. *Antennas:* There are many stories of vaporized antennas. Clearly they are especially vulnerable. Many antennas are actually used as lightning rods, especially on powerboats. The equipment at the lower end of the antenna can be given a fair amount of protection with a coaxial line transient suppressor (a *lightning arrestor*). This is connected between the coaxial (*coax*) cable and ground, shorting out the coax if high voltages occur.

However, the capacity of coax itself to conduct lightning is limited. In a direct strike it will short out internally, which has the advantage of reducing the energy reaching the equipment at the other end, but makes the coax ineffective as a lightning protector. To properly protect the coax, and in all situations where an antenna is used as a lightning rod, a lightning arrestor also must be installed at the base of the antenna, connected to ground with a minimum #8 AWG cable.

(Note: ABYC specifications allow only metal rod antennas as lightning rods. This excludes most fiberglass antennas. If the antenna has a *loading coil*—a cylinder at its base—the loading coil must be bypassed

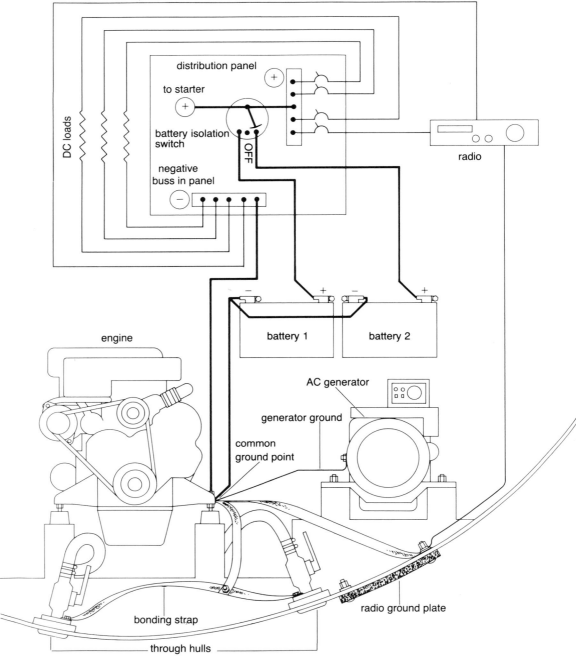

Figure 4-9. **Using a bolt on the engine as a common ground point** (see close-up in Figure 4–10). This is a common choice for the ground point, though not the best one. A substantial stud in or near the distribution panel would be better. Insulated terminal studs or posts can be purchased for this purpose.

DC loads

distribution panel

to starter

battery isolation switch

OFF

negative buss in panel

radio

battery 1

battery 2

AC generator

generator ground

common ground point

engine

bonding strap

through hulls

radio ground plate

with a *lightning gap*. Otherwise, for lightning protection purposes, the antenna is considered to be no higher than *the base of the coil*.

Ham radio antennas may present special problems. The peak voltage when transmitting is calculated as a function of the rating of the piece of equipment (peak power in watts), its SWR (standing wave ratio, which is a measure of the ratio of power reflected back from the antenna compared with output), and the resistance

(impedance in ohms) of the coaxial cable leading to the antenna. The formula is:

$$V = (P \times Z \times SWR)$$

Where V = peak voltage
             P = peak power in watts
             Z = impedance of the coax cable in ohms
   SWR = standing wave ratio

MOVs have a *clamping voltage*—the voltage level at which the device closes the circuit and starts to conduct to ground—that must be higher than the system's peak voltage but low enough to provide equipment protection. A voltage of three times the peak transmission voltage normally is selected to give an adequate margin.

Finally, ketch owners might consider mounting antennas on the mizzen mast rather than the main (assuming the main has lightning protection). The higher main is more likely to receive a direct hit. The only equipment that survived the two hits mentioned above was a mizzen-mounted VHF radio.

Compasses. After a lightning strike, compass deviation may be 20 degrees or more on certain headings. It will slowly return to normal. This means the deviation will need checking, and adjusting if necessary, at regular intervals for some time.

The Common Ground Point

The boat's common ground (earth) point has been referred to a number of times. In any given boat there may be several ground systems: the negative side of the DC system; the green or bare equipment safety ground on AC systems; and the boat's bonding system. Note that only the first actually carries current. The last two are purely for safety and/or protection against corrosion.

In order to eliminate stray currents within and between the ground systems, *it is important that they all be held at the same ground potential.* This is done by tying them together electrically. However, it is equally important that no potential circuits are created for stray-current movement around the grounding systems. For this reason they are only tied together at one point—the boat's common ground point.

The usual practice is to select a substantial bolt on the engine block, although this is not the best choice and should not be done on boats with a fully insulated ground system (see page 65). It would be preferable to set up a substantial stud somewhere else (generally in or close to the distribution panel) and to run all grounding leads and straps to this bolt. Insulated bolts (terminal studs or terminal posts) can be bought for this purpose. Typical connections to the common ground point include:

- A ground strap from the battery;
- The ground (return) line from the neg-

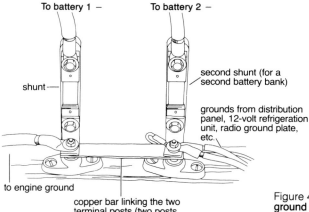

To battery 1 — To battery 2 —

shunt

second shunt (for a second battery bank)

grounds from distribution panel, 12-volt refrigeration unit, radio ground plate, etc.

to engine ground

copper bar linking the two terminal posts (two posts accommodate more ground cables)

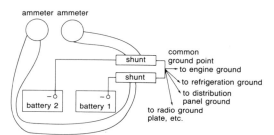

ammeter ammeter

shunt

shunt

battery 2   battery 1

common ground point
to engine ground
to refrigeration ground
to distribution panel ground
to radio ground plate, etc.

Figure 4-10. **A common ground point.** In this sophisticated configuration, current charge or draw can be measured separately to each battery bank via the shunts. In most boats the shunts are omitted and there is one common negative cable to the two battery banks. The terminal stud or studs should be mounted on insulated bases; all ground wire, cable, and strap ends should be sandwiched between nuts and washers.

ative buss bar in the DC distribution panel;

- The ground wire (green or bare) from the AC distribution panel (but never the neutral wire except on AC systems with Type-B isolation transformers; see page 74);
- The ground from an auxiliary generator;
- The central bonding strap;
- Ground connections to radio ground plates.

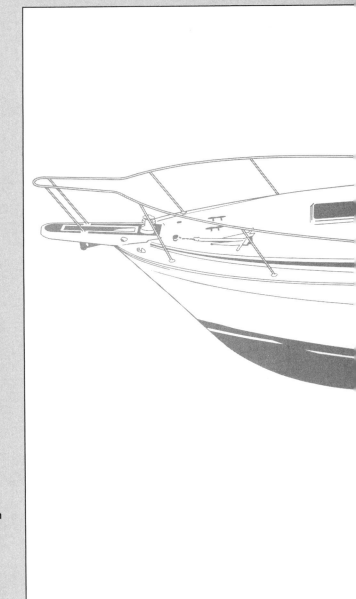

———————	12 VDC
-----------------	12 V ground (return)
— — — —	120 VAC
·················	bonding strap jumper
[hatched box]	ground
[gray box]	bonding (mass)
[crosshatched box]	grounding and bonding combined

Figure 5-1. Alternative sources of electrical power can go a long way towards easing life aboard. Become your own power company.

(1) wind generator
(2) batteries
(3) 110 VAC shoreside receptacle
(4) shunt regulator
(5) 110 VAC load center
(6) to AC appliances
(7) generator set
(8) distribution panel
(9) DC/AC inverter
(10) battery charger
(11) solar panel
(12) isolation transformer

Auxiliary Sources of Power: Converters, Inverters, Wind and Water Generators, and Solar Panels

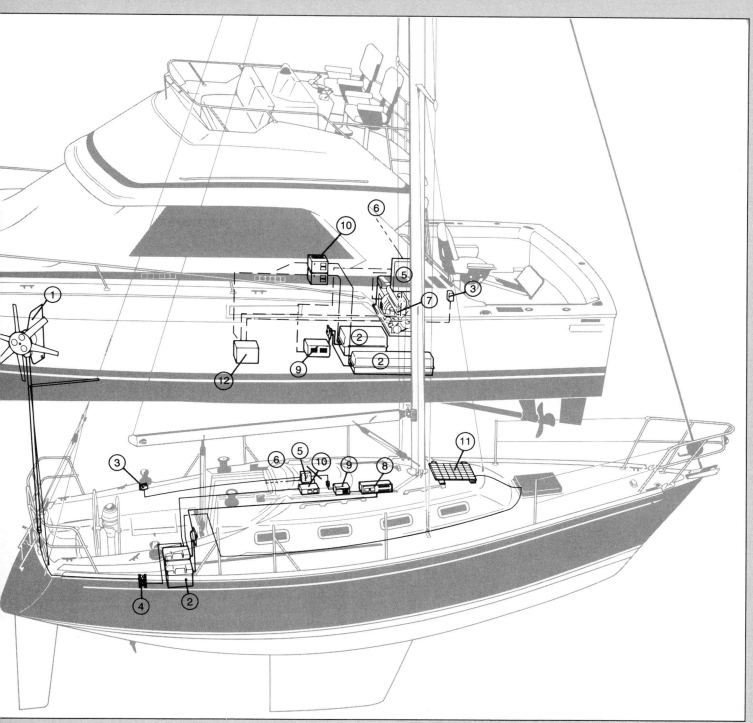

This chapter deals with various auxiliary power sources, both DC and AC. Battery chargers, often referred to as *converters,* and DC/AC inverters are opposite sides of the same coin, the one converting AC power into DC power for battery charging, the other transforming the batteries' DC power into AC power. In addition, wind and water generators and solar panels have become increasingly popular devices to produce direct current for battery charging.

Dockside Battery Chargers (Converters)

How They Work

AC power is fed into a transformer—a device for changing voltages. The incoming AC voltage (generally 115 volts in the USA and 240 volts in the UK) is stepped down to near-battery voltage—12, 24, or 32 volts, depending on the system. But this is still alternating current. To use it for battery charging, it must be *rectified* to direct current using silicon diodes (see Chapter 2).

If more than one battery is to be charged, the transformer output is split and fed to the charger output terminals through distribution *(output)* diodes. Sometimes the rectifying and distribution diodes are combined (Figure 5-2A). We now have a basic charger to which various refinements may be added (Figure 5-2B), including:

1. A circuit to compensate for variations in incoming AC voltage. This is known as *line compensation.*
2. A *thermistor* and/or *varistor* connected across the low-voltage side of the AC transformer to adjust output for changes in temperature and to protect against voltage "spikes" (more on varistors on page 111).
3. A capacitor connected across the high-voltage (incoming AC) side of the transformer.
4. Current limiting and voltage regulation circuits.
5. Automatic "OFF" and "ON" circuits.
6. An "ignition-protection" circuit, which shuts down the charger during engine cranking and running. This prevents overload from the starter motor, and

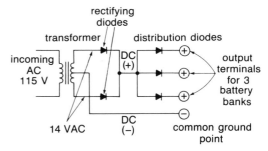

Figure 5-2A. **Basic battery charger circuit.** The transformer steps down incoming 115 VAC power to approximately 14 VAC; the rectifying diodes convert this to DC; this is then fed to the battery. If more than one battery is to be charged, the output is channeled through distribution diodes.

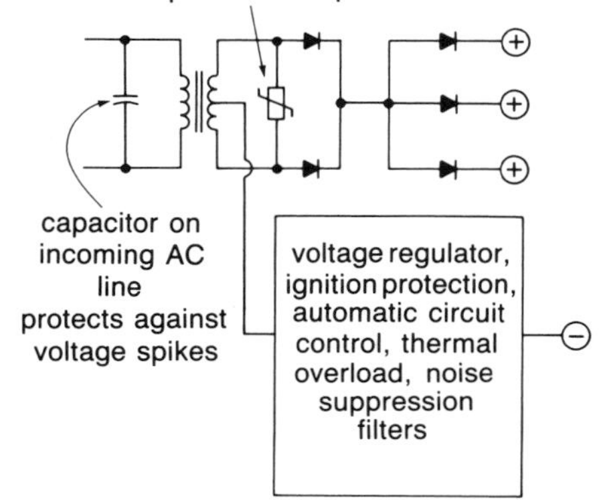

Figure 5-2B. **Battery charger refinements.**

conflict between alternator and battery-charger voltage regulators.

7. Various filters to reduce radio interference.

As with all other parts comprising the DC system, a battery charger must be matched to its function within the overall framework of battery usage and battery-charging capabilities. Some examples should make this clear:

1. **A boat with 24-hour-a-day AC power.** The battery charger needs to keep up with the boat's DC load and maintain the batteries in a state of full charge, without overcharging them (similar to an automobile's alternator).

2. **A cruising boat with occasional shore-side hook-up or generator use.** The battery charger will need to rapidly recharge large-capacity, deeply discharged batteries, and preferably have an equalization capability (see Chapter 2, "Sulfation and Equalization").

3. **A weekend sailboat with shoreside hook-up.** The charger is there to keep the batteries topped up during the week, without overcharging them.

It is important to select a battery charger appropriate to its tasks. Otherwise, at best, a lot of money is likely to be wasted; at worst, serious battery damage may occur. For example, overcharging at dockside is a major cause of premature battery death.

In selecting a battery charger, the first priority is to get a charger with a current rating (amperage output) adequate to the demands to be placed on it. A trickle charger is a useless investment for most cruising sailors. Next comes the question of voltage regulation.

Types of Battery Charger Voltage Regulation

Unregulated. Most trickle chargers are unregulated. The output is generally less than 3 amps and regulation is considered unnecessary. However, output currents as low as 1 amp, if connected permanently to unused batteries, can cause overcharging, water loss, and battery plate damage. Gel-type batteries are particularly susceptible to damage from prolonged periods of minor overcharging. Even with trickle charg-

ers, battery state of charge needs to be monitored and the charger switched off at full charge (Figure 5-3A).

Constant potential (voltage). This is the largest class of chargers, regulated in the same fashion as alternators. A constant-potential charger seeks to maintain output at a constant voltage. If battery voltage falls, the charger responds by increasing output; as battery voltage rises, the charge rate is tapered off. Constant-potential chargers suffer from the same drawbacks as voltage regulators. If the voltage is set low enough to avoid overcharging during prolonged use, the charge rate is tapered off too soon to quickly recharge deeply discharged batteries. If the voltage is high enough for rapid recharging, however, serious overcharging is likely during prolonged use. In practice, most chargers are regulated to 13.8 volts, not high enough to rapidly recharge well-discharged, deep-cycle batteries, but high enough to overcharge fully charged batteries if the charger is left on permanently, as at the dockside (Figure 5-3B). *This is a major cause of battery failures on boats.*

Many of the "cheaper" constant-potential marine chargers use a *ferro-resonant* transformer. This type reduces costs because the transformer automatically stabilizes output voltage at a certain level, eliminating the need for various control circuits. Ferro-resonant transformers provide none of the flexibility most boat owners need, however, and waste up to 45 percent of the incoming energy in internal losses.

The published amperage rating of many constant-potential battery chargers is borderline fraudulent. Since output tapers off steadily as the battery's state of charge rises, the lower the battery voltage selected for rating purposes, the higher the charger's apparent output. For example, if a manufacturer rates a charger at a battery voltage of 11.5 volts, it may put out, say, 15 amps. At 11.5 volts, however, a battery is *stone dead.* At more typical states of charge—say 50 to 60 percent of full charge—battery voltage will be 12.2 to 12.4 volts, and the charger's output will be only a trickle.

Since there are no industry standards for rating battery charger output, *it is important to know at what voltage the charger supplies its rated output.* Given two chargers with the same nominal output, the higher the rating voltage, the more powerful the

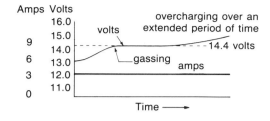

Figure 5-3A. Unregulated (constant-current trickle charger).

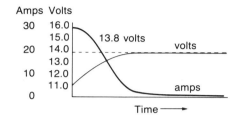

Figure 5-3B. Constant potential (preset to around 13.8 volts).

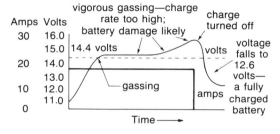

Figure 5-3C. Constant current (set to 20 amps for a 100-Ah battery).

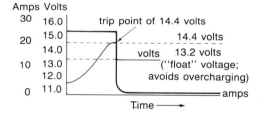

Figure 5-3D. Constant current/constant potential (set to 25 amps and 14.4 volts on a 100-Ah battery).

charger. A useful benchmark would be actual output at 13.8 volts, since this is a typical regulator setting on constant-potential chargers.

Automatic. A refinement seen on many constant-potential chargers is automatic voltage regulation. A circuit senses battery voltage and turns off the charger output when voltage reaches a certain level. After battery voltage has fallen by a set amount, charger output is switched back on. This eliminates some but not all problems with overcharging during prolonged use.

As with constant-potential chargers, charge rates tend to be too low (regulated to 13.8 volts) for fast charges, too high for "float" charging (maintaining a fully charged battery).

"Manual" switches on automatic ferro-resonant chargers do *not* in any way affect the regulated output of the charger (this is permanently established by the transformer), but merely bypass the automatic shutdown circuit, keeping the charger turned on at all times. If a battery is at full charge the voltage will stabilize more or less with the regulated voltage of the transformer and therefore very little current will flow whether the charger is in "manual" or "automatic" mode. This kind of manual override does not help a lot when equalizing sulfated batteries, and will not increase the rate of charge of discharged batteries at all. On the other hand, a ferro-resonant battery charger without an automatic shutdown circuit is quite capable of overcharging and seriously damaging batteries if left permanently connected.

Constant current. These are normally high-output "boost" chargers. The output is adjustable and can be set to a specific amperage, which in general should be limited to no more than 25 percent of the battery's Ah rating, and considerably less as a battery comes to full charge. The charger will maintain this more or less irrespective of battery voltage, much like the voltage-regulator bypass devices discussed in Chapter 2. Rapid battery charging at maximum charger output is possible, but with the inherent risk of serious overcharging and battery damage. Most chargers incorporate a timer, and switch off after a preset interval (Figure 5-3C).

Constant current/constant potential. These chargers—sometimes called *deep-cycle*—maintain a *constant current* until a certain battery voltage is reached, and then "trip" to *constant-potential* regulation. The trip point is set high enough (14.2 to 14.4 volts) to bring batteries close to a full charge, but then the voltage regulator is reset low enough (13.2 to 13.6 volts) to maintain an effective "float" voltage and avoid overcharging (Figure 5-3D).

With these chargers, it is important to limit the constant current to no more than 25 percent of the battery's Ah capacity. Otherwise the charger will drive up the battery voltage and trip to its float voltage long before the battery is fully charged. Even at 25 percent of Ah capacity, 14.2 to 14.4 volts will be reached at about the 80-percent charge level. With a float voltage of 13.2 to 13.6 volts the batteries will never be fully charged and will likely suffer some sulfation. A lower constant-current rating (e.g., 10 percent of the battery's Ah rating) will result in a more fully charged battery before the charger reaches the trip point, but obviously over a longer period of time.

At the other end of the scale, if the constant-current charge rate is too low the battery will never be driven to the trip point of 14.2 to 14.4 volts and the charger will stay in the constant-current mode. Nevertheless, the charger output might be high enough to cause overcharging and battery damage over an extended period of time.

Summary. The ideal marine battery charger would hold a constant-current charge of around 25 percent of a battery's Ah rating until battery voltage reached 14.2 to 14.4 volts. The charger would then trip to constant-potential charging *at these voltages* until battery charge acceptance fell to less than 5 percent of its Ah rating. Only then would the charger trip to a float voltage of between 13.2 and 13.6 volts. Batteries would be charged at the dockside to well over 90 percent without persistent overcharging. One or two (very expensive!) battery chargers with all these features are just now coming onto the market.

The majority of boats are best served by a high-capacity, constant-current/constant-potential charger, but these are invariably expensive. An effective substitute is a constant-current charger with a timer.

Since most boats deeply discharge large-capacity batteries periodically, any charging device gets worked hard. To guard against burning up, marine battery chargers should always include a maximum-current limiting device and a thermal-overload trip. Any charger that incorporates constant-potential regulation ideally should have a manual voltage override, together with a current-controlling capability, so that the charger can be used periodically at low amperages and high voltages for battery equalization. Chargers like this are few and far between!

Note: Regardless of the type of voltage regulation, accessories never should be run directly from a charger without a battery in the circuit. This can damage sensitive electronic circuits in both chargers and equipment.

Transformers and Rectifiers

The transformer. It is essential for a battery charger intended for boats to use an *isolation transformer.* In these, the incoming AC flows through one coil and transfers power magnetically to a totally separate coil. This second coil, which is electrically isolated from the incoming AC, supplies power to the DC side. All marine battery chargers use isolation transformers, but some automotive chargers do not: The neutral AC wire may be common to both sides of the transformer (see Figure 5-4A). Should the neutral and hot leads get crossed, *the common line will be hot!* This can happen quite easily with the insertion of a two-prong plug in a receptacle the wrong way around, creating a reverse polarity situation. In the damp marine environment this presents a serious shock hazard and also can lead to devastating stray-current corrosion (see Chapter 4).

Testing for an isolation transformer. With the battery charger completely disconnected, test with an ohmmeter (R × 100 scale) between all output terminals and all incoming AC leads, *reversing the meter leads at each test.* An isolation transformer should read an open circuit (infinite ohms) between any input wire and any output terminal.

Alternatively, take the charger ashore and plug it in. Connect a test light between a positive battery output terminal and a good ground, such as a metal pipe buried in damp earth. Do the same between the charger's negative output terminal and ground. Now reverse the polarity on the incoming AC by turning the charger's plug in its receptacle. If the charger has a three-prong grounding plug, which it most certainly should, this will require a two-prong adaptor. Repeat the two tests to ground. *If the test light glows at any time the AC supply is leaking into the DC circuits and the charger is not suitable for marine use.*

Note: It has become increasingly common to fit isolation transformers on the shoreside power connection of boats with sophisticated AC circuits (Chapter 3). In this case nonisolated-type battery chargers may be used on board.

Rectification. A rectifier is a device that conducts in one direction but not in another. During one-half of the AC cycle, it allows current to flow; during the other half, the current is blocked. In effect, this cuts off the bottom half of the sine wave (see Chapter 3, "What Is Alternating Current?"). The cheapest chargers use *half-wave rectification,* which produces 60 DC

Figure 5-4A. **Marine battery chargers utilize an isolation transformer to eliminate the direct physical connection between incoming shore power and the boat's electrical system.**

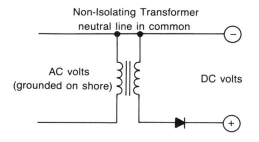

Non-Isolating Transformer
neutral line in common

AC volts
(grounded on shore)

DC volts

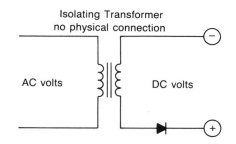

Isolating Transformer
no physical connection

AC volts

DC volts

pulses per second from the USA standard 60-cycle AC, and 50 DC pulses per second from the UK's AC. Half-wave rectifiers are inherently "noisy" electrically.

Better chargers use *full-wave rectification*, which essentially combines the outputs of two half-wave rectifiers, thus employing both halves of the AC cycle, resulting in 120 DC pulses per second (100 in the UK). In 24-and 32-volt chargers—and some higher-quality 12-volt chargers—a full-scale *bridge rectifier* is generally employed, as in an alternator. *Full-wave rectification is important to reduce radio interference* (Figure 5-4B).

Troubleshooting

SAFETY: Before attempting to open any battery charger, unplug it from the power source and disconnect all its batteries. *AC power can kill.* Accidentally shorted DC cir-

Figure 5-4B. **Half-wave and full-wave rectification.**

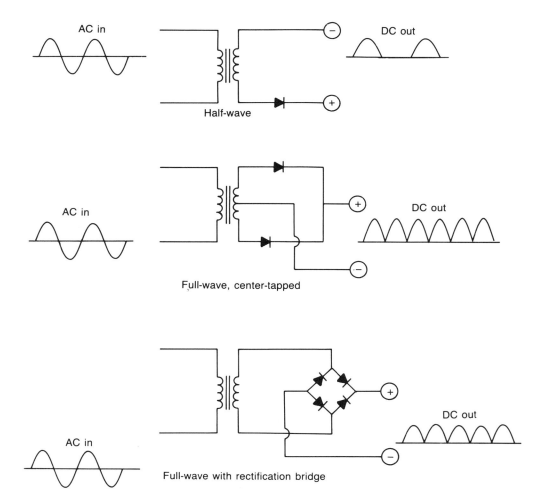

AC in

DC out

Half-wave

AC in

DC out

Full-wave, center-tapped

AC in

DC out

Full-wave with rectification bridge

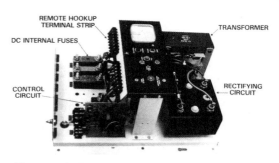

Figure 5-5A. Component lay-out of a typical marine battery charger.

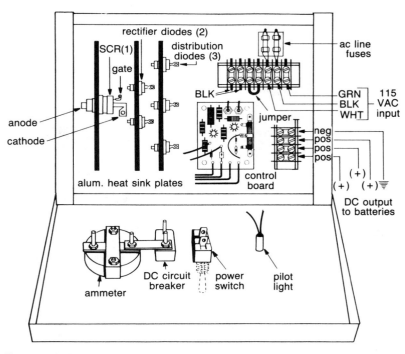

Figure 5-5B. Control panel of a charger similar to Figure 5-5A, opened to show arrangement of components.

Figure 5-5C. Yet another variation of a marine battery charger. This one has its control panel mounted integral to its casing.

cuits can blow out diodes and expensive circuits.

WARNING: Most chargers now incorporate at least some solid-state circuitry. Shorting out the battery leads to test for output (it will spark) or connecting batteries in reverse may blow out expensive circuits. Some chargers may be damaged by turning them on if they are not connected to a battery.

Before blaming the charger.

• Check the incoming AC shore power or onboard generator; you may not be receiving power.
• Check all relevant circuit breakers.
• Check the charger's incoming AC fuses. Normally there are two; see Figure 5-5 for typical component layout.
• Check the charger's AC switch.
• Double-check the two AC terminals with a voltmeter or test light to make sure the charger really is receiving juice. (See Chapter 3, "Testing AC Circuits.")

Where present, a remote control for a charger is in series with the AC "ON/OFF" switch, but will be wired into the circuit *after* the "ON" light (if fitted). If the remote control is "OFF," the "ON" light will glow, *but the charger will be off.* Check that the remote switch is "ON," and double-check for AC power across its two terminals on the charger. If in doubt, fit a jumper wire across its terminals.

AC fuses blow immediately on plugging in. Look for a shorted transformer, capacitor (if fitted), rectifying diodes, or thermistor or varistor (if fitted). The transformer is a bulky unit with two AC supply wires running into it and two or more wires running out to the rectifying diodes. A capacitor (if fitted) is a cylindrical object wired *across* the incoming AC wires; a thermistor or varistor is a much smaller electronic component, which will be wired across the output wires to the rectifier diodes (Figure 5-5).

Troubleshooting Chart 5-1.
Battery Charger Problems: No Output.
Checking the AC Side

Warning: AC power can kill. Before opening any battery charger, unplug it from the power source and disconnect all its batteries. Accidentally shorted DC circuits can blow out diodes and expensive circuits.

Is AC voltage reaching the charger? (Use a voltmeter or test light on the incoming AC terminals to check for incoming voltage. **YES ↓**	**NO ▶** Check the AC supply: the incoming shore power or onboard generator; fuses, breakers, and switches (including remote control switch if present); and wiring.
Are the charger's AC fuses blowing every time it's plugged in? **YES ↓**	**NO ▶** Go to "Checking the DC Side" below.
If a capacitor is fitted across the incoming AC lines, remove it and try again. Do the fuses still blow? **YES ↓**	**NO ▶** Fit a new capacitor.
Repeat the test above with any thermistor or varistor, and the rectifying diodes. Do the fuses still blow? **YES ↓**	**NO ▶** Fit new thermistor, varistor, or rectifying diodes.
Replace the transformer.	

Checking the DC Side

With the charger connected to a charged battery check the output voltage at the charger first with it off and then with it on. Is there a voltage increase? **NO ↓**	**YES ▶** The charger is OK. Perform the same test at the battery. If there is no voltage rise, the circuit between the charger and battery is defective—check all terminals, breakers, switches and wiring. If there is a voltage increase, the charger is working but may be suffering from voltage drop (page 80).
Does the charger have an automatic shutdown circuit? **NO ↓**	**YES ▶** Override it with a manual switch (if fitted) or discharge the battery for a few minutes and try again.
Does the charger have an ignition-protection circuit? **NO ↓**	**YES ▶** Disconnect it and try again. If the charger now works it can be used without this circuit, taking care to switch the charger off before firing up the engine.

(Chart 5-1 continued)

1. Disconnect any capacitor and try again; if the charger works install a new capacitor.
2. Disconnect the thermistor or varistor and try again; if the charger works install a new thermistor or varistor.
3. Disconnect the two wires to the rectifying diodes (they may need to be unsoldered); if the fuses still blow, the transformer is shorted. If not, the diodes are shorted.
4. To test the diodes, the circuit must be broken: Remove them from their heat sinks or unsolder their connecting wires. Test the diodes with an ohmmeter; they should show continuity in only one direction (see Chapter 2, "Diodes").

AC side OK but no output to the batteries (ammeter does not register).

1. Check that the battery selector switch is in the correct position.
2. Check the leads from the charger to the batteries, and any fuses or switches in the line.
3. To double-check, turn the charger "OFF," connect it to *a fully charged battery,* and test the battery voltage. It should be around 12.5 volts. Turn on the charger and test across its positive and negative terminals: If the voltage is now higher than the previously measured battery voltage, the charger is putting out. (Note: If the battery is fully charged, an automatic charger may have simply turned itself off. If it has a manual switch, turn it to manual. If not, put a load on the battery for a few minutes to drop its charge below the regulator kick-in voltage.)
4. If the charger is hot, let it cool down. It may simply be tripping on its "thermal-overload" protection. In this case it will cycle on and off almost inaudibly at intervals of several minutes.
5. If the charger has an ignition-protection circuit disconnect the wires leading to it and test again. When the engine is shut down these wires should be sensing no voltage; if they are sensing voltage, the charger will not come on line.
6. An overloaded charger with a DC overload circuit breaker will cycle on and off with an audible click. Reduce the load and check for shorts in the boat's wiring or DC equipment. If the circuit breaker

trips *with the AC power off*, the charger has a shorted distribution (output) diode.

7. Still no output? If the charger has an internal DC circuit breaker and/or an ammeter, bridge across them with jumper wires. Still no output? Call a specialist.

Persistent undercharging. Note: Many automatic battery chargers with multiple-battery charging capabilities have only one battery-voltage sensing line. If this line senses a fully charged battery, *no matter how dead the other batteries are, the charger will stay "OFF" until the voltage on the sensed battery falls below the kick-in point.* The battery that is used most often should be connected to the charger output terminal that has the battery-sensing capability. Alternatively, during battery charging, connect all batteries in parallel via the battery selector switch.

If problems persist, load up the batteries, then turn on the charger so that it is putting out at its full rate. Check the output voltage on the charger and at the batteries. If there is a significant difference (more than 0.3 volt), there is an unacceptable voltage drop in the wiring and switches (Figure 5-6). The battery charger will sense a higher voltage than the battery actually receives and will shut down too soon. Measure voltage both at the battery posts and the battery terminal clamps; any difference here indicates a poor connection that needs cleaning.

Voltage drop caused by inadequate wiring is a major cause of undercharging.

Situate a charger as close to the batteries as possible, no more than 10 feet away. Do not place a battery charger in or over a battery compartment, however. Gases emitted during charging will corrode sensitive electronic parts. Use Table 3-1 to determine wire size based on maximum charger output and minimum 3-percent voltage drop—the larger the wire, the better.

Now bring the batteries to full charge by one means or another, testing them with a hydrometer, then check the charger's output voltage. If it equals the rated output voltage (probably around 13.8 volts), the charger is OK. If the previous test shows no voltage drop to the batteries, the charger may be undersized for its job, or, more likely, the batteries are failing.

If charger output is low, before trying to adjust it (if it is adjustable), be certain the batteries are fully charged and check the

---

Troubleshooting Chart 5-1 (continued)	
Is the charger hot? **NO**	**YES** It may have tripped on its thermal overload protection. Reduce the DC load, allow it to cool, and try again.
Did the charger show maximum amperage before tripping off (probably with an audible click)? **NO**	**YES** It is tripping on overload. Disconnect all DC loads from the battery and try again. Check for shorts in the boat's DC equipment and wiring, or overloading of the charger. Maybe the battery itself is shorted.
Open the charger (see the warning above) and put a jumper wire across the two terminals to any internal breaker and the ammeter. Does the charger now work? **NO**	**YES** Replace the breaker or ammeter.
If all tests to this point fail to isolate the problem, call a specialist.	
Persistent Undercharging (this page).	
Persistent Overcharging (page 124).	

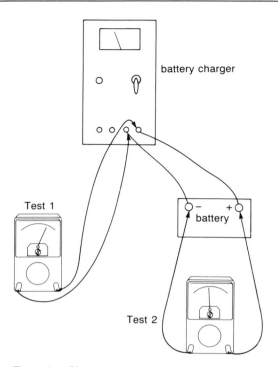

Figure 5-6. Checking battery charger output. Load up the battery so that the charger sees full output, then test between the charger's output terminals (Test 1), and between the battery's output terminals with the charger connected (Test 2). There should be no difference between Test 1 and 2. If 2 is lower there is a voltage drop in the wiring and/or connection between the battery charger and the battery.

incoming AC power *at the charger.* Low input voltage will produce low output if the charger does not have "line compensation."

Persistent overcharging. The symptom of this condition is that the batteries "boil" and lose water. This may be the result of improper manual regulation on constant-current chargers, or once again the batteries may be at fault, most likely from one or more shorted cells. Batteries will often overcharge when housed in hot locations.

If the output voltage on constant-potential chargers is higher than rated, check the incoming AC voltage; high input will produce high output unless the charger has line compensation. Continuously high output to good, cool batteries will be the result of an internal short in the voltage regulation circuit (where fitted, i.e., nonferro-resonant battery chargers), and this requires a specialist's attention.

DC/AC Inverters: Household Power from Batteries

How They Work

A DC/AC inverter essentially reverses the mechanism of a battery charger: A transformer steps up battery voltage to household voltage. The difficulty comes in translating this stepped-up voltage from direct current to the alternating current required for many household appliances—and in establishing the correct sine wave form for the alternating current.

Modern DC/AC inverters use sophisticated electronics to produce alternating current. Even so the results are mixed; some inverters produce a true sine wave virtually indistinguishable from machine-generated AC wave forms, and others produce extremely crude approximations that will affect the performance of some AC equipment, as we shall see.

Most AC equipment used on boats—for example, blenders, hand tools, or a stereo—places only a small, intermittent load on the system. AC items such as electric toasters, coffee percolators, vacuum cleaners, and hair dryers impose heavier loads but, once again, for only short periods of time. Then there are heavy-load items of intermittent use, such as microwaves, and longer term or repeated use, such as electric stoves, water heaters, air-conditioning systems, refrigerators, and freezers (Figure 5-8A).

With a little planning the overall AC load can be kept low for most of the day and the heavy loads concentrated into one or two hours, normally around mealtimes if an electric stove is used (Figure 5-8B). Running an AC generator 24 hours a day to handle such intermittent loads is not only noisy and uneconomical, but is actually harmful to the generator's engine.

Figure 5-7. **DC/AC inverters, such as these Heart Interfaces, produce standard AC power from the boat's batteries.**

Since the total power consumption during the low-load hours is not high, it can be handled by large deep-cycle batteries if their DC power can be converted to suitable AC. Generator run-time then can be restricted to a few high-load hours each day.

This is the thinking behind DC/AC inverters. On AC-loaded boats, savings in fuel and maintenance bills on the generator soon pay for the cost of an inverter. With an inverter, many powerboat owners can shut down their generators for much of the day. Boaters with smaller AC demand and no generator still can greatly improve the quality of their lives with a small DC/AC inverter and just a few low-load AC appliances.

However, inverter-based AC systems must be planned carefully to concentrate all high AC loads at times when the generator is running. In addition, the inverter must draw on adequate battery banks with adequate charging capability. The first step is to calculate electrical loads.

To size an inverter correctly, both the AC and DC loads must be considered. On the AC side, we are interested only in the maximum demand at any given point in time. On the DC side, we need to know the total demand to be met from the batteries in a 24-hour period (or between *full* battery charges if this interval is other than 24 hours) in order to determine needed battery capacity and charging capability. AC load calculations generally are made in watts, as opposed to DC loads, which are generally calculated in amps. Much of Chapter 1 is relevant to what follows.

Calculating AC loads. We need to determine what appliances are likely to be on, and when, in order to find the system's peak demand in watts. But note:

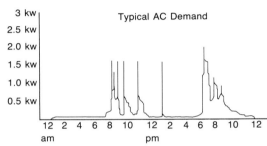

Figure 5-8A. **Patterns of AC use on board. Uncontrolled use, requiring the generator to be operated (and underutilized) 24 hours a day. Note the usage concentrated at meal times, and when AC-powered entertainment equipment is used.**

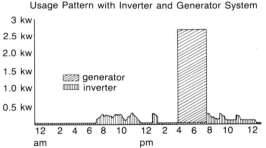

Figure 5-8B. **Controlled use, concentrating the use of high-load AC equipment into a limited period of generator operation, and running the AC system from a DC/AC inverter for the rest of the day.**

- Induction-type AC motors (AC refrigerators and air-conditioning systems, pumps, washing machines) pull three to six times their rated power on initial start-up. A 400-watt refrigeration compressor motor may draw up to 2400 watts momentarily. When making load calculations, make a separate accounting of these "surge" loads (Table 5-1). No individual surge load may be greater than the inverter's surge capacity, and two or more appliances with high surge ratings must never be switched on simultaneously if their combined rating exceeds the inverter's surge rating.
- Resistive loads (incandescent lights, heaters, toaster, electric stove) can pull sev-

Table 5-1. Typical Loads for Induction Motors.

Motor Requirements	¼ h.p.	⅓ h.p.	½ h.p.	¾ h.p.	1 h.p.	2 h.p.	3 h.p.
Starting watts (in-rush)	750	1,000	1,500	2,000	3,300	4,000	5,000
Running watts	350	400	600	750	1,100	2,000	3,000

eral times their rated load while heating up. A 100-watt light bulb can draw 700 watts when it is first switched on!

"Power Factors" (PF). In DC circuits, watts = volts × amps. Not so with many AC appliances. Here watts = volts × amps × Power Factor (PF). Resistive loads have a power factor of 1.0, so watts *really do* equal volts × amps. But induction motors and fluorescent lights, to name two common items, have a PF of less than 1.0, sometimes as low as 0.5. What this means in practice is that the rated wattage of an appliance gives a false idea of its power consumption. Consider a 60-watt fluorescent light with a PF of 0.5. At first sight it would seem to draw 60 ÷ 115 = 0.52 amp. But, watts = volts × amps × PF. Therefore, amps = watts ÷ (volts × PF). So amps = 60 ÷ (115 × 0.5) = 1.04 amps. *The amp draw is doubled.* When calculating wattage for induction motors and fluorescent lights, in the absence of specific information on power factors, it is best to take the rated watts and allow half again as much. In other words, count a 60-watt fluorescent light as a 90-watt load. Table 5-2 gives some typical AC loads.

Calculating DC loads. First list the wattage of all the AC appliances to be run off the inverter, making allowances for power factors. Next estimate each item's hours of daily use. Multiply the wattage by the hours to get a total daily load for each appliance. Add up all the loads and divide by 12 (on a 12-volt system) to find the daily total amperage draw. See Table 5-3 for an example. If the inverter is to be run off the "house" batteries, do not forget to add in the loads incurred by any DC appliances that you intend to use concurrently (see Chapter 1).

A percentage of power is lost in the conversion of DC to AC. Many inverter manufacturers claim conversion efficiencies better than 90 percent. If you look at the small print, however, this is generally over

a narrow range of inverter output, and efficiency declines sharply on both sides of this range. Some inverters are no better than 70-percent efficient. Thus a 20-percent fudge factor seems to be a pretty fair allowance. It is also worth noting that this efficiency rating is only for the conversion from DC to AC. Once the batteries are discharged, 1.2 amps must be put back for every amp drawn out due to inefficiencies in battery absorption.

Batteries and battery capacity. In most applications, the amperage draw of a DC/AC inverter places heavy demands on batteries. Good-quality deep-cycle batteries are a must (see Chapter 1). To avoid excessive discharging, battery capacity should amount to *at least 2.5 and preferably four times the anticipated need.* In the example in Table 5-3, a load of 121 Ah requires a minimum battery capacity of 300 Ah, and preferably 480.

Battery Ah ratings are based on a slow rate of discharge (over a period of 20 hours in the USA; 10 in the UK). As higher loads are introduced and the rate of discharge increases, the battery's Ah capacity declines sharply (see Chapter 1, Figure 1-5). Even a small 300-watt DC/AC inverter will impose a load of up to 30 amps (300 ÷ 12 = 25 + 20% for inefficiency = 30 amps). A 1500-watt inverter can impose a staggering load as high as 150 amps—close to that of a small starter motor. Imagine what cranking an engine continuously for half an hour would do to your batteries!

At these kinds of loads, battery capacity will only be a fraction of its rated capacity. Output voltage will fall off sharply after only a short period of time and the inverter will trip off due to low battery voltage. The battery will recover and tolerate another short burst of energy, but not quite as long as the first. *Repeated high-load discharging of batteries for prolonged periods sooner or later will cause internal damage* (Figure 5-9).

Table 5-2. Typical Loads for AC Appliances.

Electrical Appliance	Motor Start-Up Watts	Running Watts
Air conditioner, ¾ h.p.		800
Automatic pilot		150 –250
Blanket, electric		50 –250
Blender	600	300
Broiler		1,350
Can opener		100
Depthometer		25 –1,000
Drill, ⅜-inch	600	350
Dryer, hair		850 –1,200
Fan, air circulating	50 –200	25 –100
Food, mixer	400	235
Heater, space		750 –1,500
Heater, water		1,500
Iron		900 –1,200
Light bulbs		(as indicated)
Pan, frying		1,200
Percolator, coffee		600
Radar		750 –1,500
Radio		50 –100
Radiophone		100 –200
Range, electric (per element)		1,000 –1,500
Soldering gun		250
Television		300 –750
Toaster		750 –1,200
Vacuum cleaner		800
Waffle iron		1,200
Water system	500 –1,500	300 –1,250

1. Average wattage ratings, 60 Hz.

Table 5-3. Calculating Total Daily Amperage Draw.

Appliance	Watts	Hours Used in 24-Hour Period	Total Watts Used in 24 Hours
Electric lights (3)	40 each	2 each	240
Color television	100	2	200
Stereo	50	2	100
Toaster	1,100	0.1 (6 min.)	110
Vacuum cleaner	800	0.17 (10 min.)	133
Hair dryer	1,200	0.17	200
Blender	300	0.1	30
Coffee percolator	600	0.33 (20 min.)	200
Total Anticipated Daily Demand			1,213

1213 watts ÷ 12 volts = 101 amp-hours
101 Ah + 20% "fudge factor" = 121 Ah from 12-volt system

Figure 5-9. The effect of inverter (or other high-drain) use on storage batteries. **Near right:** Battery voltage for various loads; 500-Ah deep-cycle batteries. **Far right:** 200-Ah gel-type batteries.

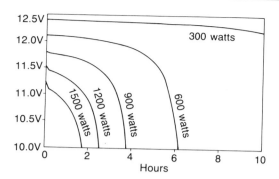

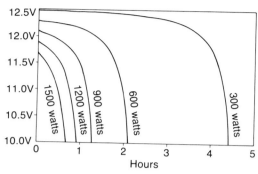

DC/AC inverters are quite useless on continuous AC loads, even if these are moderate—not because of limitations in the inverter, but because of limitations in battery capacity. A ½ h.p. AC refrigeration unit running around the clock will throw the system completely off balance. AC refrigeration should be of the holding-plate type so that refrigeration pull-down time and generator running time can coincide (see Chapter 10).

Most DC/AC inverter manufacturers advertise their products as having a microwave capability. Although this may be true of the inverter, it is not likely to be true of the batteries. We also must distinguish between sandwich-warming microwaves that draw approximately 500 to 700 watts, and full-size cooking microwaves, which draw from 1200 to 1500 watts. *If you want to use a microwave for cooking, use it during "generator hours," not "inverter hours."*

Unless a boat has enormous battery banks, large-capacity inverters should be used at their full rated output only on rare occasions and for brief periods of time. Few boats can support even a 1,000-watt inverter. Inverters really shine on light AC loads—200 to 300 watts.

Battery protection. Repeated discharging below 50 percent of full charge eventually will kill even the best deep-cycle batteries. Because inverters can discharge batteries rapidly, they invariably incorporate a low-battery-voltage shut-down circuit. Under a heavy load, however, battery voltage falls rapidly while overall capacity is not necessarily affected greatly—especially if the load is of short duration. Most inverters therefore have a low-voltage trip point of 10 to 11 volts to prevent their kicking off under heavy, short-duration loads. But under a light load, any battery that is pulled down to 10 volts will be *stone dead.* In other words, the low-voltage trip protects the inverter, not the battery. It is use-less to rely on an inverter's low-voltage cut-out to protect your batteries; you need some other means of monitoring them.

Battery charging. What comes out must go back in, plus around 20 percent (see Chapter 1). With an anticipated daily demand of 120 Ah (again using the boat in Table 5-3 as an example), we will need to recharge around 145 Ah. Batteries with a capacity of 480 Ah will accept a charge rate of up to 120 amps. To keep the alternator below 75 percent of its maximum rated capacity, a minimum 160-amp alternator will be needed (or perhaps two 80- to 100-amp alternators).

A number of the more expensive inverters incorporate excellent constant-current/constant-potential battery chargers of 40 or more amps. These maintain a high rate of charge until reaching a battery voltage of around 14.2 to 14.4 volts (approximately 80 percent of full charge). The charger then tapers off the charge rate while maintaining a constant voltage, finally tripping to a battery "float" voltage of around 13.2 volts, which avoids any overcharging during prolonged periods of generator operation or shoreside hook-up. Some inverters have a manual override in the charging mode to allow for battery equalization once a month.

Inverter miscellany. The very best inverters incorporate an AC-sensing circuit so that, should another source of AC power come on line while the inverter is in use, the inverter automatically transfers its AC load to the new source (generator or shoreside hook-up) and switches to the battery charging mode. Unless an inverter has such a circuit, *it must never be possible to switch an inverter into an AC circuit at the same time as an onboard generator or shoreside hook-up*—expensive damage will result. Inverters need to be incorporated into a *four-position* ("OFF," "GEN," "SHORE," "IN-

VERTER"), *two-pole* AC distribution switch of the break-before-make variety (see Chapter 2, "Battery Isolation Switches").

- All inverters place a small load on the DC system when on standby (i.e., switched on, but with no AC load). This varies from as little as 0.05 amp to over 1.0 amp—the latter being a significant consideration on power-conscious boats.
- Inverters need protecting against overload and high temperatures as well as low battery voltage—conditions that can damage delicate, solid-state electronic components. To my knowledge all inverters currently available have this protection, but it is worth checking further.
- Reverse polarity will blow out an inverter. Since reverse-polarity protection increases the battery drain when on standby, power-conscious inverters do not include it. When hooking up an inverter, *it is essential to make the right connections.*
- The DC wiring to an inverter must be exceptionally heavy and as short as possible to avoid overheating and voltage drop. A 1400-watt inverter will likely have a 3500-watt, one-second surge capability. With a 20-percent conversion loss or fudge factor, 3500 watts translates into 330 amps at 12 volts. *This is a starter-motor load. DC cables need to be of an equivalent size—battery cables.* The inverter should have its own battery isolation switch.
- Only the very best inverters produce true sine-wave AC. Most produce a "modified" sine wave. Depending on the degree of modification, this may closely approximate a true sine wave, or more nearly approximate a "square wave." The latter is likely to cause hum in the stereo, lines on the TV, and slower microwave cooking (if you *must* use the microwave with the inverter). Unless the inverter has a pure sine wave, most voltmeters will read 10 to 20 volts low when measuring the AC output. Only true RMS voltmeters will be accurate.

Troubleshooting

No output. If the unit has just been installed, double-check the installation for correct polarity. Reverse polarity will likely have caused irreparable damage. Check all wiring and switches; check for DC input and AC output *at the inverter.* Feel the in-

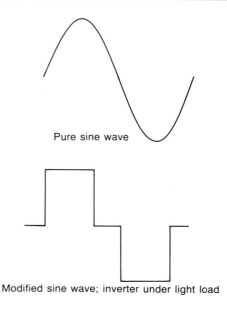

Pure sine wave

Modified sine wave; inverter under light load

Modified sine wave; inverter under heavy load

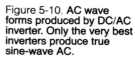

Figure 5-10. **AC wave forms produced by DC/AC inverter. Only the very best inverters produce true sine-wave AC.**

verter, and see if any of the protection devices have tripped.

Inverter is hot. Tripped on high-temperature cutoff. Allow the unit to cool and try again. If the inverter has an internal fan, check its operation. The unit may be in an area without adequate ventilation, such as an engine room.

Overload tripped. Switch off all appliances and reset (if manual trip). Bring appliances back on line one at a time and see if any trip the inverter. The overload may be a result of excessive starting surge loads or a short in an individual piece of equipment or its wiring. Also check for undersized DC cables (they will be warm) or voltage drop across loose or corroded connections (see Chapter 3).

Low voltage tripped. Most likely the battery capacity or charging capability is inadequate for the loads being placed on the system. Check battery state of charge and condition. Check also for undersized cables and loose or corroded terminals.

Table 5-4. Sizing DC/AC Inverters.

STEP	ANSWER
1) Do you know the AC load in watts for each appliance on your boat? Note: Where a power factor is appropriate, such as with induction motors or fluorescent lights, multiply the load rating by the power factor to obtain a true rating. See Table 5-2 for typical loads for AC appliances. If you have no specific power factor add half again as many watts to the rating (e.g. a 60-watt fluorescent light counts as a 90-watt load).	If your answer is no, list all onboard AC appliances and find out their rating in watts. If the surge or start-up load rating is greater than the operating load rating, list it in a separate column. Then go to Step 2. If your answer is yes, go directly to step 2.
2) How many hours a day is each appliance drawing power?	List hours of use in a column by each appliance's load rating. _____ total watts/day
3) Multiply the (true) rating by the daily use of each appliance (Answers to Question 1 times Answers to Question 2). Add all appliance sums together to get the total 24-hour AC load in watts.	
4) How often do you fully charge your battery? Give answer in days—2 times a day, 1 time every 2 days, etc.	_____ day(s)
5) If charging more than once a day, *divide* Answer 3 by Answer 4 to find the maximum AC demand between charges (e.g. divide by 2 if charging two times a day). If charging less than once a day, *multiply* Answer 3 by Answer 4 (e.g. multiply by 2 if charging once every two days). Answer 5 is your total AC load between battery charges.	_____ watts-load
6) Divide Answer 5 by 12 on a 12-volt system (24 or 32 on 24- or 32-volt systems) to get an approximate amperage demand on your DC system. Note: Multiply by 1.2 to account for converter inefficiencies.	$\dfrac{\text{watts demand of AC appliances}}{\text{system voltage}} \times 1.2 = $ _____ amps demand
7) Add to Answer 6 the amperage demand placed directly on the battery by DC appliances, as calculated from Chapter 1, to get total amperage demand.	_____ total amps demand
8) Multiply Answer 7 by a minimum of 2½, and preferably 4, to get the Ah capacity of the battery bank that will be needed to power the inverter. Note: Use only top-quality deep-cycle batteries. Answer 8 is your needed battery capacity.	_____ Ah capacity
9) Is Answer 8 totally impractical for your boat or budget?	If your answer is no, go to Step 11. If your answer is yes, go to Step 10.
10) You will have to limit your AC load based on your boat's battery bank. Determine your maximum battery bank size; *divide* this by a minimum of 2½, preferably 4; subtract the amperage demand you anticipate from those DC appliances you wish to use; and divide the quotient by 1.20 to determine a maximum amp draw; and multiply the resulting figure by 12 for 12-volt systems (24 for 24-volt systems, 32 for 32-volt systems) to give a maximum AC demand in watts. Go back to Steps 1, 2, and 3 to find ways of bringing the total AC load down to the maximum allowable level. Take high-demand AC items and arrange to use them when other sources of AC power are available so that their load is not thrown onto the DC system.	_____ watts based on _____ Ah capacity of the battery bank
11) Calculate the maximum foreseeable continuous AC load—or *peak* load—by adding the true ratings of all the AC appliances listed in Step 1 that might be used at the same time.	_____ watts peak load
12) Now calculate the maximum foreseeable AC surge rating by adding the surge ratings of all AC appliances that might come on line simultaneously. The inverter must be large enough to handle the larger of Answers 11 and 12.	_____ watts surge load
13) Take Answer 7 and multiply it by 1.2 to find the amps that must be put back in the battery bank.	_____ amps
14) Take Answer 8 and divide it by 4 to get a desired *rate of charge* from a battery charger or alternator. Add any residual DC loads when charging. Multiply the sum by 1.3 to find the minimum continuous rating of an alternator.	_____ rate of charge (amps) + _____ residual DC load (amps) _____ sum (amps) × 1.3 = _____ min. continuous rating (amp-hours)
15) Divide Answer 13 by Answer 14 and then multiply the quotient by 1.3 to get the minimum charging time.	_____ hours

Note that some trips reset automatically; others must be set manually. There also may be manual circuit breakers inside some units. Check the instruction book.

Erratic operation. The inverter trips continually on low voltage when appliances come on. Check for a starting overload (high surge), undersized cables, and loose or corroded connections. Check the voltage drop (see page 80) from one end of the DC cable to the other *when under full load*. Feel the cables to see if they are warm. Check the battery's condition.

Equipment problems. Appliance motors run slow and hot, transformers "hum," microwave is slow, TV has lines on it, etc. The inverter output is closer to a modified square wave than a modified sine wave! Moreover, the greater the load, the squarer it will get. In addition, the lower the battery voltage the squarer it will get (check the batteries). To reduce problems, it may be necessary to use sensitive equipment only at the batteries' peak state of charge and with no other AC equipment on line. If this doesn't work you will need a pure sine wave inverter.

Wind and Water Generators

Wind generators and water generators are essentially the same units fitted with different "propellers" (impellers, turbines, vanes). Wind generators in particular are making a tremendous impact on the cruising scene. The rest of this section focuses on them, although almost all is equally applicable to towed water generators.

How They Work

The most common wind generators in marine use are of two distinct types: those resembling an alternator, and those built around an off-the-shelf DC electric motor. The former have a magnetized rotor spinning inside a set of coils—the *stator*—in which alternating current is generated; this current is rectified to DC by silicon diodes and then fed to a battery. See Chapter 2, "Alternators," for a more detailed description.

Electric-motor-type wind generators reverse an alternator's mechanism. Instead of spinning a magnet inside a series of coils, a series of coils is mounted on the rotor—now called an *armature*—and spun inside a set (sometimes two sets) of fixed magnets mounted in the motor case. Alternating current is generated in the armature coils—a positive pulse every time a coil passes a positive pole, and a negative pulse whenever it passes a negative pole.

The armature coils (*windings*) each terminate in a copper bar on the end of the armature. These copper bars comprise segments of a ring (a *commutator*), each segment separated from the others by insula-

tion. Two (sometimes four) spring-loaded brushes bear against the commutator, picking up the current generated in the armature windings. Each brush is in line with one of the poles of the magnet(s) and picks up the electrical pulse generated when an armature winding passes that pole. As a result, those brushes in line with a positive pole pick up only positive pulses (which are fed to the battery's positive terminal), while those in line with a negative pole pick up only negative pulses (which are connected to the battery's negative terminal). Thus the AC output in the armature windings is rectified mechanically in the commutator without the need for any diodes.

The output of engine-driven alternators is regulated by varying the field current to the field winding, thus controlling the strength of the unit's magnetic field. Wind and water generators, however, have permanent magnets that produce a fixed magnetic field, and so this form of regulation is impossible. On alternator types the permanent magnets in the rotor eliminate the need for slip rings and brushes to feed field current to the rotor. As a general rule of thumb, alternator-type wind generators tend to be smaller and have lower outputs—up to 7 or 8 amps—than DC-motor types, which can produce up to 15 amps.

Some alternator-type units with iron-core stator coils are *self-limiting:* Regardless of operating speed they cannot produce more than their rated output and therefore will not burn up. Other stator coils are "air-filled" and do not have this self-limiting characteristic: Output increases

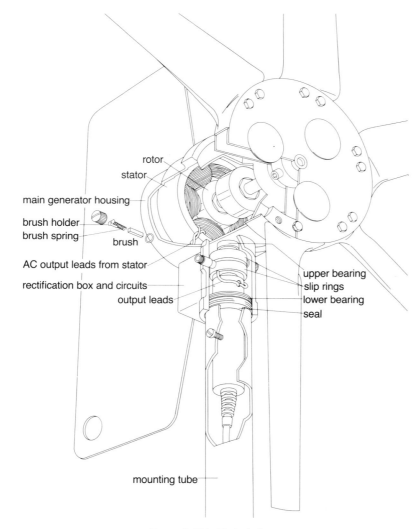

Figure 5-11. **Performance curve of one particular wind generator with a "winding protection thermostat."**

claimed output: "typical performance (cold windings)," or "voltage limiter inoperative"

winding protection thermostat cuts in

actual output in real life, with the winding protection thermostat operative

Amps Output

Windspeed (knots)

rotor
stator
main generator housing
brush holder
brush spring
brush
AC output leads from stator
rectification box and circuits
output leads

upper bearing
slip rings
lower bearing
seal

mounting tube

Figure 5-12A. **Typical slip ring-equipped wind generator.**

with operating speed, eventually burning up the coil unless some means is used to restrict output. The coils are most commonly protected with a temperature-sensitive switch (a winding protection thermostat): When the coils heat up the switch breaks the circuit and allows them to cool down.

Alternators with iron-core stator coils have a higher *breakaway torque* (they require more wind speed to get going) and take longer to rise to full output than those with air-filled coils. However, they are rugged, simple, and their performance generally approximates manufacturers' claims.

Where air-filled coils are used, as soon as the coils heat up to the preset cutoff point, output levels off or even falls. *In normal operating conditions on some models, this cutoff point may be as low as 2 amps,* whereas, the manufacturer may claim a 7-amp output as "typical performance (cold windings)"—not a real-life situation. Manufacturers also may promote misleading output with the comment, "voltage limiter inoperative" (Figure 5-11). *Buyer beware!*

In general, generators with large 2- and 3-bladed propellers put out far more power than those units with smaller 5- and 6-bladed propellers (*turbines*). However, those large blades can make an annoying racket whenever wind speeds rise much above 10 knots—especially on mast-mounted units where the blades cut through the dead air behind the mast. In addition, most of the larger units can self-destruct in high winds unless fitted with a governor to hold down operating speeds. Since few have governors, most larger units cannot be left safely in operation on an unattended boat. The smaller generators, especially those with self-limiting coils, can generally withstand any wind speed without damage. For these units, 6-bladed turbines are to be preferred over 5-bladed ones: If a blade is damaged, its opposite number can be removed and operation continued without turbine imbalance.

Some generators have a fixed mount, but others have a wind-seeking capability that allows them to rotate into the wind. These run the risk of twisting the output cable, so most have a couple of slip rings in the mount to receive the generator output, which is picked up by brushes, just as with the field current on a standard alternator's rotor. This way the output cables remain stationary and can never twist (Figure 5-12).

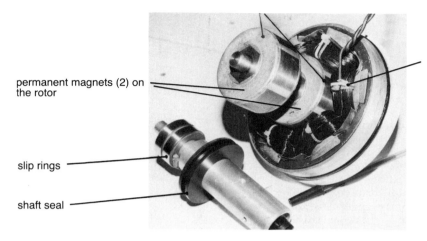

permanent magnets (2) on the rotor

one set of stator coils (another set in the other half of the generator housing goes with the second permanent magnet)

slip rings

shaft seal

Figure 5-12B. **This rotor has two permanent magnets; each has a set of stator coils. One set of coils can be seen on the right in the generator housing; the other set is in the other half of the housing, which has been removed.**

bearing

brush

brush holder

Figure 5-12C. **Looking into the base of the same generator. The output shaft and slip rings (see above) have been removed to expose the brushes.**

However, some wind generators advertised as having wind-seeking capability do not have slip rings in their mount, instead relying on the fact that the generator normally makes only one partial turn to line up with the wind before stabilizing, which makes wraparound very unlikely. This eliminates the brushes and slip rings, but carries the potential for tearing up the output cable. For example, if a boat is tied to a dock, and therefore not rotating with the wind, and the wind works around in several complete circles, the generator will follow the wind, wrapping the output cable around the generator mounting unless the generator is tied off to prevent its moving.

Voltage Regulation

Since wind generators have permanent magnets, it is not possible to regulate output by controlling the field current as in standard generators and alternators. As a

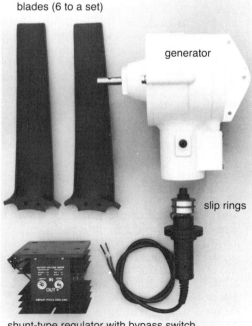

blades (6 to a set)

generator

slip rings

shunt-type regulator with bypass switch

Figure 5-12D. **A complete wind generator kit.**

result most wind generators are controlled manually: The operator monitors battery voltage until the battery is charged, then the circuit is broken and the wind generator shut down.

Never isolate the battery from a charging circuit while leaving a wind generator hooked in: Very high voltages may result, which can damage most electrical equipment.

Manual control carries obvious risks, especially where high-output wind generators are concerned. If left on line too long, a generator can drive batteries to damaging, and dangerously high, voltages. Thus, some form of automatic regulation is advisable in many situations. There are three possibilities

1. An upper limit cutout that automatically breaks the charging circuit when the battery voltage reaches a certain preset level (for appropriate levels, see Chapter 1). This removes the load from the wind generator, which in high winds may run away with damaging results. DC-motor types in particular have unlimited output as their speed increases and will burn out in high winds under no load.

2. DC-motor wind generators can be "braked" electrically: The output leads are shorted when the battery reaches a preset voltage, thus locking the generator magnetically. Most regulators of this type include a manual switch so that the generator can be stopped at any time. The problem with electric braking is that, when it is done at high speeds and levels of output, it tends to burn up the brushes and commutator, and it still may not stop the wind generator. Some other means of braking must be available. Generally this is done by turning the generator 90 degrees to the wind, which stalls it. Where this is not possible, as with a fixed mount behind a mast, an effective manual brake is a necessity.

3. Low-output generators (below 8 amps—normally alternator types) generally are regulated by switching the output to a "dummy" load. This is known as *shunt* regulation. The load consists of a fixed resistance, which dissipates the alternator's output in the form of heat—often quite a bit of heat. Thus the regulator must be in a cool place with a good airflow (Figure 5-13). Sometimes a heating element in a hot water tank is used to dissipate output,

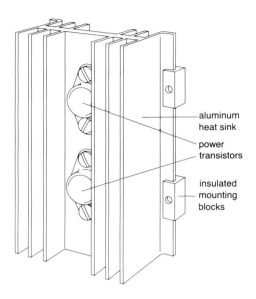

aluminum heat sink

power transistors

insulated mounting blocks

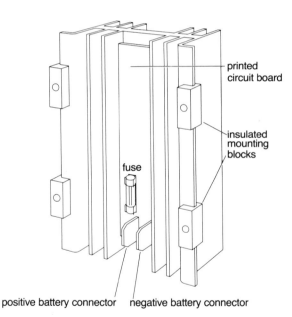

printed circuit board

insulated mounting blocks

fuse

positive battery connector   negative battery connector

Figure 5-13. **The shunt regulator is a solid-state device sensitive to battery terminal voltage. As this approaches a preset voltage (for example 13.8 volts for a 12-volt battery), the regulator allows current to be increasingly diverted from the battery and dissipated through the heat sink as heat, thus preventing overcharging and loss of electrolyte through gassing.**

thus putting the unwanted alternator capacity to good use. In theory, shunt regulators also can be used with DC-motor generators. Since these generally have higher outputs than alternator types, however, too much current (read, heat) is generated for most shunt regulators to handle.

Just as with engine-driven alternator regulators, shunt regulation generally is of the constant-potential type: The alternator output to the batteries is cut back progressively rather than just chopped as a set voltage is reached (see Chapter 2). Normally regulators are set to around 14.4 volts, which means alternator output starts to taper off around 13 volts—too low for effective fast charging of deep-cycle batteries. Shunt regulators therefore should have a manual bypass so that they can be switched out at times to maintain constant-current charging until the batteries come up to 14.0 volts or higher.

As mentioned, shunt regulators generally have a fairly low amperage rating, sufficient only to handle the loads of the wind generator in question. If the wind generator output is teed into the ship's battery-charging circuits, the engine-driven alternator can feed back through the shunt regulator, burning it up and causing a severe fire risk. A protective diode sized to handle the wind generator's full output must therefore be installed between the shunt regulator and the ship's battery-charging circuit (Figure 5-14).

Note, however, that the addition of any diode will cause a voltage drop of around 0.6 volt. Now the regulator will start to cut in at around 12.4 volts and limit output to 13.8 volts. If in addition the regular charging circuit also incorporates diodes for split charging, there will be an *additional* 0.6-volt drop, producing a cut-in voltage of 11.8 and a final voltage of 13.2—*much too low to be of any use.* In other words, the wind generator must be hooked in *downstream* from any split-charging diodes. To charge two batteries independently, the wind generator must have its own pair of split-charging diodes to avoid paralleling the batteries through its charging line (Figure 5-14).

Any regulator on a wind generator should have a manual bypass so that its full output can be used periodically for battery equalization (see Chapter 2). Wind generators are excellent for this purpose, and in fact may pay for themselves over a period of years in terms of extended battery life alone.

Finally, regardless of how a wind generator is connected to the charging circuit, it must have a fuse as close to the battery as possible. Any shorts in the wiring on the battery side of any isolation diodes will

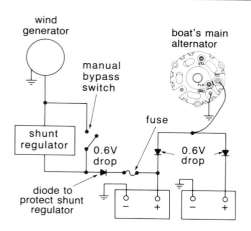

Figure 5-14A. **Schematics of voltage-regulated wind generators, set up for split charging. Charging a single battery.**

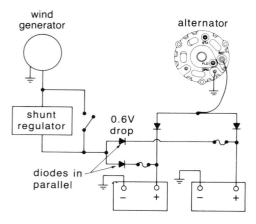

Figure 5-14B. **Charging two batteries; correct installation.**

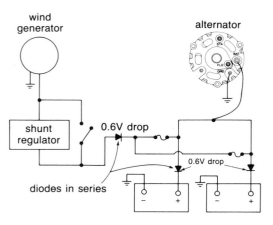

Figure 5-14C. **Charging two batteries; this approach produces excessive voltage drop.**

carry full battery output, burning up the wires and likely causing a fire.

Maintenance

Given the wide variety of wind generators available, it is possible to make only a few general points on maintenance. Brushes and brush springs are the most obvious point of failure. Alternator types will have brushes only on the slip rings, and none at all if no slip rings are present. DC motor-type generators will have brushes to collect the output from the commutator, as well as slip ring brushes if they are fitted. Some larger generators have four brushes on the commutator.

Check brushes and springs periodically for wear, corrosion, and loss of tension. If brushes or springs are defective, inspect the commutator or slip rings for burning or pitting (see page 163).

Check the shaft bearing occasionally by gripping the blades and attempting to move the shaft up and down and side to side. Any play indicates the need for bearing replacement, which will require generator disassembly. See below for one or two precautions to observe when taking the unit apart.

Check all external fasteners periodically. Most wind generators are subject to a cer-

tain amount of vibration, and fasteners will sometimes work loose. Add a drop of Loctite thread-sealing compound when replacing them.

To cure excessive vibration, if the turbine blades can be detached individually take them off in *opposite pairs*, weigh them on a postal scale, and correct any differences. Be sure to mark them so that they can go back as matched pairs.

Fiber-reinforced plastic blades are UV-degradable in sunlight. If the surface becomes crazed and powdery, sand them lightly and paint with a two-part polyurethane paint.

The leading edge of unprotected spruce blades will wear down just from the impact of bugs, rain, etc. The blades must be kept smooth for maximum efficiency and noise reduction; recoat the blades with epoxy or two-part polyurethane.

Many generators have aluminum housings with stainless steel fasteners, shafts, and bearings. Add salt spray and this is a

Figure 5-15. **To check wind generator blade alignment, place the generator, blades up, on a flat surface, with one blade tip just touching a wall. Draw a pencil mark on the wall at the blade tip, and slowly rotate the blades, checking the alignment of each as it passes the mark. If blades are out of alignment, adjust by putting pieces of tape under the blade clamp—below the blade to move blade tip up, above the blade to move blade tip** *down.*

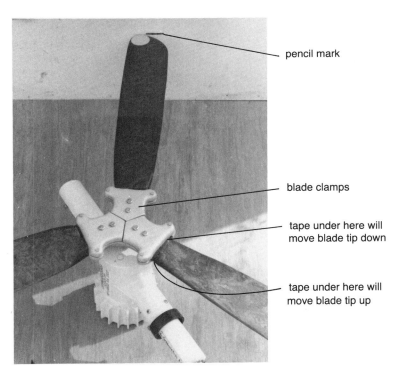

pencil mark

blade clamps

tape under here will move blade tip down

tape under here will move blade tip up

recipe for corrosion. Rinse the housings from time to time with fresh water. Watch closely for any signs of galvanic interaction. If present, remove the relevant fastener or part, apply a Teflon-based grease to inhibit further corrosion, and replace.

Troubleshooting

No output from the generator:

1. Check all fuses and switches.
2. Check the output voltage as close to the generator as possible. If it is high (it may run to 40 volts or more), the charging circuit is open at some point; check the fuses and switches once again. Open-circuited wind generators can give quite a shock at high speeds; *be careful.*
3. Check the continuity of all wiring with an ohmmeter (see Chapter 3). Be sure to disconnect the generator from the batteries first and immobilize its blades; any voltage is likely to wreck the ohmmeter.
4. With the generator still disconnected from the battery, let the blades spin and check the open-circuit voltage. It should be well above battery voltage.
5. If there is no output, disconnect any voltage regulator and try again.
6. Still no output: Check all brushes and brush springs for possible sticking.
7. Still no output: If a rectifier is fitted (alternator types), test the diodes as outlined on page 56. On DC-motor types inspect the commutator (see page 163).
8. Finally, as a crude test disconnect the output leads from the batteries, short them together, and try turning the propeller blades by hand. If everything is working they should be noticeably more difficult to turn than normal. If not, there is likely some internal fault in the generator; check the stator (alternator types) or armature (DC motors).

Disassembly

Again it is impossible to be specific, but these are a few points to watch for:

1. It is frequently crucial to align housing halves to within plus or minus one degree. Before separating any housings, mark the two halves for an exact re-

Troubleshooting Chart 5-2.
Wind Generator Output Problems.
Symptom: Generator provides no battery charging when battery voltage is below the preset cutoff level of the voltage regulator (if one is fitted).
Note: Many of the following tests involve checking the voltage on an open-circuited generator. An open-circuited (i.e., disconnected from its battery) wind generator can produce up to 100 volts and give a severe shock. Be careful.

Disconnect the generator leads at the battery and check for voltage with the generator spinning. Is voltage present? **NO**	**YES** Generator is OK.
Disconnect the output leads at the generator and check for voltage at the generator output terminals with the generator spinning. Is voltage present? **NO**	**YES** Generator is OK. The fault is in its circuit. Check all fuses, switches, breakers and terminals. Bypass any diode or voltage regulator to see if this is the problem.
Inspect all brushes and brush springs for wear, corrosion, loss of tension, or sticking. Replace as necessary and spin again. Is voltage present? **NO**	**YES** Generator is OK.
DC-motor-type generators: Inspect the commutator for burning and pitting (page 163); *Alternator-type generators:* Test the rectifying diodes (page 56); repair as necessary and spin again. Is voltage present? **NO**	**YES** Generator is OK.
Short together the output leads from the generator and turn the generator by hand. Is there more resistance to turning than normal? **NO**	**YES** The generator is probably OK. Go back to the beginning.

The generator is probably defective: Check its stator or armature (see Chapters 2 and 6).

alignment. A line scribed across the joint works best.

2. The permanent magnets used in wind generators are powerful and hold many housings together with a strong magnetic force. Some housings have threads for the addition of jacking screws to aid separation; others must be levered apart carefully with screwdrivers. When replacing them keep fingers well out of the way: The magnets may grab the housings and pull them together uncontrollably.

3. The magnets will attract any metal particles or flakes lying around. Work in a scrupulously clean environment and check the magnet before reassembling. It is particularly important to keep the air gap between the magnets and stator (armature) clean.

4. Whenever a unit is opened, pay special attention to any shaft seals where the drive shaft exits the housing. Some units rely solely on "sealed" bearings and have no additional shaft seals. These bearings do not always keep out salt water for long and may need replacing.

5. Various armature and stator tests can be carried out as outlined in the sections on universal motors (Chapter 6) and alternators (Chapter 2).

Solar Panels

How They Work

Solar panels are essentially silicon-based semiconductors that convert sunlight directly into electrical energy. The cells themselves are made from chemically treated silicon crystals that are sliced into thin wafers and mounted in a grid. Each cell produces about 0.5 volt DC in full sunlight. To produce more power, more cells are connected together into panels. The more cells in a panel, the greater its voltage.

Solar panels can be an expensive minefield for the unwary. The promise is great—"free energy from the sun"—but the reality can be extremely disappointing if an installation is not sized and mounted correctly, and if the panels themselves cannot withstand the marine environment—and many can't.

Let's deal first with this notion of "free energy from the sun." Nothing could be further from the truth. Watt for watt, solar panels are one of the most expensive ways to generate electricity, although prices are falling with improving technology. For $300 (1989), a panel can generate at best about 3 amps' output in bright sunlight. Even the Virgin Islands average only seven hours of sunlight a day. That comes to 21 amps per day maximum. In reality, problems with location and angles to the sun will reduce even this figure considerably (see below). In addition every passing cloud will cut output, usually when you want it most! Wind generators are much cheaper per amp produced.

This is not to say that solar panels do not have a place on boats, particularly for maintaining batteries at full charge when a boat is left unattended. It is just a matter of getting things in perspective.

Things to Consider When Setting Up a System

Rated panel voltage. We know that for effective charging, output voltage must be higher than battery voltage. As the two more nearly equalize, charge acceptance of the battery declines. Solar panels must have enough silicon cells present to maintain a healthy voltage differential over battery voltage for the limited panel output to charge a battery effectively. Many panels that appear fine on paper are not in practice. It is easy to be confused by competing claims of "open-circuit volts" and "load volts." Since output voltage is directly related to the number of silicon cells in a panel, panels with 36 or 37 cells will charge more effectively than those with only 32 or 33.

Temperature. Solar panels are rated (at least in the USA) by their output at 25°C (77°F). As temperatures rise, however, voltage falls and output tapers off. Since the silicon wafers, which constitute solar panels, are black and therefore absorb heat, and since they must be in bright sunlight to work, solar panels get pretty hot! In use, temperatures may climb to 50°C (122°F) or higher.

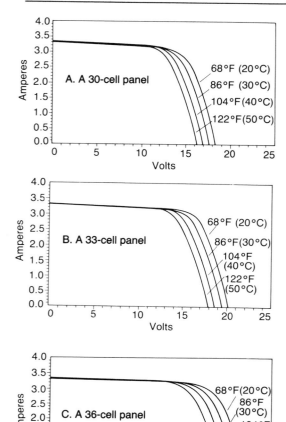

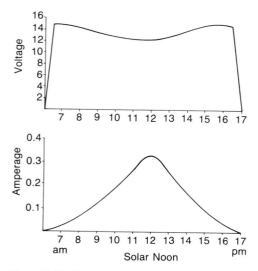

Figure 5-17. Output voltage and amperage in relation to solar noon. Note the drop in voltage as temperatures rise at solar noon and on into the early afternoon, and the relatively narrow band of time during which a panel puts out anywhere near its rated output.

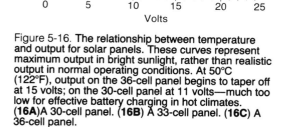

Figure 5-16. The relationship between temperature and output for solar panels. These curves represent maximum output in bright sunlight, rather than realistic output in normal operating conditions. At 50°C (122°F), output on the 36-cell panel begins to taper off at 15 volts; on the 30-cell panel at 11 volts—much too low for effective battery charging in hot climates. (**16A**)A 30-cell panel. (**16B**) A 33-cell panel. (**16C**) A 36-cell panel.

Figure 5-16 illustrates the dramatic fall in output on three different panels as temperatures climb. Note that at effective battery-charging voltages (14.0+ volts) the 30-cell panel at 50°C (122°F) has lost over 25 percent of its output.

Solar noon. Rated output is achieved only in bright, overhead sunlight. While it does not take direct sunlight to produce rated voltage, the *current* produced will be minimal without strong sunlight directly overhead (Figure 5-17).

Blocking diodes. The matter of output is further complicated by the need for blocking diodes. While a solar panel puts out in sunlight, it takes back after dark. This reverse current flow varies from panel to panel. It has become customary to fit blocking diodes on the panel output, allowing current to feed to the battery but not back. Even the best quality diodes cause a voltage drop of around 0.6 volt. All the panels in Figure 5-16 have built-in diodes, and the rated output has taken these into consideration. But some panels do not, and in this case a diode is added. If a manufacturer specifies a certain output, say 2.0 amps at 14.0 volts, without a blocking diode, this output will be available only at lower voltages—13.4 volts—once a diode is installed and not at the voltages necessary to charge a battery effectively. Output will fall off rapidly as effective charging voltages are reached. Remember, this rated output is at standard test temperatures; at realistic temperatures in many locations, it will be considerably lower, even before the diode is put in the system. If a diode does seriously affect output—e.g., in panels with a smaller number of cells—the loss in charging capability almost always will be greater than the battery drain that would occur at night if no diode were fitted. The benefits of a diode are very questionable in this situation. On the other hand, the output volt-

SOLAR PANELS AND SPLIT-CHARGING ISOLATION DIODES

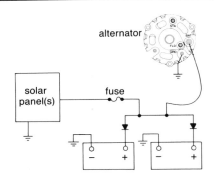

Figure 5-18A. Unregulated solar panel. If the panel is installed upstream from main blocking diodes, the solar panel will not need its own diode.

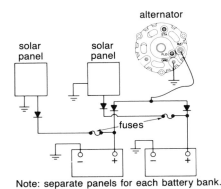

Figure 5-18B. Unregulated solar panels with a diode.

Note: separate panels for each battery bank.

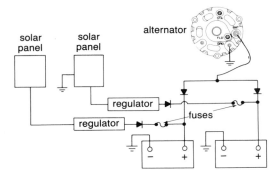

Figure 5-18C. Regulated solar panels with diodes in the regulators.

age on panels with more cells (36 on up) generally will not be pulled down enough by a diode to mar charging performance.

Note: Diodes are easily damaged and very sensitive to heat. Many small diodes come with pigtail leads attached. If you solder such a diode into a circuit—which is the best way to install it to avoid problems with connections—clamp a pair of pliers or similar tool to the diode lead to act as a heat sink and conduct heat away from the diode during soldering (see Chapter 2, "Diodes: Soldering and Connections").

Other causes of voltage drop. Since solar panel output is so sensitive even to small voltage drops, it is critical to use electrically sound, corrosion-proof connections and adequately sized wiring.

A good rule of thumb for determining wire size is to multiply the maximum short-circuit current at 47°C of all the panels in a particular circuit (this industry-standard specification should be given somewhere in the panel specifications) by 1.25 and to treat the result as the required current-carrying capacity of the panel wiring. Then refer to Table 3-1 to determine the needed wire size for any given wire length.

Multi-battery systems. As we have seen, it is crucial to keep voltage drop in solar panel outputs to a minimum. Most split charging systems (systems which charge more than one battery while keeping them isolated) use isolation diodes (see Chapters 1 and 2). These introduce a voltage drop of around 0.6 volt. If a solar panel is to be used in a split-charging system with isolation diodes, it will not need a blocking diode, which would only introduce an extra unwanted voltage drop. The panel should be installed upstream from existing diodes (see Figure 5-18A).

If a panel has a built-in diode, it should be installed downstream from any split charging diodes. But in this case its output can be fed only to one battery—if fed to two it will parallel the batteries via its wiring. Where two batteries need to be charged independently, two separate panels should be used as in Figure 5-18B.

If a panel uses a voltage regulator (see below) the regulator will quite likely include a diode of its own. In this case panel diodes are not needed and the installation should be as in Figure 5-18C.

Self-regulation. Figure 5-16A typifies the output of so-called self-regulated solar panels. The promotional literature might read: "Like a finely tuned charge controller, the (Brand X) regulates its electrical output to the needs of the battery being charged. As the battery approaches full charge, the current output decreases. . . . This is an ideal method to maintain the battery at nearly full charge." Actually, these panels are constructed with fewer silicon cells than other panels. This reduces the output voltage, with the inevitable result that as battery voltage rises and more nearly equalizes with panel voltage, panel output (amps) declines. If we add in temperature projections for warmer climates (especially the tropics) and perhaps minimal voltage drop in a circuit, self-regulating solar panels frequently will fail to charge a battery adequately, irrespective of the claimed output.

Independent regulation. Other panels have more cells in series per 12-volt unit (up to 37) than self-regulating units and produce a higher output voltage. In general, the more cells in series the better. With higher output voltages, more powerful panels (generally those with a maximum amp rating above 0.5 percent of the Ah capacity of the battery being charged) do need regulating to avoid overcharging the batteries during long periods of nonuse. A shunt regulator (charge controller) similar to that of many lower output wind generators is used. The cut-in point is generally around 13.0 volts; panel output amperage is tapered down to zero at around 14.4 volts. Any regulator should have a manual override to maintain faster charge rates when desired, and to make it possible to use larger solar panels (3 amps and up) for battery equalization (see Chapter 2).

Battery charging and battery floating. Solar panels are particularly useful for maintaining charged batteries at a float voltage when a boat is unattended. Correct float levels can easily double battery life, besides ensuring that everything is ready to go the minute you board your boat.

Conventional wet, lead-acid batteries self-discharge at a rate of around 1 percent per day at 80°F (27°C), rising to 2 percent per day at 100°F (38°C). Older batteries will discharge faster—up to twice as fast. At 80°F (27°C), this is a loss of 1 to 2 amps per day for every 100 Ah of battery capacity. Assuming about five hours of effective sun a day (no shadows, reasonable angle; see below), we need a solar panel output of 0.2 to 0.4 amp per 100 Ah of battery capacity to float the battery (0.4 to 0.8 amp at 100°F). A battery capacity of 400 Ah will need 0.8 amp to 1.6 amps of solar panel output at 80°F; 1.6 to 3.2 amps at 100°F (Figure 5-19).

Any solar panel with a rated output of up to 0.5 percent of the Ah capacity of the battery it is charging can safely be left permanently attached without regulation. Above this level of output, some form of disconnect or regulator is required.

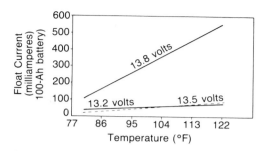

Figure 5-19. Float current vs. temperature and battery float voltage. Using 13.2 to 13.5 volts as a desirable float voltage, we see that a constant float current of 50 milliamps would suffice for a 100-Ah battery at 86°F. But 50 milliamps × 24 hours = 1.2 amps per day, and we can count on only five hours of *effective* sun per day. This calls for a panel capacity of about 0.25 amp (1.2 ÷ 5) for every 100 Ah of battery capacity to be floated. For example, 1 amp for a 400-Ah battery.

Fuses. Regardless of the capacity of a solar panel, how it is hooked into the system, or what diode protection it has, it must have a fuse in the positive cable as close to the battery as possible. Although solar panel output may be minimal, a short in the circuitry on the battery side of any diodes will cause the wires to carry full battery current, burning them up and most likely starting a fire. I know of one boat that was destroyed this way.

Solar panel location. All the preceding specifications apply only to solar panels in direct sunlight, angled to intercept the sun's rays at approximately 90 degrees. This is virtually impossible to achieve on a boat! If the panels are set up on angled mounts, as is normally the case on land, the panels will lose the sun every time the boat turns (Figure 5-20). As a result, panels are almost always flat-mounted, which is generally the best compromise. (In this case they should be mounted on blocks to keep them off the deck and maintain an air space that will help cool them.) In the tropics, with the sun nearly overhead, the panels can perform quite well; the farther north one goes the poorer the angle.

Although a solar panel does not require direct sunlight to reach its maximum voltage output, anything that restricts the impact of the sun (including poor angles) has a marked effect on the amperage produced. Even small shadows that partially shade the panels can cause a significant voltage drop, which, as we have seen, can sharply reduce output at battery-charging levels. On sailboats, mast, boom, sailcover, and even rigging shadows can ruin output completely. An outboard mount helps to get panels into the sun but may be vulner-

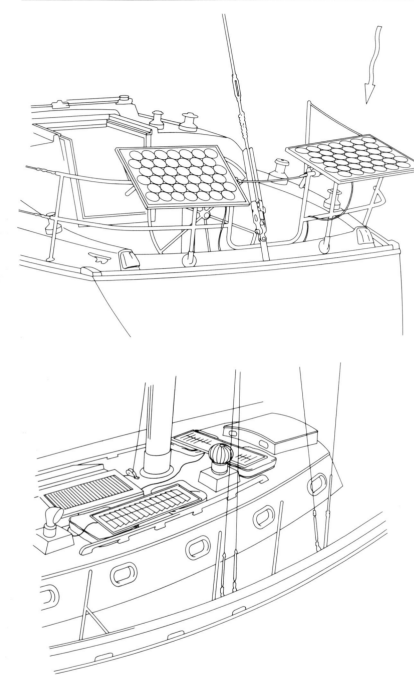

Figure 5-20. **Typical solar panel placements.**

able to pooping waves or docking damage. Outboard mounts do have another advantage: keeping panels away from onboard traffic and damage. Although many panels are advertised as being capable of withstanding the impact of feet and dropped winch handles, as often as not the fine print will contain the qualification, *occasional!* In any event, it makes sense to keep panels in protected areas when possible.

Construction. Early solar panels used silicon cells cut from "grown" crystals—a very expensive process. Some of the larger, more expensive panels still do this, and it is still the way to go for top quality. Recent advances in technology have introduced thin-film, amorphous silicon, which is what almost all small panels are made of. Amorphous silicon appears to work as well as crystals, but has yet to be proved over time. It is clear that the output of amorphous silicon panels tends to deteriorate 10 percent or so over the first two or three years before stabilizing.

Regardless of silicon type, panel construction itself is the principal factor limiting solar panel life in marine use. Some panels fall apart in a matter of months. Many more delaminate while appearing perfectly sound and allow moisture to find its way into the panel, which shorts out. Metal-backed, plastic-encased panels in particular suffer from differential expansion and contraction of the metal and plastic as the panel heats and cools, resulting in eventual delamination. Some of the new flexible, amorphous-silicon panels appear to have microscopic holes in the plastic, which admit water. Plastic cases suffer from a further problem: ultraviolet degradation.

Glass cases, of course, are highly vulnerable to being cracked or broken. Rigidly mounted, they may be damaged simply by the inevitable flexing of a boat in a seaway. Terminals on any panel are especially susceptible to corrosion, and the exit points of the cables form a frequent point of moisture ingress into the panels.

Looking at advertised panels, I wonder how many will survive as long as 10 years, let alone indefinitely. And yet with today's technology there is absolutely no reason why manufacturers cannot produce panels that will withstand the marine environment for 10 years or more. If a solar panel has a warranty in marine use of less than 10 years, I would consider its construction suspect and would look for another product.

Troubleshooting

If a panel is physically sound but appears not to be putting out amperage, disconnect it and check its open-circuit voltage in sunlight. If it is between 16 and 20 volts, the panel itself is OK. All that remains is to check the blocking diode, the wiring, and the connections (see Chapters 2 and 3). Before checking the diode and wiring, be sure to cover or otherwise disable the solar panel. Its output is perfectly capable of blowing out an ohmmeter.

Troubleshooting Chart 5-3.
Solar Panel Problem: No Apparent Output.

Disconnect the panel's leads *at the battery* and check for voltage *in bright sunlight.* Is there voltage? 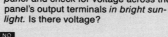	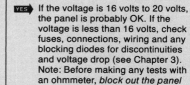 If the voltage is 16 volts to 20 volts, the panel is probably OK. If the voltage is less than 16 volts, check fuses, connections, wiring and any blocking diodes for discontinuities and voltage drop (see Chapter 3). Note: Before making any tests with an ohmmeter, *block out the panel* to avoid damaging the meter.
Disconnect the panel's leads *at the panel* and check for voltage across the panel's output terminals *in bright sunlight.* Is there voltage?	If the voltage is 16 volts to 20 volts the panel is probably OK but its wiring is defective. Check as above. If the voltage is less than 16 volts there are problems with the panel and its internal wiring.

The panel is defective: If it has a built-in diode, jump it out and test again.

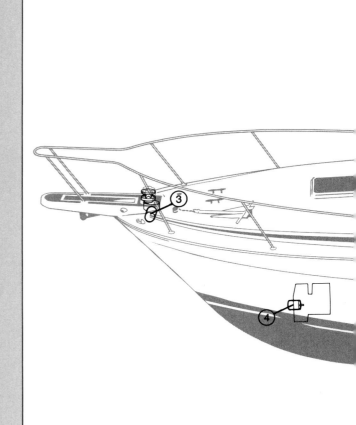

CHAPTER 6

Figure 6-1. Electric motors and generators are found throughout modern pleasure boats. Although initially mysterious, they are readily maintained and repaired.

- (1) starter motor
- (2) pump
- (3) anchor windlass
- (4) air conditioner fan motor
- (5) freezer compressor
- (6) air conditioner compressor
- (7) blower
- (8) refrigerator compressor
- (9) bilge pump
- (10) freshwater pump
- (11) macerator pump

Electric Generators and Electric Motors

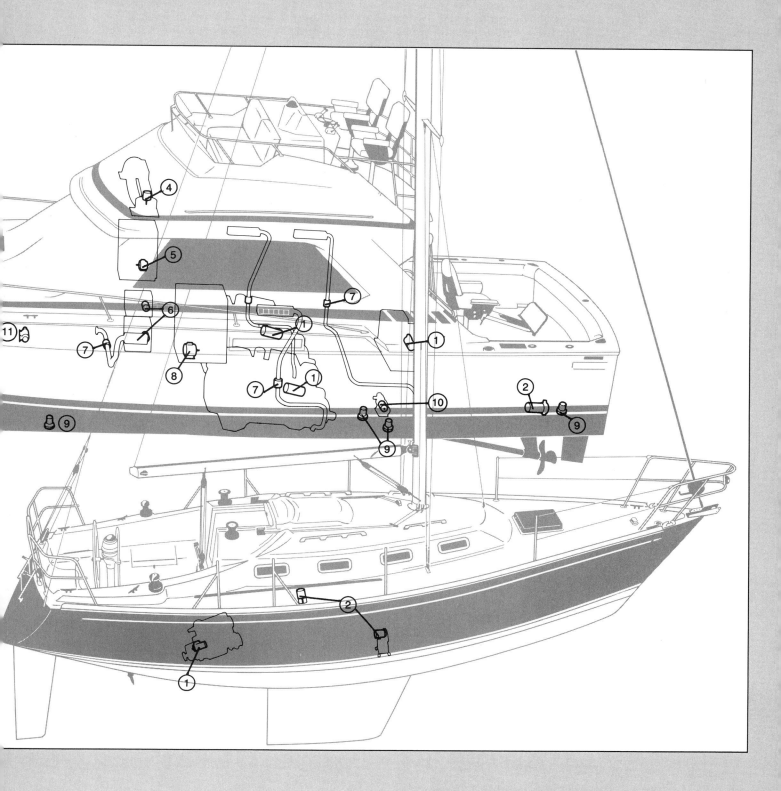

AC Generators

AC power requires a stable frequency of 50 Hz or 60 Hz, depending on the country (see Chapter 3, "Understanding AC Circuits"). This is achieved with a shore-power hook-up, with a DC/AC inverter (Chapter 5), or by running an electric generator *at a virtually constant speed* regardless of the load placed on it. Since a boat's engine speed *changes* constantly, it is generally not possible to drive an AC generator directly from a main propulsion engine (although it can be done by running the engine at an appropriate fixed speed when the generator is in operation). There are a number of different approaches to powering generators:

1. An entirely separate engine, regulated (*governed*) to a constant speed and coupled directly to a generator.
2. A variable-speed clutch, belt-driven off the boat's main engine, that compensates for changes in engine speed and imparts a constant speed of rotation to a generator (e.g., Mercantile Manufacturing Company's AutoGen).
3. A hydraulic pump, belt-driven off the main engine, that powers a constant-speed hydraulic motor coupled to a generator (e.g., Onan's Hydra-Gen).
4. A large DC electric motor driving an AC generator (e.g., Honeywell Bull's Rediline).

How They Work

Onboard AC generating sets (gensets) can be separated into two broad categories: alternator-type units, which produce AC by spinning a magnet (*rotor*) inside a set of coils, or *stator* (see Chapter 2, "Alternators, How They Work"); and *armature*-type units, which spin the coils inside magnets.

Armature-type AC generators. Multiple coils are wound around the rotor, or *armature,* while two or more electromagnets (*field windings*) are mounted inside the generator case. The AC output is generated *in the armature windings* and fed to slip rings on the end of the armature shaft, where it is picked up by spring-loaded brushes and conveyed to the boat's distribution panel. As with an alternator, output is regulated by adjusting the current to the field windings.

The generator field windings normally are designed to retain sufficient residual magnetism when the generator is at rest to reenergize the generator when the armature is spun again. The generator output then is tapped for field current. Since the output is AC and field windings require DC, this field current must first be rectified via a *bridge rectifier* (Chapter 2). A few generators, notably AutoGen, supply current to the field windings by a direct feed from

Figure 6-2. **Armature-type AC generator, with frame and field windings removed.**

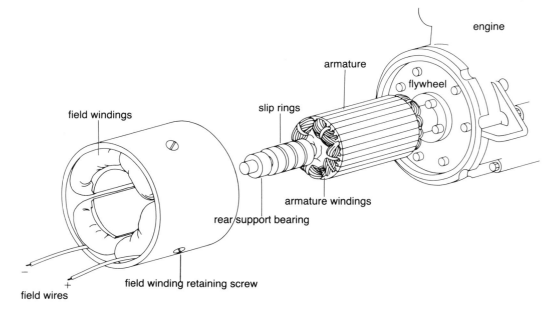

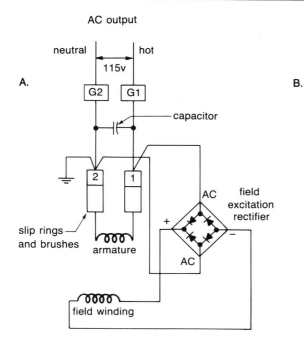

A.

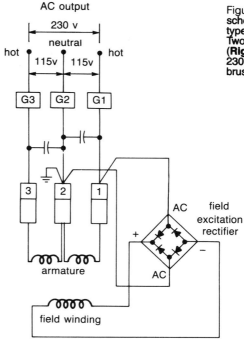

B.

Figure 6-3. **Wiring schematics for armature-type AC generator. (Left)** Two brush, 115 volts. **(Right)** Three brush, 115/230 volts. **(Below)** Four brush, 115/230 volts.

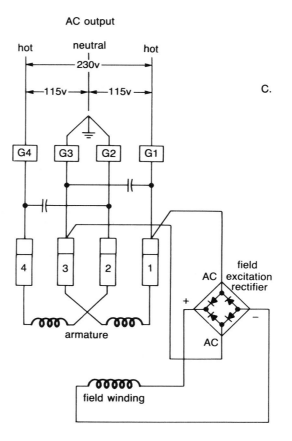

C.

the boat's batteries, thus eliminating the need for rectifiers.

This type of generator may have two, three, or four slip rings and brushes, depending on internal configuration and power output. The simplest (small, 115-volt AC generators in the USA; 240 volts, UK) have two slip rings and brushes—one hot, the other neutral (which is grounded to the generator frame; see Figure 6-3A). Small 115/230-volt AC generators (USA) have three slip rings and brushes—two hot (115 volts each), and the third neutral (which once again is grounded to the generator frame). Larger generators (both 115-volt and 115/230-volt) have four slip rings and brushes (see Figure 6-3C)—two hot and two neutral, the latter being tied together and grounded to the generator frame at some point.

The field windings are bolted to the inside of the generator case. The simplest generators have two field windings (a two-pole generator) to produce one magnetic field (north and south), but most have two sets of windings (a four-pole generator).

Alternator-type generators. Just as with an automotive alternator, the field winding (rotor) spins inside the output coils or stator. Since there is no external excitation the rotor is designed to retain some residual magnetism to provide output on initial start-up; it is *self-exciting*.

Kohler generators supply DC current to the rotor using brushes and slip rings. One of the windings on the stator supplies AC output to a rectifying diode and voltage regulator; the regulator controls the field current to the rotor, just as in an automobile alternator.

Most other makes of AC alternators are brushless: The rotor is designed in such a way that it generates its own DC input to its field windings. An extra set of *exciter windings* is needed in the stator to make this possible. A few expensive automotive alternators are built the same way, but these rarely turn up in the marine field.

A brushless generator is just that: There are no slip rings or brushes on the rotor. Since DC, and not AC, is needed to power field coils, the rotor has one or more rectifying diodes built into its circuitry.

In addition to the exciter windings and the main stator windings, many brushless generators include another set of auxiliary windings in the stator. The output from these auxiliary windings is rectified to DC, and controlled by a voltage regulator. On larger generators (8.0 kW and up) this is likely to power and control the exciter windings (Figure 6-4B). But on smaller generators it will charge the generator engine's starting battery (Figure 6-4A). If this output powers the exciter windings, failure of the auxiliary windings, the rectifier, or regulation circuit will disable the output of the generator. The failure of auxiliary windings used for battery charging, however, will have no effect on the main AC output: The auxiliary windings and associated circuitry can safely be ignored when troubleshooting the generator's AC output.

General Maintenance

Most generators have bearings that are sealed for life. A few have grease fittings,

Figure 6-4A. Simplified wiring schematic for a brushless AC generator—auxiliary windings used for battery charging. Note that: (1) The windings for the main stator (B), exciter (C), and battery-charging circuits (D) are all built into the stator. (2) The battery-charging circuit (D) is independent of the generator's AC output. (3) The rotating field, or rotor (A), has no slip rings or brushes and its diodes are built-in. (4) This generator is self-regulating—there is no voltage regulation circuit. Output voltage is determined principally by the speed of rotation, but also is affected by generator load. No-load voltage can be altered by plugging a different numbered lead (7, 8, or 9) into the capacitors in the exciter circuit (C). (5) Frequency can be changed from 60 Hz to 50 Hz by changing the engine r.p.m. Because this will alter voltage as well, it will be necessary to tap different capacitor and output terminals (on the terminal block) to get the desired voltage (e.g., in the UK, 240 volts at 50 Hz).

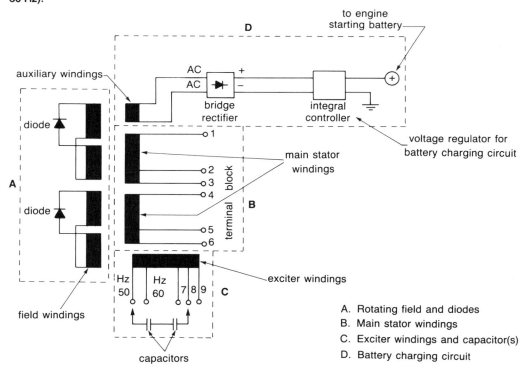

A. Rotating field and diodes
B. Main stator windings
C. Exciter windings and capacitor(s)
D. Battery charging circuit

which need one shot once or twice a year, but *no more*. The only other thing that needs attention are the brushes on armature-type generators. These brushes carry the full output current of the generator. If allowed to wear down or stick in their brush holders so that they make an imperfect contact with their slip rings, arcing will occur and expensive damage will be done to the slip rings.

Brushes need to be checked regularly (Westerbeke recommends every 200 hours) and replaced once they are worn to half their original length. They must move freely in their brush holders and have reasonable spring tension. If in doubt, *replace. Brushes must always be put back in the same holders and the same way around.* To avoid confusion, remove and replace them one at a time. New brushes are bedded in as described on page 164. (Note that the brushes on Kohler generators carry only the rotor excitation current and not generator output current. Thus they are subject to far less wear and need checking only every 500 hours.)

Occasionally, vibration will cause a field winding to work loose on armature-type generators. The windings are mounted with bolts through the outside of the generator case. These bolts will be evenly spaced on either side of the case with two-pole generators, or spaced every 90 degrees with four-pole generators. Check them for tightness from time to time.

Troubleshooting Armature-Type Generators

No output. First remove all the loads from the generator and check for output at the generator's AC terminals (see Chapter 3). The generator may be working, but there may be an open switch or broken wire to the boat's circuit. Next check the engine tachometer to see that the generator is spinning at or close to its rated speed. Still no output?

If the generator is externally excited by the boat's 12-volt battery, there will be an external field ("F" or "FIELD") terminal on the back of the generator. With the generator circuit switched on (but not necessarily running), check between this and a good ground. It should read at least sev-

Figure 6-4B. Simplified wiring schematic for a brushless AC generator—auxiliary windings used to power the generator voltage regulation circuit. Voltage regulation is found only on larger generators. Most smaller generators will be of the type illustrated in Figure 6-4A.

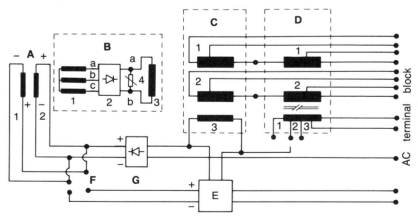

A. Exciter stator windings
B. Exciter rotor
   1. Auxiliary windings (a,b,c)
   2. Diodes (6)
   3. Rotating field windings
   4. Pozi resistor
C. Main stator
   1. Main stator windings
   2. Main stator windings
   3. Main stator auxiliary windings

D. Compound transformer
   1. Compound transformer windings
   2. Compound transformer windings
   3. Compound transformer auxiliary windings
E. Automatic voltage regulator
F. Selector switch
G. Bridge rectifier

Figure 6-5. **Checking for residual voltage.**

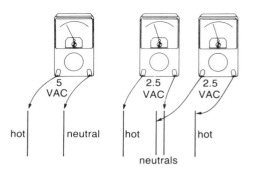

eral volts DC. If not, there is a fault in the external excitation wiring or voltage regulator. If voltage is present, there is a fault in the field windings, armature, brushes, or capacitors (see relevant sections below).

If the generator is internally excited, proceed as follows:

Residual voltage check. Remove whatever covers are necessary to expose the bridge rectifier and disconnect the field leads from the positive (+) and negative (−) terminals. Label the leads first so they can be reconnected correctly, and place them safely out of the way. (If the negative terminal is not marked, it is the one *opposite* the positive terminal.) Operate the generator with no load and measure for voltage between the hot and neutral output leads. There should be a low voltage generated by the residual magnetism in the field windings. (On Westerbeke two-brush units it is around 5 volts AC; three-and four-brush units, 2.5 volts AC.) If residual voltage is present, the armature, brushes, and capacitors (if fitted, they will bridge the output leads) are almost certainly OK and the problem lies in the rectifier, field windings, or regulation circuit. If residual voltage is *not* present, the unit may simply have lost its residual magnetism. Otherwise the problem is in the armature, brushes, or capacitors.

Residual voltage present. Connect a 12-volt battery to the field leads that were disconnected from the bridge rectifier—positive to positive, negative to negative. Run the generator without a load and measure the voltage at the output leads. If voltage is now present (50 to 70 volts on Westerbekes), the generator itself is OK, but there is a fault in the bridge rectifier. If voltage does not rise, the field windings (or their wiring) are defective.

To test a bridge rectifier: First make sure the generator is fully isolated. Leave the positive and negative leads disconnected and disconnect the two AC leads (the other two leads). Using an ohmmeter on the R × 1 scale (see Chapter 3), connect the positive meter lead to the positive terminal and touch the negative meter lead to the other terminals in turn. All should show infinite resistance (no needle deflection). Reverse the leads and repeat. All should show a circuit with a small resistance (between 5 and 50 ohms on Westerbekes). Check across the two AC terminals, then reverse the leads and recheck. Both tests should show infinite resistance. If the rectifier fails *any* of these tests, one or more diodes is defective.

To test field windings: First make a close visual inspection of the wires running into and out of each field winding, looking for broken, burned, or chafed spots. If the wiring seems intact, connect an ohmmeter (R × 1 scale) between the positive and negative field wires (previously disconnected from the bridge rectifier), or in the case of externally excited generators, between the field terminal and a good ground, such as the generator case (scratch a spot bare to make a good contact). A zero reading indicates a grounded winding; most field windings will show a resistance varying between 12 and 40 ohms—the lower the output of the generator, the higher the resistance. Switch the meter to the R × 100 scale. A very high reading indicates an open circuit in the field windings or their attendant wiring. Finally, on internally excited generators test on the R × 1 scale between each of the field wires going to the bridge rectifier (the ones previously disconnected) and the generator case. Any continuity (zero or low reading) shows a short to ground.

Residual voltage not present. The unit has lost its residual magnetism or there is a fault in the armature, brushes, or capacitors (if fitted). Residual magnetism is easily restored by *flashing the field.* Reconnect any leads to the rectifier. With the generator shut down, simply connect a 12-volt battery (or even a 6-volt flashlight battery) across the positive and negative field winding terminals—positive to positive, negative to negative—and hold for 10 seconds. *Be sure to connect the leads from the battery to the rectifier the correct way around. Reverse polarity will blow out the diodes.* Make the connections at the rectifier before making those at the battery to avoid waving around hot leads that might accidentally

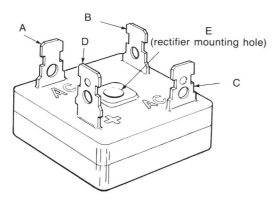

Figure 6-6. Testing a bridge rectifier. (Resistance values given are for Westerbeke "BC" generators, commonly found on boats.) (1) Set VOM scale to R × 1. Zero the meter. (2) Connect the (+) lead from the meter to D. With the (-) meter lead, momentarily contact A, B, C, and E. No deflection of the meter needle should occur, showing infinite resistance. (3) Remove the (+) lead from D and connect the (-) lead to it; with the (+) lead, momentarily touch A, B, and C. Points A and C should show an 8-ohm resistance, ±2 ohms; B should show a 40-ohm resistance, ±5 ohms. (4) Touch E with the (+) lead. No deflection of the needle should occur. (5) Place the (+) lead of the meter on A and the (-) on C. No deflection of the needle should occur (infinite resistance). Reverse the connections and the same should occur. *If the rectifier fails any of the above tests, it is defective and should be replaced.*

Figure 6-7. Capacitors store electricity. Their capacity to do so is measured in *microfarads* (abbreviated MFD, or μF). Because there often is sufficient electricity stored to administer a shock, discharge capacitors with a screwdriver as shown before working with them.

blow something out. After flashing the field, operate the generator. If output is not restored, it is time to check armature, brushes, and the capacitors (if fitted).

To test a capacitor: Capacitors must first be discharged, as they store electricity and can pack quite a punch, even when disconnected from a power source. This can be done by bridging the capacitor terminals with a screwdriver a method that can be hard on the capacitor (and the screwdriver). Better to rig a 115-volt light bulb (240 volts in the UK and Europe) with two test leads, and touch the leads to the capacitor terminals. Now set the ohmmeter on the R × 100 scale and connect it to the capacitor terminals. It should jump to zero ohms and slowly return to high. If it fails to go down, the capacitor is open circuited; if the meter goes down and stays down (zero ohms), the capacitor is shorted. Check between each capacitor terminal and its case. There should be an open circuit. If not, there is a short. Capacitors are rated in *microfarads,* and additionally are rated for continuous and intermittent duty. Replace with the same size and type.

To test an armature and brushes: Armature winding resistances are very low (typically around 1 ohm) and so can only be mea-

sured by a very accurate meter. With most meters it will be difficult to distinguish between a *low resistance* and a *short*. Nevertheless, I have included the test procedure for those with sufficiently sensitive meters.

Isolate the generator and disconnect any capacitors—the round or nearly round cylinders with one or two spade terminals. To be safe, discharge the capacitors as outlined above. Connect an ohmmeter between each brush in turn and the generator case (a good ground), first on the R × 1 scale and then on the R × 100 scale. The neutral (grounded) brushes should show a short on both tests (i.e., zero ohms) and, in fact, should be wired to the generator case at some point. If they do not show a short, the wiring to the brush is defective.

On a two-brush generator, one brush is hot and one neutral. On a three-brush generator, the two end brushes are hot and the middle one is neutral. On a four-brush generator, the two end brushes are hot and the middle two are neutral.

The hot brushes will show a low resistance (around 1 ohm) on the R × 1 scale. If they show no resistance on R × 1, the armature is shorted. If they show high resistance on R × 100, the armature is open circuited. In either case it needs rewinding. Note: An open circuit may also be the result of a brush failing to make electrical contact with its slip ring, and *not necessarily the brush being tested.* Be sure the brushes are seating properly.

Before condemning an armature, remove and inspect all the brushes and their springs. Connect the ohmmeter between the slip rings. With two slip rings, there should be a low reading (around 1 ohm) on the R × 1 scale. With three slip rings, there are three possible measurements: between 1 and 2, 1 and 3, and 2 and 3. On the R × 1 scale, 1-and-2 and 2-and-3 should give a low reading, and 1-and-3 a higher reading—approximately double.

With four slip rings, there are six possible combinations! Between 1 and 2, 3, or 4; 2 and 3 or 4; and 3 and 4. On the R × 1 scale, 1-and-3 and 2-and-4 should give approximately the same low reading; all the others, no reading (open circuit). If any continuity is found between 1-and-2, 2-and-3, 3-and-4, and 1-and-4, there is a short in the armature.

Finally, set the meter to the R × 100 scale and test between each slip ring and the armature shaft. There should be no continuity between any slip ring and the shaft. A zero reading at any time indicates a ground in the armature.

Erratic output. This may be due to a fault in the voltage regulator (see "Voltage wrong" below), or it may be the result of worn, badly seated, and arcing brushes. If the slip rings have also been burned, pitted, or worn out of round, the armature will have to be sent to a machine shop to be "turned down." A step in a slip ring is acceptable. For more on this, see the section on "Commutator Cleaning" on page 163.

Frequency wrong. A frequency meter is a necessity, not a luxury, for effective control, adjustment, and troubleshooting of any onboard generator. In the absence of a meter, frequency can be checked using an electric clock with a second hand and another *accurate* timepiece, such as the time beeps from station WWV on the 2.5 MHz single-sideband frequency. If the electric clock runs slowly, frequency is low. If it runs fast, frequency is high.

In a correctly functioning generator, frequency is directly related to speed of rotation. Depending on internal construction, a generator will come to its designed frequency at several different speeds (e.g., 1200, 1800, and 3600 r.p.m.), but *only one is correct for the designed voltage output.* If a generator comes up to its designed speed slowly, you may well see the frequency meter come up to the correct frequency, go past it and off the scale, and then come up again. It may do this as many as three times, which is quite normal.

Once the generator speed has stabilized frequency should be as designed (60 Hz

in the USA; 50 Hz in the UK). However, most boat generator governors (speed-regulating devices) are not sensitive enough to hold a constant speed from no load to full load. The governors are set to permit mild overspeeding (maximum 63.5 Hz in the USA) on no load, to be about right at half load, and to permit mild underspeeding on full load. As a result frequencies normally will vary (usually plus or minus 5 percent) from a couple of cycles over to a couple of cycles under (Table 6-1). Belt-driven variable-speed-clutch generators (AutoGen) are likely to show a wider variation with changes in engine speed.

Variations outside this range indicate improper governing or, in the case of frequency dropping off and an engine "bogging down," an overloaded generator or a malfunctioning engine. If the load is not reduced rapidly, expensive electrical damage is likely.

1. *Frequency is low:* Switch off the load and check again. If frequency returns to normal, the generator is probably overloaded (or its propulsion unit losing power through mechanical problems). Beware the starting loads of many electrical motors, which can be *several times* the motor rating and can bog a generator down. If frequency still is low, check the speed of the propulsion unit before blaming the generator. Most engines have mechanical governors that are adjusted by loosening a locknut and turning a screw—check the engine manual. With belt-driven generators, check belt tension and constant-speed clutches; on hydraulic units, check the oil level.

2. *Frequency is too high:* The propulsion unit is overspeeding. Adjust the governor accordingly.

3. *Frequency varies erratically:* Check the AC circuit for high, varying loads, such as a refrigeration compressor cycling on and off or a microwave on anything less than full power. Microwaves on defrost cycle or lower "cook-power" settings are *not* actually operating on less than full power. The microwave simply cycles on and off at timed intervals, sometimes only a second or two apart. A full-size, 1500-watt microwave will give a small 3-kW generator's governor a really hard time!

Table 6-1. Typical Generator Speeds, Frequencies, and Voltages.[1]

Load	Speed	Hz	Voltage (115)	Voltage (230)
No load	1,830	61	129	258
Half load	1,800	60	120	240
Full load	1,755	58.5	115	230

1. Generator governed to a nominal 1,800 r.p.m.

If the frequency continues to wander with all AC loads off, the governor on the propulsion unit is defective. Governors sometimes will *hunt,* a condition in which they constantly and rhythmically cycle the engine speed up and down. Refer to the engine manufacturer's manual.

Voltage wrong. Voltage is generally a function of generator speed and load: The faster the generator spins and the less the load, the higher the voltage. Unless the generator reaches its designed minimum speed, it cannot reach its designed output voltage. This is particularly true of belt-driven variable-clutch units. If the driving pulleys are sized wrong or the boat's engine turns over too slowly, the generator cannot reach its designed voltage.

A generator is rated at a certain maximum output (in kilowatts or amps) at a particular voltage (e.g., 5 kW or 44 amps at 115 volts). At anything less than full output, as the load is decreased the voltage will tend to rise. Externally excited generators prevent voltage from going too high by using a voltage regulator to reduce the current to the field windings, just as with an alternator. Internally excited generators are self-regulating via the rectifying bridge.

Since voltage is generally related to speed, if voltage is off first check the speed by checking the frequency. As previously noted, in extreme cases, frequency may be correct but at a completely wrong speed; this is not a problem likely to arise in normal use. Since generator speed is likely to vary somewhat with load, some variations in voltage are to be expected. Typical ranges from no load to full load may be as much as 130 volts down to 108 volts (on a 115-volt genset), or 260 volts down to 225 (on a 230-volt genset). Voltages above and below these levels are likely to damage onboard equipment and must be corrected. Some external voltage regulators incorporate a *potentiometer* (a variable resistor) with a small screwdriver slot in the end for fine-tuning generator voltage.

Low voltage: Always check the voltage *at the generator:* Low voltage may simply be the result of voltage drop through inadequate wiring. Before making any adjustments (where they are possible), perform all the tests outlined for low frequency. Next, feel the voltage regulator (if external) or generator to see if it is hot (hot is too hot to touch). Overheating will play havoc with some of the solid-state components and can lead to erratic regulation or a slow tapering off of output voltage—to as low as half voltage. If hot, allow the unit to cool down and hope that no damage has been done.

With external regulation, if voltage is still low adjust the potentiometer. If voltage cannot be brought up enough, do *not force the potentiometer.* Check generator speed yet again. Perhaps it really is in the wrong speed range. Otherwise the voltage regulator is probably defective.

With internally excited generators, check the bridge rectifier and field windings as previously outlined. On all generators, check the condition of brushes and brush springs and ensure they are making good contact with their slip rings.

High voltage: Check engine speed and frequency. If correct, adjust the voltage-regulator potentiometer on units with external regulation. If the voltage cannot be brought down, the voltage regulator probably has an internal short.

Disassembly and bearing replacement. Worn bearings make a distinctive rumble and should be replaced as soon as detected. If these are left unattended, armature vibration will lead to accelerated wear and ultimately to damage to the brushes and slip rings, and various wires are likely to work loose or chafe through. The field

Troubleshooting Chart 6-1.
Armature-Type AC Generators: No Output.

Is there output voltage at the generator's AC terminals? **NO** **TEST:** Check for AC volts at the terminals after disconnecting all electrical loads from the generator.	**YES** Generator is OK. The problem is in the boat's circuits. Look for a broken wire or an open switch.
If the generator is *externally* excited, is there DC voltage at the field terminal? **NO** **TEST:** Locate the field terminal on the back of the generator. With the generator switched on but not necessarily running, attach a DC voltmeter between the terminal and a good ground. It should register several volts.	**YES** **FIX:** Check the capacitors, brushes, and armature. Check the field windings. Replace any defective parts.
Check the excitation circuit and voltage regulator.	
If the generator is internally excited, is there residual voltage? **NO** **TEST:** Expose the bridge rectifier and label and disconnect the positive and negative field wires, placing them out of the way. Operate the generator with no load and measure the voltage between the hot and neutral output leads. Presence of a low voltage indicates that there was residual magnetism in the field windings.	**YES** **FIX:** Connect 12 volts to the disconnected field wires, run the generator and test for AC voltage at the output terminals. If there is voltage check the rectifier. It likely needs repair or replacement. If there is no voltage, check the field windings and replace as necessary.
Is there voltage when you flash the field? **NO** **TEST:** Reconnect all leads. With generator shut down, connect a battery across the field winding terminals and hold for 10 seconds. Try the generator again.	**YES** The generator is OK.
Check the capacitors, brushes, and armature (see text).	

windings may even work loose and start rubbing on the armature.

Generators have few parts, and disassembly is straightforward. If the generator is belt driven, begin by removing the pulley. Remove the brushes, taking care to note the position of all wires, which way around the brushes go, and in which brush holders. Unbolt and remove the end bearing retaining plate; the bearing will be a press fit in the plate or will be held with a small retaining plate. To get at the bearing in the other end, the armature will need to be withdrawn; take care not to drag it against the field windings.

This procedure leaves the field windings and any rectification and voltage regulation circuits still attached to the generator case. To reassemble the unit, reverse the process.

Troubleshooting Alternator-Type Generators with Brushes (Kohler)

No AC output. Check for AC voltage *at the generator.* If this is OK, the boat's AC circuit is at fault. If there is no voltage at the generator, shut it down, locate the voltage regulator, and check its fuse (if fitted). If OK, check the brushes and brush springs to ensure they are making contact with the slip rings. If OK, disconnect the positive and negative field leads from the voltage regulator to the brushes, first labeling them so that they can be replaced properly. Connect a 12-volt battery to the field leads—positive to positive, negative to negative—and run up the generator (Figure 6-8A). It is now being externally excited by the battery. Check for AC output. If present (it may range anywhere from 20 to 100 volts), the voltage regulator or its stator winding is probably defective. If there is no AC output, the rotor or stator is probably defective.

Testing the rotor. Make a visual inspection for damaged insulation, windings, or slip rings. Pitted or burned slip rings will have to be turned down in a lathe. Spin the rotor by hand and flex its shaft to check the bearings. Check between the slip rings with an ohmmeter (R × 1): Resistances are typically from 3 to 5 ohms. Check for continuity between each slip ring and the rotor shaft (R × 100). Any continuity indicates a short.

Testing the stator. Label and disconnect all leads from the terminal block. Test between the leads on each set of stator wind-

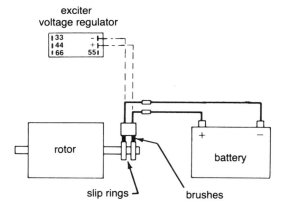

Figure 6-8A. **Externally exciting a brush-type AC alternator.**

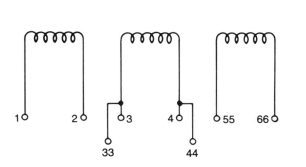

Note: New stators have the center-tapped B2 lead removed and re-identify B3 as B2.

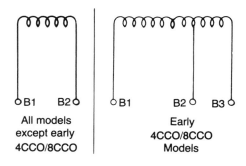

Figure 6-8B. **(Left)** Stator leads on Kohler generators. **(Below)** Stator winding resistance readings, when cold, in ohms.

Leads	4CCO	4CCFO	7CCFO	8CCO	10.5CCFO	12.5CCO	12.5CCFO	16CCO	16.5CCFO	20CCO
1-2, 3-4, 33-44	.25	.34	.18	.14	.07	.07	.07	.07	.07	.07
55-66	2.8	4.2	1.26	1.1	1.1	1.1	1.1	1.4	1.4	1.4
B1-B2 (w/o center-tapped winding)	.15	.20	.10	.08	.06	.06	.06	.06	.06	.06
B1-B2 (with center-tapped winding)	.10	—	—	.06	—	—	—	—	—	—
B1-B3 (with center-tapped winding)	.15	—	—	.08	—	—	—	—	—	—

ings (R × 1). Resistances are very low (typically from 0.06 to 0.34 ohm) and indistinguishable from a dead short on most meters. The windings that supply the voltage regulator will have a slightly higher resistance (typically from 1 to 4 ohms). Test between each lead of a winding and all other winding leads (R × 100). There should be no continuity.

Problems with frequency and voltage. Refer to the earlier discussions of frequency and voltage under "Troubleshooting Armature-Type Generators." Most of the comments are equally applicable here.

Troubleshooting Brushless Alternator-Type Generators

No AC output. Check for AC voltage *at the generator.* If this is OK, then the problem is in the boat's AC circuit. If no voltage is present at the generator, shut it down and remove its covers. Test all the windings: exciter, stator, rotor, and, for larger generators only, test the auxiliary winding if it powers the exciter windings.

Stator windings. These terminate in the main output terminal block. Disconnect all leads, grounds, and interconnections from

DIODE PLACEMENT ON BRUSHLESS GENERATORS

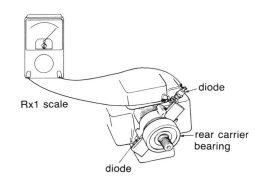

Rx1 scale

diode

rear carrier bearing

diode

Figure 6-9A. Small generators (one or two diodes). Test field winding resistance at leads shown.

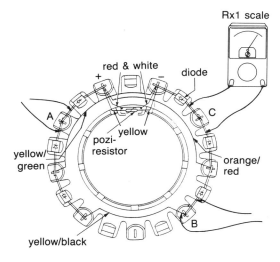

Rx1 scale

red & white

diode

+ −

A

C

yellow/green

yellow

pozi-resistor

orange/red

yellow/black

B

Figure 6-9B. Larger generators (six diodes). Check resistance of field windings A, B, and C at the points shown.

12-volt bulb glows brightly

+

12-volt battery

Figure 6-9C. Testing a diode in place, using a 12-volt battery and a lamp equipped with jumper leads.

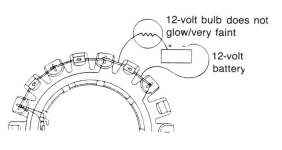

12-volt bulb does not glow/very faint

12-volt battery

Figure 6-9D. Testing a diode removed from the rotor. Use a VOM set to the R × 1 scale.

← low resistance

infinite resistance →

the terminal block, first labeling everything and noting positions so that it can all be put back correctly.

Each set of stator windings will have at least two leads—three if the generator can be used on both 50 Hz and 60 Hz. (On these units, the outermost leads on a winding are for 50 Hz; the lead tapped closer to the center of the winding is for 60 Hz.) Test the resistance between the two outermost leads on each winding (meter on R × 1). These readings will be very low—on the order of 0.2 to 0.6 ohm (smaller generators will show higher resistance). All but the most sensitive meters will show a dead short. Infinity indicates an open-circuited coil.

Now switch to the R × 100 scale and test from every stator lead to ground, and from the leads on one stator coil to another. Any continuity indicates a short to ground or between windings.

Rotor windings. The rotor may have up to three sets of windings, and as many as six diodes, located on or around the rotor. Turn the rotor over to identify the diode(s).

1. *Diodes screwed into the end of the rotor (smaller generators; Figure 6-9A).* To quickly test the winding(s), check (R × 1) between the top connection and base of the diode. It should read about 1 to 4 ohms (the smaller the generator, the lower the reading). Again, less-sensitive meters will show this as a short. If resistances are out of line and you want to test the windings more thoroughly, unsolder the wires from the top(s) of the diode(s), using the lowest heat possible; remove the diode(s), and test between the unsoldered wire(s) and the wires that were attached to the base of the diode(s). A 1- to 4-ohm resistance should be present. On the R × 100 scale, check for continuity between each lead and the rotor shaft. Any continuity indicates a short in a winding.

2. *Diodes spread around the rotor (larger generators).* The individual winding resistances can be measured with the diodes in place by measuring between each diode on each side of a winding. Do not include the diode (see Figure 6-9B).

3. *Diode testing.* Diodes cannot be checked in place with an ohmmeter. However, a test can be made using a 12-volt battery and a lamp with attached jumper leads (Figure 6-9C). The lamp should light

brightly one way and glow faintly with the leads reversed. If the lamp lights in both directions, the diode is shorted; if it doesn't light at all, the diode is open circuited.

Should diodes be removed for any reason, they can be tested with an ohmmeter (R × 1 scale). In one direction they will show infinity (open circuit); in the other, a complete circuit. Typical resistances may range from below 10 up to several hundred ohms (Figure 6-9D).

Exciter windings. This will be the only set of connections left untested, excluding any battery-charging circuit. If the terminals are bridged by one or more capacitors (Figure 6-10), then the excitation windings are *not* powered by an auxiliary circuit (smaller generators). On the other hand, if there are *no* capacitors, we have an auxiliary circuit to deal with as well (larger generators).

Capacitor-type circuit. Discharge the capacitor or capacitors as described earlier in this chapter, label all connections, and unplug.

As with the stator windings, the exciter windings will probably be tapped for both 60 Hz and 50 Hz. Measure the resistance (R × 1 scale) between the two leads farthest apart. It should be anywhere from 0.5 to 3 ohms (a short on most meters). The smaller the generator, the higher the resistance. On the R × 100 scale, measure from each lead to ground and to all stator leads. Any continuity indicates a short.

Capacitors are tested as before.

Auxiliary winding-type circuits. Small brushless generators do *not* use the auxiliary winding in the stator to feed the exciter windings. Thus the auxiliary winding and its bridge rectifier and regulation circuit can be ignored when troubleshooting generator output. In larger generators that use the auxiliary winding (no capacitors on the excitation windings), the resistance of the excitation windings can be read from the positive and negative terminals of the bridge rectifier. Resistances may be considerably higher than in capacitor circuits. Measurements from either of these points to ground (R × 100 scale) should read infinity. If not, a winding is shorted.

The bridge rectifier can be disconnected and tested as outlined earlier in the chapter.

After disconnecting its leads, the auxiliary winding in the stator can be tested across its two output leads, at least one of which will run to one of the AC terminals on the bridge rectifier. Resistances are once again low (1 to 2 ohms). No continuity (R × 100 scale) should be found between either auxiliary winding lead and ground or any other winding lead (stator windings and excitation windings). If continuity is present, there is a short.

If at this stage no problem has been found, the voltage regulation circuit needs testing. This, unfortunately, is getting too complex for this book.

Flashing the field. On rare occasions exciter windings may lose their residual magnetism. This can be restored by flashing the field with a 12-volt battery. With the engine running and all wiring in place, momentarily touch the leads from the battery to the two capacitor terminals (small generators) or the positive and negative terminals (be sure to get the correct polarity!) on the bridge rectifier (large generators). If two capacitors are fitted, touch the

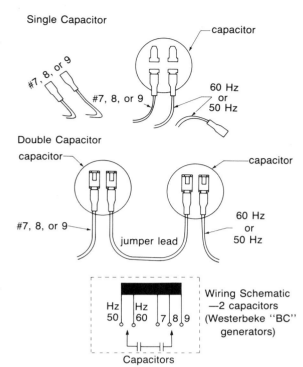

Figure 6-10. Exciter winding capacitor connections on brushless generators. The frequency of the generator is changed from 60 Hz to 50 Hz by changing the engine speed. Voltage is then adjusted by connecting the relevant lead to the capacitor and leaving the other one loose. The no-load voltage of the generator can be raised or lowered by switching leads 7, 8, and 9. The higher the number on the lead connected, the higher the no-load voltage.

two capacitor terminals that have the power leads, not the two terminals that are bridged.

No output on battery-charging circuit (if fitted). Identify the bridge rectifier. The auxiliary stator winding will have two leads running to the two AC terminals on the bridge rectifier. Disconnect these terminals and measure the winding resistance across the two leads (R × 1 scale). It should be very low (0.5 to 0.2 ohms) and indistinguishable from a dead short on most meters. Check from each lead to ground (R × 100). Any continuity indicates a short. Check to all other stator leads. Once again, any continuity indicates a short.

Remove the DC connections from the bridge rectifier (label as necessary) and test it as described earlier in the chapter.

The output from the rectifier will be regulated by a solid-state voltage regulator. About all that can be done with this is to check all wiring and terminals. It will be subject to all the same problems regarding voltage drop, undercharging, etc., outlined in Chapter 2, "Troubleshooting Voltage Regulators."

Problems with frequency and voltage. Refer to the relevant sections on pages 152–153. Most of the comments are equally applicable to brushless generators. One additional point needs to be made: Where a brushless generator with capacitor-type excitation windings (small generators) suffers from low voltage, *the capacitor may be at fault even if it checks out OK with the tests outlined.* Try changing the capacitor.

Electric Motors

How They Work

All electric motors, regardless of type, operate on the same general principles. A magnetic field is established inside the motor case, either with fixed permanent magnets, or by using electromagnets—coils of wire (field windings) wrapped around iron shoes that become magnetized when a current is passed through the windings.

An armature or rotor is mounted on bearings inside this magnetic field. An armature contains another series of windings on an iron frame that also becomes magnetized when a current is passed through the windings. A rotor contains a set of fixed metal bars. In either case, like or opposing magnetic fields between the motor case and the armature or rotor drive the armature or rotor around in its bearings—we have an electric motor. Depending on methods of construction and details of operation, electric motors fall into three broad categories: universal motors, permanent-magnet DC motors, and induction motors.

Universal motors. The magnetic field inside the motor case is created by a couple of field windings. This type of motor uses a wound armature with anywhere from four windings on up (depending on motor construction). Each armature winding terminates in a copper bar. These bars are mutually separated by insulation and ar-

ranged in a circle on the end of the armature shaft to become a *commutator*. Electricity is conducted to both the field windings (magnetizing them) and the armature windings (via the spring-loaded brushes and the commutator; Figure 6-11). The individual armature winding connected to the commutator bars in contact with the brushes is magnetized, and this magnetic attraction or repulsion (depending on direction of rotation) interacts with the magnetic field produced by the field windings, causing the armature to turn.

As the armature turns the brushes connect with another segment of the commutator, deenergizing the first winding on the armature and energizing the next. It in turn is attracted or repelled by the field windings and keeps the armature turning.

The brushes are offset slightly from the field windings so that when the energized armature winding is attracted or repelled by the field magnet, the armature is pulled (or pushed) around. Without this offset, the motor would remain locked in one position.

Some motors (*series-wound* motors) have the field and armature windings connected in series: The current flows first through a field winding, into a brush, through an armature winding, out the other brush, through the second field winding, and then back to the power

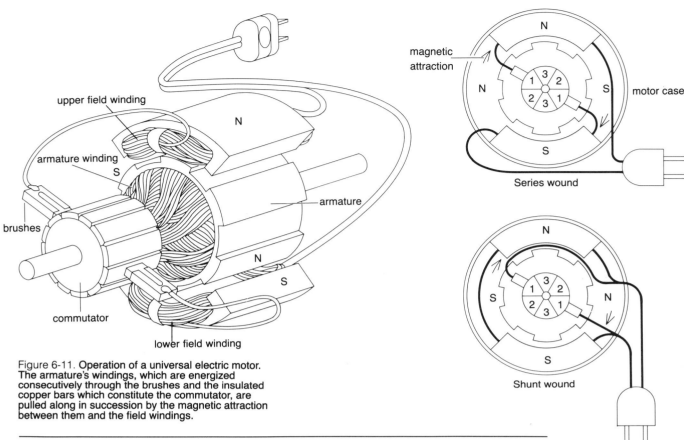

Figure 6-11. **Operation of a universal electric motor.** The armature's windings, which are energized consecutively through the brushes and the insulated copper bars which constitute the commutator, are pulled along in succession by the magnetic attraction between them and the field windings.

source. Others (*shunt-wound* motors) have the field and armature windings in parallel. The current flows from a common terminal through both the field and armature windings, then back to another common terminal.

The speed of a shunt-wound DC motor is governed by its load. Thus if this type of motor is run without a load, it will run faster and faster until it ultimately self-destructs. This is why these motors are used inside a sealed, composite unit with the load permanently attached to the shaft.

Permanent-magnet DC motors. Permanent-magnet motors replace the field windings with permanent magnets. These motors resemble universal motors in all other respects (brushes, commutators, wound armatures).

Induction motors. Induction motors work on AC power only. They contain field windings but they have no windings on the armature and therefore have no brushes or commutator. This type of armature is generally referred to as a rotor, and comprises a number of copper bars. These mo-

tors rely on the pulsating nature of AC power. The current through the field windings, alternating from positive to negative and back, sets up a pulsating magnetic force that alternately attracts and repels the copper bars in the rotor. Once an induction motor starts spinning, it will keep spinning as long as current flows. The problem is to get it moving in the first place. Two different methods are used to start induction motors:

Split-phase ("resistance") starting: A separate set of *phase* or *start* windings is added to the field windings, offset from the *run* windings and designed to generate an offset magnetic force and get the motor moving. As it comes up to speed, a centrifugal switch or a current-sensing switch generally cuts off the start windings, often with an audible click.

Capacitor-start motors further refine the starting process by the addition of one or two capacitors—round or oval cylinders with two spade terminals on one end, usually fitted under a cover on top of the motor, that store an electric charge. Some capacitor-start motors have no switch on the

Figure 6-12A. **Split-phase capacitor start induction motor.**

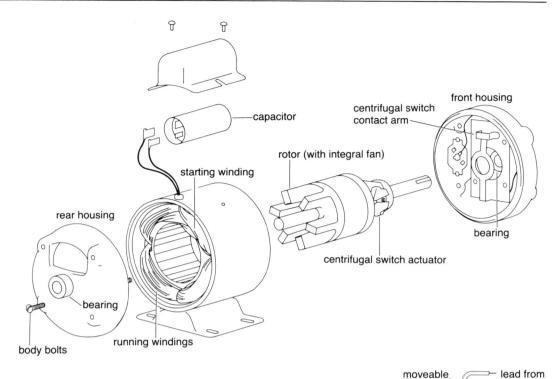

capacitor

front housing

centrifugal switch contact arm

rotor (with integral fan)

starting winding

rear housing

bearing

bearing

centrifugal switch actuator

body bolts

running windings

Figure 6-12B. **(Left)** Shaded-pole induction motor.

Figure 6-12C. **(Right)** Operation of the centrifugal switch on a split-phase motor.

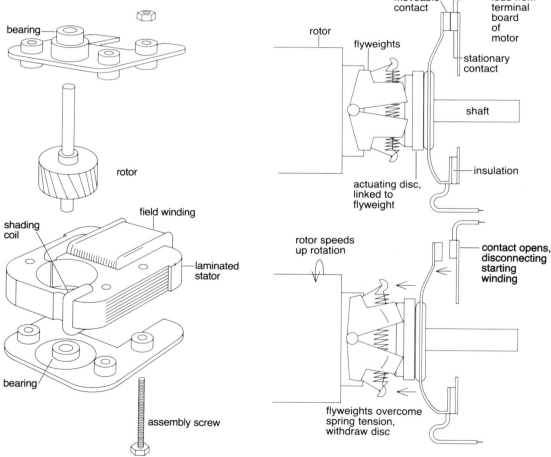

bearing

rotor

shading coil

field winding

laminated stator

bearing

assembly screw

moveable contact

lead from terminal board of motor

rotor

flyweights

stationary contact

shaft

insulation

actuating disc, linked to flyweight

rotor speeds up rotation

contact opens, disconnecting starting winding

flyweights overcome spring tension, withdraw disc

start windings, which remain energized at all times; others have a switch. Where two capacitors are fitted, the second maintains partial current to the start windings even after the main start circuit is switched off. This makes for smoother running and reduces hum.

Shaded-pole starting: Shaded-pole motors have a copper strap around a section of the field magnet that creates a magnetic asymmetry and gets the motor moving. Shaded-pole motors are simple, inexpensive, and reliable, but since the magnetic asymmetry is a permanent feature, even when running at full speed, they are also inefficient.

Speed Regulation

Universal motors. Universal motors commonly are controlled by varying the current to the field windings. This is done either by a multiposition switch or with a rheostat and knob, which permits continuous adjustment of the field current. Newer devices may have solid-state regulators similar to the voltage regulators found on alternators, but with an added manual controller to adjust output. On such devices a short circuit will result in maximum speed at all times; an open circuit will disable the motor. Motors designed to run at a single, constant speed are likely to have a governor.

Tapped-field speed control: The field winding has three to six connections at different points along its length. The closer a connection to the end of the winding, the shorter the length of winding energized when current is applied, and therefore the less the resistance (since resistance is a function of wire length). The less the resistance the greater the current flow. The greater the current flow the more the magnetism. The more the magnetism the faster the motor will spin! So, by connecting (tapping into) the field winding at different points, we vary motor speed. The different points are accessed by a multiposition selector switch (Figure 6-13A).

Rheostats: A rheostat generally consists of a circular coil with a spring-loaded contact that can be rotated to any point on the coil. Current is fed into the coil at one end and flows along it until reaching the contactor, which then becomes the exit path for the current. As more coil is included in

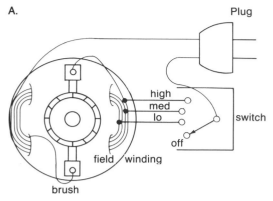

A.

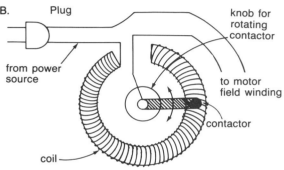

B.

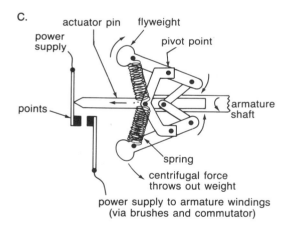

C.

Figure 6-13. Regulating the speed of universal motors. **(Top)** Multiposition switch. **(Middle)** Rheostat (variable resistor). **(Bottom)** Mechanical governor.

the circuit the resistance increases, causing less current to flow. The rheostat is placed in the supply line to the field windings, controlling the current fed to the windings and therefore motor speed (Figure 6-13B).

Governors: A governor is mounted on the end of an armature shaft. As the armature spins the governor's flyweights are thrown outward against the spring pressure by centrifugal force. As a result the various levers move the actuator pin out, and this in turn opens the points, cutting

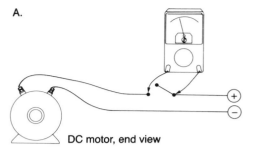

A.

DC motor, end view

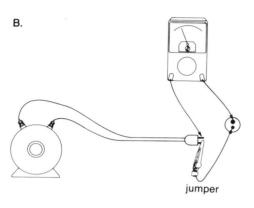

B.

jumper

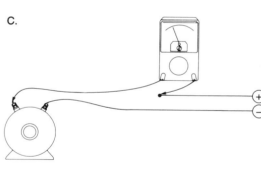

C.

off the current to the armature windings. The motor slows, centrifugal force declines, the weights are pulled back in by the springs, the points close, power is restored to the armature windings, and the motor speeds up once again. Motor speed is set by adjusting the spring pressure on the flyweights; the more pressure, the greater the centrifugal force needed to open the points, and therefore the faster the motor will spin before the points are opened. Things to look for when troubleshooting governors are burned or corroded points, a dirty or rusty shaft (interfering with the movement of the actuator pin), and any dirt or corrosion on the rest of the linkage or the springs (Figure 6-13C).

Induction motors. Since induction motors work by utilizing the pulsating nature of

AC power, their speed is tied directly to the frequency in the AC system (e.g., 60 Hz in the USA; 50 Hz in the UK). As such, speed is not variable. The motors may have anywhere from two to six or more field windings (*poles*). Speed is broadly governed by the number of poles. At 60 Hz, this will yield approximately 3500 r.p.m. with 2 poles, 1750 r.p.m. with 4 poles, and 1160 r.p.m. with 6 poles. Speed regulation of induction motors generally is available only by switching poles into or out of the circuit.

Troubleshooting

Preliminary testing: all motors.

Voltage test: Check the voltage at the motor, preferably across its input and output terminals. If these are inaccessible, check at the nearest power outlet or terminal block. Switch the motor on and off. Severe voltage drop results from a dead battery, defective wiring and switches, or a shorted motor.

Amperage test, DC motors: If you have a DC ammeter with a capacity high enough to carry the rated load of the motor, connect it *in series* with the hot lead. This can be done either by turning off the switch and jumping it out with the meter leads, or by unsoldering or otherwise breaking loose a connection. If the motor is pulling more amps than rated, it has a short; if pulling no amps, it is open-circuited. This could result from a blown fuse, tripped breaker, turned-off switch, broken or disconnected wire, brushes not contacting the commutator, or a burnt winding in the motor itself.

Amperage test, AC motors: Clip an AC ammeter around the power lead and compare the amp draw with the rated load. On 230-volt AC motors (USA), test both power leads one at a time—they should be pulling approximately the same number of amps. Induction motors are notoriously inefficient—the smaller the motor, the greater the inefficiency. If the motor is rated in watts, its *rated* amperage can be found by dividing the watts by system voltage. *Actual amperage may be more than twice this,* and on initial start-up as much as six times higher! This makes it difficult to distinguish partial shorts. Dead shorts will draw heavy amperage continuously; open circuits, no amps.

Table 6-2. Typical Running Amperages for Induction Motors.[1]

Horsepower	115-Volt Motor	230-Volt Motor
1/6	4.4 amps	2.2 amps
1/4	5.8	2.9
1/3	7.2	3.6
1/2	9.8	4.9
3/4	13.8	6.9
1	16	8
1 1/2	20	10
2	24	12

1. Starting currents for split phase are 5 to 7 times higher, for capacitor 2 to 4 times higher.

Resistance tests: Disconnect the motor from its power source and connect an ohmmeter on the R × 1 scale between the hot and ground leads (12-volt motors), the hot and neutral leads (115-volt, USA, or 240-volt, UK), or the two hot leads (230-volt, USA). The meter should show a small resistance, depending on the type and size of the motor. In general, the more powerful the motor, the lower the resistance.

If the meter shows zero ohms, the motor has an internal short. However, DC motors that have a heavy current draw, such as starter motors, may show so little resistance that only the most sensitive meters can distinguish between normal internal resistance and a short. If the meter shows infinite resistance, change to the R × 100 scale and test again. Still very high or infinite resistance? The motor is open-circuited at some point. Likely causes are an open switch, a broken wire, burnt brushes or brush springs, or a burnt winding.

Leave the meter connected on the R × 1 scale and turn the motor by hand. On motors with brushes the reading may flicker up and down uniformly, but any sudden or erratic differences probably indicate problems with the brushes or commutator.

If the motor has variable speeds, such as a food processor, switch through the range (or turn the speed adjusting knob) and observe the ohms reading. It should increase or decrease gradually. Any sudden deviations indicate a problem. An exception is when the switch is turned off: The reading should jump to infinity. If it does not, the switch is defective.

If the preceding tests indicate a problem in the motor, it needs to be dismantled. Generally this is a simple and obvious procedure. Take care not to break any wires when removing end covers and housings, especially on universal motors, where brush and field winding wires may be attached to two different parts of the casing. Motor casings and covers often must be reassembled exactly as they came apart. It is always a good idea to make a couple of punch marks or scratches in the paint across a joint so that they can be realigned exactly. Universal and permanent-magnet motors with spring-loaded brushes are likely to launch them during incautious disassembly. Extra care is needed.

Electrical problems.

Universal motors. The most likely problem areas are the brushes and commutator.

The brushes must be free-moving in their holders, have sufficient spring tension, and as a general rule, should be at least as long as they are wide.

When worn beyond this point they need replacing. The commutator must be clean, shiny, and smooth (a step worn by the brushes is OK). Any pitted or darkened segments indicate a short or open circuit in one of the armature windings (Figure 6-15A), and the armature needs replacing or rewinding.

Commutator testing: The armature and commutator can be tested using the ohms scale of a VOM. Set the meter to the R × 1 scale, touch one probe to one commutator segment and the other probe to the adjacent segment. The ohms reading should be low, but not zero. Test adjacent segments all around the commutator; all should read about the same. No ohms (needle all the way to the *right*) indicates a short between windings (except with some cheap meters insufficiently sensitive to distinguish normal readings from a short). High ohms (needle all the way to the *left*) indicates an open circuit (a burned winding). Finally, set the meter to the R × 100 scale and test between the armature shaft and each commutator segment. A zero reading at any time indicates a short to ground (Figure 6-15B).

Commutator cleaning: A dirty commutator that checks out OK and is in reasonable shape (not pitted, out of round, or excessively worn) can be cleaned by pulling a strip of fine sandpaper (600 or 400 wet-or-dry) lightly back and forth until all the seg-

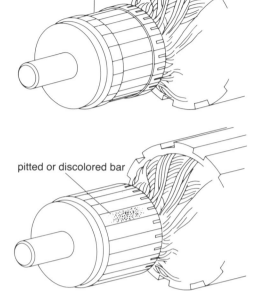

Figure 6-15A.
Maintenance procedures for universal motors. Worn and grooved commutator is OK as long as the ring is shiny. A pitted or dark bar results from an open or short circuit in the armature winding.

OK

pitted or discolored bar

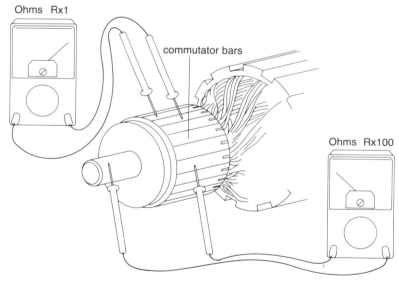

Ohms Rx1

commutator bars

Ohms Rx100

Figure 6-15B. Testing an armature. Testing between adjacent bars on the commutator should give a low ohms reading; all readings about the same. Testing from each commutator bar to the shaft should show infinity, indicating an open circuit.

ments are uniformly shiny. Cut back the insulation between each segment of the commutator to just below the level of the copper segments by drawing a knife or sharp screwdriver across each strip of insulation. Take care not to scratch the copper or burr its edges (Figure 6-15D and E). Use a triangular file to bevel the edges of the copper bars. Always renew the brushes at this time.

Brush renewal: Pull out the old brushes and thoroughly clean away all traces of carbon from the commutator and motor housing with a proprietary cleaner, such as Electroclean or WD40. Dry thoroughly afterward. Slip in the new brushes, *which must slide in and out of their holders without binding*. The *commutator* ends of the new brushes will need "bedding in": Wrap some fine sandpaper (600 or 400 wet-or-dry; *not emery cloth*) around the commutator under the brushes (Figure 6-15F), with the sanding surface facing *out*. Spin the armature until the brushes are bedded to the commutator; they should be almost shiny over their whole surface. Remove the sandpaper and blow out the carbon dust.

Field winding testing: The field windings will have a wire running into one winding, around to the other(s), and out.

One end may or may not be grounded to the motor case. Test with a VOM, set to the R × 1 scale, between the ungrounded end of the field winding wire and the other wire or the motor case (scratch around to get a good ground). If the meter reads zero (needle all the way to the *right*), the field windings or wires are shorted to ground (except on large motors being tested with a cheap meter not sensitive enough to read field-winding resistances). Now set the meter to the R × 100 scale. A high reading (needle all the way to the *left*) indicates the field windings or their wiring are open-circuited (burned through like a fuse, or a broken wire).

On those motors with governor-type speed controls, check the governor for free movement, the springs for reasonable tension, and the points for any signs of pitting and corrosion.

Permanent-magnet motors. These are tested and repaired in exactly the same way as universal motors, with the exception that there are no field windings to worry about.

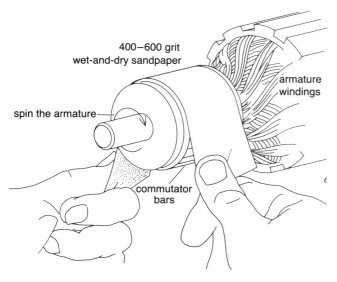

400–600 grit
wet-and-dry sandpaper

spin the armature

armature
windings

commutator
bars

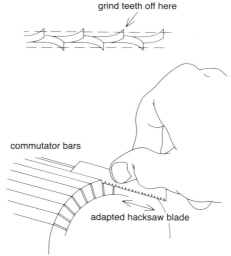

grind teeth off here

commutator bars

adapted hacksaw blade

Figure 6-15C. (**Top Left**) Polishing a commutator.

Figure 6-15D. (**Top Right**) Cutting back the insulation on a commutator. Modify a hacksaw blade as shown.

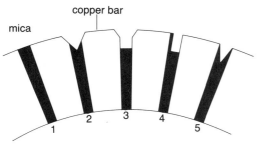

mica

copper bar

1 2 3 4 5

400–600 grit wet-and-dry
sandpaper

spin the armature

brush holder complete
with brush and spring

Figure 6-15E. (**Bottom Left**) Cutting back the insulation on a commutator. At 1, the mica insulation is flush with the commutator bars. Cut back as in 2 (good) or 3 (better). Avoid cutting back as in 4 or 5.

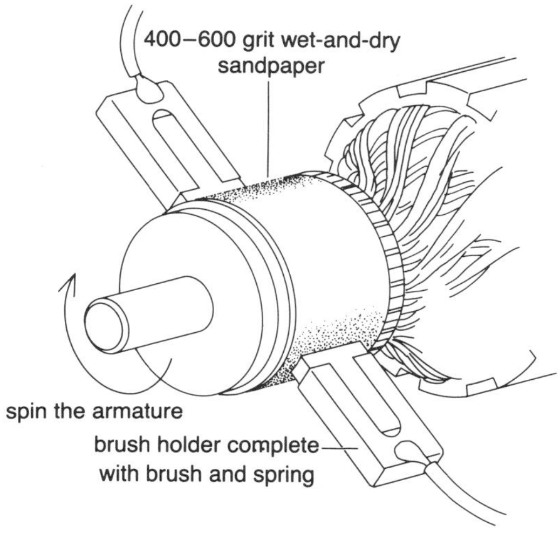

Figure 6-15F. (**Bottom Right**) Bedding in new brushes.

Induction motors. Induction motors have no brushes, commutator, or armature windings to concern us. Field windings are tested as for universal motors. Shaded-pole motors have little else to go wrong electrically. Split-phase motors have one or two special problem areas.

Thermal overload trip: If the motor is very hot (too hot to touch), let it cool down. Some thermal overload trips reset themselves; others have to be reset by pushing a button on the motor housing.

Motor hums but does not start: The start windings probably are not energizing. Spin the motor by hand (switch turned on). If it goes, the start circuit is bad. Check for a centrifugal switch in the open position or one that has dirty or corroded points. If present, the switch will be on the end of the rotor shaft. Clean it and ensure free movement. If the motor has capacitors, test these also.

Capacitors must be discharged before being tested, as they store electricity and can pack quite a punch hours after a motor has been switched off. Discharging can be done by bridging the capacitor terminals with a screwdriver, but this can be hard on the capacitor. Better to rig up a light bulb (115 volts USA, 240 volts UK) with two test leads and touch the leads to the capacitor terminals.

Now set the ohmmeter on the R × 100 scale and connect it to the capacitor terminals. It should jump to zero ohms and then slowly return to high. If it fails to go down, the capacitor is open-circuited; if the meter goes down and stays down (zero ohms), the capacitor is short-circuited. Capacitors are rated in microfarads of capacity, and are different for continuous duty

Figure 6-16. **Testing capacitors. Discharge first (see Figure 6-7). Test across the capacitor terminals with an ohmmeter on R × 100. The meter should jump to zero ohms and slowly return to high. If it fails to go down, the capacitor is open-circuited. If it goes down and stays down (zero ohms), the capacitor is shorted. Testing from any terminal (or lead) to the case on R × 100 must show infinity. If not, the capacitor is shorted.**

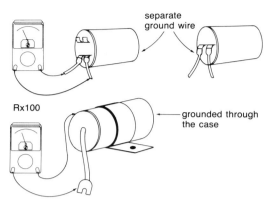

separate ground wire

Rx100

grounded through the case

and intermittent duty. Replace any capacitors with the same size and type.

Motor starts and kicks off: The start windings are not switcning off when the motor comes up to speed. Check the centrifugal switch, if fitted.

Mechanical problems.

Motors are mechanically very simple. A bearing supports the armature (rotor) at both ends. Sometimes a fan is added to the shaft.

Small motors have bushings for bearings (brass or bronze sleeves) which require a very little light machine oil periodically. Do not overdo it: Excess oil will carry dirt into the motor windings.

Larger motors have ball bearings. Most are sealed for life, but a few older ones have external grease nipples (one shot of grease occasionally). Worn bearings produce distinctive rattles and rumbles. With the power off, armatures (rotors) should turn freely by hand with no catches or rough spots. There should be no up and down or sideways movement, and almost no in and out movement (end play).

The clearance between an armature (rotor) and its field winding shoes (or magnets) is quite small. Any misalignment or serious bearing wear will cause the armature to rub on the shoes (magnets). This will produce a shiny spot on both the armature and shoe and must be fixed. If the armature and its bearings appear to be in good shape, check any fastenings to the field windings. On some motors the windings are bolted through the motor case and can work loose with vibration.

Starter Motors

Starter motors are universal motors, but with one or two special quirks that merit attention.

Starter motor circuits.

The heavy amperage draw of a starter motor requires heavy supply cables. Ignition switches frequently are located some distance from the battery and starter motor. To keep cable runs to a minimum, a remotely operated switch—a *solenoid*—that is operated by the ignition switch turns the starter motor on and off (Figure 6-17A and B).

A solenoid contains a plunger and an electromagnet. When the ignition switch is turned on it energizes the magnet, which pulls down the plunger, which closes a couple of heavy-duty contacts, thus making the circuit to the starter motor (Figure 6-17C).

Some starting circuits utilize a *neutral start* switch, or solenoid, which prevents the engine from being cranked when it is in gear. Some circuits fit a second solenoid, which, when energized by the ignition switch, closes a set of points to energize the first solenoid, which then closes the starter-motor points.

The ground side of a starter-motor circuit almost always runs through the starter-motor case and engine block to a ground strap, which is connected directly to the battery's negative terminal post. However, sometimes an insulated ground is used, in which case the starter motor is isolated electrically from the engine block; a separate cable grounds it to the battery. This is very much the recommended practice in marine use to eliminate risk of stray currents and corrosion (see Chapter 4).

Inertia and pre-engaged starters.

Starter motors are of two basic kinds: inertia and pre-engaged. The solenoid for an inertia motor is mounted independently, at a convenient location. The starter-motor drive gear that turns the engine over—the *pinion*—is keyed into a helical groove on the motor drive shaft. When the solenoid is energized the motor spins. Inertia in the gear causes it to spin out along the helical groove and into contact with the engine flywheel, which then is turned over (Figure 6-18A).

The solenoid of a pre-engaged starter is *always* mounted on the starter itself (a surefire indicator!). When the solenoid is energized the electromagnet pulls a lever, which pushes the starter-motor pinion into engagement with the engine flywheel; the main solenoid points now close, allowing current to flow to the motor, which spins at full speed, and (we hope) starts the engine. Pre-engaged starters mesh the drive gear with the flywheel *before* the motor

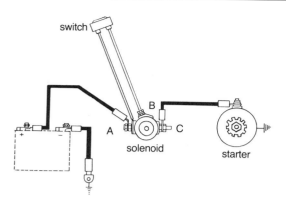

Figure 6-17A. Starting circuit with an inertia starter. To bypass the switch, connect a jumper from A to B. To bypass the switch and the solenoid, connect a heavy-duty jumper (for example, a screwdriver) from A to C.

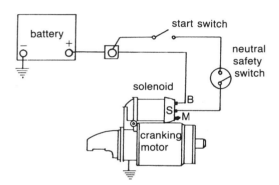

Figure 6-17B. Starting circuit with a pre-engaged starter. To bypass the switch, connect a jumper from terminal B to terminal S on the solenoid. To bypass the solenoid and switch, connect a heavy-duty jumper (for example, a screwdriver) from terminal B to terminal M. See also Figure 6-19A.

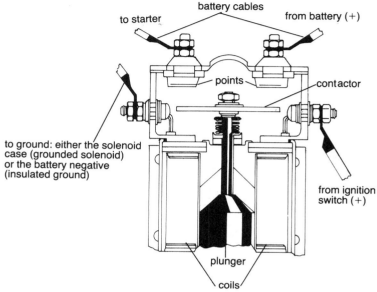

Figure 6-17C. Solenoid operation. Upon closing the ignition switch, a small current passing through the solenoid's electromagnet pushes the contactor up against spring tension, completing the circuit from the battery to the starter motor.

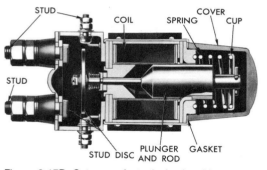

Figure 6-17D. Cutaway of a typical solenoid.

spins, greatly reducing overall wear (Figure 6-18B).

Sometimes an inertia starter's pinion will stick to its shaft and not be thrown into engagement with the flywheel. In this case the motor will "whirr" loudly without turning the engine over. A smart tap on its case while it is spinning may free it up (don't do this too often; it's hard on the gear teeth). At other times the pinion may jam in the flywheel and not disengage. In this case access can be gained to the end of the armature shaft via a cover, normally located in the center of the rear housing of the starter motor. Turning the squared-off end of the shaft back and forth with a wrench should free the pinion.

Circuit testing. Remember: A battery that is in reality almost dead may show nearly full voltage on an open-circuit voltage test.

Figure 6-18A. **Inertia-type starter motor.**

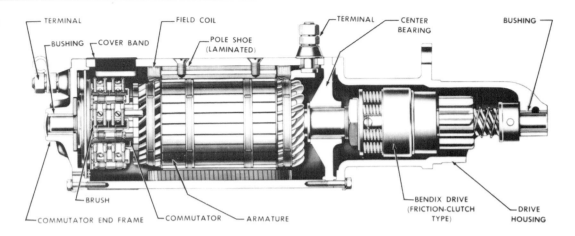

TERMINAL — FIELD COIL — TERMINAL — CENTER BEARING — BUSHING

BUSHING — COVER BAND — POLE SHOE (LAMINATED)

BENDIX DRIVE (FRICTION-CLUTCH TYPE) — DRIVE HOUSING

BRUSH

COMMUTATOR END FRAME — COMMUTATOR — ARMATURE

Figure 6-18B. **Pre-engaged starter motor with solenoid mounted on it.**

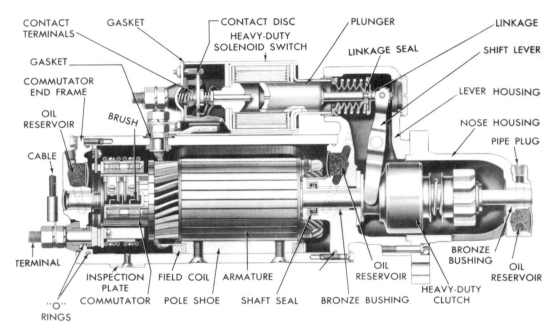

CONTACT TERMINALS — GASKET — CONTACT DISC HEAVY-DUTY SOLENOID SWITCH — PLUNGER — LINKAGE

LINKAGE SEAL — SHIFT LEVER

GASKET — LEVER HOUSING

COMMUTATOR END FRAME — NOSE HOUSING

OIL RESERVOIR — BRUSH — PIPE PLUG

CABLE

TERMINAL — BRONZE BUSHING — OIL RESERVOIR

INSPECTION PLATE — FIELD COIL — ARMATURE — OIL RESERVOIR — HEAVY-DUTY CLUTCH

"O" RINGS — COMMUTATOR — POLE SHOE — SHAFT SEAL — BRONZE BUSHING

Turn on a couple of lights and try to crank the engine. The lights should dim but still stay lit. If the lights remain unchanged, no current is flowing to the starter; if the lights go out, the battery is dead or the starter is shorted. Check the battery first; test all cells with a hydrometer (see Chapter 2, "Testing Your Battery").

Never crank a starter motor for more than 15 seconds continuously when performing any of the following tests. Because starter motors are only designed for brief and infrequent use, they generally have no fans or cooling devices. *Continuous cranking will burn them up.*

Note: Some of these tests will create sparks. Be sure to vent the engine room properly, especially with gasoline engines.

Preliminary tests. A couple of quick steps will isolate problems in the starting circuit. First switch off the battery isolation switch. The solenoid will have two heavy-duty terminals: one attached to the battery's positive cable, the other with a second cable (or short strap in the case of pre-engaged starters) running to the starter itself. There also will be one or two small terminals. If only one of the small terminals has a wire attached, this is the one we need. If both small terminals have wires attached, one is a ground wire; we need *the other one* (it goes to the ignition switch). If in doubt turn off the ignition and battery switch and test from both to ground with an ohmmeter on the R × 1 scale. The ignition switch wire should give a small reading; the ground wire will read zero ohms.

Switch the battery isolation switch back on. Bypass the ignition switch circuit (and neutral start switch if fitted) by connecting a jumper wire or screwdriver blade from the *battery terminal* on the solenoid to the *ignition switch* terminal. If the motor cranks, the ignition switch or its circuit is faulty. If the solenoid clicks but nothing else happens the starter is probably bad (or the battery really is dead; check it again). If nothing at all happens there is either no juice to the solenoid (check the battery isolation switch) or the solenoid is defective.

If the starter failed to work use the screwdriver to jump out the *two heavy-duty terminals* on the solenoid (Figure 6-19C). Be warned: *The full battery current will be flowing through the screwdriver blade.* Consid-

Figure 6-19A. Typical pre-engaged starter motor and solenoid. Jumping across 1 and 2 bypasses the ignition switch; 1 and 3 bypasses both the ignition switch and the solenoid. The starter should spin but will not engage the engine's flywheel.

Figure 6-19B. **Bypassing the ignition switch by jumping out the two smaller wires.**

Figure 6-19C. Bypassing the solenoid altogether by jumping out the two main cable terminals.

Troubleshooting Chart 6-2.
Starting Circuit Problems: Engine Fails to Crank.

Note: Before jumping out solenoid terminals, completely vent the engine compartment, especially with gasoline engines, since sparks will be created.

Turn on some lights and try to crank the engine. Do the lights *go out?* **NO**	**YES** If the solenoid makes a rapid "clicking" the battery is probably dead—replace it. If the solenoid makes one loud click the starter motor is probably jammed or shorted—free it up or replace it as necessary. While the starter is out, try turning the engine over by placing a wrench on the crankshaft pulley nut. If the engine won't turn this is the problem—there may be water in the cylinders (page 206) or it may be seized up.
When cranking, do the lights *dim?* **NO**	**YES** Check for voltage drop from poor connections or undersized cables. Try cranking for a few seconds, then feel all connections and cables in the circuit—battery and solenoid terminals, and battery ground attachment on engine block. If any are warm to the touch, they need cleaning. If this fails to show a problem set VOM to 12 volts DC. Place the probes according to Figure 6-20, then try to crank the engine. If there is no evidence of voltage drop, check for a jammed or shorted starter.
Is the ignition switch circuit faulty? **NO** **TEST:** With a jumper wire or screwdriver blade, bridge the battery and ignition switch terminals on the solenoid. If the starter motor now cranks, the ignition circuit is defective.	**YES** Replace ignition switch or its wiring as needed.
Is the solenoid defective? **NO** **TEST:** Use a screwdriver blade to jump out the two heavy-duty terminals on the solenoid. (This procedure is tricky: Observe all precautions outlined in accompanying text.) If the starter now spins, the solenoid is defective.	**YES** Replace the solenoid.
Is there full battery voltage at starter motor when cranking? **NO** **TEST:** Check with VOM between the starter positive terminal and the engine block when cranking.	**YES** The starter is open-circuited and needs replacing. First check its brushes for excessive wear or sticking in their brush holders.
The battery isolation switch is probably turned "OFF"!	

erable arcing is likely. A big chunk may be melted out of the screwdriver blade. Do not touch the solenoid or starter case with the screwdriver: This will create a dead short. Hold the screwdriver *firmly* to the terminals. If the starter now spins, the solenoid is defective. If the motor does not spin, *it* is probably faulty. If no arcing occurred, there is no juice to the solenoid.

You can crank a motor with an inertia starter by jumping a defective solenoid. A pre-engaged starter, however, will merely spin without engaging the engine flywheel since the solenoid is needed to push the starter pinion into engagement with the flywheel.

Voltage drop tests. The above tests will quickly and crudely determine whether there is juice to the starter motor and whether or not it is functional. More insidious is the effect of poor connections and undersized cables—these create voltage drop in the circuits, rob the starter motor of power, and result in sluggish cranking or failure to crank at all—especially when cold. A potential result is a burnt-out starter motor.

A quick test for voltage drop can be made by cranking (or trying to crank) for a few seconds and then feeling all the connections and cables in the circuit: both battery terminals, both isolation switch terminals, solenoid terminals, and the battery ground attachment point on the engine block. If any of these are warm, there is resistance and voltage drop; the connection needs cleaning.

More accurate tests can be made with a VOM set to read 12 volts DC. Run the positive meter probe to the battery positive post (not the cable clamp), and the other to the solenoid positive terminal, and crank the engine. Switch down the voltage scales. *Any voltage reading shows voltage drop in this part of the circuit.* Clean all connections and repeat the test.

Switch back up the voltage scales and perform the same test (cranking the engine) across the two main solenoid terminals. Switch down the scales. Any voltage indicates resistance in the solenoid (see below for cleaning dirty and pitted points).

Repeat the same tests from the solenoid outlet terminal to the starter motor hot terminal; from the starter motor to the engine block; and from the engine block back to the battery negative post (not the cable clamp). The latter test frequently reveals poor ground connections.

Motor disassembly, inspection, and repair.

Before removing a starter motor from an engine, isolate its hot lead, or better still, disconnect it from the battery. The starter will be held to the engine by two or three nuts or bolts. If it sticks in the flywheel housing, a smart tap will jar it loose (but check first to see that you didn't miss any mounting bolts).

Inertia starters. Remove the metal band from the rear of the motor case. Undo the locknut from the terminal stud in the rear housing. Do not let the stud turn; if necessary, grip it carefully with Vise-Grips (Mole wrenches). Note the order of all washers. These insulate the stud, and it is essential that they go back the same way.

Undo the two (or four) retaining screws in the rear housing. If tight, grip with a pair of Vise-Grips from the *side* to break them loose. Lift off the rear housing with care; it will be attached to the motor case by two brush wires. Lift the springs off the relevant brushes and slide the brushes out of their holders to free the housing.

Pre-engaged starters. To check the solenoid points on a pre-engaged starter, remove the battery cable, the screw or nut retaining the hot strap to the motor, and all other nuts on the stud(s) for the ignition circuit wiring. Undo the two retaining screws at the very back of the solenoid. The end housing (plastic) will pull off to expose the contactor and points. (Note: The spring in here that will probably fall out goes on the center of the contactor.) Check the points and contactor for pitting and burning and clean or replace as necessary.

To remove the solenoid *coil* (electromagnet), undo the two screws at the flywheel end of the solenoid and turn the coil housing through 90 degrees. The coil now will pull straight off the piston. The piston and fork assembly generally can only be removed by separating the starter motor case from its front housing (see below).

If you find it necessary to undo the pivot pin bolt on the solenoid fork, mark its head so that it can be put back in the same position. Often, turning this pin adjusts how far the pinion is "thrown" when it engages the flywheel.

Remove the two starter-motor retaining screws from the rear housing and lift off the rear cover; it comes straight off and contains no brushes. This will expose the brushes and commutator.

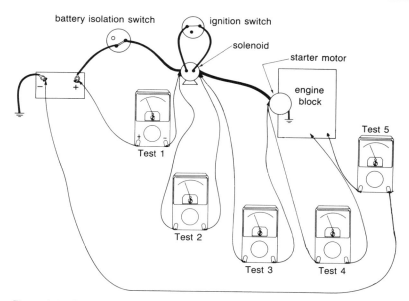

Figure 6-20. **Testing for voltage drop on starter motor circuits. Use a VOM set to read 12 VDC; test while the engine is cranking to identify areas of excessive resistance.**

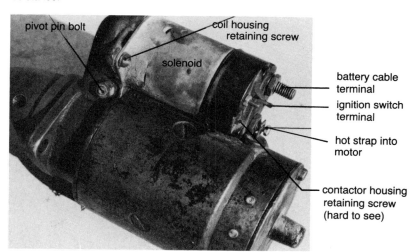

Figure 6-21A. **Disassembling a pre-engaged starter.**

All starters. The motor case, complete with field windings, now can be pulled off to expose the armature. If the end cover was held with four short screws as opposed to two long ones, there will be four more screws holding the motor case at the other end. Note that both end housings will probably have small lugs so that they can be refitted to the motor case in only one position.

Inspect the commutator and brushes for wear as previously detailed in the section on universal motors. Without a very sensitive ohmmeter, it will be impossible to dis-

Figure 6-21B. **Removing stubborn end-plate bolts.**

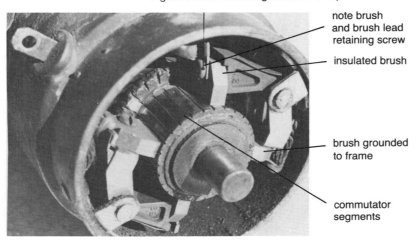

note brush and brush lead retaining screw

insulated brush

brush grounded to frame

commutator segments

Figure 6-21C. **End housing removed.**

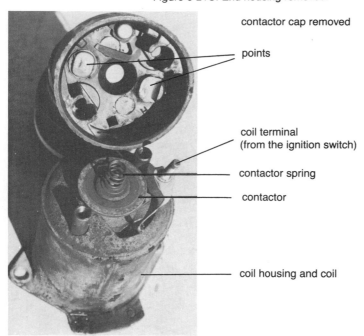

contactor cap removed

points

coil terminal (from the ignition switch)

contactor spring

contactor

coil housing and coil

Figure 6-21D. **Solenoid disassembly.**

tinguish between normal resistances and a short when doing the various winding and resistance tests. Any high resistances indicate an open circuit.

There will be four brushes instead of two, to handle the higher loads. Some brush leads are soldered in place; other brushes are retained with screws. If replacing soldered brushes, cut the old leads, *leaving a tail long enough to solder to.* Tin this tail and the end of the new brush wire and solder them together (see Chapter 3 for more on soldering).

The brushes attached to the field windings are insulated; those to the end housing or motor case are uninsulated. When replacing the end housing of an inertia starter, push the brushes back in their holders and jam them in place by lodging the brush springs against the *side* of the brushes. Once the plate is on, slip the springs into position with a small screwdriver, and then put the metal band back on the motor case.

The pinion. Given the intermittent use of boat engines and the hostile marine environment, the pinion (or drive gear, often known as a *bendix*) can be especially troublesome. Pinions are particularly prone to rusting, especially where salt water in the bilges has contacted the flywheel and been thrown all around the flywheel housing.

Inertia starters are more prone to trouble than pre-engaged starters. Dirt or rust in the helical grooves on the armature shaft will prevent the pinion from moving freely in and out of engagement with the flywheel.

A small, resistance spring in the unit keeps the pinion away from the flywheel when the engine is running. If this spring rusts and breaks, the gear will keep vibrating up against the flywheel with a distinctive rattle.

In automotive use the shaft and helical grooves are not oiled or greased since the lubricant picks up dust from the clutch plates and causes the pinion to stick. In marine use, however, there are no clutch plates in the flywheel housing and the shaft should be greased lightly to prevent rusting.

The pinion assembly is usually retained by a spring clip (a snap ring or circlip) on the end of the armature shaft—occasionally by a *reverse-threaded* nut and cotter pin (split pin). An inertia starter has a powerful "buffer" spring that must be com-

Electric Generators and Electric Motors

plunger

pivot pin bolt

contactor

coil

commutator

armature

Figure 6-21F. (**Above**) Starter motor armature and commutator.

Figure 6-21E. (**Left**) Coil unit removed.

Figure 6-21G. Pre-engaged starter motor disassembled.

case with field coils and brushes

end housing with bushing

solenoid coil with contactor and spring

solenoid contactor housing

solenoid plunger

pinion

clutch

solenoid plunger forks

armature and commutator

Figure 6-21H. (**Far Left**) Testing between bars on a commutator (R × 1 scale). Very low resistance (indistinguishable from a short with this meter).

Figure 6-21I. (**Near Left**) Testing from commutator bars to the armature shaft (R × 100 scale). Very high resistance—no continuity.

pressed before the clip can be removed. Special tools are available for this, but a couple of small C-clamps or two pairs of adroitly handled Vise-Grips usually will do the trick.

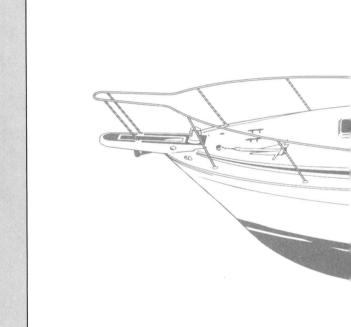

CHAPTER 7

Figure 7-1. Trouble-free marine electronics depend to a large extent on proper installation practices.

——————— 12 VDC

------------- 12 V ground (return)

— — — — 120 VAC

················ bonding strap jumper

ground

bonding (mass)

grounding and bonding combined

(1) Satnav antenna
(2) loran antenna
(3) insulated backstay SSB antenna
(4) copper mesh ground plane
(5) radar
(6) VHF antenna
(7) wind indicator
(8) weatherfax
(9) radios
(10) antenna tuner
(11) copper foil ground plane
(12) depth sounder/speed/log transducers
(13) instruments
(14) battery isolation switch
(15) batteries

Marine Electronics

Troubleshooting Electronic Equipment

Troubleshooting printed circuit boards (pc-boards) and solid-state electronics is a highly skilled and specialized field far above the heads of the average layperson. As more and more computerized technology worms its way into every aspect of our lives, we find ourselves increasingly at the mercy of electronics manufacturers and repair technicians. Fortunately, most electronic equipment is highly reliable *as long as it is kept cool and dry*. Place equipment in well-ventilated areas, and do not obstruct cooling vents. Difficulties that do arise are more often than not external to the equipment. These we can often do something about, and this is the focus of this chapter.

Preliminary Troubleshooting

Unit will not come on-line. As with all other electrical equipment, the primary suspect is always the voltage supply. Check all switches, breakers, and fuses. Check the manual to see if there are any internal fuses that might have blown. Some units—most notably radar—may have more than one fuse. Check for voltage drop at the equipment terminals *with the unit switched on*. Check radios in the transmit mode, since this draws the most current.

If voltage drop is present, check the battery first. Do a specific gravity test on all cells with a hydrometer. If the battery is OK, check all connections, terminal blocks, fuse holders, and switches for voltage drop as outlined in Chapter 3.

An example: After seven years of flawless operation, our VHF radio started to act up. The problem turned out to be no more than a buildup of a thin layer of corrosive residue on the tip of one of the contacts in the in-line fuse holder.

Unit comes on but gives no data (or obviously incorrect data). In this situation the number one suspect *is the operator*, especially with more sophisticated devices such as Lorans and satnavs. Failure to study owner's manuals and memory lapses from infrequent use contribute to such problems. But perhaps the most difficult errors to spot are those that arise from a firm but faulty memory of how to operate a piece of equipment, since we are convinced we are doing things right!

Difficulties also arise from entering incorrect data. For example, common satnav errors include confusion between local time, daylight savings time, and GMT; entering latitudes as South instead of North; entering longitudes as East instead of West; and punching in the wrong coordinates on waypoints.

A number of problems are associated with low- or high-voltage conditions. Engine cranking frequently will pull system voltage levels below a critical minimum needed to maintain internal memories, which become corrupted and must be reset and reprogrammed. Some large electric winches may affect memory-based equipment the same way. The solution is to connect the electronic equipment to a separate, isolated battery, which is not subjected to these loads, or to turn it off during periods of high battery demand.

Voltage spikes and surges from alternators and generators can have a similar effect. In normal circumstances the boat's batteries act as a giant filter to absorb such transient voltages, but not always. For instance, on our boat if we switch our engine over to the battery that powers the satnav, the GMT clock in the satnav runs slow. The longer the engine is on, the wilder our fixes. One time when we were in the Caribbean, a fix placed us in the Indian Ocean! The answer? We keep the satnav on a separate battery, which we charge when the satnav is not in use.

Most 12-volt electronic equipment will digest a wide range of input voltages—from 10 to as much as 40 volts. Some equipment—most notably some depth sounders—cannot tolerate voltages even as high as 16 volts. To be on the safe side, *whenever equalizing batteries at high voltage levels be sure to isolate electronic circuits*.

Much electronic gear depends on internal memories powered by small NiCad (nickel cadmium) batteries that maintain the equipment in a user-ready state when shut off. These batteries have a life expectancy of two to three years (When did you last change yours?). As they begin to die memory lapses will occur, especially when units are switched off for longer periods of time. The equipment normally will still be usable, but only by reprogramming at every use. If dead batteries are left in place, they may begin to weep and corrode expensive circuit boards.

Then there is a host of problems associated with antennas, ground planes, and electrical interference ("noise")—the subjects of the next three sections.

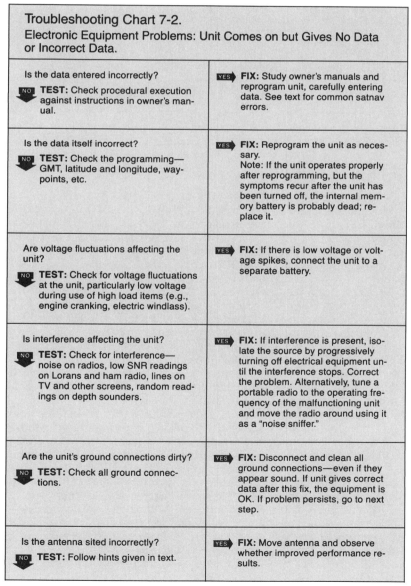

Troubleshooting Chart 7-1.

Electronic Equipment Problems: Unit Will Not Come on Line.

Symptom: No lights, no beeps, etc.

Is there a problem with the voltage supply? **NO** **TEST:** Check the voltage at the equipment when it is turned on.	**YES** **FIX:** If no volts or low volts, check the battery, switches, fuses, connections, etc., for voltage drop as outlined in Chapter 3.
Are there blown fuses or tripped circuit breakers within the unit? **NO**	**YES** **FIX:** Replace or reset as necessary.

If unit still will not come on line, call a specialist.

Troubleshooting Chart 7-2.

Electronic Equipment Problems: Unit Comes on but Gives No Data or Incorrect Data.

Is the data entered incorrectly? **NO** **TEST:** Check procedural execution against instructions in owner's manual.	**YES** **FIX:** Study owner's manuals and reprogram unit, carefully entering data. See text for common satnav errors.
Is the data itself incorrect? **NO** **TEST:** Check the programming—GMT, latitude and longitude, waypoints, etc.	**YES** **FIX:** Reprogram the unit as necessary. Note: If the unit operates properly after reprogramming, but the symptoms recur after the unit has been turned off, the internal memory battery is probably dead; replace it.
Are voltage fluctuations affecting the unit? **NO** **TEST:** Check for voltage fluctuations at the unit, particularly low voltage during use of high load items (e.g., engine cranking, electric windlass).	**YES** **FIX:** If there is low voltage or voltage spikes, connect the unit to a separate battery.
Is interference affecting the unit? **NO** **TEST:** Check for interference—noise on radios, low SNR readings on Lorans and ham radio, lines on TV and other screens, random readings on depth sounders.	**YES** **FIX:** If interference is present, isolate the source by progressively turning off electrical equipment until the interference stops. Correct the problem. Alternatively, tune a portable radio to the operating frequency of the malfunctioning unit and move the radio around using it as a "noise sniffer."
Are the unit's ground connections dirty? **NO** **TEST:** Check all ground connections.	**YES** **FIX:** Disconnect and clean all ground connections—even if they appear sound. If unit gives correct data after this fix, the equipment is OK. If problem persists, go to next step.
Is the antenna sited incorrectly? **NO** **TEST:** Follow hints given in text.	**YES** **FIX:** Move antenna and observe whether improved performance results.

(Chart 7-2 continued)

Troubleshooting Chart 7-2 (continued).	
Is the coaxial cable or its connectors faulty? **NO** **TEST:** Remove the coax connection from the back of the equipment and inspect closely for corrosion; repeat for any other in-line connectors. Just behind the coax connection to the equipment (or any other in-line connectors) carefully peel back a small piece of the outer coax insulation and inspect the braid for tarnishing and corrosion. If both ends of the coaxial cable can be disconnected, test with an ohmmeter set to the R × 100 scale from the center pin of one connector to its case. Any reading less than infinity indicates an internal short (probably in one of the connectors). Now short the center pin on the connector to its case and test between the pin and the case on the other connector, using the R × 1 scale. Any reading of more than 2 or 3 ohms indicates excessive resistance.	**YES** **FIX:** Clean connections. Replace shorted or defective cable and connectors. If the braid is corroded, replace the coax and its connection. If the braid is clean and shiny, replace the insulation and seal with 3M 5200 or some other sealant.
Is the problem persisting?	**YES** **FIX:** Call a specialist.

Antennas

Antennas come in a bewildering array of shapes and sizes. Except in special circumstances, it is best to follow the equipment manufacturer's recommendations. Since most antennas look pretty much alike externally, it is hard to judge one brand against another. Internal construction varies markedly in quality, however. Such features as all-soldered connections, high-quality brass sleeves, rugged mounting brackets, etc., serve to differentiate antennas for the long haul from antennas you will probably have to replace in a few years. *Always buy a quality antenna from a reputable manufacturer.* Radio equipment is only as good as the antenna to which it is fitted (Figure 7-2).

Optimizing Your Antenna System

Gain. The principal yardstick for measuring relative antenna performance is *gain,* expressed in decibels, or "dB." A 3-dB gain antenna doubles the power of outgoing and incoming signals, 6 dB quadruples it, 9 dB magnifies it eight times.

Increased performance (decibel rating) is achieved by concentrating the signal into a narrower beam width. A 0-dB antenna radiates uniformly in all directions, including straight up. A 3-dB antenna concentrates horizontal radiation at the expense of the vertical, but still radiates in a 360-degree arc around the antenna. This horizontal concentration is carried even further in 6 dB and 9 dB antennas (Figure 7-3A).

However, if a boat is rolling heavily, a more compressed signal may well undershoot or overshoot other stations: The signal will fade in and out. For this reason sailboats rarely use antennas with a higher gain than 6 dB, and 3 dB is the norm (Figure 7-3B).

With VHF radios, radio transmission is *line-of-sight,* making antenna height a more important factor in determining antenna performance than gain. Since high-gain antennas generally are longer and more expensive antennas, a small, 3-dB masthead antenna often will outperform a deck-level, 14-foot, 6-dB-gain antenna— and at considerable savings (Table 7-1). Of course if the mast ever goes over the side, the antenna goes with it.

The signals collected by antennas are measured in *millionths* of a volt. Only an-

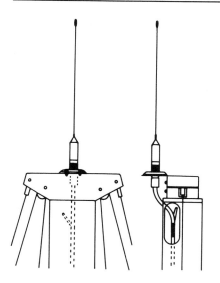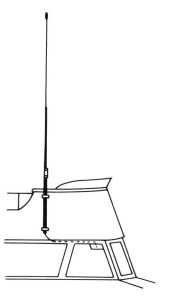

Figure 7-2. **Correct antenna mount and placement.**

tennas correctly sited, with perfect electrical connections, will work properly. Poor performance on newly installed equipment is nearly always a result of inadequate antenna installation, particularly with SSB, ham radios, and Lorans. Deteriorating performance on older units is likely to result from corrosion in coax cables and connectors.

Coax cable. Coaxial cable consists of an inner core of copper wire surrounded by a substantial insulating sleeve (the *dielectric*), which is further enclosed in metal braid and topped with another insulating sheath (Figure 7-4). The signal received by an antenna is trapped between the wire core and the braid and conducted to the receiver. The braid also excludes unwanted signals radiating from other sources, such as rigging, wiring circuits in the boat, etc.

Coax cable comes in different sizes, qualities and resistances. The latter is very important. Almost all marine antennas require 50-ohm coax, but TV antennas use 72-ohm coax. *TV antenna cable, regardless of its quality, is not suitable for marine antennas.*

Insulation is important. Many coax cables have a "foam-core" dielectric, which reduces power losses in the line. However, it also will act as a wick, allowing any moisture that finds its way through improperly sealed connections to corrode the core conductor and the braid. In marine applications, use only cable with *solid polyethylene dielectric.*

The external insulation on most cable is moisture-proof but not necessarily weatherproof. Better-quality cable is fitted with a PVC jacket for increased protection (designated *non-contaminating*), but even this frequently will break down in direct sunlight. Some cheaper—and older—cables have a simple vinyl jacket that will break down after just four or five years (sooner in a hot climate). Buy only non-contaminating cable.

The braid is equally important. Some coax uses aluminum braid—out of the question for marine use. *It must be copper.*

Table 7-1. VHF Antenna Range in Nautical Miles.

Receiver Antenna Height (feet)	Transmitter Antenna Height (feet)							
	8	12	24	40	60	120	200	400
8	8	9	11	13	15	19	23	32
12	9	10	12	14	16	20	24	33
24	11	12	14	16	18	22	26	35
40	13	14	16	18	20	24	28	37
60	15	16	18	20	22	26	30	39

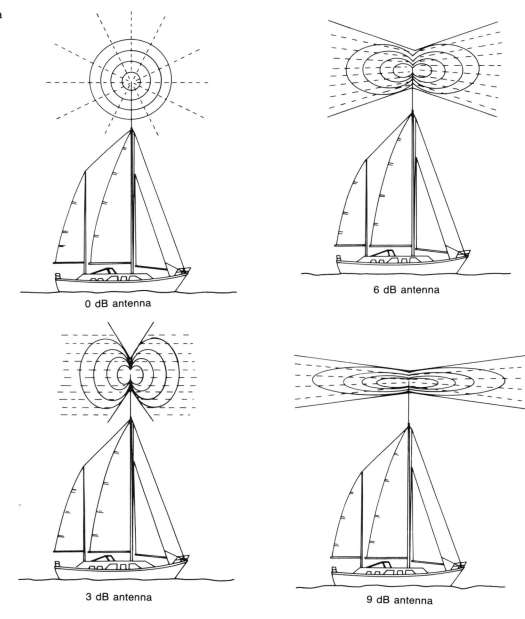

Figure 7-3A. **VHF antenna gain.** Signal radiation patterns—the higher the antenna gain, the more concentrated and far-reaching the signal.

0 dB antenna

6 dB antenna

3 dB antenna

9 dB antenna

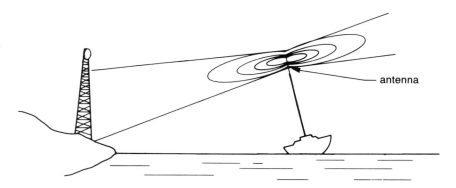

Figure 7-3B. **Antenna gain vs. boat stability.** A very high-gain antenna is not suited for a small boat; the narrow signal pattern can overshoot or undershoot distant stations when the boat rolls.

antenna

There are further differences in the *tightness of the weave*. Cheap coax has loosely woven braid, which is electrically "leaky," leading to signal loss, distortion, and interference. Braid is described by a percentage figure: 98 percent is the best.

So where does this leave us? *Buy only from quality stores and ask for their best coax.* Coax shipped with equipment is likely to be RG-58, or RG-8X (RG-8 "mini"). This cable is a little less than ¼ inch (0.195 inch, or 5 mm) in diameter. If it has "foam" printed on the side, discard it. (Note: The cable supplied with some antennas *cannot be cut or shortened;* read the instructions carefully.) Where any long cable runs are needed—over 30 feet (10 meters) or so—use the larger (lower loss) RG-8A/U, which is just under ½ inch (0.410 inch, or 11 mm) in diameter. Note that RG-8U, the same size as RG-8A/U, frequently does not have a non-contaminating jacket and therefore should not be used.

At the top of the line in normal boat use is RG-213U, the same size as RG-8 and RG-8A/U but with completely waterproof and ultraviolet-resistant insulation. Twice the price but twice the quality. It's a good investment, although a little hard to work with. Even professionals have to struggle with connectors on RG-213U. Belden is considered to be the premier coax manufacturer, and their version of RG-213U, Belden 9913, is your best bet for a long-lived and troublefree antenna installation.

Coax connections. Faulty antenna connections rank right up there with power supply deficiencies and operator error as a principal cause of electronic malfunctions. Anytime equipment performance is unsatisfactory, check all connections, particularly those exposed to the weather.

Although non-contaminating cable is waterproof, it still can wick up considerable amounts of water through its ends, just from humidity in the air—never mind rainwater and salt spray. The water is sucked along the copper braid by capillary action, corroding the braid and ruining line efficiency. Coax connections must be made with proper connectors and then sealed to keep out all moisture. Make all connections with the following points in mind:

• The connector must match the cable. The standard terminal is a PL-259, which fits RG-8U, RG-8A/U, and RG-213U cable. RG-58 and other small cables use an UG-175U adaptor to neck

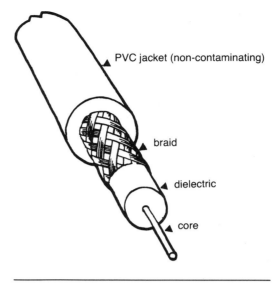

Figure 7-4. Coaxial cable construction. Coax cable consists of an inner core of copper wire surrounded by a substantial insulating sleeve (the dielectric), which is further enclosed in a metal braid and topped with another insulating sheath.

PVC jacket (non-contaminating)

braid

dielectric

core

the PL-259 down to cable size. Two cables are connected screwing their respective PL-259s into a *barrel connector,* sometimes numbered PL-258. More esoteric types of connectors are available, such as SO-239 chassis connectors and BNC connectors, but these rarely find an application on board. Any good electronics store should have all these connectors.

• *Coax connectors should always be soldered.* Because of installation errors with soldered connections, many manufacturers now include pressure-crimped terminals with their equipment. These are *not* recommended for marine use. Sooner or later (generally sooner) corrosion will develop in the terminal, creating resistance and interfering with the signal.

• Installation procedures are illustrated in Figure 7-5. Before fitting the connector, tin the core cable and the braid, and make absolutely certain that no stray wires from the braid can short the core cable. (This would make the antenna inoperative and might do expensive damage to your equipment.) The braid must make a clean fit inside the connector, all the way around. Any gaps in the braid will produce a leaky connection. When soldering the braid, avoid excessive heat, which may melt the dielectric. If you doubt your soldering abilities, get help.

• Coat the connector with a waterproof silicone sealant (RTV) or with an electrician's putty, such as Coax Seal; then seal the whole joint with heat-shrink or self-amalgamating tape. (Allow the silicone, if used, to partially set before adding the tape.) Install drip loops (Figure 7-5C)

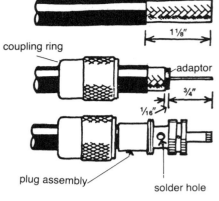

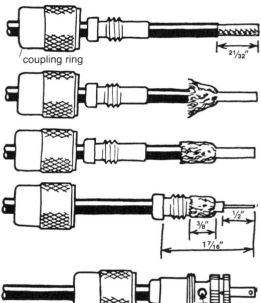

Figure 7-5A. **Method of installing coax connectors without adaptors. (RG-8U, RG-8A/U, RG-213U, RG-213A/U). (1)** Cut the end of the cable even. Remove the vinyl jacket 1⅛ inches—do not nick the braid. Make sure the braid is evenly distributed. **(2)** Bare ¾ inch of center conductor—do not nick the conductor. Trim the braided shield 9/16 inch and *tin the braid.* Slide the coupling ring onto the cable. **(3)** Screw the plug assembly onto the cable. Solder the plug assembly to the braid through the solder holes. Solder the conductor to the contact sleeve. Make sure no loose strands of braid can short out the core.

coupling ring

adaptor

plug assembly

solder hole

Figure 7-5B. **Method of installing coax connectors with adaptors (RG-58, RG-58X (mini 8). (1)** Cut the end of the cable even. Remove the vinyl jacket ²¹/₃₂ inch—do not nick the braid. Slide the coupling ring and the adaptor onto the cable. **(2)** Fan the braid slightly and fold back over the cable. **(3)** Compress the braid around the cable. **(4)** Position the adaptor to the dimension shown. Press the braid down over the body of the adaptor and trim. Bare ½ inch of the center conductor—do not nick the conductor. Pre-tin the exposed center conductor. **(5)** Screw the plug assembly onto the adaptor. Solder the braid to the shell through the solder holes. Solder the conductor to the contact sleeve. **(6)** Screw the coupling ring onto the back of the shell.

coupling ring

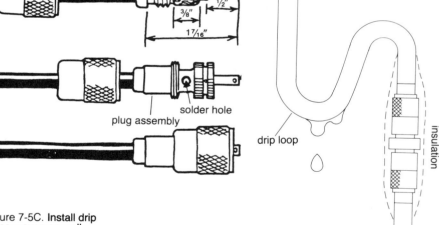

solder hole

plug assembly

Figure 7-5C. **Install drip loops—even on well-insulated connections.**

insulation

drip loop

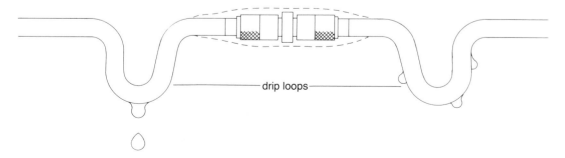

drip loops

even on well-insulated connections. When checking a connector look for corrosion around the center pin and tarnish on the braid.

Testing coax and connections. Never short the center pin and connector housing on a cable connected to an antenna or electronic equipment. Expensive damage may result.

If the coax can be disconnected at both ends, test with an ohmmeter on its highest scale (R × 100) from the case of one of the connectors to its center pin. Anything less than infinite resistance shows a short (probably in the connector installation). Now clip a jumper wire from the pin to the case on one connector and test at the other end on the R × 1 scale. Resistance should be close to zero (depending on the length of the cable). Higher readings show unwanted resistance, such as corroded wire or poor connections.

Using the ohmmeter, some tests can be made with the cable connected to its antenna. With most antennas, testing from the connector case to the center pin at the equipment end of the cable will reveal very low resistance; without a sensitive meter, it will not be possible to distinguish between normal resistance and a short.

Such a test will reveal an open circuit or excessive resistance. But there is a catch. Some antennas—especially those that utilize *loading coils*—will show an open circuit *in normal use* and a short circuit when failed! As most people do not know which type of antenna they have, these tests are of limited practical use.

Emergency VHF antenna. A serviceable temporary antenna can be made from any 19-inch (480-mm) length of wire (a coat hanger, for example) stuck in the antenna socket in the back of a radio. Range will be extremely limited due to its minimal height above sea level. Be very careful not to short the antenna to the outside of the terminal socket, as this might damage the radio. The radio should be used only on low power and as little as possible. Lengthy transmissions eventually will damage output transistors in the radio.

Grounds

Although not critical with VHFs and satnavs, a good ground is essential for effective SSB and Loran performance. The ground system complements the antenna, and one will not function without the other. This relationship, known as a *counterpoise,* is somewhat analogous to a diver (the radio signal) on a springboard (the ground). A better spring makes for a better dive; a better ground makes for a better signal.

Metal boats have a wonderful ground in the hull, but what constitutes a good ground in wood and fiberglass boats is debatable. Experts call for anywhere from 9 to 100 square feet of flat metal surface (copper mesh, metal foil tape, aluminum plate, etc.). Anything made of metal that is flat and close to the water will do.

A tremendous ground can be bonded directly into the hull or placed under internal ballast of boats under construction. Any boat with a solid ballast casting—internal or external—can use this as a ground either by tapping directly into the casting or by connecting to a keel bolt. On bonded boats a ground is sometimes established by running copper foil tape—available in 3- and 6-inch (8- and 15-cm) rolls from good marine electronics stores—in parallel with the bonding wires, and connecting this to all through hulls, the engine, etc.

On unbonded boats, where a common ground strap may invite the risk of electrolytic corrosion, isolating capacitors can be placed in the ground system. These block stray DC currents but allow radio frequency ground currents to flow. Consult a knowledgeable electronics technician about details of the installation.

Ground areas can be distributed throughout the boat, and need not be in actual contact with the seawater. Grounds spread out in different locations should be tied together with copper foil tape, with joints that are mechanically sound *and soldered.*

Always choose flat tape over round cables in a ground system, since round surfaces are less effective as a ground counterpoise. The tape itself should be folded rather than rolled around corners. Make all equipment connections to ground with the same tape. To connect to a single terminal on the back of a piece of

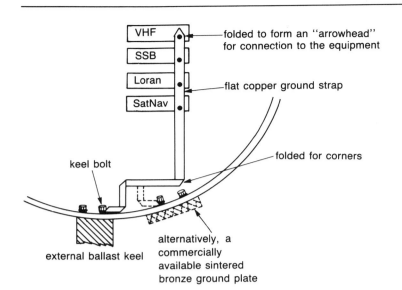

Figure 7-6. **Radio grounds.** Any boat with a solid ballast casting—internal or external—can use this as a ground by connecting to a keel bolt as shown here, or by tapping directly into the casting. Boats with an inadequate ground plane can use a sintered bronze ground plate—always get the largest practical size plate. You can't have too much ground plane.

equipment, fold the tape into an arrowhead and drill it to fit over the terminal. Ground *all* pieces of radio equipment in this fashion—receivers, transmitters, antenna tuners, radar, etc.

For boats with an inadequate ground plane, *sintered*-bronze ground plates are available. These are made of a porous bronze that allows seawater to permeate the whole plate, increasing its actual surface area many times over its external dimensions. A relatively small plate (12 by 3 inches, or 300 by 75 mm) theoretically has a total surface area of several square feet. There is some debate as to the efficacy of these plates in real use, so it is always best to get the largest practical size. You can't have too much ground plane.

Radio Interference

The abundance of radio-based equipment on modern pleasureboats and the plethora of circuits in close proximity to one another (antenna cables, power cables, engine-charging circuits, AC circuits, etc.) make interference problems increasingly commonplace.

Interference is caused by unwanted radio frequency energy, much of it generated on board, although a small proportion can be traced to external origins. This energy is picked up by antenna systems and wiring circuits and fed to receivers, which will not be able to distinguish between noise and signal if they share similar frequencies. Hissing, buzzing, crackling, popping, and other undesirable noises on radios will compete with the true signal, perhaps making it unintelligible. Depth sounders and radio direction finders (RDF) may give false readings, and lines and ripples are likely on TV screens. The SNR (signal-to-noise ratio) meter on a Loran will show a loss of signal when equipment generates interference on its wavelength.

Interference is transmitted principally by conduction and radiation. Conducted interference flows from its source through wiring circuits directly to receivers; radiated interference is picked up by wiring circuits acting as antennas and then con-

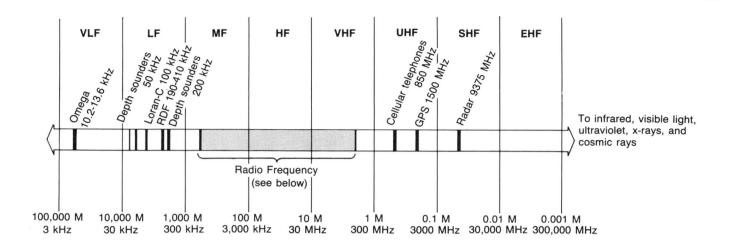

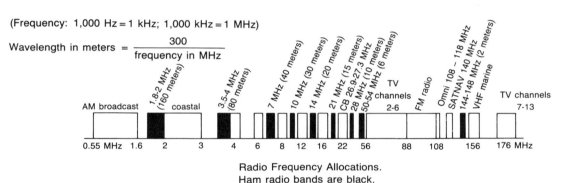

(Frequency: 1,000 Hz = 1 kHz; 1,000 kHz = 1 MHz)

$$\text{Wavelength in meters} = \frac{300}{\text{frequency in MHz}}$$

Radio Frequency Allocations.
Ham radio bands are black.

Figure 7-7. **The frequency spectrum, including the radio frequencies commonly used by boats.**

ducted to receivers. Wires conducting interference can themselves act as antennas, re-radiating the signal and creating a complex of radiated and conducted signals (Figure 7-8).

Sources of Interference

The principal sources of onboard interference are:

- Alternators and generators (dynamos)
- Mechanical and solid-state voltage regulators
- Ignition systems on gasoline engines
- Electric tachometers
- Static electricity from rotating propeller shafts
- Electric motors, especially those with commutators and brushes (DC motors used in pumps, electric winches, etc.)
- Sparks at switch contacts

- AC voltage peaks superimposed on DC circuits (mostly through alternators, battery chargers, and fluorescent lights)
- Televisions, microcomputers, radar inverters, and modulators

Anything that generates sparks or voltage pulses—even loose rigging—can generate interference.

Tracking Down Interference

To track down interference in a radio or some other electronic gear, leave it switched on (or tune a hand-held RDF to the interference frequency) and shut off all the boat's circuits one at a time: fluorescent lights, the engine, AC circuits, etc. If the interference ceases at any point, the offending circuit has been pinpointed. If it continues when all circuits are shut down, the interference probably is coming from adjacent boats or shoreside. But note: Radio interference, particularly as affects

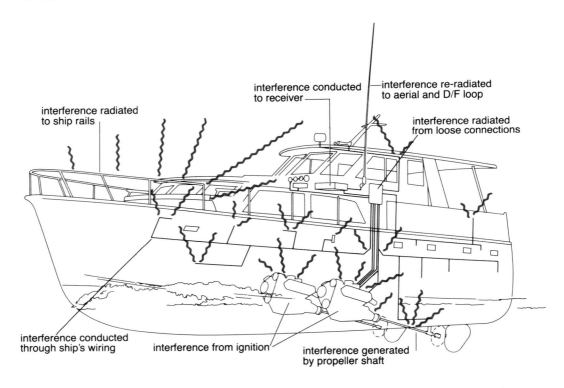

Figure 7-8. Interference is caused by unwanted radio frequencies; receivers cannot distinguish between noise and signal if they share a similar frequency.

interference conducted to receiver

interference re-radiated to aerial and D/F loop

interference radiated to ship rails

interference radiated from loose connections

interference conducted through ship's wiring

interference from ignition

interference generated by propeller shaft

medium-frequency units such as SSB, Loran, or ham radios, may be generated by sources about which we can do nothing, including sunspots, solar flares, the aurora borealis—even a distant thunderstorm.

A cheap transistor radio can become an effective noise sniffer. Tune it between stations, so that it only picks up interference, and move around the boat close to suspect items. The radio will crackle and hiss louder where interference is generated.

Engines have a number of potential noisemakers (especially gasoline engines), and it will be necessary to precisely pinpoint the culprit. Start with the alternator or generator (dynamo). If it has external field leads, disconnect these and the main output terminal to disable it; otherwise remove its belt. Crank the engine. If the interference has ceased, it is in the charging circuit. If it persists, it is either in the ignition circuit (gasoline engines) or the result of static electricity generated by the rotating propeller shaft. The latter generally produces intermittent "crackles" as the static discharges, rather than the rhythmic interference keyed to engine r.p.m. associated with alternators and ignition circuits.

Propeller shaft interference can be eliminated by fitting a bronze brush to the pro-

peller shaft and wiring it to ground or to the boat's bonding system. This is a good practice in any case to reduce the risk of galvanic corrosion. Flexible couplings should be bridged with a jumper wire (Figure 7-9).

Preventing (Suppressing) Interference

Since receivers cannot distinguish between a useful signal and noise at the same frequency, interference needs to be suppressed at its source rather than in the receiver. Suppression measures fall into three broad categories: shielding, filtering, and bonding. In addition, certain measures can be taken with the electronic equipment itself.

Shielding. Any wire carrying a fluctuating current (AC or DC) will radiate interference. If the wire forms a loop, the signal will be magnified. But if the wire is encased in metal braid (*shielded*), the unwanted signals will be trapped inside (just as with coax cable, which in fact makes excellent shielded cable in certain applications). Shorting the braid to ground should eliminate the interference, but the

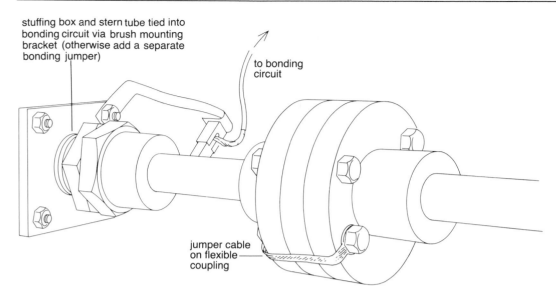

stuffing box and stern tube tied into bonding circuit via brush mounting bracket (otherwise add a separate bonding jumper)

to bonding circuit

jumper cable on flexible coupling

Figure 7-9. **Propeller shaft interference can be eliminated by fitting a bronze brush to the propeller shaft and wiring it to ground (or the boat's bonding system). Flexible couplings should be bridged with a jumper wire.**

braid itself may become an antenna, receiving and radiating signals. Thus it must be grounded *at regular points along its length* to a boat's bonding system. Where shielded cables leave and enter equipment, the braid must make a good electrical contact with the equipment case at both ends to avoid leaks. If individual wires need shielding, it is sometimes possible to slide a piece of soft copper tubing over the wire. The copper tube is then grounded.

Since alternators and voltage regulators are major contributors to interference, many of the more expensive alternator installations are shielded. The alternator's metal case grounds out radiated noise produced within; the various leads to and from the regulator are run through a shielded cable; and the regulator itself is placed in a metal box. A special ferrule ensures adequate grounding where the braided cable enters the alternator and regulator housings. The cable run is kept as short as possible (no loops!) and grounded at points along its length if necessary. The engine, alternator, regulator box, and screened wiring harness are all grounded.

Filtering. Shielding will take care of radiated noise, but conducted noise is another matter. For this, special *filters* are needed, which are a combination of coils (*inductors*) and capacitors.

Radio frequency energy is alternating current; it forms waves of different lengths. An inductor provides a high resistance path to alternating current but of-

fers very little resistance to direct current, depending on the size and length of the wire used to wind the coil. An inductor installed in series in a DC line will tend to block radio frequency energy while passing direct current.

A capacitor, on the other hand, conducts alternating current but blocks direct current. So if we combine an inductor with a capacitor we can "hold up" radio frequencies with the inductor and then short them safely to ground with the capacitor without causing a short in the DC circuit. This is the principle behind filters.

Filters are fitted in hot (positive) leads as close to offending equipment as possible to reduce the potential area for conducting and radiating unwanted frequencies. The filters then are connected to a ground.

Bonding. Note that both shielding and filtering take unwanted frequencies and *short them to a ground.* Bonding all equipment cases and metal objects to a common ground helps to reduce interference by holding everything at the same voltage potential. If there are no voltage differences and a good ground with seawater, there will be no arcing or buildup of static electricity (hence the brush on propeller shafts). Proper bonding is an important part of any electrical installation.

Radio installations. Antennas, antenna cables, and power leads to equipment should be routed as far as possible from likely interference sources, especially engine-charging circuits, fluorescent

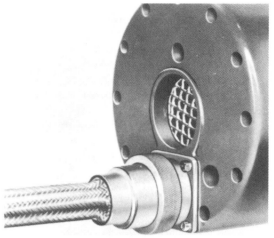

Figure 7-10A. **Voltage regulator screening box.** Since voltage regulators are a major contributor to interference, some are shielded with a metal box. The large threaded fitting (**A**) is where a screened cable screws onto the box. This cable carries all the wiring to the alternator. Any wiring coming into the box acts as an antenna both inside and outside the box, unless effectively filtered where it enters the box. The round protrusions (**B**) are built-in filters for all unscreened incoming wires, such as the battery positive wire. The nut (**C**) is the grounding connection for the screening box itself.

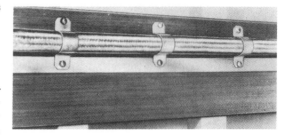

lights, and TVs. The power leads themselves are a potential source of interference. Those supplying electric motors in particular should maintain a three-foot separation from the antenna cables. Ideally, power leads should run at right angles to antenna leads. This may not be feasible, but they at least should not be bundled up with antenna leads. Power leads should be short and large enough to prevent significant voltage drop. Equipment cases should be thoroughly grounded to the bonding system. Finally, an antenna matched correctly to its equipment and tuned efficiently will give the best possible signal-to-noise ratio (SNR) and enable much unwanted noise to be filtered out at the equipment itself.

Specific Measures for Noise Suppression

Effective radio interference suppression involves good design and good discipline in the manufacture and installation of equipment, especially charging equipment. A fully screened, isolated-ground marine alternator fitted properly as original equipment will be far more effective in reducing electrical noise than any number of filters and other devices tacked onto the system at a later date. Motto: Do it right in the first place. It may seem to cost more,

Figure 7-10B. **Screening or shielding techniques.**

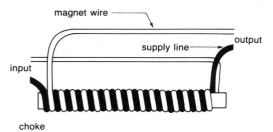

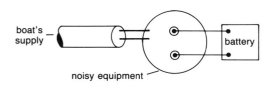

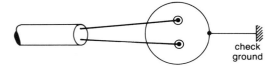

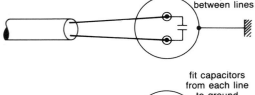

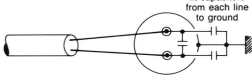

Figure 7-11B. **Making a choke.** (**1**) Use insulated magnet wire (copper) obtainable at radio supply stores. The size depends on the current drawn by the appliance as indicated on the table below. (**2**) Take a length of 3/8-inch ferrite rod (used for portable radio antennas, also obtainable at radio supply stores) as indicated below. The rod can be cut to length by filing a groove in it and breaking over a sharp edge. (**3**) Make 20 turns around the rod with the equipment supply line and magnet wire as shown in the illustration. (**4**) Slip a piece of PVC tubing over the choke and dip it in varnish to seal it. (**5**) Connect both ends of the magnet wire to ground.

Equipment current rating (amps)	Wire size (AWG)	Ferrite rod length (inches)	(mm)
1	23	1.5	40
2	20	2	50
5	17	3	75
10	14	4	100
15	12	5	130
20	11	6	150
25	10	6	150

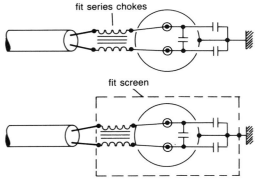

Figure 7-11A. **Specific ways to reduce interference.** (**1**) If possible disconnect the piece of equipment suffering from interference from its power supply and provide power via a separate battery with short leads. If this reduces interference, supply line filters will be effective. (**2**) Next if the equipment has a metal case, make sure it is effectively grounded. (**3**) Try a 1-μF capacitor between the supply leads (positive and negative). (**4**) Connect a 1-μF capacitor from each terminal to ground. (**5**) Make up chokes as outlined in Figure 7-11B and fit these in the supply lines. (**6**) Place the equipment in a screening box and use feed-through filters on all lines. (**7**) If all else fails, try moving the equipment and/or its leads.

but in the long run it not only will be cheaper, but performance always will be better than trying to patch up electrical circuits that aren't working quite right. This will become even more true given the explosive growth in onboard electronic equipment and microprocessors. Having said that, if problems *are* being experienced with interference, one of the following measures may help to bring it under control.

Note: Frequent use is made of pigtail capacitors, which have one "hot" lead and a mounting plate that serves as a ground connection. The lead is connected to the wiring as indicated in the text; the mounting plate is fastened firmly to ground. Leads must be kept as short as possible. *Cut them down if you can;* it will improve the operating characteristics of the capacitor.

Gasoline engines. Ignition systems produce a distinct popping synchronized with engine speed. Specific measures to reduce interference are:

- Fit resistor-type spark plugs (autoparts store).
- If copper-cored (wire-cored) high-tension (HT) leads are used between the distributor and spark plugs, fit *suppressed*

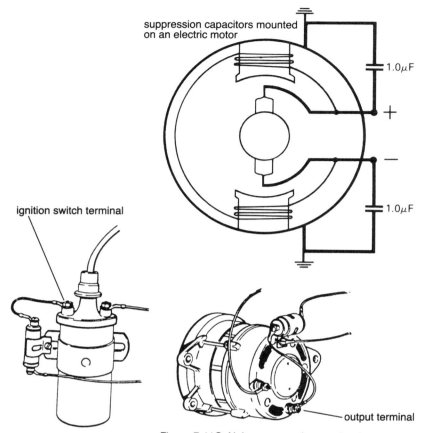

suppression capacitors mounted
on an electric motor

1.0μF

+

—

1.0μF

ignition switch terminal

suppression capacitors
mounted on an
ignition coil

output terminal

Figure 7-11C. Noise suppression on electric motors,
alternators, and coils. Note that radio interference
from ignition systems produces a distinct popping that
is synchronized with the engine speed. Alternator
interference produces whining, whistling, and howling
noises that are tied to the alternator output rather than
the engine speed.

plug caps and distributor end caps, or
else change to suppression/resistance
HT leads.

- If suppression/resistance (resistive) HT
  leads are used, fit *screened* plug caps and
  distributor end caps (autoparts store).
- Install a suppressor resistor (autoparts
  store) in the HT cable from the coil to
  the distributor cap. Mount the coil on
  the engine to keep the lead to the distributor as short as possible. Keep the low-
  tension (LT) and high-tension (HT)
  leads as far apart as possible.
- Put a 1.0-μF (microfarad), 200-volt capacitor (electronics store) between the ignition coil's hot terminal (the one from
  the ignition switch, *not* the one going to
  the distributor) and ground (the engine
  block), or . . .
- Fit a filter at the coil *in series* with the wire
  from the ignition switch. A suitable filter

is a low-pass PI-type LC filter rated at 5
amps (autoparts store).

- Make sure the coil case is well-grounded
  to the engine block.
- If the engine has an electric tachometer
  (taking its pulses from the alternator)
  make sure the tachometer wire is
  shielded properly and the shield
  grounded at both ends.

**Alternators, generators, and voltage reg-
ulators.** These produce whining,
whistling, and howling noises, the intensity
varying with alternator or generator (dynamo) output rather than engine speed.
As mentioned, proper suppression calls
for a fully screened alternator and regulator—an expensive proposition. Failing
this, try the following:

- Clean the commutator and brushes on a
  generator.
- Clean the points on a mechanical voltage
  regulator.
- If the alternator or generator is
  grounded through its mount to the engine block (most are), clean the mounting hinge, which can make an electrically
  noisy connection. Better yet, fit a separate ground strap from the generator or
  alternator to the engine block.
- Connect a 1.0-μF, 200-volt capacitor between the output terminal on the alternator or generator and ground, or . . .
- Fit a filter rated at 60 amps continuous
  (except on high-output alternators,
  where a higher capacity filter will be
  needed), in series with the output line.
- Connect a 1.0-μF, 200-volt capacitor
  from the voltage regulator's battery connection to ground.
- Alternator "ripple" requires heavy med-
  icine: A 10,000- to 20,000-μF capacitor
  (readily available for computers) in parallel with the previous capacitor.

**Electric motors (brush-type; universal,
and permanent-magnet DC).**

- Clean the commutator and brushes.
- Connect a 1.0-μF, 200-volt capacitor
  across the input and output leads as
  close to the motor as possible (inside the
  case if it can be done).
- If this fails, connect a 1.0-μF, 200-volt capacitor from each brush lead to the motor case (Figure 7-11C).

TVs and fluorescent lights.

- Turn off the offending equipment. Newer fluorescent lights have built-in noise suppression circuits; notwithstanding any claims made for them, however, fluorescent lights are still a major source of interference, especially where Lorans are concerned. Two fluorescent lights mounted within 10 feet of one another can set up "harmonics," which magnify problems. Power line filters are available (Marine Technology Inc., Long Beach, CA); these are fitted on the power supply to the light. A screening material can go inside the light cover to block interference radiated from the tubes (see below under "Video displays").

Battery charger hum. Some chargers (particularly cheap, half-wave rectified ferro-resonant chargers; see Chapter 5) can be quite noisy. While experimenting with various chokes and filters sometimes will help, a better approach is to check the battery charger installation itself; in particular, make sure the charger is close to the batteries—no more than 10 feet away—and wired to the batteries with adequately sized cables for minimal voltage drop. Check all terminals, switches, and connections to see that they are clean and tight.

Video displays. CRT display tubes (video depth sounders, raster-scan radars) radiate interference *through the face of the tube* that affects Loran reception in particular. If you suspect this is a source of trouble, cover the display tube temporarily with aluminum foil. If the tube is at fault, the interference will cease. CRT-produced interference can be eliminated by installing a transparent conductive shield in front of the tube. These are made from plastic coated with a very thin metal film and will reduce light transmissions from the tube by around five percent—hardly noticeable—and impart a slight tint. Two brands are Tekfilm, from the Tecknit Corporation, and Altair-M, from Southwall Technologies. Shielding is also available from Marine Technology, Inc.

Loose rigging. Tighten, and if necessary, connect jumper cables across turnbuckles (rigging screws) and shackles.

Saving Soaked Equipment

Salt is the big problem. Salt is hygroscopic—it attracts moisture. Salt combines with this moisture to form an electrolyte that promotes electrolytic reactions between dissimilar metals, such as a piece of wire and its soldered terminal.

In the humid marine environment, any electrical equipment into which salt has insinuated itself is more or less doomed—sooner rather than later. For instance, after a particularly wet and wild beat from Venezuela to Grenada, our autopilot went haywire, making all kinds of random responses. A day later it seemed to be working fine, but then developed a random tendency to go nuts. Although I'm generally reluctant to tear into electronic units, circumstances forced me to take it apart. Eventually I found one tiny grain of salt, no bigger than a small pinhead, which had been left behind by an evaporating drop of water. Every time the humidity rose this speck of salt absorbed moisture and shorted out a sensitive circuit board. I was able to rinse it out with a cotton swab dipped in fresh water, and we and the autopilot have been in business ever since.

Electrical equipment that has suffered saltwater intrusion will need to be opened and flushed thoroughly with clean fresh water. As long as the unit is dried completely before reconnecting to a power source, the fresh water will do no harm—certainly less harm than the salt! If you can't work on a unit immediately, better to store it in fresh water than to let the salt go to work. The problem comes in drying out some of the labyrinthine passages in electronic equipment, and in drawing the water from encased components, such as capacitors.

A good air flow will drive water from many inaccessible areas. An air compressor is best; failing that, use a fan or a vacuum cleaner's exhaust. A prolonged period of low heat—bright sunshine, or perhaps an oven, no higher than 150°F (65.6°C)—may be needed to draw out all the water from individual components. The part *must be dry* before reentering service. Any moisture is likely to create internal shorts and cause rapid and irreparable damage. Before placing the unit on line, test for normal resistances (meter on R × 1 scale); then test between the power leads and equipment case for any signs of shorts.

CHAPTER **8**

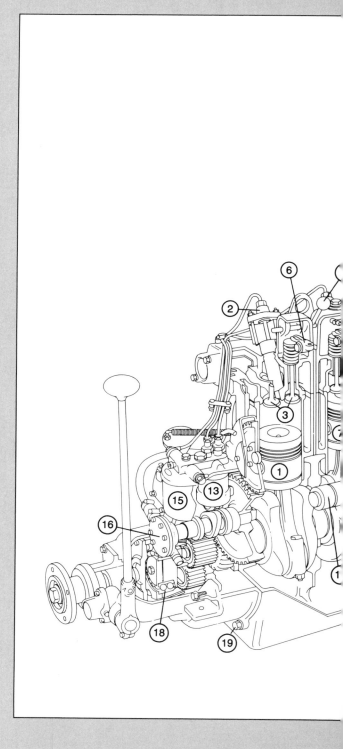

Figure 8-1. Diesel engines can deliver years of trouble-free service—given proper preventative maintenance procedures.

(1) piston
(2) injector
(3) valve
(4) turbocharger
(5) oil filter
(6) valve rocker
(7) pushrod
(8) cam follower
(9) air intake
(10) camshaft
(11) starter
(12) lube oil pump
(13) fuel injection pump
(14) compression release
(15) fuel filter
(16) water pump
(17) crankshaft
(18) cone clutch
(19) oil drain

Diesel Engines

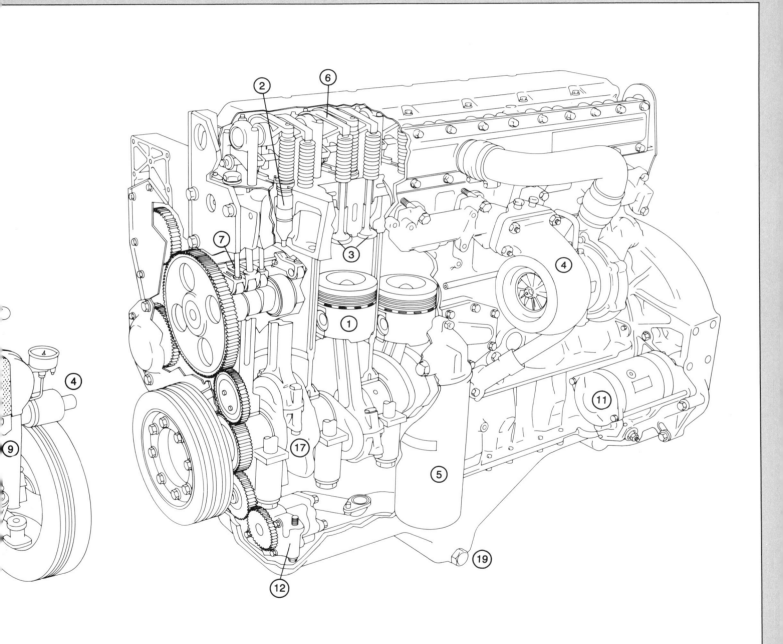

How They Work

Diesel engines are remarkably simple in principle. A piston compresses air in a cylinder, and the more the air is compressed the hotter it becomes. Compression is measured in terms of the *compression ratio,* the cylinder volume with the piston at the bottom of the cylinder compared with the smallest volume (piston at the top of its stroke). At compression ratios between 16:1 and 23:1, air temperature rises to over 1,000°F (580°C), well above diesel fuel's spontaneous ignition temperature of 750°F (400°C).

When the piston is near the top of its stroke, diesel is sprayed (injected) into the cylinder of compressed, superheated air and ignites immediately, raising temperatures and pressures even higher, which drives the piston forcefully back down the cylinder—*a power stroke.*

Four-cycle engines have two more piston strokes in the cycle. On its next upward stroke the piston expels the burned gases through an *exhaust valve;* on its next downward stroke it sucks clean air into the cylinder via an *inlet valve.* The cylinder now is filled with clean air, and the piston is at the bottom of its stroke, ready to start over.

Some diesel engines operate on *two cycles,* compressing the four cycles described into two strokes of the piston, once up and once down the cylinder. The best known are the Detroit Diesel models, widely used in powerboats.

Detroit Diesels have a mechanically driven supercharger mounted in the air inlet; this compresses the incoming air. As the piston nears the bottom of its power stroke, exhaust valves are opened and most of the exhaust gases exit the cylinder. A moment later the descending piston uncovers a series of *ports* in the cylinder wall, and the pressurized inlet air rushes in, driving the remaining exhaust gases out the exhaust valves and refilling the cylinder with fresh air. The piston now has reached the bottom of its stroke and is on its way back up the cylinder. The exhaust valves close and then the ascending piston blocks off the inlet ports in the cylinder wall. The cylinder is full of clean air and a new compression stroke is underway.

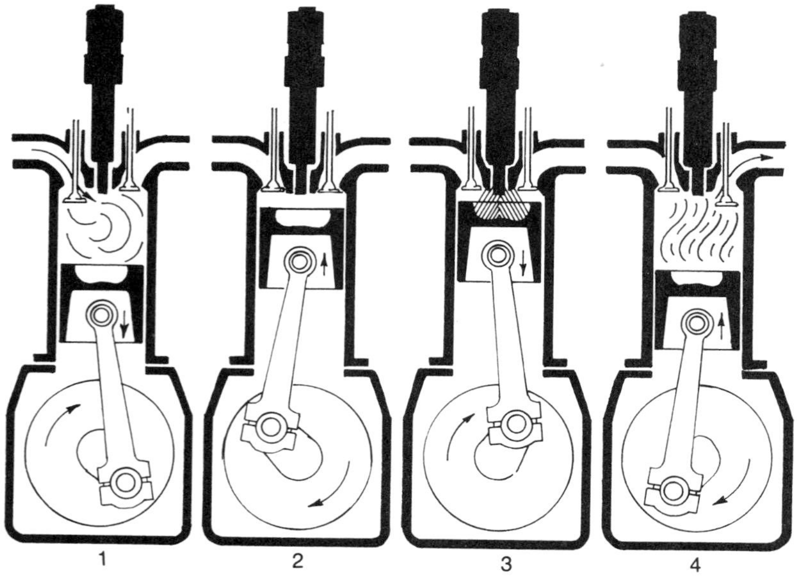

Temperature is Critical

Diesels are frequently called compression-ignition (CI) engines. They do not have a true ignition system. The diesel fuel is ignited solely by the high temperatures attained by compressing air. A diesel engine will never run if the compressed air does not reach ignition temperatures.

Air Supply

Given ignition temperature, all it takes to make a diesel engine run is a supply of clean air and a correctly timed and *atomized* injection of fuel dispersed into a cloud of tiny particles.

A diesel is hungry for air (Table 8-1). Even a small diesel will consume *every hour* enough air to fill a 20- by 20-foot room! An inadequate air supply will produce incomplete combustion, causing the engine to lose power, overheat, and emit black smoke.

Air filters are sorely neglected. A plugged filter restricts airflow through the engine, reducing performance. A ruptured air filter will admit tiny particles of dirt. These become embedded in all the soft metal surfaces of the engine, notably pistons and bearings, accelerating engine wear. Once embedded, no amount of oil changing and flushing will get them out. As little as two tablespoons of fine dust can mean a major overhaul!

The marine environment is moderately free of airborne pollutants, but nevertheless, *check the air filter from time to time.* (See the section on "Air Intake Maintenance.")

Figure 8-2. The four cycles of a 4-stroke diesel engine. (1) Inlet stroke. Air is drawn into the cylinder. (2) Compression. The air is compressed and becomes hot. (3) Injection. Fuel is sprayed into the hot air, ignites, and burns. The high pressure forces down the piston. (4) Exhaust. The burnt gases are exhausted.

1   2   3   4

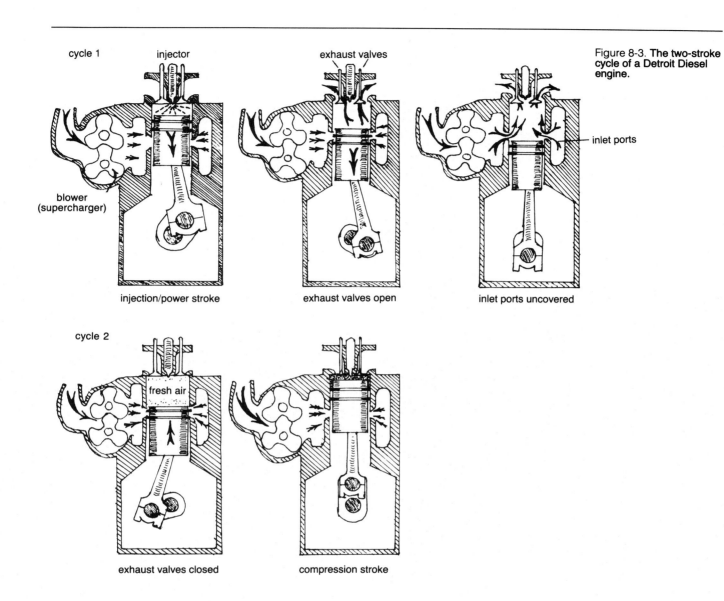

cycle 1

injector

exhaust valves

Figure 8-3. **The two-stroke cycle of a Detroit Diesel engine.**

inlet ports

blower (supercharger)

injection/power stroke

exhaust valves open

inlet ports uncovered

cycle 2

fresh air

exhaust valves closed

compression stroke

Table 8-1. Air Consumption in Four-cycle Diesel Engines. (cubic feet/minute)

The volume of air required by a naturally aspirated
four-cycle engine running at 83 percent volumetric efficiency.

CID[1]/liters	Engine Speed (r.p.m.)					
	500	1000	1500	2000	2500	3000
50/0.8	6	12	18	24	30	36
75/1.25	9	18	27	36	45	54
100/1.6	12	24	36	48	60	72
125/2.0	15	30	45	60	75	90
150/2.5	18	36	54	72	90	108

1. CID = Cubic Inches of Displacement

These figures are calculated with the following formula: $\dfrac{\text{CID} \times (\text{½ engine speed}) \times 0.83}{12 \times 12 \times 12}$

Fuel Systems

A diesel fuel system is a miracle of modern technology. It must meter quantities of fuel as small as a few millionths of a gallon, raise this to a pressure as high as 5,000 psi, and inject it into the engine at a moment in time precise to 0.000015 second—incredibly precise engineering.

Given the close tolerances in the machining of all fuel injection pumps and injectors, a minuscule piece of dirt can do extensive damage. Lucas/CAV, one of the world's largest manufacturers of fuel-injection equipment, estimates that "if right from the start the owner gets rid of dirt and water in the fuel, then *90 percent* of potential engine problems will be avoided."

Regular attention to fuel filters will do more to prolong the life of a marine diesel engine than anything else. Neglected fuel filters can destroy an engine in minutes. When a friend of mine took on dirty fuel, it plugged his filters, which ruptured. The dirt destroyed his fuel-injection pump and injectors, but not before the abnormal injection patterns caused a couple of cylinders to overheat and seize. The repair bill was close to the cost of a new engine—not unusual where fuel-injection systems are concerned.

Water can be as damaging as dirt. During shutdowns, it corrodes precisely machined surfaces; when the engine is running, the superheated air in a cylinder under compression will turn a drop of water in the tip of an injector into explosive steam. Enough force can be generated to blow the tip off the injector!

Oil Changes

Modern diesels run faster, hotter, and at higher pressures than their forebears. They generally have smaller oil capacities; a smaller amount of oil is working much harder. Diesel engine oils are specially formulated to deal with the tougher operating conditions, but even so must be changed far more regularly than gasoline engine oils. Failure to carry out oil changes will lead to a buildup of carbon sludge, dirt, and acids in the crankcase; this buildup is difficult to remove even after repeated flushing.

Sad but true: Almost 50 percent of all bearing failures are due to dirty oil or a lack of oil. Use the best available grade of diesel engine oil and change it at least as often as the engine manual suggests. Whenever changing the oil, change the oil filter.

Preventive Maintenance

Most diesels will run troublefree for thousands of hours given clean fuel, oil, and air. The actual procedures for changing filters are detailed below. There also may be one or two grease points needing regular attention (the engine manual will indicate where) and belts to auxiliary equipment that need to be kept tight (no more than ½ inch or 13 mm of deflection under moderate finger pressure in the center of the longest belt run). Any zinc anodes in the cooling system (the raw-water side—see this chapter's section, "Overheating") need replacing well before they are consumed. If this turns out to be more than once a season, an electrolysis problem needs solving before a heat exchanger corrodes through or some other expensive damage is done.

Most engine manufacturers lay down specific schedules for overhaul procedures; Table 8-2 shows realistic maintenance intervals and can serve as a general guide. The marine environment and engine use are so varied, however, that one engine may need work much sooner than another. For this reason I tend to subscribe to the philosophy, "If it ain't broke, don't fix it!" At the first sign of trouble, however—whether it be difficult starting, changes in oil pressure or water temperature, a smoky exhaust, vibration, or a new noise—get on top of the situation right away; delay may cause expensive repair bills. The section on troubleshooting deals with most common problems.

Air System Maintenance

The air system comprises both the inlet and exhaust sides of an engine. Any obstruction in either side will interfere with the air and gas flow through the engine, thereby reducing performance.

Table 8-2. Basic Preventive Maintenance for Marine Diesel Engines.

Immediately after start-up	Daily (when in regular use)	Weekly (when in regular use)	Semi-annually (or more often)	Annually (or more often)
· Check oil pressure. · Check raw water flow from the exhaust (unless engine has dry exhaust).	· Check engine oil level. · Check fresh-water coolant level in the header tank. (Do not open when hot!)	· Check transmission oil level. · Check pulley belt tensions. · Check any grease points. · Clean raw water strainer, if necessary. · When in dusty environments, check air filter and replace if necessary. · **Change the engine oil and filters** every 100 to 150 operating hours (including any turbocharger oil filter).	· Take a sample of fuel from the base of the fuel tank. Check for water and/or sediment. · Check cooling system zinc anodes and replace as needed. · When in clean environments, check air filter and replace as necessary. · **Change the fuel filters** every 300 operating hours or more frequently as needed.	· Check all coolant hoses for softening, cracking, and bulging. · Check all hose clamps for tightness. · Check the raw water injection elbow on the exhaust for signs of corrosion. Replace as needed.

Some engines do not have an air filter, but most do. Where fitted, the filter needs checking periodically. Just as with an automobile, it is not possible to lay down hard and fast rules on when to change a filter element—in dusty environments, filters need replacing regularly, but in most marine environments, changes will be rare.

Note that the oil in oil-bath air filters (many Detroit Diesels) must be changed regularly. Although it may appear clean, trapped dirt increases oil viscosity and makes the filter less effective. On no account overfill an oil bath—if excess oil is sucked into an engine, it may cause it to "run away" uncontrollably.

Exhaust systems will tend to carbon up over time. When an engine is used for long hours at low loads and engine speeds (e.g., battery charging at anchor), this may happen quite rapidly. Periodically the exhaust pipe or hose should be broken loose from the exhaust manifold or turbocharger and inspected. If carbon is building up to more than a light coat, the whole exhaust system will need cleaning.

Fuel System Maintenance

Clean fuel starts at the dockside. Regardless of the source, fuel should always be filtered. There are some excellent multistage

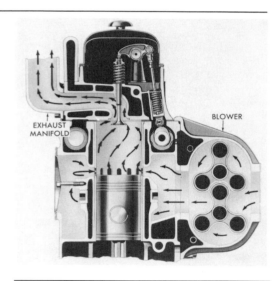

Figure 8-4. **Operation of a two-cycle Detroit Diesel.**

EXHAUST MANIFOLD

BLOWER

filter funnels on the market. Buy one and *use it!* At the first sign of contamination, stop refueling.

The fuel, even if clean when taken on board, can become contaminated in the fuel tank. Moisture from the marine environment condenses and mixes with the fuel. Bacteria can grow in diesel, *so samples must be taken at regular intervals from the bottom of every tank,* either via a drain or by inserting a pump through the tank top.

If water is present, the tank must be drained or pumped. If bacteria are present, the fuel will smell and there will be slimy deposits on the tank sides and in the filters. To combat this, various bactericides can be added. Caution: *Use no additives containing alcohol or any alcohol-based substances (e.g., methanol),* since these will swell the O-rings in the fuel filters and pumps.

Any respectable marine diesel fuel system should have two filters—a *primary filter* (probably with a see-through bowl) mounted between the fuel tank and the engine, and a *secondary filter* mounted on the engine between the fuel lift pump (also known as the *feed pump*) and the fuel-injection pump.

The primary filter is designed to remove water and larger particles from the fuel; the secondary filter should catch any remaining microscopic dirt particles and suspended water droplets. *If your engine doesn't have a primary filter, get one fitted.*

Changing fuel filters. Changing filters is straightforward. First, scrupulously clean the outside of the filter with a lint-free cloth. Next unscrew the filter housing (some have a central bolt; on others the whole filter unscrews). Remove the old element, taking a good look at both it and the bowl for any signs of contamination. If it isn't spotless—as it should be in a well-maintained fuel system—find out where the contamination is coming from and stop it before it stops you.

The filter, its housing, or both will seat on a rubber seal; fit a new seal or make sure the old one is clean, undamaged, and

Figure 8-5. **A simple water trap primary fuel filter.**

Figure 8-6. **A similar filter to Figure 8-5.**

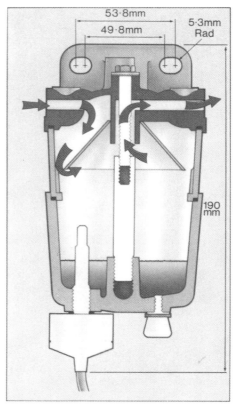

Figure 8-7. **CAV waterscan filters.** Fuel enters around the sedimenter cone, through the narrow gap between the cone and the body, and then passes to the center of the unit and out through the head and outlet connections. This radial flow causes water and heavy abrasive particles to separate out by gravity and collect in the bowl of the unit. There are no moving parts. The electronic probe, fitted in the base of the unit, contains two electrodes. As the level of water increases, it completes the circuit between the electrodes and a warning signal goes off. This signal can be used to trigger a light, buzzer, or other device to advise the operator of the need to drain the unit. A simple thumbscrew drain is provided. The system provides an automatic circuit check that triggers the warning device for a period of 2 to 4 seconds when the system is first energized.

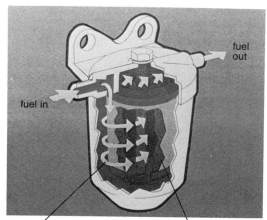

swirling motion
causes larger
particles of dirt
to be thrown out by
centrifugal force

replaceable paper
element

Figure 8-8. Primary fuel filter with 9-micron mesh. This filter differs from the Lucas/CAV filter in Figure 8-7 in that it has a paper element as well.

in place (it may have slipped). Fill the new filter and the filter bowl with clean diesel and screw back on. Snug up tight.

There is a third filter on many engines that is frequently overlooked. It is in the top of the fuel lift pump (feed pump); to get at it, undo the screw in the center of the top housing, and lift the housing off (Figure 8-14).

Bleeding (purging) a fuel system. Anytime a fuel system is opened up it must be bled (purged) of all air before the engine

Figure 8-9. Cleaning a watertrap filter. Before you begin, clean off all external dirt. If the sedimenter uses a gravity feed supply, turn off the fuel before dismantling the unit. Slacken off the thumbscrew in the base and drain the accumulated water and sludge.
(1) Unscrew the center bolt and at the same time hold the base to prevent it rotating.
(2) Detach and separate the base and the sedimenter element. Inspect the center sealing ring for damage and renew if imperfect.
(3) Clean the base and rinse it out with clean fuel oil. Clean and rinse the metal sedimenter element.
(4) Clean out the sedimenter head and inspect the upper sealing ring for damage. Renew the sealing ring if imperfect in any way. New sealing rings may be obtained from the supplier of the filter elements.
(5) Ensure that the center sealing ring is correctly positioned and place the sedimenter element (with the cone pointing upward) on the base.
(6) See that the upper sealing ring is correctly placed in the head and offer up to the head the assembled element and base. (7) Engage the center bolt with the central tube and make sure the top rim of the sedimenter element is seating correctly before tightening the center bolt to a torque figure of 6 to 8 lbs. ft. (0.830 to 1.106 kg. m.). Do not overtighten the center bolt in an attempt to cure leaks. Tighten the drain thumbscrew hand tight only.

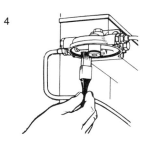

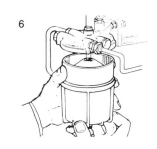

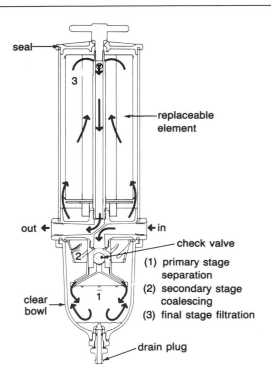

seal

3

replaceable element

out ← ← in

check valve

2

(1) primary stage separation

(2) secondary stage coalescing

(3) final stage filtration

clear bowl

1

drain plug

Figures 8–10A and 8–10B. **Combined primary and secondary filters.**

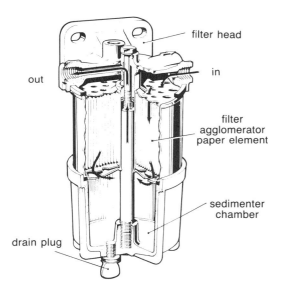

filter head

out

in

filter agglomerator paper element

sedimenter chamber

drain plug

Figures 8–11A and 8–11B. **More secondary fuel filters with agglomeration (coalescing) capabilities.**

200   Diesel Engines

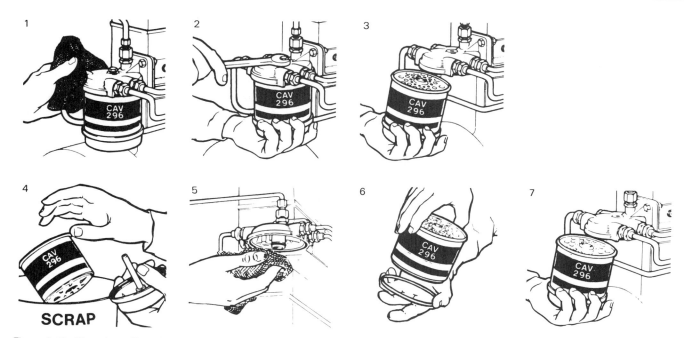

Figure 8-12. Changing a filter element with a replaceable element.
(1) Clean off all external dirt from the unit before attempting to service. Unscrew the thumbscrew in the base and drain off accumulated water and sludge.
(2) Unscrew the center bolt and at the same time hold the base of the unit to prevent it rotating.
(3) Release the filter element complete with base, by pulling the element downward and at the same time turning it slightly so that it comes free from the internal O-ring.
(4) Detach and discard the element. Detach and inspect the lower sealing ring for damage. Renew the ring if defective.
(5) Clean out the sedimenter base. Complete cleaning by rinsing with clean fuel oil. Clean the unit head and inspect both the upper sealing ring and the O-ring for damage. Renew any imperfect sealing ring.
(6) Replacement sealing rings may be obtained from the suppliers of the filter element.
(7) Check that the upper sealing ring and O-ring are positioned correctly in the head and fit a new filter element to the head. Rotate the element slightly when fitting to enable it to slide easily over the O-ring. Ensure that the lower sealing ring is positioned correctly in the base and offer up the base to the assembled head and element. Guide the center stud through the center tube of the element and engage it with the center bolt. Make sure that the rims of the element and base are seating correctly before tightening the center bolt. Do not overtighten.

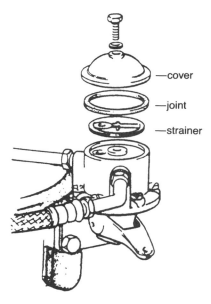

Figure 8-13. (Left) The fuel filter in a lift pump.

Figure 8-14. (Right) Cleaning the lift pump. (1) Remove the cover and joint from the top of the fuel lift pump and remove the gauze strainer. (2) Carefully wash any sediment from the lift pump. (3) Clean the gauze strainer, joint, and cover. (4) Reassemble the lift pump. Ensure that a good joint is made between the lift pump body and the cover because any leakage here will let air into the fuel system.

—cover
—joint
—strainer

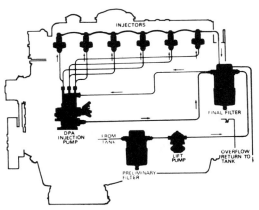

Distributor-type pump

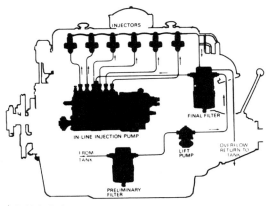

Multiple-jerk pump

Figures 8–15A and 8–15B. **Fuel system schematics.**
Note the two different types of fuel-injection pumps in
common use on four-cycle engines—distributor type
and jerk type. They are easily distinguished since the
fuel lines are arranged in a circle on the former and in
a straight line on the latter.

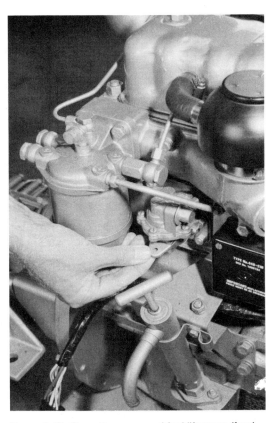

Figure 8-16. **Operating a manual fuel lift pump (feed pump).**

can be run. Some engines, notably Detroit Diesels, are self-purging (see the next section), but most engines require manual purging.

Typical fuel systems are shown in Figure 8-15. The fuel is drawn from the tank by a lift pump (feed pump) and passes through the primary filter. The lift pump pushes the fuel on at low pressure through the secondary filter to the injection pump. The injection pump meters it and pumps exact amounts of fuel at precise times and at very high pressures, down the injection lines to the injectors and then into the cylinders. Any surplus fuel at the injectors is returned to the secondary filter or the tank via leak-off, or return, pipes.

There will be an injection line (also called delivery pipe) from the injection pump to every injector (i.e., to each cylinder) on the engine, but the leak-off pipes go from one injector to the next and then down a common pipe back to the secondary filter or tank. This makes it easy to distinguish delivery pipes and leak-off pipes on most engines. A few, however (notably many Caterpillars), have *internal* fuel lines and injectors which are hidden by the valve cover. In this case each delivery pipe runs from the fuel-injection pump to a fitting on the side of the cylinder head and from there all is hidden (see Figure 8-18A). Detroit Diesels are completely different; see the next section.

The lift pump may have a handle on its base for manual operation. If it doesn't work, turn the engine over half a revolution to free its mechanism. If there is no separate lift pump (it may be incorporated with the injection pump) or no handle on the lift pump, there may be another hand pump, probably attached to the secondary filter.

Between the lift pump and the injection pump there may be one or two bleed nip-

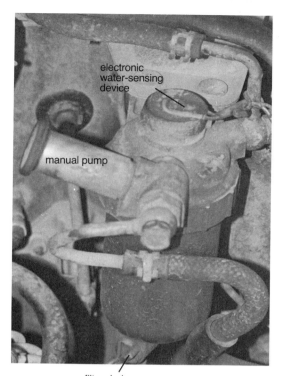

electronic
water-sensing
device

manual pump

filter drain

Figure 8-17A. **Manual fuel pump mounted on a filter.**

Figure 8-17B. **Bleeding a secondary fuel filter.**

Figure 8-17C. **Bleeding the fuel inlet pipe to a distributor-type fuel-injection pump.**

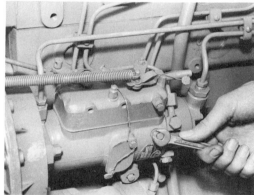

Figure 8-17D. **Bleeding the lower nipple on a CAV DPA distributor-type fuel-injection pump.**

Figure 8-17E. **Bleeding the upper nipple on a CAV DPA distributor-type fuel-injection pump.**

Preventive Maintenance   203

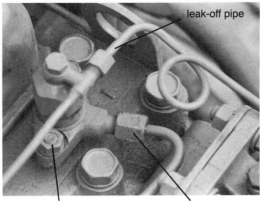

Figure 8-17G. **The location of the injector nut.**

Figure 8-17F. **The bleed points on a Volvo MD 17C.**

ples or nozzles—probably on the top of the secondary filter and on the injection pump itself (it may have two). Open the first in line after the lift pump—i.e., the one on the secondary filter; if it doesn't have one, loosen the connection on the fuel line coming out of the filter. Stroke the lift pump by hand.

Fuel should come out of the nipple or loosened fuel line. It must be pumped out *until absolutely free of air bubbles.* At this point tighten the nipple or fuel line and move on to the next one, on the fuel-injection pump. Repeat the procedure. (If the injection pump has two nipples, do the lower one first.)

Take the trouble to catch or mop up all vented fuel. Diesel fuel will soften and eventually destroy most wire insulation and also the rubber feet on flexibly mounted engines.

The process to date should have bled the system to the injection pump. *Set the throttle wide open* and crank the engine. Within a few seconds it should fire. If not, loosen one of the injector nuts holding the fuel lines to the injectors, and crank again. Fuel free of air should spurt out of this connection at every injection stroke for this cylinder (every second engine revolution on four-cycle engines). If there is no fuel, or if there is air in the fuel, the bleeding process has not been done adequately and needs repeating. On engines with internal fuel lines where the injector nuts are not easily accessible, loosen the nuts on the delivery pipes where they enter the cylinder head.

Detroit Diesel ("common rail") fuel systems. Detroit Diesels do not have a separate fuel-injection pump. Instead, each injector has its own built-in pump. An engine-driven fuel lift pump pushes fuel at moderate pressure into a manifold built into the cylinder head. A pressure relief valve on the manifold outlet maintains constant pressure in the manifold and allows excess fuel to flow back to the fuel tank. Fuel flows continuously through all the injectors. Each injector is actuated at a precisely controlled moment, driving fuel into its cylinder.

A common rail system is self-purging. As long as there is fuel in the tank, a break-free suction line, and a working fuel pump, the diesel flowing through the system will drive out any air. To check fuel flow, undo the return line from the cylinder head to the tank and then crank the engine—a steady flow should come out (not the little dribbles you would see from four-cycle injection lines).

Changing Oil Filters

Most oil filters are of the spin-on variety and require a special filter wrench. These come in different sizes, so get the right one. Clean around the filter housing be-

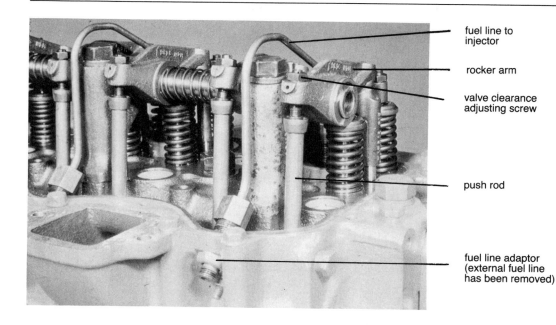

Figure 8-18A. Internal fuel lines. Shown here are fuel lines inside a valve cover and their point of entry into the engine.

fuel line to injector

rocker arm

valve clearance adjusting screw

push rod

fuel line adaptor (external fuel line has been removed)

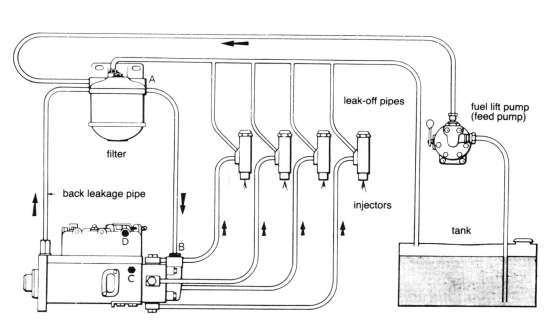

Figure 8-18B. A typical four-cycle diesel engine fuel system with distributor pump.

A

filter

back leakage pipe

D

B

C

leak-off pipes

injectors

fuel lift pump (feed pump)

tank

fore taking the old filter off, and check the sealing ring before fitting a new one. If the ring is built into the filter (most are) make sure the old one is not stuck to the engine. Lightly oil the new one before installing it. Hand tighten and then do up another three-quarters of a turn.

If you do not have the necessary filter wrench (spanner), try wrapping an engine belt around the filter and grasping tightly—it will give you a surprisingly strong grip. Failing this—and in an emergency—hammer a large screwdriver through the filter; it invariably will provide enough leverage to get the filter moving.

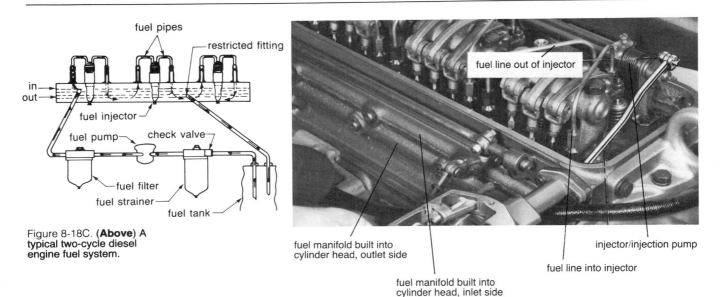

Figure 8-18C. **(Above)** A typical two-cycle diesel engine fuel system.

Figure 8-18D. **(Right)** A Detroit Diesel or common rail fuel system.

Labels on diagram (left): fuel pipes · restricted fitting · in · out · fuel injector · fuel pump · check valve · fuel filter · fuel strainer · fuel tank

Labels on photo (right): fuel line out of injector · fuel manifold built into cylinder head, outlet side · fuel manifold built into cylinder head, inlet side · fuel line into injector · injector/injection pump

Troubleshooting

Engine Won't Crank at All

Starter motor problems. Refer to Chapter 6, "Starter Motor Circuits."

Water in engine. If the starter motor and starting circuit give every indication of being OK, but the engine is locked up solidly or almost solidly, there may be water in the cylinders. *Stop cranking!*

In the past too many raw-water-cooled exhaust systems (see the section on engine exhausts in this chapter) were installed improperly. In certain circumstances, the errors allow salt water to siphon into the engine, filling the cylinders. If the water remains for any length of time, it will do expensive damage to bearing and cylinder surfaces, requiring a complete engine overhaul. If caught in time, the water can be eased out of the exhaust and the engine will continue to operate. If the engine has decompression levers and a hand crank, turn it over slowly several times. Otherwise, just flick the starter motor on and off, turning the engine over slightly and pausing between each crank. Take it slowly—if the process is rushed, piston rings and connecting rods may be damaged. (The engine can be eased over by hand with more control by placing a wrench on the crankshaft pulley nut, or by putting it in gear and using a pipe wrench on the propeller shaft.) Once the engine has turned through two complete revolutions, it basically should be free of water. Spin it a couple of times *without starting it.* Now check the crankcase for water in the oil. If any is present, change the oil and filter. Start the engine and run it for a few minutes to warm it, shut it down, and *change the oil and filter again.* Now give it a good run to drive out any remaining moisture. After 25 hours of normal operation, or at the first sign of any more water in the oil, *change the oil and filter for a third time.*

Put appropriate siphon breaks in the cooling system (see this chapter's section on "Problems with Exhaust Systems").

Engine Cranks But Won't Fire

Problems with starting almost always fall into one of two categories: failure to attain ignition temperatures and lack of fuel.

Failure to attain ignition temperatures.

Cranking speed: No diesel will start without a brisk cranking speed. The engine just will not attain sufficient compression temperatures to ignite the injected diesel. If the motor is turning over sluggishly *stop cranking and save the battery;* you will need all the energy it has.

The techniques outlined in the sections on "Compression" and "Heat" will help generate that first vital power stroke. Sometimes the following tricks also will boost cranking speeds:

- If fitted with decompression levers and a hand crank, turn the engine over a few times by hand to break the grip of the cold oil on the bearings. Assist the starter motor by hand cranking until the engine gains momentum and then knock down the decompression levers.
- Disconnect any belt-driven auxiliary equipment (refrigeration compressors, pumps, etc.) to reduce the starting load.
- Place a hand over the air inlet while cranking. Restricting the airflow will reduce compression levels and help the engine build up speed. Once moving smartly, remove your hand—hopefully the motor will fire. *Never block the air inlet on an operating engine—the high suction pressures generated may damage both the engine and your hand.*
- In *a dire emergency* on an engine with no decompression levers, loosen one or two injectors in the cylinder head so that these cylinders "blow by," allowing the engine to pick up momentum. Once started, tighten them down immediately. On some engines—Volvos, for example—this procedure may loosen the injector sleeves in the cylinder head as well as the injector, which will let cooling water into the engine; this problem demands special tools for its repair.
- An additional trick *for those under sail* is to sail the boat hard with the propeller freewheeling in neutral, then start cranking and throw the transmission into forward. The added momentum of the propeller may "bump start" the engine.

Compression: An engine that grows harder to start over time, especially when cold, is probably losing compression due to poorly seated valves and blow-by down the sides of pistons. The air in the cylinders is not compressed enough to produce ignition temperatures. Short of a "top end" overhaul, there is not a lot that can be done with valves. Piston blow-by, however, can be cured temporarily by adding a little oil to the cylinders. The oil dribbles down and settles on the piston rings, sealing them against the cylinder walls.

Troubleshooting Chart 8-1.
Diesel Engine Problems: Engine Cranks but Won't Fire.
Note: See Chart 6-2 if engine won't crank.

Is the engine cranking slowly? Note: Stop cranking and save the battery! [NO]	[YES] Try the five methods for boosting speed listed in the text under "Cranking Speed". If slow cranking is due to cold, see below. If these fail, recharge the batteries.
Is the engine too cold? [NO] Check cold-start devices. If glow plugs and manifold heaters are working, the cylinder head will be noticeably warmer. Plugs can be tested by using a multimeter, or unscrewing the plug and holding it against a good ground. See text under "Heat" for details.	[YES] Replace faulty glow plugs or manifold heaters; warm the engine, inlet manifold, fuel lines, and battery using a hair dryer, light bulb or kerosene lantern. Raise temperature slowly and evenly—concentrated heat can crack the engine castings.
Is the air supply obstructed? Check any air flaps, air filter, and exhaust seacock for blockage or closure. [NO]	[YES] Open air flap; replace air filter element; open exhaust seacock.
Is the fuel level too low? Check the fuel level in the tank. [NO]	[YES] Add fuel. It will probably also be necessary to bleed the fuel system (see page 199).
Is the fuel delivery to the engine obstructed? [NO] Check to see that no kill devices are in operation; all fuel valves are open; no fuel filters are plugged; the remote throttle is actually advancing the throttle lever on the engine; and any fuel solenoid valve is functioning.	[YES] If stop or kill control has been pulled out, push it in. Check power supply to and operation of fuel shutdown solenoid valve by connecting it directly to the battery with a jumper wire. If see-through fuel filters are plugged, change filters. Open the throttle wide.
Is the fuel delivery to the injectors obstructed? [NO] TEST: Open throttle wide, loosen an injector nut and crank the engine.	[YES] If no fuel spurts out, check primary, secondary, and lift pump filters and bleed the system (Figure 8–17). Check fuel lift pump for diaphragm failure. If fuel still does not flow, go back and check system for fuel level, blockages, and air leaks. Only after all else has been eliminated, suspect injection pump failure.
Note: If fluid spurts out when conducting previous test, make sure it is fuel, not water.	
Is the compression inadequate to achieve ignition temperature? [NO] (a) Suspect inadequate cylinder lubrication or piston blow-by. . . . (b) Suspect valve blow-by. . . .	[YES] FIX: On engines with custom-fitted oil cups in the inlet manifold, fill cups with oil and then crank engine. On others remove air filter and squirt oil into the inlet manifold as close to the cylinders as possible *while* cranking. See "Compression" in text. FIX: If valves are poorly seated, a top-end overhaul is needed.
If you have exhausted these tests, you can suspect incorrect timing, a worn fuel-injection pump, worn or damaged injectors.	[YES] FIX: Replace pump or injectors. Timing problems indicate a serious mechanical failure; correction requires a specialist.

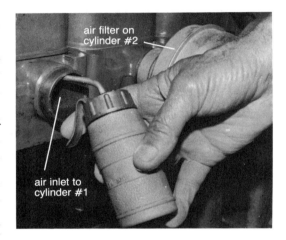

Figure 8-19. **Adding oil to the inlet manifold to increase combustion chamber pressure.**

If there is plenty of battery reserve, *set the throttle wide open* and crank for a few seconds. Then let the engine rest for a minute. Three things will be happening: the injected diesel will be dribbling down onto the piston rings; the initial heat of compression will be taking the chill off the cylinders; the battery will be catching its breath. Try cranking again.

If this fails, or if there is little battery reserve left, introduce a small amount of oil directly into the engine cylinders.

On engines with custom-fitted oil cups on the inlet manifold (for example, many Sabbs), fill the cups with oil, then crank the engine. On others, remove the air filter and squirt oil into the inlet manifold as close to the cylinders as possible, while cranking the engine. The oil will be sucked in when the engine cranks. Then let the engine sit for a minute or two to allow the oil to settle on the piston rings. The engine will smoke abominably for a few seconds after starting as it burns off the oil—this is OK. Put the air filter back in place as soon as the engine fires.

When applying oil to the cylinders, use only a couple of squirts in each cylinder. Oil is incompressible; too much will damage piston rings and connecting rods. Also take care to keep the oil can clear of any turbocharger blades—a touch of the can will result in expensive damage.

Oil used in this fashion is often a magic—albeit temporary—cure for poor starting, but the engine needs attention to *solve* the starting problem.

Heat. The colder the ambient air temperature the lower its temperature when compressed and the harder it is to achieve ignition temperatures. As if this were not problem enough, cold weather thickens engine oil, which makes the engine crank sluggishly. Slower cranking gives the air in the cylinders more time to dissipate heat to cold engine surfaces, and more time to escape past poorly seated valves and piston rings. A battery that puts out 100 percent at 80°F (27°C) will put out at 65 percent at 32°F (0°C), and only 40 percent at 0°F (−18°C). Cold is a major obstacle to reliable engine starting, therefore most engines incorporate some sort of cold-start device to boost engine temperatures during initial cranking.

There is a whole variety of cold-start devices, the most common being *glow plugs* and inlet manifold heaters. Glow plugs are heaters placed directly in the combustion chamber; inlet manifold heaters heat the incoming air via an electric heating coil or via flame primers, which ignite some diesel in the inlet manifold. Additional heat is sometimes provided by heaters in the oil sump, fuel filters and fuel lines.

If glow plugs and manifold heaters are working, the cylinder head or manifold will be noticeably warmer near the individual heating devices. Glow plugs can be checked further by unscrewing, holding against a good ground (the engine block), and turning on; they should glow red hot. Alternatively, use a multimeter (see Chapter 3). Typical amp draw is 5 to 6 amps per plug; typical resistance is 1.5 ohms per plug.

Test amperage by placing a suitable DC ammeter in the power supply line *between the main hot wire and each glow plug* (not in the main hot wire itself, since this may carry up to 40 amps on a six-cylinder engine). Test resistances by disconnecting the hot wire from each glow plug and testing from the hot terminal on the plugs to a ground, using the most sensitive ohms scale. Only a good ohmmeter will be accurate enough to distinguish between a functioning glow plug and a shorted plug.

Any safe means used to boost engine, battery, and inlet air temperatures will help with difficult starting. This includes using a hair dryer, light bulb, or kerosene lantern to warm fuel lines, filters, manifolds, and the incoming air; removing oil and water, warming them on the galley stove, and returning them; heating battery compartments with a light bulb; or removing the battery, putting it in a heated crew compartment, and returning it once it is warm.

A propane torch flame also can be used to boost temperatures by gently playing the flame over the inlet manifold and fuel lines and across the air inlet when the engine is cranked to heat incoming air. *A torch cannot be used in the presence of gasoline or propane vapors.* Do not play the torch flame over electrical harnesses, plastic fuel lines and fittings, or any combustibles.

Raise temperatures slowly and evenly, playing the heat source over a broad surface area. Concentrated heat may crack the engine castings. Boiling water or very hot oil also may cause cracks.

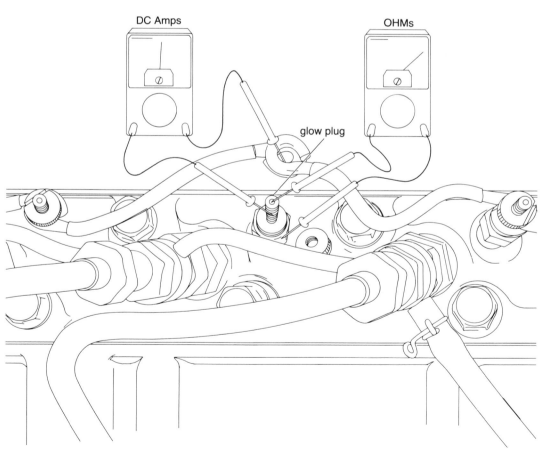

Figure 8-20. **Using a multimeter to test glow plugs.**

Lack of fuel.

Check the obvious. Is the throttle open? A diesel never will start with the throttle closed. Is the remote throttle actually advancing the throttle lever on the engine? Is the cold-start device set properly? If the engine has a "kill" lever, has it been left in the "kill" position? Have any emergency shutdown devices, such as air flaps on Detroit Diesels, been tripped inadvertently?

Is there plenty of diesel in the tank? The fuel suction line invariably is set an inch or two off the bottom of the tank; if the boat is heeling, air can be sucked in even when there appears to be adequate fuel on board. Is the fuel valve (if fitted) open?

Fuel supply to the injectors. Does the engine have an electrically operated fuel shutdown solenoid? If so, it will have either one or two wires coming out of the back of the fuel-injection pump, or a cylinder with one or two wires coming from it mounted close to the pump and operating a lever on the pump. Check the power supply to the solenoid (with the ignition on). If in doubt as to its operation, connect a jumper directly from the battery positive terminal to the solenoid positive terminal. If there is only one wire, it is positive; if two, one will be a ground wire and we want the other one (see Figure 8-21).

Now check any see-through filters and take samples where possible—many filters have a little drain for this purpose. Be careful not to let air into the system, especially with primary filters. If the fuel shows any signs of contamination, change the filters. Remember to check the filter in the lift pump if fitted.

Bleed the fuel system.
Make sure the throttle is wide open, loosen an injector nut (see Figure 8-17G) and crank the engine. Clean fuel, completely free of air, should spurt out of the loosened connection. If not, go back and methodically check the fuel system for fuel, blockages, and air leaks. A complete failure of the injection pump is not likely unless the fuel system has been greatly mistreated; suspect everything else first.

Persistent air. One of the more aggravating problems on many four-cycle diesels can be persistent air in the fuel system. Some fuel-injection pumps (particularly rotary [distributor-type] pumps) are self-purging to a degree; others (notably "jerk-

Figure 8-21. **A solenoid-operated fuel shutdown valve.**

type" pumps) will cease to operate with even small amounts of air. As noted, Detroit Diesels can handle considerable amounts of air.

Sources of air can be poor connections, improperly seated filter housings (especially if the problem occurs after a filter change), and pinholes in fuel lines due to corrosion and vibration against bulkheads and the engine block. Since the only part of the fuel system under a suction pressure is that from the tank to the lift pump, this is the most likely problem area. Sometimes fuel tanks are deeper than the lifting capacity of the lift pump; the pump may fail to raise the fuel when the tank is almost empty, or to raise enough fuel (called fuel starvation) at higher engine loadings.

If the primary filter has a see-through bowl, loosen the bleed nipple on the secondary filter, operate the hand pump on the lift pump if fitted, and watch the bowl. Air bubbles indicate a leak between the fuel tank and the primary filter, or in the filter gasket itself. No air: The leak is probably between the filter and the pump.

In the absence of a see-through bowl, disconnect the fuel line from the lift pump to the secondary filter *at the filter* and place it in a jar of clean diesel. Pump. If there is a leak on the suction side, there will be bubbles in the jar.

Any air source on the lift pump's discharge side should show itself as a fuel leak when the engine is running. When the engine is shut down, the fuel may suck

Figure 8-22. **The diaphragm on a fuel lift pump (feed pump).**

diaphragm cover screw

diaphragm

manual operation lever

in air as it siphons back to the tank. Next time the engine is cranked, it will probably start and die. On rare occasions fuel may siphon back through a defective injector, the injection pump, and the lift pump, but a number of things have to be out of order for this to happen. In this situation there will be no external evidence of the air source, making for frustrating detective work!

Lift pump (feed pump) failure. Most small, four-cycle diesel engines found in boats use a diaphragm-type lift pump (see Figure 8-22). These are basically foolproof, but eventually the diaphragm will fail, in which case little or no fuel will be pumped out of the fuel system bleed nipples when the lift pump is operated manually. Older pumps often have a drain hole in the base (fuel will drip out if the diaphragm has failed), but recent Coast Guard regulations have banned this.

For boats doing extensive cruising, a spare diaphragm—or better still a complete pump unit—should be part of the engine spares kit. Diaphragms are accessible by undoing a number of screws (generally six) around the body of the pump,

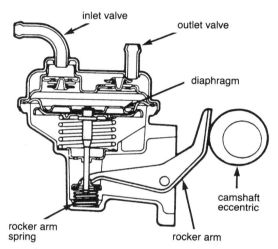

inlet valve

outlet valve

diaphragm

camshaft eccentric

rocker arm spring

rocker arm

Figure 8-23. **A typical mechanical fuel pump.**

Figure 8-24. **A gear-type lift pump (transfer pump).** This pump is fitted to Caterpillar engines and performs the same function as a diaphragm lift pump; since there is no provision for hand pumping, a hand pump is incorporated on one of the fuel filters. Unlike a diaphragm pump, a gear pump will always put out more fuel than the engine requires. The excess is bled back to the inlet side of the pump or fuel tank via a pressure relief valve built into the pump itself, or installed elsewhere in the fuel system.

and lifting off the top half. The method of attaching the diaphragm to its operating lever varies—it may be necessary to remove the whole pump from the engine (two nuts or bolts) and play with, or remove, the operating lever.

Larger engines, and Detroit Diesels, use a gear-driven fuel pump. These rarely fail.

Smoke

Diesel engine exhaust should be clear with the possible exceptions of:

- Sudden acceleration or extra loading (e.g., switching on a belt-driven refrigeration compressor). The engine may give off a little black smoke for a second or two until it settles down.
- Idling or running under low loads. The fuel pump may have problems metering out the minute quantities of fuel needed, resulting in an uneven idle and a little smoke. *Diesels should not be idled or run at low loads for prolonged periods, as they tend to carbon up.* If the engine must be used for battery charging at anchor or dockside, buy a high-output alternator to keep the time to a minimum and, if possible, switch in other loads (e.g., refrigeration) or put the engine in gear. Give the engine some work to do.

Any other smoke is a sure sign of problems. The color of the smoke is a useful guide to the source of the trouble.

Black smoke. Black smoke results from inadequate combustion of the injected diesel. This can arise from a restricted airflow through the engine (plugged air filter, defective turbocharger, or blocked exhaust); too much fuel injected (generally due to overloading—the governor responds by opening up the fuel rack and pumping in more fuel), or improper fuel injection (an injector fails to atomize the fuel correctly, dribbles fuel into a cylinder after the main injection pulse, or injects too late).

Check the air filter first. If the engine has a turbocharger, check all the ducting for airtightness. Remove an inspection cover and check the compressor assembly for carbon buildup. If you find buildup, clean the assembly (see "Turbochargers" later in this chapter), making sure it spins freely with no binding. Open up the exhaust system and look for excessive carbon. Check the exhaust line for any kinks or other restrictions.

Table 8-3. Smoke Color and Its Causes.

Color	Possible Causes

Black	Restricted air flow
	    Dirty air filter
	    Defective turbo/supercharger
	    Plugged exhaust
	Overload
	Improper injection
	    Poor atomization
	    Injector dribble
	    Late injection

Blue	Worn or stuck piston rings Worn valve guides and stems Worn turbo/supercharger oil seals High crankcase pressure

White	Misfiring cylinders
	Water in fuel
	Air in fuel
	Water in the cylinders
	    Blown head gasket
	    Cracked cylinder head or liner
	Lack of compression

Figure 8-25. **An air filter with a replaceable paper element.**

If the airflow is deemed adequate, what about overloading? Is a line wrapped around the propeller? Is the bottom particularly fouled? Are you powering hard into headwind and seas? Has any extra load been placed on the engine recently, such as belt-driven auxiliary equipment, a high-output alternator, or a new propeller?

In the case of faulty fuel injection, remove the defective injectors (following directions in the engine manual) and send them in for servicing. *Make no attempt to work on the injectors.*

Black smoke can also be the result of high exhaust back pressure (see this chapter's section, "Problems with Exhaust Systems").

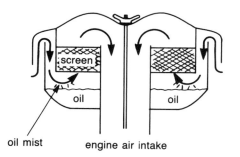

oil mist   engine air intake

Figure 8-26. **An oil-bath-type air cleaner.**

Blue smoke. Blue smoke comes from burning oil. There are only a few paths by which oil can find its way into the combustion chambers—up past piston rings; down valve stems; through defective turbocharger or supercharger oil seals; and out of crankcase ventilators, when there is high crankcase pressure as a result of defective piston rings. Replacing defective piston rings, valves, and turbocharger oil seals responsible for these paths are all beyond the scope of this book.

White smoke. White smoke is indicative of one or more cylinders misfiring, water or air in the fuel, or water in the cylinders (most likely from a blown head gasket or cracked cylinder head). If the smoke occurs on start-up and at light loads but clears when the engine warms, it may be due to condensation or water vapor formed in combustion and is acceptable, but then again one or more cylinders also may have a compression problem and be failing to reach ignition temperatures until the engine warms up. If the smoke develops during normal operation, generally accompanied by erratic misfiring, the engine is running out of diesel or has water in the fuel.

Misfiring

Most diesels run unevenly at idle speeds, even though not "missing," with a fair amount of knocking and clattering. This is normal. Under load, however, the engine should perform smoothly. Rhythmical misfiring indicates one or more cylinders missing all the time; erratic and random misfiring, a generalized engine problem. If the missing is more pronounced at high loads, the fuel filters are probably plugged; if it is accompanied by black smoke, the air filter also is likely plugged.

In the case of rhythmical misfiring, the offending cylinder(s) can be isolated by loosening the injector nuts in turn (with the engine running) until fuel spurts out (see Figure 8-17G). If the engine slows or changes its note, this cylinder is OK. If no change occurs (or no fuel comes out) this cylinder is missing. Note: Don't do this with a Detroit Diesel; fuel will *flood* out.

Overheating

Engines are air cooled (rare in marine use); raw-water cooled (the seawater is circulated directly through the engine—also rare); or heat-exchanger cooled. Engines with heat exchangers have an enclosed ("fresh" water) cooling circuit with a header tank. The cooling water passes through a heat exchanger, which has seawater on its other side, carrying off the engine heat.

Heat exchangers are either inside the boat, complete with their own raw-water circuit and pump, or fitted to the outside of the boat in direct contact with the seawater (called a "keel cooler") and so requiring no raw-water pump.

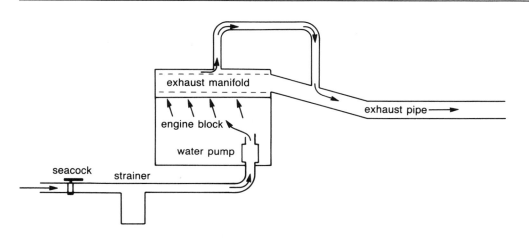

Figure 8-27. **Raw-water cooling.**

Almost all engines with a raw-water pump and circuit pass the raw water through any oil coolers (in the engine and hydraulic gearbox, if fitted) and then discharge it into the exhaust to cool and silence the exhaust (see the next section). (Detroit Diesels include the engine oil cooler and transmission oil cooler in the freshwater circuit.) Even some keel-cooled engines have an extra raw-water circuit specifically to cool the engine oil and exhaust.

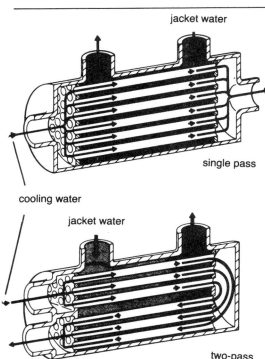

Figure 8-28. **Single-pass and two-pass heat exchangers.**

jacket water

single pass

cooling water

jacket water

two-pass

Overheating on initial start-up. The seacock on the raw-water circuit is probably closed! Almost all raw-water pumps are the rubber impeller (vane) type, most made by Jabsco. If the pumps are run dry, the impellers tear up.

Check the pump drive belt. If this is OK, remove the pump cover (usually six screws) and check the impeller. Make sure that when the pump turns, the impeller is not slipping on its shaft. If the impeller is damaged, pull it out with needle-nosed pliers or pry it out with two screwdrivers; a few have a locking screw. Any missing vanes need tracking down—they will most likely be found in the heat exchanger (if fitted).

If the engine is freshwater cooled, check the water level in the expansion tank. *Never remove the cap when hot;* serious burns are likely.

If the level is low, find out where the water is going.

Overheating during normal operation. Check the oil level. If a low oil level is causing the engine to overheat, expensive damage may be in the making.

The raw-water inlet screen (if fitted) on the outside of the hull may be blocked with a piece of plastic. Throttle down, put the boat in reverse, and throttle up. With any luck the reverse propeller thrust will wash it away. To confirm, loosen a hose below the waterline and see if water flows into the boat. Check the raw-water filter. If there is a lot of silt, the heat exchanger (or engine itself on raw-water-cooled boats) may well be silted up. Many heat exchang-

Figure 8-29. **Heat exchanger schematic.**

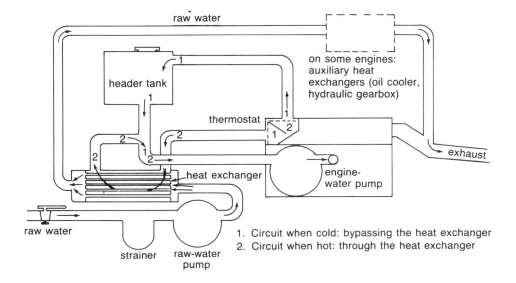

raw water

header tank

thermostat

on some engines: auxiliary heat exchangers (oil cooler, hydraulic gearbox)

exhaust

heat exchanger

engine-water pump

raw water

strainer

raw-water pump

1. Circuit when cold: bypassing the heat exchanger
2. Circuit when hot: through the heat exchanger

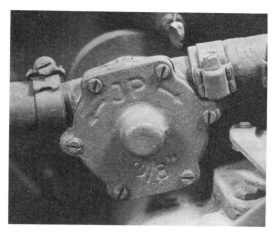

Figure 8-30. **A raw-water pump from a Volvo MD 17C.**

Figure 8-31. **A raw-water filter.**

ers have removable end caps and can be rodded out with a suitable wooden dowel.

Perhaps the engine is overloaded (a rope around the propeller; a badly fouled bottom; too much auxiliary equipment). Maybe the ambient water temperature is higher than normal; a boat moving into the tropics may experience a 40°F (22°C) rise in water temperature, and engine temperatures may rise a little.

The thermostat may be malfunctioning (some raw-water-cooled engines don't have thermostats). It will be found under a bell housing near the top and front of the engine. Take it out and try operating without it. To test, put it in water and heat it. It should open at around 165°F to 180°F (74°C to 82°C) except on raw-water-cooled engines, in which case it should be set to open between 140°F and 160°F (60°C and 71°C).

All raw-water circuits should incorporate zinc "pencils" or anodes to keep corrosion at bay. These must be replaced at regular intervals (see Table 8-2). Failure to do so will lead to electrolysis in heat exchangers and oil coolers, and excess scale formation in raw-water circuits.

Where the raw water is injected into the exhaust (in both raw-water- and heat-exchanger-cooled engines) a relatively small nozzle is sometimes used to direct the water down the exhaust pipe and away from the exhaust manifold. When scale forms in the raw-water circuit, these nozzles tend to plug.

If a boat has been operating in salt water and then moves into fresh water, scale formed in salt water will swell and the engine will gradually overheat. On heat-exchanger-cooled engines with galvanized exhaust piping, check the pipes for a par-

Figure 8-32. **An impeller-type water pump**

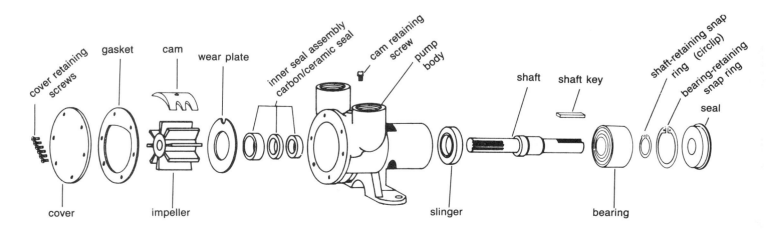

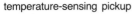
temperature-sensing pickup

thermostat housing bolts

Figure 8-33. **The thermostat housing on a Volvo MD 17C.**

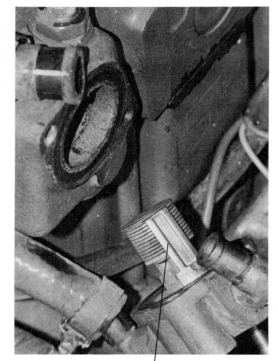

thermostat

Figure 8-34. **The thermostat removed from a Volvo MD 17C.**

Figure 8-35. **A zinc anode in the cooling system of a Yamaha diesel engine.**

ZINC

anode

tial blockage. On raw-water-cooled engines, first look at the water side of the exhaust manifold—a major descaling may be in order!

Raw-water-cooled engines are likely to develop scale around the cylinders over time, especially if run above 160°F (71°C). According to Detroit Diesel, $\frac{1}{16}$ inch of scale on cylinder walls has the insulating effect of $4\frac{1}{2}$ inches of cast iron! Descaling requires professional advice.

Finally, problems with temperature gauges are rare. If suspected, consult this chapter's section on "Engine Instrumentation."

Problems with Exhaust Systems

The exhaust is an integral part of the air-flow through an engine. Any restriction will generate *back pressure*. This will cause the engine to lose power, overheat, and probably smoke (black). Many cruising boats run their engines long hours at light loads, battery charging and refrigerating at anchor. The result: The exhausts carbon up. An exhaust should be broken loose and inspected annually. A heavily sooted exhaust will need cleaning—so will the exhaust passages on the engine, and the turbocharger if fitted.

The exhaust is also a major component of the cooling system, removing about one-third of the engine's excess heat. Raw water from the cooling system is almost always injected into the exhaust. This cools the gases rapidly, which in turn reduces their volume and quite effectively silences them. Silencing is further improved with water-lift-type mufflers (silencers, see Figure 8-37) or in-line mufflers, but these add to back pressure. The alternative is a *stand pipe* (see Figure 8-38) but it requires adequate insulation because the exhaust is hot all the way to the muffler.

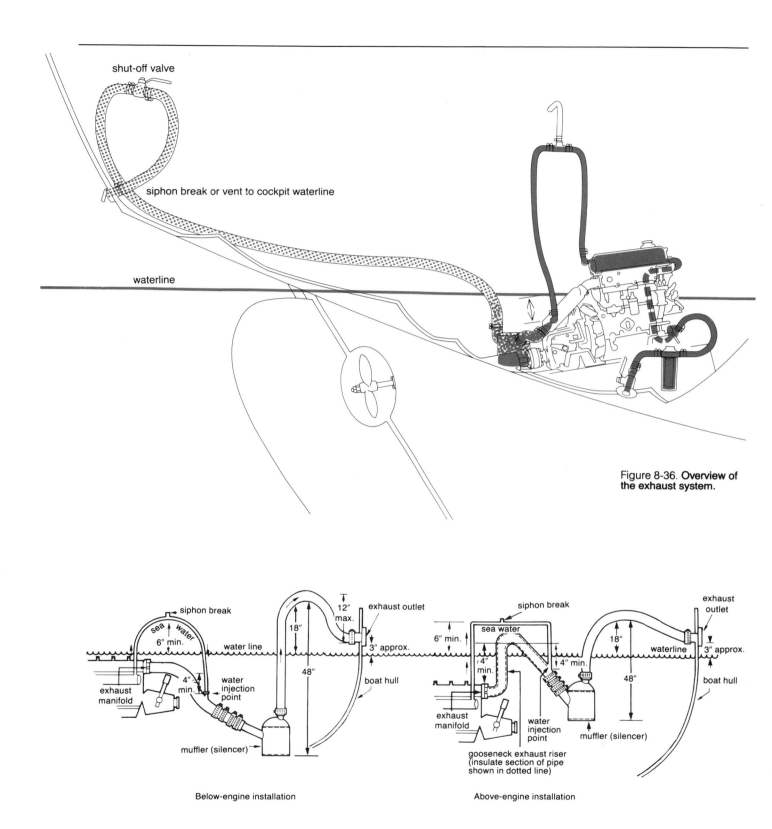

shut-off valve

siphon break or vent to cockpit waterline

waterline

Figure 8-36. **Overview of the exhaust system.**

siphon break

sea water

6″ min.

water line

12″ max.

exhaust outlet

18″

3″ approx.

48″

boat hull

exhaust manifold

4″ min.

water injection point

muffler (silencer)

Below-engine installation

siphon break

6″ min.

sea water

4″ min.

4″ min.

18″

waterline

exhaust outlet

3″ approx.

48″

boat hull

exhaust manifold

water injection point

gooseneck exhaust riser (insulate section of pipe shown in dotted line)

muffler (silencer)

Above-engine installation

Figure 8-37. **Water lift muffler installations.** Note: It would be preferable to fit a shut-off valve in the exhaust line, especially on sailboats, so that following seas can be prevented from driving up the exhaust pipe when the engine is shut down.

Figure 8-38. **A modified wet muffler.**

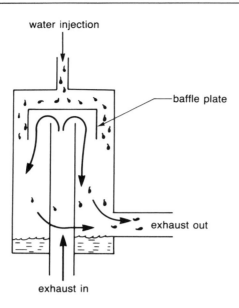

water injection

baffle plate

exhaust out

exhaust in

Figure 8-39A. **A corroded galvanized exhaust elbow. The hot gases and water from the engine exhaust have eaten right through it.**

Figure 8-39B. **The same corroded exhaust elbow patched with rubber inner tube and hose clamps. This repair held for 200 hours of engine running time.**

The combination of hot exhaust gases and salt water is a potent one for corrosion. *Once the water is injected,* good-quality, wire-reinforced steam hose is the best material for exhaust pipes, and fire-retardant fiberglass for water-lift mufflers. However, if the raw-water circuit fails, both materials are likely to burn up, although any high-temperature engine alarm (if fitted) should sound before this happens.

On most engines, the cooling water is injected at an elbow coming out of the exhaust manifold. This water must be fed in the direction of gas flow to prevent splash onto the exhaust valves. The valve closest to the elbow will have a tendency to corrode from water vapor coming back up the exhaust when the engine is shut down.

Sooner or later the elbow itself will corrode through, and so it should be inspected periodically. Carry a spare. A temporary repair can be made by wrapping a strip of rubber cut from an inner tube tightly around the elbow and clamping with two hose clamps or jubilee clips (see Figure 8-39).

On any engine that is below the waterline, both the water injection line and the exhaust pipe present the potential for water to siphon back into the exhaust, fill it, and flow into the engine via open exhaust valves. The injection line must have an effective siphon break. The exhaust pipe can be looped up above the waterline and discharged well up in the hull, and in sailboats, the exhaust should have an *accessible* positive shut-off valve to close it, in case following seas threaten to drive up the back of the boat.

Siphon breaks tend to plug up with salt crystals. Once plugged they are inoperative. They also spray salt water all over the running engine and its electrical systems, adding insult to injury. It is better to remove the valve element (or fit a tee in the first place), add a hose to the top, and vent this well above the waterline (into the cockpit works well).

The higher an exhaust is looped above the waterline, the greater the security from siphonic action, but the greater the back pressure since the cooling water has to be lifted farther. The vertical lift of the cooling water should not exceed 40 inches (one meter) on naturally aspirated engines (i.e., without turbochargers). This corresponds to a back pressure at full load of somewhere around 1.5 psi. On turbocharged engines the water lift should be kept down to 20 inches (half a meter) to give a full-load back pressure of around 0.75 psi.

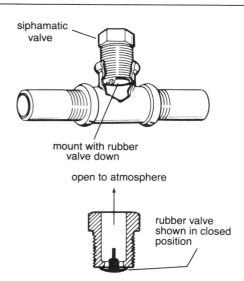

Figure 8-40. **A Kohler siphon break.**

Figure 8-41. **A vented loop on an engine cooling circuit. The hose (top) discharges into the cockpit so that if the vent fails in the open position it will not spray cooling water all over the engine.**

Low Oil Pressure

Low oil pressure is generally the result of worn bearings, but all too often it is the result of a low oil level. Terrible, but true. Other causes may be overheating, which lowers the viscosity of the oil, or putting the wrong viscosity oil in the engine in the first place.

In engines with internal fuel lines, oil pressure will drop if a leak allows diesel to dilute the oil. By the time there is enough diesel to make an appreciable difference to the oil pressure, the oil level should be noticeably higher and the oil will smell of diesel (take a drop of oil off the dipstick, rub it on your fingers, and sniff it). The leak needs fixing and the oil changing.

Note: On a well-heeled sailboat, the oil suction pipe will sometimes come out of the oil and suck in a slug of air. Pressure will drop suddenly and erratically, accompanied by a sudden, alarming clatter from the bearings. Shut down the engine immediately, or put the boat on an even keel. Any sudden bearing failure will cause a similar knock and a sudden pressure drop; immediate shut-down is indicated. Gradual pressure loss over a long time will result from general engine and bearing wear.

A sudden loss of oil—and pressure—from a ruptured hose or blown gasket will be easy to spot. Less obvious is oil loss through corroded oil coolers—the oil will be pumped out of the exhaust, and sometimes water will be pumped into the crankcase. When the engine is shut down, water may enter the oil side. If fittings can be found to bypass the cooler (on the oil side) the engine can still be run until a replacement is found, but keep a close eye on the temperature and pressure gauges.

Oil gauges do malfunction occasionally, but this is the last thing to suspect. This chapter's "Engine Instrumentation" explains troubleshooting procedures.

Turbochargers

Poor turbocharger performance will cause engine symptoms similar to those caused by a plugged air filter: reduced power, overheating, and black smoke. Turbochargers spin at up to 120,000 r.p.m.; the speed of the blade tips exceeds the speed of sound; temperatures are as high as 1200°F (650°C)—hot enough to melt glass. The degree of precision necessary to make all this possible means that turbochargers are strictly items for specialists.

A turbocharged engine should never be raced on start-up—the oil needs time to be pumped up to the bearings. Similarly, never race the engine before shutting it down; the turbine will continue to spin for some time but without any oil supply to

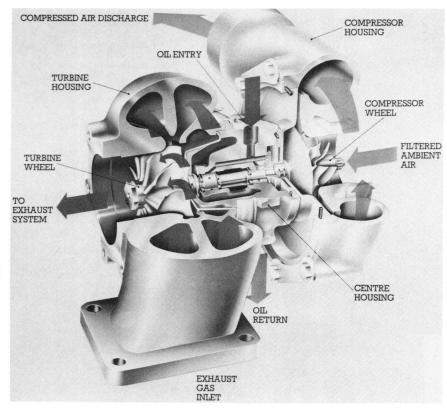

Figure 8-42. **Cutaway view of a turbocharger.**

Labels on figure 8-42:
COMPRESSED AIR DISCHARGE
OIL ENTRY
COMPRESSOR HOUSING
TURBINE HOUSING
COMPRESSOR WHEEL
TURBINE WHEEL
FILTERED AMBIENT AIR
TO EXHAUST SYSTEM
CENTRE HOUSING
OIL RETURN
EXHAUST GAS INLET

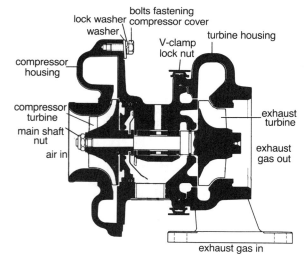

Figure 8-43. **A Holset 3LD/ 3LE turbocharger.**

Labels on figure 8-43:
lock washer
washer
bolts fastening compressor cover
turbine housing
V-clamp lock nut
compressor housing
compressor turbine
main shaft nut
air in
exhaust turbine
exhaust gas out
exhaust gas in

the bearings. Clean oil is critical to turbocharger life—the bearings will be one of the first things to suffer from poor oil change procedures. (Note: Some turbochargers have their own oil filters, which should be changed at the same time as the engine oil filter.)

Before condemning a turbocharger you can make the following tests:

1. Start the engine and listen to it. If a turbocharger is cycling up and down in pitch, there is probably a restriction in the air inlet (most likely a plugged filter). A whistling sound is quite likely produced by a leak in the inlet or exhaust piping.

2. Stop the engine and remove the inlet and exhaust pipes from the turbine housings. (These are the pipes going into the *center* of the turbine housings.) This will give a view of the turbine wheels. With a flashlight check for chipped or bent blades, rub marks on the wheels or housings, excessive dirt on the wheels, or oil in the housings. The latter may indicate oil-seal failure, but first check for other possible sources, such as oil coming up a crankcase breather into the air inlet, or a plugged oil drain from the turbocharger itself, which will cause oil to leak into the turbine housings.

3. Push in on the wheels and turn them to feel for any rubbing or binding. Do this from both sides.

If these tests reveal no problems, the turbocharger is probably OK. If it failed on any count (except dirty turbine blades), it should be removed as a unit and sent in for repair.

Cleaning turbine blades. Mark both housings and the center unit with scribed lines so that they can be put back together in the same relationship to one another. Allow the unit to cool before removing any fasteners or it may warp. If the housings are held on with large snap rings (circlips), leave them alone—they will come apart easily enough but will require a hydraulic press to put back together! Those held with bolts and large clamps can be taken apart.

If the housings are difficult to break loose, tap them with a soft hammer or mallet. Pull them off squarely to avoid bending any turbine blades. Turbines can be cleaned with noncaustic solutions only (de-

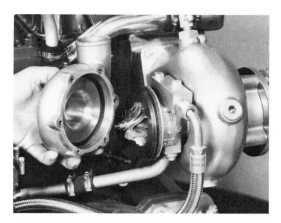

Figure 8-44. **Removing a turbocharger housing.**

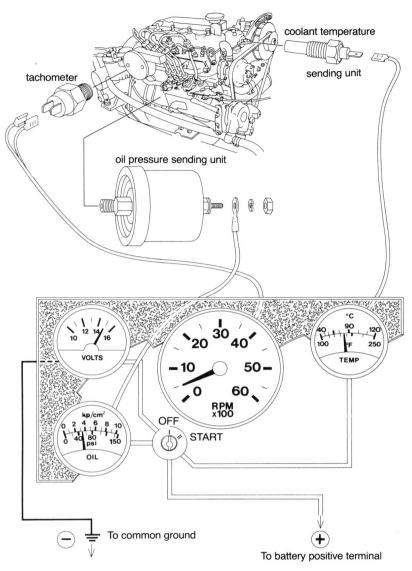

Figure 8-45. **How the typical instrument panel receives information from the engine.**

greasers work well) using soft bristle brushes and plastic scrapers. Do not use abrasives; resultant damage to the blades will upset the critical balance of the turbines. Make no attempt to straighten bent blades—the turbocharger demands a specialist's help.

After reassembly spin the turbines by hand to make sure they are turning freely. Before starting the engine, crank it for a while to get oil up to the turbocharger bearings.

Engine Instrumentation

Some engines are still found with thermometer-type temperature gauges and mechanical pressure gauges and tachometers. All will have some kind of a metal tube from the engine block to the back of the gauge. Gauge failure is normally self-evident—the gauge generally sticks in one position. Temperature gauges and their sensing bulbs have to be replaced as a complete unit; oil pressure gauges may just have a kinked sensing line; tachometers a broken inner cable.

Most engines today use *electronic* instruments comprising a *sending unit* on the engine block, transmitting a signal to a gauge, warning light, or alarm. Problems are not quite so straightforward.

Warning lights and alarms. Ignition warning lights are explained on page 45. All other alarms and warning lights use a simple switch. Positive current from the battery is fed via the ignition switch to the alarm or warning light and down to a switch on the engine block. If the engine reaches a preset temperature, or oil pressure drops below a preset level, the switch closes and completes the circuit.

Most switches (sending units) are the earth-return type—i.e., grounded through the engine block. However, some are for use in insulated circuits, in which case they have a separate ground wire. An insulated return is preferred in marine use, especially when connected to gauges (as opposed to warning lights or alarms). Anytime the ignition is "ON" a small current is flowing through a gauge circuit, which may contribute to stray-current corrosion if grounded through the engine block. A warning light or alarm circuit is different

W = warning light or alarm wire
G = gauge wire

Sending Units

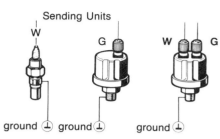

ground ⏚   ground ⏚   ground ⏚

Figure 8-46. Sending units for alarms and gauges. **Left:** Simple sensor with a warning contact "W," as used, for example, for oil pressure warning lights in engines. **Middle:** Sensor with measuring contact "G" for a display instrument. This provides continuous value for a given operational condition. **Right:** Sensor with both W and G contacts for continuous instrument display and for warning when a critical value has been reached.

Warning light or alarm

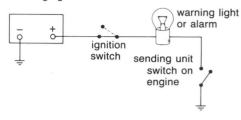

Gauge

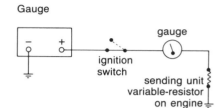

Combined alarm and gauge

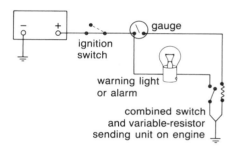

Combined alarm and gauge (another approach)

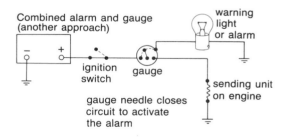

Figure 8-47A. Warning light, alarm, and gauge circuits; electronic gauges.

in that the circuit only conducts when the light or alarm is activated and therefore in normal circumstances will not contribute to stray-current corrosion. Many sending units incorporate both an alarm switch and a variable resistor, which connects to a gauge. In this case there will be two wires on an earth-return unit, and three on an insulated unit. If problems are suspected with an alarm or warning light, *turn on the ignition switch and:*

1. Test for 12 volts between the alarm or light positive terminal and its negative terminal (or a good ground on the engine block if there is no negative connection). No volts: The ignition circuit is faulty. 12 volts: Proceed to the next step.

2. To test the alarm or light itself disconnect the wire from the sending unit and short it to a good ground. The alarm or light should come on. If not, make the same test from the second terminal on the back of the alarm or light (the one with the wire going to the sending unit) to a good ground. No response: The alarm or light is faulty. Response: The wiring to the sending unit is bad.

3. If the alarm or light and its wiring are in order, the sending unit itself may be shorted (the alarm or light stays on all the time) or open-circuited (it never comes on, even when it should). Switch off the ignition, disconnect all wires from the sending unit, and test with an ohmmeter on the R × 1 scale from the

sending unit terminal to a good ground. A temperature warning unit should read infinite ohms unless the engine is overheated, in which case it reads zero. An oil warning unit reads zero with the engine shut down and infinite ohms at normal operating pressures.

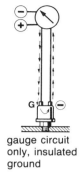

Figure 8-47B. **An insulated-return gauge circuit, similar to the gauge circuit in Figure 8-47A, but with a separate ground wire. This reduces the potential for stray-current corrosion.**

gauge circuit only, insulated ground

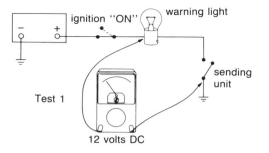

Test 1

12 volts DC

Figure 8-48. **Testing a warning light or alarm circuit.**

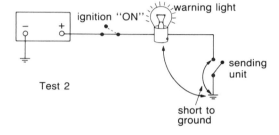

Test 2

short to ground

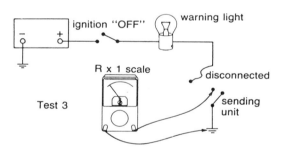

Test 3

R x 1 scale

disconnected

Temperature and oil pressure gauges.

Positive current is fed from the battery via the ignition switch to the gauge and from there down to a variable resistor on the engine block and then to ground.

To test a gauge: Turn on the ignition switch and:

1. Test for 12 volts from the gauge positive terminal to a good ground. No volts: The ignition switch circuit is faulty. 12 volts: Proceed to the next step.
2. Disconnect the sensing line that goes to the sending unit *from the back of the gauge.* A temperature gauge should go to its lowest reading; an oil pressure gauge to its highest reading.
3. Connect a jumper (a screwdriver will do) from the sensing line terminal on the gauge to the negative terminal on the gauge (or a good ground on the engine block if there is no negative terminal). A temperature gauge should go to its highest reading; an oil pressure gauge to its lowest reading.

If the gauge passed these tests it is OK. Reconnect the sensing line and disconnect it at the sending unit on the engine. A *temperature gauge* should go to its lowest reading, an oil pressure gauge to its highest reading. Short the sensing line to the engine block. A temperature gauge should go to its highest reading, an oil pressure gauge to its lowest reading. If not, the sensing line is faulty (shorted or open-circuited).

To test sending unit: Switch off the ignition, disconnect all wires, and test with an ohmmeter on the R × 1 scale from the sending unit terminal to a good ground. A temperature sender varies from around 700 ohms at low temperatures through 200 to 300 ohms at around 100°F (40°C), down to almost zero ohms at high temperatures: 250°F (120°C). An oil pressure sender varies from around zero ohms at no pressure to around 200 ohms at high pressure.

Tank level gauges (electronic).

A float is put in the tank either in a tube or on a hinged arm. As the level comes up, the float or arm rises, moving a contact arm on a variable resistance (a kind of rheostat). Positive current is fed from the battery via the ignition switch to the gauge, down to the resistor, and from there to ground. The gauge registers the changing resistance.

The same tests apply to the gauge, the sensing line, and the sending unit as for an

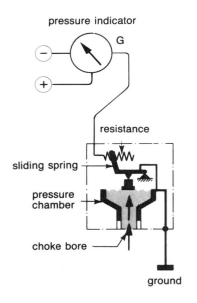

pressure indicator

G

resistance

sliding spring

pressure chamber

choke bore

ground

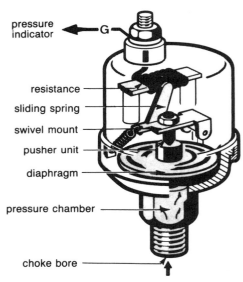

pressure indicator ◄— G

resistance

sliding spring

swivel mount

pusher unit

diaphragm

pressure chamber

choke bore

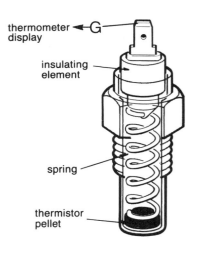

thermometer display ◄— G

insulating element

spring

thermistor pellet

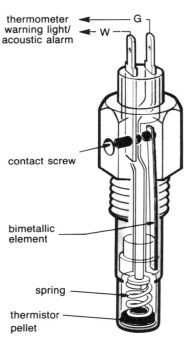

thermometer warning light/ acoustic alarm ◄— G
◄— W

contact screw

bimetallic element

spring

thermistor pellet

Figure 8-49. **How pressure is measured.** As in all indirect systems of measurement, this system consists of a sensor, a sensor transmission line, and a display instrument. An almost "stepless" resistance is picked up by a sliding contact and then transmitted to the display device. The sliding arm is activated by a pressure membrane, which is in turn acted on by the pressurized medium (oil, water, etc.). By means of a choke bore at the inlet of the pressure sensor, an adequate level of damping is achieved. The display instrument is a cross-coil measuring device. Here too there is a possible combination with a warning contact for visual or acoustic alarm systems. For more information please refer to the section on measuring oil pressure. **Top:** schematic representation of the pressure sensor. The membrane is actuated by the pressure. The movement is transmitted via a lever system to the sliding spring, which scans a resistance and transmits the value to a measuring system. **Bottom:** section through a pressure sensor of the type used for engine oil, transmission oil, and coolant pressure measurement. It can also be fitted with a warning contact.

Figure 8-50. **How temperature is measured.** The temperature measuring system comprises a sensor, a sensor transmission line, and a display device, and it functions on the principle of resistance measurement. An appropriate resistance is placed in the temperature sensor. This resistance (known as thermistor pellet) changes considerably as temperature changes. This method of measuring is ideal for the temperature range of $-40°C$ to $+200°C$ ($-40°F$ to $+328°F$) as the entire spectrum of temperature measurements (air, water, coolant, oil, etc.) can be carried out. The thermistor pellet is connected in sequence to the display instrument, a cross-coil measuring device, the scale of which is shown in degrees Centigrade/ Fahrenheit. In addition, the sensor also can be fitted with a warning contact. This warning contact is in the form of a switch activated by a bimetal element, which at a predetermined critical temperature level closes a circuit actuating either an acoustic alarm or a warning light (lamp).

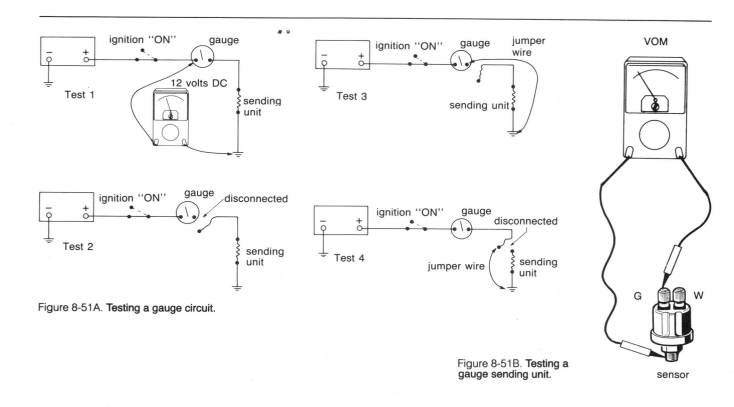

Figure 8-51A. **Testing a gauge circuit.**

Figure 8-51B. **Testing a gauge sending unit.**

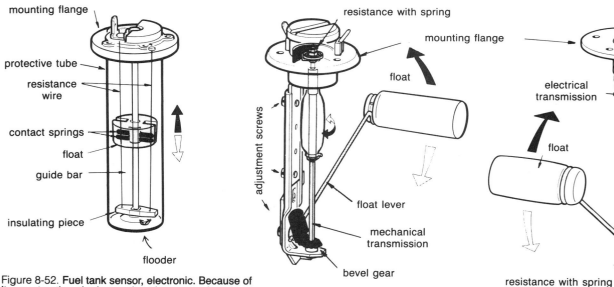

Figure 8-52. **Fuel tank sensor, electronic.** Because of its construction, the immersion pipe sensor is only suitable for use with fuel tanks. The float unit is mounted on the guide bar and makes contact with the two resistance wires by the contact springs. In this way, the resistance will vary in proportion to the level of the liquid and this variation is displayed in an analog converted form at the fuel gauge. The protective tube and the flooder provide excellent damping.

Also shown here are the typical differences between the water tank sensor (**left**) and the fuel tank sensor (**right**). For electrically conductive media, the electrical resistance element must be positioned in the assembly flange. The level of the liquid is then transmitted mechanically up to the element.

Figure 8-53. Pneumatic
tank level sensor.

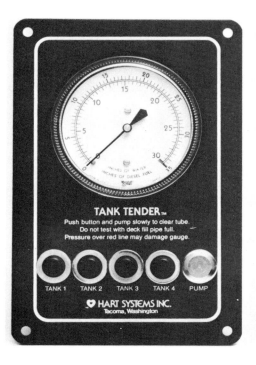
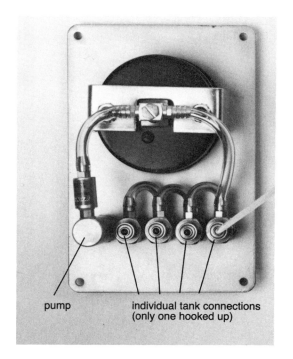

pump   individual tank connections
                        (only one hooked up)

oil pressure gauge. Sending unit resistances are also similar—near zero ohms on an empty tank, up to around 200 ohms for a full tank.

Should everything check out OK, but the unit always reads "empty," the float on the sending unit is probably saturated or else there is a mechanical failure—for instance, a broken or jammed arm. A saturated float can be made temporarily serviceable by strapping a piece of *closed-cell* foam to it.

Pneumatic level sensors. These are relative newcomers on the market but are likely to become very popular due to their versatility and simplicity. A tube is inserted to the bottom of the tank and connected to a small hand pump mounted on the tank gauge panel. The gauge itself is teed into the tube just below the pump.

When the pump is operated, air is forced down the tube and bubbles out into the tank. Depending on the level in the tank (and hence in the tube) more or less pressure is needed to drive all the fluid out of the tube. The gauge registers this pressure in "inches of water" (in the tank) or

"inches of diesel." The gauge only works while the hand pump is being stroked slowly. A table is drawn up converting the gauge reading to gallons. (The conversion will vary from tank to tank depending on tank size and shape.) The gauges come with instructions on how to draw up this table. Where the instructions are missing, or with odd-shaped tanks, the best bet is simply to empty the tank, then to keep adding known quantities of fluid (e.g., five gallons at a time), stroking the hand pump and noting the gauge reading after each addition.

Pneumatic level gauges are more accurate than electronic gauges. What is more, apart from leaking connections or kinked tubes there is nothing to go wrong. As many as 10 tanks can be measured with one gauge by simply switching the gauge and pump into the individual tank tubes. Since there is no fluid in the tubes beyond the level in the tank itself, there is no possibility of cross-contamination from one tank to another. This means diesel and water tanks both can be measured with the same unit.

Troubleshooting Chart 8-2. Diesel Engine Problems: An Overview

Cause	Poor starting	Low compression	Lack of fuel	Low cranking speed	Knocks	Black Smoke	Blue smoke	White smoke	Misfiring	Poor idle	Overheating	Loss of power	High exhaust back pressure	Low oil pressure	Rising oil level	Excessive oil consumption	Seizure
Throttle closed	●																
Fuel shut-off solenoid inoperative	●																
Lift pump diaphragm holed	●		●												●		
Plugged fuel filters	●		●														
Air in fuel lines	●		●														
Empty fuel tank	●		●														
Dirty fuel	●		●		●	●											
Defective injectors	●					●		●	●	●		●					
Poor fuel quality	●							●									
Injection pump leaking by	●					●											
Injection timing incorrect	●				●			●				●					
Too much fuel injected						●						●					
Piston blow-by	●	●					●		●	●		●				●	
Dry cylinder walls	●	●					●									●	
Valve blow-by	●	●							●			●					
Decompressor levers on	●	●															
Valve clearances wrong	●	●							●	●		●					
Valves sticking in guides	●	●							●	●						●	
Preheat device inoperative	●							●									
Worn valve stems							●		●							●	
Plugged air filter	●					●						●	●				
Plugged exhaust / turbocharger						●					●	●	●				
Kink in exhaust hose													●				
Oil level low							●							●		●	●
Wrong viscosity oil				●										●		●	●
Diesel dilution of oil							●							●	●		
Dirt in oil														●			●
Defective oil pressure relief valve														●			
Defective pressure gauge														●			
Defective water pump											●						●
Air bound pump valves											●						●
Closed sea cock											●						●
Plugged raw water filter											●						●
Plugged cooling system											●						●
Blown head gasket / cracked head		●				●		●	●		●				●		●
Water in cylinders							●	●	●						●	●	
Uneven load on cylinders					●						●						
Worn bearings				●													
Seized piston	●			●													●
Auxiliary equipment engaged				●													
Battery low / loose connections	●			●													
Engine overload / rope in prop.											●						●

Figure 8-54. **Winter lay-up.**

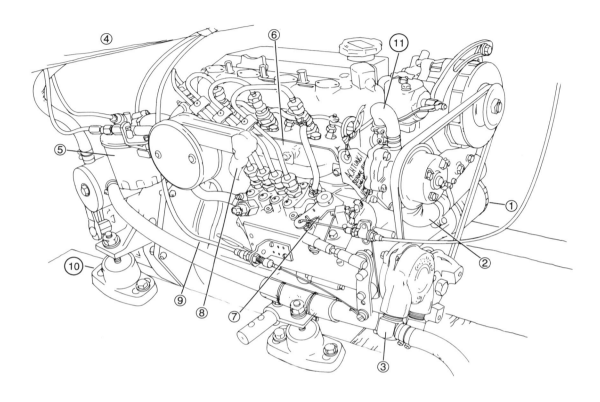

Winter Lay-Up

1. Change the oil at the *beginning* of the winter, not the end. The oil will contain all kinds of harmful acids and contaminants. You don't want them going to work on the engine all winter long! While you're at it, change the transmission oil.

2. Change the antifreeze on freshwater-cooled engines. The antifreeze itself does not wear out, but it has various additives to fight corrosion which do.

3. Drain the raw-water system, taking particular care to empty all low spots. Remove rubber pump impellers, grease lightly with petroleum jelly, and replace. Leave the pump cover screws loose; otherwise the impellers have a tendency to stick in the pump housings.

Leave yourself a prominent note to remind you that you've done this! Run the engine for *a few seconds* to drive any remaining water out of the exhaust.

4. Wash the valves on any vented loops in warm water to clean out salt crystals.

5. Check the primary fuel filter and fuel tank for water and sediment, and clean as necessary. If the tank is kept full, it will cut down on condensation.

6. Squirt some oil into the inlet manifold and turn the engine over a few times (without starting) to spread the oil around the cylinder walls.

7. Grease all grease points.

8. Seal all openings into the engine (air inlet, breathers, exhaust) and the fuel tank vent. Put a conspicuous notice somewhere that you have done this so that you remember to unseal everything at the start of the next season.

9. Remove the inner wires of all engine control cables from their outer sheaths. Clean, inspect, grease, and replace them. Check the sheathing as outlined on page 239.

10. Inspect all flexible feet and couplings for signs of softening (generally from oil and diesel leaks) and replace as necessary.

11. Inspect all hoses for signs of softening, cracking, or bulging, especially those on the hot side of the cooling and exhaust systems.

CHAPTER 9

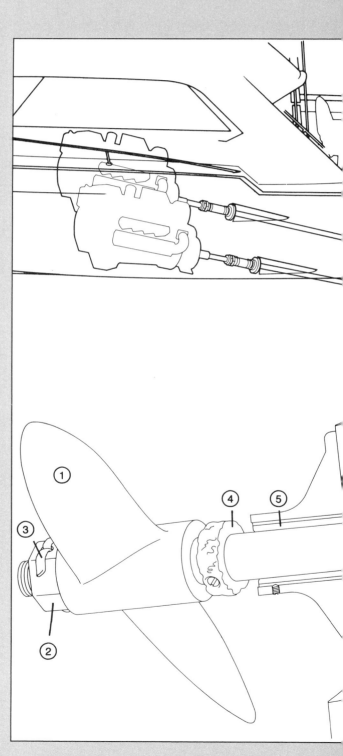

Figure 9-1. **The mysterious space between engine and propeller is easily maintained, yet is all too often neglected.**

(1) propeller
(2) retaining nut
(3) cotter pin
(4) zinc
(5) cutless bearing
(6) bearing
(7) stern tube
(8) propeller shaft
(9) flexible stuffing box
(10) packing rings
(11) locking nut
(12) compression spacer
(13) adjusting nut
(14) shaft coupling
(15) output shaft
(16) gearbox
(17) input shaft
(18) clutch discs

From Transmission to Propeller

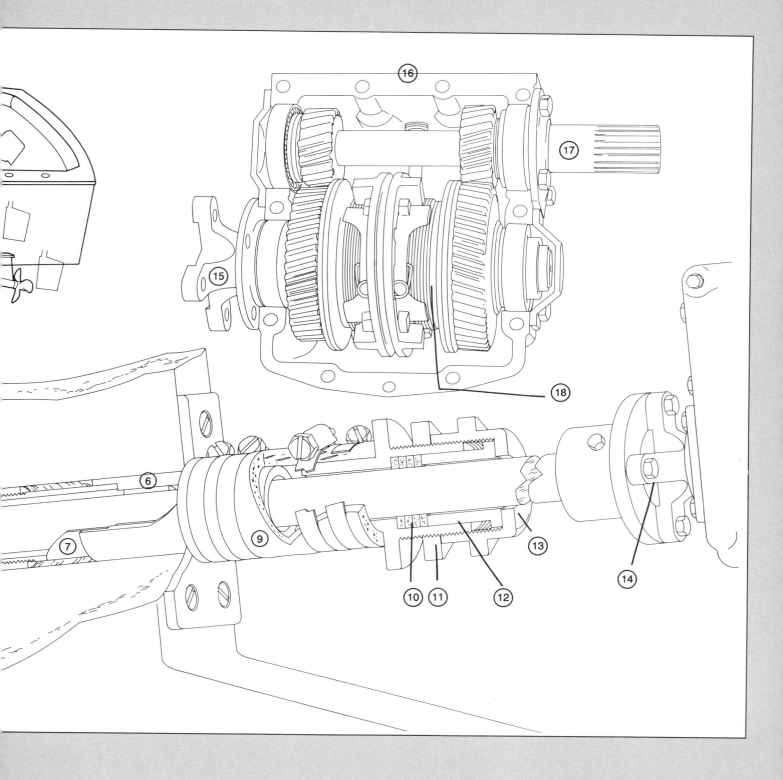

Most boats have an inboard diesel with an attached transmission, or gearbox, coupled directly to the propeller shaft. The propeller shaft is sealed in the boat with a *stuffing box* (also called a *packing gland*) and then supported just in front of the propeller with a Cutless-type bearing. (Cutless is a registered trademark of L. Q. Moffitt.) Depending on the hull and propeller shaft configuration, the Cutless bearing may be installed either inside the hull or in an external strut ("A" or "P" frame).

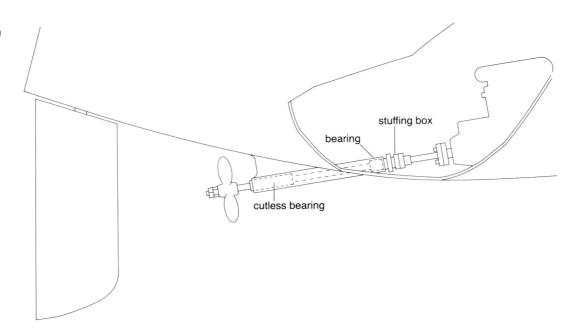

Figure 9-2A. **Variations on stuffing boxes and stern tubes. This boat has a spade rudder with a propeller shaft supported in a stern tube.**

stuffing box

bearing

cutless bearing

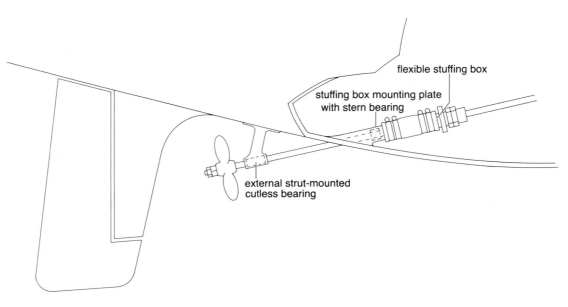

Figure 9-2B. **The propeller shaft on this boat is supported by an external strut.**

flexible stuffing box

stuffing box mounting plate with stern bearing

external strut-mounted cutless bearing

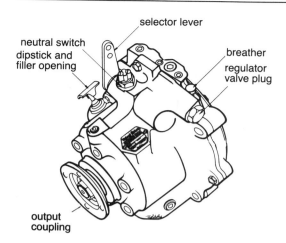

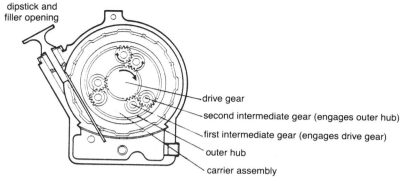

Figure 9-3A. Typical hydraulic gearbox. This one is a "Velvet Drive" by Borg Warner.

Figure 9-3B. An internal view of a similar transmission. The transmission gears actually have teeth all the way around; to simplify things, the artist has drawn teeth only where they contact others.

Transmissions: How They Work

A few manual transmissions (gearboxes) are still found, generally of the *planetary,* or *epicyclic,* type. Far more common are *hydraulic planetary* boxes, many of which are made by Borg Warner, and *two-shaft* boxes, servohydraulically operated. Many of the latter are manufactured by Hurth. Between them Borg-Warner and Hurth have a major share of the worldwide market in marine transmissions. Other makes are very similar to these two.

Planetary Transmissions

In this type the engine turns a geared drive shaft (the drive gear), which rotates constantly in the same direction as the engine. Deployed around and meshed with this gear are two or three gears on a carrier assembly. Each of these gears is also meshed with another gear, which in turn engages a large, outer, geared hub. The carrier assembly with its collection of intermediate gears and gear shafts is keyed to the output shaft of the transmission.

On one end of the drive shaft is the *forward clutch.* Engaging forward locks the drive shaft and carrier assembly together. The whole assembly rotates as one, imparting engine rotation to the output shaft of the transmission via the carrier assembly.

Reverse is a little more complicated. The forward clutch is released and a second clutch engaged, which locks the outer, geared hub in a stationary position. The drive gear spins the intermediate gears of the carrier assembly around the inside of the hub, but in the *opposite* direction of rotation to the drive gear. The carrier assembly imparts this reverse rotation to the output shaft.

Manual and hydraulic versions of a planetary box are very similar; the principal difference is that on a manual box the reverse clutch consists of a *brake band* that is clamped down around the hub, whereas in a hydraulic box a second clutch, similar to the forward clutch, is used.

A manual box uses pressure from the gear shift lever to engage and disengage the clutches. A hydraulic box incorporates an oil pump: The gearshift lever merely directs oil flow to one or the other clutch; the oil pressure is used to do the actual work. While quite a bit of pressure is needed to operate a manual transmission, gear shifting with a hydraulic transmission is a fingertip affair.

Two-Shaft Transmissions

In this type the engine is coupled to one shaft (the input shaft) to which two gears are keyed, one at either end. A second shaft, the output shaft, has two more gears riding on it; one of these engages one of the input gears directly, and the other engages the second input gear via an intermediate gear. These two output gears are

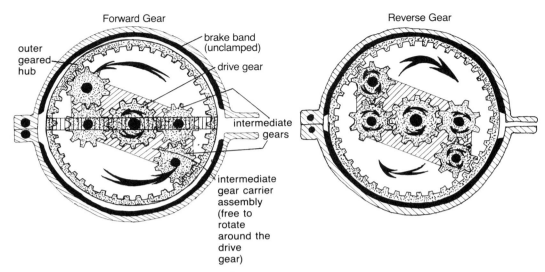

Forward Gear

outer
geared
hub

brake band
(unclamped)

drive gear

intermediate
gears

intermediate
gear carrier
assembly
(free to
rotate
around the
drive
gear)

Reverse Gear

Figure 9-4. **Forward and reverse in an epicyclic gearbox.** At left, in forward gear, the brake band is unclamped, while the forward clutch locks the drive gear and carrier assembly together so that they rotate as one. (The band across the center of the drawing symbolizes the clutch locking up all the gears.) In reverse gear, on the right, the forward clutch is released, leaving the carrier assembly free to rotate around the drive gear while the brake band is clamped down, locking up the geared hub. The carrier gear assembly is driven around the hub in the opposite direction to the drive gear.

Figure 9-5. **A hydraulic planetary transmission.**

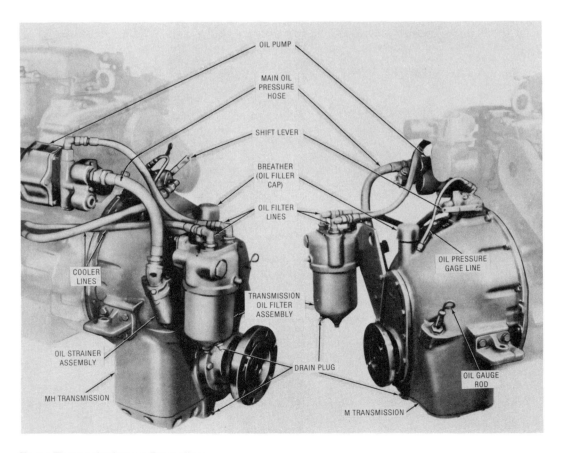

OIL PUMP

MAIN OIL
PRESSURE
HOSE

SHIFT LEVER

BREATHER
(OIL FILLER
CAP)

OIL FILTER
LINES

OIL PRESSURE
GAGE LINE

COOLER
LINES

TRANSMISSION
OIL FILTER
ASSEMBLY

OIL STRAINER
ASSEMBLY

DRAIN PLUG

OIL GAUGE
ROD

MH TRANSMISSION

M TRANSMISSION

From Transmission to Propeller

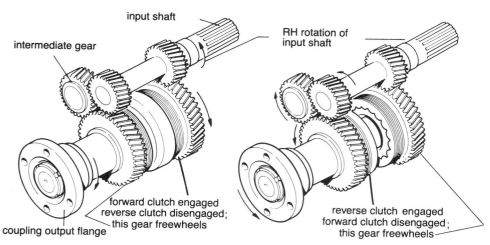

input shaft

intermediate gear

RH rotation of input shaft

forward clutch engaged
reverse clutch disengaged;
this gear freewheels

coupling output flange

reverse clutch engaged
forward clutch disengaged;
this gear freewheels

Figure 9-6A. Two-shaft transmission. With the forward clutch engaged (**left**), the output shaft rotates in the opposite direction to the input shaft.
With the reverse clutch engaged (**right**), the input shaft drives the output shaft in the same direction via the intermediate gear.

Figure 9-6B. A two-shaft Hurth transmission with the top cover removed for visibility.

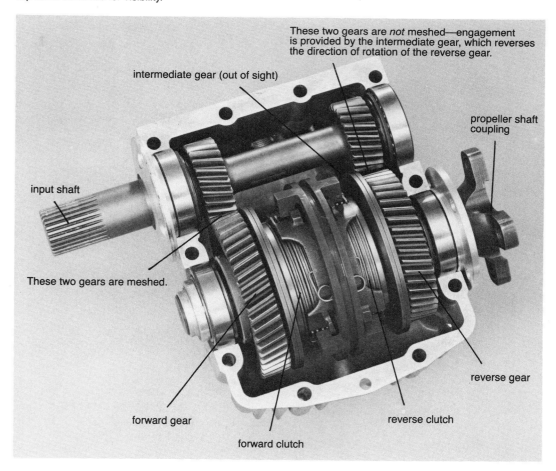

These two gears are *not* meshed—engagement is provided by the intermediate gear, which reverses the direction of rotation of the reverse gear.

intermediate gear (out of sight)

propeller shaft coupling

input shaft

These two gears are meshed.

reverse gear

forward gear

reverse clutch

forward clutch

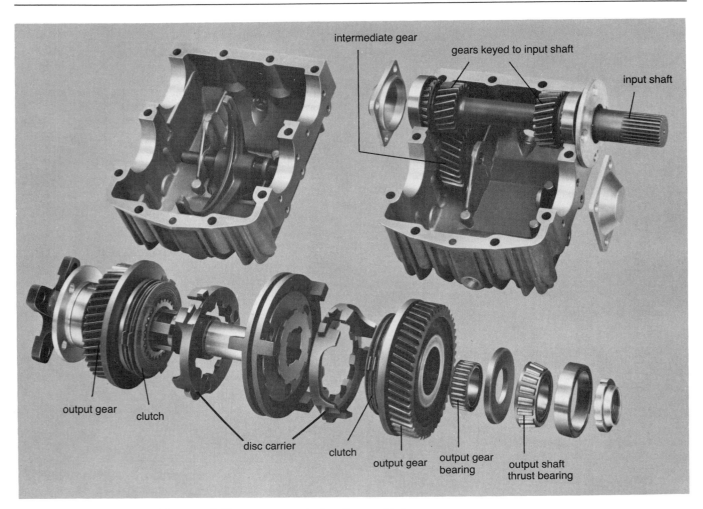

Figure 9-6C. **The same transmission, disassembled.**

mounted on bearings and are free to rotate around the output shaft.

The drive gears impart continuous forward and reverse rotation to the output gears. Each output gear has its own clutch, and between the two clutches is an engaging mechanism. Moving the engaging mechanism one way locks one gear to the output shaft, giving forward rotation; moving the mechanism the other way locks the other gear, giving reverse rotation.

When the clutch engaging mechanism is first moved to either forward or reverse, a gentle pressure is brought to bear on the relevant clutch. This initial friction spins a "disc carrier," which holds some steel balls in tapered grooves, and the rotation drives the balls up the grooves. Because of the taper in the grooves, the balls exert increasing pressure on the clutch and thus complete the clutch engagement. In other words, only minimal pressure is needed to set things in motion, and thereafter a clever design supplies the requisite pressure to make the clutch work without the necessity for oil pumps or oil circuits. Gear shifting is once again a fingertip affair.

Transmissions: Maintenance and Troubleshooting

Transmission maintenance is minimal: It generally boils down to keeping exterior surfaces clean (important for detecting oil leaks); periodically checking the oil level (unless there is a leak, it should need no topping up); checking for signs of water

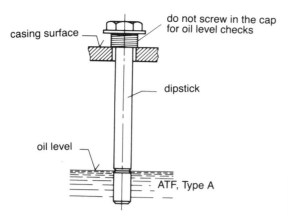

Figure 9-7. **Checking oil level on Hurth gearboxes.**

contamination (water emulsified in oil imparts a creamy color); and changing the oil annually. Most transmissions will operate on 30-weight engine oil or F-type transmission fluid. (Many manufacturers prefer the latter; see your manual.) If you have a hydraulic transmission, run the engine for a couple of minutes and then shut it down before checking the oil level. If there is an oil screen, a magnetic plug, or both in the base of the transmission, make an inspection when changing the oil for any signs of metal particles or other internal damage.

Operating Cables

Except for manual boxes, which have a gear shift handle, most transmissions today use a "push-pull" cable to move the gear shift lever on the box. A push-pull cable is one that pushes the lever in one direction and pulls it in the other. *More transmission problems are caused by cable malfunctions than anything else. Faced with difficulties, always suspect the cable before blaming the box.*

If the transmission operates stiffly, fails to go into either or both gears, stays in one gear, or slowly turns the propeller when in neutral ("clutch drag"), make the following checks:

1. See that the transmission actuating lever is in the neutral position when the remote control lever is in neutral.
2. Ensure that the actuating lever is moving *fully* forward and backward when the remote control is put in forward and reverse. (This is particularly important on Hurth boxes.)

Troubleshooting Chart 9-1.

Transmission Problems.

Symptoms: Failure to engage forward or reverse; clutch drag in neutral; or tendency to stick in one gear.

Move the remote control lever through its full range a couple of times. Does it move the operating lever on the transmission itself through its full range? **YES** ⬇	**NO** ➤ Check for a broken, disconnected, slipping, or kinked cable.
Is the remote control lever free-moving? **YES** ⬇	**NO** ➤ Break the cable loose at the transmission and try again. If still stiff, remove the cable from its conduit, clean, grease, and replace. If the cable moves freely when disconnected from the transmission, move the transmission lever itself through its full range. If binding, the transmission needs professional attention.
When the remote control is placed in neutral, is the transmission lever in neutral? **YES** ⬇	**NO** ➤ Adjust the cable length.
Is the transmission oil level correct? (Most transmissions have a dipstick; hydraulic transmissions frequently make a buzzing noise when low on oil). **YES** ⬇	**NO** ➤ Add oil and run the engine in neutral to clear out any air.
Does the transmission output coupling turn when the transmission is placed in gear? **YES** ⬇	**NO** ➤ The transmission needs professional attention.
Does the propeller shaft turn when the transmission coupling turns? **YES** ⬇	**NO** ➤ The coupling bolts are sheared or the coupling is slipping on the propeller shaft. Tighten or replace set screws, keys, pins and coupling bolts as necessary.

There must be a fault with the propeller:
1. It may be missing or damaged;
2. A folding propeller may be jammed shut;
3. A variable pitch propeller may be in the "no pitch" position;
4. If this is the first trial of a propeller, it may simply be too small and/or have insufficient pitch.

Figure 9-8A. **(Left)** Typical remote engine and transmission controls. These can comprise three sections: (1) the pilothouse control; (2) the cable system; and (3) the engine control unit. Input motion is transmitted from the pilothouse control via the cables to the actuating mechanisms on the engine and transmission. This setup uses Morse's enclosed cable-over-pulley system.

Figure 9-8B. **(Right)** A dual-station installation, with the main station controlled by push-pull cables, and the remote station using cable-over-pulley.

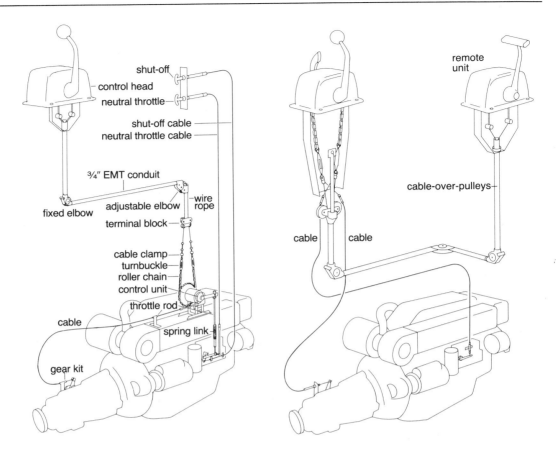

Figure 9-8C. **A** dual-station installation using remote bellcrank units and single-lever controls.

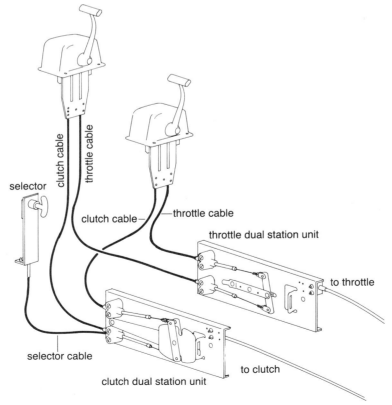

3. Break the cable loose at the transmission and double-check that the actuating lever on the box is "clicking" into neutral, forward, and reverse. On Hurth boxes there is no distinct "click" when a clutch is engaged, but the lever must move through a minimum arc of 30 degrees in either direction. Less movement will cause the clutches to slip; more is OK. As the clutches wear, the lever must be free to travel farther. If the transmission actuating lever is stiff or not traveling far enough in either direction, make sure that it is not rubbing on the transmission housing or snagging any boltheads.

4. While the cable is loose, operate the remote to see if the cable is stiff. If so, replace the cable.

5. Inspect the whole cable annually, checking for the following: seizure of the swivel at the box end of the cable conduit; bending of any actuating rods; corrosion of the end fittings at either end; cracks or cuts in the conduit jacket; burned or melted spots; excessively tight curves or kinks (the minimum radius of any bend should be 8 inches); separation of the conduit jacket from its end fittings; or corrosion under the jacket (it will swell up). If at all possible, remove the inner cable, inspect it, and grease it with a Teflon-based waterproof grease before replacing. Cables should be replaced at least every five years. An old one should be kept as a spare.

Oil Leaks

A sudden major oil loss is likely to be the result of a ruptured oil line (in which case it will be obvious) or a holed oil cooler (in which case it will not be obvious; see below). The oil seal around the clutch actuating shaft is sometimes the source of a slow leak.

However, the most likely source of an oil leak is the output-shaft oil seal, particularly if the engine and propeller shaft are

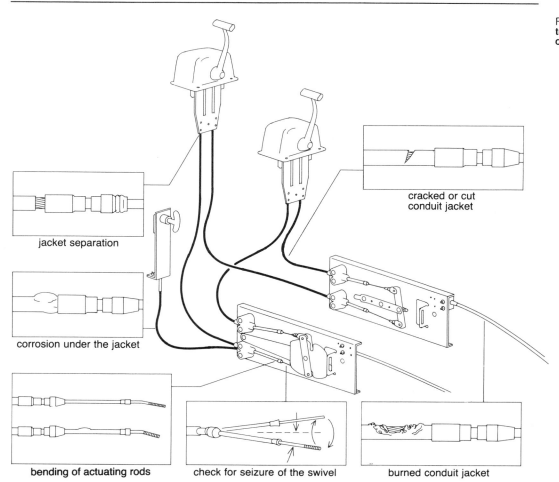

Figure 9-9. **Checking transmission control cables.**

cracked or cut conduit jacket

jacket separation

corrosion under the jacket

bending of actuating rods

check for seizure of the swivel

burned conduit jacket

poorly aligned and there is excessive vibration. For alignment checks, see page 245. Seal replacement varies from reasonably straightforward to difficult. Here is the procedure:

1. Unbolt and separate the two halves of the propeller coupling. It is a good practice to mark both halves so they can be bolted back together in the same relation to one another.

2. The coupling half attached to the transmission output shaft must be removed. This coupling is held in place with a central nut, which is done up tightly on most modern boxes but on some older boxes is just pinched up and then locked in place with a cotter pin.

   The coupling rides on either a splined shaft (one with lengthwise ridges all the way around) or a keyed shaft (one with a single square locking bar inserted in a slot in the shaft and a slot in the coupling). In the latter case, care must be taken when removing the coupling not to lose the key down in the bilges. What is more likely, however, is that the key will stick in the shaft. If there is no risk of its falling out and getting lost it can be left there; otherwise a screwdriver should be held up against one end and tapped gently until the end can be pried up and the key removed.

   Some couplings are a friction fit on their shafts and should be removed with a proper puller (Figure 9-10). This

Figure 9-10. **Removing the output shaft coupling with a coupling puller.**

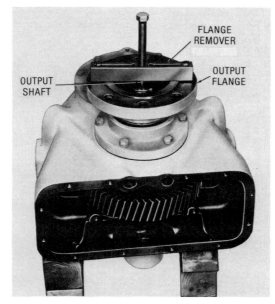

FLANGE REMOVER

OUTPUT FLANGE

OUTPUT SHAFT

is nothing more than a flat metal bar bolted to the coupling and tapped to take a bolt in its center. The bolt screws down against the gearbox output shaft, forcing off the coupling. It's worth noting that on some boats with vertical rudderposts, the propeller shaft cannot be pushed far enough aft to provide the necessary room to slide the gearbox coupling off its shaft! The propeller hits the rudder stock and will go no farther. In this case the rudder has to be removed or the engine lifted off its mounts to provide the necessary space—an awful lot of work to change an oil seal. In such a case, you may want to consider having the propeller shaft shortened and installing a small stub shaft in line between the transmission and propeller shaft.

3. Transmission oil seals make a press fit into the rear transmission housing. The seals consist of a rubber-coated steel case with a flat face on the rear end and a rubber lip on the front end (the end inside the gearbox). Inside a seal is a spring which holds this lip against the coupling face to be sealed.

   Removing a seal from its housing is not easy. If at all possible, the housing should be unbolted from the transmission and taken to a convenient workbench. (This is often fairly simple on older boxes and boxes with reduction gears, but may not be feasible on many modern hydraulic boxes.) The seal may be dug out with chisels, screwdrivers, steel hooks, or any other implement that comes to hand; it doesn't matter if the seal gets chewed up, *as long as the housing and shaft (if still in place) are unscratched.*

4. New seals are placed into a housing with the rubber lip facing into the gearbox, and the flat face outside. It is critical to place a seal in squarely and then to tap it in evenly using a block of wood and a hammer. *If a seal is forced in cockeyed it will be damaged.* The block of wood is necessary to maintain an even pressure over the whole seal face—*hitting a seal directly will distort it.* A seal is pushed in until the rear end is flush with the face of the gearbox housing. Once in place, some seals will require greasing (there will be a grease fitting on the back of the gearbox), but most need no further attention.

5. Reassembly of a coupling and propeller shaft is a reversal of disassembly. Pro-

peller shaft alignment should be checked anytime the coupling halves are broken loose and reassembled. Many gearboxes with tight coupling nuts have what are called "preloaded" thrust bearings. The gearbox output shaft, on which the coupling is mounted, turns in two sets of tapered roller bearings—one facing in each direction. Between the two is a steel sleeve. When the coupling nut is pulled up this sleeve is compressed, maintaining tension on the bearings and eliminating any play. Anytime the coupling nut is undone, a torque wrench should be used and the pressure needed to break the nut loose noted. When the nut is done back up, it should be pulled to the same torque plus *2 to 5 foot-pounds,* in order to maintain the correct bearing preloading. In any event, the torque should be at least 160 foot-pounds on most Borg-Warner boxes, but the coupling should still turn freely by hand with only minimal drag. Should a new bearing spacer be fitted between the thrust bearings, a special jig and procedure are called for, and the whole transmission reduction unit will have to go to a professional.

On an older transmission in which the coupling nut is done up less tightly and restrained with a cotter pin, it is essential that the nut be properly replaced. The best approach is to pull the nut to a moderate tightness to make sure everything is properly seated, and then back it off an eighth of a turn or so before inserting the cotter pin. The transmission then should be put in neutral and the coupling turned by hand to make sure there is no binding.

Oil Coolers and Overheating

Most modern transmissions are fitted with oil coolers. The water generally comes from the engine's raw-water circuit, although Detroit Diesels use the freshwater circuit. *It is essential to fit sacrificial zinc anodes in the water side and to inspect and change them regularly.* Failure to do so will likely result in galvanic corrosion eventually eating through the cooling tubes, which will allow transmission oil to be pumped out of the engine exhaust and water to enter the transmission. If the transmission shows signs of overheating, the most likely causes are plugged cooling tubes on the water side or a slipping clutch. Restricted water

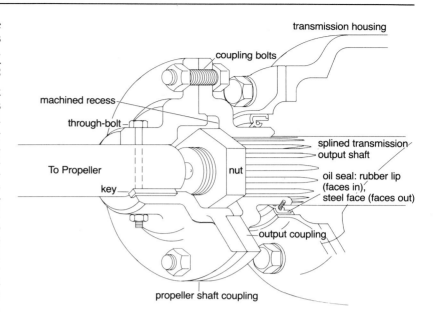

Figure 9-11. **Transmission oil seal and output coupling arrangement. The recesses machined into the face of the two coupling halves assist shaft alignment.**

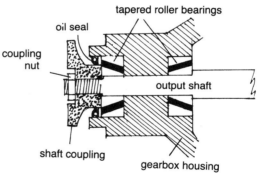

Figure 9-12A. **Typical thrust-bearing arrangement.**

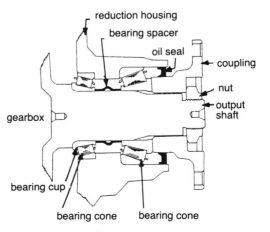

Figure 9-12B. **Pre-loaded thrust bearings.**

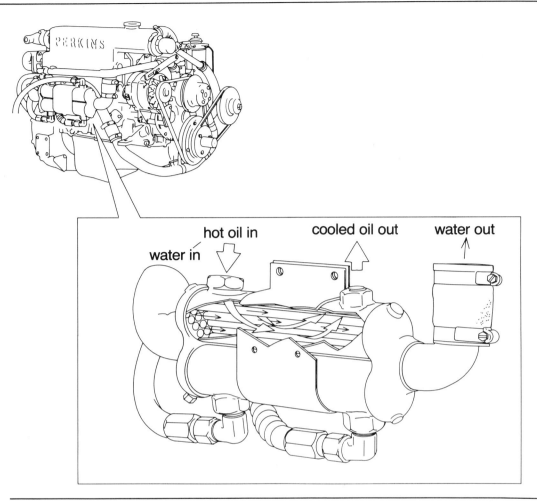

Figure 9-13. Oil coolers greatly increase engine life. Cooling water passes through the oil reservoir through small-diameter copper tubing. This dual-section unit from Perkins cools both gearbox and engine oil.

water in   hot oil in   cooled oil out   water out

flow through the cooling tubes means that they should be opened up and cleaned as described on page 215.

If the cooling tubes are not at fault, the clutch may be slipping, which will generate considerable friction and heat. Make sure the operating cable is moving the operating lever the full amount to engage the clutch (see above). If it is, the clutch is most likely worn out. Since there is no adjustment, except on manual boxes (see below), the transmission will need rebuilding. Do not run a box with a slipping clutch; the heat buildup can do extensive damage.

Clutch Adjustments: Manual Planetary Transmissions

In these transmissions the top of the box generally unbolts and lifts off. Inside are adjustments for both the forward and reverse gears. Reverse is easier.

Move the gear lever in and out of reverse—the brake band will be clearly visible as it clamps down on the hub and unclamps (see Figure 9-4). On one side of the band will be an adjusting bolt. If the transmission is slipping in reverse, tighten the bolt a little at a time, engaging reverse between each adjustment. When the gear lever requires good firm pressure to go into gear, and clicks in with a nice, clean feel, adjustment is correct.

It is important not to overdo things. Put the box in neutral and spin the propeller shaft by hand. If the brake band is dragging on the hub, *it is too tight; the box is going to heat up and seriously accelerate wear.* If no amount of adjustment produces a clean, crisp engagement, the brake band is worn out and needs replacing—or at least relining.

To adjust the forward clutch, first put the transmission in and out of gear a few times to see what is going on. The main plate on the back of the clutch unit (it pushes everything together) will have one central adjusting nut or between three and six adjusting nuts around it. Put the box in

Figure 9-14. Operating principles of a Paragon *S-A-O*—a common planetary gearbox. To engage engine forward; (1) push lever; (2) *shift yoke* pushes back; (3) *shift cone* slides along *output shaft* (3A), thus movintg (4) the *cam levers,* which press on (5) the *pressure plate* that compresses the *friction discs* (6) in the clutch. These in turn press against the near surface of (7) the *gear carrier,* thus completing the transmission of motion from the (8) *input shaft,* to the *output shaft* (3A). The pressure plate is adjusted by backing out the lock bolt (5A), screwing up the castelated nut (10) and retightening the lock bolt. To reverse directions, pull lever back to compress (9) the *reverse band,* locking it around the gear carrier like a huge hose clamp.

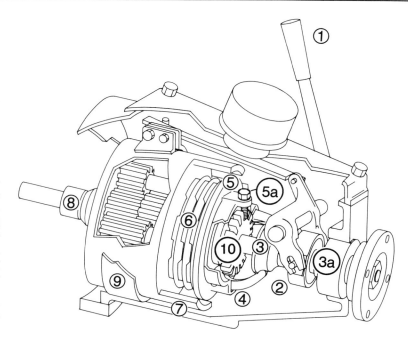

neutral and turn it over by hand, tightening each adjustment nut, as it becomes accessible, by one-sixth turn. After going all the way around, try engaging the gear again. Repeat until the gear lever goes in firmly and cleanly. Lock the adjusting nuts. Once again, do not tighten to the point at which the clutch drags in neutral; if overtightening seems necessary, the friction pads on the clutch plates probably are worn out and need replacing.

Hydraulic Transmissions: Special Problems

There are a couple of problems peculiar to hydraulic boxes. A "buzzing" noise indicates air in the system, generally due to a low oil level.

Most transmissions have an oil pressure regulating valve, which passes oil back to the suction side of the pump if excess pressures develop. In the event of a low oil level, or should the regulator valve stick open, the clutches may slip or not engage at all. On the other hand, if the engine is running too fast, or the regulator valve is stuck closed, the clutches will engage roughly. The valve is generally a spring-loaded ball or piston screwed into the side of the box and easily accessible for removing and cleaning (Figure 9-15).

Couplings and Engine Alignment

Couplings should always be keyed to their shafts and then pinned or through-bolted so that they cannot slip off. The practice of locking a coupling with set screws is not very seaworthy. If you find a coupling held this way, be sure the set screws seat in good-sized dimples in the shaft, and preferably are tapped into the shaft a thread or two so that there is no risk of slipping. *Should they slip, the propeller and shaft are liable to pull straight out of the boat in reverse, leaving the ocean pouring in through the open shaft hole!* Just for insurance it is a good idea to place a stainless steel hose clamp (Jubilee clip) around the shaft in front of the stuffing box; if the coupling should ever work loose, the hose clamp will stop the shaft from leaving the boat. Check those set screws at least once a year.

Most engines use conventional couplings, either solid or flexible, between transmission and the propeller shaft. Accurate alignment is critical to smooth, vibration-free running and a long life for the transmission bearings and oil seal and the Cutless bearing. Alignment cannot be checked, however, unless the propeller shaft is straight and the two coupling halves are exactly centered on and square to their shafts. A coupling should be fitted to its shaft and machined to a true fit in a lathe before putting the shaft in the boat.

To check the alignment on your engine, undo the coupling bolts and separate the coupling halves. There should be a machined step on one coupling that fits closely into a recess on the other (see Figure 9-11). Bring the two halves back to-

Figure 9-15. **Oil pressure regulating valve.**

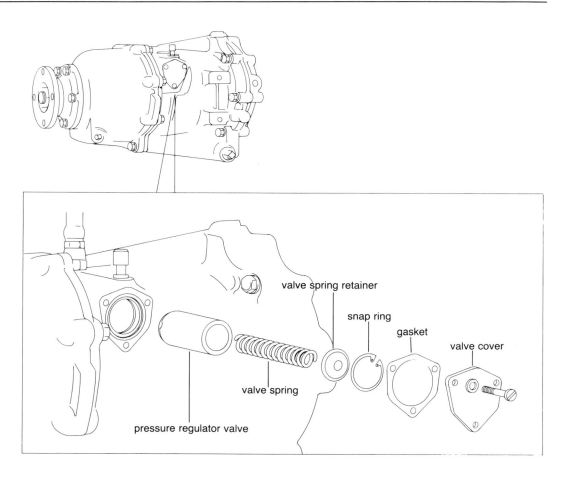

Figure 9-16. **Shaft couplings may be keyed and pinned in place (left and center), or restrained by set screws seated in dimples in the propeller shaft (right).**

gether—the step should slip into the recess cleanly and without snagging at any point. If it does not, the shafts are seriously misaligned (see below).

Note that in cases where a long run of propeller shaft is unsupported by a bearing, the shaft will sag down under its own weight and the weight of its coupling half. The correct procedure is to calculate half

the weight of the protruding shaft, add to it the weight of the coupling, and then pull up on the shaft by this amount with a spring scale of the type used for weighing fish. In practice, on smaller shafts you can generally flex the shaft up and down by hand to get a very good idea of the centerpoint, and then support the shaft with an appropriately sized block of wood. A notch in the wood will hold the shaft and allow it to be rotated.

Assuming the two halves come together cleanly, bring them almost into contact and then measure the gap at the top with a feeler, or thickness, gauge. Repeat at the bottom and on both sides. The difference from any one point to another should not exceed 0.001 inch per inch of coupling diameter (for example, 0.003 inch on a 3-inch-diameter coupling, or 0.06 mm on a 6-cm diameter).

If the difference exceeds tolerable limits, turn the propeller shaft coupling through 180 degrees while holding the transmission coupling stationary, and then measure the clearances again. If the widest gap is still in the same place the engine alignment needs correcting (see below). If the widest gap also has rotated 180 degrees, either the propeller shaft is bent, or its coupling is not squarely on the shaft, or both. The shaft and coupling should really be removed from the boat and "trued up" by a machine shop.

Adjusting Engine Alignment

Engine alignment should be checked once a year, always in the water; the hull may well have a different shape there than on land. It is preferable to wait a few days to a week after launching a boat to give the hull time to settle—especially a wooden hull. The engine must be jacked around and moved from side to side until the clearances all around the coupling are in tolerance. Some engines have adjustable feet, which greatly simplifies things; others need thin strips of metal (shims) placed under the feet until acceptable measurements are reached. Make sure that all feet take an equal load, or else when the mounting bolts are tightened there is a risk of distorting the engine block and causing serious damage. Engine alignment can be a time-consuming and frustrating business. When everything looks fine, tightening down the engine bolts may throw the alignment out again. Patience is the order of the day.

Flexible Feet and Couplings

Most engines today are mounted with flexible feet and couplings. (It is essential to fit a flexible coupling if flexible feet are used.) *These are not substitutes for accurate engine*

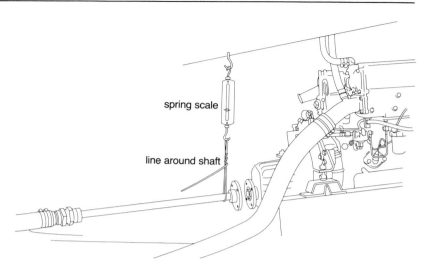

spring scale

line around shaft

Figure 9-17. Eliminating shaft droop. Attach a spring scale to the overhead; fix a line to the shaft and the scale and tension it until the scale reads one-half the weight of the shaft plus the weight of the coupling.

alignment. Modern, lightweight hulls tend to "work" in a seaway, whereas engines are necessarily extremely rigid. The principal reason for flexible feet is to absorb hull movements and lessen hull-transmitted engine vibrations, not to compensate for inadequate alignment.

Constant-Velocity Joints

Back in the 1950s, constant-velocity joints (CVJs) were developed for front-wheel drive cars. These are a special refinement of a universal joint, allowing a limited amount of shaft play in all directions. CVJs have since been adapted for marine installations, notably by Aquadrive, a Swedish company.

CVJs are used in pairs, one joint having a short, splined shaft that slides into a splined collar on the other. The entire unit is bolted between the transmission and propeller shaft, and, according to the makers, will permit misalignment of up to ½ inch or 13 mm! Since reverse thrust of the propeller would pull the two sliding shafts apart, the unit has to be combined with a *thrust bearing.* The propeller shaft is locked into this bearing, which in turn is fastened to a hull-bonded bulkhead, absorbing all forward and reverse thrust from the propeller and leaving the CVJs to cope solely with misalignment.

CVJs require no maintenance; the various bearings are packed in grease and sealed in rubber boots. Since all the main components are steel, however, a careful eye will have to be kept out for corrosion,

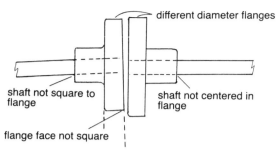

different diameter flanges

shaft not square to flange

flange face not square

shaft not centered in flange

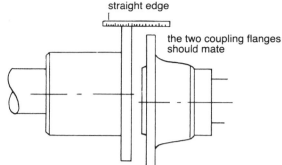

straight edge

the two coupling flanges should mate

Figure 9-18B. **Bore alignment. The machined step on one coupling half must slip easily into the recess on the other.**

runout

hub

hub

shaft

Flange Face Runout

hub centerline

hub

shaft

shaft centerline

Flange Bore Runout

Figure 9-18A. **Shaft and coupling problems that will make accurate engine alignment impossible. For effective alignment: (1) Both shafts must be square to their couplings. (2) The shafts must be centered exactly in their couplings. (3) The coupling faces must be square. (4) The coupling diameters must be exactly the same.**

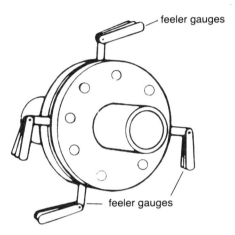

feeler gauges

feeler gauges

Figure 9-18C. **Engine alignment. Once the coupling flanges match and the machined step fits into its recess, check the gap between the two flanges with a feeler gauge on all four sides.**

especially on boats with wet bilges. Should the rubber bearing boots ever get damaged, they will need immediate replacement. In spite of the tolerance of CVJs for extreme misalignment, their life expectancy will be increased if alignment is kept fairly accurate.

Shaft Seals

Almost all boats still have a traditional stuffing box, or packing gland, either rigidly fastened to the hull where the shaft exits through the *sterntube* (and often incorporating a stern bearing) or mounted on a short length of hose that is fastened to the sterntube to form a "flexible" stuffing box. Here, however, as in so many other areas of boating equipment, some innovative new approaches have been tried in recent years. Notable among these are rotating seals, discussed below.

Stuffing Boxes (Packing Glands)

A small cylinder is fitted around the propeller shaft, forming a close fit at its lower end (and frequently incorporating a shaft bearing at this point in rigid stuffing boxes). A large packing nut or clamp plate makes another close fit around the shaft and closes off the top end of the stuffing box. A metal sleeve (the *compression spacer*) in the cylinder around the shaft is held in place by the nut or incorporated in the

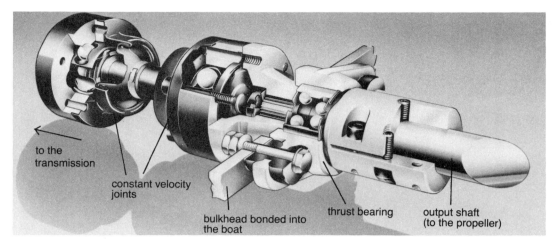

Figure 9-19. Constant velocity joints, such as this Aquadrive unit, compensate for shaft misalignment.

to the transmission

constant velocity joints

bulkhead bonded into the boat

thrust bearing

output shaft (to the propeller)

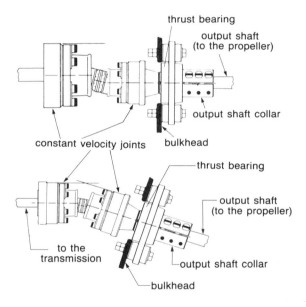

thrust bearing

output shaft (to the propeller)

output shaft collar

constant velocity joints

bulkhead

thrust bearing

output shaft (to the propeller)

to the transmission

output shaft collar

bulkhead

Figure 9-20. **How constant velocity joints handle different types of misalignment.**

underside of the clamp plate.

Rings of greased flax are pushed down into the cylinder around the shaft (generally three or four rings). This is the "packing." The compression spacer is placed on top. The nut or clamp plate is tightened to compress the packing, squeezing it out against the sides of the cylinder and up against the shaft, effectively sealing the shaft.

Some stuffing boxes have grease fittings, and in this case a bronze spacer ring is generally incorporated between the second and third rings of packing and directly below the grease fitting, allowing the grease to be distributed around the stuff-

ing box. A shot of grease (or one turn on the grease cup) should be put in about every eight hours of engine running time. Packing itself comes as a square-sided rope in different sizes—$\frac{3}{16}$ inch (4 mm), $\frac{1}{4}$ inch (6 mm), $\frac{3}{8}$ inch (8 mm), etc. It is important to match the packing to the gap between the shaft and cylinder wall. Packing can be bought as preformed rings to match the stuffing box (the best option for most people), or by the roll. When cutting rings off a roll, make about five tight wraps around the propeller shaft at some convenient point and then cut across the wraps with a very sharp knife, making a diagonal cut.

Packing Adjustment and Replacement

A stuffing box is meant to leak. When the shaft is turning, two or three drops a minute are needed to keep the shaft lubricated. If the leak is worse than this the nut or clamp plate is tightened down to compress the packing a little more. If a greaser is fitted, pump in a little grease first. Tighten down the nuts no more than one-quarter turn at a time. With a clamp plate, tighten the two nuts evenly.

Start the engine and put the transmission in gear for a minute or so. *Shut down the engine.* Feel the stuffing box and adjacent shaft: If they are hot, the packing is too tight. A little warmth is acceptable for a short while as the packing beds in, but any real heat is completely unacceptable— it is quite possible (and common) to score grooves in shafts by overtightening the packing, in which case the shaft will never seal and will have to be replaced. (Some-

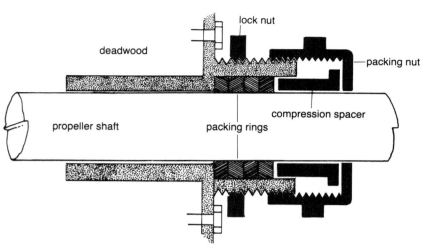

Figure 9-21A. Cross-section of a rigid stuffing box.

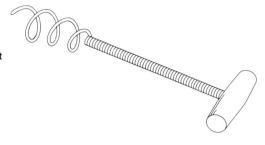

Figure 9-22. Removing the packing from a deep, awkwardly placed stuffing box should be reserved for this special tool. Screwdrivers and other substitutes may not remove the last few turns of packing.

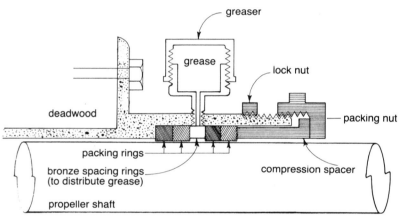

Figure 9-21B. Cross-section of a stuffing box equipped with a grease fitting. The screwdown cap-style cup greaser could be replaced with a standard grease nipple or a remote greaser.

times it can be turned end for end to place a different section in the stuffing box.)

If the shaft cannot be sealed without heating, the packing needs to be replaced. It should, in any case, be renewed every year, since old packing hardens and will score a shaft when tightened up. The hardest part of the job is generally getting the old packing out. *It is essential to remove all traces of the old packing or the new wraps will never seat properly.* With a deep, awkwardly placed stuffing box, it is next to impossible to pick out the inner wraps of packing with screwdrivers and ice picks; a special tool is needed, consisting of a corkscrew on a flexible shaft. Unless this tool is available it is not advisable to start digging into the packing, especially if the boat is in the water. Appreciable quantities of seawater will start to come into the boat as the packing is removed, and speed is of the essence.

When fitting new rings of packing, grease each with a Teflon-based waterproof grease before installation, and tamp each ring down before putting in the next. I use some short pieces of pipe slit lengthwise, slipped around the shaft, and pulled down with the packing nut or clamp plate to *gently* pinch up the inner wraps (not too tight, or the shaft will "burn"). Stagger the joints from one wrap to another by about 120 degrees. Don't forget the greasing spacer (if one is fitted) between the second and third wraps.

Graphite Packing Tape

Graphite packing tape is sometimes used instead of flax. It comes as a fragile reel of tape that is wrapped around and around the shaft until a sufficient thickness is built up to fill the space between the shaft and the stuffing box cylinder. These wraps are then slid into the stuffing box, and the tape is run around and around again to form another set of wraps. When the stuffing box is full, the nut or clamp plate is used to compress the graphite, and more is added. The total uncompressed width of the rings of tape should be about one and one-half times the depth of the stuffing box to impart an adequate degree of compression.

Graphite packing tape is far superior to conventional greased flax. The graphite crushes to form an excellent seal and, since graphite is a lubricant, there is little risk of burning the shaft. If extra packing is needed, it is simply added to the existing packing; there is no need to clean out the stuffing box. Graphite tape does have two drawbacks, however: It is expensive, and more important, graphite is high on the galvanic table and may promote corrosion.

Having said that, I should add that I have been using graphite for seven years without problems.

Flexible Stuffing Boxes

Flexible stuffing boxes are attached to the sterntube with a length of hose. *If this hose fails, water will pour into the boat at an alarming rate.* The hose must have two *all* stainless steel hose clamps at each end. Annually, inspect the hose for any signs of cracking or bulging, and tighten the screws on the hose clamps. Should it be necessary to replace the hose, the propeller shaft coupling will have to be broken loose and the coupling removed from the shaft.

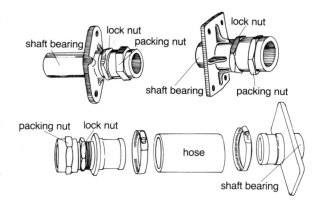

Figure 9-23. **Rigid stuffing boxes (top)** and a flexible stuffing box (**bottom**).

Rotary Seals

Stuffing boxes soon will be a thing of the past on many boats, replaced by rotary seals. These operate as follows: A rubber boot, in which is embedded a solid (phosphor bronze) stationary seat, is clamped to the sterntube. A second rubber boot with a hard ring (the *rotating seal*) molded into it is slid up the propeller shaft (the coupling must come off) until the rotating seal mates with the stationary seat. This boot is pushed up a little more to maintain a gentle pressure between the seal and seat. The boot is then clamped to the propeller shaft.

As the shaft turns, so too does the rotating seal. The smooth faces of the seal and the seat prevent any leaks into the boat, just as with a carbon/ceramic seal on a pump (see Chapter 12). A small amount of water (the occasional drop) is necessary to lubricate the faces of the seal; without it the seal will heat up and self-destruct. If

lubrication is inadequate there is provision for water injection into the seal assembly using water from the engine's raw-water system. The lubrication should be checked *when underway* by feeling the seal to see if it is heating up: Sometimes the motion of a boat through the water will create a vacuum around the sterntube, which draws the water out of the sterntube.

When a boat is put back in the water after being hauled out, it is essential to ensure that a rotary seal is properly lubricated before cranking the engine (see step 6 in Figure 9-25). If this is not done, the seal may burn up.

There is no maintenance on a rotary seal, aside from checking the hose clamps annually and inspecting the rubber boots to make sure there is no deterioration. Just as with a flexible stuffing box, failure of the boots will let in an alarming amount of water. With proper lubrication, however, the seal faces last almost indefinitely.

Cutless Bearings and Struts

Most Cutless bearings consist of a metal or fiberglass pipe with a ribbed rubber insert in which the shaft rides. Water circulates up the grooves to lubricate the bearing. Externally mounted bearings (in a strut, see Figure 9-2B) need no added lubrication, but some installed in hull bottoms and deadwoods have an additional lubrication channel into the sterntube. In place of the ribbed rubber, various plastics are sometimes used.

With a properly aligned engine most Cutless bearings will last for years, as long as they are lubricated adequately. They require no maintenance. At the annual haulout, flex the propeller shaft at the propeller; if there is more than minimal movement, the bearing needs replacing. If not renewed, a worn Cutless bearing will cause excessive shaft vibration, which will rapidly wear stuffing box and transmission bearings and seals. A Cutless bearing worn

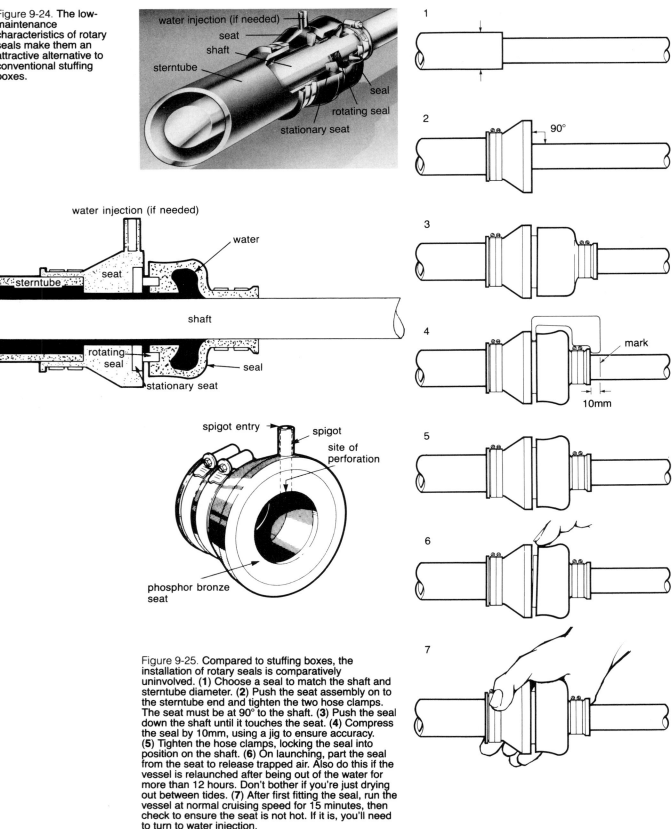

Figure 9-24. **The low-maintenance characteristics of rotary seals make them an attractive alternative to conventional stuffing boxes.**

water injection (if needed)
seat
shaft
sterntube
seal
rotating seal
stationary seat

water injection (if needed)
water
seat
sterntube
shaft
rotating seal
seal
stationary seat

spigot entry
spigot
site of perforation
phosphor bronze seat

1

2   90°

3

4   mark
     10mm

5

6

7

Figure 9-25. Compared to stuffing boxes, the installation of rotary seals is comparatively uninvolved. (**1**) Choose a seal to match the shaft and sterntube diameter. (**2**) Push the seat assembly on to the sterntube end and tighten the two hose clamps. The seat must be at 90° to the shaft. (**3**) Push the seal down the shaft until it touches the seat. (**4**) Compress the seal by 10mm, using a jig to ensure accuracy. (**5**) Tighten the hose clamps, locking the seal into position on the shaft. (**6**) On launching, part the seal from the seat to release trapped air. Also do this if the vessel is relaunched after being out of the water for more than 12 hours. Don't bother if you're just drying out between tides. (**7**) After first fitting the seal, run the vessel at normal cruising speed for 15 minutes, then check to ensure the seat is not hot. If it is, you'll need to turn to water injection.

rubber insert
metal sleeve

Figure 9-26. **Cutless bearings.**

flexed inward. Take care not to cut through the bearing into the surrounding strut or sterntube. A new bearing is then lightly greased and pushed in, using a block of wood and *gentle* hammer taps if necessary. The bearing should not be a tight (interference) fit, since it may distort.

The retaining set screws must tighten into dimples in the bearing case, and should be locked in place with Loctite or something similar. They must *not* press on the bearing case, since this would distort it, causing friction between the rubber bearing and the propeller shaft. The shaft itself should *not* be a tight fit in the bearing sleeve.

Most bearing cases are made of naval brass or stainless steel. Fiberglass/epoxy (FE) cases are becoming more common, however. This material works just as well as the metals and is especially recommended for steel and aluminum hulls, where it will eliminate the risk of galvanic corrosion.

Struts are all too often inadequately mounted. The stresses from a fouled propeller or bent shaft will work them loose. Check the fasteners annually, and tighten as necessary. If the bolts are a loose fit in the hull due to elongated holes, a good dollop of bedding compound combined with a good-sized, well-bedded backing block will tighten things.

on only one side is a sure sign of engine misalignment.

The shaft must come out to renew a Cutless bearing. Most bearings are a simple sliding fit, locked in place with set screws. Once the set screws are loosened, a strut-mounted bearing can generally be knocked out from the inner side of the strut. To do the same on a hull-mounted bearing, the stuffing box will have to be removed from the inner end of the sterntube.

Not infrequently the Cutless bearing refuses to dislodge. In this case two longitudinal slits will have to be made in the bearing with a hacksaw blade so that a section can be pried out, allowing the rest to be

Propellers

The number one problem with propellers is fouled lines, generally your own! These can be a devil of a job to clear. Before resorting to snorkeling gear and a hacksaw, put the transmission in neutral and have someone pull on the fouled line while a second person rotates the propeller shaft by hand in the opposite direction to which it was turning when the line was caught. Often the line will simply unwind.

Bent propeller blades can cause quite a bit of vibration. It is advisable to check them at the annual haulout. Set up a pointer (a piece of wood or a pencil) on the hull side or strut so that it nearly touches the tip of one propeller blade. Rotate the propeller by hand. Any differences in the blade clearances will immediately become apparent.

Standard Propellers

Propellers are mounted on keyed and tapered shafts, retained by a propeller nut with either a second locking nut or else a cotter pin (split pin). There may or may not be a "fairing piece" over the top of the nut to smooth out the water flow.

To remove a propeller, back off the retaining nut (*but not all the way*) and use a piece of hardwood and a hammer to hit the propeller smartly behind its boss and jar it loose from the taper on the shaft. If it won't come, concentrate on the spot with the keyway—this is the most likely point of binding. If it still won't move, it will be necessary to heat the propeller hub with a propane torch. Move the torch around the

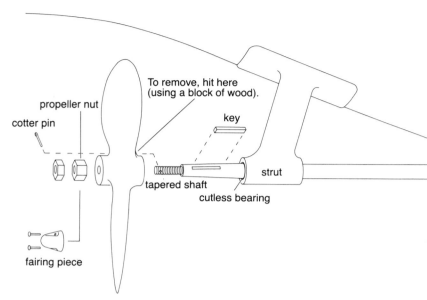

Figure 9-27. **Propeller installation. Note that the half-nut, which would be between the blades and the locking nut, can be dispensed with when a fairing nut is used.**

propeller nut

cotter pin

To remove, hit here (using a block of wood).

key

strut

tapered shaft

cutless bearing

fairing piece

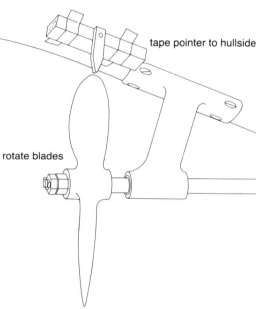

tape pointer to hullside

rotate blades

Figure 9-28. **Using a pointer to check for propeller blade misalignment.**

hub in a circular fashion to avoid excessive localized heating.

When refitting a propeller, grease the shaft to help in future removal and *be sure to put the key back!* Lock the retaining nut securely.

Variable-Pitch Propellers

My boat has a Sabb variable-pitch propeller, and with it I once hit a log at full speed.

The log jammed on a propeller blade, hit the hull, and stopped the motor dead. The blade was badly bent, the hub cracked away from the hull. We moved all heavy equipment forward, hung the dinghy from the bowsprit, and pumped it full of water. This brought the propeller unit out of the water.

We repaired the hull and disassembled the propeller. The force of the blow had distorted the propeller blade mounting flange and most of the operating parts in the internal mechanism. Several hours of painstaking work with a file and an emery cloth got everything moving freely again. Some gentle work with a hammer straightened the blade. Since then we've put on another 1,000 hours of engine running time and been to Venezuela and back, and haven't done another bit of maintenance on the propeller. I am of the opinion variable-pitch propellers are virtually indestructible!

The blades on a variable-pitch propeller can be rotated in the propeller case to vary the angle of attack of the blades in the water. The usual mechanism (in a Sabb propeller, for example) incorporates an offset pin on the base of each propeller blade. This pin keys into a slot in a block on the end of the propeller shaft (Figure 9-30).

The whole unit is enclosed in a case. This revolves on bearings around a mounting hub bolted firmly to the boat. To change the pitch the shaft *moves in and out,* rotating the blades via their offset pins.

On some units the pitch is adjusted with a hand crank, and on others with a cable-operated pitch-control lever.

Pitch should always be changed at low engine speeds when the blades are under a light load. High-load pitch changes severely stress the whole mechanism, particularly the cables (if fitted). If any unusual stiffness is encountered, do not force a cable; irreparable damage may result. Check for a bent propeller shaft or blades.

Maintenance is minimal. A shot of grease is pumped into the propeller case via a remote greaser every eight hours of running time or so.

Should the unit malfunction (excessive slop in the blades and mechanism, or excessive friction), removing two bolts from the case will enable its two halves to be pried apart, giving access to all the parts. Separate the case halves evenly on both sides; don't just jam a screwdriver in one side and force the two halves apart. Check the wear of the propeller blade pins in

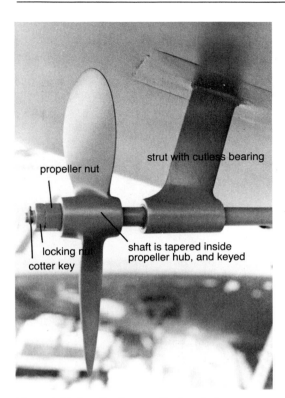

propeller nut

strut with cutless bearing

locking nut
cotter key

shaft is tapered inside
propeller hub, and keyed

Figure 9-29. **Details of a propeller installation.**

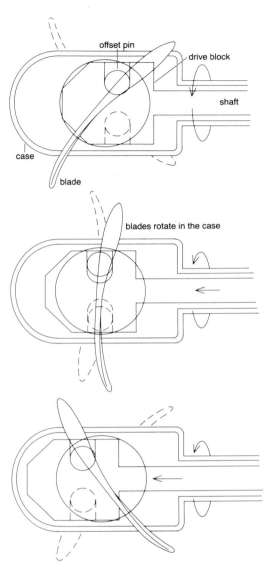

offset pin

drive block

shaft

case

blade

Figure 9-30. **The mysterious workings of the variable-pitch propeller. The shaft and its attached drive block move in and out. Recesses in the drive block catch an offset pin at the base of the blades and cause them to rotate.**

blades rotate in the case

their mounting blocks, and the state of the bearings.

If the propeller blades have hit anything, check their mounting flanges and bearing surfaces for damage and "dress up" as necessary with a file or emery cloth. To check their operation for rough spots or sticking, reassemble the case with the blades in it (without putting it back on the hub) and rotate the blades in the case by hand. To check the movement of the case around the hub, reassemble it to the hub without the blades, and turn by hand.

If the pitch-control mechanism uses a cable, operate the mechanism while the blades and case are off the unit to check for stiffness in the cable and linkage. If present, disconnect the cable from the linkage to determine which of these two is at fault. The cable is made of spirally wound spring steel and engages a gear at the control end. Should it need regreasing (unlikely), disassemble the gear case to get it out.

While the cable is out, rotate the control lever; the stiffness may be due to dirt and a buildup of salt or corrosion between the control lever shaft and its housing. Similarly, if the engine throttle control lever is mounted through the center of the pitch

control lever (Sabb) and becomes stiff, disconnect the throttle cable to the engine and check for binding between the throttle lever and the variable-pitch lever. If present, disassemble, clean, lubricate, and reassemble.

Folding Propellers

By their very nature, folding propellers are sailboat specific—the idea being that the propeller can be made less intrusive when the boat is under sail. There are two styles of folding propeller.

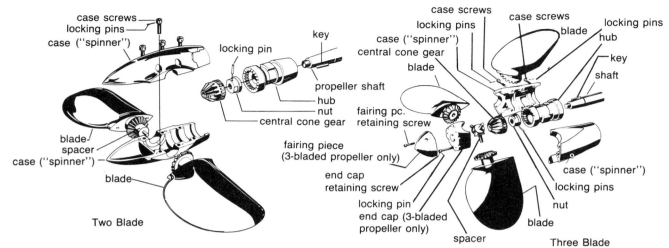

Figure 9-31. **Max-Prop**
fully feathering propeller.

The old style. This folding propeller (e.g., Luke) has two hinged blades, which are held in the closed position when sailing by the flow of water over the propeller. When the engine is cranked and put in forward the centrifugal force opens the blades partway, and then the developed thrust drives them all the way open, sometimes with considerable force. In reverse, any thrust developed tends to close the blades. This tendency is counteracted by centrifugal force, but efficiency is minimal.

The most common problem with this type of propeller is a failure to open at all due to weeds or barnacles in the hinge. These propellers must be kept clean.

The new style. Recently a completely different kind of folding propeller, the Max-Prop, has been taking the sailboat market by storm. Each blade has a bevel gear on its base engaging a central, beveled cone gear mounted on the propeller shaft. The whole unit is enclosed in a case (the "spinner").

When the engine is cranked and put in gear, the propeller shaft turns while the case and blades tend to lag due to inertia. The blades will be in a feathered position. The initial torque of the turning shaft drives the cone gear, which in turn rotates the propeller blades in the case via the bevel gears. The blades have a preset "stop" such that they cannot rotate beyond a certain point. Once this stop is reached the propeller shaft spins the whole unit, including the case.

When the engine is shut down, water pressure on the blades forces them back to the feathered position.

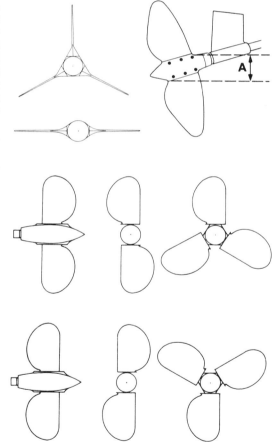

Figure 9-32. The operation of Max-Prop propellers. Under sail, the Max-Prop feathers to a low drag shape. In forward, the torque of the prop shaft acts on the differential-type blade design to force the blades open to a preset pitch at any throttle setting. In reverse, as in forward, the torque of the shaft will rotate the blades 180 degrees, presenting the same leading edge and pitch in reverse.

When put in reverse the propeller shaft once again drives the blades to their full pitch before spinning the whole unit, thus ensuring maximum efficiency in reverse. (Note that the blade pitch can be adjusted by altering the position of the stops, but this can only be done by disassembling the case. In other words, although the mechanism looks broadly similar to a variable-pitch propeller, this is in fact a fixed-pitch blade with a fully feathering characteristic.)

Maintenance is simply a matter of checking sacrificial zinc anodes regularly and renewing the grease every one or two years. To renew the grease you must take apart the unit. Make a careful note of where everything goes and put it all back the same way. A waterproof bearing grease such as Lubriplate Marine A works well. Lighter Teflon greases will be washed away.

If the propeller blades are stiff to rotate by hand, or have "hard" spots, it may simply be the result of too much grease—take a little out. Otherwise, check for small burrs on the gears or minor damage on any of the bearing surfaces (the propeller blade bases; bearing surfaces in the case; and the hub). Remove the cone gear and reassemble the unit. Now each blade can be checked for stiffness individually, and the rotation of the case around the hub tested; this should enable problem areas to be isolated. "Dressing up" with emery cloth or a fine file will solve most problems.

I once met cruising sailors with twin Max-Props driven by hydraulic motors (with a central hydraulic pump on the boat's main engine). Gear shifting was done by remotely controlled solenoids. On one occasion someone accidentally hit the reverse solenoid to one propeller, abruptly reversing the oil flow at full speed. Something had to give, and the bevel gears stripped off. *Each Max-Prop is built as a balanced unit at the factory. Parts are not interchangeable.* In cases of serious damage such as this, the whole unit must be returned to the factory.

Shaft Locks

When a boat is under sail or tow (powerboats take note!), propeller drag will cause the propeller to freewheel unless the shaft is braked. A freewheeling propeller will, in many instances, create more drag than a locked one. *Some transmissions, such as Detroit Diesels', will burn out due to a lack of oil circulation,* while in all installations additional and unnecessary wear will occur to Cutless bearings, stuffing boxes, transmission oil seals and bearings. Freewheeling propellers can also make quite a racket.

When the engine has a manual transmission the shaft can be locked simply by putting it in gear. This will not work with a hydraulic box, however, since there is no oil pressure for gear shifting when the engine is shut down. A shaft brake is needed, and there are essentially two choices.

Automatic (Hydraulic) Units

Hydraulically operated units all have a spring-loaded piston. The spring is opposed by oil pressure, and the oil line is connected to the hydraulic transmission. When the engine is at rest the spring

Figure 9-33. **A manual propeller shaft lock.**

Figure 9-34. **The anatomy of a manual shaft lock.**

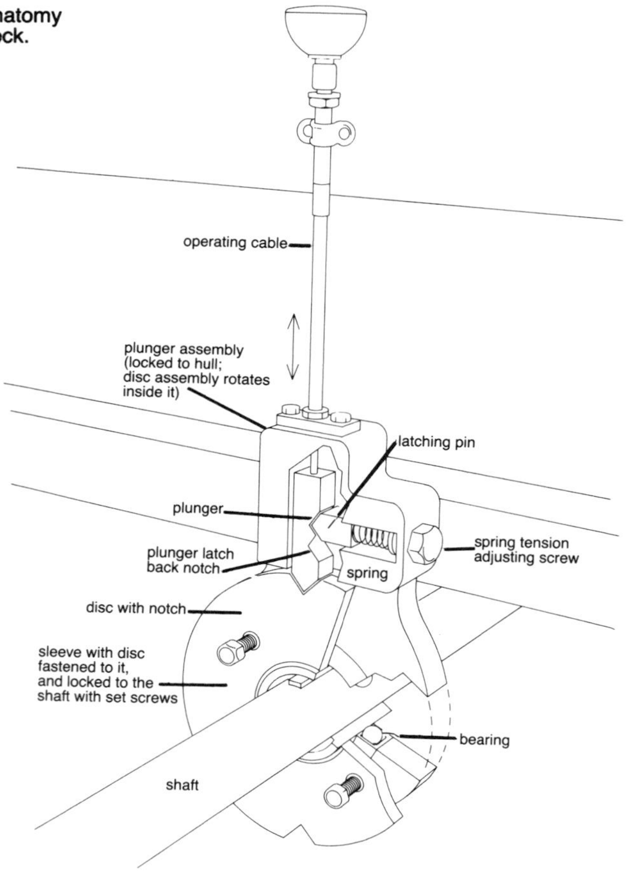

operating cable

plunger assembly
(locked to hull;
disc assembly rotates
inside it)

latching pin

plunger

plunger latch
back notch

spring tension
adjusting screw

spring

disc with notch

sleeve with disc
fastened to it,
and locked to the
shaft with set screws

bearing

shaft

forces out the piston and operates the brake. When the engine is started, oil pressure from the transmission oil pump forces the piston back against the spring pressure, releasing the brake. These units are thus automatic in operation, overcoming the main objection to older manual units—which is the probability of leaving the brake on at some time, putting the transmission in gear, and burning up the brake.

Four variations on the hydraulic theme are widely available:

1. *Caliper disc brakes*, operating as on a car. A disc is bolted between the two propeller-shaft coupling halves. A hydraulically operated caliper grips the disc to stop rotation.

2. *Cam disc*. Similar to the above except that the disc has several cams. A hydraulically operated arm locks into the cams.

3. *Brake band*. A hydraulically operated brake band clamps around the propeller shaft coupling.

4. *Plunger type*. A slotted sleeve is clamped around the shaft, and a hydraulically operated plunger locks into one of the slots.

Manual Units

In the older manual units, a brake pad simply clamps around a block on the shaft or coupling. There is the obvious inherent risk that the owner will forget the brake when next the engine is started and, as a result, burn up the brake. Newer manual units, however, have a notched disc clamped to the propeller shaft, with a plunger engaging the notch. If the brake is left engaged while the engine is started and put in gear, the plunger is simply forced out of the notch and held back by another spring-loaded pin until it is manually set once again (Figure 9-34).

Problem Areas

• If the engine is required for battery charging or refrigeration rather than propulsion, the automatic hydraulic devices become an annoyance, unlocking when the engine is cranked despite the fact that we don't want them to. A manual valve or an electric solenoid valve has to be installed in the hydraulic line to close it off and prevent pressure reaching the piston, but then we must face the quandary posed by the old-style manual units: If we put the engine in gear while forgetting to reopen the hydraulic line, the shaft brake will burn up.

• Hydraulic oil leaks through faulty piston seals, connections, or hoses on the automatic units will cause the loss of the transmission oil and ultimately transmission failure. Adding a hydraulic shaft lock may, in fact, void any warranty on the transmission.

• The manual plunger types have a tendency to jump out during hard sailing. Spring tension on the latching pin can be increased to hold the plunger in place, but then it becomes more difficult to disengage the plunger.

• The cam disc, the hydraulic plunger, and the manual notched-disc plunger-style units can only be set at low propeller speeds. Ignoring this rule is likely to result in damage to the former unit; in the latter two cases the plunger will just jump out. It may be necessary to slow the boat and reduce propeller freewheeling before engaging the device; in other words, these devices are shaft locks rather than shaft brakes.

Maintenance

Hydraulic units. Pay close attention to the hydraulic lines and inspect them regularly for any signs of leaks around the piston seals. Check the brake linings on caliper and brake band units for wear. *Don't allow them to slip*—a lot of heat will be generated. Check any sleeve mounting bolts from time to time.

Manual units. The control cable is a Morse-type. Figure 9-9 shows a number of points to watch for with Morse cables. The plunger unit is mounted on a bearing within which the propeller shaft rotates. The bearing is sealed for life. Check for undue play once in a while, and while at it check the set screws that lock the central sleeve to the propeller shaft.

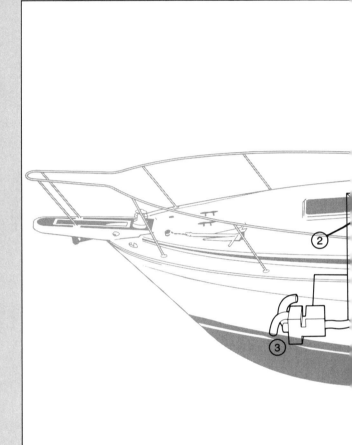

CHAPTER 10

Figure 10-1. Problems aboard can crop up almost anywhere, but most can be ignored as long as the beverages and the mahi-mahi are kept cold.

(1) compressor
(2) plenum
(3) air conditioner
(4) freezer
(5) refrigerator
(6) pump
(7) strainer
(8) air conditioner raw-water intake
(9) holding plate in icebox
(10) belt-driven compressor
(11) condenser (in engine raw-water intake line)

Refrigeration and Air Conditioning

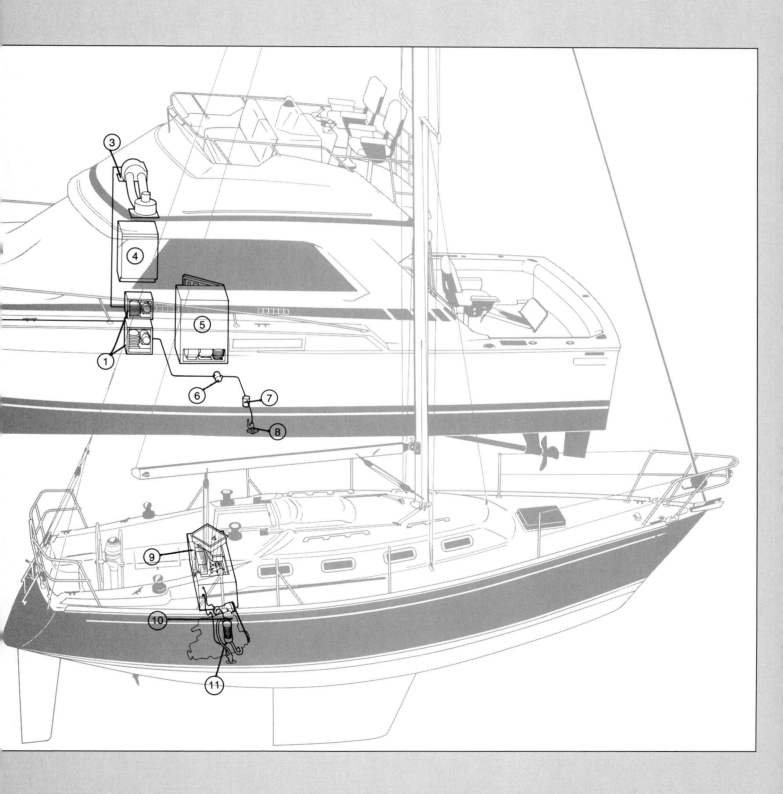

Few things provide more creature comfort than a decent refrigeration/freezer system. Many operate faultlessly for years; others are a source of perpetual problems. Almost all refrigerators, freezers, and air conditioners operate on the same principles, and a grasp of these principles is essential to effective troubleshooting.

It should be noted that virtually all refrigeration, freezer, and air-conditioning systems on boats use one of two similar gases known as R-12 and R-22. Either, when allowed to escape into the atmosphere, attacks the earth's ozone layer; leaking refrigeration and air-conditioning systems are a major contributor to the depletion of the ozone layer. Many of the procedures outlined in this chapter, in conformity with current industry and trade practice, involve deliberately venting R-12 or R-22 into the atmosphere. Clearly every effort should be made to minimize all such releases, but this is not enough. Environmentally safe refrigerant gases have been developed, and there is no reason why these should not replace R-12 and R-22. We should all be pressing for a worldwide ban on these substances and for the manufacture and distribution of refrigeration and air-conditioning units, both for the boat and ashore, that will be compatible with safer refrigerants. Europe is ahead of the USA in this regard. Clearly the current dependence on R-12 and R-22 is reckless and irresponsible.

How They Work

We all know that water boils at 212°F (100°C). Or does it? In a pressure cooker water boils at over 240°F (116°C), which is why food cooks so much faster. The reason for this is that anytime pressure is increased the boiling temperature goes up, and conversely, when pressure is decreased the boiling temperature goes down. Water boils at 212°F only at sea level atmospheric pressure. At any other pressure the boiling temperature is higher or lower.

Let's look at this from another angle. If we raise the temperature to over 212°F (100°C) at normal atmospheric pressure, any water present will form steam. If the temperature drops back below 212°F (100°C), however, the steam will condense back into water. Since the boiling temperature rises with pressure, raising the pressure while holding the temperature at 212°F (100°C) also will condense the steam into water. At higher pressures the condensation temperature of steam is higher; at lower pressures it is lower.

When water turns into steam at sea level atmospheric pressure the water is at 212°F (100°C) and so too is the steam. But quite a bit of energy is needed to bring about this change of state from water to steam, even though no change of temperature occurs. This is easily seen. Put a thermometer in a pot of water, bring it to a boil, and then boil it all away. It will start to boil quite quickly but will take some time to boil away, even though there will be no further

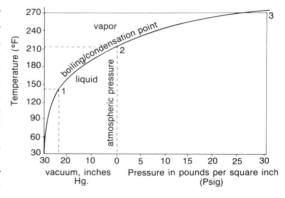

Figure 10-2. **The relationship between pressure and the boiling point of water. At 1 (24" Hg vacuum) water boils at 142°F. At 2 (atmospheric pressure) water boils at 212°F. At 3 (30 psig) water boils at 272°F.**

rise in temperature. The converse also applies: When steam condenses into water, even though the steam and water are both at 212°F (100°C), the steam *gives up* a large amount of heat.

Because heat absorbed and lost during changes of state does not result in a change in temperature (and cannot be measured with a thermometer) it is called *latent heat*. For a vapor (or gas) to condense into a liquid it must give up latent heat of condensation; for a liquid to boil into a vapor or gas it must absorb latent heat of vaporization.

These two concepts—the changing of boiling or condensation temperatures with changes in pressure, and the latent heat of vaporization and condensation—are at the heart of almost all refrigeration and air-conditioning systems. Let us see how it works.

All boat refrigeration systems circulate a substance known as R-12 (also known as Freon 12, the trade name of the Du Pont company). At atmospheric pressure liquid R-12 vaporizes, or boils, into a gas at $-21.6°F$ ($-29.7°C$), just as water boils at $212°F$. When R-12 is pressurized its boiling temperature rises. At 100 psi (pounds per square inch), R-12 boils at $90°F$ ($32.2°C$), or, put another way, if it is already in gaseous (vapor) form at 100 psi and if its temperature falls below $90°F$ ($32.2°C$) it will condense into a liquid. At 170 psi its boiling/condensation temperature is $125°F$ ($51.7°C$). At 220 psi the boiling/condensation temperature is $145°F$ ($62.8°C$). (Note: Air conditioners generally use R-22 as a refrigerant; R-22 operates the same way as R-12, but with different boiling/condensation temperatures.)

In a refrigeration system R-12 gas is pulled into a compressor and compressed, generally to between 125 and 175 psi. The gas will condense at 125 psi if its temperature falls below $104°F$ ($40°C$); at 175 psi, below $127°F$ ($52.8°C$). The hot gas is cooled in a "condenser"; its temperature falls below its condensation point at this pressure and it turns into a liquid. In liquefying it gives up a large latent heat of condensation to the condenser.

The pressurized liquid enters a receiver/filter/drier (RFD for short; sometimes the receiver and filter/drier are two separate units). The RFD is nothing more than a tank with a fine screen and some dessicant (water-absorbing substance). The RFD filters out trash, absorbs moisture, and acts as a reservoir of liquid R-12. It is worth noting that most RFDs have a sight glass on top (more on this later), or one located nearby.

From the RFD the pressurized liquid R-12 goes to the refrigerator or freezer. There it is sprayed through a very small orifice into a length of finned tubing known as an *evaporator,* much like the radiator of a car. The orifice may consist of nothing more than a very small piece of capillary tubing, or it may be incorporated in a special valve that regulates the size of the orifice according to the needs of the system—a *thermostatic expansion valve* (TXV for short).

The evaporator tubing is connected directly to the suction side of the compressor

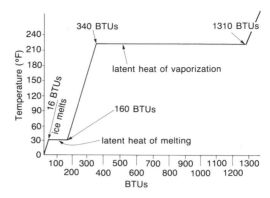

Figure 10-3. Latent heat graph for water. Graph shows the amount of heat required to turn one pound of ice at 0°F into steam at 212°F.

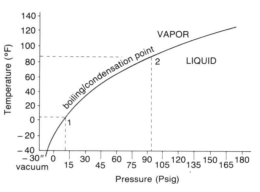

Figure 10-4. Temperature/pressure curve for R-12 refrigerant. Example: for R-12 the vaporization/condensation point at 5°F is 11.79 psig (1), at 86°F it is 93.34 psig (2).

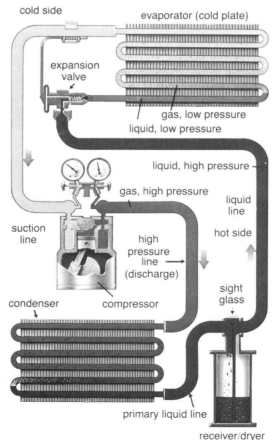

Figure 10-5. Typical refrigeration cycle. Follow the arrows from the compressor, through the condenser, receiver/dryer, expansion valve, and evaporator, then back to the compressor. (Water side of condenser not shown.)

Figure 10-6. **The refrigeration cycle.**

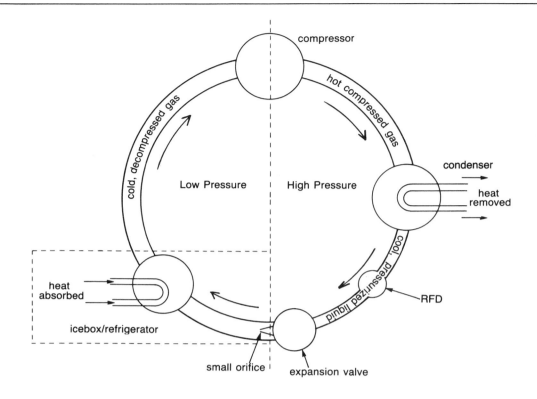

so that its pressure is held well down—typically anything from 30 psi down to a substantial vacuum, maybe as low as −10 inches of mercury. At 30 psi, liquid R-12 evaporates at 32°F (0°C); at −10 inches of mercury it evaporates at around −40°F (−40°C). (Sea level atmospheric pressure is in reality 14.7 psi, but is treated as 0 psi on most gauges. Any pressure less than atmospheric is then considered as a partial vacuum, which is commonly measured as inches of mercury pulled down in a mercury barometer. Two inches of mercury equals about 1 psi; −10 inches of mercury is approximately 5 psi below atmospheric pressure. See Figure 10-2.)

The sudden pressure drop from one side of the capillary tube or expansion valve to the other lowers the vaporization point of the liquid R-12 below the temperature in the evaporator. As a result, the liquid boils off into a gas. In doing so it absorbs large amounts of latent heat, pulling this heat out of the refrigerator or freezer and so cooling it down. The gas returns to the compressor, is recompressed, and goes back to the condenser where it is converted back into a liquid. The latent heat of condensation given up in the condenser is the same latent heat of vaporization that was absorbed in the evaporator; the heat

has been taken from the food compartment of the refrigerator or freezer and transferred to the condenser.

The condenser dissipates the heat it has gained in one of two ways: Either a fan blows air over a radiator and the air carries the heat off (just as with a car radiator), or seawater is pumped through the condenser, carrying the heat overboard (just as with a heat exchanger on an engine's cooling circuit). Water-cooled condensers are up to 25 times more effective than air-cooled. Only small constant-cycling refrigeration units (see below) will have air-cooled condensers, and many of these would be better off with water cooling. All other systems are water-cooled.

An air conditioner works in exactly the same fashion, except that it uses R-22. All refrigeration and air-conditioning units are lubricated by oil, which circulates with the refrigerant. Refrigerant oil is specially blended for extremely low temperatures, and no other type can be used.

Pressures

Suction and discharge pressures are affected by a dozen different factors. Nevertheless, a few broad generalizations may

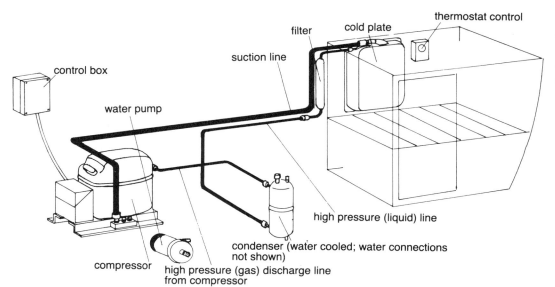

Figure 10-7. Hermetically sealed AC compressor with cold plate. This is a "shell"-type condenser (see page 284). A tube-in-tube condenser would be preferable.

control box

filter

cold plate

thermostat control

suction line

water pump

high pressure (liquid) line

condenser (water cooled; water connections not shown)

compressor

high pressure (gas) discharge line from compressor

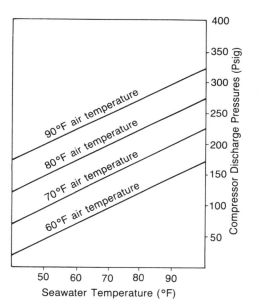

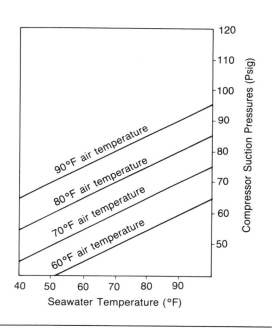

Figure 10-8. Typical operating pressures for an air-conditioning unit using R-22 with a water-cooled condenser.

help. Let's look first at refrigerators and freezers, which are usually R-12 systems. If the icebox and evaporator are warm to start with, initial suction pressures probably will run around 30 psi, discharge pressures around 175 psi. Small, constant-cycling water-cooled units will come down gradually, perhaps to about 20 psi and 150 psi (air-cooled units in hot climates may have discharge pressures as high as 180 psi). Large-capacity units with holding plates (see below) will keep coming down steadily. Suction pressures at the cold part of the cycle may range anywhere from 10 psi down to −10 inches of mercury (a considerable vacuum); discharge pressures range from 125 psi to as low as 100 psi.

Air conditioners with R-22 run at higher pressures and temperatures. They should stabilize fairly rapidly (after a few minutes) with suction pressures of 60 to 80 psi and discharge (head) pressures anywhere from 150 to 250 psi (the warmer the ambient air temperature and the cooling water, the higher the pressures). In extremely hot conditions pressures may go as high as 90 psi and 300 psi. If the unit is started on a freezing day, the ranges will be lower.

Different Types of Refrigerators, Freezers, and Air Conditioners

AC Units

A household refrigerator or freezer has a small, 115-volt (240-volt in the UK) compressor with an air-cooled condenser, a capillary-tube expansion valve, and either a finned evaporator or, in smaller fridges, a small ice cube-*cum*-freezer compartment in the form of an aluminum box with the evaporator tubing built into its sides and bottom, forming little ridges in the box. Never defrost this or any other type of fridge or freezer using a knife or ice pick; one pinhole through the evaporator tubing will destroy the whole unit. Such units are *constant cycling:* They are kept turned on the whole time, and the compressor will kick in up to 45 minutes of every hour in hot climates. They are frequently used on boats with a shoreside hook-up. When shore power is unavailable, these units require that an onboard generator run 24 hours a day.

Larger AC units on boat refrigerators and freezers (1/2 h.p. on up) generally use *cold plates,* or *holding plates,* in place of an evaporator box. The finned evaporator coil is placed in a sealed tank containing a solution to which chemicals are added to lower its freezing point—for example, to 20°F (−6.7°C) or 0°F (−17.8°C). The evaporator freezes the solution in the cold plate, and then the compressor is shut down. Over time the cold plate slowly thaws out, absorbing heat from the refrigerator or freezer. When the cold plate has almost defrosted, the compressor is turned back on and freezes it again. In a well-

Figure 10-9. **Cold plate construction.**

designed unit this should not have to be done more than once a day.

Air-conditioning units use a good-sized compressor and evaporator. A fan blows air through the cold, finned evaporator, cooling the air. This cold air then circulates around the boat. Air-conditioning units must be constant cycling and are only available with continuous AC power.

All AC units (large and small) use hermetically sealed compressors. The compressor and its drive motor are sealed in a metal canister so that there can be no refrigerant leaked from the compressor, a common problem with most other systems.

Figure 10-10A. **(Left)** Small AC air conditioning unit, front view.

Figure 10-10B. **(Right)** Small AC air conditioning unit, back view.

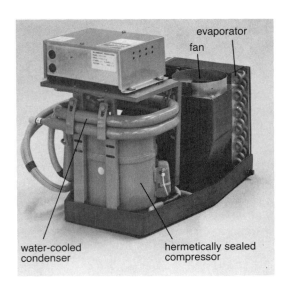

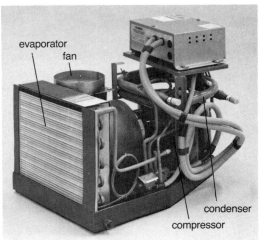

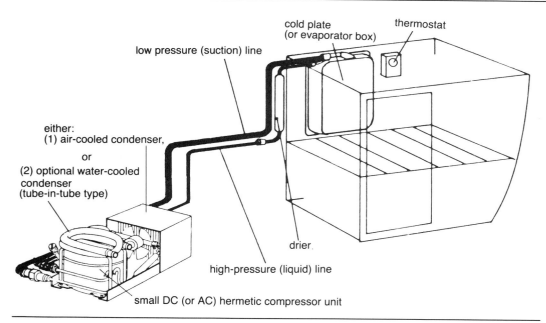

low pressure (suction) line

cold plate
(or evaporator box)

thermostat

Figure 10-11. **Small
(constant-cycling) DC
refrigeration system.**

either:
(1) air-cooled condenser,

or

(2) optional water-cooled
condenser
(tube-in-tube type)

drier

high-pressure (liquid) line

small DC (or AC) hermetic compressor unit

DC Refrigerators and Freezers

AC units require a shoreside hook-up or an onboard generator, and in the case of constant-cycling units, the generator must run 24 hours a day. To get around this, three types of DC system are used:

1. Small,constant-cycling DC units: A small electric motor powered by the ship's batteries drives a small compressor. In all other respects this is the same as a small, constant-cycling AC unit. The power drain over a 24-hour period will be considerable—more so than with larger DC units, since small compressors are less efficient than larger ones, consuming more power to produce the same overall result. An adequate bank of good-quality deep-cycle batteries is a must, and if prolonged engine running for battery charging is to be avoided, a high-capacity alternator and marine voltage regulator (or regulator bypass) also will be needed. See Chapters 1 and 2. The alternative is a large-array solar panel or high-output wind generator, which may allow a boat to refrigerate and meet all its other power needs for days on end without running its engine.

2. Intermediate DC units coupled to cold plates: Given adequate batteries, DC refrigeration units of up to ½ h.p. can be run directly from the batteries, although the larger units will pull upward of 40 amps when running. These units must be coupled to cold plates—if they are allowed to cycle on and off, the high starting loads and heavy drain soon will pull batteries down.

Some form of battery protection is required—a low battery cutout, a timer to limit compressor running, or both. Just as with constant-cycling units, deep-cycle batteries and efficient charging systems are necessary. When coupled to cold plates, a larger compressor will actually use less power for the same daily refrigeration output than will a small, constant-cycling unit.

3. Large-capacity DC motors and compressors coupled to cold plates: These are well beyond the capability of boat batteries, and can only be powered via a powerful alternator while the engine is running, or by a large battery charger with a shoreside hook-up. Such a system should need running only once a day to pull down the cold plates.

Since the compressor will be less powerful than an engine-driven compressor (see below), engine running time is likely to be longer than with an engine-driven unit. Then there are the extra costs of the alternator, battery, battery charger, and DC motor—a high price to pay for a shoreside capability.

Engine-Driven Refrigerators and Freezers

For most boat owners, these are the most powerful units of all. An automotive air-

Figure 10-12A.
Intermediate-and large-capacity DC refrigeration system.

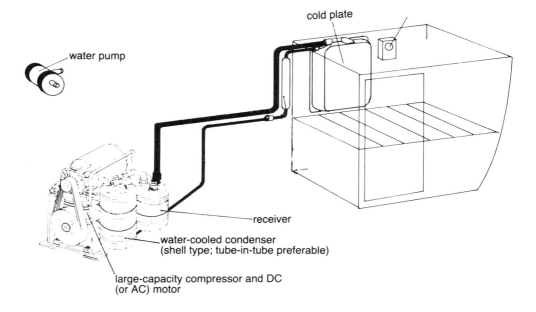

water pump

cold plate

receiver

water-cooled condenser
(shell type; tube-in-tube preferable)

large-capacity compressor and DC
(or AC) motor

Figure 10-12B.
Intermediate-sized DC refrigeration unit for use with cold plates.

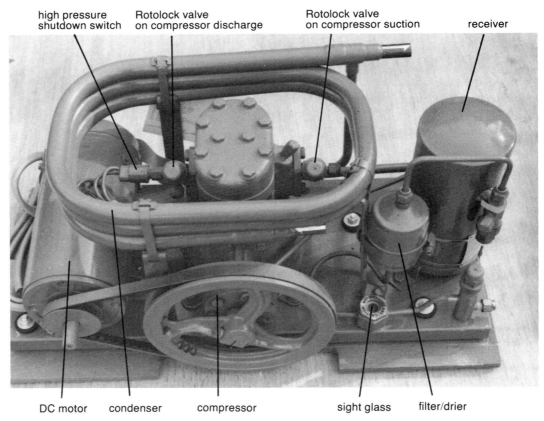

high pressure
shutdown switch

Rotolock valve
on compressor discharge

Rotolock valve
on compressor suction

receiver

DC motor   condenser   compressor   sight glass   filter/drier

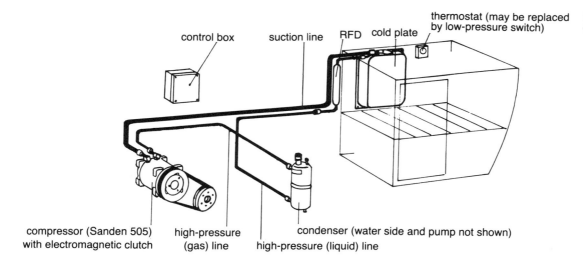

Figure 10-13A. **Engine-driven refrigeration.**

control box

suction line

RFD

cold plate

thermostat (may be replaced by low-pressure switch)

compressor (Sanden 505) with electromagnetic clutch

high-pressure (gas) line

high-pressure (liquid) line

condenser (water side and pump not shown)

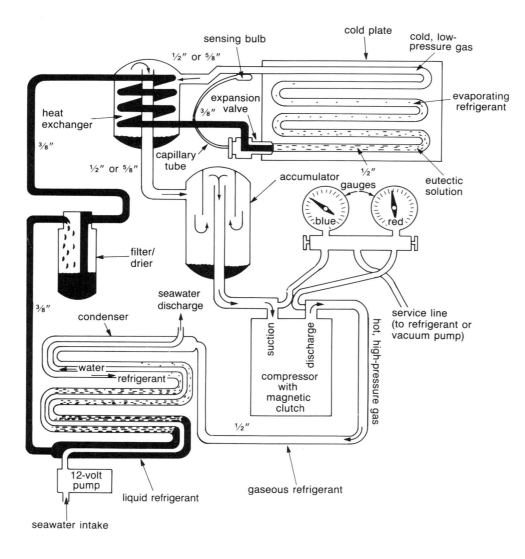

Figure 10-13B. **Engine-driven cold plate refrigeration (shown with gauge set attached).**

sensing bulb

½" or ⅝"

cold plate

cold, low-pressure gas

heat exchanger

⅜"

expansion valve

⅜"

capillary tube

½" or ⅝"

evaporating refrigerant

½"

eutectic solution

accumulator

gauges

blue

red

filter/ drier

⅜"

seawater discharge

service line (to refrigerant or vacuum pump)

condenser

suction

discharge

hot, high-pressure gas

water

refrigerant

compressor with magnetic clutch

½"

12-volt pump

liquid refrigerant

gaseous refrigerant

seawater intake

Different Types of Refrigerators, Freezers, and Air Conditioners

267

conditioning compressor is belt-driven directly off the boat's engine and used to pull down cold plates in a short time, typically one hour per day in a well set-up system. The cold plates should hold over for at least 24 hours. Some engine-driven units install the condenser in the engine cooling circuit, using the engine's water pump, but most condensers have their own water pump.

Hybrid Refrigerators and Freezers

It is quite common to find an engine-driven unit together with a small constant-cycling AC or DC unit. The small unit is used at dockside with a shore-power hookup (a DC unit runs off a battery charger), thus avoiding the need to run the engine. The small unit may have its own evaporator box or be plumbed into a small, secondary coil in the cold plates. In either case, it is completely independent of the main unit.

Thermoelectric Refrigeration

In this type refrigeration is achieved electronically, without the use of compressors or condensers. There are no moving parts. Thermoelectric units have low capacity and are used for small fridges. They will not freeze. If they go wrong, check the battery voltage, cable connections, and so on, as with any other electronic equipment (see Chapter 3).

Kerosene (Paraffin) and Propane Refrigeration

Onboard refrigerators occasionally are powered by kerosene or propane. These are inefficient, especially in the tropics, and neither work properly nor remain safe when the boat is heeled. They should be replaced with proper marine refrigeration units.

The rest of this chapter deals with all types of mechanical refrigeration—everything except thermoelectric, kerosene, and propane.

Handling Refrigerant

R–12 and R–22 are reasonably safe and inert gases, but a few precautions must be observed:

1. Both gases are heavier than air and in large quantities will displace the oxygen needed to breathe. In the small enclosed space of a boat, leaks will sink into the bilges and gradually displace the air in the cabin. Any serious leaks need to be dispersed with a good airflow through the cabin.

2. It is not safe to solder or braze on a system with refrigerant in it. At high temperatures R-12 will produce a gas similar to phosgene, which was used in the trenches in World War I. If any soldering or brazing has to be done the unit should be discharged and purged, if possible with carbon dioxide.

3. No refrigerant ever should be added to the high-pressure side of a unit when it is running. The high pressures may blow up the can of refrigerant.

4. Refrigerant containers should not be left in direct sunlight or allowed to heat up beyond 125°F (52°C).

5. Cans of refrigerant contain liquid in the bottom, gas in the top. If the can is inverted when charging a system, liquid will come out. This is sometimes done by professionals, but amateurs should always play safe: Charge with gas; never invert the can.

6. Evaporating refrigerant is extremely cold. It can cause frostbite and permanent damage to eyes. Always bleed a system right down with the gauge set (see below) before opening it up, and keep fingers away from the venting refrigerant. Wear safety glasses.

R-12 and R-22

Almost all refrigeration units use R-12; almost all air-conditioning units use R-22. The two operate in a similar fashion but at different pressures and temperatures. *They are not compatible. In particular, R-22 placed in a system designed for R-12 will wreck the system.* Be very careful to put the right gas in a system. R-12 generally comes in white cans; R-22, in green.

Refrigerant can be bought in one-pound cans from most automotive stores. These are expensive and need a special adaptor to put the refrigerant in the system. More than one can will be needed to charge even the smallest unit. On my boat I carry a 15- or 30-pound can and keep it on board. These too can be bought at automotive stores. The cost should be between $1 and $2 per pound—shop around. Even if you

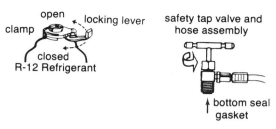

open · locking lever
clamp
closed
R-12 Refrigerant

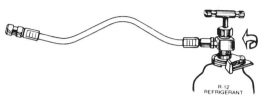

safety tap valve and
hose assembly

↑ bottom seal
gasket

R-12
REFRIGERANT

Figure 10-14. Using small cans of R-12 refrigerant to recharge your system. (1) With lever in open position, seat clamp into place on top of can of R-12 refrigerant. (2) Rotate clamp lever to fully closed position.(3) Examine valve assembly. Make sure that penetrator is completely retracted by turning valve handle counterclockwise. Check that bottom seal gasket is in place. Do not force beyond initial stop. (4) Screw valve and hose assembly into clamp until valve bottoms. Do not overtighten. (5) Attach charging hose loosely to low pressure service connection, or to the service hose connection on a gauge set. (6) Screw in safety tap valve handle until seated. This will cause the needle to pierce the can and at the same time close the valve. (7) If using a gauge set, close both gauge valves. (8) Open the valve on the can of refrigerant. Gas will blow out of the loose charging hose connection. After a second or two snug up this connection by hand only. (9) If using a gauge set, refer to "Purging a Gauge Set" (see below). If connection is directly to the compressor low side (suction) service valve, see "Charging a System." Caution: Never remove the adapter assembly from a can of refrigerant until the can is completely empty, otherwise the remaining contents will be vented uncontrollably.

never need it yourself, someone you meet along the way will be eternally grateful for a topping up from your can! A gauge set will be needed to put the refrigerant in the system.

Use of Gauges to Add Refrigerant

A refrigeration gauge set is not expensive ($20 to $50—again, shop around) and *is an essential troubleshooting tool.*

A gauge set includes one red and one blue gauge screwed into a "manifold," and below each gauge is a hose. On either side of the manifold is a valve. A third hose, the service hose, is located between the two gauge hoses. When the gauge valves are closed, the gauges will register the pressure in their respective hoses. When either valve is opened, its hose is connected with the service hose. When both valves are opened at the same time, all three hoses equalize with one another. The blue side of a gauge set always connects to the suction (low-pressure) side of a compressor, the red side to the discharge (high-pressure) side. Suction and discharge connections will be found on the suction and discharge fittings on the compressor. Belt-driven compressors generally have the cylinder head stamped "SUCT" and "DISCH"; hermetically sealed compressors may not be labeled, but it doesn't mat-

Figure 10-15. **(Left)** A refrigerant gauge set: an essential tool for self-sufficient, refrigeration-equipped boats. **(Right)** Suction-side gauge. The outer band indicates pressure; the inner bands the evaporation/condensation temperature of R-22, R-12, and R-502 refrigerants at any given pressure.

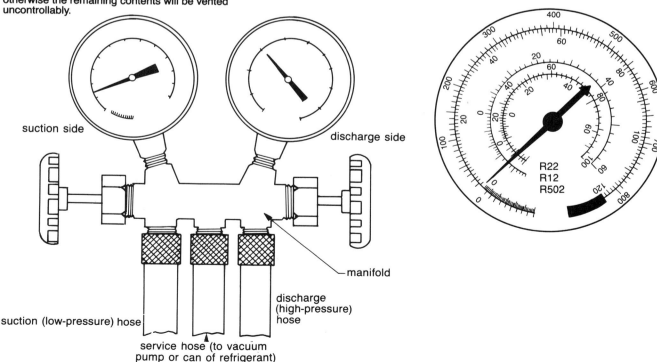

suction side

discharge side

manifold

discharge
(high-pressure)
hose

suction (low-pressure) hose

service hose (to vacuum
pump or can of refrigerant)

R22
R12
R502

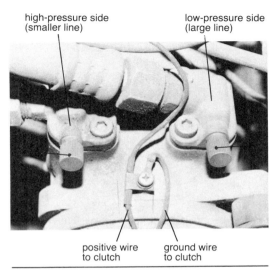

Figure 10-16. **Engine-driven compressor gauge connections.**

high-pressure side (smaller line)

low-pressure side (large line)

positive wire to clutch

ground wire to clutch

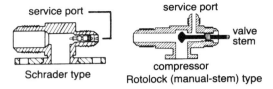

service port

service port

valve stem

Schrader type

compressor
Rotolock (manual-stem) type

Figure 10-17A. **The two most commonly found types of service valves.**

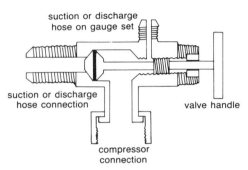

suction or discharge hose on gauge set

suction or discharge hose connection

valve handle

compressor connection

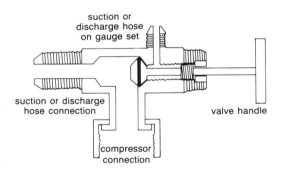

suction or discharge hose on gauge set

suction or discharge hose connection

valve handle

compressor connection

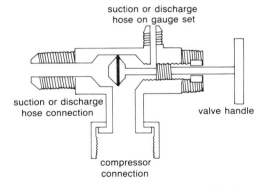

suction or discharge hose on gauge set

suction or discharge hose connection

valve handle

compressor connection

Figure 10-17B. Rotolock (manual stem-type) valve operation. **(Top)** Valve is closed to system but open to gauge set (for compressor removal, etc.). **(Middle)** Valve is closed to gauge set but open to system (for normal operation). **(Bottom)** Valve is open to both system and gauge set (for monitoring performance, etc.).

ter. *The suction line is always larger than the discharge line.* There may also be other hose connections around the system, but the two closest to the compressor are the ones you want. The discharge connection is *only* needed when troubleshooting. Routine procedures such as evacuating and charging a system (see below) can all be done with just the suction side connected.

Compressor Connections

It is vitally important that no dirt enter a system. Before making any connections make sure that everything is spotlessly clean. Tighten the hose fittings by hand only.

The hose connections on the compressor will be fitted with service valves. There are two kinds: Schrader valves and screw-type (Rotolock or "manual-stem") valves. Schrader valves are the same as valves on bicycle and car tires, with a spring-loaded pin. One end of each hose on the gauge set has a metal piece for depressing the pin in a Schrader valve—this end must always go on the valve.

Rotolock valves have a squared-off stem, which is screwed in and out to open and close the valve. There are three possible positions: all the way out (counterclockwise or anticlockwise) closes off the gauge hose to the system but leaves the compressor hooked in; the mid-position (a turn or so clockwise) opens the gauge hose to the system while still leaving the compressor hooked in; and all the way in (clockwise) closes off the compressor to the system but leaves the gauge hose connected to the compressor (Figure 10-17). A proper 1/4-inch square ratchet wrench—obtainable from refrigeration supply houses—is highly recommended for Rotolock valves. The use of adjustable wrenches or pliers soon messes up valve stems.

Purging a Gauge Set

Once a refrigeration or air-conditioning unit is charged *it is essential that no air be allowed to enter the system.* What this means in practice is that anytime a gauge set is hooked up for charging, all air must be purged from the gauge set hoses and replaced with refrigerant before making the final connections. To do this, shut down the unit (if it is running). There are then two methods:

1. This method uses refrigerant already in the system (presupposing it has at least a partial charge). Close both gauge valves, loosen the hoses below the gauges, and prepare to screw the hoses onto their compressor connections.

   If the compressor has Schrader valves, as each hose is done up it will open the Schrader valve and refrigerant gas will blow out of the loosened connection at the gauge manifold. The connection is then snugged up. This hose is purged.

   If the compressor has Rotolock valves, turn the valves fully counterclockwise before making any connections. Attach the hoses at the compressor, then turn the Rotolock valves clockwise one-half to one turn. Refrigerant will blow out of the loosened connections at the gauge manifold. These connections are then snugged up. The hoses are purged.

   Connect a can of refrigerant to the service hose, leaving the hose loose at the can. Crack open either one of the gauge valves—refrigerant will blow out of the loose connection at the can. Snug up the connection. Purging is complete. (Note that if the can has a Schrader valve, the pin on the service hose must go on the can.)

2. This method uses a can of refrigerant. Close the valve on the can, then connect the can to the gauge manifold with the service hose and tighten both connections. Tighten the other two hoses at the manifold and connect them *loosely* at the compressor (we do not want to open a Schrader valve at this stage). Close both gauge valves and open the valve on the can of refrigerant. Crack

each gauge valve in turn, blowing refrigerant out of the loose hose connection at the compressor before tightening the connection. Close the gauge valves or you will be adding refrigerant to the system if it has Schrader valves. Purging is complete. On a unit with Schrader valves, once the hoses are tightened the gauges are always open to the system, but where Rotolock valves are fitted the valves must be opened one-half to one turn clockwise.

Charging a System

Purge the hoses. (If the unit has just been vacuumed, as described below, and the gauge set is still connected, just purge the hose from the can of refrigerant to the gauge manifold.) Check to see that both gauge valves are closed and the Rotolock valves on the compressor (if fitted) are open one turn. Make sure the can of refrigerant is upright. Open the valve on the can of refrigerant. Open the suction-side gauge valve. Refrigerant will enter the unit. Wait until the pressure in the system has settled down (probably at around 60 to 70 psi, but this depends on ambient temperatures). If you are using a small can of refrigerant and the can runs out, close the gauge valve, put on a new can, purge the service hose, and continue. *Then close the suction valve on the gauge set.*

Locate the sight glass on the system. It will probably be on top of or next to the RFD. (Some air-conditioning units do not have a sight glass—see below.) Take a look in it; it will be clear. Now start the unit and watch the sight glass. Fairly soon foamy, fast-moving bubbles will appear as the first liquid refrigerant comes out of the condenser mixed with gas bubbles. The bubbles should steadily decrease. In a fully charged, fully cold system they will disappear altogether, leaving a sight glass that is once again completely clear, but this time filled with liquid.

The initial charge of refrigerant, however, is not going to be enough to clear the sight glass. The problem is to determine how much more to put in—too much will damage the compressor. *The final charge can only be determined with the unit cold.* In the case of air conditioners and refrigeration units without cold plates this will take only 5 minutes or so, but where cold plates are fitted, if the plates are warm, it may take 20 minutes to a half hour, perhaps even longer.

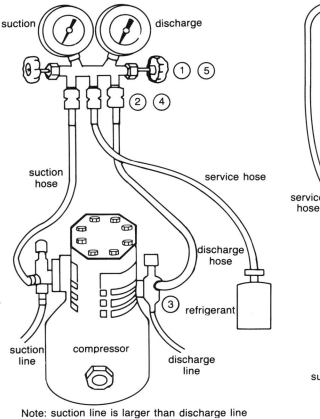

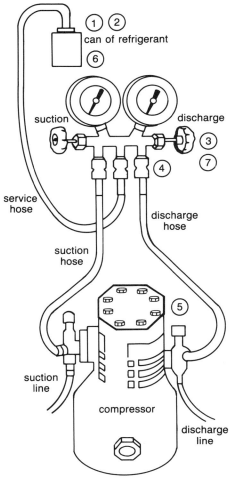

Note: suction line is larger than discharge line

Figure 10-18A. Purging a gauge set using refrigerant already in the system. **Preliminary step:** If the system has Rotolock valves, fully backseat the valves. (1) Close both gauge valves. (2) Loosen the suction and discharge hose connections at the gauge set; tighten the service hose connection. (3) Tighten the suction and discharge hose connections at the compressor one at a time. (4) Schrader valves: Allow refrigerant to blow out of the loosened connections at the gauge set for a second or two and then snug up. Rotolock valves: Turn the valves clockwise one-half to one turn; allow refrigerant to blow out of the loosened connections at the gauge set for a second or two and then snug up. (5) Connect the service hose loosely to a can of refrigerant; crack open either gauge valve; allow refrigerant to blow out of the loosened connection at the can of refrigerant for a second or two and then snug up. Purging is complete.

Figure 10-18B. Purging a gauge set using a can of refrigerant. **Preliminary step:** If the system has Rotolock valves, fully backseat the valves. (1) Close the valve on the can of refrigerant. (2) Tighten the service hose at the can of refrigerant. (3) Close the gauge valves. (4) Tighten all three hose connections at the gauge manifold. (5) Fit the hoses loosely at the compressor. (6) Open the valve on the can of refrigerant. (7) Crack each gauge valve in turn; allow refrigerant to blow out of the loosened connection at the compressor for a second or two then snug up. Now close the gauge valve if the compressor has Schrader valves or you will be adding refrigerant to the system. Purging is complete.

Monitor the sight glass continually. If the stream of bubbles is still pretty steady once the unit has cooled down, open the suction-side gauge valve to let in more refrigerant. The bubbles will start to decrease. After a while there may be just one big bubble hovering in the top of the sight glass. Close the gauge valve and let the unit stabilize. If more bubbles appear, add more refrigerant. Let the unit get really cold—don't rush things—before doing the final topping off. Eventually the sight glass should be completely clear (all liquid). *Don't add any more refrigerant.* If compressor discharge pressures become excessively high (much over 200 psi on a refrigeration unit or 250 psi on an air conditioner), and/or the suction line on a refrigeration unit starts to frost heavily all the way back to the compressor, the system is almost certainly overcharged. There should be no frosting of the suction line in an air conditioner.

Charging a unit without a sight glass. If the owner's manual is around it will probably specify the weight of refrigerant (in pounds) required for a full charge. Hang the can of refrigerant from a set of scales and weigh off this amount (this goes for any system where the weight is known). Alternatively, many air-conditioning manuals specify a set of operating pressures at certain ambient air and cooling water temperatures. Measure the air and water temperatures, enter the graphs provided, and read off the suction and discharge ("head") pressures. Continue adding refrigerant until these pressures, or something close to them, is reached. When charged and in operation the compressor suction line will be cool and probably sweating. If it is warm, the charge is inadequate; if it is frosting, the charge is excessive. (This applies to air conditioners only; many refrigeration and freezer units run colder, and some frosting of the suction line is acceptable.)

Removing a Gauge Set

Shut down the unit. Close off any can of refrigerant, but leave its hose connections tight. Open both gauge valves until the system equalizes, with both gauges reading the same pressure. Close both gauge valves. Loosen the hose connection at the can of refrigerant, allow the hose pressure to bleed off, and remove it.

1. *Schrader valves.* Remove each hose in turn at the compressor *as fast as possible.* Refrigerant will vent as long as the valve stem is depressed, which is why the hoses must be undone quickly.
2. *Rotolock valves.* Backseat the valves counterclockwise. Crack one of the gauge valves and bleed off its hose through the service hose. Close the valve and observe the pressure—if it climbs back up, the Rotolock valve is not properly seated (the high-pressure side may show a slight rise initially but then should stabilize). When the Rotolock valve is holding, bleed off the hose and remove it.

Cap all valves and hose ends to make sure that no dirt can enter the system.

Vacuuming ("Evacuating") a System

In most troubleshooting situations the unit should still have some refrigerant in it, even if it has a slow leak. But if it has bled down completely, or if it has had to be broken open for any reason, it must be completely cleared of air before it is recharged with refrigerant. This is normally done by hiring a refrigeration expert, who will use a vacuum pump. The pump is connected via the gauge set and sucks the unit down to a complete vacuum, removing all air. Refrigerant then is put in.

Sometimes when a unit is bled down or loses its charge due to a leak, the lubricating oil will be lost from the system. Before evacuating and recharging a system, always ensure that it has adequate oil (see below), or the compressor will burn out quite rapidly in use. In the absence of a vacuum pump it is possible to evacuate a system using the compressor, but *this procedure should be carried out only if there is no other choice.* It is not as effective as a vacuum pump and carries the risk of damaging the compressor.

1. Connect the gauge set to the compressor. Close the gauge valves. Loosen the discharge hose at the gauge set. Open the compressor Rotolock valves (if fitted) one turn. Connect a can of refrigerant to the service hose. Open the can's valve wide and then the suction-side gauge valve wide. Refrigerant will blow around the system and out through the discharge hose at the loose connection on the gauge manifold. Let it blow for a few seconds and then close the valve on the can of refrigerant, tighten the discharge hose while it is still venting, and close the suction-side gauge valve (both valves will now be closed). Disconnect the service hose at the can of refrigerant. At this point most of the moisture and air will have been blown out of the system.
2. Put an inch or two of clean *refrigeration oil* (which can be bought from most automotive parts stores) in a jam jar. Start the unit and turn on the compressor. Keep the compressor speed down if possible (for example, idle the engine on an engine-driven unit). Open the discharge-side gauge valve—the compressor will pump down the system through the open service hose. When the gas flow from the service hose slows (this won't take long, and the slowing will be audible to the ear or touch) dip the hose into the jar of refrigeration oil so that no air can be sucked back in. Watch the suction gauge.

3. The service hose in the oil will stop bubbling and the suction gauge will go into a vacuum quite quickly (within a minute or two). If it doesn't there is a bad leak on the system (the service hose will continue to bubble) or the compressor is defective. Engine-driven compressors should pull a vacuum of up to −28 inches of mercury; smaller units will pull less. Once the system is at its deepest vacuum, close the discharge gauge valve and *shut down the compressor.* The unit is now evacuated.

4. Reconnect the can of refrigerant. Loosen the service hose at the manifold. Open the valve on the can of refrigerant and purge the service hose. Tighten the hose at the gauge manifold. Open the suction-side valve and fill the unit with refrigerant. Loosen the discharge hose at the gauge manifold and blow off refrigerant again—we are back at step 1. Close the valve on the can of refrigerant, tighten the discharge hose while it is still venting, and close the suction-side gauge valve (both valves will now be closed). Disconnect the can of refrigerant.

5. Repeat steps 2 and 3.

6. Reconnect the can of refrigerant, purge the service hose as in step 4, and charge the unit as described above. *On no account remove the gauge set until enough refrigerant has been put in to give positive pressure in the unit, or you will have wasted your efforts!*

Note: There are two types of belt-driven compressors in widespread use on engine-driven systems—*reciprocal* and *swash-plate* ("wobble") compressors. The former tend to be square, the latter round (see below). Neither type likes to be used for evacuating a unit, but *swash-plate compressors are especially prone to burnout due to oil starvation.* Use a compressor to pump a system down only when there is no other choice, and *never run the compressor like this for more than two or three minutes.*

New compressors come fully charged with oil. If you're fitting a new engine-driven compressor and evacuating the system as described above, don't fit the drive belt before you've turned the compressor over by hand a dozen times to drive any oil out of the cylinders. If oil still dribbles out of the discharge hose during step 1 above, replace what is lost with an equal amount of clean refrigeration oil.

Maintenance and Repair: Component-by-Component Guide

Iceboxes

A refrigeration or freezer system is only as good as the icebox it is cooling. If the box has inadequate insulation and seals, the unit is never likely to operate satisfactorily. Things to check for are:

1. A minimum of 3 inches of closed-cell foam (polyurethane, not Styrofoam or polystyrene) on refrigerators; 4 to 6 inches on freezers, all around (the tops can be thinner).

2. Tightly fitting lids or doors with proper seals—excessive frosting may indicate leaking seals. Try placing a dollar bill all around the lid or door and pulling it out. It should be gripped at all points.

3. Any drains must have a U-trap or valve to prevent cold air sinking out of the box. Drains frequently are overlooked and can cause major heat losses.

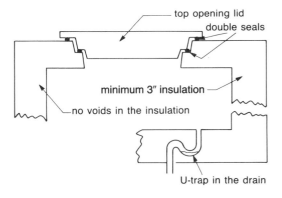

Figure 10-19. **A proper icebox should have a double-sealed, top-opening lid, a minimum of three inches of closed-cell foam insulation, and a U-trap drain to prevent the escape of cold air.**

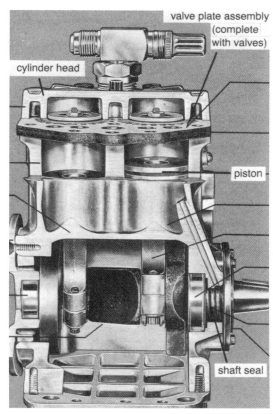

valve plate assembly (complete with valves)

cylinder head

piston

shaft seal

Figure 10-20. **Reciprocal compressor.**

Compressors

Hermetically sealed compressors are inaccessible and either work or don't work. Among belt-driven compressors, two types predominate, as mentioned above: reciprocal and swash-plate ("wobble"). Reciprocal compressors use a crankshaft-driven piston, just as in an engine. Almost all those used in boat refrigeration are made by either Tecumseh or York, the two being almost identical except that the Tecumsehs have a cast iron block and the Yorks an aluminum block.

Swash-plate compressors have multiple pistons (normally five or six) that are all connected to a "wobble" plate, beneath which is a lob-sided rotor (it has a cam built into it). As the cam on the rotor passes beneath the wobble plate the plate is moved up and down, which in turn moves the pistons up and down. Most swash-plate compressors in boat use are made by Sankyo/Sanden.

Belts on compressors must be correctly aligned. With the belt off, a length of 1/2-inch (13-mm) doweling should drop cleanly into the grooves on the two pulleys. The belts should be set up moderately tight—tighter than alternator belts. Compressors must be extremely rigidly mounted. Without a solid mount, correct alignment, and adequate tension the compressor will chew up belts at regular intervals. If the belts vibrate excessively, particularly when long belt runs are involved, an idler pulley is needed to bear against the center stretch of the belt.

Compressors are lubricated by oil circulating with the refrigerant. Reciprocal compressors also have a sizable oil sump, but swash-plate compressors do not. *If a swash-plate compressor is run without refrigerant in the system (for example, if it has leaked out), it will burn up.* These compressors should be protected by a low-pressure cutout switch and/or a high-temperature cutout switch *on the compressor body* (this de-energizes the clutch if the compressor overheats).

Notwithstanding the practice of some refrigeration companies, swash-plate compressors should not be used on systems with more than two cold plates, since the oil in the system may puddle out in the long cold-plate coils and lead to compressor burnout. Extra oil should always be added to the system to provide a margin of safety (up to seven ounces on a medium-sized two-plate unit).

The colder the temperature on a system the lower the suction pressure at the compressor. Some freezer units may pull down to a vacuum of more than –10 inches of mercury. The lower the suction pressure the less refrigerant is circulated, and therefore the less oil as well. Swash-plate compressors should not be pulled into a vacuum for prolonged periods—they are likely to burn up. The valves are also susceptible to damage.

Swash-plate compressors should not really be used where cold plates are run in parallel, with shutdown solenoids on each plate. As the plates freeze and shut down, the full compressor output is concentrated on the last plate, frequently pulling it into a vacuum.

Almost all engine-driven refrigeration units marketed today use swash-plate compressors because they are cheaper and lighter than reciprocal compressors. The buyer should know that the failure rate is higher. Where possible, anyone contemplating offshore cruising would be well advised to spend the extra on a reciprocal compressor. However, this may not be pos-

Figure 10-21. **Swash-plate ("wobble") engine-driven compressor.**

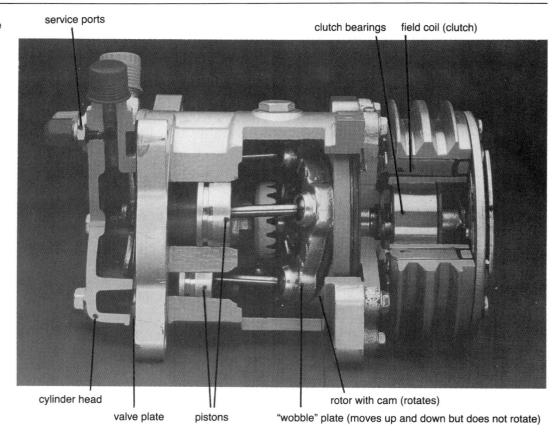

service ports

clutch bearings   field coil (clutch)

cylinder head

valve plate   pistons

rotor with cam (rotates)

"wobble" plate (moves up and down but does not rotate)

Table 10-1. Pulley Sizes[1].

| Engine Speed (r.p.m.) | Pulley Ratio | Engine Pulley Size for: | |
		6-inch Compressor Pulley (inches)	4½-inch Compressor Pulley (inches)
1,000	1 : 1	6	4½
1,500	1 : 1½	4	3
2,000	1 : 2	3	2¼
2,500	1 : 2½	2⅖	1⅘
3,000	1 : 3	2	1½
3,500	1 : 3½	1⁷⁄₁₀	1³⁄₁₀

1. For compressor speed of 1,000 r.p.m.

sible on smaller one-and two-plate units, since the larger reciprocal compressors may simply be too powerful for the system, dragging it into a deep vacuum, which will sooner or later damage any compressor.

Compressors can only handle gases. If a unit is overcharged or the expansion valve incorrectly adjusted (see below), there is a danger of *liquid* refrigerant entering the compressor—a condition known as "liquid slugging." The compressor is likely to start knocking, and the engine may bog down. Liquid slugging can do extensive damage to a compressor.

Compressor valves and the seal behind the pulley are the two most common problem areas.

Valves. Valves are reasonably easy to replace, but be sure you have the two gaskets needed and a new valve plate assembly before starting. The compressor must be bled of all refrigerant. Clean all exterior surfaces. Remove the suction and discharge hoses, Rotolock valves (if fitted), and the compressor suction and discharge connections if they are *bolted* to the cylinder head. Undo the cylinder head's retaining bolts.

Figure 10-23A. **(Opposite)** Replacing valves on York and Tecumseh compressors. The service ports have been removed (only necessary if they have been through-bolted) and the cylinder head bolts undone. The "S" cast into the right hand side of the cylinder head denotes the suction side.

Figure 10-23B. **(Below Left)** The cylinder head has been tapped loose to reveal the valve plate. The two locating dowels ensure the valve assembly will be replaced correctly.

Figure 10-23C. **(Below Right)** The valve plate itself has now been tapped loose to reveal the pistons. The gasket material adhering to both faces will need to be scrupulously cleaned off. Take care not to scratch the soft aluminum surfaces or allow anything to fall into the compressor.

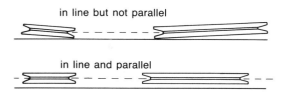

in line but not parallel

in line and parallel

Figure 10-22. **Pulley alignment**

Figure 10-24. **An exploded view of a Sanden (Sankyo) compressor. The pulley, clutch bearing, and field coil assembly** *(top)* **mount on the end of the shaft** *(bottom, left).*

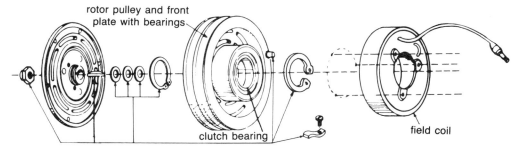

rotor pulley and front plate with bearings

clutch bearing

field coil

accessory kit: nut, key, shims, snap rings, coil, lead wire clamp with screw, retainer screws

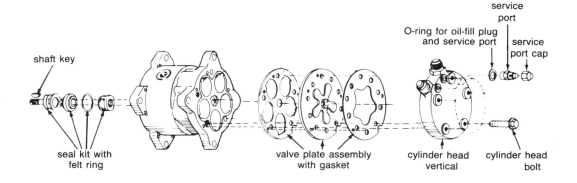

shaft key

seal kit with felt ring

valve plate assembly with gasket

O-ring for oil-fill plug and service port

service port

service port cap

cylinder head vertical

cylinder head bolt

Beneath the cylinder head is a gasket; beneath that, a thin metal plate (the valve plate); and beneath that another gasket. The head and then the valve plate must be pried off. *Do not scratch any aluminum surfaces. Note which way around and which way up the various pieces go. Scrupulously clean all surfaces. Make sure no bits of dirt or old gasket fall in the cylinders.*

Clean everything again. Lightly oil the cylinder block with refrigeration oil and set the new lower gasket in place. Use no gasket cement of any kind. Lightly oil both faces of the valve plate and set it in place. Put on the new head gasket, lightly oil the cylinder head, and set it in place. Lightly oil the threads on the cylinder head bolts and run them in by hand. If they won't go in all the way, find out why—take them out and clean the threads. Check the lengths—sometimes some are longer than others and must go back in specific holes. Don't force them down—it is easy to crack or strip off aluminum castings. When all are an easy fit by hand, torque to the manufacturer's specifications (or 20 foot pounds if in doubt). Torque in two stages

(e.g., 15 foot pounds and then 20 foot pounds) and work from side to side.

Shaft Seals. Small leaks around shaft seals are inevitable, so don't be too hasty to condemn a seal. Many leaks picked up by ultrasensitive electronic leak detectors are quite acceptable (see below), but anytime a leak is picked up by a Halide leak tester or soap solutions, the seal is gone.

Some compressor shaft seals are not too hard to replace; others require specialized equipment. But in any case, seal repairs frequently do not hold up too well. It is best to replace the compressor, or at least exchange it for a rebuilt one (these are not too expensive). The most important thing that can be done to prolong seal life is to run the unit frequently. This keeps the seal lubricated.

Clutches. Engine-driven compressors employ an electromagnetic clutch using 12 volts from the boat's battery. The drive pulley freewheels around the clutch unit, which is keyed to the drive shaft. Energizing the clutch locks the unit and drives the

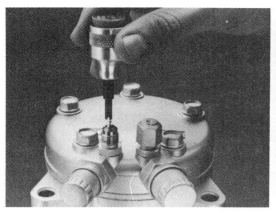

Figure 10-25A. **(Left)** Cylinder head and valve plate service for Sanden (Sankyo) Compressors. Inspect cylinder head for fitting or thread damage; discard if damaged. Inspect the two service ports on the back of the cylinder head. The valve core can be removed by using Sanden's Valve Core Tool.

Figure 10-25B. **(Right)** The complete service port can be removed with a 14mm wrench. Inspect the service port O-ring (same as oil filler plug O-ring); replace if damaged.

Figure 10-25C. **(Left)** Remove the five cylinder head cap screws using a 13mm socket.

Figure 10-25D. **(Right)** Tap the outer edge of the cylinder head with a small hammer and a gasket scraper until it is freed from the valve plate. Inspect for damage. (The cylinder head gasket normally sticks to the valve plate.)

Figure 10-25E, F. Position gasket scraper between the outside edge of the valve plate and the cylinder block and lightly tap the valve plate loose. Inspect reed valves and discharge retainer. Discard assembly if any portion is damaged.

Figure 10-25G, H. If valve plate and/or cylinder head are to be reused, carefully remove gasket materials using the gasket scraper. Do not damage cylinder block or valve plate surfaces.

Figure 10-25I, J. **Installing the cylinder head only:** Check valve plate again for damage and removal of all old gasket material. Coat valve plate top with clean refrigerant oil. Position new gasket. Set cylinder head inplace and torque as shown in Figure 10-25M.

Figure 10-25K. **Installing valve plate and cylinder head:** (1) Coat new valve plate gasket with clean refrigerant oil. (2) Install valve plate gasket. Align valve plate gasket with locating pin holes and oil orifice in cylinder block (the gaskets have a notch at the bottom outside edge to aid alignment).

Figure 10-25L. (3) Install valve plate. With the discharge valve, retainer, and nut pointing away from the cylinder block, align valve plate locating pins to the pin holes in the block and position valve plate. (4) Install cylinder head. (refer to cylinder head installation, Figures 10-25I and 10-25J).

Figure 10-25M.
IMPORTANT NOTE:
Torque cylinder head to 22 to 25 foot pounds (3.0–3.4 kg) using the "star" configuration as shown.

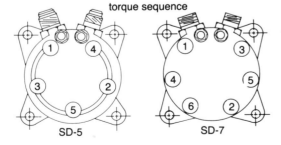

torque sequence

SD-5   SD-7

compressor. When the engine is running with the clutch disengaged, the pulley turns but its center hub remains stationary. When the clutch is energized the center hub turns with the pulley.

If the compressor fails to operate, energize the clutch and make sure the center hub is turning. If it is not, or if it is slipping, check the voltage at the clutch and check its ground wire. (A slipping clutch also may be the result of oil on the clutch.) If there is no voltage, or a severe voltage drop, test the clutch by jumping it out directly from the positive terminal on the battery. If the clutch still fails to work it needs replacing. Those on Tecumsehs and Yorks are reasonably easy. Sankyo/Sanden require two special tools, which cruising sailors are well advised to buy: a clutch front-plate wrench (spanner) and a front-plate puller. A couple of other tools—a rotor puller and installer set, and a clutch plate installer—are useful but not necessary.

To remove a York or Tecumseh clutch assembly, a special tool is normally used to lock the pulley hub so that the pulley retaining nut can be undone. Some means of holding the hub will have to be devised. A universal deck plate key works well. Place a wrench on the bolt and hit it smartly to jar it loose. Take out the bolt. *Do not hit the pulley rim to break it loose from its tapered shaft.* Find a 5/8-inch NC (coarse thread) bolt to fit the threads in the center of the pulley and wind in the bolt to back the pulley off. Unbolt the clutch retaining plate from the compressor block (four bolts). Replace the whole clutch and pulley assembly as one.

Figure 10-26A. **(Left)** 1. Replacing a clutch on Sanden (Sankyo) compressors. Insert the two pins of the front plate spanner into any two threaded holes of the clutch front plate. Hold clutch plate stationary. Remove hex nut with 3/4-inch (19mm) socket.

Figure 10-26B. **(Right)** 2. Remove clutch front plate using puller. Align puller center bolt to compressor shaft. Thumb tighten the three puller bolts into the threaded holes. Turn center bolt clockwise with 3/4-inch (19mm) socket until front plate is loosened.
NOTE: Steps 1 and 2 must be performed before servicing either the shaft seal or clutch assembly.

Figure 10-26C. **(Left)** For HD-series compressors, remove bearing dust cover as shown.

Figure 10-26D. **(Right)** 3. Remove shaft key by lightly tapping it loose with a screwdriver and hammer.

Figure 10-26E. **(Left)** 4. Remove the internal bearing snap ring by using snap ring pliers (pinch type).

Figure 10-26F. **(Right)** Note: On some later model clutches, the snap ring is below the bearing, and step 4 will not be necessary.

Figure 10-26G. **(Left)** 5. Remove the external front housing snap ring by using snap ring pliers (spread type).

Figure 10-26H. **(Right)** 6. Remove rotor pulley assembly. First insert the lip of the jaws into the snap ring grove (snap ring removed in step 4). Then place rotor puller shaft protector (puller set) over the exposed shaft.

Figure 10-26I. **Align thumb-head bolts with puller jaws and finger tighten.**

Figure 10-26J, K. **Turn puller center bolt clockwise using 3/4-inch socket until rotor pulley is free.**

Figure 10-26L. **(Left)** 7. Remove field winding; loosen winding lead wire from its clip on top of compressor front housing. (Early models do not use this clip; 1979 and later models use a snap-ring retainer for the field coil; 1978 and prior model 508s are held with screws.)

Figure 10-26M. **(Right)** Use spread-type snap ring pliers to remove snap ring and field coil.

Figure 10-26N. **(Left)** Clutch installation: (1) Install field coil. Reverse the procedure outlined in step 7, "Removing Clutch." Coil flange protrusion must match hole in front housing to prevent coil movement and correctly locate lead wire. (2) Replace rotor pulley: Support the compressor on the four mounting ears at the compressor rear. If using a vise, clamp only on the mounting ears—never on the compressor body. Then align rotor assembly squarely on the front housing hub.

Figure 10-26O. Using rotor installer set, place the ring part of the set into the bearing cavity. Make certain the outer edge rests firmly on the outer race of the rotor bearing. Now place the tool set driver into the ring as shown.

Figure 10-26P. Tap the end of the driver with a hammer while guiding the rotor to prevent binding. Tap until the rotor bottoms against the compressor's front housing hub (there will be a a distinct change of sound during the tapping process).(3) Reinstall internal bearing snap ring with pinch-type pliers.(4) Reinstall external front housing snap ring with spread-type pliers.(5) Replace front plate assembly. Check that the original clutch shims are in place on the compressor shaft. Next replace compressor shaft key. Then align front plate keyway with compressor shaft key.

Figure 10-26Q. Using shaft protector, tap front plate onto shaft until it bottoms on the clutch shims (there will be a distinct sound change).(6) Replace shaft hex nut. Torque to 25 to 30 foot pounds. Note: SD–505 torque is 156 ± 26 in./lbs.; 180 ± 30 kg./cm.

Figure 10-26R. (7) Check air gap with feeler gauge to 0.016 to 0.031 inch. If air gap is not consistent around the circumference, lightly pry up at the minimum variations; lightly tap down at points of maximum variation. Note: The air gap is determined by the spacer shims. When reinstalling or installing a new clutch assembly, try the original shims first. When installing a new clutch onto a compressor that previously did not have a clutch, use 0.040, 0.020, and 0.005 shims from the clutch accessory kit. If the air gap does not meet the specification in step 7, add or subtract shims by repeating steps 5 and 6.

clutch front plate spanner

front plate puller

rotor puller set

clutch rotor installer set

clutch plate installer

dipstick

Figure 10-27. **Special tools used in servicing Sanden (Sankyo) compressors.**

Condensers

Air-cooled condensors. Air-cooled condensers are totally dependent on a good flow of cool air over the condenser fins. If the condenser is in an enclosed space or an engine room, ambient air temperatures will climb, and condenser efficiency will fall dramatically. Likewise, if the cooling fins are plugged with dust, efficiency will fall. Make sure any air-cooled condenser has an adequate flow of cool air. If necessary, duct air into the bottom of the condenser compartment (minimum 4-inch or 100-mm duct) and vent the top of the compartment (minimum 4-inch-diameter vent). Never obstruct the ducts. Fan motors require no maintenance but an occasional light oiling of shafts and bearings. Note that DC fans, if connected with reverse polarity, will run in reverse, greatly reducing efficiency. If the motor fails to operate make all the usual voltage tests at the motor before condemning it.

Water-cooled condensers. Two types of water-cooled condensers are commonly found: "tube-in-tube" and "shell" condensers (see Figures 10-29 and 10-30). The latter are cheaper and increasingly fitted as standard equipment, but the former are more efficient and are preferred. *The water tube in any condenser must always be made of cupronickel rather than copper,* since cupronickel is more resistant to corrosion. The efficiency of a water-cooled condenser is directly related to the rate of water flow through it and the temperature of the cooling water. Any decrease in flow or rise in water temperature will have a marked effect on performance. Many condensers that work just fine in cooler climates prove inadequate in the tropics.

It helps to have a separate overboard discharge for the condenser cooling water. (It must have its own supply and pump for this, rather than share the engine circuit.) This way the flow rate can be accurately measured. Hold a gallon jug below the discharge and time how long it takes to fill—for example, one gallon in 15 seconds represents a flow rate of four gallons a minute. Anytime system performance declines, measure the flow rate. If it has fallen, inspect the intake strainer for plugging and all hoses for kinking or collapsing. Next check the pump impeller (see Chapter 12). Finally, some condensers have a removable cover, which allows the water tubes to be "rodded out" (use a wooden dowel with care), but most do not.

If a condenser is proving inadequate due to higher ambient water temperatures, before condemning it try increasing the water flow through it. If it is using the engine's water pump, the flow rate may be only one to two gallons a minute, especially at engine idle. Installing a separate pump could easily increase this to four to six gallons a minute.

Condensers require no routine maintenance apart from renewing any sacrificial zinc anodes that are fitted. These must be inspected on a regular basis and replaced as necessary. Should a water tube in a condenser corrode through, water will enter the refrigeration circuit and do extensive damage.

During a winter lay-up be sure to drain the condenser, or it is likely to freeze and burst. The drain must be at the lowest point and effectively remove all water. Alternatively, mix up a 50-percent antifreeze solution, break the pump suction loose, and pump this through the water circuit.

Figure 10-28A. **Replacing a clutch on York and Tecumseh compressors. Using a universal deck plate key to hold the pulley stationary while undoing its retaining bolt.**

Figure 10-28B. **Screwing off the pulley with a 5/8-inch NC (coarse-thread) bolt.**

Figure 10-28D. **The clutch has been removed to reveal the shaft seal assembly.**

Figure 10-28C. **The pulley has been removed to reveal the clutch coil. This is held by four bolts—one in each corner of its base plate.**

clutch coil retaining bolt

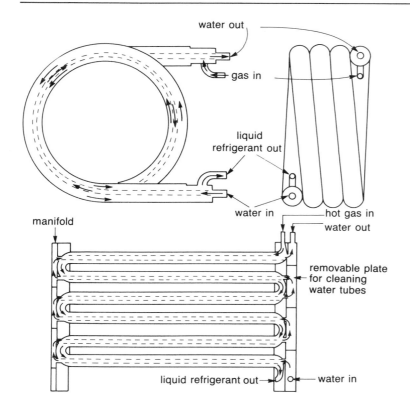

Figure 10-29. **Tube-in-tube condenser.**

Figure 10-30. **Shell-type condensers.**

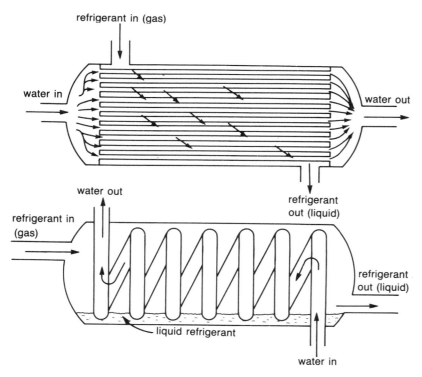

Receiver/Filter/Driers (RFDs)

During operation of a refrigeration or air-conditioning unit the RFD acts as a reservoir for liquid refrigerant, cleaning and drying it of moisture. Anytime a unit is opened up, the RFD should be replaced as a basic insurance measure. If problems are experienced with moisture in the system (see below), fit a new RFD and vacuum the unit.

Feel the inlet and outlet lines to the RFD, as well as its body, periodically during normal operation. They should all be uniformly warm. If there is a temperature drop across the RFD, it is plugged and needs replacing. It will also need replacing periodically as a part of routine maintenance. *A filter/drier should always be fitted with a valve on each side so that it can be isolated and changed without bleeding the refrigerant from the whole system.* Not only will this make servicing easier and cheaper, but it also will reduce considerably the volume of refrigerant vented into the atmosphere. Since escaping refrigerant gases contribute to the depletion of the earth's ozone layer, any environmentally conscious government would make unvalved filter/driers illegal. Without valves, the whole unit must be bled down to replace a filter/drier. It must then be vacuumed and recharged following installation of the replacement.

Expansion Valves

Capillary tubes either work or they don't. There is no adjustment. The tube needs to be warm where the liquid refrigerant goes in, and cold where it sprays out.

Expansion valves have a remote sensing bulb, which is strapped to the exit pipe from the evaporator or cold plate and connected to the top of the expansion valve with a length of capillary tubing. The bulb controls expansion valve operation. If the capillary tube is broken or kinked the whole valve needs replacing. To test the operation of a remote bulb, run the unit until it is cold, then warm the bulb with your hand. After a few seconds the suction pressure gauge should show a slight rise (a pound or two) as the expansion valve opens and admits more refrigerant. The suction line to the compressor will probably start frosting up. *Let the bulb cool back down* or else excess liquid refrigerant may pass through the evaporator and cause liquid slugging at the compressor. The suction pressure should drop again.

An expansion valve should be warm where the liquid refrigerant enters it and cold where the evaporator tubing exits. There generally will be a filter screen on the inlet side. If the valve is frosted all the way up the body and close to the inlet, the filter is probably plugged. The gauges will show an abnormally low suction pressure and the unit will not cool down properly. The unit will have to be bled, broken open, and the screen cleaned (wash it in kerosene or paraffin and blow-dry). The system must then be vacuumed and charged.

Any moisture in the system will freeze in the expansion valve orifice and plug it up. The gauges will show an abnormally low suction pressure, and the unit will not cool down. The compressor discharge line will run cooler than normal, and the evaporator side of the expansion valve will be warmer than normal. These symptoms are similar to those accompanying a plugged filter. To distinguish the two, allow the whole system to warm up and then restart it. With a plugged filter, the suction gauge immediately will show abnormally low pressures; if moisture is the problem, it will take a minute or two to produce abnormally low pressures. To combat frozen moisture, repeatedly shut down the unit and allow the expansion valve to warm up. Start the unit again. With any luck the ice will thaw out and be picked up by the RFD. If the expansion valve still freezes, the unit will have to be bled down and the RFD will need replacing (see above) before vacuuming and recharging. Allow a holding-plate unit to thaw completely before vacuuming. Vacuum on as warm a day as possible; this will help clear any moisture. If using a vacuum pump, hold a complete vacuum for at least 30 minutes, preferably longer; several hours would not be unreasonable.

Superheat. Superheat is not an easy concept to grasp at first. When the liquid refrigerant boils off in an evaporator it absorbs latent heat of vaporization, thus cooling the evaporator. At any given compressor suction pressure, there is a specific temperature above which the liquid refrigerant will boil. *Once the evaporator cools down to this temperature no more refrigerant will boil off.* If the expansion valve continues to let in liquid refrigerant, it will pass straight through the evaporator in liquid form with a risk of liquid slugging at the compressor. The purpose of an expansion valve is to limit the flow of refrigerant to just a tiny bit less than will cool the evaporator to the boiling point, thus preserving a small margin of safety to prevent liquid

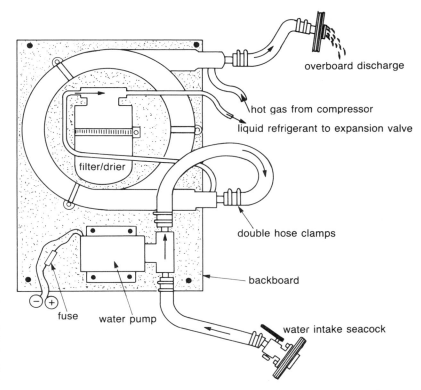

overboard discharge

hot gas from compressor

liquid refrigerant to expansion valve

filter/drier

double hose clamps

backboard

fuse   water pump

water intake seacock

Figure 10-31. **Condenser installation.**

Figure 10-32. **Cutaway view of an expansion valve.**

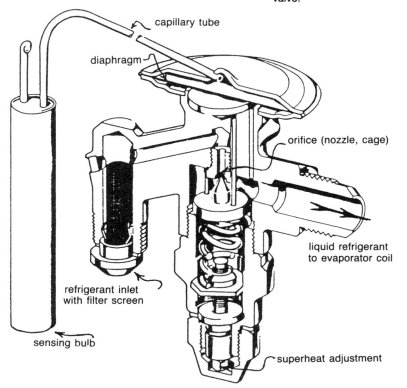

capillary tube

diaphragm

orifice (nozzle, cage)

liquid refrigerant to evaporator coil

refrigerant inlet with filter screen

sensing bulb

superheat adjustment

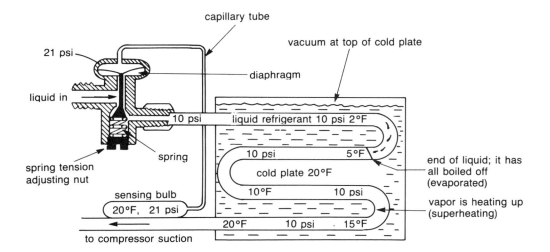

Figure 10-33. **Expansion valve operation.**

slugging at the compressor. *The evaporator never quite cools to the boiling temperature of the refrigerant at the given compressor suction pressure.* The difference between the boiling temperature of the refrigerant at this pressure and the actual temperature of the evaporator is known as superheat. In a well set-up system it is generally maintained at 6°F to 10°F (3.3°C to 5.5°C).

To check superheat settings, find the compressor suction pressure and then move across the gauge needle to the various temperature scales in the center of the gauge. Select the appropriate scale for the refrigerant in use (R–12 or R–22) and then read off the temperature given. This is the boiling temperature of this refrigerant at this pressure. Next precisely measure the temperature of the compressor suction line where it exits the evaporator (this is generally where the sensing bulb is strapped on). This temperature measurement requires a sensitive electronic thermometer. The amount by which this temperature exceeds the temperature read off the suction pressure gauge is the degree of superheat in the system.

A problem arises at this point. Frequently the compressor may have a long suction line containing bends and restrictions. The pressure measured at the compressor will be lower than that at the evaporator outlet, and it is this latter pressure that is needed to determine the superheat.

Some idea of the pressure drop in the suction line can be gained by watching the suction gauge while the unit is running and then cutting off the compressor. The pressure will jump and then slowly climb until it equalizes with the high side. This initial little jump is fairly indicative of the pressure drop to the evaporator. If this jump is more than a pound or two, the suction lines are undersized—a relatively common problem.

All this is rather academic, since equipment sensitive enough to measure evaporator temperatures accurately is unlikely to be available. Cruder methods for setting up the superheat generally have to be used in practice.

Superheat adjustments. Most expansion valves have a screw or squared-off stem in the body of the valve, covered with a 3/4-inch cap nut. Remove the nut. Moving the screw beneath it in and out alters the amount of fluid passing through the expansion valve. (If there is no external superheat adjusting screw, it will be inside the discharge port of the expansion valve, and the valve must be taken out of the system to get at it! These valves should be avoided like the plague.)

A system must be properly charged before making superheat adjustments.

Superheat adjustments are made while the unit is running, but only on a cold unit. To do otherwise is to invite liquid slugging at the compressor when the unit cools.

When making superheat adjustments, *never move the screw more than a half-turn at a time, and wait several minutes for the system to stabilize* (up to 20 minutes on a large-capacity holding plate unit).

If the flow of refrigerant increases, the suction pressure will rise slightly and the suction line at the evaporator outlet will cool. If the flow of refrigerant decreases the opposite happens. If at any time the suction line frosts heavily all the way back to the compressor and down the compressor side, excessive refrigerant is passing through the system and the compressor is in danger of liquid slugging. (This situation also arises with overcharging of refrigerant.) Restrict the flow or shut down the unit before damage occurs.

When a refrigeration or freezer system is cold, superheat can be adjusted to permit frosting of the suction line where it exits the evaporator. No damage to the compressor will occur as long as this frosting does not reach the compressor. (Even if it does, there is generally a degree of safety built in.)

Cold-plate units with multiple plates *in series* (one after the other) should be adjusted to permit frosting of the suction line where it exits the last plate. If the plates are in parallel, each will have its own expansion valve, which should be adjusted to permit mild frosting of the suction line where it exits the cold plate.

Air-conditioning units operate at higher pressures and temperatures, and the suction line should be cool at the compressor. If it is not, the expansion valve should be opened further. *The suction line should never frost;* if it does there is danger of liquid slugging at the compressor.

Refrigeration Oil

Refrigeration oil is specially blended to deal with extremely low temperatures and to remove all traces of moisture. It can be bought at automotive parts stores. *No other oil should ever be used.*

When a system is first set up the correct amount of oil should be put in. Subsequently, anytime oil is lost it must be replaced. In particular, whenever components are replaced, oil must be added to compensate for that lost with the old component. The following amounts should be added: with an RFD, one ounce; with an accumulator (if fitted), one ounce; with an evaporator or cold plate, two ounces; with a compressor, whatever is specified in the manual.

Most compressors leave the factory precharged with oil, and it should not be necessary to add more. If for any reason a compressor is dry, eight ounces will suffice for all Tecumseh and York compressors; the Sanden/Sankyo compressors require five ounces.

Oil can be added when a unit is bled down and opened up; alternatively, it can be added to systems using R–12 (but not R–22) from pressurized cans obtained at an autoparts store. The cans require use of the adaptor (See Figure 10-14). The oil is added to the low-pressure side of a unit while it is running.

Since oil-check procedures vary from compressor to compressor, it would be misleading to lay down a general approach. You would be well advised to write to the compressor manufacturer and get the relevant manual, especially if your unit has a swash-plate compressor and has been opened up to be worked on; loss of oil may endanger the compressor.

Troubleshooting

General Analysis

Troubleshooting starts long before a problem develops. Learn your way around the unit; identify all the components; get a feel for normal operating temperatures at different points. If you feel confident, hook up the gauges and get an idea of normal operating pressures in different conditions.

Find the sight glass and observe it during a number of starts—from a warm unit and from an already cold unit. See how quickly the stream of bubbles appears and then disappears as the condenser produces liquid. Check the sight glass at least monthly: If the bubbles begin to take

longer to clear, or refuse to clear at all, the unit is losing refrigerant and the compressor (especially a swash-plate compressor) may be in danger of burning up.

If the condenser has its own overboard discharge, measure the cooling water flow. Get a thermometer and measure the temperature of the seawater and then the temperature of the overboard discharge. Do this at different points of the cycle for a cold-plate refrigeration unit to gain some idea of typical in-and-out cooling water differentials. You can use these figures to crudely calculate the efficiency of the system as follows:

Troubleshooting Chart 10-1.
Refrigeration and Air-Conditioning Problems: Brief Overview.

Unit fails to run: Is there a fault in the AC or DC circuit to the compressor or compressor clutch? **NO** ▶ **TEST:** Check the voltage *at the compressor or clutch.*	**YES** ▶ **FIX:** Check all fuses and shutdown devices. Reset or bypass any over-temperature or over-current shut-down device mounted on the compressor itself. Jump out the compressor or clutch directly to check its operation. If OK, jump out individual shutdowns to find the problem in the circuit.
Unit still fails to run: The compressor or clutch is faulty. Test motors as outlined in Chapter 6, or replace the clutch unit (pages 278–285). Hermetically sealed compressor will need replacing.	
Unit cycles on and off: Is the condenser hot? **NO** ▶ **TEST:** Feel the condenser (water cooled) or inspect the fan and fins (air cooled). Check water flow or air ducting.	**YES** ▶ Check the flow of cooling water and its temperature. If the condenser is air-cooled, check its fans and fins. If the boat has recently moved into warmer ambient conditions the condenser may be undersized.
Unit cycles on and off: Is it undercharged? **NO** ▶ **TEST:** Check the sight glass—a mass of bubbles indicates a low refrigerant charge. If the sight glass is clear, switch off the unit, wait 15 minutes, and turn it back on. Watch closely: If the sight glass remains clear, the unit is out of refrigerant.	**YES** ▶ Recharge as necessary. If the unit is completely out of refrigerant it must first be vacuumed down (page 273).
Unit cycles on and off: Is it overcharged? **TEST:** Inspect the suction line which will frost heavily to the compressor; the sight glass will be clear; listen to the compressor which may knock loudly (if so, shut down immediately).	**YES** ▶ Bleed off excess refrigerant as necessary.
The unit runs but fails to cool the icebox or boat properly: Is the condenser hot? **NO** ▶ **TEST:** See above.	**YES** ▶ See above.
The unit runs but fails to cool the icebox or boat properly: Is it undercharged? **NO** ▶ **TEST:** See above.	**YES** ▶ See above.
The unit runs but fails to cool the icebox or boat properly: Is the compressor vibrating or excessively noisy? **NO** ▶ **TEST:** Listen to the compressor.	**YES** ▶ Run the compressor tests outlined in the text (page 291) and repair as necessary.
The unit runs but fails to cool the icebox or boat properly: Is there a temperature differential across the RFD or at any point in the lines? **NO** ▶ **TEST:** Feel with your hand.	**YES** ▶ The RFD or line is blocked. Replace. The unit will need bleeding down, vacuuming, and recharging.
The expansion valve may be plugged or frozen, or its superheat setting too high (see the text). The unit may simply be undersized for the demands being placed on it.	

1. Take the cooling water flow rate in gallons per minute and multiply this by 7.5 (U.S. gallons) or 8.3 (Imperial gallons) to convert it into pounds.

2. Find the temperature differential between the cooling water coming out of the condenser and going into it in *degrees Fahrenheit.*

3. Multiply (1) by (2), and then multiply the result by 60. This will give the approximate rate of heat removal in Btus per hour. (The British thermal unit, or Btu, is the standard for rating refrigeration and air-conditioning equipment.) The figure you get will overstate performance; to improve your accuracy multiply by 0.9 if the cooling water is salt water, and then by 0.75 to take account of various extraneous heat sources. This will give a fairly conservative approximation of system performance. You probably will find the unit is well short of its advertised capabilities—this is quite normal!

Leak Detection

Refrigerant leaks are the number one problem in boat refrigeration and air conditioning. There are three ways of detecting leaks:

1. *Electronic leak detectors.* These are ultra-sensitive, in fact too much so around belt-driven compressor seals, where a small leak is both normal and permissible.

2. *Halide leak detectors.* A fitting screws onto a standard propane torch. The flame heats a catalyst, and a hose is used to "sniff" around the refrigeration unit. If refrigerant is present the flame will change color: no leak—pale blue; slight leak—pale green; medium leak—brilliant green; serious leak—brilliant peacock blue. Halide leak detectors are ideal for boats and reasonably cheap (around $25). If *any* leak is detected it needs fixing.

3. *Soap solutions* (50-percent dishwashing liquid). Sponge or brush the solution onto the part in question. If the solution bubbles there is a bad leak.

Note that leaks often leave a telltale trace of refrigeration oil.

Sometimes a unit will lose efficiency slowly over a month or two, and no leak can be found. Suspect the hoses. Neoprene and hydraulic hoses have been found to leak several ounces per foot per year through pores in the hose itself, but since the leak is not concentrated at any one point, leak detection equipment very often will not pick it up. Only proper refrigeration hose (obtainable from auto-parts stores) should be used.

Failure to Run

On AC and DC units check the voltage at the compressor as described in Chapter 3. Remember, AC voltages can kill. Many electrically powered compressors have overload (high-temperature) and low-voltage cutouts. If tripped, these may require manual resetting, or the unit may have to cool down (or undergo voltage correction) before it will reset automatically. If the unit can be made to run, check for voltage drop at the compressor during operation.

Larger AC compressors have starting capacitors. If the motor hums but won't start, the capacitor may be faulty. Test as outlined in Chapter 6 or replace with a good one.

Hermetically sealed compressors that will not work despite adequate voltage will have to be replaced as a unit. On engine-driven compressors check the operation of the clutch and replace as necessary (see page 280).

If there does prove to be an electrical problem, trace it back through the circuit. Primary suspects, as always, are fuses, circuit breakers, and connections (Figure 10-34). Additionally, there is likely to be one or more high-and low-pressure or temperature cutout switches or solenoids on the system itself (as opposed to the compressor) and maybe a relay or two. Bypass each in turn to see if it is causing a problem. If it is, before condemning it make sure it is not performing its proper function (for example, cutting out because of genuinely low pressure due to a loss of refrigerant).

Unit Fails to Cool Down or Cools Too Slowly

1. Check the sight glass. A steady stream of fast-moving bubbles indicates the unit is low on refrigerant. If the sight glass is completely clear, it is filled either with air (completely out of refrigerant) or liquid (functioning OK).

Faced with a clear sight glass, shut things down and give the unit 15 minutes to equalize. Restart it while watching the sight glass. If no bubbles appear, there is no refrigerant. Watch closely: The bubbles may appear for just a few seconds, and then only as a large, slow-moving bubble hovering in the top of the sight glass; if this happens the refrigerant charge is OK.

Hook up the gauge set. When *not running*, a *warm* unit low on refrigerant will show pressures of 50 psi or less on both gauges. (Note: A fully charged cold unit also will show low pressures, so make sure the unit is warm.) When running, a unit low on refrigerant will have generally low pressures on both the suction and discharge side, and the compressor discharge temperature will be lower than normal.

2. Condenser problems. If the condenser is operating inefficiently, the compressor discharge and suction temperatures and pressures will be abnormally high. On a water-cooled condenser, check the flow rate and the ambient temperature of the water (see the section on condensers above). On an air-cooled condenser check the fan, the ambient air temperature, and the condenser fins to make sure they are clean.

3. Compressor problems. If the valves are leaking, or the head gasket is blown between the high and low sides, the compressor will run hot. A failed valve often will make a "clacking" noise at idle speeds. If the compressor has Rotolock stem-type service valves (as opposed to Schrader valves), make the following tests:

• Run the compressor, closing the suction-side service valve *to the system* (all the way in, clockwise). The compressor should rapidly pull a complete vacuum (-28 to -30 inches of mercury). Shut down the compressor.

• If a vacuum of -28 inches of mercury cannot be pulled, the suction valve or head gasket is bad (or the Rotolock valve is not properly closed).

• If a vacuum of -28 inches of mercury can be pulled, but it rises fairly rapidly to atmospheric pressure (0 psi) after the compressor is shut down, the shaft seal is leaking.

• If a vacuum of -28 inches of mercury can be pulled, but it rises fairly rapidly to a positive pressure after the

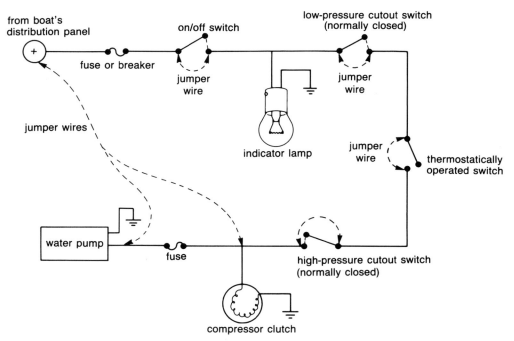

Figure 10-34A. **(Above)** Schematic of a simple engine-driven refrigeration system. To operate, all switches and breakers must be closed and any fuses intact. To troubleshoot the clutch or water pump, first check the ground connection, then connect a jumper wire from the positive terminal, as shown. If the unit now works there is a problem in the circuit. Jump out individual switches to isolate the problem as shown, starting from the positive supply end of the circuit.

Figure 10-34B. **(Below)** Schematic for a unit with dual cold plates and thermostats. The thermostats supply power to close a solenoid, which then supplies power to the clutch and water pump circuit. With either thermostatic switch closed, power is supplied to close the solenoid; when both are open the circuit is broken.

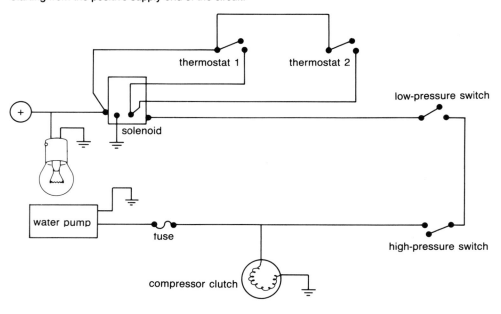

compressor is shut down, the discharge valve or head gasket is leaking.

• If the compressor has Schrader-type service valves, run it normally for five minutes and then shut it down. If the suction and discharge pressures equalize in less than two minutes, the head gasket or valves are almost certainly bad.

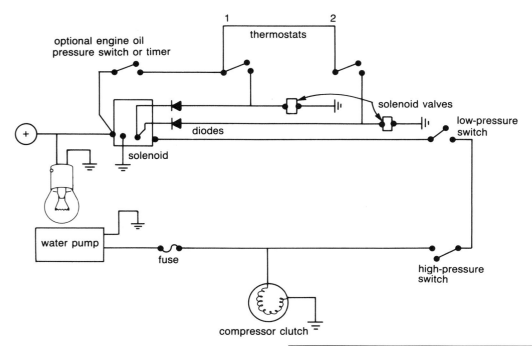

Figure 10-34C. Schematic of a more complex system, with dual cold plates and thermostats, and individual shutdown solenoids on each cold plate to close off the flow of refrigerant to that plate. The thermostats supply power to close the main solenoid, and also open individual solenoid valves on the liquid lines to each expansion valve. When a thermostat opens (i.e., breaks the circuit) its liquid line solenoid closes and shuts down its cold plate. The diodes prevent power from one thermostat feeding back via the common connection on the main solenoid to the other thermostat's liquid line solenoid valve, which would keep the solenoid valve open when it should be closed. When both thermostatic switches open the circuit is broken and the unit shuts down.

4. Expansion valve problems. Check the expansion valve for signs of a plugged filter or freezing (see the section on expansion valves).

5. Blockages. Check all lines, and in particular the RFD, for any sudden temperature drops indicating a blockage (see the section on RFDs).

Unit Cuts On and Off

One of the temperature or pressure switches is cutting in and out. The switch is probably working correctly, indicating a fault in the system. If the unit is cutting out on high pressures, check the condenser. If it is cutting out on low pressures, check the refrigerant charge.

If high pressures are combined with heavy frosting on the suction line back to the compressor and a clear sight glass, and refrigerant has just been added, the unit is probably dangerously overcharged, and the compressor is at risk of serious damage.

Compressor Is Noisy

It is hard to distinguish compressor noises. At certain speeds compressors sometimes will set up harmonic vibrations, which are amplified through the compressor mounts, bulkheads, etc. The belt may well dance or jump. There is nothing wrong with the compressor. Try tightening the drive belt a little; perhaps add an idler pulley on the slack side of the belt. Check the alignment of the pulleys, and stiffen the compressor mount.

At idle speeds and low loads, defective valves will sometimes clatter. Check suction and discharge pressures and perform the compressor tests outlined above.

Compressor noise will increase with higher pressures. If noise levels are above normal, check discharge temperatures and pressures. If these are high, check the condenser.

Overcharging or improper superheat adjustments can cause liquid slugging at the compressor. The compressor will knock quite loudly, and the engine will bog down a little. *Shut the compressor down immediately* until the problem is resolved.

Finally, general wear on bearings, pistons, connecting rods, and so on over time will produce a gradual increase in com-

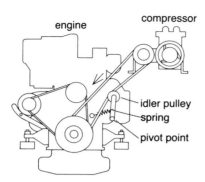

Figure 10-35. **Idler pulley arrangements.** The idler pulley goes on the slack side of the belt. (In most setups the belt from the engine pulley would drive the compressor directly, without the intermediate pulley shown here.)

engine
compressor
idler pulley
spring
pivot point

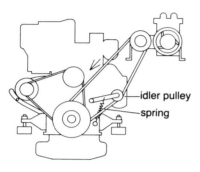

idler pulley
spring

Table 10-2. Size Relationships.

Nominal Copper Fitting Size (inches)	Fits Refrigeration Tubing with OD of (inches)
1/8	1/4
1/4	3/8
3/8	1/2
1/2	5/8
3/4	7/8
1	1 1/8

pressor noise. Discharge pressures will decline slowly and suction pressures will rise. The compressor will run hot. It is time to replace it.

Cold Plates Fail to Hold Over

If this has always been the case, the icebox may have inadequate insulation or the unit and cold plate may just be too small. If the failure is a new problem, check the items covered above under "Unit Fails to Cool Down or Cools Too Slowly." In addition:

1. Consider whether a recent change in operating conditions (such as a move to warmer waters) is showing up a basic weakness for the first time.
2. Check the seal on the icebox lid or door (see page 274);
3. Has the icebox usage changed? For example, are some recently arrived heavy beer drinkers continually putting fresh cans of warm beer into the fridge? This is the WB (warm beer) factor!
4. Are the cold plates heavily iced? This will insulate them and reduce the rate of heat removal from the icebox.

Air Conditioners

Check the filter on the air inlet to the evaporator at regular intervals. A plugged filter will result in rising pressures and temperatures, with a general loss of performance. Check also that the drain in the drip pan below the evaporator is clear—in hotter, humid climates a steady trickle of water will condense on the evaporator, and if not properly drained away can cause considerable damage to surrounding woodwork.

If the fan goes out make all the usual voltage tests. *Remember, this is AC voltage. It can kill!*

Refrigeration (and Gas) Plumbing

Apart from flexible connections to compressors on some units, almost all refrigeration plumbing is done with soft copper tubing and compression (not very common), flared, or soldered fittings.

All tubing for refrigeration use should be purchased from a refrigeration supply house. It comes in 50-foot coils, and is specially cleaned, dehydrated, and capped to keep out moisture. Cut it with tube cutters, not a hacksaw; take extreme care to keep dirt and metal filings out of the tubing; and always cap all open ends immediately after cutting.

Refrigeration tubing is measured in the USA by its outside diameter (OD), and thus is sized differently from the copper tubing commonly found in hardware stores (see Table 10-2). In the UK and Europe, all copper tubing is standardized in metric sizes—8, 10, 15, 22 and 28 mm.

When making tubing runs, bend the copper *as little as possible;* with constant flexing it "work-hardens" and then is more prone to kink or crack. If tubing does become hard, it can be resoftened by heating to a cherry red color with a propane torch and then dousing with cold water.

Tight bends are liable to flatten out, kink, or both, unless made with proper bending tools or springs. The springs fit outside the tubing; these are quite cheap, and available from plumbing suppliers.

As noted, tubing (and pipe, for that matter) should always be cut with tubing cutters since this is the only way to ensure a smooth and square cut. Clamp the cutters *lightly* around the tubing and make a full turn. Tighten the handle a half turn after each turn until the cut is complete. On the back of the cutters will be a hinged arrowhead fitting—use this to clean any burr on the inside of the tubing.

Compression Fittings

1. Slide a nut up the tubing and then slip on a compression ring, or "olive."
2. The tubing fits into a recess in the compression fitting. The fit must be perfectly square.
3. The nut slides up onto the fitting and is tightened, keeping the tubing pressed into the recess at all times.
4. The compression ring is squeezed against the fitting and into the soft metal of the tubing, forming an effective seal.

Flare Fittings

Tubing flares are made with a special tool. There are a number of relatively inexpensive flaring kits on the market, and one or two real Cadillacs for around $80. The cheaper kits consist of a clamp that fits around the tube and has a machined bevel in its face. A horseshoe-shaped bracket with a threaded bolt in its center fits over the clamp. On the base of this bolt is a *spinner*—a block of metal cut to the same taper as the bevel in the clamp. The spinner is screwed into the mouth of the tubing and forces its sides out against the bevel. The flare is complete.

Here are some tips:

1. The nut must be put on the line before making the flare! If possible, use long-nosed flare nuts (as opposed to the more common short ones), since they provide more support to the tubing and reduce the chances of cracking due to vibration.

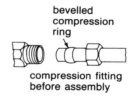

bevelled compression ring

compression fitting before assembly

Figure 10-36A. **(Above)** A compression fitting.

Figure 10-36B. **Making a flare fitting. Use a tubing cutter to make a straight, even cut on the tubing. Then clean off the burrs inside and out. Put the flare nut on the tubing and then use the flaring kit—clamping the tube, fitting the bracket, and screwing down the spinner. Finally, slide the flair nut to the now-flared end of the tube and tighten the nut to the flare fitting.**

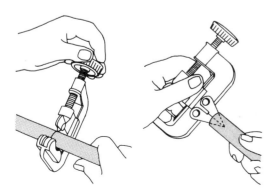

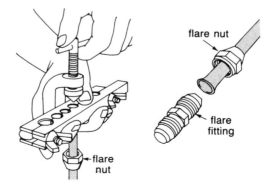

flare nut

flare nut

flare fitting

2. The end of the tube must be *cut square and cleaned of all burrs inside and out.* Any dirt, trash, or metal filings left in the tubing will come back to haunt refrigeration and gas systems.

3. Warming the tube before screwing down the spinner will help prevent cracking.

4. Depending on clamp configuration, the tubing may need to protrude above the face of the clamp by one-third to one-half the depth of the bevel to permit an adequate flare. If it is set flush with the face of the clamp, the resulting flare will be skimpy and prone to leak. When made, the flare should only just fit into, but not hang up on, the flare nut.

5. The spinner should be oiled when making the flare.

6. The spinner should not be screwed down too tightly—it will weaken the flare. When the joint is done up, the flare nut will pull the tubing snugly onto the flared fitting.

7. If the flare looks uneven or in any other way unsatisfactory, it must be cut off and remade. Doing so right away will be a lot easier than doing so later.

Soldering

Tubing can be soldered using fittings (sweat fittings) available for use on hard copper pipe. Because refrigeration tubing is sized differently from other copper pipe in the USA, the correlation shown in Table 10-2 is necessary. In the UK and Europe, sweat fittings match tubing of the same metric dimension. A wide range of fittings is readily available. Some fittings are pre-soldered (omit steps 4 and 5 below), but most are not.

1. Clean both surfaces to be soldered with fine (#400-to #600-grit) wet-or-dry sandpaper until shiny (see Figure 10-37). Do not use emery cloth—oils in the cloth backing will spoil the soldering.

2. Apply soldering flux immediately but sparingly to both surfaces. Push the fitting onto the pipe and twist to spread the flux evenly. The flux is there to keep out oxygen and contaminants *once the joint is clean.* Flux is no substitute for cleaning.

3. Heat the joint evenly with a propane torch.

Figure 10-37. **Soldering.** Refer to the text for a step-by-step detailing of the process.

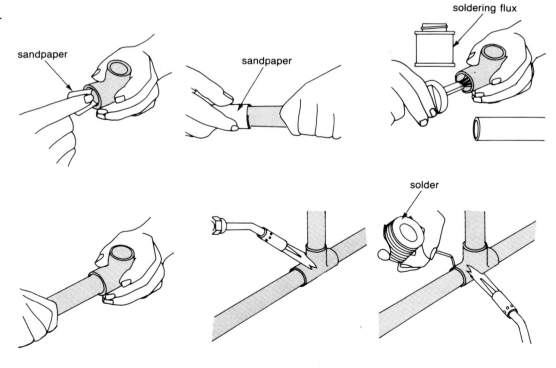

Refrigeration and Air Conditioning

4. Touch solid solder to the joint periodically until the pipe and fittings are hot enough to melt the solder. *The solder itself is not heated by the torch*—if the metal in the joint is not hot enough to melt the solder, it will not flow properly.

5. Let solder flow into the joint. Apply only enough heat to keep the solder melting; more will overheat the joint. Generally the flame can be held at some distance or turned away from the joint and passed quickly over it a couple of times.

6. When solder shows all around the fitting, the joint is complete. Remove the heat. Any more solder added to the joint will merely flow out the other side and into the pipe, causing a partial blockage.

7. When the joint is cool, thoroughly clean away the excess flux.

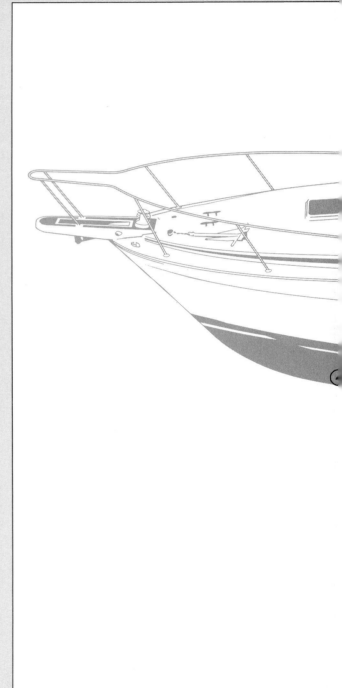

CHAPTER 11

Figure 11-1. Problems with onboard plumbing can ruin a cruise faster than anything else. A familiarity with the system—and where everything is located—is highly recommended.

(1) Y-valve
(2) macerator pump
(3) toilet pump
(4) shower sump
(5) lavatory basin
(6) vented loop
(7) galley sink
(8) icemaker
(9) shower
(10) freshwater fill
(11) head overboard discharge
(12) head raw-water intake
(13) holding tank
(14) lavatory basin drain
(15) galley sink drain
(16) water heater
(17) air conditioner raw-water intake
(18) engine cooling water intake
(19) auxiliary raw-water intake
(20) freshwater tank
(21) freshwater pump
(22) washdown system
(23) holding tank pump-out
(24) bilge pump
(25) bilge pump strainer
(26) collection box
(27) foot pump

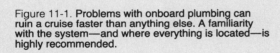

———— cold water

----------- hot water

Toilets, Through-Hull Fittings, and Seacocks

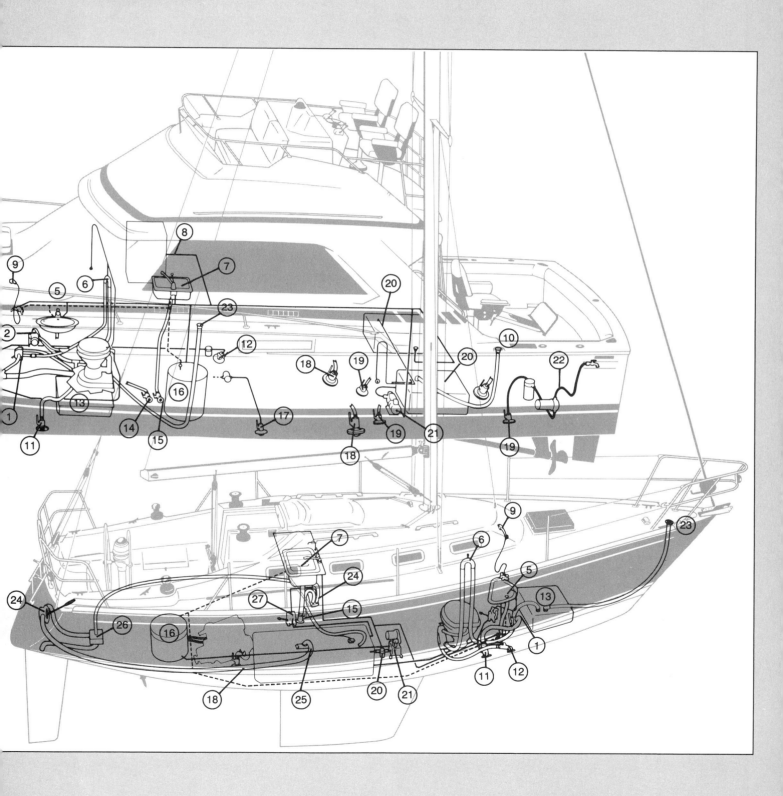

Discharge Regulations

Discharge of untreated raw sewage is illegal anywhere within the United States' 3-mile limit. Any installed toilet (marine sanitation device or MSD, in Coast Guard jargon) in a vessel shorter than 65 feet must conform to one of three types. (The regulations for vessels over 65 feet are even more stringent.)

- *Type I MSDs* break up the sewage so that no visible floating solids remain. The sewage is treated chemically to kill bacteria and then discharged overboard.
- *Type II MSDs* are similar but treat the sewage to more exacting standards.

- *Type III MSDs* (including portable toilets) eliminate overboard discharge in prohibited areas. The usual method is to store the sewage in a holding tank and then discharge it either through a dockside pump-out facility or overboard beyond the 3-mile limit.

Type I and II devices must be properly certified and have a certification label. Holding tanks require no certification provided they store sewage only at ambient temperatures and pressures (usually provided by venting the tank to atmosphere via a through-hull fitting). It is perfectly legal to have a toilet and holding tank with a Y-valve such that the toilet can be pumped directly overboard (beyond the 3-mile limit) or into the holding tank. The valve must be secured in the holding tank position when in territorial waters. Padlocking, removal of the valve handle, or use of a plastic wire tie are all considered adequate methods of securing the valve.

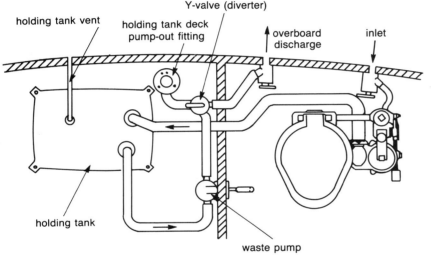

Figure 11-2A. **Typical arrangement of onboard waste disposal system with holding tank and overboard discharge. With this configuration, all effluent first passes through the holding tank before being pumped overboard. The inlet and discharge lines should be looped above the waterline and fitted with vented loops.**

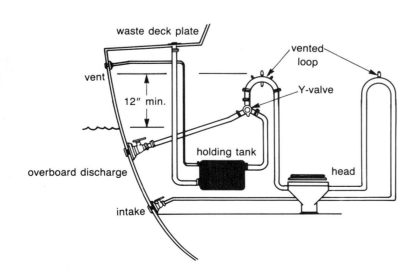

Figure 11-2B. **An alternative approach, with a Y-valve (diverter) before the holding tank. On all onboard plumbing systems, ensure that access to through-hulls and seacocks is quick and easy.**

Heading Off Toilet Problems

Proper Installation Practices

Hoses. Almost all marine toilets use a ¾-inch (19-mm) ID (inside diameter) suction hose (supplying water for flushing) and a 1½-inch (38-mm) ID discharge hose. Suction hoses must be noncollapsible—any good-quality, reasonably firm hose will do (automotive heater hose; reinforced PVC hose). Discharge hoses are more critical. Many of the thin-walled, spirally ribbed (frequently wire-reinforced) industrial vacuum cleaner-type hoses will allow sewage gas to permeate the hose wall. What is needed is a proper *sanitation hose* or a fabric-reinforced neoprene hose. Standard automotive radiator hose is 1½-inch (38-mm) ID and works well, especially where tight bends are needed, since it can be bought in a variety of preformed shapes.

It is difficult to make leakproof connections with ribbed hoses. Some hoses have special end fittings known as *cuffs*, which screw up onto the hose and provide a smooth inner face. These hoses come with both left- and right-handed "threads," and it is essential to match the cuff to the hose. A little PVC cement between the hose and cuff will help to make a good seal, but be sure to screw up the cuff tightly as fast as possible; the cement sets up rapidly.

In general a close fit between a smooth hose and a smooth piece of pipe or adaptor will provide a better seal than a ribbed hose barb. Where fits are poor a little caulking (a polyurethane adhesive such as 3M 5200 works well) smeared over the surface of the adaptor will spread out on the inside of the hose and make a good joint, but once this sets the hose will be very hard to get off. The caulking should not be applied to the inside of the hose since the adaptor merely will push it up inside the hose where it will cause a blockage. If the hose is a little too small to fit its adaptor, dip the end in boiling water for a minute to soften it, then smear the adaptor with dishwashing liquid as a lubricant. The hose should slide on with a little pushing.

Two all-stainless steel hose clamps (Jubilee clips) should be used on all connections. Watch out for hose clamps with nickel-plated screws: These soon rust out. Do not overtighten to the point at which the clamps cut the hose. If this is the only way to stop a leak, the hose-to-adaptor fit is just not good enough, and one or the other must be changed.

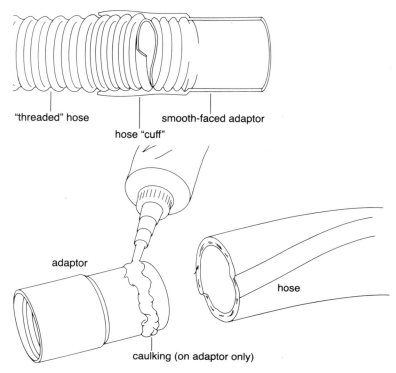

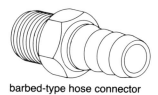

Figure 11-3. **Leakproof connections between fittings and pipes are essential, and easily obtained by attention to detail.**

PVC pipe. Hard plastic (PVC) piping, available from any hardware store, is excellent for any plumbing job on board. It is easily cut with a hacksaw, comes with a tremendous range of fittings, and can be glued together in seconds with PVC cement. Prior to gluing, the end of the pipe and the inside of the fitting should be lightly sanded with 400-grit wet-and-dry paper, then cleaned with a solvent cleaner (available from any hardware store), and finally coated with the cement. *Immediately* press the pipe home, twisting a half turn or so as you go to spread the glue evenly. Hold for about 30 seconds to give the glue a chance to grip, and do not subject the joint to pressure for at least half an hour. Once installed, PVC piping is maintenance-free, and it is easily cut up and glued back together for later modifications.

Table 11-1. Table of Pipe Sizes.[1]

| Nominal Outside Diameter (inches) | Actual Outside Diameter (inches) | | | | | Wall Thickness (copper tubing, in inches) | | | | |
| | Schedule 40 Pipe | | | Copper Tubing | | Water Tubing | | | Refrigeration | |
	Metal: Brass, Bronze, Galvanized	PVC	CPVC	Water	Refrigeration	K	L	M	K	L
⅛ (0.125)	¹³⁄₃₂	—	—	¼	N.A.	0.032	0.025	0.025	N.A.	N.A.
¼ (0.250)	³⁵⁄₆₄	—	—	⅜	N.A.	0.035	0.030	0.025	N.A.	N.A.
⅜ (0.375)	⁴³⁄₆₄	—	—	½	⅜	0.049	0.035	0.025	0.032	0.032
½ (0.500)	²⁷⁄₃₂	0.840	⅝	⅝	½	0.049	0.040	0.028	0.049	0.032
⅝ (0.625)	N.A.	—	—	¾	⅝	0.049	0.042	0.030	0.049	0.035
¾ (0.750)	1³⁄₆₄	1.050	⅞	⅞	¾	0.065	0.045	0.032	0.049	0.035
⅞ (0.875)	N.A.	—	—	N.A.	⅞	N.A.	N.A.	N.A.	0.065	0.045
1 (1.0)	1⁵⁄₁₆	1.315	—	1⅛	N.A.	0.065	0.050	0.035	N.A.	N.A.
1⅛ (1.125)	N.A.	1.660	—	N.A.	1⅛	N.A.	N.A.	N.A.	0.065	0.050
1¼ (1.250)	1²¹⁄₃₂	—	—	1⅜	N.A.	0.065	0.055	0.042	N.A.	N.A.
1⅜ (1.375)	N.A.	—	—	N.A.	1⅜	N.A.	N.A.	N.A.	0.065	0.060
1½ (1.500)	1²⁹⁄₃₂	1.900	—	—	—	—	—	—	—	—
2 (2.0)	2⅜	2.375	—	—	—	—	—	—	—	—
2½ (2.500)	2⅞	—	—	—	—	—	—	—	—	—

1. N.A. = Not Applicable.

The snag for the uninitiated is that the "nominal" pipe sizes one sees on the label or in the catalog differ considerably from actual sizes, which can be very confusing. This is compounded by the fact that different plastics are used for cold water (PVC) and hot water (CPVC). PVC and CPVC pipes with the same nominal size (½ inch, for example) also differ in size! PVC pipe is generally preferred for all but hot water applications.

Pipes, both metal and plastic, come in different thicknesses (that is, strengths) known as *schedules*. Schedule 20 is the thinnest and is not suitable for any plumbing on board. Schedule 40 is standard and works well; schedules 80 and 160 are heavy-duty and very heavy-duty respectively, and find no application on board. Hoses are generally specified by inside diameter: 1-inch hose has an ID of 1 inch (25 mm).

Vented loops. Almost all sailboat toilets, and many powerboat toilets, are installed below the waterline. The toilets have valves on both the suction and discharge sides, but even so any leakage past either a suction or discharge valve can siphon water into the toilet, eventually sinking the boat if not discovered in time. Many boats have sunk this way. *It is absolutely essential to fit some form of a siphon break on both suction and discharge lines.*

A siphon break is formed by looping the line above the water level and installing at the high point of the loop a valve that allows air to be drawn into the line. This valve must be above the water level at all angles of heel.

The usual configuration consists of a U-bend with a small T containing a rubber flap. Several problems may arise:

1. The vent will sometimes plug up, notably with salt crystal in the suction line, rendering the loop inoperative. The vent valve should be periodically unscrewed and washed in warm fresh water.

2. Air can be drawn into the suction pump through the vented loop in the suction line. This will reduce the water flow to the toilet and in extreme cases can lead to a loss of prime and subsequent air locking in the suction pump. A U-trap in the suction line, close to the toilet, will retain some water and keep the pump wetted. This simple measure may not suffice for some electric pumps, however, in which case a solenoid valve should be wired to the vent in such a way that the solenoid closes when the toilet is flushed, and opens when flushing is completed (i.e., a "normally open" solenoid valve).

3. A vented loop in the discharge line will allow foul odors into the boat. It is best to attach a small hose to the vent and run this overboard. Its exit must be above the waterline at all times or it will siphon into the boat and negate the purpose of the vented loop.

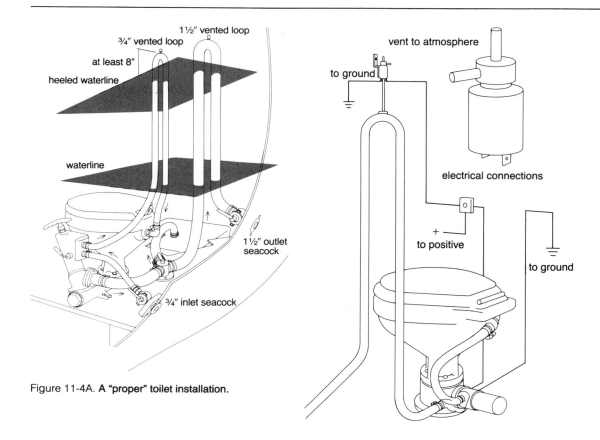

Figure 11-4A. **A "proper" toilet installation.**

General Maintenance

Marine toilets require little maintenance. It is worthwhile to half-fill the bowl periodically with warm water, add some biodegradable laundry detergent, and flush this through the system. Follow with another half-bowl of warm water containing approximately two ounces of mineral or baby oil—the oil will help keep all rubber parts (valves, impellers, and seals) supple and in good condition. A little Teflon-based waterproof grease smeared on the pump piston rod prolongs the life of the piston rod seal on a manual toilet.

Never use toilet bowl cleaners, drain cleaners, bleach, or deodorants unless these are made specifically for marine toilets. Most will attack and swell up rubber parts.

All wire terminals on electric toilets should be checked periodically for corrosion and cleaned when necessary. Keep a sharp eye for external signs of leaking pump seals, since these are a major cause of pump failures.

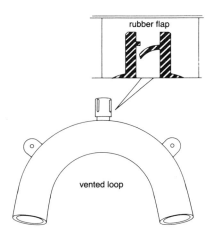

Figure 11-4B. **Above:** A vented loop: a simple rubber "flap" valve, or even just a very small hole, to prevent water being siphoned into the boat through a leaking inlet valve. **Top:** A vented loop with a solenoid valve, which prevents excess air from being sucked into the system by the head's pump.

Winterizing

Improper winterization is a leading cause of toilet failure. It is not enough just to pump the toilet dry and leave it. Water remains trapped in low spots in both the suction and discharge lines as well as in the pump housing.

1. Close the suction seacock, disconnect the hose, and dip it in a can of antifreeze. Use ethylene glycol only; alcohol will swell up rubber parts. Pump the toilet until the antifreeze washes down the bowl sides and flows out the discharge.
2. Close the discharge seacock, disconnect the hose, and drain it.
3. The toilet can either be pumped dry or left with the antifreeze in it. Holding tanks and treatment systems (if present) must be drained and winterized separately. Some specialized types (such as Raritan's LectraSan) should be disconnected *before* putting antifreeze in the system, since the antifreeze will cause problems.

Troubleshooting

Problems Common to All Marine Toilets

Odors. The obvious source of odor is a leak. Less obvious are the following:

1. Permeable hose. Rub a cloth on the hose and then sniff it. If the cloth smells, the hose is permeable and should be replaced with proper sanitation hose.
2. Marine life, especially eel grass, in the flushing water. This gets caught on the underside of the toilet bowl rim and gives off a rotten-egg smell. Where this is a constant problem, a strainer may be needed on the suction line seacock.
3. The discharge line vented loop. A piece of hose should be attached to the vent and led outside cabin areas, but *be sure the hose is never underwater at any angle of heel.*
4. Clogged vent on the holding tank. This generally results from overfilling the tank and driving solid waste up the vent.
5. Low spots in the holding tank vent lines. These may fill with liquid and act as a U-trap, effectively plugging the vent.
6. Defective discharge valve. The result can be raw sewage backing into the toilet bowl, a problem that may not be obvious since the water in the bowl may appear clean. However, the bacteria present will cause the bowl to stain rapidly—overnight in warm climates.
7. A worn O-ring, or piston rings, on a manual toilet with a double-acting piston. This will allow raw sewage to work up past the piston into the flushing side of the pump. The pump must be dismantled and rebuilt.

Clogging. Marine toilets use little water (commonly as little as one quart per flush) and contain pumps, impellers, and valves that cannot handle solid objects and are not found in household toilets. Clogging is an ever-present problem, so much so that many experienced cruising sailors keep a separate receptacle for waste toilet paper and put *only* human waste down the toilet.

There are special short-fiber toilet papers on the market for use on boats. These break down quickly, reducing the risk of clogging. But the key is to keep paper usage to a minimum. No fibrous substances (rags, sanitary napkins) should ever be put down a marine toilet. In fact, nothing that hasn't been eaten first should be put down the head!

Never combat a blockage with drain cleaners; these will attack sensitive parts in the toilet. The best bet is to add water to the toilet bowl and leave it overnight. Usually the waste will break down enough to pump out the following morning.

Sooner or later, however, we all have to face a clogged toilet that won't clear (such as when our daughter threw a piece of coconut down the toilet!). There is nothing to be done but take it apart.

Calcium buildup. Calcium deposits, similar to the deposits in tea kettles, build up in time, primarily on discharge valves, lines, and seacocks. In extreme cases the calcium can pretty well plug a toilet. If a toilet has become progressively harder to

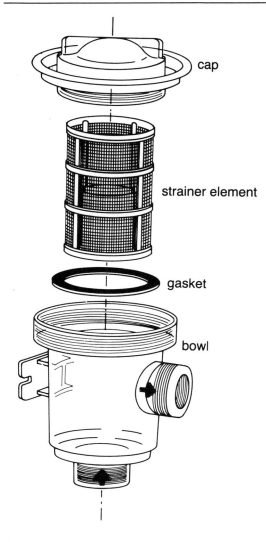

cap

strainer element

gasket

bowl

Figure 11-5. A raw-water strainer such as this may be needed in the inlet to exclude marine life—such as eel grass or mussels—which may want to colonize your waste disposal system. These need frequent checking, as the strainers themselves often become colonized and plugged.

flush over a period of time, with an ever-increasing tendency to clog, or if its discharge line is constantly leaking back into the bowl, calcium is a likely culprit.

A good dose of vinegar (acetic acid) on a regular basis —say, once a month—will go a long way toward keeping things free, but if the lines begin to clog, stronger treatment is needed. Muriatic (hydrochloric) acid, obtainable from many boat chandleries and hardware stores, dissolves the calcium but also will attack metal parts in the toilet, albeit at a much slower rate. Place a 10-percent solution in the bowl, observing all the warnings on the bottle. The solution

will "fizz" as it works, until the bowl and its immediate drain are free of calcium.

When the bubbling has ceased, pump the bowl almost dry. This will move the acid solution into the pump and the first part of the discharge line. Wait awhile and then flush the toilet a few strokes more to move the solution farther through the line. Continue in this manner until the entire discharge line has been covered. Thoroughly flush the system to remove all traces of acid.

The acid is used up as it bubbles. In severe cases of calcification it may be necessary to treat the system several times. Once it is clear, a small dosage at irregular intervals should keep it clear. If the acid treatment fails, the only recourse is to break down the toilet and discharge lines and chip out the calcium. Hoses can be beaten on the dockside to break loose the deposits, but replacing them would be preferable.

Manual and Electrified Manual Toilets

How they work. The central component in these toilets is a double-acting piston pump, either operated by hand or, in the electrified manual toilets, driven by an electric motor. The suction water is led to the top of the pump cylinder and from there to the toilet bowl rim. The discharge line leads to the bottom of the pump cylinder and from there to a holding tank or overboard discharge. There are "in" and "out" valves on the suction and discharge sides. (A few toilets—notably Baby Blakes—have separate suction and discharge pumps and pump cylinders, but the majority are as described.)

On its downward stroke the pump piston pulls flushing water into the top of the pump cylinder while driving sewage out the bottom end. On its upward stroke the piston forces the flushing water into the toilet while sucking effluent into the base of the cylinder.

Since the piston rod is attached to the top of the piston and therefore passes through the flush-water end of the pump cylinder, the flushing side volume is less than the waste discharge side by the amount of space occupied by the piston rod. In theory the pump will always pump out more than it sucks in, thus keeping the bowl dry. To make sure, a manual valve is invariably fitted on the suction side enabling the flushing water to be turned off while the bowl is evacuated.

Internal suction and discharge valves may be one of three types: spring-loaded ball valves; flapper valves; and joker ("duckbill") valves.

Ball valves are held against a seat by a weak spring. Pressure from the opposite side of the seat lifts the ball off the seat, allowing water to flow past; pressure from the other direction combines with the spring pressure to push the ball against the seat and hold the valve closed. A flapper valve is nothing more than a weighted flap resting on a baseplate. Fluid can flow one way, lifting it off its seat, but flow in the other direction forces the flap down onto its seat. A joker valve is a slitted rubber hemisphere to the convex surface of which is attached a rubber sleeve (the "duck's bill"). Fluid pushing through the base of the hemisphere opens the slit and sleeve; fluid approaching the hemisphere from the other side collapses and closes it.

Leaking seals. Where the piston rod exits the top of its cylinder on a manual toilet there is a seal—the familiar grease-type seal consisting of a metal case and a rubber lip to grip the rod. Sooner or later these seals always seem to start leaking and have to be replaced. Note that what is leaking is clean water, not effluent; a minor leak is annoying but can safely be left until a repair is convenient.

Most seals are accessible from the outside, but some can only be reached by dismantling the pump, which is a very poor design and extremely aggravating. When buying, avoid these toilets.

External seals. Close the seacocks. Lift the pump handle, wrap the piston rod with tape, and grip gently with Vise-Grips (Mole wrench). Unscrew the handle, knob, or yoke (depending on make and type of pump action), *taking great care not to let go of the rod, since it may drop down inside the pump!* Unscrew the seal assembly (or remove the retaining snap ring or circlip) and slide the assembly off the piston rod, temporarily removing the Vise-Grips to let the assembly past. Before installing a new seal, lightly tape the threads on the top of

Figure 11-6A. **A simple, double-acting piston toilet.**

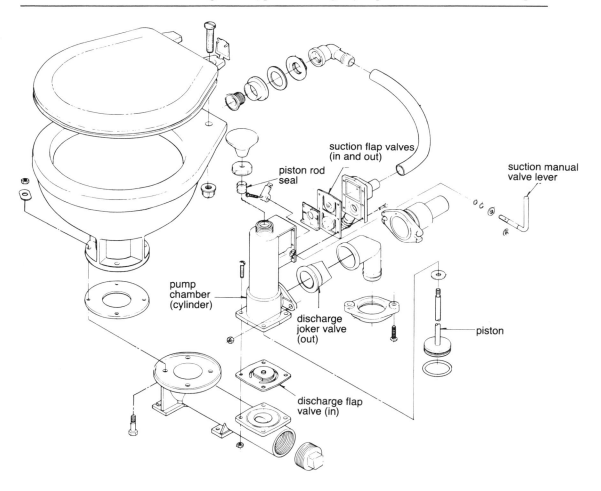

suction flap valves (in and out)

piston rod seal

suction manual valve lever

pump chamber (cylinder)

discharge joker valve (out)

piston

discharge flap valve (in)

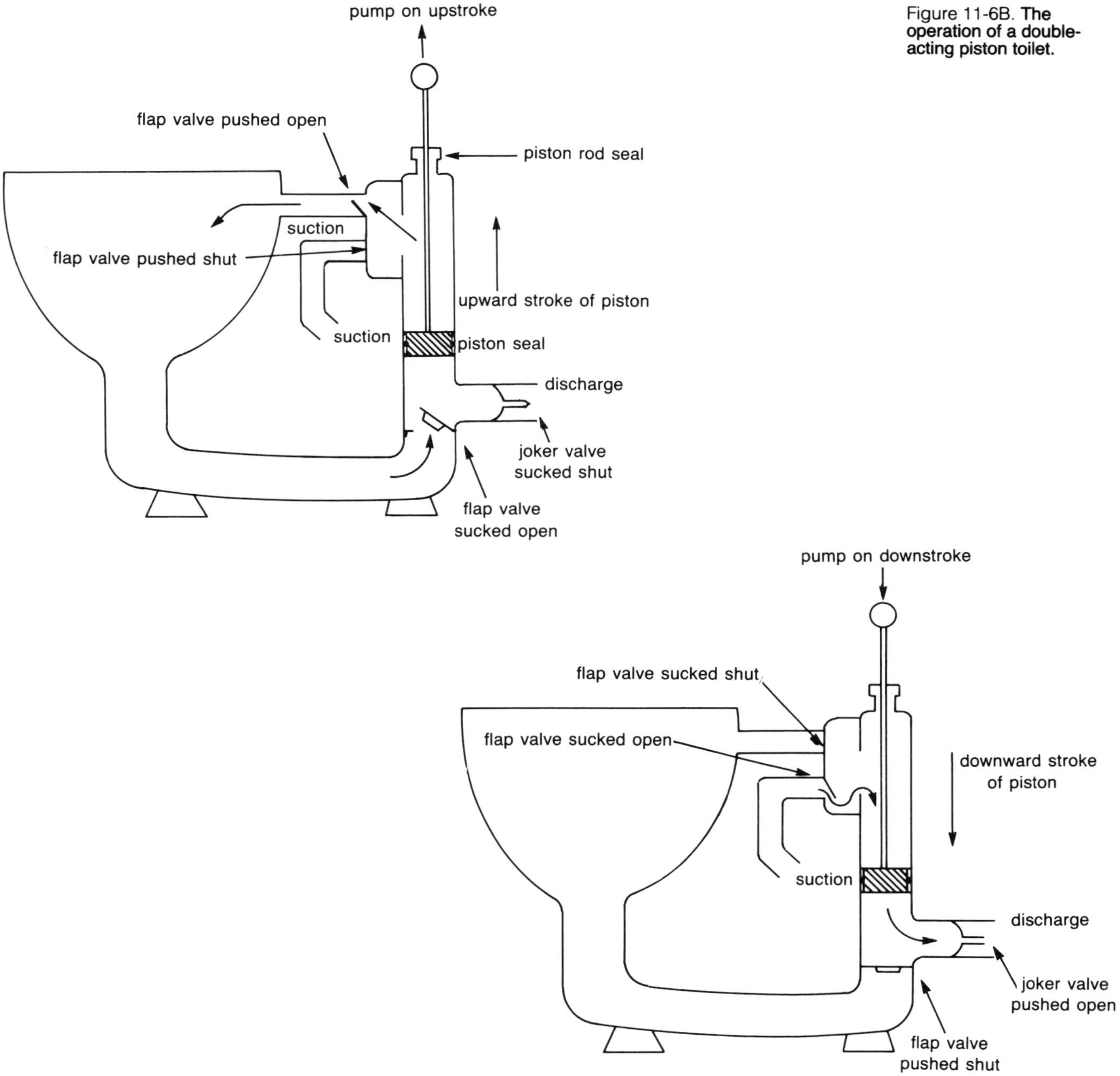

Figure 11-6B. **The operation of a double-acting piston toilet.**

pump on upstroke

flap valve pushed open

piston rod seal

suction

flap valve pushed shut

suction

upward stroke of piston

piston seal

discharge

joker valve sucked shut

flap valve sucked open

pump on downstroke

flap valve sucked shut

flap valve sucked open

downward stroke of piston

suction

discharge

joker valve pushed open

flap valve pushed shut

the piston rod to avoid damaging the seal when it slides over. The lip of the seal, if present, faces toward the pump cylinder (i.e., down).

Internal seals. Remove the pump body from the toilet by unscrewing it from its base and disconnecting the suction and discharge hoses. Wrap a piece of tape around the piston rod, gently grip the rod with Vise-Grips, and unscrew the handle

or knob. The piston and rod then can be knocked out of the bottom of the pump (after removing any calcium deposits as described above).

The seal fits into a recess at the top of the pump housing and must be pried out, which is frequently a time-consuming and frustrating business. The best approach is to straighten a piece of stiff wire (such as a coat hanger), file a point in its end, and bend the last ¼ inch (6 mm) in at 90 de-

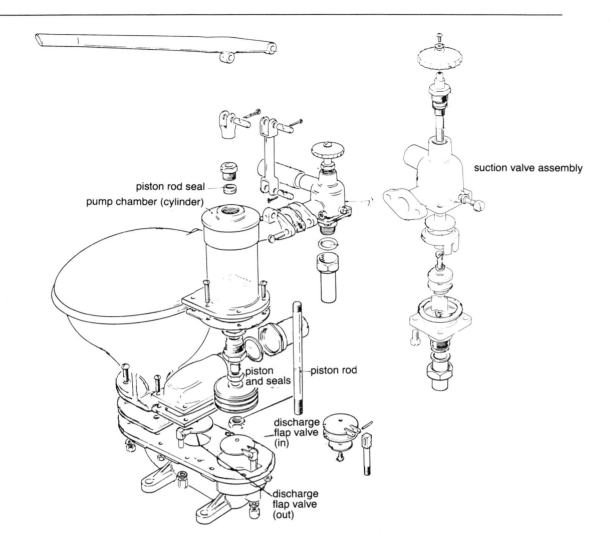

Figure 11-6C. **A better quality double-acting piston toilet.**

piston rod seal

pump chamber (cylinder)

suction valve assembly

piston and seals

piston rod

discharge flap valve (in)

discharge flap valve (out)

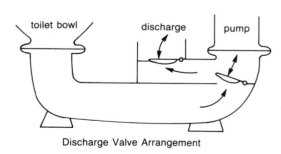

toilet bowl

discharge

pump

Discharge Valve Arrangement

grees. Poke this through the top of the piston housing and try to force it between the seal and its seat. Once the seal starts to work loose, it is important to work it from side to side or it will get cockeyed and jam.

Tape the threads at the top of the piston rod and slide on a new seal with its lip facing down (toward the piston). Put the piston rod back in the pump housing and use the piston to push the new seal gently into place.

In time, the plastic bore around the piston rod (at the top of the cylinder) wears, and the rod action becomes sloppy. Once this happens, the seal fails more quickly. One solution is to add a small length of hose to the top of the pump housing and clamp a second seal into this to form a flexible stuffing box (packing gland). It may be

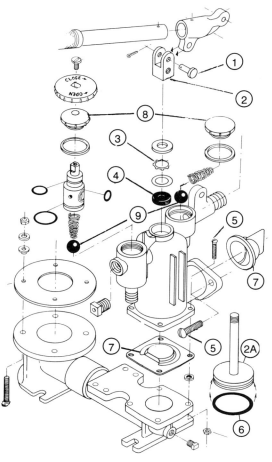

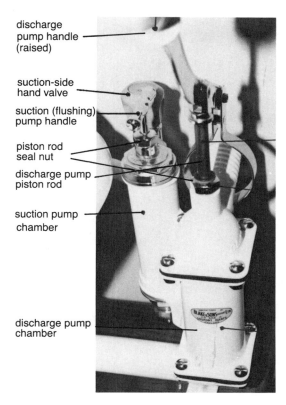

discharge
pump handle
(raised)

suction-side
hand valve

suction (flushing)
pump handle

piston rod
seal nut

discharge pump
piston rod

suction pump
chamber

discharge pump
chamber

Figure 11-6E. Blake toilet,
with independent
discharge and flushing
pumps.

Figure 11-6D. Replacing an external piston rod seal. Remove the pump handle (**1**). Remove the yoke (**2**) from the piston rod (**2A**). Remove the star washer or packing nut (**3**). Replace the seal (**4**).

To replace discharge valves and the piston seal (**6**): Remove the cylinder retaining screws and hoses (**5**). Check the piston O-ring (**6**) and the discharge valves (**7**).

To check the suction in-and-out valves, remove the two covers (**8**) to provide access to the springs and ball valves (**9**).

necessary to file down the top of the housing to get the hose to fit. The pump stroke (and therefore capacity) will be reduced by the length of the hose, and the toilet therefore will require a little more pumping.

Bowl fills faster than it drains.
As noted, pumps are designed to empty the bowl faster than it fills. If the reverse happens, it is almost always because a discharge flapper or joker valve is stuck partially open. Vigorous pumping will generally clear it unless the problem is a result of scale buildup or valve failure. Try the muriatic acid treatment. If all else fails you will have to dismantle the toilet and replace the valves (see below).

Bowl fills when not in use.
Either the suction or the discharge valve or valves are leaking. Close first one seacock and then the other, observing the bowl level, to find out on which side the problem lies. You will have to dismantle the toilet to check the valves. In addition to the internal suction valve, many toilets have a handwheel-type manual valve on the suction line (e.g., Blakes). These often seem to leak after a few years. They are not repairable and must be replaced.

Handle is pumped but nothing happens.
If strong resistance is felt, check that the seacocks are open and that the inlet valve is in the correct position. Check also that the holding tank is not full. If little or no resistance is felt, the piston nut has probably fallen off, allowing the piston to drop off its shaft. The pump needs dismantling.

Electric pump operates slowly or not at all.
First check the voltage *at the motor, while it is running*. If there is no voltage (it will not be running!) check all fuses, breakers,

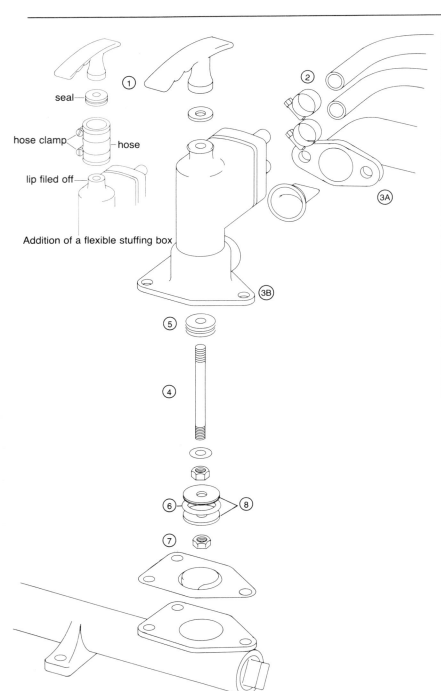

Figure 11-7B. Manual toilet (**above**) and electrified manual toilet (**top**).

Figure 11-7A. Replacing an internal piston rod seal. Remove the pump handle or knob (**1**). Remove the suction hoses (**2**). Remove the pump cylinder retaining screws. Knock the piston rod (**4**) out of the base of the cylinder. Remove the old seal (**5**) and put in a new one. If necessary, replace the piston seal O-ring (**6**) by taking off the piston retaining nut (**7**) and separating the two halves of the piston (**8**). {INSET} Alleviate wear-induced slop in the piston rod's action by adding a flexible stuffing box.

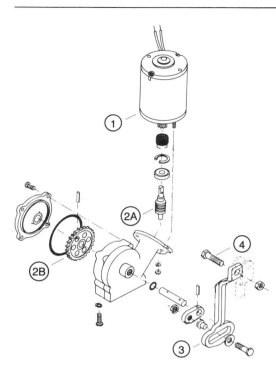

Figure 11-7C. Electrified toilet drive mechanism. To disconnect, remove the drive bolt (**4**) and operate the toilet manually. Check the connecting rod (**3**) and worm gears (**2A** and **2B**) for binding. Test the motor (**1**) for voltage drop, shorts, etc. (see Chapter 3).

Inspect flapper valves for damage, swelling, or dirt and calcium buildup, any of which could prevent them from seating properly. Inspect joker valves for obstructions in the sleeve (duckbill). Calcium deposits can be broken up by flexing the rubber or by putting the valves in a 10-percent muriatic acid solution. (Observe all cautions on the acid bottle.) Check ball-valve springs for corrosion and adequate tension, and the balls and their seats for trash and pitting.

Flapper valves are replaced with the weight uppermost. Make sure the side of the valve that hinges is matched to the belled outside of its housing; otherwise the valve will fail to open or will hang up in operation.

Joker valves are fitted with the sleeve or duckbill facing *away* from the toilet, *toward* the holding tank and seacock.

Pistons generally consist of two dished washers trapping an O-ring, and held to the end of the piston rod with a nut. If the O-ring needs replacing simply undo the nut and separate the washers. Make sure the new O-ring is mounted squarely, and be sure the piston retaining nut is adequately locked to its shaft with a lock washer, liquid adhesive (such as Loctite), or by peening (hammering) the shaft threads over once the nut is on. Grease the cylinder wall with petroleum jelly before replacing the piston.

Scrupulously clean all mating surfaces before reassembly; otherwise leaks are almost certain. Do not overtighten screws, especially on plastic toilets. A little silicone gasket cement or sealing compound smeared on mating surfaces before reassembly will prevent most minor leaks.

connections, etc. If the voltage is low, check the ship's battery and recharge as necessary. If the battery is OK, there must be excessive voltage drop between the battery and the motor (no more than 10 percent is permissible). Refer to Chapter 3.

Because of the heavy electrical loads and long wiring runs, some pumps use a solenoid ("relay") to close the motor circuit, with a remotely operated switch at the toilet. The principle is the same as that of an engine-starting circuit. Check the solenoid for voltage drop (see page 167 for troubleshooting this type of circuit).

If the voltage is adequate, disconnect the electric drive (normally one bolt) and operate the toilet manually. If it works normally, check the electric drive gears (normally a worm gear arrangement) and linkage for binding.

Repairing valves and pistons. Disassembly and reassembly are simple. Two to four screws remove the pump from its base; two or more screws undo the discharge manifold; suction hoses are generally held with hose clamps.

Lavac Toilets

Lavacs (made by Blake) are beautifully simple. The toilet lid is designed to make a seal with the bowl. When the waste is pumped out (with the lid down), a vacuum is pulled in the bowl, which sucks in the flushing water. No inlet pump or valves are needed. There is almost nothing to go wrong. Lavacs use diaphragm pumps on the discharge (see Chapter 12). These are far less troublesome than piston pumps. Where an electric diaphragm pump is fitted it is advisable to install a manual diaphragm pump *in series* with it as a backup. This is the same pump minus the motor drive, so only one set of spare pump valves

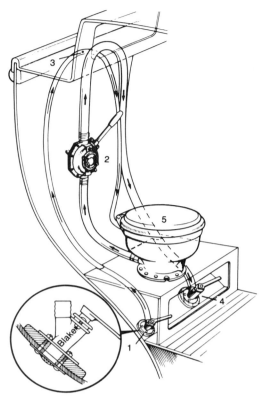

Figure 11-8A. Blake's Lavac toilet. As the waste is pumped overboard (or to the holding tank; not shown), the resulting vacuum draws in water through the inlet. (**1**) Inlet seacock. (**2**) Diaphragm discharge pump. (**3**) Air bleed valve—a simple plastic plug with a small hole drilled in it. The size of the hole controls the level of water remaining in the bowl. The larger the hole, the less water remains. (**4**) Discharge seacock. (**5**) Bowl.

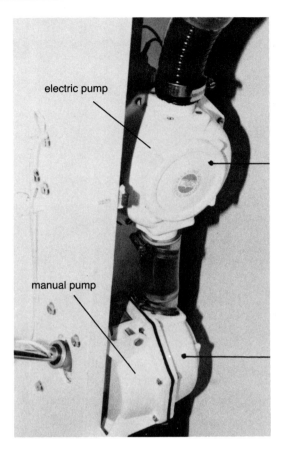

electric pump

manual pump

Figure 11-8B. Lavac toilet with electric and manual diaphragm pumps in series.

Figure 11-9A. **Typical electric toilet.**

and diaphragm is needed. The suction line has no valves—merely a vented loop. Should it start siphoning into the bowl, the vented loop must be plugged. The bowl can always be pumped dry with the lid open.

The most likely problem is a loss of vacuum in the bowl leading to a reduction or complete loss of the flushing water. Older Lavacs have plastic-coated aluminum bowls. Once they start to corrode and the seal fails between the bowl and lid, the bowl will need replacing with one of the newer (post-1981) porcelain bowls.

If the bowl is OK, check the sealing face on the underside of the lid. If this is sound, check all the suction hose connections for an air leak.

Electric Toilets

How they work. At the base of these toilets is a multipurpose pump, usually compris-

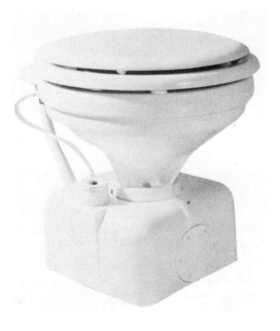

Toilets, Through-Hull Fittings, and Seacocks

ing the following components mounted on a common shaft: a small rubber impeller pump, supplying flushing water to the toilet bowl; a macerator pump (a device that breaks up the sewage into tiny particles); and a good-sized rubber impeller or centrifugal pump to discharge the waste.

The bowl fills faster than it drains. Waste is probably caught in the discharge valves. Close the inlet, pump down, and then open the inlet and flush through to clear the discharge lines. If the problem persists, check the discharge pump impeller, valves, and lines for wear, obstructions, or calcification.

Inadequate flushing. The suction pump may be running slowly due to a variety of electrical problems that usually involve low voltage; the pump impeller may be worn; or the pump may be sucking air through a loose connection or through the vented loop (see above, page 302). The suction seacock may even be coming out of the water when the boat is heeled.

Motor runs, but either suction or discharge fails to operate. The pump impeller, particularly if it is the rubber-impeller type, is probably stripped. *Most pumps cannot tolerate being run dry for more than a few seconds without damage.* But before pulling the pump apart, check that all valves and seacocks are open and the pump is primed. Note that when a pump is run dry not only the impeller(s) but also the seal(s) are likely to be damaged.

Motor repeatedly blows fuses. This is especially likely at the start of a new season. During the winter, rubber impellers frequently get stuck to their pump housings; they then overload the motor and fuse on startup. Try lubricating the pump (pour some water in the bowl and suction lines), and if possible turn it by hand. The other common problem is the swelling of pump impellers caused by inappropriate chemicals (toilet bowl cleaners; deodorants; drain openers) put down the toilet. In this case the pump will need to be dismantled and the impeller replaced.

Loud noises from the pump. There may be a solid object jammed in the macerator, or the motor bearings may be worn out. The latter is generally due to leaking seals allowing water into the bearings. In either case the pump needs disassembling (see below).

Water leaks around pump housings. One of the pump seals is leaking. (Some pumps have one seal; others have a central motor with pumps on both ends of the shaft, in which case there is a seal at both ends.) *Any defective seal needs immediate corrective action. Seal leaks are one of the principal causes of bearing and motor failures.*

Figure 11-9B. **An exploded view of an electric toilet.**

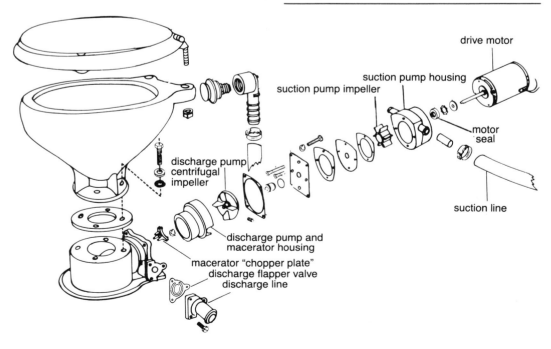

discharge pump centrifugal impeller

discharge pump and macerator housing

macerator "chopper plate"
discharge flapper valve
discharge line

suction pump impeller

suction pump housing

drive motor

motor seal

suction line

Motor operates sluggishly or erratically.
Check for low voltage at the motor. If the voltage is OK, the pumps may be partially plugged, or the motor brushes may be worn or hanging up in their holders. The brushes should be accessible after a couple of covers are removed. Check the brush springs and the free movement of the brushes in their holders. While the brushes are out, check the commutator for excessive carbon and signs of arcing and burning (see Chapter 6).

Motor burnout. The principal causes of burned-out motors are:

1. Seal leaks into the motor causing a short circuit.
2. Overheating as a result of low voltage; pump clogging; or *extended running*. Motors are rated for intermittent use— some as little as two minutes at a time; some as long as 15 minutes. Motors should have momentary-type switches—switches that must be held against a spring pressure—to guard against accidentally leaving them on.

Overhauling the pump and motor. Disassembly is usually reasonably obvious and straightforward. There will be one or more flap and/or joker valves on the discharge side. The first unit encountered is generally the macerator, with the discharge pump behind it. (The latter may be either a centrifugal pump or a rubber-impeller pump.) PAR toilets have the suction pump mounted behind this, followed by a seal and the motor. Raritan toilets have a double-ended motor shaft, with the suction pump on one end and the macerator and discharge pump on the opposite end. In this case both ends of the motor shaft have a seal.

Nearly all suction pumps are the rubber-impeller type. Inspect the vanes for wear on their outer edges (they should be rounded and not flat) and for adequate flexibility with no signs of distortion or cracking.

Seal replacement. Old seals can be pried and pushed out with bent coat hangers, screwdrivers, etc.; take great care not to score the seal housing. The housing must then be scrupulously cleaned. New seals must be pressed into position with equal care; this is the most important part of any rebuilding job. If the seal is at all cocked, bent, or distorted it will leak and the motor will fail in a short time.

New seals are placed in their housings with the lip that encloses the motor shaft facing *toward* the pump chamber that is being sealed. A piece of dowel or a socket of the same diameter as the seal should be used to push it home; use the minimum pressure and keep the seal square to the housing at all times.

Testing the motor. Motors are the universal type (see Chapter 6). Older motors usually have field windings; newer motors are the permanent-magnet type. The various tests outlined in Chapter 6 can be applied to armatures, commutators, field windings, and brushes. The armature should be flexed and spun to check the bearings and make sure it is not rubbing on the field winding shoes or magnets.

If there is any problem with the armature, field windings, or bearings, it is better to replace the entire motor than disassemble it. Motors are constructed to very close tolerances in order to eliminate vibration and shaft seal leaks. It is impossible to meet these standards without specialized bench equipment.

When refitting pumps, be sure to get the positive and negative wires the right way around. Polarity is not necessarily critical on motors with wound field coils, but it is absolutely critical on the more common permanent-magnet types. The usual color coding on DC motors comprises a red or orange wire for the positive, and a black wire for the negative. On AC motors a black wire is normally positive, a white wire neutral, and a green wire ground (USA color codes; see Chapter 3 for UK and European equivalents).

Other Types of Systems

Macerator pumps. These are used to break up and pump out the waste from many holding tanks, and are almost the same as the pumps on electric toilets, with the exception that there is no flushing pump built into the unit. Pumps may be inside or on top of the holding tank, or may be mounted separately. In the event of a problem, make all the usual voltage tests. If a pump mounted above the holding tank spins but fails to pump, before pulling it apart disconnect the discharge hose and pour in some water to make sure it is primed. It may just be airbound.

Never run a macerator pump dry; the seal and impeller will burn up. Never run

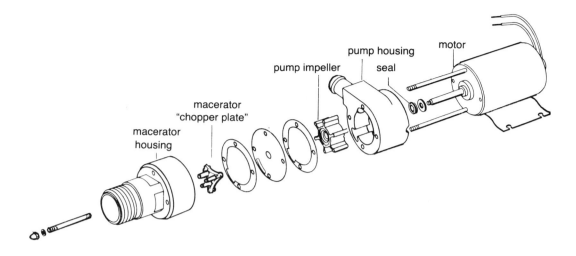

Figure 11-10. **A macerator pump.**

it continuously; the motor will burn up. Motors are rated for intermittent use only—2 to 15 minutes, depending on the make of the pump. It is best to fit only momentary-type switches—i.e., spring-loaded buttons or switches that must be held in the "ON" position.

LectraSan holding tanks. LectraSan is a sewage treatment system manufactured by Raritan. Waste is pumped into a small holding tank that has approximately a four-flush capacity using the discharge pump on the toilet. There the waste is chopped up by a macerator pump in one chamber, and stirred by a mixer in another chamber. In between, through an electrolytic process, two electrodes immersed in the suspension manufacture hypochlorous acid from the seawater used for flushing. This is done without the addition of chemicals. The acid kills bacteria, and further toilet flushes push the treated waste out of the tank and overboard.

The LectraSan system must be used *every time the toilet is flushed.* Failure to do so will overload the macerator and clog the system. The unit goes through a pretreat cycle of approximately 30 seconds and then a treatment cycle of two minutes. The unit must be turned on *before flushing,* it must be flushed *during the pretreat cycle,* and it must *not* be flushed, or flushed again, during the treatment cycle. In other words, once the toilet is flushed the unit must be allowed to complete the cycle before reflushing.

LectraSans have a high current draw (45 amps on 12 volts) but for only two minutes.

In the event of a problem, make all the usual voltage drop tests *at the unit while in operation.* Check previous sections of this book for macerator pump and electric motor tests.

The control unit has a meter indicating low, normal, and high treatment levels. Treatment levels are related to battery voltage, water salinity, and temperature—the higher the voltage, salinity, and temperature the higher the meter reading. In fresh or brackish water salt must be added to maintain salinity, either manually when flushing or via a special tank. If meter readings are low, check first for voltage drop during operation. If the voltage is OK, try adding salt. If meter readings are too high, quite likely excessive salt is being added.

The holding tank and electrodes may become calcium encrusted in time. Flush muriatic acid through the unit as described previously. Rinse well before reusing. If more extensive inspection and cleaning is needed, lift off the whole top and lift out the electrode pack.

Never allow toilet bowl cleaners, drain openers, or deodorants into LectraSan units. If any of these chemicals should enter a unit, flush it repeatedly before turning it on again. Damaging chemical reactions with the hypochlorous acid formed during operation are otherwise likely.

VacuFlush toilets. VacuFlush toilets are manufactured by SeaLand Technology Inc. These toilets utilize a vacuum pump and a vacuum chamber. Depressing a foot pedal in the base of the toilet opens a ball

main unit

control panel

salt feed tank

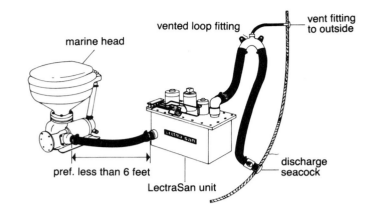

marine head

vented loop fitting

vent fitting to outside

discharge seacock

pref. less than 6 feet

LectraSan unit

Figure 11-11A. **An alternative to holding tanks, units such as Raritan's LectraSan—acting much as a municipal sewage treatment plant—macerate and chlorinate waste and discharge it directly overboard.**

Figure 11-11B. **Installation options for LectraSan systems. Top right:** Basic electric toilet. **Second from top:** Basic manual toilet. **Next:** Electric toilet with salt feed tank. **Bottom left:** Manual toilet with salt feed tank. **Bottom right:** The LectraSan unit itself.

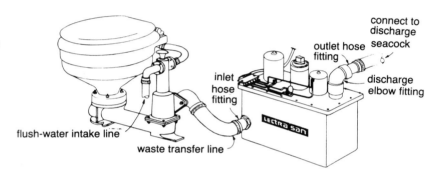

connect to discharge seacock

outlet hose fitting

inlet hose fitting

discharge elbow fitting

flush-water intake line

waste transfer line

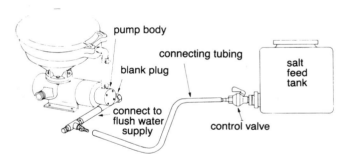

pump body

connecting tubing

salt feed tank

blank plug

connect to flush water supply

control valve

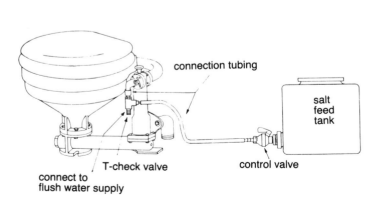

connection tubing

salt feed tank

T-check valve

control valve

connect to flush water supply

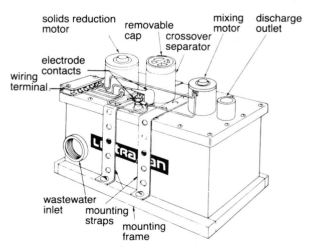

solids reduction motor

removable cap

crossover separator

mixing motor

discharge outlet

electrode contacts

wiring terminal

wastewater inlet

mounting straps

mounting frame

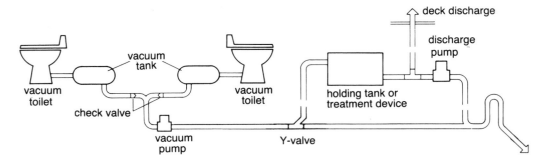

Figure 11-12A. **VacuFlush** toilets, from Sealand Technology, use a central vacuum pump to transfer waste to the holding tank or treatment device.

deck discharge

discharge pump

vacuum tank

holding tank or treatment device

vacuum toilet

vacuum toilet

check valve

vacuum pump

Y-valve

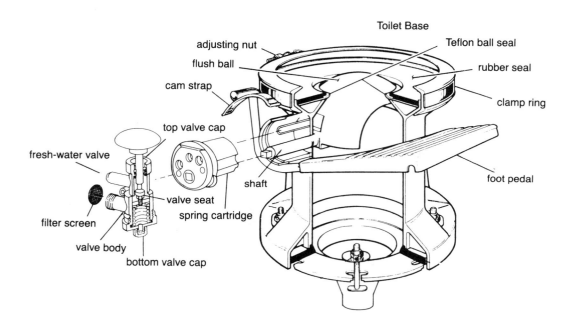

Figure 11-12B. **Parts arrangement for VacuFlush toilets.**

Toilet Base

adjusting nut

Teflon ball seal

flush ball

rubber seal

cam strap

clamp ring

top valve cap

fresh-water valve

foot pedal

filter screen

shaft

valve seat

valve body

spring cartridge

bottom valve cap

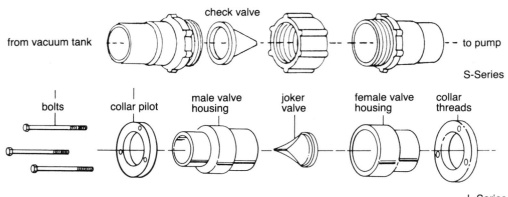

In-Line Check Valve

check valve

from vacuum tank

to pump

S-Series

bolts

collar pilot

male valve housing

joker valve

female valve housing

collar threads

L-Series

Figure 11-13. Raritan's Jet Head toilets are found primarily on larger, sea-going vessels.

valve. The waste is sucked out and passed to a holding tank or overboard. The vacuum pump then kicks in and pulls down the vacuum chamber, ready for the next flush. Water for rinsing the bowl is taken from the boat's pressurized freshwater supply—the rinsing valve is connected to the foot pedal, opening just before the main ball valve and closing just after it. It takes 60 to 90 seconds for the vacuum pump to pull down the vacuum chamber ready for use. The pump will then kick in after every flush. Because of a slow loss of vacuum, the pump can be expected to come on once an hour even if the toilet is not flushed.

If the pump runs longer than 90 seconds or more frequently than once an hour between flushes, a more serious vacuum leak is present. Likely sources include faulty hose connections, poor seals on the main ball valve, and leaking check valves. (There are several joker-type valves in the system.) Tighten all hose clamps. Pour a little water in the bowl; if it is sucked away the seals are leaking. In this case, try tightening the main clamp ring, but beware of overtightening, which will jam the valve or prevent it from closing properly. If check valves are suspected, try repeated flushings. If this fails, add muriatic acid to dissolve calcium deposits (see page 305). If all else fails, take the valves apart and inspect.

A lack of flushing water will arise from low pressure on the freshwater system, a plugged freshwater valve (there is a filter screen on the inlet), or a defective water valve. If the water will not turn off, the valve may be stuck open due to a bent operating lever or dirt on the valve seat, or the valve itself may be defective.

The pump is a bellows or diaphragm type. These are covered in Chapter 12.

Jet Head toilets. Jet Head toilets, built by Raritan, are for seagoing vessels only. A high-capacity centrifugal pump directs a powerful jet of water into the toilet bowl, breaking up waste and flushing it away. These toilets use far more water than conventional marine toilets and are not suitable for use with holding tanks.

Through Hulls and Seacocks

Traditionally, all seacocks and through hulls (skin fittings) were bronze, the seacocks having a tapered plug generally held in place with a ring and two bolts or screws. Now there is a much greater diversity of types and materials. Common alternatives include gate valves and ball valves, and materials such as plastics, stainless steel, brass, and rubber.

Traditional seacocks. It takes but a quarter-turn on the handle to open or close a seacock, and it is instantly obvious whether it is open or shut. When it is open the handle lines up with the tailpiece; when shut, the handle is at right angles to the tailpiece. Construction is simple, rugged, and more or less chemical-proof (Figure 11-14A).

The tapered plug and seat have a high surface area with the potential for considerable friction. A traditional seacock needs regreasing annually, and the keeper nuts or plug retaining nut should only be tightened enough to stop the seacock from leaking. Overtightening will squeeze out the grease, and the resulting metal-to-metal contact will lead to accelerated wear and seizure.

A seized plug generally can be freed by tapping on the handle with a hammer. Many plugs are installed *across* the barrel of the seacock (see Figure 11-15A) and can be tapped from the base after loosening the plug retaining nut.

In time the plug tends to become wasp-waisted, and water leaks around the plug sides. The seacock fails to hold. Overtightening keeper nuts or the plug retaining nut will not solve this problem, but merely will create others. The plug should be removed, smeared with grinding paste (available from automotive parts stores) and then worked around and around in its seat until a smooth metal-to-metal contact is reestablished on all surfaces. Clean away all traces of the grinding paste, then regrease the plug.

If the plug and its seat are worn beyond restoration, a new seacock is called for. Plugs and seats come in matched pairs, and it generally is not possible to replace one without the other.

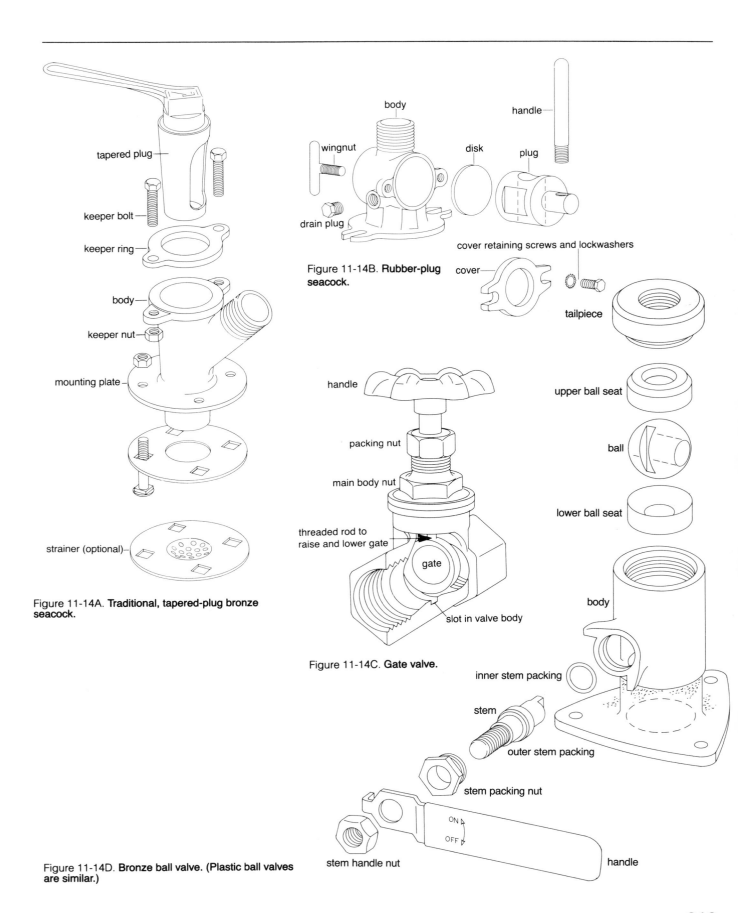

tapered plug

keeper bolt

keeper ring

body

keeper nut

mounting plate

strainer (optional)

Figure 11-14A. **Traditional, tapered-plug bronze seacock.**

body

wingnut

drain plug

disk

plug

handle

Figure 11-14B. **Rubber-plug seacock.**

cover retaining screws and lockwashers

cover

tailpiece

upper ball seat

ball

lower ball seat

body

handle

packing nut

main body nut

threaded rod to raise and lower gate

gate

slot in valve body

Figure 11-14C. **Gate valve.**

inner stem packing

stem

outer stem packing

stem packing nut

ON

OFF

Figure 11-14D. **Bronze ball valve. (Plastic ball valves are similar.)**

stem handle nut

handle

Rubber-plug seacocks. This popular variation is sold by Groco, among others. Replacing the tapered plug is a solid rubber bung, through which is a metal-lined hole. The bung seats on a metal plate, or disk. A threaded locking handle (wingnut) is set into the body of the seacock. When the handle is tightened it forces the metal plate against the bung, compressing the rubber, squeezing it against the sides of the seacock, and sealing it (Figure 11-14B).

To operate the seacock, loosen the locking handle until the seacock can be turned, and then tighten it just until the seacock stops dripping from around its plug retaining (keeper) ring, also called simply a cover. Overtightening will deform the rubber, especially when the seacock is closed, forcing the sides of the bung up into the seacock inlet and discharge ports.

These seacocks are not suitable for applications where chemicals may be present (e.g., toilets and sinks). The rubber swells, jamming the bung and making it next to impossible to turn. Maintenance involves annual regreasing.

Gate valves. This type features a gate that moves in a slot in the body of the valve. The gate rides on a threaded rod; turning the rod via a handle raises and lowers the gate (Figure 11-14C).

Gate valves have no place on boats. Most are made of brass and will de-zincify in time (see page 100), falling apart. Even when made of bronze they suffer from several drawbacks. It is not possible to tell by looking at the handle whether the valve is open or shut. Trash is easily trapped under the gate, and then the valve won't seal. The threaded rod on which the gate rides is relatively thin and easily sheared if the valve jams. Lacking a mounting flange, the valve cannot be independently fastened to the hull (see installation below).

When opening a gate valve, open it fully and then turn the handle back a half turn so that it is free. There is then likely to be less confusion as to whether the valve is open or shut (when closed the handle will be tight, when open, loose) and less likelihood of forcing the handle the wrong way and shearing the stem.

It is advisable to disassemble gate valves annually, inspect them closely for corrosion, and regrease stems and threads. To do this, unscrew the main housing nut on the valve body. When reassembling, screw the gate partially up before tightening the main housing nut, otherwise the gate may bottom out in its slot and suffer damage. The small nut around the stem is a packing nut; tighten it gently if the stem leaks, and repack if necessary.

Ball valves. A ball with a hole through it fits into a spherical seat with inlet and discharge ports. Turned one way the hole in the ball lines up with the ports and allows flow; turned the other way it closes the ports (Figure 11-14D).

Ball valves are efficient and foolproof. The metal versions generally have bronze bodies with chrome-plated bronze balls riding in Teflon seals. Plastic ones have reinforced-plastic bodies and balls once again riding in Teflon seals.

To disassemble a ball valve, undo the main body nut. The balls, whether plastic or bronze, should be greased annually. In my experience the plastic stems on many plastic valves are the weak spot, tending to harden and become brittle with age. *Do not force them or they will break.* Plastic seacocks have one other major disadvantage: In a fire they will melt. On the other hand, they will not succumb to electrolysis, which is probably the greater threat to most underwater hardware.

Seacock and Through-Hull Installation

Wood and fiberglass hulls. Through hulls are fitted as shown in Figure 11-15A. Note the substantial backing block. The through hull is retained by an external mushroom or flush-mount fitting.

Seacocks are installed in a similar fashion, with the exception that all seacocks should be flanged and independently fastened. That is, they should not merely rely on the external mushroom or flush-mount fitting. Be sure the drain plug in the housing faces down.

Metal hulls. Plastic through hulls can be installed as above. *Metal through hulls must be insulated from the hull to prevent galvanic interaction.* The seacock then must be electrically isolated from the piping attached to it by means of an intervening length of rubber hose (Figure 11-15B).

Hose attachments. These should be made with properly matched adaptors, hose barbs, or tailpieces. Use *two all-stainless steel* hose clamps. (Make sure the screws are stainless and not just nickel-plated.) Check

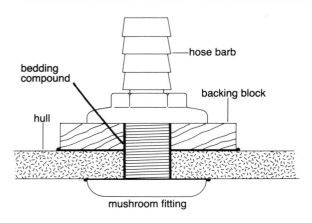

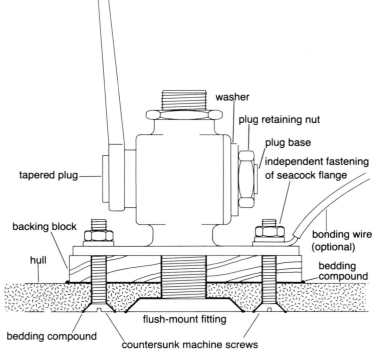

all hoses and clamps at least once a year. The clamps should be undone for inspection, since they frequently rust and fail inside the worm screw unit, where the rust is not visible.

Fids. Keep on board one or two fids (tapered softwood plugs) of a suitable size to (a) ram into seacocks and (b) ram into hull openings occupied by seacocks. In the event of a catastrophic failure of the hose or seacock, or the complete loss of a seacock, the hole can be rapidly plugged.

Figure 11-15A. **Proper through-hull and seacock installation, wood and fiberglass hulls.**

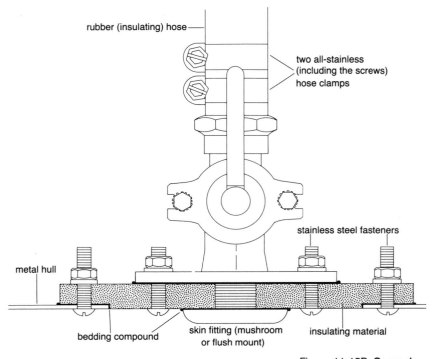

Figure 11-15B. **Seacock installation, metal hulls.**

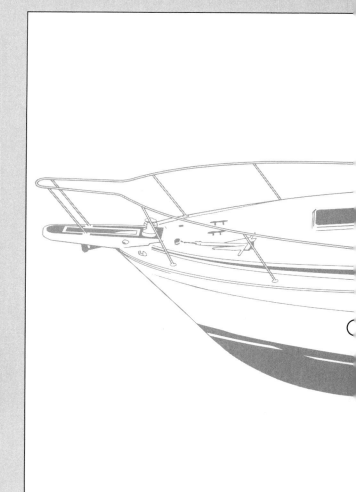

CHAPTER 12

Figure 12-1. **A thorough understanding of pumps and their repair could someday keep your vessel afloat in an emergency.**

(1) toilet pump
(2) bilge pump
(3) macerator pump
(4) collection box
(5) foot pump
(6) engine cooling pump
(7) freshwater pump

Pumps

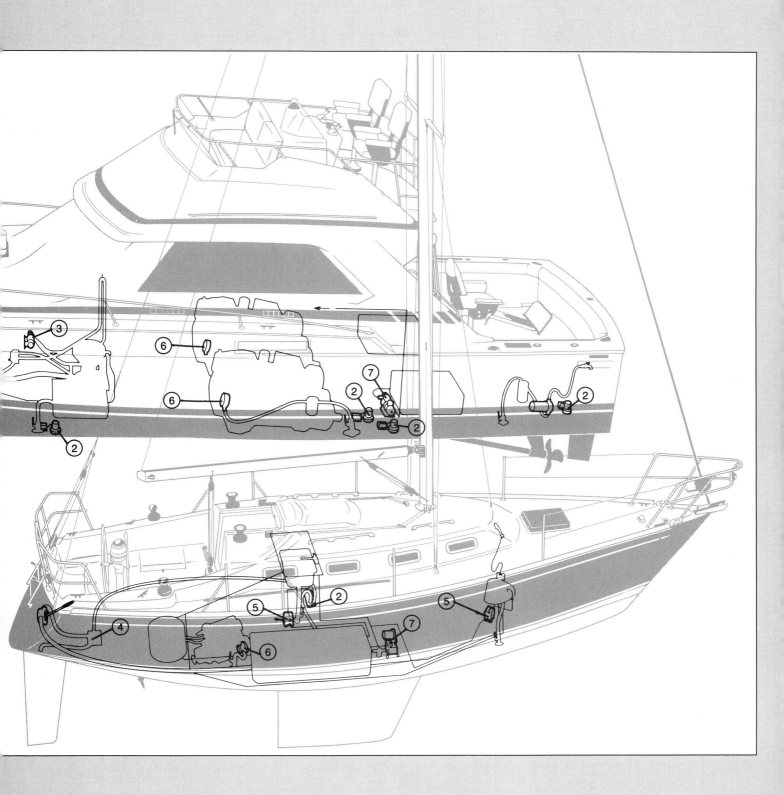

This chapter deals with the mechanical (pumping) end of pumps. If problems are experienced with electric motors, refer to Chapter 6, bearing in mind that most old motors are *wound field-coil* universal motors, while most new ones are *permanent magnet* universal motors. Note also that the biggest possible contribution to avoiding electrical problems will be made by installing the pump in such a way that the motor is on top, so that if the pump seal leaks, the fluid will not run into the pump motor.

How They Work

Pumps on boats fall into three broad categories: *variable-volume impeller* pumps; *centrifugal* pumps; and *positive-displacement* pumps. (These are my categories.)

Variable-Volume Impeller Pumps

These work on the principle of a change in the displaced volume of the impeller from one side of a pump chamber to another. The most common variety has a flexible impeller turning in a pump body that has one side flattened by screwing a blanking piece (a *cam*) into the body. As the vanes on the impeller reach the cam, they are squeezed down, expelling any fluid trapped between them. As the vanes pass the cam, they spring back up, drawing in more fluid.

Less common variations on the same theme are vane and rotary pumps. On vane pumps, the drive shaft is permanently offset in the pump housing such that the impeller ("rotor") is always closer to the pump body at some points than others. Set in slots in the rotor are hard vanes, which are held against the pump body. As the rotor spins the vanes move in and out of their slots, thus maintaining contact with the pump body. The changing volume between the vanes alternately draws in and expels fluid in much the same manner as the vane action in a flexible impeller pump.

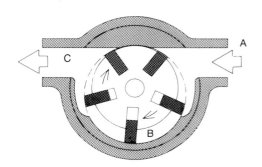

Figure 12-2. **(Below)** Operation of a variable volume, flexible impeller pump. **(A)** Upon leaving the offset cam, the flexible impeller blades expand, creating a vacuum which draws liquid into the pump body. **(B)** As the impeller rotates, each successive blade draws in liquid and carries it to the outlet port. **(C)** The remaining liquid is expelled when the flexible impeller blades are again compressed by the offset cam, creating a continuous, uniform flow.

Figure 12-3. **(Above)** Operation of a variable-volume vane pump. **(A)** Upon leaving the eccentric portion of the pump body's liner, the vanes create a partial vacuum, which draws in fluid. **(B)** As the rotor rotates, each successive vane draws in liquid and carries it to the discharge port. **(C)** When the vanes again contact the eccentric portion of the liner, they force liquid out the discharge port.

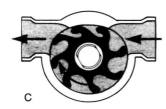

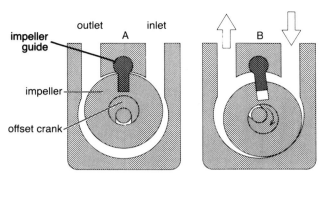

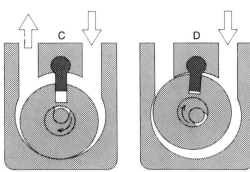

Figure 12-4. Operation of a rotary pump. (**A**) The pump at rest. (**B**) The impeller oscillates over and down, opening a space between the impeller and impeller guide, which draws in fluid through the inlet port. (**C**) Suction-side volume increases steadily, drawing in more fluid. At the same time, the discharge-side volume decreases, expelling fluid. (**D**) Discharge-side volume near minimum; most fluid is expelled. Suction-side volume is still increasing, drawing in more fluid.

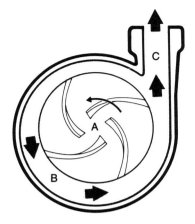

Figure 12-5. Operation of a centrifugal pump. (**A**) Liquid enters the inlet port in the center of the pump. The level of liquid must be high enough above the pump for gravity to push it into the pump, or the pump must receive initial priming. (**B**) Centrifugal force generated by rotating and curved impeller forces fluid to periphery of the pump casing, thence toward the discharge port. (**C**) The velocity of fluid discharge translates into hydraulic pressure in the system downstream from the pump. The flow rate is dependent upon restrictions in the inlet and outlet piping, and the height that the liquid must be lifted.

Figure 12-6. A manual diaphragm pump.

In rotary pumps the impeller does not actually rotate! Instead it is mounted on, but not keyed to, an "eccentric" shaft. The shaft is centered in the pump housing but with an offset section where it passes through the impeller bearing, much as a crankshaft is offset where it passes through a rod end (big end) bearing. The impeller is kept from spinning by an impeller guide (Figure 12-4) held in the pump body and fitting in a slot in the impeller. As the shaft turns the impeller oscillates in a circular pattern but without actually turning, pulling in and expelling fluid as it goes (just as a connecting rod oscillates without actually turning).

Centrifugal Pumps

These have an impeller with vanes designed in such a way that fluid drawn into the center of the impeller is thrown out by centrifugal force (Figure 12-5). The momentum generated in the fluid keeps it moving and is what makes the pump work. A less common variation on the same principle is a "turbine" pump, which has a somewhat different arrangement of the vanes on the impeller but is otherwise the same.

Positive-Displacement Pumps

This type moves a diaphragm, "bellows," or piston in and out of a pump chamber, alternately increasing and decreasing its volume (Figures 12-6, 12-7A, and 12-7B). These pumps, unlike the others, only can work with a set of valves—one valve lets the fluid into the chamber and traps it; an-

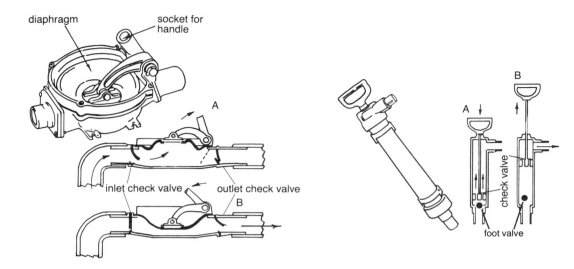

Figure 12-7A. **Operation of a manual diaphragm pump. (A)** As the handle is pulled back, the flexible diaphragm expands, creating a vacuum which pulls back the check valve and draws fluid into the pump chamber. **(B)** When the handle is pushed down, hydraulic pressure forces the inlet check valve closed, at the same time opening the outlet check valve and expelling fluid through the outlet.

Figure 12-7B. Operation of a lift pump. **(A)** The handle is depressed. Fluid is trapped between the base of the piston and the foot valve and forced up into the pump body through the check valve in the base of the piston. (Several pump cycles must be repeated before the vacuum formed below the check valve draws the fluid to the level of the pump.) **(B)** As the handle is lifted, the check valve closes, and the fluid is lifted to the outlet. At the same time, a vacuum is formed below the check valve, which draws more fluid into the pump chamber through the foot valve.

other lets it out and stops it from being sucked back in. Since there is no impeller, there is no shaft entering the pump chamber and therefore no shaft seal and asso-ciated leaks (except on some piston pumps; see section on piston pumps at the end of this chapter).

Choosing a Pump

If a pump is to be successful and trouble-free, it must be correctly matched to its application. Given the multiplicity of pumps on the market, it is sometimes hard to pick the best one for a particular use—frequently two different types will do equally well. The following are some of the questions to be considered.

Self-Priming or Not

All pumps, excluding the centrifugal ones, are self-priming—in other words, they have the capability to draw fluid up to themselves. Centrifugal pumps have no self-priming capability whatsoever and must always be installed below the liquid level they are to pump, at all angles of heel.

Pressure Range

Almost all pumps will work with discharge pressures up to 25 psi (pounds per square inch), although frequently the motors on small electric pumps will not handle the same loads (some less than 10 psi). Most flexible impeller pumps should not be used above 25 psi. Rotary, vane, and centrifugal pumps usually will go safely to 40 psi. Centrifugal pumps, in particular, will not be damaged by raising discharge pressures, but the pump output will be sharply curtailed until it ceases altogether. Positive-displacement pumps are limited solely by the strength of their diaphragms, valves, and other parts; they rarely are built to go above 50 psi, and most require pressures well below this.

Restrictions in the Flow

The more restricted the discharge—or the greater the *head* (the vertical distance a pump has to lift fluid)—the higher the discharge pressure. Pumps respond differently to this situation. Variable-volume impeller pumps and positive-displacement pumps attempt to move the same volume of fluid and therefore work harder and harder until something fails (e.g., vanes strip off impellers; diaphragms rupture; etc.). Centrifugal pumps, on the other hand, are not bothered by an increase in discharge pressure—the pump just responds by moving less and less fluid. In fact, the greater the pressure and the less the flow, the less the load on the pump (and the less current it will draw if it has an electric motor).

Any variable-volume impeller pump or positive-displacement pump used in a system where the flow gets cut off while the pump is running (e.g., a freshwater system; a saltwater wash-down system with a garden-hose-type shutoff nozzle) must protect the pump with a built-in pressure switch to limit the load on the pump.

Running Dry

Diaphragm and bellows pumps can run dry indefinitely without damage. Piston pumps are less tolerant, generally depending on the nature of the piston seals. On all other pumps there are two considerations: the impeller and the pump shaft seals.

No flexible impeller or vane pump can run dry for more than a few seconds without damage—the fluid pumped is critical for lubrication. All centrifugal pump impellers can run dry indefinitely. Most rotary pumps fall somewhere between these two extremes.

However, even where an impeller can tolerate running dry, the shaft seal probably cannot. No lip-type seal can run dry for very long without heating up its shaft and damaging the seal. Carbon/ceramic seals are more tolerant, but again there are very definite limits (see below for more information on seals).

If a pump is likely to run dry, use a diaphragm or bellows pump.

Chemical Tolerance

This is an important consideration in many applications even if it is not obvious at first. Galley sinks and shower drains handle many kinds of soap, detergents, and bleach; bilges contain traces of oil and diesel; effluent systems are frequently subjected to powerful toilet bowl cleaners, drain openers, deodorants, and bleaches (though they most definitely should *not* be—see Chapter 11); even freshwater systems handle traces of chlorine and other chemicals.

Flexible impellers are the most susceptible to chemical damage—they swell up and bind in their pump housings. Fuses blow and/or vanes strip off. The standard impeller is normally made of neoprene, but nitrile, polyurethane and Viton are all available for special applications (see Table 12-1). Positive-displacement pumps also have diaphragms and valves that are susceptible to chemical damage. Centrifugal pumps and many vane and rotary pumps have relatively inert bronze and plastic (phenolic or epoxy) impellers and vanes; however, they may still have chemical tolerance problems with lip-type shaft seals. (Note: Carbon/ceramic seals are far more tolerant, but generally are sealed in pump housings and on shafts with rubber "boots" and O-rings that may not be tolerant.)

Passing Solids

Impeller pumps can handle only the smallest particles of solid material, whereas positive-displacement pumps have a moderate solids-handling capability—largely dependent on the type of valves fitted. Ball valves are not tolerant, while flap and joker valves can pass some solids; see Chapter 11 for a description of these valves.

Temperature Range

This is seldom significant. Flexible impeller pumps are the most restrictive, with a temperature range of around 45°F to 180°F (7°C to 82°C). Most other pumps will handle both colder and hotter temperatures.

Direction of Rotation

Almost all variable-volume impeller pumps can be run in either direction, the exception being those with manual clutches. These are generally designed to

Table 12-1. Chemical Compatibility for Impellers.[1]

Chemical or Compound	Bronze	316 Stainless	Phenolic	Epoxy	Poly-propylene	Neoprene	Nitrile	Viton
Acetone	1	1	1	3	1	3	3	3
Alcohol, ethyl	1	1	1	1	1	1	2	2
Alcohol, isopropyl	1	1	1	1	1	1	2	1
Alcohol, methyl	1	1	1	1	1	2	3	3
Ammonia	3	1	1	1	1	1	2	3
Antifreeze, Most brands	1	1	1	1	1	1	1	1
Prestone	1	1	1	1	1	3	1	2
Pyro Super	1	1	1	1	1	3	1	—
Valvoline	1	1	1	1	1	2	2	—
Beer	1	1	1	1	3	1	—	—
Butter	3	1	3	1	1	2	1	1
Carbolic acid	1	1	3	1	1	2	—	—
Chlorox (bleach)	1	1	3	1	1	1	2	2
Citric acid (lemon juice, etc.)	2	1	1	1	1	1	2	—
Corn oil	2	1	1	1	—	2	1	1
Cottonseed oil	1	1	1	1	1	2	1	1
Deodorants, some	1	1	1	1	1	3	3	—
Detergents	1	1	—	1	1	1	1	—
Diesel fuel	1	1	—	1	2	3	2	1
Disinfectant deodorant	1	1	1	1	—	2	1	1
Gasoline	1	1	1	1	2	3	3	1
Grease	1	1	2	1	—	3	3	1
Horseradish	—	—	—	1	—	1	3	—
Hydraulic oil	1	1	3	1	3	3	2	1
Hydrogen peroxide	3	2	3	1	1	3	1	—
Kerosene, paraffin	1	1	1	1	1	3	2	1
Ketchup	2	1	3	1	—	2	1	1
Lard	1	1	3	1	1	2	1	—
Lemon oil	—	1	1	1	—	2	—	1
Linseed oil	1	1	3	1	—	3	1	—
Mayonnaise	3	1	—	1	—	1	2	1
Mineral oil	1	1	1	1	1	2	1	1
Muriatic acid	2	3	1	1	2	1	2	1
Phosphoric acid	2	1	3	1	2	1	1	1
Pine oil	3	1	2	1	—	3	3	1
Propylene glycol	1	1	1	1	1	2	1	—
Rapeseed oil	1	1	—	1	—	2	—	1
Refrigeration gases, R-12	1	3	—	1	1	2	2	2
R-22	1	2	—	1	1	2	2	3
Sesame seed oil	1	1	—	1	1	2	1	1
Soap solutions	2	1	1	1	1	2	1	1
Soybean oil	1	1	3	1	1	3	1	1
Starch	1	1	1	1	1	1	2	1
Toothpaste	1	1	3	1	—	2	1	1
Turpentine	2	1	—	1	2	3	1	1
Urine	2	1	1	1	1	3	1	—
Varnish	1	1	1	1	1	3	2	—
Vegetable juice	2	2	1	1	1	2	2	—
Vegetable oil	1	1	2	1	1	2	1	1
Vinegar	2	1	—	1	1	2	2	3

1. Note how poorly neoprene performs and yet this is the standard flexible pump impeller!
Key: 1 = OK; 2 = Proceed with caution; flush after use; 3 = Rapid deterioration; — = no information.

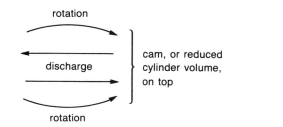

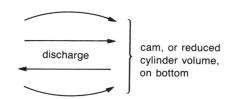
Figure 12-8. **Reversing the direction of flow of a variable-volume impeller pump.**

run clockwise (looking at the pump from the end cover). Flexible impellers are normally factory-installed for clockwise rotation; if you are adding or replacing these pumps and they are to run counterclockwise (anticlockwise), it is preferable—but by no means necessary—to remove the impeller and bend the vanes down the other way before starting. The suction and discharge ports also will be reversed.

Centrifugal pumps are not reversible. Positive-displacement pumps pump the same way regardless of the direction of the drive motor's rotation.

Continuous Duty

Most pump motors are designed for *intermittent* use only—sometimes as little as two minutes at a time. The motor must then be allowed to cool down or it may burn up. Other motors can run indefinitely without damage. Check the manuals that came with your pump to ascertain which type you have.

Maintenance, Troubleshooting, and Repair

Flexible Impeller Pumps

The principal causes of failure are running dry and swelled impellers from chemicals. In the former case, the impeller vanes are likely to strip off; in the latter, the impeller jams in the pump body. In either case, a new impeller is needed.

Flexible impeller pumps like to be used often. If left for long periods without running (e.g., over the winter) the impeller vanes have a tendency to stick to the pump housing. When the pump is restarted, it may blow fuses or strip off its vanes. If this is a constant problem, try fitting an over-thick gasket (see "Reassembly"—this technique results in a small loss of pump efficiency). Otherwise the pump cover will need loosening until the pump starts spinning.

Other common problems are leaking seals (again quite likely a result of running dry) and worn or corroded bearings. Apart from normal wear, bearings will be damaged by water (from leaking seals), improper belt tension (too tight), and misalignment of drive pulleys or couplings. Optimum belt tension permits the longest stretch of a belt to be depressed ⅓ inch to ½ inch with moderate finger pressure.

Figure 12-9. **A typical flexible impeller pump.**

Pulley alignment can be checked by removing the belt and placing a rod in the groove of the two pulleys; any misalignment will be clearly visible.

Disassembly. Despite the thousands of different flexible impeller pumps, most share many construction similarities. Removal of the end cover (four to six screws) will expose the impeller. Almost all impellers are a sliding fit on the drive shaft (either with splines, square keys, Woodruff keys, one or two flats on the shaft, or a slotted shaft). Using a pair of needle-nose pliers, grip the impeller and pull it out. Note that some impellers are sealed to

Troubleshooting Chart 12-1.
Flexible Impeller, Vane, and Rotary Pump Problems: No Flow.

If the pump is belt-driven, is the pump pulley turning? **YES ↓**	**NO ➤** Tighten or replace the drive belt.
If a clutch is fitted, is it working? (The center of the pulley will be turning with the pulley itself.) **YES ↓**	**NO ➤** Adjust or replace the clutch.
For gear-driven pumps and for belt-driven pumps on which the pulley is turning, proceed as follows:	
Remove the pump cover: Are the impeller vanes intact? **YES ↓**	**NO ➤** Replace the impeller and track down any missing vanes. The pump probably ran dry; find out why. Check for a closed seacock, plugged filter, collapsed suction hose, or excessive heeling that causes the suction line on a raw-water pump to come out of the water. Less likely is a blockage on the discharge side causing the pump to overload.
Are the vanes making good contact with the pump body? **YES ↓**	**NO ➤** The impeller is badly worn and needs replacing. On vane and rotary pumps the vanes may be jammed in the impeller and just need cleaning.
Does the impeller turn when the pump drive gear or pulley turns? **YES ↓**	**NO ➤** The impeller, drive gear, or pulley is slipping on its shaft, or the clutch (if fitted) is inoperative. Repair as necessary.
If the impeller turns, the pump may just need priming. Otherwise the suction or discharge line must be blocked. Check for a closed seacock, plugged filter, collapsed suction hose, or excessive heeling that causes the suction line on a raw-water pump to come out of the water.	

their shafts with O-rings; most are not. If the impeller will not come, it may be one of the few locked in place with a set, or allen, screw (some Volvo and Atomic Four engines in particular). If the screw is inaccessible, the drive side of the impeller will have to be disassembled and the impeller knocked out on its shaft.

Inspect the impeller. The vanes should have rounded tips (not worn flat), with no signs of swelling, distortion, or cracking of the vanes. If in any doubt, replace the impeller. If an O-ring is fitted to the shaft, check it for damage. If the impeller has a tapered metal sleeve on its inner end ("extended insert" impellers), inspect the sleeve and discard the impeller if there is any sign of a step where the sleeve slides into the shaft seal.

If it is necessary to remove the cam (e.g., to replace a *wear plate*—see next paragraph), loosen the cam retaining screw, tap the screw until the cam breaks loose, and then remove the screw and cam. Clean all surfaces of sealing compound.

Some impellers have a wear plate at the back of the pump chamber. If fitted, the plate can be hooked out with a piece of bent wire. Note the notch in its top; this aligns with a dowel in the pump body. If the wear plate is grooved or scored, replace it.

Shaft seals are of three types:

1. Lip-type seals, which press into the pump housing and have a rubber lip that grips the shaft.
2. Carbon/ceramic seals, in which a ceramic disc with a smooth face seats in a rubber "boot" in the pump housing and a spring-loaded carbon disc, also with a smooth face, is sealed to the pump shaft with a rubber sleeve or O-ring. The spring holds the carbon disc against the ceramic disc and the extremely smooth faces of the two provide a seal.
3. An external packing gland (stuffing box), which is the same as a propeller shaft packing gland. These are not very common. For care and maintenance see page 246.

Although it is possible to hook out and replace some carbon/ceramic seals with the shaft still in place (this cannot be done with lip-type seals), in most cases the shaft must be taken out. To do this, take apart the drive end of the shaft. First unbolt the pump from its engine or remove the drive pulley if belt driven; then proceed as follows:

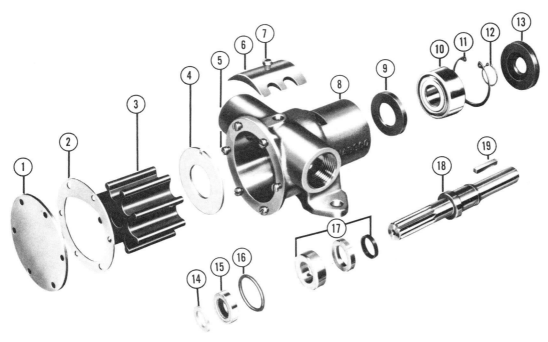

Figure 12-10. An exploded view of the pump shown in Figure 12-9. 1. Pump cover. 2. Gasket. 3. Impeller (splined type). 4. Wear plate. 5. Pump cover retaining screws. 6. Cam (mounted inside pump body). 7. Cam retaining screw. 8. Pump body. 9. Slinger (to deflect any leaks away from the bearing). 10. Bearing. 11. Bearing retaining circlip. 12. Shaft retaining circlip. 13. Outer seal. 14, 15, 16. Inner seal assembly, lip-type, or 17. Inner seal assembly, carbon-ceramic type. 18. Pump shaft. 19. Drive key.

If the pump has a seal at the drive end of the shaft (part number 13 in Figure 12-10), hook it out. When removing any seals, be extremely careful not to scratch the seal seat. Behind the seal in the body of the pump usually will be a bearing retaining circlip (pumps bolted directly to an engine housing may not have one). Remove the circlip, flexing it the minimum amount necessary to get it out. If it gets bent, it should be replaced rather than straightened out.

Support the pump body on a couple of blocks of wood and tap out the shaft, hitting it on its *impeller* end. (Exception: those pumps with impellers fastened to the shaft—these must be driven out the other way.) Do not hit the shaft hard; be especially careful not to burr or flatten the end of the shaft. It is best to use a block of wood between the hammer and the shaft, rather than to hit the shaft directly.

If the shaft won't move, take another look for a bearing retaining circlip. If there truly is none, try hitting a little harder. If the shaft remains fast, try heating the pump body in the area of the bear-

ings with hot water or gentle use of a propane torch. The shaft will come out complete with bearings.

The main shaft seal now can be picked out from the impeller side of the body with a piece of bent wire. There may well be another bearing seal on the drive side, and quite probably a "slinger" washer between the two. If the washer drops down inside the body, retrieve it through the drain slot.

To remove the bearings from the shaft take the small bearing retaining circlip off the shaft, support the bearing with a couple of blocks of wood placed *under the inner bearing race*, and tap out the shaft, hitting it on its drive end.

Inspect the shaft for any signs of wear, especially in the area of the shaft seal. Spin the bearings and discard if they are rough, uneven, or if the outer race is loose. Scrupulously clean the pump body, paying special attention to all seals and bearing seats. *Do not scratch any bearing, seal, or seating surfaces.*

Reassembly. To fit new bearings to a shaft, support the inner race of the bearing and tap the shaft home. To make the job easy, first heat the bearing (e.g., in an oven to around 200°F [93°C] but no more) and cool the shaft (in the icebox). The shaft should just about drop into place. Replace the bearing retaining circlip, flat side toward the bearing.

Figure 12-11. Removing a pump shaft. Remove the end cover and impeller. Support the pump body with a couple of blocks of wood, impeller end up. Protect the end of the impeller shaft with a block of wood, and lightly tap the shaft free.

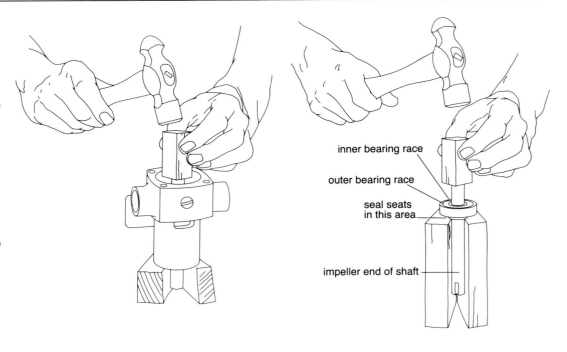

Figure 12-12. **Far right:** Removing a bearing from the pump shaft. Remove the bearing-retaining circlip from the shaft; support the bearing with a couple of blocks of wood placed under the inner bearing race; protect the shaft end with a block of wood; and lightly tap the shaft free from the bearing.

Figure 12-13. Replacing a pump seal. Seat the seal squarely in its housing. Using very soft hammer taps and a piece of hardwood doweling the same or larger diameter as the seal, push the seal down until flush with the pump chamber.

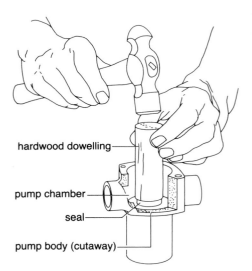

Figure 12-14. When replacing a pump seal, make sure the hardwood doweling seats on the seal's metal rim and not the rubber lip. The seal goes in with the rubber lip towards the pump chamber.

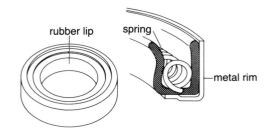

Now is the time to put the new shaft seal in the pump body—also the inner bearing seal (if fitted). Lip-type seals have the lip *toward the impeller.* Carbon/ceramic seals have the ceramic part in the pump body, set in its rubber boot with the shiny surface facing the impeller.

Lip-type seals are lightly greased (petroleum jelly or a Teflon-based, waterproof grease), but *carbon/ceramic seals must not be greased.* The seal faces must be wiped spotlessly clean—even finger grease must be kept off them—and the seals lubricated with water.

All seals must be centered squarely and pushed in evenly. If the seal is bent, distorted, or cockeyed in any way, it is certain to leak. A piece of hardwood doweling the same diameter as, or a little bigger than, the seal makes a good drift. The seal is pushed down until it is flush with the pump chamber.

If the pump has a slinger washer, slide it up through the body drain and maneuver the shaft in from the drive side of the body, easing it through the slinger and into the shaft seal. Pass the shaft through any seals very carefully.

Seat the bearings squarely in the pump housing, support the pump body, and drive the bearings home evenly, applying pressure to the *outer* race (a socket with just a little smaller diameter than the bearing works well). Once again, heating the pump body and cooling bearings will help tre-

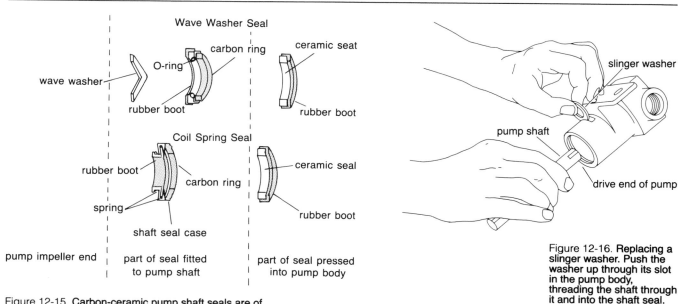

Figure 12-15. **Carbon-ceramic pump shaft seals are of two basic types: wave-washer seals (uncommon), and coil-spring seals. In either case, the ceramic seal and rubber boot are pressed into place in the pump body, and the carbon-ring seal and retainer are fitted to the pump shaft.**

Figure 12-16. **Replacing a slinger washer. Push the washer up through its slot in the pump body, threading the shaft through it and into the shaft seal.**

mendously. Refit the bearing retaining ring (circlip) with the flat side to the bearing, and press home the outer bearing seal (if fitted), lip side toward the pump impeller.

Turn now to the pump end (refer to Figure 12-10). If the pump has a carbon/ceramic seal, clean the seal face, lubricate it with water, and slide the carbon part up the pump shaft, with the smooth face toward the ceramic seat. Some seals use "wave" washers to maintain tension between carbon seal and seat; most use springs. (If the seal has both, discard the wave washer.) Replace the wear plate, locating its notch on the dowel pin. Lightly apply some sealing compound (e.g., Permatex) to the back of the cam and to its retaining screw. *Loosely* fit the cam. Lightly grease the impeller with petroleum jelly or a Teflon-based, waterproof grease and push it home, bending down the vanes in the opposite direction to pump rotation. Replace the gasket and pump cover. Tighten the cam screw.

The correct gasket is important—too thin, and the impeller will bind; too thick, and pumping efficiency is lost. Most pump gaskets are 0.010 inch (ten thousandths of an inch) thick, but on larger pumps this may be 0.015 inch. As noted previously, some impellers on pumps used only intermittently have a tendency to stick in their housings and, if electrically driven, blow

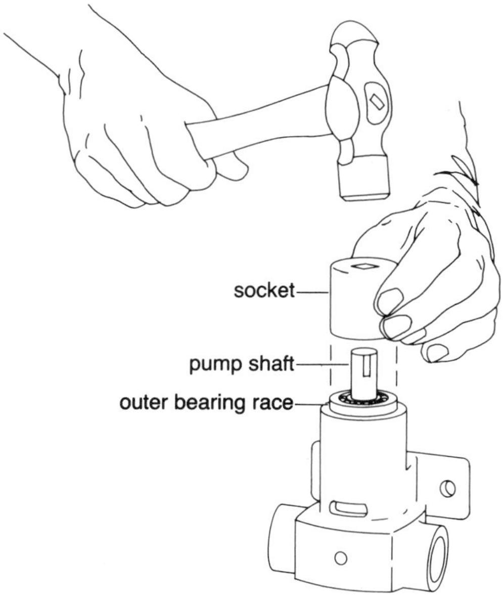

Figure 12-17. **Driving home a bearing. Use a ratchet-drive-type socket with a diameter slightly smaller than the outer bearing race.**

fuses when the pump is started. To stop this, loosen the pump cover on initial start-up, and then tighten it back down. However, you can achieve the same result with a small loss in pumping efficiency without loosening the cover screws if you fit an overthick gasket.

When refitting a flanged pump to an engine, be sure the slot in the pump shaft, or the drive gear, correctly engages the tang

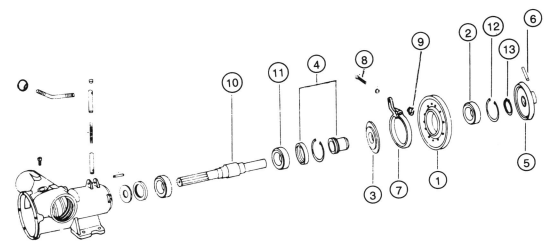

Figure 12-18. **An exploded view of a manual clutch for a pump. 1.** Pulley. **2.** Pulley bearing. **3.** Adaptor ring. **4.** Body plug and engaging sleeve. **5.** Clutch cone. **6.** Clutch-cone locking pin. **7.** Clutch-operating ring. **8.** Clutch-operating-ring securing bolt. **9.** Clutch-operating-ring securing nut. **10.** Pump shaft. **11.** Bearing. **12.** Pulley-to-bearing retaining ring. **13.** Engaging-sleeve-to-bearing retaining ring.

To adjust this type of clutch: (**A**) Engage the clutch. (**B**) Loosen nut (**9**) and the clutch-operating-ring securing bolt (**8**). (**C**) Open up the slot in the operating ring by prying with a screwdriver. (**D**) Hold the adaptor ring (**3**) stationary and rotate the clutch-operating ring backward 20 degrees. (**E**) Retighten the operating ring nut and bolt.

Figure 12-19. **An exploded view of a pump with an electromagnetic clutch.**

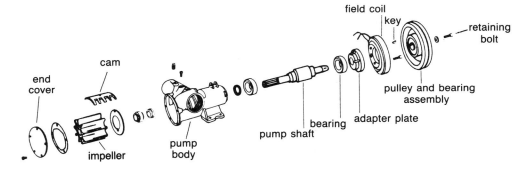

or gear on the engine, and make sure the pump flange seats squarely *without pressure.* Pulley-driven pumps must be properly aligned with their drive pulleys, and the belt correctly tensioned.

Manual clutches. Some pump pulleys are turned on and off via manually operated clutches. The pulley spins on a bearing mounted on an *adaptor ring.* The adaptor ring in turn fits on an assembly known as a *body plug and engaging sleeve.* The engaging sleeve is threaded (screwed) onto the body plug. On the back of the pulley, a tapered friction surface fits loosely inside a tapered housing, called the clutch cone, which is locked to the pump shaft. The pulley freewheels and the pump remains stationary until the clutch lever is operated. Then the operating lever turns the

adaptor ring, which in turn "backs out" the engaging sleeve on the threaded body plug, forcing the pulley's tapered friction surface into contact with the clutch cone; this locks up the whole assembly and the pump turns.

In time the clutch wears and begins to slip. You can adjust it by unscrewing the engaging sleeve a little more from the body plug, but this solution is limited by the number of threads between plug and sleeve. The engaging sleeve (and therefore the pulley) will start to wobble, accelerating wear, if it is unscrewed too much.

Adjustment is made by engaging the clutch and then loosening the clutch-operating ring (also called the "lever ring" and the "engaging clamp ring") where it fits around the adaptor ring. Jam the adaptor ring in place with a screwdriver

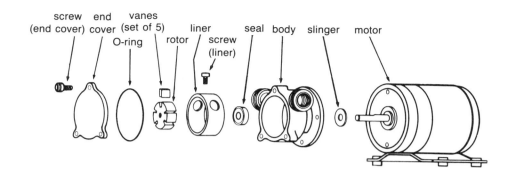

screw end vanes
(end cover) cover (set of 5) liner seal body slinger motor
O-ring rotor screw
(liner)

Figure 12-20. **An exploded view of a vane pump.**

and rotate the operating ring backward around the adaptor ring (it may be necessary to wedge open the slit in the operating ring with a second screwdriver). Move the operating ring 20 degrees or so, retighten its securing bolt, and try the clutch. Repeat if necessary, but if the ring has to be moved more than a total of 45 degrees, the clutch is badly worn and needs replacing.

Clutch kits contain the body plug and engaging sleeve assembly, pulley, bearing, adaptor ring, and instructions for fitting. Note that the body plug and engaging sleeve are a matched set and should always be replaced together.

Electric clutches. The device here that locks a pulley to its shaft is a *field coil* (see Figure 12-19), which is energized electrically and locks a freewheeling pulley to its hub by electromagnetic force. You cannot adjust an electric clutch—it either works or it doesn't. If it fails, first check that there is full voltage at the coil and that it is grounded properly.

To replace either a pulley and bearing assembly, or the field coil, remove the pulley. Undo its center retaining bolt (it will probably be necessary to remove the pump cover and hold the impeller to stop the shaft from turning). If the bolt proves tough to break loose, place a correctly sized wrench (spanner) on it and hit the wrench smartly with a hammer—the shock should do the trick.

The end of the pump shaft, where the pulley fits on, is tapered. Between the shaft and the pulley is a key. Tap the pulley loose with a soft-faced mallet or a hammer and a block of wood. Watch out for the key; don't let it fall into the bilges. The field coil is unbolted from either an adaptor or the pump body. To reassemble the clutch reverse these steps—be sure to put the key back.

Winterizing. Loosen the end cover to drain the pump. It is best to leave it loose in case any more fluid finds its way in. The impeller should be withdrawn, lightly greased (petroleum jelly or Teflon-based waterproof grease) and put back. This will keep the impeller from sticking to the pump body and aid in priming the pump the next time it is run.

Rotary and Vane Pumps

Running dry will destroy rotors, vanes, and seals (with the possible exception of some rotary pumps that have Teflon impellers). Dirt particles in the fluid being pumped will score the pump chamber and accelerate wear on vanes. Dirt lodged in vane slots eventually will jam them into the rotor and pumping will cease.

In most cases removing an end cover provides access to the impeller, which will slide off its shaft. The vanes on vane pumps tend to fall out of the rotor. Since it is best to put them back in the same slots and the same way around, slip a rubber band around the rotor when it is half out. This holds the vanes in place.

Aside from the usual seal, shaft, and bearing inspections, check old vanes against a new vane (spares should always be carried on board) for signs of wear. If any are worn down more than one-third of their original length, replace the whole set. If the new vanes have a radiused edge, this faces out (toward the pump wall). Some vane pumps have removable liners; replace the liner if the one in place is excessively scored.

Seal and bearing replacement for vane and rotary pumps is similar to this procedure for flexible impeller pumps.

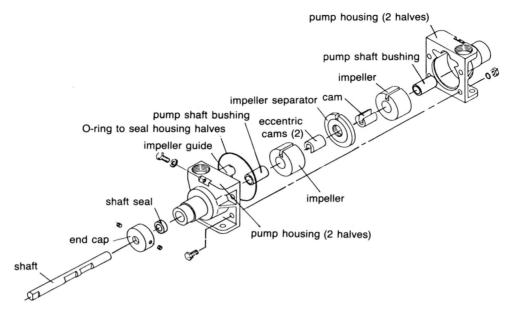

Figure 12-21. **An exploded view of a rotary pump. This particular one has twin impellers.**

pump housing (2 halves)

pump shaft bushing

impeller

impeller separator cam

eccentric cams (2)

pump shaft bushing

O-ring to seal housing halves

impeller guide

shaft seal

end cap

shaft

impeller

pump housing (2 halves)

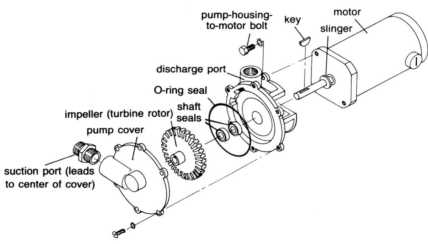

Figure 12-22A. **An exploded view of a centrifugal pump with a turbine impeller.**

pump-housing-to-motor bolt

key

motor

slinger

discharge port

O-ring seal

shaft seals

impeller (turbine rotor)

pump cover

suction port (leads to center of cover)

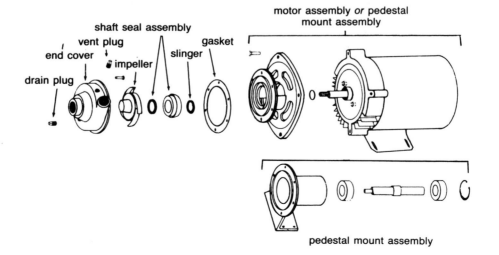

Figure 12-22B. **A spiral-vane centrifugal pump.**

motor assembly *or* pedestal mount assembly

shaft seal assembly

vent plug

gasket

end cover

slinger

impeller

drain plug

pedestal mount assembly

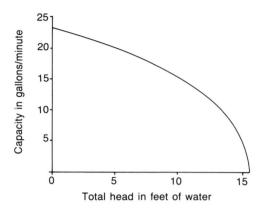

Figure 12-23. Typical performance curve for a centrifugal pump.

Centrifugal Pumps

Properly installed, centrifugal pumps are largely troublefree. The most common problem is loss of prime. These pumps work best when they are installed below the level of the fluid being pumped, but they can become airbound if for any reason the pump chamber fills with air. Installations *above* the fluid level depend on a check valve in the suction line to hold the prime. Any fluid leaking back through the valve will put the pump out of action.

Gradual wear of the impeller blades increases clearances between the impeller and its housing, resulting in a slow loss of pumping efficiency. If the pump is installed in a pressurized system, it will run for longer periods until finally its output pressure cannot reach the cutout point of the pressure switch; the pump then stays on all the time. Wear will cause centrifugal bilge pumps with a considerable lift to pump at a slower and slower rate.

(Note that where a centrifugal bilge pump lists a capacity of, for example, "1800 GPH" [gallons per hour], the pump probably has been rated with zero feet of head [lift] and no hoses attached! Give the same pump a six-foot head [quite usual] and a couple of bends in the discharge line and, even when new, the capacity will be cut in half. Centrifugal pumps are very sensitive to head pressures and wear.)

Removal of the end housing gives access to the pump impeller. Some impellers are held on with set screws (allen screws); others are screwed onto their shafts. To undo the latter, tape the drive shaft and grip it with Vise-Grips; unscrew the impeller (generally counterclockwise when viewed from the impeller end).

Troubleshooting Chart 12-2.
Centrifugal Pump Problems: No Flow or Reduced Flow.

Is the pump refusing to spin?

NO ▼ **TEST:** Check the voltage at electric motors while switched on, or the drive mechanism on other pumps (gears, belt, pulley, clutch); check for trash jammed in the impeller on a bilge pump.

YES ▶ Remove trash. Repair or replace belt, or refer to Chapter 6 for problems with electric motors. (Note: Most old motors are wound, field-coil universal motors; newer ones are permanent-magnet universal motors.)

Has the pump lost its prime?

NO ▼ **TEST:** Prime the pump by disconnecting a discharge line and pouring in fluid to fill the pump chamber. Run the unit again. If there is flow, the pump is OK.

YES ▶ 1. Check that the pump is below the waterline (including when the boat is heeled) or, if above the waterline, that it has a check valve in the suction line. If the valve is fitted, check that it is not leaking back.
2. Check that the suction line is not kinked or blocked (by a closed seacock or plugged filter, for example).
3. Check that the suction line makes a continuous run up to the pump with no U-bends that can trap air.
4. Check that all suction line connections are tight and not sucking air.

Are there obstructions in the discharge line?

NO ▼ **TEST:** Check for common obstructions in the discharge line, such as a kinked hose or closed seacock.

YES ▶ **FIX:** Straighten hose or open seacock and try running the unit again. If there is flow, the pump is OK.

Is the head pressure too high?

NO ▼ **TEST:** Disconnect the discharge line at its overboard discharge, lower it in relation to the pump, and try running the unit again.

YES ▶ Reduce the head or get a more powerful pump. If the pump has worked previously as installed, the loss of pumping ability is likely due to a worn impeller. Replace the impeller.

The procedure for seal and bearing replacement for centrifugal pumps is similar to that for flexible impeller pumps.

Electric Diaphragm Pumps

These pumps are used widely in pressurized freshwater systems, and sometimes as bilge, shower, and effluent pumps. In a pressurized system, the pumps are likely to be fitted with a check valve on the discharge side, a pressure switch, an accumulator tank, and possibly a low tank level switch. None of these is likely in other applications. The following troubleshooting sections refer specifically to pressurized freshwater systems, but cover most other situations.

Pump fails to operate. Check the voltage at the motor (see Chapter 3). If there is no voltage, check the pressure switch. The points may be open, pitted, burned, or corroded (see the section on "Pressure and Level Switches"). If the pressure switch is OK, maybe there is a low tank level switch that has cut out. If the voltage at the motor is OK, check the motor itself (Chapter 6).

Some motors have a high-temperature switch which may have "tripped"—if so, push the reset button, which will be somewhere on the motor housing.

Pump operates but no water flows. First check to see if the motor is turning the pump—the drive belt or coupling may be broken; the connecting rod loose; etc. If the pump itself is operating, open all faucets to reduce any back pressure on the pump. Check the water tank level, especially if the boat is heeled. If the pump has a suction strainer, inspect it. In some situations, the suction line may have an in-line check valve or foot valve—make sure it is not plugged or stuck shut. The suction hose may be kinked or plugged up. Any air leaks (loose connections) will stop the pump from priming. Finally, there may be problems with the pump itself—most probably trash stuck under the valves, but perhaps a hole in the diaphragm (see the section on dismantling and repairing). Break loose the discharge line and try blowing back through the pump. If this can be done there is definitely a problem with the valves or diaphragm.

Table 12-2. Pump Types and Common Applications.

Common Application	Flexible Impeller	Vane	Rotary	Centrifugal[1]	Electric Diaphragm	Manual Diaphragm	Piston
Engine cooling,							
Raw water	X	—	—	X	—	—	—
Fresh water	—	—	—	X	—	—	—
Refrigeration condensers	X	—	—	X	—	—	—
Deck wash down	X	—	—	X	—	—	—
Bilge,							
Electric	—	—	—	X	X	—	—
Manual	—	—	—	—	—	X	X
Sink discharge	—	—	—	—	X	X	—
Toilets,							
Electric	X	—	—	X	—	—	—
Manual	—	—	—	—	—	X	X
Showers	—	—	—	—	X	—	—
Fresh water,							
Pressurized	X	—	—	—	X	—	—
Manual	—	—	—	—	—	X	X
Fuel transfer[2]	—	X	X	—	—	—	—

1. Must be installed below the waterline.
2. Must be compatible with diesel.

Pump operates roughly, noisily, and vibrates. The suction line may be kinked, plugged, or too small, thus restricting flow, but more likely the pump itself is the problem. The pump must be securely mounted with vibration-absorbing pads. Loose drive pulleys and/or excessive play in the connecting rod and various bearings could be causing the noisy vibration; check them and tighten them if necessary. The pump probably has a rubber "pulsation dampener" or a "surge chamber," either of which is designed to smooth out flow through the pump; as a last resort, take the bottom plate off the pump and check this dampener to see if it is deformed or ruptured (see "Pulsation Dampener Replacement").

Pump fails to cut off when faucets (taps) are closed. Check the water tank; it is probably empty! If not, the pump may be airbound; open a faucet, allow enough water to flow through so that the pump is primed, and then close the faucet. The pressure switch may be stuck on—make sure its points are open. Lastly, check the voltage at the motor—a low voltage will cause the pump to operate slowly and perhaps not come to pressure. This means the motor is in danger of burning up.

Pump cycles on and off when faucets are closed. Water may be leaking from a loose connection, an open faucet, or perhaps a toilet if fresh water is used for flushing (e.g., VacuFlush). Otherwise pressure is bleeding off the system *back through the pump*—the discharge check valve (if fitted) or valves are leaking (see "Valve Replacement").

Pump cycles rapidly on and off in use; water "knocks" in the piping. Most pressurized water systems use an *accumulator tank*. This is an air-filled tank that tees into the discharge side of the pump. As the pump operates it fills the tank with water, compressing the air within it, until it reaches the cutout setting on the pump pressure switch. When a faucet is opened, the compressed air forces water back out of the tank and through the faucet until pressure has fallen to the cut-in point on the pump pressure switch. The pump then kicks in and recharges the accumulator tank. The net effect is to reduce the amount of cycling on and off that the pump does, which reduces wear on both the pump and the pressure switch points.

Two types of accumulator tank are in use. The first is just a simple tank. The second has a built-in rubber diaphragm with a tire valve on the outside of the tank. Air is pumped in through the valve to pressurize the tank (generally to around 20 psi, but the pressure should be approximately the same as the cut-in pressure setting on the pressure switch). Water enters the tank on the other side of the diaphragm, forcing in the diaphragm against the air cushion.

Both tanks can become "waterlogged." The simple tank becomes so when the initial tankful of air is slowly dissolved and carried away by the water entering and leaving the tank; the diaphragm tank is affected if the pressure bleeds off the air side of the diaphragm or the diaphragm ruptures. In either case, the pump will cycle on and off at shorter and shorter intervals. This causes sudden pressure changes in the plumbing, which, in turn, not only damages pumps but can produce some surprisingly loud knocks (sometimes called "water hammer").

Turn off the pump and *open a faucet to bleed all pressure off the system.* The simple tank must be completely drained to renew the air charge; if it has no drain plug, it may be necessary to break the connection loose at its base. The diaphragm type is pumped back up again, generally with a bicycle pump.

Excessive pressure. Some shoreside hook-ups have pressures that will damage valves and diaphragms. Most pumps are protected with a built-in check valve in the discharge fitting. Even so a pressure regulator (to around 35 psi) always should be fitted on the shoreside connection.

Dismantling and repairing.

Valve replacement. Turn off the power and bleed down the system through the faucets. Removing four screws on most pumps allows the complete drive and diaphragm assembly to be lifted off, providing access to the valves. Inspect the new valves carefully—if one has a small hole in it, this is the intake valve. The intake valve goes in with the rubber disc uppermost; the discharge valve, with the disc down. When replacing the diaphragm assembly, make sure the surfaces are clean, and tighten the screws evenly.

The discharge fitting in some pumps has a check valve, which generally cannot be repaired. In the event of failure the whole fitting must be replaced. Remove the old fitting, carefully noting its orientation so

Figure 12-24A.
Accumulator tanks
(pressure tanks), like the
one shown in this
schematic of a typical
onboard pressurized water
system, serve as a water
reservoir, providing
pressurized water between
pump cycles, and reducing
the frequency with which
the pump must run. These
tanks are susceptible to
waterlogging—a reduction
in tank air volume as the
initial charge of air
dissolves into the water.
This increases pump
cycling, and can lead to
system damage.

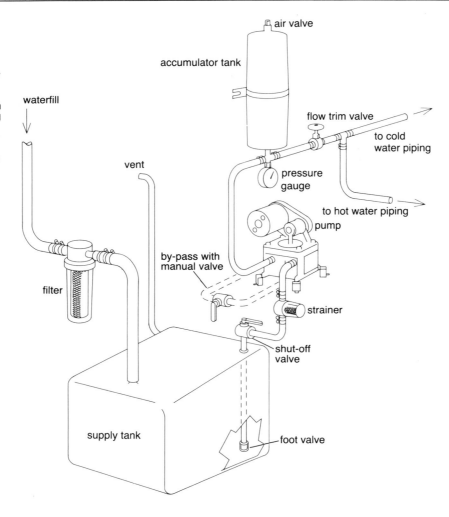

Figure 12-24B. A captive-
air, or pre-pressurized
accumulator tank. When
the pump starts, water
enters the reservoir. At
maximum preset pressure,
the system is filled and the
pump shuts off. When
water is used, pressure in
the air chamber forces
water into the system. The
pump stays off until the
minimum pressure setting
is reached; then the pump
turns on. By isolating the
water within a rubber
bladder, water-logging is
largely eliminated. The air
charge is readily renewed
with a bicycle pump.

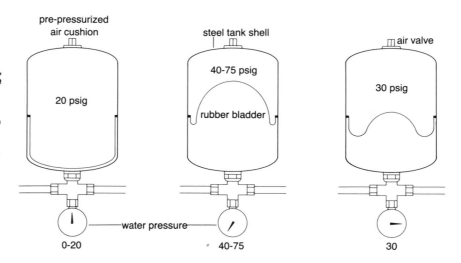

340   Pumps

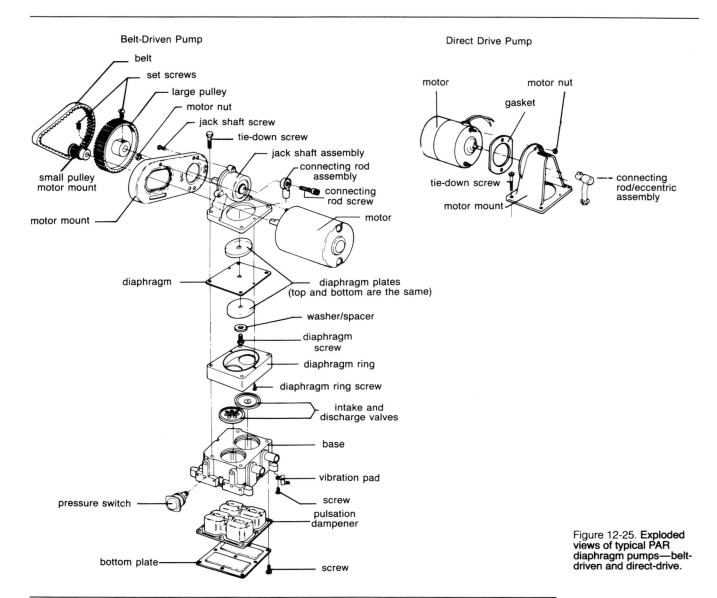

Belt-Driven Pump

- belt
- set screws
- large pulley
- motor nut
- jack shaft screw
- tie-down screw
- jack shaft assembly
- connecting rod assembly
- connecting rod screw
- motor
- small pulley
- motor mount
- motor mount
- diaphragm
- diaphragm plates (top and bottom are the same)
- washer/spacer
- diaphragm screw
- diaphragm ring
- diaphragm ring screw
- intake and discharge valves
- base
- vibration pad
- pressure switch
- screw
- pulsation dampener
- bottom plate
- screw

Direct Drive Pump

- motor
- motor nut
- gasket
- tie-down screw
- motor mount
- connecting rod/eccentric assembly

Figure 12-25. **Exploded views of typical PAR diaphragm pumps—belt-driven and direct-drive.**

that you can put the new one in the right way around!

Diaphragm replacement. Once again, undo and lift off the complete diaphragm assembly. Turn it over, take out the screws holding the diaphragm retaining ring, and pull off the ring. Undo the central screw or bolt holding the diaphragm and its plates together. When fitting anything other than a circular diaphragm, take care to align it properly so that it does not get twisted in use.

Connecting rod replacement. Remove the diaphragm as above. Undo the connecting rod screw and take off the connecting rod. Connecting rod bearings need to be oiled lightly once a year (3-in-1; Marvel Mystery

Oil). When replacing drive belts, the tension should be adjusted so that moderate finger pressure depresses the belt ¼ inch between the pulleys.

Pulsation dampener replacement. Mark the baseplate(s), also called bottom plates, and pump body so that they can be put back properly. Remove all the screws from the baseplate(s). Pull out the rubber pulsation dampener(s) and check for deformation, ruptures, or cuts. When doing the baseplate screws back up, first tighten the center screws on each side and then work out toward the corners. Do not overtighten.

Winterizing. Pumps with pulsation dampeners generally can freeze without dam-

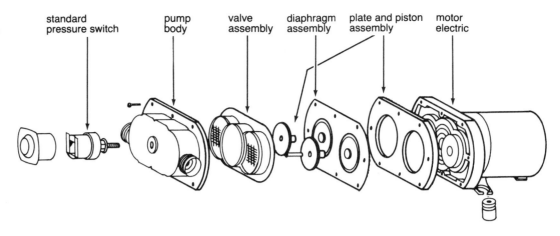

Figure 12-26. **In-line electric double-diaphragm pump.**

standard pressure switch   pump body   valve assembly   diaphragm assembly   plate and piston assembly   motor electric

age, but the rest of the water system cannot, so winterize the whole system. Either drain the pump and all its piping, or disconnect the suction line from the tank and pump *propylene glycol antifreeze* through it.

Note: Automotive antifreeze is made from ethylene glycol and is poisonous—*do not use it in freshwater systems.* Propylene glycol has almost identical antifreeze properties and is safe to use. Flush the system at the start of the new season.

Pressure and Level Switches (on automatic, electric pumps)

High-Low pressure cutout and cut-in switches. Many of the newer pumps have sealed pressure switches screwed into the body of the pump. In the event of problems the switch must be discarded and replaced.

In an emergency, bypass the switch by wiring the pump directly to its supply line, turning it on and off manually with its main switch or breaker. But remember, if you fail to turn it off after use *just one time,* it will keep on pumping until something breaks or burns out. Older and larger pumps tend to have adjustable switches. A central retaining screw allows the cover to be lifted off, exposing the points and two adjusting screws.

Dirty, pitted, and/or corroded points are a frequent source of trouble; inspect them and all wire terminals closely. The points can be cleaned with a fine grade of wet-or-dry sandpaper (400-grit). Points operation can be checked by prying them apart, and pushing them together, with a screwdriver. There may be a small spark; a large spark indicates a problem with the points or with the pump motor (it may be shorted). If the

points close but the pump fails to come on, bridge the wire terminals with a jumper wire to see if it is the switch that is defective.

The two adjusting screws control the pump cut-in and cutout pressures. Generally, turning down one screw increases both pressures; turning down the other raises the cutout pressure without altering the cut-in pressure. Adjustment procedure, therefore, is to set the cut-in pressure with the first screw, and then to fine-tune the cutout pressure with the second screw.

Level switches.

Mercury float switches. Commonly used on bilge pumps, mercury float switches consist of a drop of mercury in a sealed glass vial that is attached to a hinged arm with a float. As the fluid level rises, the float comes up until the mercury runs from one end of the vial to the other, where it forms an electrical connection across two points, turning on the pump. When the fluid level drops, the mercury runs back to the other end of the vial, breaking the circuit.

There is no adjustment on these switches. The float must be set high enough so that the switch cuts off before a bilge pump runs dry, at any angle of heel, or else the pump will not shut down. It is best to mount pumps and switches on the centerline of the boat. All wiring connections must be made well above the water level to avoid shorts and corrosion.

Common problems are dirt and/or debris jamming the hinge on the float so that the switch fails either to come on or go off; corrosion forming on wire connections, which causes a voltage drop at the pump;

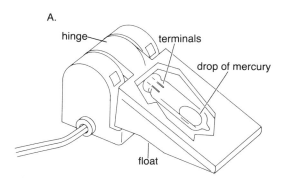

A.

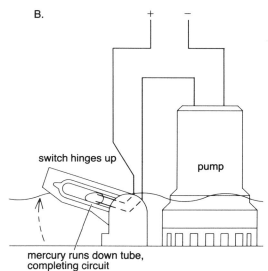

B.

Figure 12-27A, B. **Mercury float switches: How they work.** A rise in fluid level causes the buoyant end of the switch to rise. The electrically conductive mercury contained in the switch cavity flows to the bottom of the switch, where it bridges two terminals, completing the circuit, and turning on the pump.

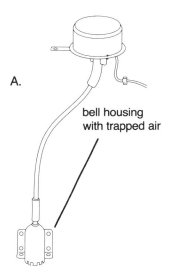

A.

bell housing with trapped air

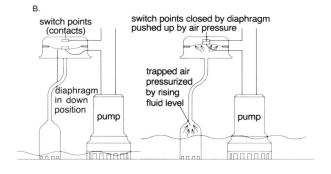

B.

Figure 12-28A,B. **Pneumatic level switches: How they work.** When the fluid level rises, air trapped in the bell housing is pressurized and pushes in the diaphragm. This closes the switch points and completes the circuit, turning on the pump.

and overloading of the switch, causing it to burn up. Some switches on the market are extremely lightweight both electrically and mechanically; they are a poor investment for such a potentially important piece of hardware.

Pneumatic switches. These are another type of bilge switch, readily adaptable as a low-level cutout switch for tanks. A *bell housing*, set in the bilge, has a tube communicating with a pressure-sensitive switch. Rising fluid levels increase air pressure in the bell housing and tube, triggering the switch. Falling fluid levels reduce pressure, cutting off the switch.

The height of the bell housing in the bilge is critical; it must turn a pump off before it runs dry, regardless of the angle of heel. (Again, it is best to mount pumps and switches on the centerline of the boat.) Most switches are adjustable via a screw on the switch unit. Remove the switch cover to gain access to this screw.

Problems will arise if sloshing water slowly replaces the air in the bell housing. The switch will cut on and off at higher and higher levels. Any air leaks in the tube between the bell housing and the switch will put the pump entirely out of action, as

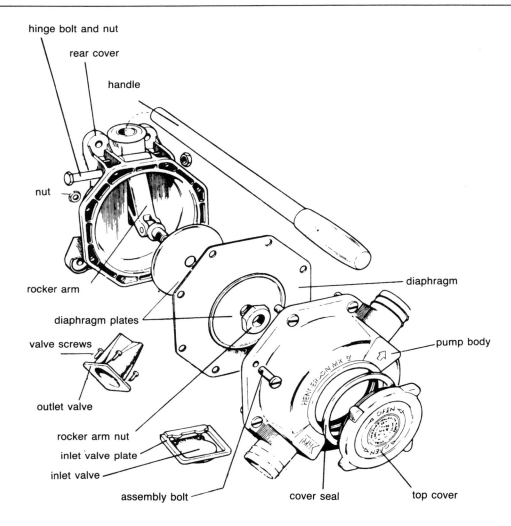

Figure 12-29A. **A manual diaphragm pump with an internally mounted handle.**

hinge bolt and nut

rear cover

handle

nut

rocker arm

diaphragm plates

valve screws

outlet valve

rocker arm nut

inlet valve plate

inlet valve

assembly bolt

diaphragm

pump body

cover seal

top cover

will a blockage of the air tube (dirt from the bilges; a crimped tube; etc.). At the other end of the scale, high temperatures (e.g., in an engine room) will cause the air in the bell housing to expand and the pump to cut in and out at abnormally low fluid levels, with a danger of burning up the pump.

Timer switches. Some freshwater pumps have a simple timer switch in the circuit. Every time the pump kicks in it resets the timer. If the pump runs for more than a preset period (say five minutes), which would happen if the tank ran dry, the timer breaks the circuit. The pump will not restart until the timer is reset, generally by tripping the breaker on the pump circuit. There may or may not be adjustments on the time interval.

Electronic switches. Two types of low-tank-level electronic switches are in use. One employs a set of electrodes immersed in the tank to measure the conductivity of the tank fluid. When the tank runs dry, the loss of conductivity between the electrodes causes the switch to trip. The second type of electronic switch senses pump temperatures. When most pumps run dry, they heat up due to the added friction and the loss of the cooling effect of the fluid passing through them. The switch senses this rise in temperature and breaks the circuit. Neither switch is user-repairable. If they fail in the open position, they will have to be bypassed until a replacement can be fitted. Heat-sensitive switches should not be put on pumps in engine rooms or other hot locations.

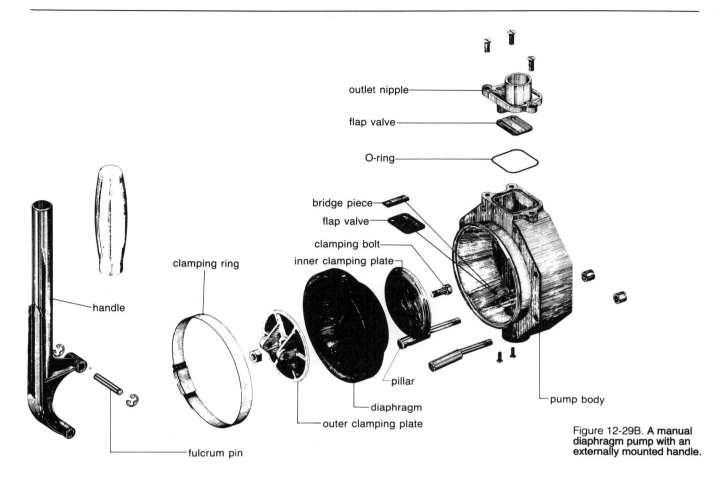

outlet nipple

flap valve

O-ring

bridge piece

flap valve

clamping bolt

inner clamping plate

clamping ring

handle

pillar

diaphragm

pump body

outer clamping plate

fulcrum pin

Figure 12-29B. **A manual diaphragm pump with an externally mounted handle.**

Low-pressure cutout switches. These units are mechanically similar to high-pressure switches, although their function is different. They are mounted on the discharge side of a pump. They break the circuit when pressures are abnormally low, as would happen if a tank ran dry (e.g., 6 psi on a system set to maintain 20 to 40 psi). A low-pressure shutdown switch may well be built into the same unit as a pressure-regulating switch. Adjustment and points maintenance follow pressure switch procedures. Once tripped, or on initial start-up of a system (before pressure has built up), most have to be reset manually.

Manual Diaphragm Pumps

A handle moves a lever (rocker arm or "fork") which arcs backward and forward around a pivot point or fulcrum. Attached to the lever is a diaphragm. As the diaphragm moves out, it draws fluid into a pump chamber; as it moves in, it expels the fluid. Simple flap or joker valves on the inlet and outlet allow the fluid in and out.

Double-diaphragm pumps. These pumps have a diaphragm and pump chamber on both sides of the lever—as one diaphragm moves in, the other moves out, and vice versa. Each pump chamber has its own inlet and outlet valves; the two suction and discharge ports feed into common suction and discharge manifolds. Some double-diaphragm pumps have a spring in one chamber to return the operating handle unfailingly to the same position. Foot-operated diaphragm pumps have a spring-loaded plunger instead of an operating handle and lever. Standing on the plunger moves the diaphragm in; the spring brings it back out.

Problems. There is almost nothing to go wrong with a diaphragm pump. If the pump fails to prime, suspect an air leak in the suction hose or improperly seated valves. A less likely possibility is a ruptured diaphragm.

Valves. Problems generally arise as a result of pieces of trash lodging in the valves and holding them open. Chemicals also

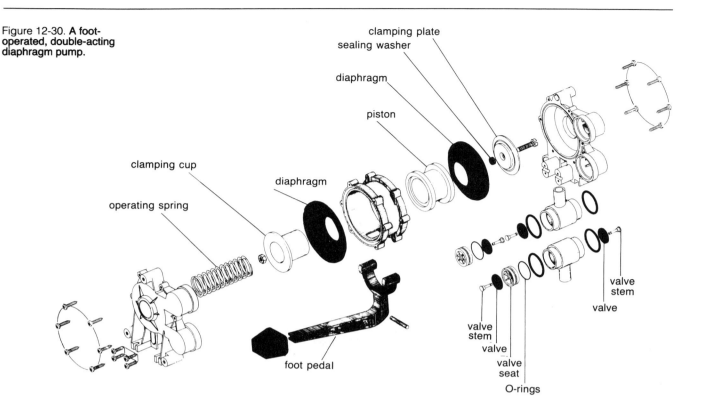

Figure 12-30. **A foot-operated, double-acting diaphragm pump.**

clamping plate

sealing washer

diaphragm

piston

clamping cup

diaphragm

operating spring

foot pedal

valve stem

valve

valve stem

valve

valve seat

O-rings

Figure 12-31. **A foot-operated, single-diaphragm pump.**

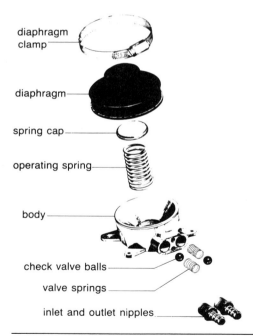

diaphragm clamp

diaphragm

spring cap

operating spring

body

check valve balls

valve springs

inlet and outlet nipples

swell up the rubber flaps, which either fail to seat properly or hang up in an open position on the side of the valve housing. In some applications, calcium builds up on valve seats (see Chapter 11). Eventually fatigue will cause the flaps to tear and come loose.

Diaphragms rupture. Many diaphragms are constructed of several layers of fabric. Before a complete failure occurs, the layers may delaminate, trapping fluid in between. Complete failure is close. Rarely, one of the diaphragm plates (on each side of the diaphragm) will fracture, and the broken pieces will punch a hole in the diaphragm.

Galvanic corrosion. Many pump housings and levers are cast aluminum; hinge pins are stainless steel. Galvanic corrosion and seizure may occur, especially if the pump is rarely used. On some models, pump handles have a nasty habit of collapsing and breaking where they slot into, or over, the rocker arm (lever arm). Always carry a spare handle.

Overhaul and repair. Almost all diaphragm pumps are very simple to dismantle and reassemble. The greatest problems arise with stainless steel fasteners frozen in aluminum housings; they often shear off when you try to undo them (see the section on "Freeing Frozen Fasteners," Appendix B).

Diaphragms are variously retained by screwed-in retaining plates, slotted clamping rings, and large hose clamps (Jubilee clips). On either side of a diaphragm is a plate, held together with one central bolt or with several screws. Two things are important when fitting a new diaphragm: (1) make sure that all seating surfaces are spotlessly clean; and (2) properly line up the lever (fork) pivot point on the outer plate with the lever (fork) before tightening down the diaphragm retaining device. Where a diaphragm is held with a retaining ring and a number of screws, tighten the screws evenly, alternating from side to side.

Some valves are changed by unscrewing the valve ports from the outside of the pump body (the hoses must first come off); access to others is from inside the pump body (the diaphragm normally must be removed). Valves are variously retained by valve plates, "bridge pieces," and clips. Remember, the key points are: (1) scrupulously clean all mating surfaces; (2) make sure the valves are inserted the *right way up* (inlet valves flapping inward; outlet valves outward; joker valves on the discharge side with the "duck's bill" facing *away* from the pump); and finally (3) make sure the valves are in the *right way around* (some valve housings are asymmetrical; if the valves are inserted improperly, they either will not open or will hang up on the valve housing).

Piston Pumps

A piston fits in a cylinder, with a valve on the base of the piston and one in the cylinder (or else an "in and out" valve in the cylinder). When the piston is pulled up, it draws fluid into the cylinder. When it is pushed down, the valve in the cylinder (the inlet valve) closes and the trapped fluid pushes past the valve in the piston, or out of a second valve in the cylinder (the discharge valve). If the fluid has moved past the piston into the upper side of the cylinder, the next upward stroke of the piston drives it out of the discharge port. On this type of pump, the piston rod must be sealed where it enters the cylinder in order to prevent leaks.

Many different valve types are used on both pistons and cylinders. Older pistons may have a dished leather washer screwed to the lower end. As the piston descends its cylinder, trapped fluid in the cylinder pushes in the sides of the washer and forces its way up past the piston. When the piston is withdrawn, the fluid pressure pushes the sides of the washer out against the cylinder wall to form a seal. Modern pistons of this type are sealed with a neoprene cup washer. Another approach is to use an O-ring to seal the piston in its cylinder and fit a ball or flapper valve into the piston's base.

Cylinder valves may be simple rubber or metal flaps, balls, or a rubber disc with a central retaining valve stem. As fluid is sucked in, the valves, regardless of type, are lifted off their seats. When fluid is discharged, the valves are forced down against their seats.

Foot-operated piston-type galley pumps have spring-loaded pistons. Foot pressure

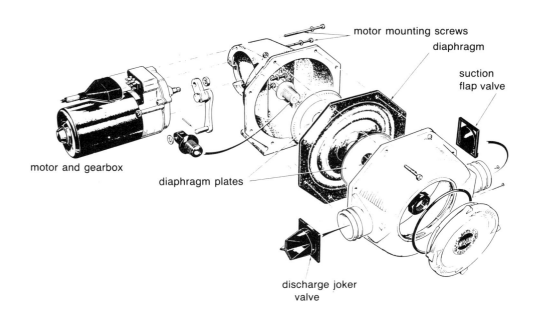

motor mounting screws
diaphragm
suction flap valve
motor and gearbox
diaphragm plates
discharge joker valve

Figure 12-32. **An electrified manual diaphragm pump. This is essentially the same pump as shown in Figure 12-29A, with the exception of a modified rocker arm and a rear housing adapted to take a motor.**

Maintenance, Troubleshooting and Repair   347

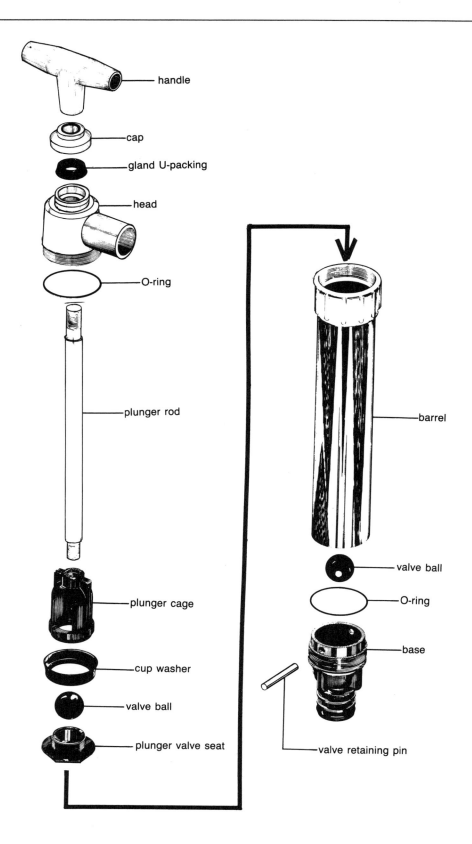

Figure 12-33A. **A piston pump with ball valves.**

handle

cap

gland U-packing

head

O-ring

plunger rod

barrel

valve ball

O-ring

plunger cage

base

cup washer

valve ball

plunger valve seat

valve retaining pin

pushes the piston in; the spring brings it back out.

Problems. The most common piston pump problem is trash in valve seats; this causes a loss of prime and ability to pump. A failure of a piston's dished washer or O-ring will have the same result. Before blaming the pump, check for air leaks in the suction line. Vigorous pumping will sometimes restore prime and clear valves.

The piston rod seals will leak eventually, especially after a winter shutdown. Most have a cap, which can be tightened to improve the seal.

Overhaul and repair. Most pistons are withdrawn by unscrewing the piston rod seal from the top of the cylinder. Damaged dish washers can be replaced with a piece of thin leather (e.g., from an old wallet) if no spares are available. Cut the washer a little larger in diameter than the cylinder bore, screw it to the piston, and then lubricate with water. Form the edges up around the base of the piston until the washer fits the cylinder.

Cylinder valves generally unscrew from the base of the cylinder—although on cheaper pumps they are housed in a rubber boot that simply pushes on and pulls off. If the valve consists of a rubber disc, inspect it closely for small tears and nicks, which might not be immediately apparent. Look for and remove pieces of trash between all valves and seats.

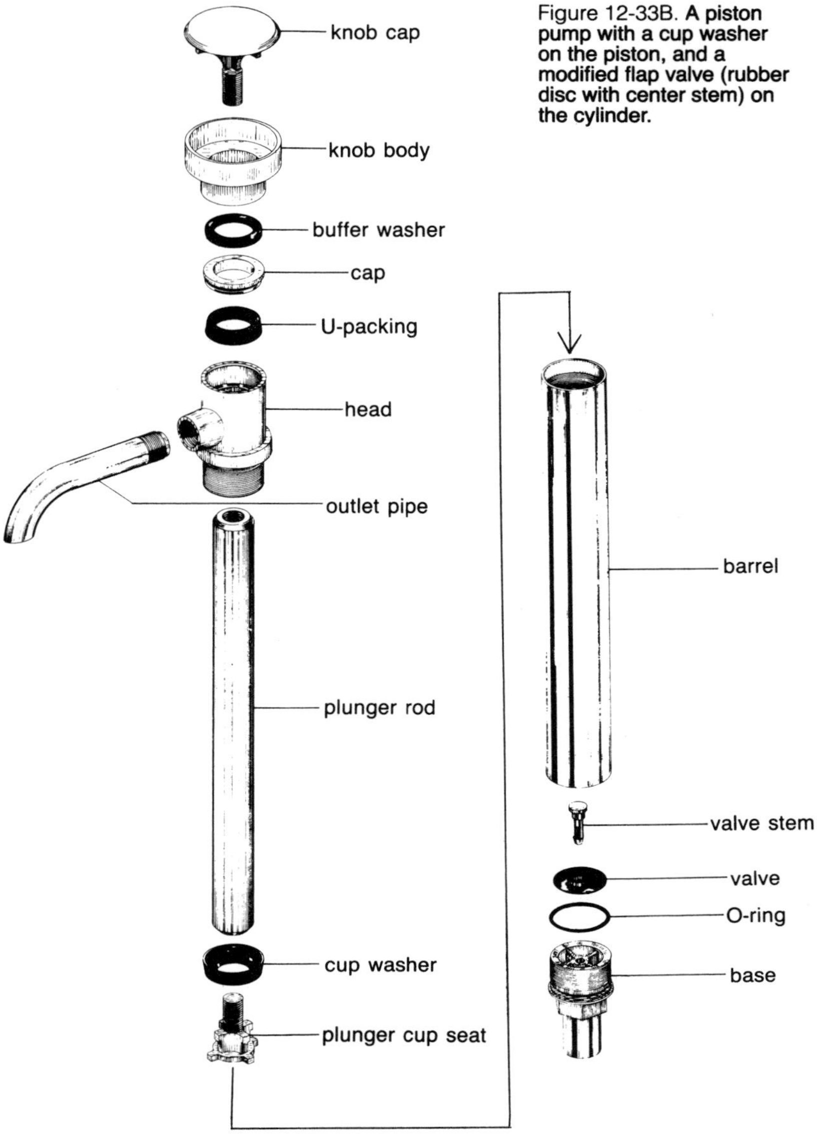

Figure 12-33B. A piston pump with a cup washer on the piston, and a modified flap valve (rubber disc with center stem) on the cylinder.

knob cap
knob body
buffer washer
cap
U-packing
head
outlet pipe
plunger rod
cup washer
plunger cup seat

barrel
valve stem
valve
O-ring
base

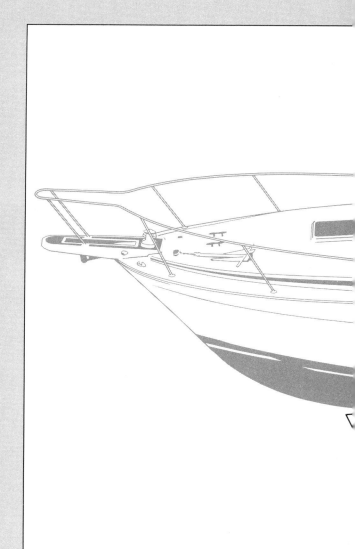

Figure 13-1. **Types of steering and self-steering systems are as diverse as types of boats, but all follow logical installation and maintenance procedures.**

(1) windvane self-steering
(2) rudder
(3) pedestal
(4) wheel
(5) autopilot
(6) hydraulic steering station with integral pump
(7) check valve
(8) hydraulic reservoir
(9) steering cylinder

Steering Systems

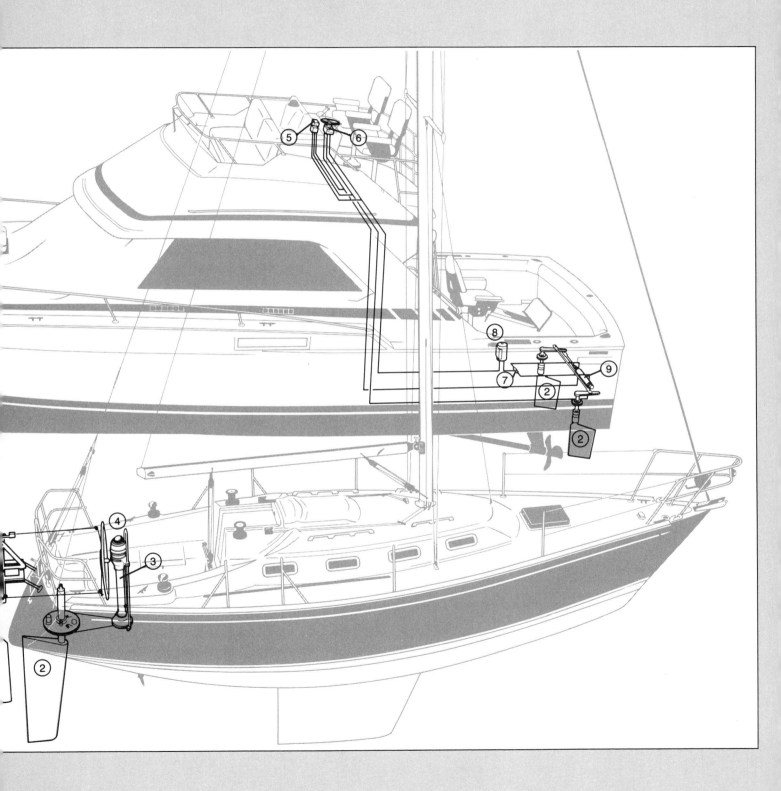

Main Steering Systems

Types of Steering

How they work. It used to be that most rudders were hinged either to the stern of the boat and a full-length keel (aft-hung rudders) or else underneath the boat to the trailing edge of a shorter keel or separate skeg (or half skeg). The hinge used is known as a *gudgeon* (the strap part, generally on the rudder) and *pintle* (the hinge pin, generally fastened to the keel, skeg, or transom). At the base of the rudder is a *heel* bearing to support the weight of the rudder (Figure 13-2A).

A rudder hinged by its forward edge like this is "unbalanced." When turned, the force of the water acting on it is all in one direction. By pivoting a rudder at a point set back from its forward face, the forces are counterbalanced and the rudder becomes much easier to turn. Such rudders are known as "balanced" and have become extremely popular. On sailboats a bal-

Figure 13-2A. Despite the bewildering diversity of rudders, all work on the same principle: Water flowing by the boat is deflected by the rudder when it deviates from the boat's centerline, forcing the boat's stern in the opposite direction from which the rudder is turned. This boat's rudder is mounted on the trailing edge of the skeg, its weight carried by the heel bearing.

Figure 13-2B. A transom-mounted, or outboard rudder.

Figure 13-2C. A half-skeg rudder.

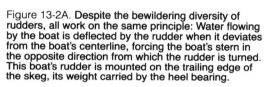

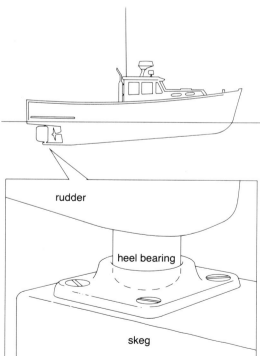

rudder

heel bearing

skeg

Figure 13-2D. **A full-skeg rudder.**

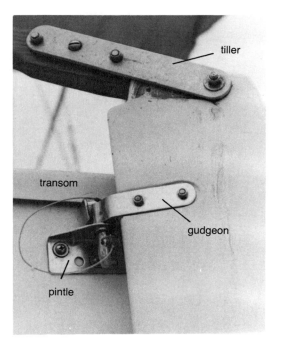

Figure 13-2E. **A typical spade rudder.**

radial-drive wheel

stuffing box

bearing
bearing tube
bearing

rudder
reinforcing web

Figure 13-2F. **This pintle and gudgeon is inverted to lock the rudder in place. To remove the rudder, the pintle must be unbolted from the boat. Right:** A more typical arrangement than shown below, with a locking pin through the top pintle.

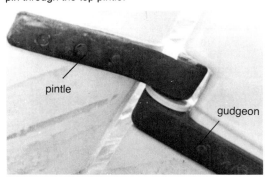

pintle

gudgeon

tiller

transom

gudgeon

pintle

Figure 13-3A. **There are even more ways to control rudders than there are types of rudders. This tiller installation shows a support ring to accept the weight of the rudder.**

support ring

Figure 13-3B. **Mechanical-linkage wheel steerers, although not inexpensive, are easily maintained and provide positive steering action. Shown here is rack-and-pinion steering.**

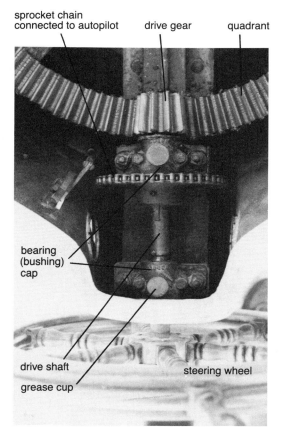

sprocket chain connected to autopilot   drive gear   quadrant

bearing (bushing) cap

drive shaft

grease cup

steering wheel

Figure 13-3C. **Rack-and-pinion, pedestal-drive steering.**

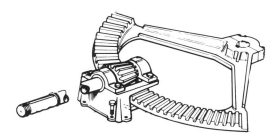

anced rudder usually appears with a fin keel that is set well forward; the skeg is dispensed with, and the rudder—here called a *spade rudder*—is simply suspended beneath the boat (Figure 13-2E). This is also the typical way of mounting a powerboat rudder.

Most aft-hung rudders are extended above deck level with a reinforcing pad on either side (cheek blocks) and a tiller slotted between the pads. Most other rudders have a hollow or solid pipe (the *rudderstock* or *post*) with a framework welded or bonded to it (the web), around which the rudder is built.

Where a rudderstock enters a boat there is a bearing, and at the top of the stock another bearing. In order to prevent the entry of seawater around the stock, either a seal (a *stuffing box* or *packing gland*) is placed on top of the lower bearing, or the

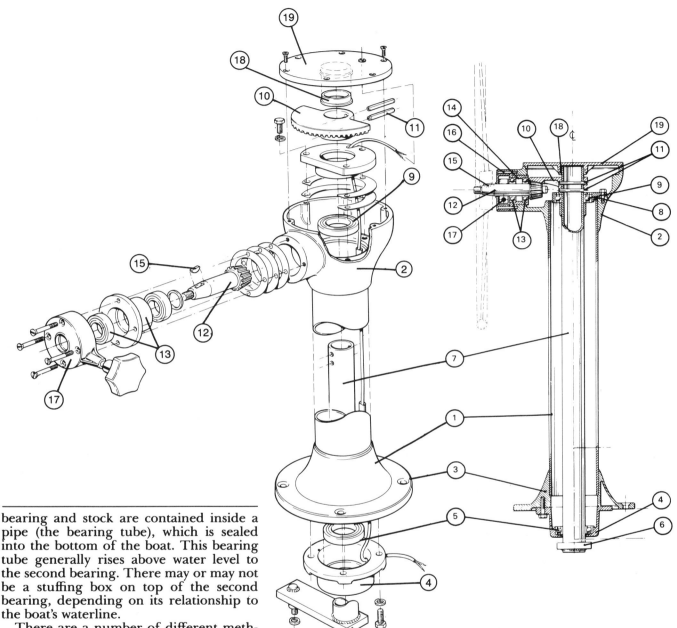

bearing and stock are contained inside a pipe (the bearing tube), which is sealed into the bottom of the boat. This bearing tube generally rises above water level to the second bearing. There may or may not be a stuffing box on top of the second bearing, depending on its relationship to the boat's waterline.

There are a number of different methods used to turn rudders, some of the most popular being:

Tiller steering. A piece of wood simply slots in between the cheek blocks on aft-hung rudders, or between two metal straps attached to the head of the rudderstock (Figure 13-3A). For maximum strength, it is important that the tiller be constructed of straight grained wood, or better still, laminated of several thin layers of wood.

All other steering configurations use a wheel.

Figure 13-3D. An exploded view of the steering pedestal from a rack-and-pinion steering system. 1. Pedestal tube. 2. Pedestal bowl. 3. Pedestal base. 4. Lower bearing housing. 5. Sealed ball bearing. 6. Output lever. 7. Down-tube assembly. 8. Output socket. 9. Sealed ball bearing. 10. Gear quadrant. 11. Pin. 12. Input pinion. 13. Sealed ball bearing. 14. Input socket. 15. Woodruff key. 16. Brake cover. 17. Brake clamp assembly. 18. Top cover bearing. 19. Top cover.

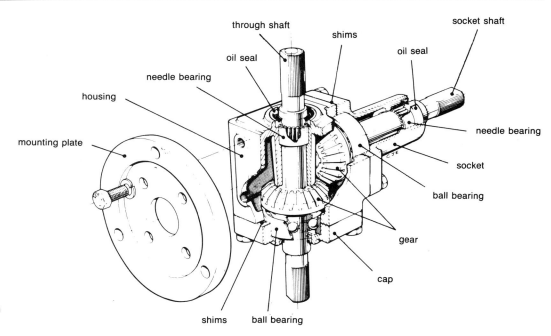

Figure 13-3E. For large boats and boats with power-assisted steering, a bevel box such as this often replaces the rack-and-pinion pedestal shown in Figure 13-3D.

through shaft
shims
socket shaft
oil seal
oil seal
needle bearing
housing
needle bearing
mounting plate
socket
ball bearing
gear
cap
shims
ball bearing

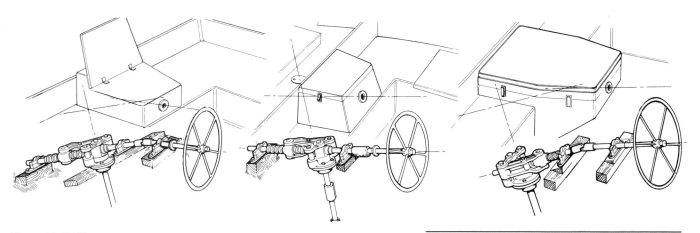

Figure 13-3F. Three different configurations of a worm-drive pedestal steering mechanism. The unit can be adapted to a variety of boats by the use of U-joints. Should the worm seize in operation, the steerer can be unbolted from the rudderhead and the emergency tiller substituted.

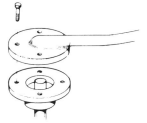

emergency steering tiller

Direct-drive steering. An arrangement of solid shafts and gears connects the wheel to the rudder. There are several options:

Rack and pinion. The steering wheel is keyed to a shaft (drive shaft) on the other end of which is a beveled gear (the *pinion*). This gear engages a circular bevel-geared *quadrant* (the *rack*), which is fastened to the rudderstock and turns the rudder (Figure 13-3B). There is generally a universal joint between the wheel and the quadrant.

Rack and pinion: pedestal options. Traditional rack-and-pinion steering has to be set up close to, and at roughly the same height as, the rudderhead. In order to make the use of a pedestal possible, another "dummy" ruddershaft is set up in the pedestal. The steering wheel, drive shaft, and rack-and-pinion gear are mounted to the top of this dummy shaft just as in a traditional rack-and-pinion setup. An output lever keyed to the bottom of the dummy shaft is connected by a solid rod to a second lever on the ruddershaft (Figure 13-3C).

Another type of rack-and-pinion pedestal assembly is sometimes used, with a non-beveled pinion and a straight, rather than circular, rack. The wheel turns a sprocket. An "endless" roller chain (joined at both ends like a bicycle chain) turns a second sprocket in the base of the unit. This sprocket drives the pinion gear, moving the rack. The rack turns the rudder via a solid link and lever arm.

Worm drive. The drive shaft has a *worm gear* fastened along it. A *traversing nut* rides up and down the worm gear, connected to the rudderhead by various linkages (Figure 13-3F). Moving the traversing nut is what turns the rudder.

Cable steering. The wheel turns a sprocket, driving a length of roller chain, to which wire cables are attached at each end (Figure 13-4C). There are two methods of running these cables to the rudderhead—open-cable steering uses a series of sheaves (pulley blocks); "pull-pull" steering uses enclosed cable conduits (Figure 13-4D). Some systems combine both. Open-cable steering is best where there is a clear cable run from the pedestal to the rudderhead (e.g., aft-cockpit boats); pull-pull works better where there are complex routing problems (e.g., center cockpit boats). On smaller boats the two cables of a pull-pull system are sometimes replaced with a single "push-pull" cable.

At the rudderhead the cables are attached either to a circular fitting (*radial* or *disc-drive steering*) or to a quadrant (Figures 13-4A and D). Once again, the determination of which to use is largely a matter of space and accessibility.

Note that radial steering on an aft-cockpit boat eliminates the outboard sheaves that are necessary with the more traditional quadrant steering. This greatly simplifies installation and removes a couple of potential problem areas.

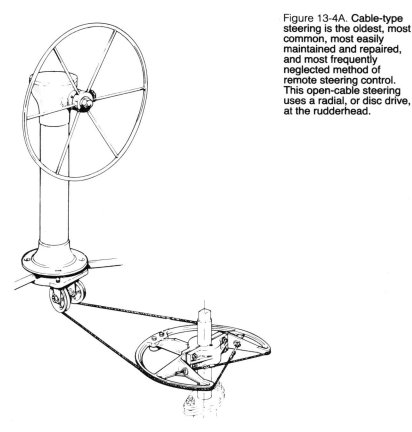

Figure 13-4A. Cable-type steering is the oldest, most common, most easily maintained and repaired, and most frequently neglected method of remote steering control. This open-cable steering uses a radial, or disc drive, at the rudderhead.

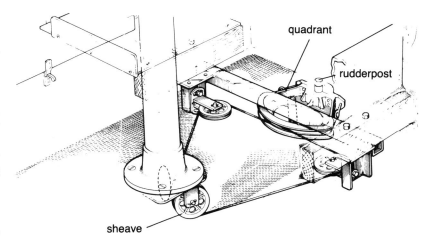

quadrant

rudderpost

sheave

Figure 13-4B. This open-cable steering system uses a quadrant at the rudderhead.

Figure 13-4C. **Open-cable steering pedestal arrangements.**

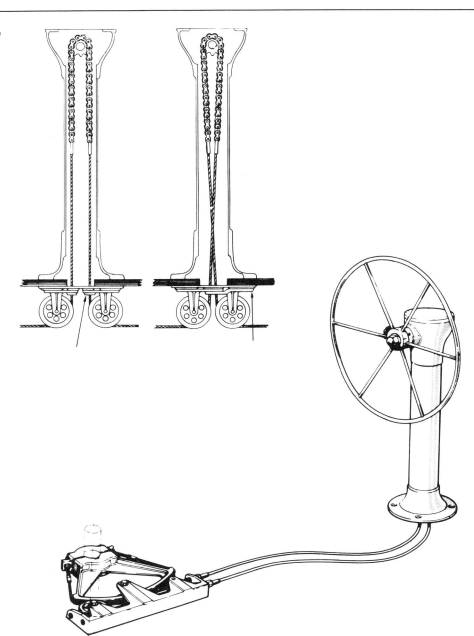

Figure 13-4D. **Pull-pull cable steering via a quadrant mounted on the rudderhead.**

Figure 13-4E. **Detail of the quadrant from Figure 13-4D.**

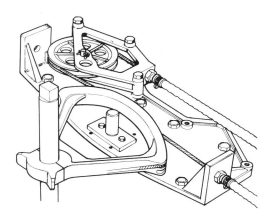

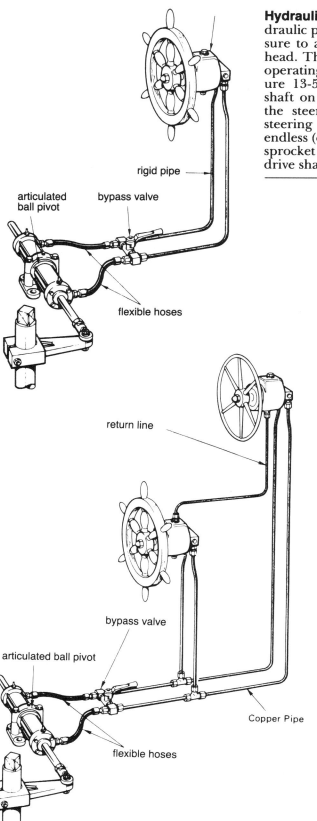

rigid pipe

articulated ball pivot

bypass valve

flexible hoses

Hydraulic steering. The wheel turns a hydraulic pump, which sends oil under pressure to a hydraulic piston at the rudderhead. This piston turns the rudder via an operating lever on the rudderstock (Figure 13-5A and B). Sometimes the drive shaft on the pump is coupled directly to the steering wheel. At other times the steering wheel turns a sprocket, and an endless (circular) roller chain connects this sprocket to another one on the pump drive shaft.

Figure 13-5A. Powerboats, and not a few sailboats, increasingly rely on hydraulic steering. The steering wheel powers a hydraulic pump connected via high-pressure tubing to a hydraulic cylinder, or ram, mounted at the rudderhead. This is a typical single-station hydraulic steering assembly (**top**); and a representative dual-station assembly (**bottom**).

Figure 13-5B. A hydraulic steering system designed for use with pedestal steering.

return line

bypass valve

articulated ball pivot

flexible hoses

Copper Pipe

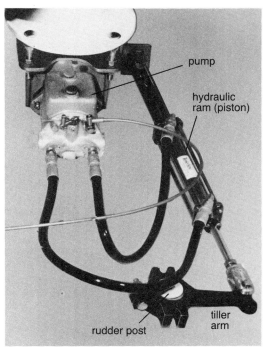

pump

hydraulic ram (piston)

rudder post

tiller arm

Maintenance and Troubleshooting

Gudgeons and Pintles

At every annual haulout flex the rudder up and down and from side to side vigorously, to check for wear and loose fasteners. If the rudder is fastened with stainless steel gudgeons, *remove it and inspect the pintles closely for any signs of crevice corrosion* (see Chapter 4). Many gudgeons ride on Delrin washers—these too need checking and replacing if worn.

Loose fasteners can be a problem with both wood and fiberglass rudders. In wood, if the surrounding area is damaged or rotted, it is best to remove the gudgeon; drill an oversized hole out to undamaged wood; plug this with epoxy; and then refit the gudgeon, drilling a new hole for the fastener through the epoxy plug. See Figure 15-5 for details.

Most fiberglass rudders have a foam, balsa, or wood core. Entry of water into this core through loose or improperly bedded fasteners, or around loose shafts (see below), can lead to various problems, including delamination, cracking along mold lines, and corrosion of the internal web. If the rudder has become waterlogged it will be necessary to drill a hole in its base and leave it to drain until there is no sign of moisture around the drain hole (this may take weeks) before sealing up the hole and rebedding the fasteners properly with polyurethane caulking (e.g. 3M 5200).

When refitting a rudder be sure to secure it properly. Some have a cotter pin (split pin) through a pintle; others have a threaded pintle with a retaining nut; on a few, one pintle is reversed and must be unbolted to remove and replace the rudder. Be especially careful to lock off nuts. This can be done by tightening two nuts against each other or using a Nyloc nut, but it is preferable to drill through the pintle and insert a cotter pin. Many years ago we had a rudder float away in the middle of the North Sea when the retaining nut came off, and we ended up having to be rescued by a Dutch lifeboat.

Rudderstocks, Tubes, Bearings, and Stuffing Boxes

Rudder construction. A number of poorly constructed rudders have either inadequate or improperly fastened internal webs.

Under a severe load the rudderstock will break loose from the web, causing a complete failure of the rudder. Before this happens the stock may start to twist inside the rudder; failure is imminent. Whenever the boat is hauled, tie off the wheel or tiller and flex the rudder as hard as possible. If there is any movement between the rudder and rudderstock the whole rudder must be replaced immediately.

Many rudderstocks are hollow. These are not built to withstand any kind of a serious grounding shock. Consequently any grounding of a spade rudder with a hollow stock is liable to bend the stock at the point where it enters the base of the hull. *Bent hollow stock rudders should be replaced, not straightened.* Any straightening reduces the strength of the most highly stressed point of the rudder. If the rudder absolutely cannot be replaced, straighten it and insert a second tube down into the stock to reinforce it at the point of the bend. Mildly bent *solid* stocks *can* be straightened.

Bearings. The bearings on smaller boats generally consist of a plastic bushing (Delrin, etc.). On larger boats various roller bearings are used. During a haulout, if the rudder flexing described above reveals more than minimal play, *the bearings need replacing.* (Should they be left and fail in a seaway the rudder will start banging around quite violently and do a considerable amount of damage. If this cracks or breaks the bearing tube, it could even sink the boat.)

On the other hand, some plastics swell in salt water. Delrin, and especially nylon, suffer from this problem. Dimensional changes of up to 6 percent are well known and have been responsible for a number of seized or tight systems. Two materials that have zero water absorption are PTFE (Teflon) and UHMWPE (ultrahigh molecular weight polyethylene). PTFE is far too soft for bearing use and has a very low compressive strength in its natural state. Therefore it normally is combined with copper or fiberglass. UHMWPE is now readily available from plastics distributors, has zero water absorption, a very low coefficient of friction, and a high compressive strength, making it one of the best materials to use.

If the steering on a new boat becomes stiff, break the cables loose at the rudderhead and turn the rudder. If it is binding, the bearings probably need reaming.

Most bearing tubes are fiberglass pipes bonded into the base of the hull (Figure 13-7A). The lower bearing (bushing) is pushed up from below and either held with a couple of set screws or a bead of sealing compound *around its base* (3M 5200 caulk or similar). Do not put caulking up *inside* the bearing tube as it will make later bearing removal very difficult. The bearing tube may terminate in a stuffing box, or be carried up and bonded to the underside of the deck.

The upper bearing (bushing) not only absorbs sideways loading, but also holds the weight of the rudder in spade rudder installations. Either a collar or the rudder-head fitting (quadrant, radial drive wheel or disc, or tiller strap fitting) rests on the bearing and keeps the rudder in the boat. *Note that loosening this fitting may allow the rudder to fall out of the bottom of the boat, so be warned*!

Bearing tubes. The bearing-tube-to-hull joint is critical. If it should fail, the boat is in danger of sinking. Bearing tubes in fiberglass hulls are bonded fiberglass; in steel and aluminum hulls they are welded pipes. Inspect the joint annually for any signs of cracking.

Repairing a fiberglass tube.

1. Clean and abrade the hull for 4 to 6 inches (100 to 150 mm) around the bearing tube and up its sides. Be sure to remove all traces of paint, gelcoat, and dirt. Abrade the surface of the fiberglass with a coarse sander. Liberally swab the area with acetone. (Note: Ace-

tone fumes are powerful; if working in confined spaces ensure adequate ventilation.)

2. If the tube-to-hull joint has a tight radius, this is probably why it is cracking. Fair it out with a paste made from catalyzed polyester resin and a filler such as microballoons or talc. (Prefilled putties are available from chandleries.) In a pinch, use talcum powder for a filler. Cut a piece of stiff cardboard to the desired curvature (in profile) and use this to shave off the excess putty and impart a smooth finish. Practice on a scrap piece before you apply the putty on your boat.

Figure 13-6. Bent (**left**) and broken spade rudders. Their unsupported heels and unprotected leading edges make this type of rudder particularly susceptible to damage.

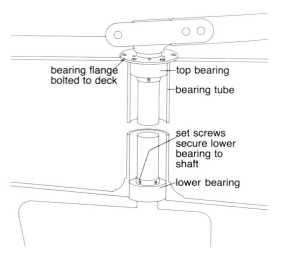

bearing flange bolted to deck

top bearing

bearing tube

set screws secure lower bearing to shaft

lower bearing

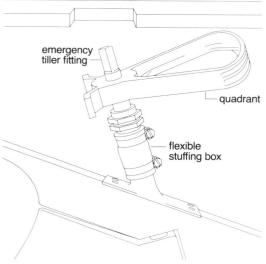

Figure 13-7A. Typical layout of rudder support bearings for tiller steering with a top bearing.

emergency tiller fitting

quadrant

flexible stuffing box

Figure 13-7B. Typical arrangement for wheel steering without a top bearing.

3. Fiberglass *cloth* is easier to work into compound curves than either mat or woven roving, and pound for pound is also stronger. However, it is best laid up over a layer of mat, which holds more resin. This helps to fill in any air spaces in the cloth and provides a better bond with the existing laminate. Cut the mat and cloth into manageable strips (say 3 inches wide by 8 inches long, or 75 by 200 mm). When laying up the strips, use a disposable brush to apply the resin, *saturating the mat or cloth* and mopping up excess later. The fiberglass becomes completely transparent when fully saturated.

4. Try to lay up successive layers of fiberglass before earlier layers have completely gelled. Stagger all joints to avoid any "hard" edges, which will concentrate stresses. If more than one layer is laid up, use alternate layers of mat and cloth and cut the successive layers longer so that the top layer of cloth makes a smooth transition to the hull and tube sides.

Note that polyester resin is normally used on fiberglass because it does the job and is relatively cheap. Various epoxies, however, will provide a better bond to old fiberglass, and make a stronger and more flexible repair.

Stuffing boxes. See the section on stuffing boxes in Chapter 9.

Rudderhead Fittings

The rudderhead fitting is subjected to tremendous loads from time to time, notably when the rudder is slammed around in heavy seas. Should any play develop between the rudderhead fitting and rudderstock, the movement of the rudder will ceaselessly work away at this weakness until something fails. At the annual haulout, when flexing the rudder with the tiller or wheel tied off (see above), check closely for any play. *No play at all is acceptable.*

Rudderhead fittings are clamped to rudderstocks and locked with keys, set screws, or through-bolts. A key is a length of square metal that fits in matching slots machined in the rudderstock and rudderhead clamp (Figure 13-8). Keys both here and elsewhere in the steering system *must be stainless steel and not brass,* since brass will not only de-zincify and fail, but also cause galvanic corrosion on aluminum quadrants and discs (radial drive wheels), causing them to fail. (Note that aluminum rudderhead fittings should be used only on aluminum and stainless steel ruddershafts and never on bronze, for the same reason.) Set screws are frequently threaded into the rudderhead clamp and seated in dimples in the shaft. *This is not adequate.* It is far better to drill out and tap (thread) the seat in the shaft so that the set screw will positively screw into the shaft. This way the screws cannot slip. Be sure to use some locking compound on the screws so that they cannot work their way out (e.g., Loctite).

Many rudderhead fittings on hollow stocks are through-bolted. If the bolt holes become stretched (elongated), allowing some movement of the bolt, drill out the holes and fit a larger diameter bolt. Do not take this too far since the loss of metal will weaken the clamp and shaft.

Once again, *remember that the rudderhead clamp may be the only thing holding a spade rudder in the boat. Before loosening it, secure the rudder!* (If there is room to fit a hose clamp around the shaft somewhere else, this should be done as a security measure in case the rudderhead fitting ever slips.)

Direct-Drive Steering

Rack and pinion (mounted on rudderstock). Rack-and-pinion steering is just about foolproof. The critical factors are to keep the drive shaft at 90 degrees to the quadrant, and to keep the quadrant and pinion gears closed up so that the teeth cannot jump. Where the wheel is not mounted at right angles to the quadrant, a universal joint will be fitted to the shaft.

The pinion gear is generally supported in a couple of bronze bushings, which will need lubricating two or three times a season. Some have grease cups or fittings for this purpose (use Teflon-based waterproof grease); if not, engine oil will do. The gears and rack need greasing. The pinion-gear-to-quadrant clearance can often be adjusted by loosening the quadrant clamps on the rudderstock and moving the quadrant slightly up and down its keyway (this *cannot* be done with set screws or through-bolts on hollow shafts). If the pinion gear mounting bracket has a "contact arm" on which the quadrant rests, worn pinion and quadrant gears can be temporarily closed up by "shimming" the contact arm (sliding a piece of thin metal between it and the quadrant).

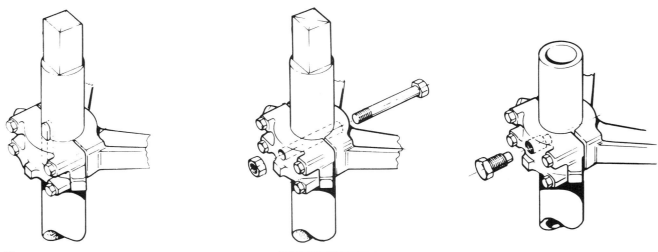

Figure 13-8. Variations on a rudderhead fitting theme. **Left:** Keyway machined into rudderstock and quadrant. **Center:** Through-bolted, using a high-tensile bolt. **Right:** Drilled and pinned, using a high-tensile peg. Because of the extreme point loading at the end of the peg, this method is not recommended.

The mounting bracket for the pinion gear takes *all* the steering loads—check its fasteners carefully at the annual inspection. Lubricate any universal joint and check for play in the joint, its keyways, or the pins locking it to its shafts. Note that many universal joints are steel and not stainless steel. These should be covered with a grease-filled rubber boot (obtainable from large tool supply houses). In the absence of a boot, grease the universal joint and wrap a length of inner tubing around it, securing the tubing with two stainless steel hose clamps.

Rack and pinion (pedestal type). The top plate and input socket screws (see Figure 13-3D) tend to freeze if not removed annually, cleaned, and refitted, preferably with an antiseize compound.

The fit of the rack-and-pinion gears is adjusted at the factory by placing shims (thin metal spacers) under the face of the pedestal input and output sockets. Any wear that takes place can be removed by taking away a shim *from the input socket only*. This will close up the gears, eliminating play.

Some (older) pedestals use needle bearings (see Figure 13-3E) on the output shaft. These will need greasing annually and even when properly maintained have been found to lead to premature wear of the shaft and bearing. Other (newer) pedestals use sealed carbon steel ball bearings, which are essentially maintenance-free. These are liberally coated with a water-repellent grease on assembly to prevent corrosion, but should still be inspected annually for any signs of rust, which, if present, should occasion cleaning and re-coating.

A lack of rudderstops (see below) and/or incorrect installation of the output lever, operating linkage, and tiller arm will sometimes allow the linkage to come close to, or actually "cam over" center; in the latter event steering reverses! This results in excessive loads on pedestal and rudder bearings and on the linkage. Check to see that, with the rudder straight ahead, the pinion is centered on the rack and the output lever and tiller arm are both at right angles to the rudder.

Worm steering. Most of the same considerations apply as above. The wheel must be at 90 degrees to the rudderhead, or else a universal joint is needed. The worm gear and traversing nut need greasing two or three times a year. Worm gears are frequently steel (not bronze). Without adequate and regular greasing they will freeze solid when not in use and prove very hard to free. There are also a number of links, hinge pins, and clevis pins, all of which need lubricating (with engine oil), and probably a central grease fitting on the top of the shaft assembly.

In time, wear between the worm gear and traversing nut and in the various hinges will allow the rudder to rock ceaselessly from side to side, especially at anchor, accelerating the rate of wear. The traversing nut normally has relatively soft threads of babbitt (the white metal found in many bearings), and is designed to wear,

Troubleshooting Chart 13-1.
Wheel Steering Failures: Rack-and-Pinion.

Does the drive shaft turn when the wheel is turned? **YES** ↓	**NO** → Check for a disengaged clutch or slipping wheel (loose and/or sheared off key).
Does the rack-and-pinion gear turn when the shaft turns? **YES** ↓	**NO** → Check for a sheared pin locking the rack-and-pinion gear to its shaft, or a slipping universal joint (if fitted). Repair as necessary.
Does the quadrant turn when the gear turns? **YES** ↓	**NO** → Check for a jumping or stripped gear. Close up the clearance between the gear and quadrant (page 362).
Does the rudderstock turn when the quadrant turns? **YES** ↓	**NO** → The quadrant clamp is slipping on the rudderstock. Tighten or replace bolts and set screws or shim as necessary (page 362).

The internal webs in the rudder itself have sheared. Rig a jury rudder. On sailboats, balance the rig.

thus protecting the worm gear. The threads are renewable at the factory. The various links and clevis pins will need rebushing and renewing as necessary.

Correct alignment on a worm steerer is critical to smooth operation and long life. Once a year separate the two coupling halves at the rudderhead and check the alignment just as for a propeller shaft (see Chapter 9).

Cable Steering

Galvanized, brass, bronze, aluminum, and plastic sheaves are all in use on cable steering systems. The metal sheaves generally have bronze bushings running on stainless steel or brass shafts, though some have stainless steel needle bearings. There is an obvious potential for galvanic interaction; thus it is important to keep the sheaves clean and lubricated. Use engine oil two to three times a season and at the winter haulout.

Plastic sheaves have plastic bearings; the better ones also incorporate extra ball races to absorb side loading. These bearings do not corrode and need no lubrication, although they will attract dirt and thus need flushing with fresh water periodically.

Once a year slack off the cables and check all sheaves to make sure they are free-spinning without excessive play. Replace sheaves and shafts as necessary.

Mounting and aligning sheaves. Sheaves are sometimes subjected to tremendous loads. All sheaves must be rigidly mounted so that no movement that causes loss of cable tension or alignment can occur. *Screws are not acceptable;* the sheave mounting plate should always be through-bolted. Annually or before a trip check all fasteners to make sure they are tight and that the bolt holes are not elongating.

The two final sheaves leading the cables onto a steering quadrant take the highest loads of all. These are normally incorporated into one solid fixture, but if they are mounted independently on either side of the quadrant a rigid brace should be placed between the two bulkheads to which they are fastened (Figure 13-9A).

Accurate alignment of sheaves, rudderhead fittings, and the final lead-in of push-pull and pull-pull cables to a rudderhead fitting is essential to minimize binding,

Table 13-1. Wire Rope and Roller Chain Breaking Strengths.[1]

Size		Stainless Steel Wire Rope			Stainless Steel Roller Chain	
Inches	MM	Pounds	Kilograms	#	Pounds	Kilograms
3/16	4.76	2,827	1,285	—	—	—
7/32	5.56	3,857	1,753	—	—	—
1/4	6.35	5,031	2,287	—	—	—
5/16	8.00	7,986	3,630	—	—	—
3/8	9.53	11,330	5,150	—	—	—
7/16	11.00	—	—	—	—	—
1/2	12.70	—	—	40	3,000	—
5/8	16.00	—	—	50	4,700	—
3/4	19.00	—	—	60	6,750	—
1	26.00	—	—	80	—	—

1. Wire strengths are those given in Norseman tables. Other companies differ somewhat.

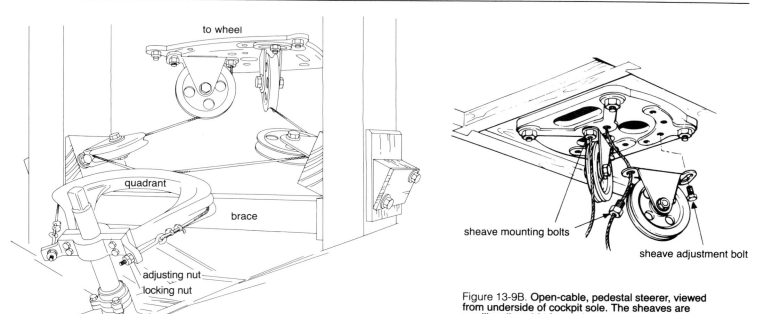

Figure 13-9A. To provide trouble-free service, open-cable steering must be designed carefully. The sheaves must be mounted rigidly and aligned accurately with one another. Alignment can be checked by laying a thin steel rod in the grooves of two connecting sheaves; the rod should lie absolutely fair. A solid brace should be used between the last pair of sheaves before the rudderhead. The tremendous forces generated can easily collapse sheave-bearing bulkheads in heavy-weather conditions.

Figure 13-9B. Open-cable, pedestal steerer, viewed from underside of cockpit sole. The sheaves are readily adjustable for angle.

cable wear, and the risk of a cable jumping off a sheave. Most sheaves have adjustable bases (Figures 13-9 A and B); some are self-aligning. As an alignment check, a length of doweling placed in one sheave groove should drop cleanly into the next. When the system is all set up put the wheel hard over from port to starboard, observing all sheaves, etc. Sometimes with angled rudderstocks and sheaves, some surprising and unexpected changes in alignment can occur. Take the boat out under full engine power and have someone observe all the sheaves and other system components while the rudder is thrown hard over and back a few times. This should reveal any weaknesses.

Cables. Stainless steel 7 × 19 cables are used universally; 1 × 19 cable is not flexible enough to withstand the constant bending around sheaves, discs, quadrants, etc. The cable needs lubricating: When oiling the sheaves (two or three times a season) soak a rag in the same oil (engine oil) and rub it along the whole length of the cables. If this reveals even one "fish hook"

(broken strands of wire), *the cables need immediate replacing.* They should, in any case, be replaced routinely every few years, and a spare set—perhaps an old set taken out of service—kept on board.

Wear on cables is greatly accelerated if they are forced through too tight a radius. For example, 3/16-inch (approximately 4-mm) cable should have sheaves with a minimum diameter of 4 inches; 1/4-inch (6-mm) cable, 6 inches. This gives a ratio of cable diameter to sheave diameter of a little over 1 to 20. Far better would be 1 to 40—i.e., 7½-inch sheaves on 3/16-inch cable and 10-inch sheaves on 1/4-inch cable—but nobody ever does this! Push-pull and pull-pull cable conduit should never be turned through a radius of less than 8 inches. The minimum possible number of bends and sheaves should be used in routing cables. If a sheave ever freezes up, inspect the cable closely where it has been dragging over the sheave.

Tension. Cable tension needs to be checked regularly. The frequency depends on the type of steering (open-cable or pull-pull), the length of the steering run, and the amount of boat usage. Six to 12 times a season would not be unreasonable on heavily used open-cable systems. If tension is loose, the steering will be sloppy, with a risk of cables jumping off sheaves and rudderhead fittings; too tight and the steering will be stiff, with greatly accelerated wear.

Troubleshooting Chart 13-2.
Wheel Steering Failures: Cable and Pull-Pull.

Do the cables at the base of the pedestal move when the wheel is turned? [YES ↓]	[NO ►] Check for a disengaged clutch, slipping wheel or sprocket, stripped sprocket teeth, or a jumped chain. Repair as necessary.
Does the quadrant (or wheel) turn at the rudderhead when the steering wheel is turned? [YES ↓]	[NO ►] **FIX:** Check for broken or jumped cables between the pedestal and rudderhead. See "Cables" in text.
Does the rudderstock turn when the quadrant (or wheel) turns? [YES ↓]	[NO ►] The quadrant clamp is slipping on the rudderstock. Tighten or replace bolts and set screws or shim as necessary (page 362).
The internal webs in the rudder itself have sheared. Rig a jury rudder. On sailboats, balance the rig.	

With the wheel tied off, it should not be possible to turn the rudderhead fitting by grasping it and applying torque. As a general rule of thumb for an open-cable system, with moderate finger pressure it should be possible to depress the cable between sheaves one inch per foot of cable run, but no more. Because of the inherent friction between cable and conduit in pull-pull systems, cables are kept looser than in open-cable systems; cable tensioners should only be hand tight. A certain amount of slack in the feel of the steering is unavoidable. Cable adjustments are made at the rudderhead by tightening a tensioning nut on each cable (Figure 13-9A). First, the chain in the pedestal must be centered on its sprocket with the rudder pointing dead ahead. This is hard to check without taking the compass off the top of the binnacle, which should be done in any event once a year to lubricate the pedestal bearings (see below), so this may be a good time to do both.

Before removing a compass make some kind of a mark on the compass and pedestal so that the two can be exactly realigned. Two or three pieces of masking tape stuck across the joint and then slit works well. The compass should be "swung" by a compass adjuster after it is put back, since its characteristics may have changed. (This too should be done annually.)

Some chains have a removable link in the center. On others the central link should be determined and identified with a piece of string. Line this up on the center of the sprocket and tie off the wheel. Now adjust the cable tensioners in such a way as to make sure the rudderhead fitting is also centered in the boat. Be sure to lock off the cable adjusting nuts when finished.

Cables in conduits. Pay particular attention to the point where the cables exit the conduits; any misalignment will result in cable and conduit wear. Inspect the conduits closely for any signs of cracking in the jacket, cuts, burned or melted spots, kinks, corrosion under the jacket, or separation of the end fittings from the jacket (see Chapter 9). Cables and conduits are not repairable; if any problems exist, replace them both.

Turn the wheel hard over from port to starboard. If any binding, jerking, or stickiness is felt, break the cables loose at the rudderhead and try again. If operation is still rough, the cables probably need replacing (unless there are problems in the pedestal or bulkhead steering; see below).

Once a year remove the cables from their conduits and inspect them closely. Refit with a liberal smearing of Teflon-based grease.

Cable-end fittings. Almost all cables terminate in a thimble and two clamps at the rudderhead. Points to check are: the area of the thimble that bears on the cable tensioner; that the cable is snugged up tightly around the thimble; that the "saddle" of the cable clamp is over the *standing* part of the cable, and the 'U' over the bitter end (see Figure 13-10C); and that the cable clamps are tight.

A variety of fittings can be used at the wheel end for joining cables and chains (Nicopress or Talurit sleeves around thimbles; swaged terminals; etc.). The section in Chapter 15, "Standing Rigging," gives points to look for. Remove clevis pins and check for wear; be sure to refit the cotter pins (split pins).

Wheels, Pedestals, and Bulkhead Stations

Wheels are keyed to drive shafts and retained with a wheel nut. In some instances, where wheel and shaft do not match, a brass adaptor will be fitted between the two. The wheel may or may not have both a clutch and a brake (Figure 13-11).

Clutch units employ a sliding coupling keyed to the drive shaft that can be pushed in and out of engagement with the wheel hub and locked in place with a spring-loaded pin. The wheel is disengaged when certain types of autopilots or a second steering station is in use. Brakes are simply a friction band that clamps around the drive shaft.

Drive shafts run in bronze bushings or needle bearings. The latter are either stainless steel or plastic. A brass or bronze (much preferred) sprocket is keyed to the drive shaft turning a stainless steel chain, except on rack-and-pinion pedestal steering (see previous section).

Clutch hubs, pedestal bearings, and chains all need lubricating at least annually, preferably two or three times a season. The compass will need to be removed from the binnacle (see above). Engine oil is fine for the clutch where it slides on the drive shaft, and for bronze bushings and chain. Grease should *not* be used on chain since it merely sits on the surface of the links collecting dirt. It *is* used, however, on *stainless steel* needle bearings (Teflon-based waterproof grease, such as Lubriplate A). *Plastic* roller bearings need no lubrication but will benefit from a shot of Teflon spray.

Pedestals are made from various grades of aluminum with different kinds of surface treatment (anodizing, painting, etc.). They merely need washing and waxing with a good-quality boat or car polish.

Trouble spots. Apart from routine wear of all components, galvanic interaction sometimes occurs between stainless steel bearings and aluminum pedestals, causing corrosion and blistering of painted surfaces. If a bulkhead steerer starts to stiffen up, check the shaft where it passes through the bulkhead; the problem may be nothing more than damp wood swelling and binding on the shaft. In this case, the hole will just need enlarging.

If a rudder is not fitted with rudderstops (see below), or if the rudderstops fail, there is a danger of the chain-to-wire adaptors running up onto the sprocket, breaking teeth, damaging adaptors, and possibly throwing the chain off the sprocket. Units that have an endless chain driving a second sprocket must be kept tensioned and aligned to stop the chain jumping off the sprockets; the lower unit will be adjustable.

Pedestal overhaul. Remove the compass, wheel nut, wheel, and clutch (if fitted). Slack off the cables at the rudderhead, lift the chain off the sprocket, and tie it off out

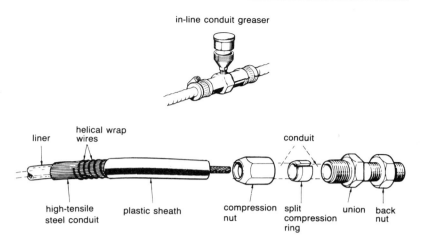

Conduit-end Compression Fitting

Figure 13-10A. **Various methods of terminating steering cables. End fitting used with cables in conduit, commonly used in pull-pull or push-pull steering systems. Less common are in-line conduit greasers, which greatly extend cable life.**

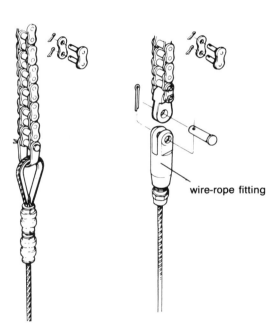

Figure 13-10B. **Chain-to-cable connections. On the left, a thimble retained by two compression sleeves (Nicopress, Talurit); on the right, a mechanical end fitting (Norseman, Stalok).**

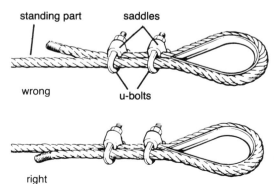

Figure 13-10C. **Bulldog grips: a less elegant, but strong and easily adjusted and repaired end fitting. Make sure the clamp's saddle rests on the standing part of the cable.**

Maintenance and Troubleshooting   367

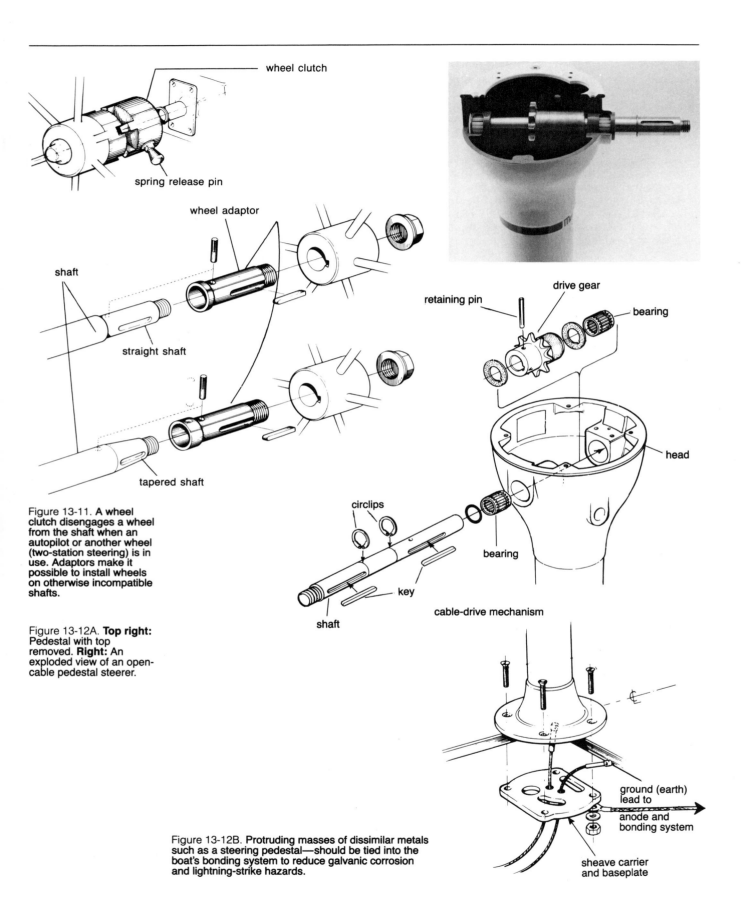

wheel clutch

spring release pin

wheel adaptor

shaft

straight shaft

tapered shaft

retaining pin

drive gear

bearing

head

circlips

bearing

key

shaft

cable-drive mechanism

ground (earth) lead to anode and bonding system

sheave carrier and baseplate

Figure 13-11. **A wheel clutch disengages a wheel from the shaft when an autopilot or another wheel (two-station steering) is in use. Adaptors make it possible to install wheels on otherwise incompatible shafts.**

Figure 13-12A. **Top right:** Pedestal with top removed. **Right:** An exploded view of an open-cable pedestal steerer.

Figure 13-12B. **Protruding masses of dissimilar metals such as a steering pedestal—should be tied into the boat's bonding system to reduce galvanic corrosion and lightning-strike hazards.**

of the way. Place some rags in the pedestal to catch any dropped fittings. In most instances the drive shaft is retained in the pedestal solely by the locking pin through the sprocket. Drive this pin out with a hammer and punch (carefully, it may only come out one way). Place a nut back on the shaft and use a block of wood behind the nut to drive the shaft assembly out of the pedestal. Worn or broken parts are replaced at this time. Reassembly is a reversal of disassembly.

Hydraulic Steering

A simple hydraulic system has a single helm station pumping hydraulic fluid to a single steering cylinder. The piston in the cylinder moves a tiller arm fastened to the rudderstock. Sometimes a single helm pump is installed without check valves. In this case, if the rudder is turned (e.g., by a wave hitting it), the wheel will turn. Most pumps, however, incorporate check valves, which prevent the rudder from turning the wheel. Where two or more helming stations or an autopilot are teed into the same hydraulic circuit, check valves are essential to prevent one helm station from "motoring" another, rather than turning the rudder.

A typical check valve assembly's operation is illustrated in Figure 13-13. *All hydraulic steering systems with built-in check valves should have either a manually operated or solenoid-operated bypass valve,* as shown in Figure 13-13; in reality many do not. In the event of a steering failure the bypass valve is opened, allowing oil to pass freely from one side of the steering cylinder to the other. An emergency tiller then can be installed on the rudderpost and used to steer the boat.

Routine maintenance. If the pump is chain-driven, check the alignment and tension on the chain every three or four months. Raise or lower the pump on its mount to adjust tension. Pumps are best installed with chain sprockets in a vertical plane; if they are not, loose chains tend to work their way off.

The oil level in pump reservoirs also should be checked every three or four months, and topped up as necessary. *Hydraulic systems are extremely sensitive to dirt; before removing any filler plugs, scrupulously clean the external surfaces of the pump.* If any oil has been lost, check all connections, seals, hoses, and lines. Make sure there is no chafing where hoses and lines pass through bulkheads.

Where two or more helm stations (or an autopilot) are teed into the same hydraulic circuit, the normal practice is to tie all the pump reservoirs together. A line is run from the fill plug on the lowest pump to the drain plug on the next highest, etc. The whole system is topped via *the fill plug on the highest pump.*

When topping up, use only the specified hydraulic oil, *never engine oil or brake fluid.* Table 13-2 gives a list of hydraulic oils obtainable worldwide and suitable for most systems. Once a year drain a sample of oil *from the lowest pump* and check for any signs of contamination such as water or dirt. (Moisture can form from condensation in reservoirs—it will cause rust to form on sensitive valves and spools, leading to failure.) If any moisture or dirt is present, drain the system until only clean oil comes out, and then refill and bleed as necessary (see below).

Bleeding a hydraulic system. Oil leaks are the main cause of problems on hydraulic systems. Small leaks can be handled by regular topping up of the reservior until repairs can be made. Any air in the system will cause the steering to feel spongy or even fail altogether. Put the wheel hard over in both directions: if it bounces back when released, you have a pretty good indication of trapped air. To remove it, or after draining and refilling a system, use the following procedure:

1. Fill all pump reservoirs, starting at the lowest (if you have more than one pump) and working to the highest. Replace the fill plugs on the lower reservoirs but leave the upper (or only) one open. Find a length of tubing that will screw into the upper reservoir fill fitting, and a clean funnel that will jam in the tubing. *Maintain a good oil level in the funnel at all times.*
2. Fit two lengths of clear plastic tubing to the bleed nipples on the steering cylinder(s) and place the free ends in a container with a little oil in it. Keep the tubing immersed in the oil to prevent air being sucked up the lines. (Note that pistons must be installed with the bleed nipples facing up.)

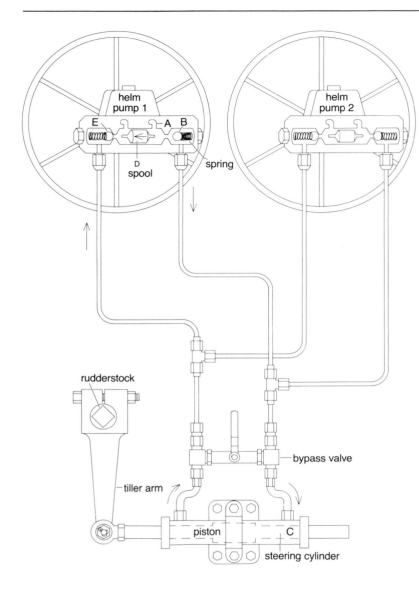

Figure 13-13A. **The operation of hydraulic steering systems.** Imagine the wheel on helm pump 1 is turned clockwise. Oil is pushed down line A; the oil pressure lifts ball valve B off its seat against its spring pressure, and sends oil to piston C. At the same time, the oil pressure moves piston D—the spool—to the left, and the pin on the end of this spool pushes the second ball valve, E, off its seat. This allows return oil from the other side of the steering cylinder back into the helm pump reservoir. The oil pressure pushes both ball valves in the check valve at helm pump 2 against their seats so that no oil flows through the auxiliary steering station.

3. Close any cylinder bypass lines. Determine which side of a cylinder will be pressurized when the wheel is turned clockwise, and open the bleed screw on that side.

4. Turn the wheel (the highest wheel, if there is more than one) slowly clockwise. Air and oil will be vented from the cylinder bleed screw. *Keep the funnel topped up.* When no more air is vented, tighten the bleed screw, open the bleed screw on the other end of the cylinder, and turn the wheel slowly counterclockwise (anticlockwise) until all air is expelled.

5. If the system has more than one wheel, repeat the procedure at each helm station while keeping the funnel on the highest reservoir filled with oil. If the system has twin steering cylinders, open the bleed screws on the same side of both cylinders at the same time, and close each when all the air is vented.

6. The steering may still be spongy due to residual air. This should work its way up into the top reservoir over time. Check its level periodically. If the sponginess persists, the bleeding procedure will have to be repeated.

Tests at the annual haulout. In time—especially if dirt has entered and scored pumps and cylinders—wear on pumps, check valves, and steering cylinders will lead to hydraulic "creep" or "slip"; the rudder will slowly turn independently of the wheel, or it will be possible to keep turning the wheel slowly when the rudder is hard over. This poses no immediate problem, but the unit will need rebuilding at the next haulout.

To determine where the problem lies, close any bypass valves (but not any valves on lines to helm stations), fit the emergency tiller (this will be good practice!) or

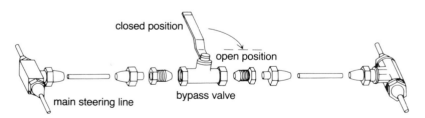

Figure 13-13B. **Detail of hydraulic steering bypass valve assembly, essential to enable an emergency tiller to be fitted (see page 374).**

Table 13-2. Hydraulic Oil Recommendations.[1]

Manufacturer	ISO 32 Centistokes Grade Mineral-Based Hydraulic Oil
BP	Energol HLP22
Castrol	Hyspin AWS32
Chevron	EP Hydraulic 32, MV, AW Machine 32
Exxon	Nuto H32
Fina	Hydron 32
Gulf	Mechanism LP32, Harmony AW32, Harmony HVI36
Mobil	DTE24, DTE13
Shell	Tellus Oil T32, Tellus Oil 32, Tellus Oil T37, Tellus Oil 37
Texaco	Rondo 32, HD 32, Rondo HDAZ

1. Do not use brake fluid.

grasp the rudderhead by hand if there is no emergency tiller, and push the rudder hard in both directions.

1. If the rudder moves but the wheel(s) remains stationary, fluid is seeping down the sides of the piston in the steering cylinder, and it needs rebuilding.
2. If the rudder and steering wheel(s) both move, the check valves in the helm pump are leaking and need rebuilding. (In a single-pump installation with no check valves the wheel will turn; this is OK.)

Amateurs should not attempt pump and piston disassembly; pumps, check valves, and steering cylinders are built to very close tolerances. Seek professional help.

Troubleshooting.

Wheel is stiff. Disconnect the steering cylinder from the tiller arm at the rudderpost and try again. If this eliminates the stiffness, the problem is in the rudder installation (see previous sections) and not the steering system. If the stiffness persists, check the wheel itself for binding (maybe the brake is on!). Other potential sources of trouble are the wrong oil in the system (too viscous) or undersized piping.

Wheel turns but rudder does not respond. Check first to see that a cylinder bypass valve is not open! Check for a mechanical failure (tiller arm slipping on rudderpost, etc.), or a loss of hydraulic oil. If the system has more than one helm station, check to see whether the other wheel (or autopi-

Troubleshooting Chart 13-3.
Wheel Steering Failures: Hydraulic.

Does the hydraulic pump drive shaft turn when the wheel is turned? **YES**	**NO** → **FIX:** Check for disengaged clutch; slipping wheel or sprockets; or broken or jumped chain, if fitted.
Does the pump have oil? (Check the reservoir.) **YES**	**NO** → If the oil is low, fill and bleed (pages 369–370). Check all connections, hoses, and seals for leaks.
Does the piston at the rudderhead move when the wheel is turned? **YES**	**NO** → Make sure no bypass valve or solenoid is open. Double-check the oil level and bleed again. If this fails to restore steering, the piston and/or pump need rebuilding, or the check valves (if fitted).
Does the rudderstock turn when the piston moves the tiller arm? **YES**	**NO** → The tiller arm clamp is slipping on the rudderstock. Tighten or replace bolts and set screws or shim as necessary (page 362).

The internal webs in the rudder itself have sheared. Rig a jury rudder. On sailboats, balance the rig.

lot motor) is turning. If so, its check valves are defective.

If none of these checks reveals a problem, break the steering cylinder loose at the tiller arm and try moving the cylinder rod in and out by hand. If it can be moved, the internal piston seals have gone and the cylinder needs rebuilding. If the cylinder checks out OK, then the helm pump itself may have failed, though this is uncommon. In any event, ship an emergency tiller (see below) and seek professional help.

Hydraulic plumbing. Hydraulic systems—particularly hydraulic winches and windlasses—may experience pressures of up to 2,000 pounds per square inch (psi). It is essential to use only the correct tubing, hoses, and fittings, and to put things together very carefully. Since hydraulic service technicians are few and far between outside large Western cities, it is also important for a boat owner with hydraulics on board to be able to do some basic troubleshooting, and have the spares on board to replace the longest run of hose or tubing should it fail or blow out.

In general, hydraulic steering systems are best plumbed with hard tubing (steel, stainless steel, or copper), since even the best hoses will stretch a little under pres-

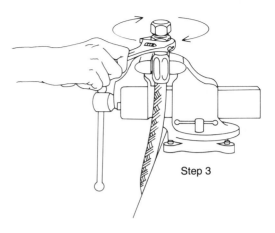

Step 3

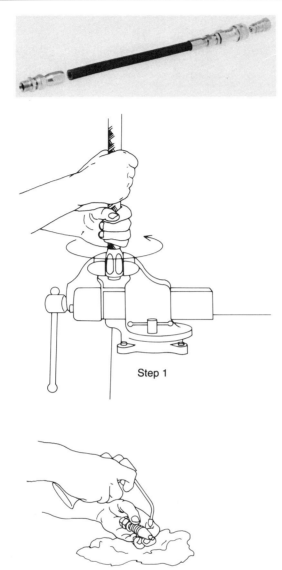

Step 1

Step 2

Figure 13-14. Making up hydraulic hoses. A special assembly tool—a mandrel—eases assembly, but is not absolutely necessary. **Step 1.** Cut hose square with fine-tooth hacksaw or cutoff wheel. Clean hose bore. Put socket in vise and screw hose counterclockwise into socket until it bottoms. Back off one-quarter turn. **Step 2.** Liberally oil nipple threads, assembly tool mandrel (if used), and inside of hose. Use heavy oil, STP, or Aeroquip Lube Oil. **Step 3.** Push assembly tool (if used) into nipple. Add a few drops of oil, and screw nipple clockwise into socket and hose. Tighten nipple, leaving .031" to .062" (.8 to 1.6mm) clearance between nipple hex and socket. Now clean the assembly by blowing out with air or washing out with warm water. Inspect the hose assembly internally for cut or bulged tube, obstructions, and general cleanliness. The smallest bit of debris can put a hydraulic system out of business. Check for proper gap (see above) between nut and socket or hex and socket. Nuts should swivel freely. Check to see that the hose assembly is not twisted, and cap the ends with plastic covers to keep the assembly clean.

sure and introduce a degree of sponginess. However, the final connection to the steering cylinder(s) must be made with a short length of flexible hose, since the cylinder(s) pivot(s) when the rudder turns.

Pipe and tubing connections are generally made with flare fittings. These are covered in Chapter 10, "Refrigeration Plumbing."

Hose should be Aeroquip 2651 or similar (or meet standard SAE 100 R7—ISOD 15349). As a rule of thumb, hose runs of up to 50 feet (16 meters) should be ½ inch (13 mm) ID; over 50 feet, ⅝ inch (15 or 17 mm) ID. Hoses should never have tight bends, and should be fastened at regular intervals (sudden pressure changes can cause hoses to move around). Hose makeup is illustrated in Figure 13-14. Various hose end fittings are available with different threads—swiveling and nonswiveling, male and female, and quick-connect. The latter have a spring-loaded, knurled ring. This is pulled back while a hose is being connected, and then springs forward, locking the fitting. *Always check a quick-connect for dirt before making a connection, and keep it capped when not in use.*

Absolute cleanliness is necessary on all hydraulic systems. In particular, watch out for rubber particles when cutting hoses and making up end fittings. Always cap hoses when not connected, especially when passing them through bulkheads and lockers where they might pick up sawdust and dirt; and always thoroughly flush new hoses and lines with hydraulic oil before connecting to the system.

Rudderstops

Good, strong rudderstops capable of absorbing sudden heavy shock loads (such as

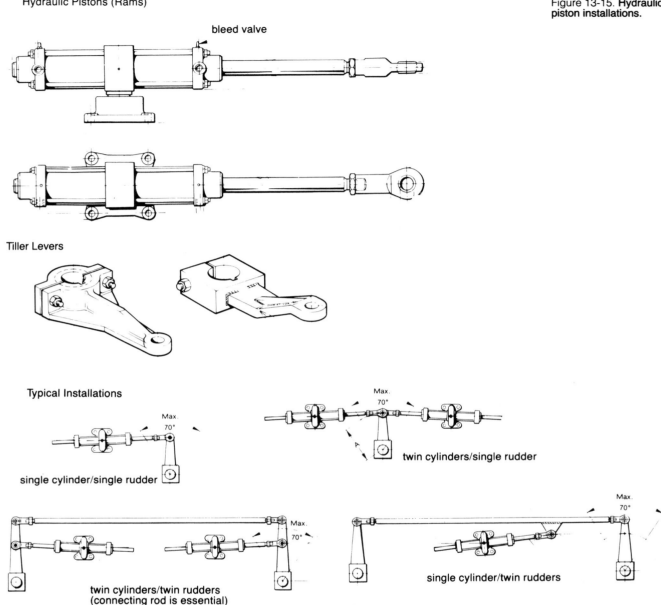

Hydraulic Pistons (Rams)

bleed valve

Figure 13-15. **Hydraulic piston installations.**

Tiller Levers

Typical Installations

Max. 70°

single cylinder/single rudder

Max. 70°

twin cylinders/single rudder

twin cylinders/twin rudders
(connecting rod is essential)

Max. 70°

Max. 70°

single cylinder/twin rudders

when a rudder is slammed over by a following wave) are essential to protect both the rudder and steering system. Insofar as possible, mount rudderstops *independently* of the rest of the steering system, rather than building them into quadrants and radial drive wheels and discs (Figure 13-16).

Always tie off the steering at a marina or at anchor so that there is no risk of waves slamming the rudder against the rudderstops.

Annually check that the rudderstops are secure and that they engage the relevant fitting on the rudderstock cleanly and fully.

Autopilot Hook-Ups on Wheel Steering

Cockpit-mounted autopilots turn the wheel via a belt and pulley. Below-deck autopilots frequently are fitted by piecing a length of chain into one of the drive cables and running this over a sprocket driven by the autopilot motor. Many different con-

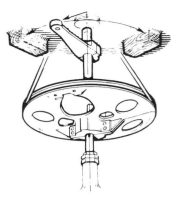

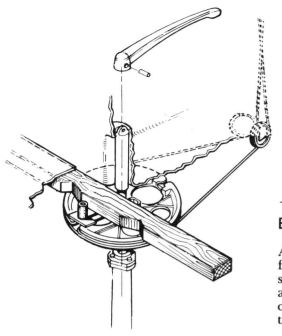

figurations can be built into such a setup (Figure 13-17A). Hydraulic autopilots generally tie into the existing lines just as an additional helm pump would (see Figure 13-28). However, all autopilots using existing steering systems suffer from a major drawback: Any steering failure will put both the wheel *and* autopilot out of action.

A preferred approach to below-deck autopilot installation is to connect the autopilot directly to the rudderhead fitting or even provide it with its own fitting, making it completely independent (Figure 13-17B). This creates a separate steering system that can be used if the main system fails. With rack-and-pinion and worm steering the autopilot sprocket is fitted directly to the steering wheel drive shaft (Figure 13-17C). With hydraulic steering, the main circuit will need a bypass valve (see Figure 13-13), and the autopilot itself will need a bypass valve for when it is not in use.

It is always best to mount sprockets *vertically* so that there is no tendency for slack chains to derail. Chains need lubricating with engine oil whenever sheaves and cables are lubricated. Autopilots are covered in more detail later in this chapter.

Emergency Steering

All wheel-steered boats *must* have some form of emergency tiller that can be installed readily if the steering fails. What is almost as important is that the skipper and crew practice fitting it *before* an emergency; there may be some surprises.

A solid rudderstock is usually squared off to accept the emergency tiller. Hollow shafts with through-bolted rudderhead fittings take a slotted tiller fitting over the bolt (Figure 13-18). Since the wheel pedestal is frequently in the way of the tiller, three approaches can be taken to get around it:

1. A very short tiller: this will be of little use in large seas.
2. A very tall tiller coming over the top of the pedestal. This too will be hard to control, with a serious tendency to bend sideways.
3. A curved tiller bending around the pedestal. This is the preferred solution.

It is extremely hard to fit a long tiller to a rudderstock when the seas are causing the rudder to weave around. Far better to have a tiller in two sections: a short stub to be fitted to the rudder to bring it under control, and the main tiller slotting onto the stub to provide leverage for effective steering. Note that any tiller passing close to a compass should be nonmagnetic.

If hydraulic steering has internal check valves and no bypass valve, the drive cylinder actuating arm will have to be disconnected from the tiller arm before an emergency tiller can be used (unless the hydraulic circuit has failed). Where worm steering is used, the whole steering assembly will have to be unbolted from the rudderstock flange, and a separate, flanged tiller bolted on.

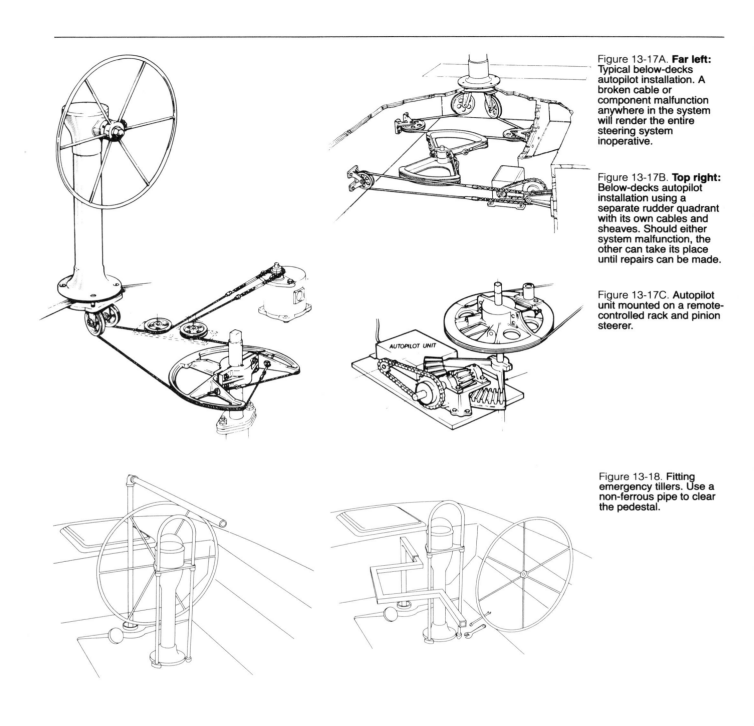

Figure 13-17A. **Far left:** Typical below-decks autopilot installation. A broken cable or component malfunction anywhere in the system will render the entire steering system inoperative.

Figure 13-17B. **Top right:** Below-decks autopilot installation using a separate rudder quadrant with its own cables and sheaves. Should either system malfunction, the other can take its place until repairs can be made.

Figure 13-17C. Autopilot unit mounted on a remote-controlled rack and pinion steerer.

Figure 13-18. Fitting emergency tillers. Use a non-ferrous pipe to clear the pedestal.

Self-Steering

There are a number of devices on the market that in theory can be fitted to any boat—power or sail—to make it hold a constant course *in relation to the wind* (i.e., if the wind changes direction, the course changes). These devices use no power and as such are attractive to sailboat owners; in practice they are not used on powerboats, which generally rely on autopilots for automatic steering (see below). This section on self-steering is therefore aimed at sailboats.

How It Works

Self-steering holds a boat on a certain course *in relation to the wind*. If the wind changes, the course will change to maintain the same relationship. A small "sail"—the *wind vane*—is aligned with the wind. If the boat veers off course the wind continues to hold the vane in alignment. The boat is thus turning in relation to the vane, and this movement is used to correct the steering. The main problem is the extremely limited amount of force generated by a vane, especially if the boat has changed its relationship to the wind by only a few degrees. This force needs amplifying. Two approaches are used: *trim tabs,* and *servopendulum* units. Both utilize water pressure and the boat's speed through the water to produce considerable steering force.

Trim tabs. An auxiliary rudder is generally fitted to the stern of the boat with a small rudder (the trim tab) hinged to its trailing edge; this trim tab is occasionally tacked onto the boat's main rudder, in which case the auxiliary rudder is not needed. The main rudder is tied off (except in cases where the trim tab is attached to it). The boat is put on its chosen course and the wind vane allowed to align with the wind. Then a clutch is engaged to connect the vane to the trim tab (Figure 13-19A). Any movement of the vane (such as happens when the boat veers off course) turns the trim tab. This requires little force because of the small size of the trim tab. For various reasons beyond the scope of this book,

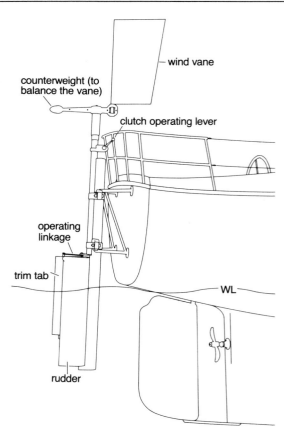

Figure 13-19A. **The operation of trim-tab type wind vane self-steering.**

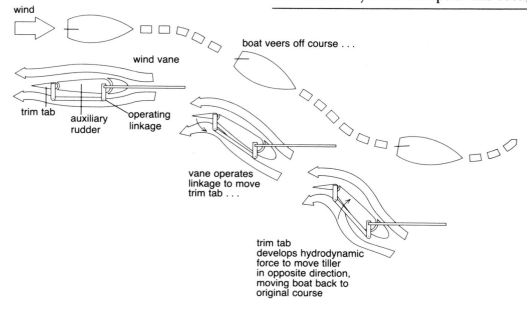

this small trim tab can develop sufficient hydrodynamic force to turn the auxiliary rudder and correct the boat's course.

Servopendulum units.

The wind vane on a trim tab pivots around a vertical axis that, on a servopendulum unit, pivots around a *horizontal* axis just slightly up from the base of the vane (Figure 13-19B). The vane itself is generally a piece of thin plywood (as opposed to a small sail), weighted at its lower end so that it remains *just* vertical.

The boat is put on its chosen course and the thin, leading edge of the vane is aligned with the wind. A clutch is engaged, connecting the vane with a *servo-rudder* in the water, which has *its* leading edge lined up with the flow of water past the boat (i.e., more or less fore and aft). If the boat veers off course, the wind vane is brought increasingly broadside to the wind, and the wind blows it down around its pivot point. The base of the vane is connected via linkage to the shaft holding the servo-rudder. As the wind vane is knocked down this linkage *pivots* the servo-rudder; this in turn creates hydrodynamic forces that cause the servo-rudder to swing sideways with considerable force. Lines attached to the servo-rudder are fastened either to the tiller or to a special drum on the wheel. When the servo-rudder swings, these lines turn the boat's own rudder and correct the course.

Control and adjustment.

On many self-steerers the wind vane shaft pivots on a bearing with a toothed gear keyed to the shaft (Figure 13-21A). When the clutch is disengaged the vane turns to align with the wind. When the clutch is engaged a ratchet engages the gear and locks the vane to the trim tab or servo-rudder. The principal disadvantage of such a system is that course corrections cannot be made in less than 5- to 10-degree increments, since this is the effect of moving from one gear tooth to the next. Finer adjustment is generally made where the control lines attach to the tiller or wheel drum.

More accurate course adjustments can be made where a *worm gear* is used on the wind vane (Figure 13-21B). The gear is disengaged to allow the vane to line up with the wind, and then fine-tuned by rotating the gears; infinite corrections are possible.

A somewhat different approach, which also allows infinite adjustment of the vane's "angle of attack" (its alignment with the wind), is to use a *cone clutch*. The vane shaft pivots around an output shaft and has a tapered seat attached to it. A tapered friction pad is keyed to the output shaft. The vane is allowed to freewheel and align with the wind. The tapered friction pad then is pushed into the tapered seat on the vane shaft, locking the vane to its trim tab or servo-rudder. Regardless of clutch type, the mechanism needs to be kept clean and

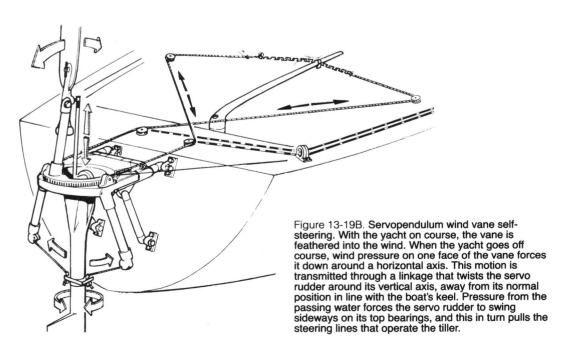

Figure 13-19B. Servopendulum wind vane self-steering. With the yacht on course, the vane is feathered into the wind. When the yacht goes off course, wind pressure on one face of the vane forces it down around a horizontal axis. This motion is transmitted through a linkage that twists the servo rudder around its vertical axis, away from its normal position in line with the boat's keel. Pressure from the passing water forces the servo rudder to swing sideways on its top bearings, and this in turn pulls the steering lines that operate the tiller.

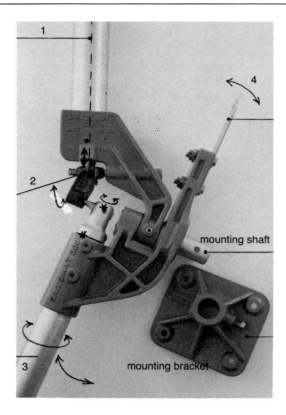

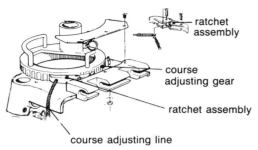

Fig 13–21A. **Controlling and adjusting wind vanes:** Gear-type clutch. The course adjusting line disengages the ratchet, allowing the vane to align with the wind. Fine-tuning the system is done where the control lines attach to the tiller or wheel drum.

Figure 13-20. Critical maintenance points on wind vane self-steerers. Friction at any of these points will greatly reduce system performance. (1) Linkage inside this shaft connects to the base of the wind vane. When the vane is blown over around its axis, this linkage moves up or down. (2) The linkage is connected here to an offset cam, causing this lever to push from side to side around its axis. (3) This in turn rotates the servo-rudder shaft as shown, causing the rudder to swing sideways. (4) Control lines attached here, and through blocks to the rudder or wheel, translate the sideways swing of the servo rudder into a pull on the helm.

lubricated. *It is a matter of basic safety to be able to disengage the wind vane quickly and without difficulty in emergency situations.*

Maintenance and Troubleshooting

Friction. The initial force developed by a wind vane on any system is quite small. Before this force can be amplified, it must be transmitted to the trim tab or servo-rudder. Any friction or sloppiness in the linkage between vane and trim tab or servo-rudder will dramatically lessen the unit's performance. The gear's exposed location ensures the accumulation of salt crystals in bearings and linkages, and if poorly chosen materials are used in con-

struction, corrosion is inevitable. The linkage needs regular cleaning of dirt or corrosion and should be checked often for free movement. Sloppy movement will allow the boat to wander around the course line before any correction is made. Where adjustment is possible any sloppiness needs to be taken out, but stop your adjustment just short of the point at which friction and binding set in.

A self-steerer's exposed location renders it vulnerable to damage both from large waves and collision, such as when docking. Fishing lines can snarl the auxiliary rudder or servo-rudder. Most vanes rely on a combination of brute strength and designed-in weak links to deal with these situations (Figure 13-22).

Wind vanes are mostly thin plywood and easily replaced. *Spares should always be carried.* Auxiliary rudders are permanent installations and take all the steering loads: *they need to be built as strongly as the boat's main rudder.* Servo-rudders will sometimes be thrown violently sideways. Some—such

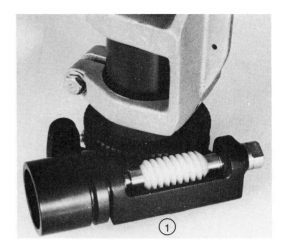

Figure 13-21B. Course is adjusted via the cable from the worm gear (1) to the helm or by pointing vane into wind using a simple friction clamp (2). Both provide infinite adjustment. Vane axis adjusted here (3). The vane axis angle can be tilted from the vertical for less sensitivity in strong winds. Rudder ratio is adjusted here (4). This varies the amount of rudder movement for any given vane movement, and therefore the degree of steering correction.

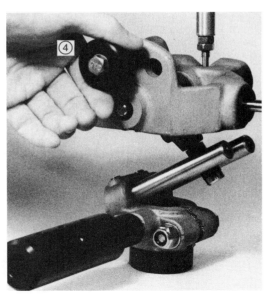

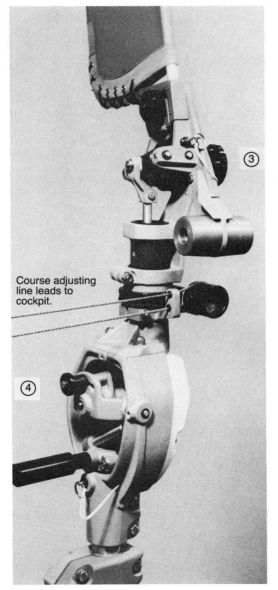

Course adjusting line leads to cockpit.

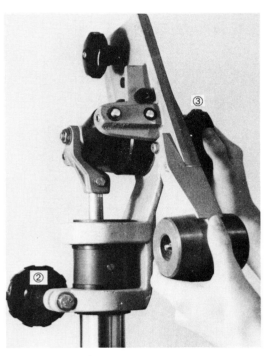

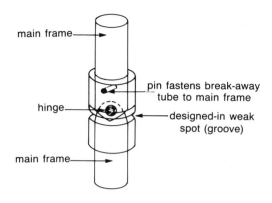

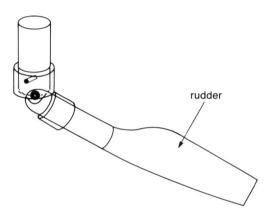

Figure 13-22. Break-away tubes and other designed-in weak links protect vulnerable and expensive wind vanes from collision damage. Shock loading shears the break-away tube and allows the main frame to pivot safely out of the way of flotsam.

main frame

pin fastens break-away tube to main frame

hinge

designed-in weak spot (groove)

main frame

rudder

as Sailomat—can pivot 90 degrees from the vertical without damage, but most can't. Whatever happens, the shock loads must not be thrown on the delicate control linkage. The unit may have break-away tubes to relieve stress. If so, carry spares. In any event, think about these things before leaving the dock. Be prepared.

In the past there have been problems with fiberglass auxiliary rudders and trim tabs delaminating (they are generally built in two halves, and the halves will sometimes separate). Watch for telltale cracks in the gelcoat. Many newer rudders—Hydrovane, for example—are built of nylon and are virtually indestructible.

Finally, perhaps the greatest problem comes from installing too small a unit for a given boat in order to cut costs. Not only will performance be unsatisfactory, but the unit will be overstressed and likely to fail. It is far better to err on the conservative side, especially if you are contemplating ocean crossings. Once you have become

used to a self-steerer, a return to steering by hand on long passages becomes a monumental chore.

Balancing a boat. Despite the dramatic force amplification achieved hydrodynamically, the end forces generated by self-steerers are still not that powerful, especially in light winds and at slow boat speeds. *No self-steering apparatus will operate effectively unless the boat is balanced first.* This is largely a matter of sail trim, although where an auxiliary rudder and trim tab are used the main rudder can be tied off in such a way as to correct for helm imbalance (e.g., weather helm).

Most boats will self-steer hard on the wind without a self-steerer. But as the boat comes off the wind, balance is harder and harder to achieve. Few boats can be balanced on a beam reach, and it may be necessary to sacrifice optimum sail trim (e.g., by letting the mainsail luff somewhat) in order not to overpower the self-steerer.

When broad-reaching and running, the more the center of effort can be concentrated in the headsails the easier the boat will be to control. The ideal situation on a downwind run is to drop the main (and mizzen) altogether and set two poled-out jibs. Since *apparent* wind speed is much reduced when running, the wind vane exerts less force than on any other point of sail; combine this with the fact that, when headed downwind, sea conditions are generally at their most difficult to handle, and it is easy to see that the self-steerer will need all the help it can get. Downwind sailing in ocean swells is the acid test of any self-steerer.

Yaw. A self-steerer *reacts* to a change in course and can never *anticipate* wind shifts or wave action. It has therefore, a built-in tendency to cause the boat to yaw from side to side around the course line. The further the boat is off the wind, the greater the tendency to yaw. Better steerers have a degree of yaw-damping capability; the gear is designed in such a way that as the auxiliary rudder (or boat's rudder) turns in response to "instructions" from the trim tab or servo-rudder, the force exerted by the trim tab or servo-rudder is lessened (*dampened*). This helps to reduce violent rudder movements and sharp course changes. But even so, no self-steerer will hold a downwind course in following or quartering seas without a fair degree of yawing—just as no helmsperson can. The best that can be hoped for with self-steering is to approximate the performance of a helmsperson.

To deal with yaw and poor downwind performance, a new breed of hybrid self-steerer is appearing on the market. These operate as straight self-steerers when *on the wind;* on a reach or run, however, the trim tab or servo-rudder is turned directly by an autopilot (see below).

Autopilots

While a self-steering device uses the wind to hold a boat on a constant course in relation to the wind, an autopilot uses the boat's DC power to hold a boat *on a constant compass course* irrespective of wind direction. Autopilots are used extensively on both sail and power boats.

How They Work

The boat's course is set on a compass. Two types are used: *fluxgate* compasses, which operate electronically, and *photo-optic* compasses, which utilize a light beam to read the compass. Extensive troubleshooting of either is beyond the scope of this book. The best procedure is to contact a compass adjuster or the manufacturer if necessary.

Any deviation from the preset course is transmitted to a central processing unit (CPU)—a minicomputer. This unit then switches power to an electric motor that drives an actuator in order to effect a course correction. The control unit's sophisticated circuitry smooths out rhythmical fluctuations in the course, such as arise from following seas. There also may be a rudder control, which alters the degree of response to any change in the boat's heading: A low rudder control setting will result in small rudder movements; a high setting causes large rudder movements. Some units have a sea-state or deadband control. This simply determines how far off course the boat may wander before the autopilot responds with a course correction.

All autopilots use an electric motor to move the rudder and make course corrections. Some motors drive a belt or chain (rotary autopilots); others move an arm in and out (linear). This may be done mechanically (via a set of gears) or hydraulically (via a pump and hydraulic piston or *ram*). Almost all motors are geared down: the reduction box may be a *worm* type or a *planetary* type (see Figure 13-23). Mechanical linear drive units must also convert rotary motion to an in-and-out motion; this is generally done via a "recirculating-ball lead screw"—a gear mounted on a worm shaft similar to the worm steering already covered in this chapter, though obviously on a much more compact scale.

Cockpit-mounted units are either rotary, using a belt to turn the boat's steering wheel, or mechanical linear, using an arm to move the tiller backward and forward (Figures 13-23A and B). Below-deck units may be rotary, mechanical linear, or hydraulic linear. Below-deck rotary units use a chain to drive another sprocket and chain linked into existing cable steering, or else operate a completely independent cable system with its own quadrant on the rudder shaft. Mechanical linear and hydraulic units either turn the existing quadrant via an operating arm or else are connected to an independent lever mounted on the rudder shaft (Figure 13-24).

Problems With Autopilots

Problems common to all autopilots.

The boat slowly veers off to one side. There is insufficient rudder reaction to course changes. Increase the *rudder* setting.

The boat oversteers and follows an S course. There is too much rudder reaction to course changes. Decrease the *rudder* setting.

Course corrections are delayed. The boat continually wanders off course before the autopilot reacts. The deadband (sea-state) setting is too high (this may not be adjustable). There may be too much slack in the steering cables, loose linkages, or air in a hydraulic unit. The rudder is weaving independently of the steering system. This will be more pronounced in calm conditions. Tighten cables as necessary. Check the oil level on hydraulic circuits and bleed the circuits of all air. Find out where the oil is going. In particular, check the shaft seals on rams.

The boat heads onto a different course or turns in circles. This is almost certainly the

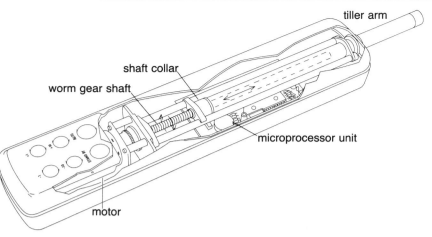

tiller arm

shaft collar

worm gear shaft

microprocessor unit

motor

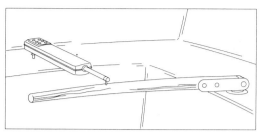

Figure 13-23A. **Worm gear and planetary gear autopilots.** This tiller-mounted unit extends and retracts the tiller-actuating arm by turning a recirculating lead ball screw—a gear on the inside and a ball bearing on the outside—that is attached to the actuating arm.

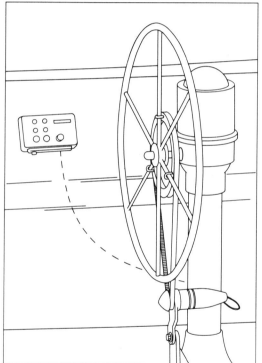

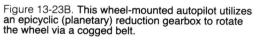

cogged belt

epicyclic gears

motor

microprocessor unit

Figure 13-23B. **This wheel-mounted autopilot utilizes an epicyclic (planetary) reduction gearbox to rotate the wheel via a cogged belt.**

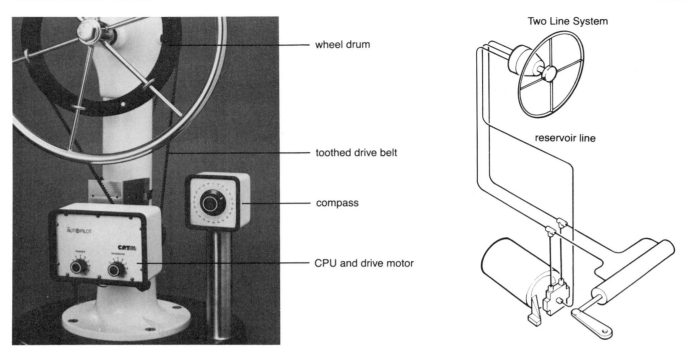

wheel drum

toothed drive belt

compass

CPU and drive motor

Figure 13-24A. **Rotary-drive, cockpit-mounted autopilot.**

Two Line System

reservoir line

Figure 13-24C. **Hydraulic autopilot teed into existing hydraulic steering system.**

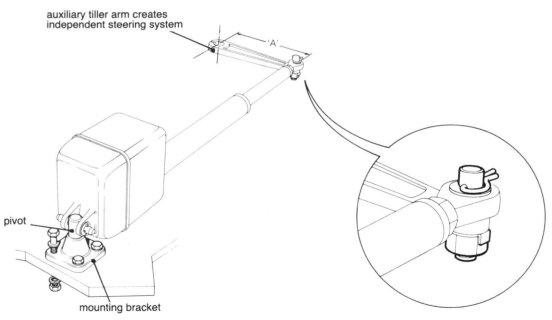

auxiliary tiller arm creates independent steering system

'A'

pivot

mounting bracket

Figure 13-24B. **Mechanical linear actuator-type autopilot.**

Figure 13-24D. **Independently mounted hydraulic autopilot.**

result of electrical interference, probably from a "noisy" alternator or SSB (especially when transmitting). If it only happens when the engine is running, it is almost certainly the alternator or its regulator; see Chapter 7, on radio interference. It also could be the result of interaction between the autopilot compass and the boat's compass. They should be at least 39 inches (1 meter) apart; try moving one. Perhaps someone has just placed a radio or other source of magnetic interference close to the autopilot's compass.

The autopilot trips off. This is likely to be the result of either voltage spikes (high-voltage transients) or low voltage. In either case the CPU trips. Does it only happen when a large load kicks in, such as when cranking the engine or using an electric winch? Check for voltage drop *at the CPU when the rudder actuator is in operation* (see Chapter 3). Check all wiring connections, especially terminals and plugs on cockpit-mounted units.

Voltage spikes can be generated by alternators, especially if batteries are in poor shape, or can occur when large loads kick off. It may be necessary to move the CPU power leads to their own battery and/or increase the size of the leads to combat voltage drop.

The autopilot fails to work at all. Check for voltage *at the CPU*. If present, check the polarity (see Chapter 3); reverse polarity may have done irreparable damage. If the unit has power and correct polarity, disconnect the leads to the drive motor, set a course, turn the boat, and check to see if there is any output voltage from the CPU. If not, it has an internal problem.

Be advised that there is a "bathtub" phenomenon associated with electronic failures (Figure 13-25). Statistically, most failures occur either soon after installation or much later, after long use. Quality manufacturers can almost entirely eliminate the early failures, primarily through testing at elevated temperatures during manufacture.

If the CPU is putting out, connect a 12-volt battery (or 24 volts on 24-volt systems) directly to the motor and see if it spins. Reverse the leads; the motor should reverse. Larger motors have a solenoid-operated clutch; if the motor fails to work, identify the solenoid and jump it out to see which item is defective (see Chapter 6, "Starter Motor Circuits"). If the motor still fails to work, *disconnect it from any actuating mechanism* (since this may be seized) and try again. If the motor is bad, various motor tests can be performed as outlined in Chapter 6, "Permanent-Magnet DC Motors."

The autopilot operates sluggishly. Check for low voltage at the drive motor when in operation. Check for binding in the parts of the steering system driven by the motor, such as a wheel brake accidentally left engaged. If necessary, disconnect the motor to check its no-load operation; while doing this check the free movement of all relevant linkages in the steering system.

The unit operates backward. The power leads from the CPU to the motor are crossed; reverse them. Some units have an internal changeover switch that serves the same function.

Cockpit-mounted units.

Water in the CPU. All cockpit-mounted units are susceptible to water in the electronics. As far as I know, only one (the Autopilot II) is genuinely waterproof. The rest are merely spray-proof. A good dunking in green water—such as when pooped—may penetrate the seals. CPUs should not be mounted in wet locations, and when stored must be kept in a dry place.

Water in the drive motor. The most likely point of ingress is through the cable gland. If the unit is likely to be subjected to a lot of spray or solid water, check this seal before use, and improve it as necessary—with silicone sealant or 3M 5200 caulking, for example.

Corrosion in the power supply socket. Another likely source of trouble! Keep the pins and plugs liberally greased with petroleum jelly. I have found that even when clean some plugs make a poor contact with the pins; knocking the plug or twisting it slightly will break the power supply and cause the CPU to trip off. A bit of judicious bending of pins or plug sockets generally solves the problem.

Lack of power. A perennial problem on sailboats. The only answer is to *balance* the sails, even at the expense of performance. For tiller autopilots, see below.

Cockpit wheel steerers.

Wheel drum centering and motor alignment. Wheel drums are bolted to the center of steering wheels. If the drum is not centered exactly, it will alternately tighten and loosen belt tension as the wheel turns. If not bolted squarely to the wheel, or if the motor is not mounted *directly in line with and square to* the wheel drum, alignment will be out, stressing belts and tending to throw them off. Motor mounting must be solid and inflexible.

Slipping belts. Most belts are toothed (i.e., have ridges across them); the teeth mate with a spline on the end of the motor drive shaft. While some, such as the Autopilot II, have good-sized teeth, others (e.g., Autohelm and Navico) do not; the latter are especially prone to slip when wet and when under a load, or whenever the drum is not properly centered or aligned. Beware of overtightening belts to stop slipping; this will lead to premature bearing failures in the motor. Tension of small-

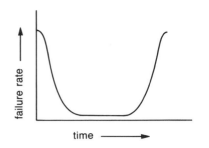

Figure 13-25. The "bathtub" concept of electronic equipment failure.

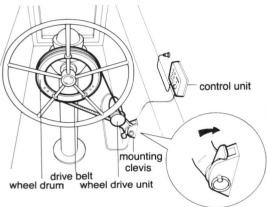

Figure 13-26. Autopilot drive arrangement on a cockpit-mounted wheel steerer. To work properly, the wheel drum must be centered exactly in relation to the wheel's axis, and the drum must be in line with and square to the wheel drive unit.

toothed belts should be sufficient to prevent slipping when the steering wheel is turned by hand with the clutch engaged; when the clutch is disengaged, however, the steering wheel should spin freely with no belt drag (Figure 13-26).

Broken belts. Like paper, belts are strong in tension but tear easily if nicked or damaged. Rough spots on wheel drums and poor alignment will shorten belt life.

Stripped drive gears. Most units incorporate a planetary-type reduction gearbox. These will allow the motor to be turned over by the wheel and so absorb some shock loads from the rudder. Nevertheless, a good number of gears are plastic and will strip off under heavy loads.

Note: It seems that most small autopilots are made for the weekend market and not designed for continuous cruising. Manufacturers accept a small percentage of failures from heavy use in order to hold down cost for the majority of the market. It is my opinion that in most cases one should not take too seriously the manufacturer's claims as to what boat sizes their autopilots can handle.

Some units, however, incorporate larger motors and worm gearing. The motors

Autopilots   385

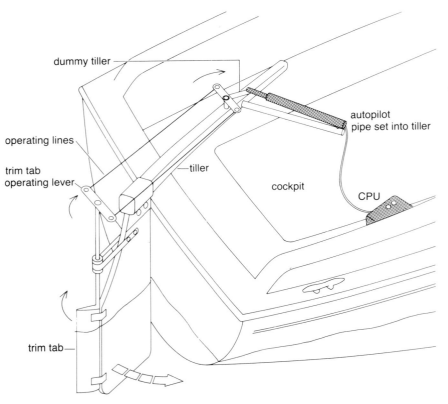

dummy tiller

operating lines

trim tab
operating lever

tiller

autopilot
pipe set into tiller

cockpit

CPU

trim tab

Figure 13-27. Autopilot performance can be improved by the use of a trim tab. The autopilot is tiller-mounted, and controls the trim tab through a dummy tiller and bell crank assembly.

some heat from a propane torch, and a judicious application of force! Clean all threads and bearings, grease with a high-quality marine grease, such as Lubriplate A, and *regrease every time the unit is put away for more than a day or two*. Better get a spare; this actuator won't last long.

Autopilot is overpowered by the waves. If the actuating unit is continually overpowered, with the arm being driven in and out against its end stops, sooner or later something will give. The unit had better be unshipped.

We have a heavy-displacement (30,000 pounds), 39-foot ketch, steered by a tiller. Our Autohelm 2000 was repeatedly overwhelmed, and the mounting units at both ends broke at different times. We solved the problem by installing a trim tab on the trailing edge of the rudder with an operating arm at the rudderhead (Figure 13-27). Two cables come forward to a "dummy" operating arm on the tiller. The autopilot actuating unit is mounted on a stainless steel pipe and hooked onto the dummy operating arm. The pipe slots into a hole drilled through the tiller and is locked into place at right angles to the tiller by a pin pushed down through the tiller and the pipe. The autopilot steers the boat *via the trim tab*, which takes minimal effort—never more than a pound or two of thrust—and uses minimal power.

Every time a wave hits the rudder, the whole unit is free to swing and go with the flow; the autopilot is *never* stressed. It has taken us to Venezuela and back in all kinds of conditions. It even holds a pretty fair course in sizable quartering and following seas. Given the right size trim tab, this setup can be used to control tiller-steered boats *of any size*. Note that such a setup can be used only where the CPU is mounted independently of the actuating unit. Where the CPU is built into the actuator, every time the tiller moves it confuses the CPU!

Below-deck linear actuators (mechanical and hydraulic).

Quadrant failures. Many times a linear actuator is attached to an existing quadrant by simply drilling a hole in the quadrant and through-bolting. Most quadrants, especially lightweight ones, are simply not designed for this kind of point loading. If the actuator must be attached to the quadrant, *a plate of the same material as the quadrant* should be bolted firmly to the quadrant and the actuator bolted to the plate to

cannot be turned over by the steering wheel (the worm gears exert too much braking action). In this case, the drive pulley will be installed with shear pins, and if overloaded the pins will give. If the motor shaft turns, but the pulley does not, check the shear pins.

Tiller steerers.

Seizure of the operating arm. All units use a worm gear driving a recirculating-ball lead screw, which in turn moves the actuating arm in and out through a seal. Many units, such as older Autohelms, use a *steel* lead screw, which is likely to rust if not properly lubricated and kept dry. Newer Autohelms are stainless steel.

When the actuating arm moves in and out, minor pressure changes occur inside the unit that can draw in humid, salt-laden air. (Some units have a pressure compensation chamber to reduce this effect; newer Autohelms have improved seals.) The next time the unit is left unused for an extended period it may seize up solid. If this happens, remove the motor and check motor operation and actuator movement independently of one another to confirm that the actuator is at fault.

It may be possible to free a frozen actuator with liberal doses of WD–40, perhaps

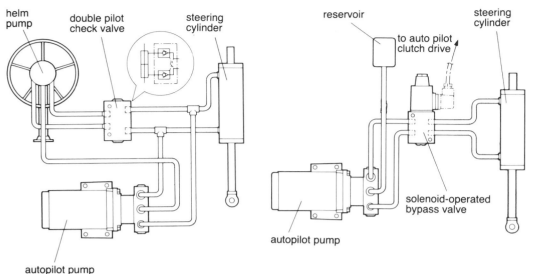

Figure 13-28. Typical hydraulic autopilot circuits. Autopilot teed into existing steering system (**left**). Most helm pumps have built-in check valves, but if these are not fitted, the double-check-valve unit shown will have to be installed to enable the wheel to override the autopilot pump. Independent hydraulic autopilot (**right**). The solenoid bypass valve allows the wheel to override the autopilot, either on command by the helmsman, or if power fails.

spread the stresses. The preferred system incorporates an independent operating lever; this provides a completely independent steering system if the main system fails.

Reduction gear failure (mechanical actuators). In all instances a rudder installation must be so designed that the rudder hits its stops before the autopilot actuator is driven into its stops. Otherwise, powerful following seas can slam the rudder over and destroy the actuator.

Actuator jams. Check all mounting bolts. Full steering loads taken by the actuator require it to be mounted as solidly as any other part of the steering system. Note that unless the quadrant or lever arm on the rudderpost and the actuator are in the same plane (mounted at the same angle), their angle to one another will change as the rudder turns. *The actuator installation must accommodate this changing angle.* If it does not, the unit will jam and/or the actuator will be bent or torn from its mounting.

Hydraulic creep. Hydraulic steering may have a pump teed into an existing hydraulic circuit, or it may have a separate pump, reservoir, and actuator operating an independent lever arm at the rudderpost (the latter being highly preferred; see above).

When an autopilot (teed into an existing circuit) is in use, check valves on the steering-wheel-mounted pump prevent flow through that pump; when the steering wheel is in use, check valves on the autopilot pump close off the autopilot circuit.

If any of the check valves fail to seat properly, the steering will creep (i.e., the rudder will move slowly even when the wheel is locked).

Creep may also be the result of fluid bleeding down the sides of the piston that drives the actuating arm. This can happen in both teed units and independently mounted units.

Hydraulic emergency override. When an *independently mounted* hydraulic unit is in operation, *it is almost impossible to override it.* Such units should have an emergency bypass solenoid remotely controlled from the steering station so that at the push of a button the hydraulic pump is bypassed, restoring full control to the steering wheel (Figure 13-28). The solenoid should be the *normally open* type so that any power failure (and therefore autopilot failure) will *automatically* open the circuit.

Below-deck rotary autopilots.

Alignment, tension, and mounting. As in other installations, full steering loads are taken by the motor. It must be rigidly bolted down with its chain sprocket correctly aligned and chain tension maintained. Any flex in the motor mounts will accelerate chain wear and run the risk of driving the chain off a sprocket.

Centering of chains and rudderstops. In cases where the autopilot drives a length of chain fitted into a cable system, it is obviously essential that the chain be centered over the motor sprocket when the rudder is centered, and that the rudder hit its stops before the sprocket runs onto the chain-to-wire-rope adaptors.

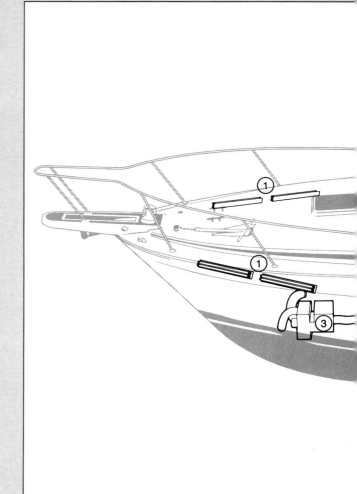

CHAPTER 14

Figure 14-1. Properly maintained, fueled appliances such as these make life aboard a pleasure; poorly maintained they can have quite the opposite effect.

(1) fluorescent lights
(2) incandescent lights
(3) air conditioner
(4) range
(5) water heater
(6) propane tank
(7) propane stove
(8) propane cabin heater
(9) navigation lights
(10) kerosene lantern

Heat- and Light-Producing Fueled Appliances: Stoves, Heaters, Water Heaters, and Lanterns

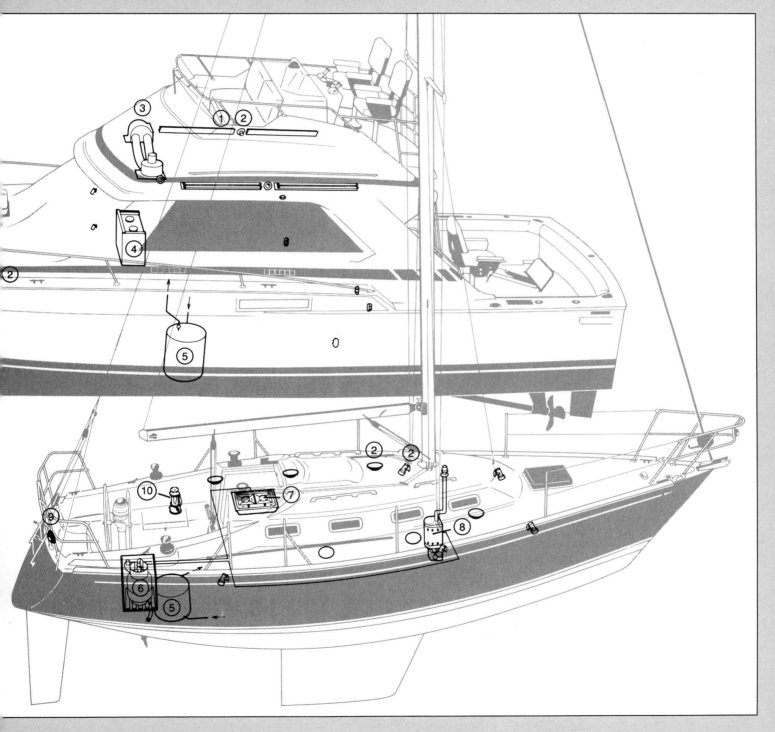

Introduction

The method of burning any given fuel—whether it be electricity, LPG, kerosene/paraffin, or some other—is more or less the same regardless of the appliance to which a burner is fitted. A kerosene stove operates similarly to a kerosene water heater. It therefore makes sense to focus on fuel types and the methods of burning them, rather than on specific appliances (with the exception of some comments on water heaters at the end of the chapter).

Any fuel that produces a flame consumes oxygen when burning and gives off carbon dioxide (CO_2) and water vapor. Boat interiors have little volume, and cabin spaces are well sealed (they must be to be watertight). The oxygen available in a closed cabin can be consumed quite rap-idly. Insufficient oxygen makes the fuel burn improperly and, instead of producing carbon dioxide, it begins to form deadly carbon monoxide (CO).

The combination of oxygen loss and carbon monoxide buildup can be fatal—it has caused a number of deaths over the years. *Always ensure adequate ventilation when burning any fuels;* this includes running diesel engines, which sometimes obtain their air via living spaces in spite of the fact that they should be independently vented. Do not use an appliance for heating unless it is so designed. Never leave a heater on overnight unless it is vented outside the cabin area and adequate air supplies are assured.

Gas

Liquefied Petroleum Gas (LPG) and Compressed Natural Gas (CNG)

The three types of gas in widespread use are propane, butane, and compressed natural gas (CNG). The first two are broadly interchangeable and generally lumped together as liquefied petroleum gas (LPG).

Butane and propane both liquefy at low pressures and temperatures (under 200 psi at 100°F [38°C]). As gas is pumped into a cylinder at ambient temperatures, these pressures are reached quickly. Then, as more gas is pumped in, it liquefies—with temperatures and pressure remaining relatively stable. When a full cylinder is rocked from side to side, the liquid can be heard sloshing around inside. In higher ambient temperatures, pressure in an LPG cylinder will increase somewhat, but never beyond 250 psi; in lower temperatures, it will decrease (for a fuller explanation of these phenomena, see Chapter 10, "Refrigeration and Air Conditioning").

As long as an LPG cylinder is kept upright, there will always be gas at the top, liquid at the bottom, and stable pressures—until the cylinder is almost empty. At this point, the pressure begins to fall as the last of the liquid evaporates.

The principal difference between butane and propane is that the former liquefies at higher temperatures and lower pressures than the latter. In extremely cold weather, liquid butane's rate of evaporation from a cylinder can slow to the point at which appliances fail to work properly. In these conditions propane should be substituted.

Compressed natural gas only liquefies at very high pressures, not found in boat applications. CNG is just that—compressed gas. Consequently, as gas is pumped into a cylinder, pressures rise continuously—a full cylinder at 100°F (38°C) has a pressure of 2,250 psi. As gas is used, the pressure declines steadily.

LPG and CNG are not interchangeable without modification of appliance burners. LPG has a much higher heat output (approximately 21,000 Btus/lb as opposed to approximately 9,000 Btus). Its burners therefore have much smaller orifices than those used with CNG. CNG used in LPG burners will produce less than half the designed output, while LPG used in CNG burners will cause high flames and dangerous overheating.

Safety precautions. LPG and CNG both form dangerously explosive mixtures when combined with oxygen in the air. LPG is considerably heavier than air—gas leaks sink to the bilges. CNG is lighter—leaks rise to the cabintop. A popular fallacy holds that since CNG rises, leaks will dissipate safely through hatches and ventilators. I am living proof that this is not so: I still bear the scars from second degree burns to my face and hands incurred when I was engulfed by a natural gas explosion on an oil platform.

LPG leaks are particularly dangerous on boats: Small leaks can remain undetected in deep bilges. A tiny spark (which can be generated by static electricity on any boat) can blow the boat apart.

Boat owners with gas on board would be well advised to invest in a good-quality "sniffer"—a device that will detect small concentrations of gas (well below the explosion point) and sound an alarm. Be sure that the sniffer is totally enclosed, and that it and all associated wiring and switches are sparkproof. I know of one boat that blew up when the sniffer was switched on for a safety check!

Both LPG and CNG have smelly gases added. Regardless of safety devices, gas "sniffers," and so on, the boat owner with gas on board should place his or her nose regularly into all potential gas-trapping spaces.

Installation practices (Figure 14-2).

Compartment requirements. Gas bottles, both in use and in storage, must be kept well secured in compartments that are sealed from all machinery and living spaces, and vented overboard. LPG compartments need to be vented *from the base,* with a minimum 1/2-inch (13-mm) interior-diameter (ID) vent (preferably 1-inch), *which slopes continuously downward so that no water can form a U-trap, and which ex-*

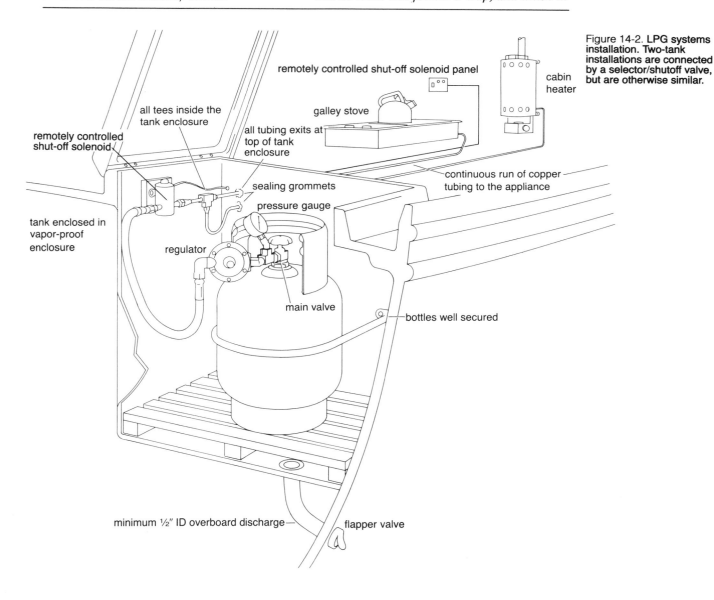

Figure 14-2. **LPG systems installation. Two-tank installations are connected by a selector/shutoff valve, but are otherwise similar.**

remotely controlled shut-off solenoid panel

galley stove

cabin heater

all tees inside the tank enclosure

all tubing exits at top of tank enclosure

remotely controlled shut-off solenoid

sealing grommets

continuous run of copper tubing to the appliance

tank enclosed in vapor-proof enclosure

pressure gauge

regulator

main valve

bottles well secured

minimum ½″ ID overboard discharge

flapper valve

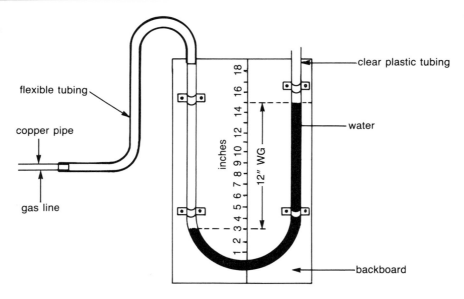

Figure 14-3. A simple, homemade manometer for measuring gas pressure in an LPG system.

Labels in figure: flexible tubing, copper pipe, gas line, inches, 12" WG, clear plastic tubing, water, backboard

its the hull above the waterline at all angles of heel. All gas vents must exit well clear of engine exhausts, ventilators, and air intakes. Gas cylinders must be secured in an upright position: If LPG bottles tip over, *liquid,* instead of gas, might come out—with potentially dangerous results.

Pressure gauge. A pressure gauge should be installed immediately "downstream" from the main cylinder valve and *before* the gas regulator (the valve that reduces cylinder pressure to operating pressure). The gauge then will be measuring *cylinder* pressure—a 300-psi gauge is needed on LPG, a 3,000-psi gauge on CNG. The gauge is an essential leak-testing tool (see "Periodic Testing" below).

Step-down regulator. Regulators should be installed with the vent port facing down so that water cannot collect in the vent and enter the system. Different gases are regulated to different pressures. Measurements are made on the low (downstream) side of the regulator in "inches of water column," using a manometer.

The boat owner can construct a manometer (Figure 14-3) quite simply. Take a board two feet long and a few inches wide. Mark it off in inches. Attach a U-shaped piece of 1/4-inch (6-mm) or larger (the size is irrelevant) clear plastic tubing. This is a manometer. To use it, set it on end, fill it half full of water, and then connect one end to the gas line being tested, leaving the other end open to atmosphere. Open the gas valve.

The gas pressure will push the water up the other side of the manometer. The difference, in inches, between the two columns of water is the pressure of the gas, given in inches of water.

Most LPG appliances are designed to run off a pressure of around 11 inches water gauge (WG, also called water column). Propane can be run a little higher than butane, sometimes up to 15 inches WG. *Pressures should never exceed 18 inches WG.* (ABYC specifications limit LPG systems to 12 inches, 0.433 psi.) *CNG operates at much lower pressures*—6.5 inches WG is normal.

(Note: A manometer is also a very useful engine troubleshooting tool [see Chapter 8]. Hook it into an exhaust line as close to the manifold as possible, after any turbocharger but before any water-lift box or muffler. Turbocharged engines should not show pressures above 20 inches WG; other engines, above 40 inches WG. The latter measurements will require a 3-foot, 6-inch manometer.)

Master shut-off valve. Next should come a normally closed, solenoid-operated, master shut-off valve wired to a remote switch close to the appliance using the gas. The remote switch makes it possible to close off the cylinder (without having to get at it) anytime the appliance is not in use. The cylinder valve still should be closed manually when leaving the boat. Tripping the battery isolation switch will close the master shut-off valve and provide a pretty fair measure of safety for those who forget to

USE LPG FUEL AT 0.433 psi ONLY

1. PLEASE READ INSTRUCTION BOOKLET PROVIDED BEFORE USING THIS GAS SYSTEM.
2. THIS SYSTEM IS DESIGNED FOR USE WITH LPG, LIQUIFIED PETROLEUM GAS (PROPANE OR BUTANE) AT 0.433 psi (7 OUNCES PER SQUARE INCH OR 12 INCHES WATER COLUMN) PRESSURE ONLY.
3. KEEP CYLINDER VALVES CLOSED WHEN BOAT IS UNATTENDED. CLOSE THEM IMMEDIATELY IN ANY EMERGENCY. IT IS RECOMMENDED THAT CYLINDER VALVES BE CLOSED WHEN APPLIANCE IS NOT IN USE.
4. BE SURE APPLIANCE VALVES ARE CLOSED BEFORE OPENING CYLINDER VALVES.
5. TEST SYSTEM FOR LEAKS AT LEAST EVERY TWO WEEKS AND AFTER ANY EMERGENCY.
   THE METHOD OF TESTING IS AS FOLLOWS:
   CLOSE ALL APPLIANCE VALVES.
   OPEN CYLINDER VALVE AND CLOSE IT IMMEDIATELY.
   WATCH THE GAUGE PRESSURE. IT SHOULD REMAIN CONSTANT FOR 15 MINUTES.
   IF ANY LEAKAGE IS DETECTED, CHECK THE ENTIRE SYSTEM WITH SOAPY WATER OR DETERGENT SOLUTION. NO LEAKAGE SHALL BE PERMITTED. PERFORM THIS TEST FOR EACH CYLINDER IN THE SYSTEM.

NEVER USE FLAME TO CHECK FOR LEAKS

(TO BE POSTED NEAR CYLINDERS)

Figure 14-4. **ABYC-recommended warning label for LPG systems.**

close the cylinder valve manually. (Note that although some stove manufacturers suggest the master solenoid valve be installed upstream in the line from the regulator, many solenoids (such as the popular Marinetics) are designed to be installed *downstream* of the regulator as described here. If the valve is to be installed upstream, first make sure it is suitable.)

Tee fittings. If more than one appliance is to be run from one gas cylinder, the necessary tees should be fitted after the solenoid but *still inside the gas bottle compartment.* Unbroken (without fittings), soft copper tubing is run to each appliance.

Securing tubing runs. Any tubing run must be securely fastened at least every 18 inches (50 cm). It needs to be protected from abrasion, flexing, pinching, or knocks where equipment may bounce around in lockers. Where tubing passes through bulkheads or decks, the hole needs to be sealed. Clean, soft copper refrigeration tubing is used for gas plumbing. Connections are made with compression fittings or flare fittings, the latter being preferable. Refer to Chapter 10, "Refrigeration," for installation tips.

Periodic testing. The system should be tested at least every two weeks as follows:

1. Close all appliance valves.
2. Open the cylinder valve and master solenoid valve.
3. Observe the pressure on the cylinder gauge and let it stabilize. Make a note of the pressure.
4. Close the cylinder valve, but not the solenoid valve, and wait 15 minutes.
5. Check the cylinder gauge. *If the pressure has fallen at all there is a leak somewhere.*

Never use a flame for leak testing! Mix a fifty-fifty solution of dishwashing liquid and water; brush this liberally onto all connections between the cylinder valve and the appliance. Any leak will cause the solution to form a mass of tiny bubbles.

Unattended operation. Any appliance designed for unattended operation (e.g., cabin heaters and water heaters) should have a sealed combustion chamber that is

Table 14-1. LPG Cylinder Pressures.[1]

	Ambient Temperature (°F/°C)														
Gas Composition	−30°F −34.4°C	−20°F −28.9°C	−10°F −23.3°C	0°F −17.8°C	10°F −12.2°C	20°F −6.7°C	30°F −1.1°C	40°F 4.4°C	50° 10°C	60°F 15.6°C	70°F 21.1°C	80°F 26.7°C	90°F 32.2°C	100°F 37.8°C	110°F 43.3°C
100% propane	6.8	11.5	17.5	24.5	34	42	53	65	78	93	110	128	150	177	204
70% propane 30% butane	—	4.7	9	15	20.5	28	36.5	46	56	68	82	96	114	134	158
50% propane 50% butane	—	—	3.5	7.6	12.3	17.8	24.5	32.4	41	50	61	74	88	104	122
30% propane 70% butane	—	—	—	2.3	5.9	10.2	15.4	21.5	28.5	36.5	45	54	66	79	93
100% butane	—	—	—	—	—	—	—	3.1	6.9	11.5	17	23	30	38	47

1. Cylinder pressure in psi as a function of ambient temperature and gas composition.

Figure 14-5A. Gas stove burner, showing gas shut-off thermocouple and spark igniter.

thermocouple

spark igniter

Figure 14-5B. The same burner with burner cap removed to show spark igniter, which works (and looks) just like a spark plug.

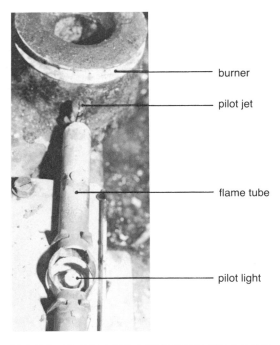

Figure 14-5C. Constantly burning pilot light. When the burner is turned on, gas is directed into the flame tube and ignites.

burner

pilot jet

flame tube

pilot light

externally vented through a flue so that there is complete separation of the combustion chamber from the air in the boat. Stove ovens must have a flame-failure safety device, which cuts off the gas supply

if the oven flame goes out. These measures are designed to prevent gas buildup in the boat.

Troubleshooting Gas Appliances

Gas odors. Immediately extinguish all open flames and smoking materials, close the manual and solenoid cylinder valves, and shut down any engines. Check to see that all appliance valves are closed. Thoroughly ventilate all interior compartments, especially the bilges if LPG is used; do not use any "blowers" that are not sparkproof (ignition protected). LPG can be "bailed" with a bucket or pumped out with a manual bilge pump if the pump is sucking air. When the boat is free of gas odors, perform a leak test as outlined above and fix any leaks.

No gas at an appliance. Make sure the cylinder valve is wide open (counter- or anticlockwise) and check the pressure on the cylinder gauge. If a new cylinder has just been put on, air may have entered the line and will need purging by leaving an appliance valve open. Keep a match or light on the burner so that when the gas starts to come through it will burn and not collect in the boat.

Check the voltage at the master solenoid valve. If the voltage is OK, close the solenoid, loosen its downstream connection, reopen the solenoid, and check for gas coming out of the loosened connection. If there is no gas, the solenoid is defective and needs replacing. After tightening, test the connection for leaks.

The line may be kinked or crushed. Inspect its entire length.

The burner may be plugged, especially on a stove where something has boiled over. Remove the burner cap and unscrew the nipple in the center of the burner (use a deep socket). It may be necessary to remove the burner from the appliance to get at the nipple. Clean out the nipple orifice with a piece of wire.

On stovetops with multiple burners but only one central pilot light, if the thermocouple fails (see "Thermocouples" in this chapter), none of the burners will light.

Some of the newer gas appliances have sophisticated electronic controls that may operate another solenoid valve at the appliance. For example, on-demand water heaters operate when a faucet (tap) is turned on. On older models with a constantly burning pilot light, a flow switch on the water line opens a solenoid on the gas line; on newer models with no pilot light, the flow switch initiates an electronic cycle—first an igniter of some sort is activated, and then the gas solenoid valve is opened. Consult any available manuals. Things to look for are: power to the solenoid valve/electronic panel, and correct polarity. With an on-demand water heater, check the water flow by opening a faucet; the flow switch may be plugged up. Even if the flow is adequate, try jumping out the switch—it may be defective. If the heater has just been installed and never has worked, make sure the hot and cold water lines are hooked up properly.

Igniter fails to work. Light the burner with a match to make sure there is gas flow. If the flame is low, inadequate flow may be the problem (see "Unit Ignites Improperly" later in this chapter).

Three types of igniter are in common use: constantly burning pilot lights, spark igniters, and filament (glow wire) igniters. Pilot lights themselves may be ignited with sparkers or filaments.

Pilot lights. Generally lit by holding in a button and then operating a sparker. If the pilot fails to light, try a match. If it still fails, check the gas supply. The pilot light orifice may be plugged and need cleaning.

If the pilot lights, but fails to ignite the main burner when it is turned on, check for obstructions between the pilot light and burner. If the pilot light is some distance away, there is often a small tube along which the flame must travel, or a hole in the burner surround through which it must pass (Figure 14-5). This may be incorrectly aligned. A low flame height also may be the cause of this problem. To increase the pilot flame height, trace the pilot line to the main valve. There probably will be a screw underneath a cap on this valve; adjust the screw and check flame height. Both procedures (alignment and adjustment) may be necessary.

Spark igniters. Pressing a button moves a magnet rapidly between coils, generating a spark. Some units have a battery; others do not. If fitted, check the battery voltage and connections. The unit may have a remote spark plug with an ignition lead from the sparker. If there is no spark, inspect the lead and its connection. At the pilot light or burner end, there may be a rigid spark plug or flexible terminals. If there is a spark plug, the plug head should be ap-

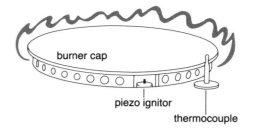

Figure 14-6A. **Typical fuel shut-off thermocouple.**

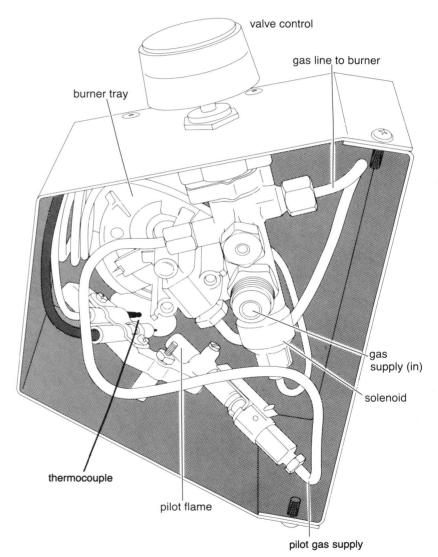

Figure 14-6B. **A mouse's view of a burner assembly.**

proximately $\frac{1}{16}$ inch to $\frac{1}{8}$ inch from the burner rim to which the spark jumps; it may be necessary to adjust its position. If the terminals are flexible, bending the sparker more directly into the gas path may provide more consistent ignition. Note that grease buildup in the area of a sparker will stop it from working.

Filament igniters. A short length of high-resistance wire, the filament, glows red hot, igniting the burner. An external power source is needed, sometimes provided by a flashlight (torch) battery and sometimes the ship's battery (where the unit is electronically controlled). If the igniter fails to work, check the battery voltage and connections (see Chapter 3, "Troubleshooting Electrical Circuits"). To check the filament, *turn off the gas*, remove any covers to provide a view of the igniter, and activate it—it must glow brightly. If the filament is heating up but still fails to ignite the burner, check its position in relation to the gas flow and bend it gently into a better position if necessary. Filaments wear out and should be replaced every one or two seasons.

Unit ignites improperly. Ignition is delayed, and then accompanied by a "pop" and a flare-up. What is happening is that excess gas is collecting, due to the delayed ignition, and then exploding.

Table 14-2. Propane Flow[1] as a Function of Tubing Diameter and Length.

Tubing Length (feet)	Tubing Outside Diameter, Type L (refrigeration tubing; inches)			
	$\frac{3}{8}$	$\frac{1}{2}$	$\frac{5}{8}$	$\frac{3}{4}$
10	39	92	199	329
20	26	62	131	216
30	21	50	107	181
40	19	41	90	145
50	18	37	79	131
60	16	35	72	121

1. Output in thousands of Btus; maximum output at 11 inches W.C., based on a ½-inch W.C. pressure drop in the tubing.
To determine the tubing size you need, measure the distance from the tank to the appliance farthest from it. Add up the total Btu requirements of all the appliances hooked into the system. (With galley stoves, add all the burners and oven together.) For example, if your tubing run is 30 feet and your appliances use 25,000 Btus, use ½-inch outside-diameter tubing.
Note that some safety shut-off solenoids have only ¼-inch ports. When fitted downstream from the regulator, regardless of tubing size, the entire system essentially has been downgraded to ¼-inch—about one-third the figures given for ⅜-inch tubing.

Gas flow over the igniter may be inadequate (see "Inadequate Heat or Flame"). Alternatively, the pilot light flame, igniter spark, or filament heat may be weak or improperly placed (see "Igniter Fails to Work").

Once lit, unit fails to stay on. All units for marine use should have some kind of safety device that closes the gas valve if the flame goes out. By far the most common cutout is a thermocouple, but some electronically controlled units use an optical sensor in its stead.

Thermocouples. A thermocouple is a device incorporating two dissimilar metals that, when heated, generate a very small amount of electricity (on the order of 1½ millivolts). This power is used to open a solenoid valve. If the burner goes out, the thermocouple cools and stops generating electricity; the solenoid valve closes.

A thermocouple must get hot before it works—hence the need to hold the gas valve open manually for up to 30 seconds after a unit lights—until the thermocouple heats up and takes over. If, after this, the unit goes out when the manual override is released, the thermocouple is defective.

Check first that the tip of the thermocouple (a small bulb-like protrusion) is in the center of the pilot light or burner flame (Figures 14-6A and 14-6B). Two wires from the thermocouple terminate in a fitting screwed into the solenoid valve; check that this fitting is not loose. However, do not overtighten it; this will short-circuit the wires and a new thermostat will be needed. If the valve still fails to open, unscrew the wire fitting and clean the terminals with very fine sandpaper (400-to 600-grit wet-or-dry). If the unit still will not stay on line, replace the thermocouple.

Optical sensors. An optical sensor picks up the burner or pilot light flame. Loss of the light from the flame causes the sensor to close a solenoid valve. If the unit will not stay on line, make sure that the optical sensor is clean. Some manufacturers that formerly used optical sensors have found them to be unreliable and no longer use them. Before buying an appliance with this type of cutout, *check its reliability record in actual boat use.*

Inadequate heat or flame. Make sure the cylinder valve is wide open and check the cylinder pressure. Inspect the gas lines for kinking or crushing. If the problem occurs on initial start-up of new equipment, the gas lines are probably undersized. Check the burners for blockages. Make sure any air vents or chimneys are not obstructed. In extremely cold weather, switch from butane to propane. Make sure CNG has not been inadvertently connected to an LPG system. Use a manometer to check the regulator pressure.

Additional safety devices. Various appliances have safety devices in addition to those already mentioned—an oven-temperature cutout or an oxygen-depletion cutout, for example. Almost all are self-resetting when the problem is resolved (i.e., the unit cools down or oxygen levels recover). Consult the manuals.

Alcohol, Kerosene, and Diesel-Adapted Kerosene

Fuel Quality

The vast majority of problems with kerosene (paraffin), diesel-adapted kerosene, and alcohol burning stoves and heaters can be traced to improper or dirty fuel. The orifices in the burners are very small and easily plugged. There are thus two requirements of a fuel:

- It must be spotlessly clean.
- It must contain no contaminants that can form carbon or other deposits in the burner.

We ran a kerosene stove for seven years *without a single blockage* until we ran out of kerosene in Venezuela. We were forced to buy inferior fuel. Within weeks all our burners were plugged. I was cleaning them once a week, then once a day, and finally once every 10 minutes! Then they failed completely and left us without a stove.

Cleanliness. All fuel taken on board needs to be scrupulously filtered through a very fine mesh. In the absence of a suitable filter, use a pair of pantyhose.

Contaminants.

In alcohol. There are a number of different types of alcohol on the market, notably butyl alcohol (butanol), methyl alcohol (methanol or wood alcohol), ethyl alcohol (grain alcohol), and isopropyl alcohol (a synthetic alcohol from petroleum gases, not a fermentation product). *Alcohol stoves are designed to run on ethyl alcohol. Both butanol and methanol have a low heat production and impurities that clog burners.*

Unfortunately for boat users, the taxation of alcohol in drinks is a major source of revenue for all governments. Ethyl alcohol is what is being taxed. In order to free ethyl alcohol, which is available for sale in other applications, of excise duties, it must be rendered unfit for human consumption—a process known as *denaturing*. In the USA, there are currently about 600 recognized ways of doing this, many of which introduce impurities that will plug up stove burners! (Note: Alcohol in liquor also contains impurities and cannot substitute for fuel.)

Straight ethyl alcohol is best as stove fuel, but it is illegal almost everywhere! The common way to denature ethyl alcohol is to add 5 percent methyl alcohol (which forms "methylated spirits"), but then other trace elements are put in. Alcohol stove fuel available at marine stores is 95-percent ethyl alcohol that has been denatured using a process to make it compatible with alcohol burners. Various shellac thinners commonly available in hardware stores are made from denatured alcohol; many of these thinners work well in alcohol stoves.

A simple test of alcohol purity can be made by pouring some in an open dish and lighting it. If there is *any* residue after the fuel has burned away, it is not suitable.

Isopropyl alcohol—the solvent, not the rubbing alcohol —is not readily available but also works well as a stove fuel. It burns hotter than ethyl alcohol, and is slightly smokier. Rubbing alcohol (surgical spirits) cannot be used as fuel because it contains various oils, which will clog burners, and frequently quite a bit of water. Isopropyl alcohol must be a minimum 91-percent concentration to work properly.

For preheating kerosene (paraffin) burners, any 95-percent denatured ethyl alcohol, or 91-percent isopropyl alcohol, will work fine. In the absence of alcohol a small propane torch played over the burner for 30 to 40 seconds works well.

In kerosene (paraffin). The *yellower* the kerosene, the higher its carbon content,

Figure 14-7. Pressure
tanks are an essential
component of the majority
of alcohol and kerosene
burners.

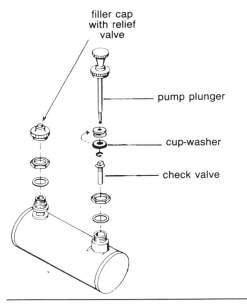

filler cap
with relief
valve

— pump plunger

— cup-washer

— check valve

and the worse it will be as a stove fuel. Ideally, kerosene should be colorless (except where artificial colors have been added, as in Esso Blue). (Note that in Spanish-speaking countries *kerosena* is diesel, while kerosene is *gasolina blanca*, which translates to "white gas").

In the USA, any good-quality, colorless kerosene is OK. In the UK, both "pink" and "blue" paraffin are suitable; in Europe and Scandanavia, Esso Blue and Esso Exsol D 60.

In diesel. The same considerations apply as for kerosene (the two are very similar). Buy the clearest possible. Number 1 diesel is a cold-weather formulation; it is better for stove use year-round.

In all fuels. Old fuel will collect a certain amount of water. Periodically empty all tanks and start again. Three to five percent of isopropyl alcohol in kerosene tanks will take care of any residual moisture.

At low temperatures (below 5°F or − 15°C) kerosene or diesel may separate out, producing a wax that will plug lines, filters, and burners. The addition of 3 to 5 percent isopropyl alcohol also will help to prevent this. Should blockage occur, run neat alcohol through the circuit—without lighting it—to flush out the wax.

Some cruising people add various carburetor cleaning solutions (such as Carb Out) to their kerosene, believing that it prevents carbon formation. Whether it does or not I cannot say, but I certainly know from bitter experience that no amount of additives will handle truly low-grade fuel. *The only way to have a troublefree kerosene stove is to use clean fuel.*

Troubleshooting

The vast majority of alcohol, kerosene, and diesel-adapted kerosene burners have a tank in which fuel is pressurized. Pressurization is achieved by manually pumping with a bicycle pump or small hand pump built into the tank. The pressurized fuel is led to channels set in the burner head. When the burner is primed, the fuel in the burner is heated and vaporizes. The burner is then lit and the fuel *vapor* is burned.

Fuel tanks. Kerosene tanks are pressurized up to 1 atmosphere (approximately 15 psi), alcohol tanks to 6 or 7 psi, by pumping air (15 to 25 strokes on most tanks and pumps). Tanks that use bicycle pumps just have a check valve built into the tank to which the pump attaches. Tanks with integral pumps have a bicycle-type pump built in, with a check valve at its base (Figure 14-7).

Wallas Marin has introduced a kerosene stove line that dispenses with the pressure tank and priming operations. A small pump supplies fuel to the burner and maintains fuel pressure, while a glow wire on the burner generates enough heat to produce initial vaporization. These stoves need a 12-volt hook-up to work: The glow wire will draw about 6 amps for two minutes. In the event of a failure to light, check for voltage drop at the stove during the ignition cycle; see Chapter 3 for this procedure.

Kenyon recently produced an alcohol stove that also does away with the pressure pump and priming. The small tank (enough fuel to burn for one hour) is built into the stove pan. A wick in the center of the burner is lit and heats alcohol in the burner. When this boils, the pressure generated forces vaporized alcohol into the burner where it is ignited by the burning wick. Heat produced by the burner keeps the process going.

Pressure tanks. If a pump bounces back when you pump, or if the pump handle is pushed all the way back out after a stroke, the check valve is not holding.

The check valve is usually a spring-loaded ball. On tanks with external (bicycle) pumps, it is simply unscrewed from the tank. On tanks with integral pumps, the check valve is at the base of the pump cylinder—the piston must be taken out to gain access, and a special long-handled wrench is needed to unscrew the valve (Figure 14-8). This is an essential tool.

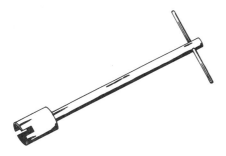

Figure 14-8. An essential tool for boat owners with pressurized fuel systems equipped with integral pumps: a wrench for removing the check valve located at the pump's base.

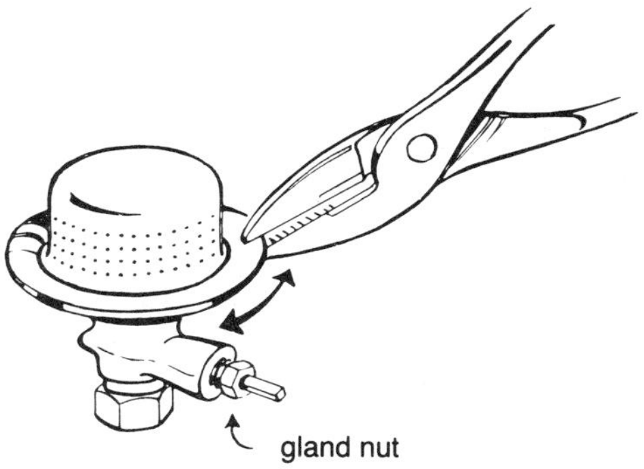

Figure 14-9. **Adjusting the air-to-fuel ratio of an alcohol stove by turning the burner flange.**

gland nut

Examine the valve for dirt on its seat. Clean with a lint-free rag and/or replace as necessary.

Pump cup washer. If the pump requires an excessive amount of stroking to build up pressure, but the tank then holds this pressure, the pump cup washer needs replacing.

To remove the pump cup washer, unscrew the top of the pump and pull the piston straight out. On the bottom, held with a nut and washer, is a dish-shaped leather or neoprene washer, the cup washer. When the pump handle is raised, air is pulled down the sides of this washer. When the pump is stroked, the washer's sides push out and seal on the cylinder wall. The cup washer needs periodic lubrication with a little silicone spray or something similar. Keep a spare on board.

Install the new washer with the sides facing down into the cylinder. In a pinch, a new one can be made from a piece of thin leather cut a little larger than the cylinder bore, bolted to the end of the pump rod, lubricated, and worked down over the lower washer until it can be slid into the cylinder.

Tank filler cap. If the tank loses pressure and needs continual pumping, but the pump handle stays in, the seals around the filler cap or the pump unit are leaking. Some filler caps incorporate a pressure relief valve (safety valve)—this too may be leaking. If the valve can be disassembled, check any seals and make sure the valve seat is clean. If the leak continues, replace the valve.

Burners.

No fuel at the burner. Check for fuel in the tank, for tank pressure, and that any valve fitted in the fuel line is open. Alcohol burners have filters in the burner, which may plug up; kerosene and diesel burners have no filters but some may have a restrictor fitting and others an in-line fuel filter, both of which can plug up.

Yellow smokey flame on start-up. Inadequate preheating is one cause. Shut off the burner, let it cool down, and start again. If the burner is difficult to preheat because of drafts, remove both ends of a three-to four-inch diameter can and place this can around the burner to contain the heat while preheating.

Extremely fierce flames when lit, which then die. The unit has a tank valve that was closed while the tank was under pressure and has not been reopened. The priming process vaporized fuel in the burner and generated very high pressures, which caused the initial fierce flame, but now the fuel is running out.

Priming a pressurized burner with a closed tank valve can build up enough force to blow up the burner. For this reason some manufacturers will not fit tank valves. Even if a valve is fitted, it is far better to bleed pressure off the tank after use rather than close the valve.

Some yellow flames occur during operation. This is a result of improper combustion, either from a lack of oxygen (air) or an excess of fuel.

On alcohol burners, hold the burner flange with a pair of pliers and rotate it slightly to adjust the air-to-fuel ratio (Figure 14-9). On all burners check for obstructions to the air supply (*or exhaust* on vented burners) and, if found, remove them.

Let the burners cool down and then check the outer and inner caps for proper seating—misalignment will impede the airflow. While doing this, inspect the caps for any carbon deposits and clean as necessary.

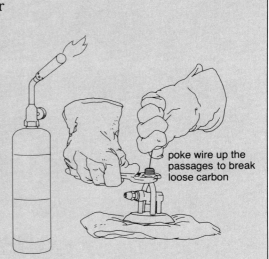

Salvaging a Carbon-Seized Burner

I have used the following procedure with marginal success; it offers a possible means of salvaging a burner when it can't be replaced right away.

Remove the old burner and heat it to a *dull red* on a working burner or with a propane torch. Don't overdo it; burners are silver soldered and brazed together—excessive heat will melt the welds. Let the burner cool slowly, and then poke a piece of wire up all the passages. The carbon should break loose and then can be shaken out.

poke wire up the passages to break loose carbon

Figure 14-10. **Salvaging a carboned-up burner.**

A lack of pressure, blockage in the fuel lines, or excessive restriction of flow with the control knob makes a burner run cool, which can cause improper vaporization of the incoming fuel. Then slugs of unvaporized fuel cause spurts of yellow flame. (Systems without pressurized tanks also can suffer from inadequate pressure; in these systems a lack of pressure signifies a need for a new pump.) Problems exacerbate in colder, draftier conditions.

If the orifice in the nipple is enlarged by improper cleaning, too much fuel comes through and combustion is incomplete. Replace the nipple.

The flame burns correctly but "dances" away from the burner. This signifies too much oxygen (air). Check the outer and inner caps for proper seating. If they are OK, file three or four notches around the bottom edge of the outer cap. The notches allow some air to bypass the combustion process.

Flame gets progressively smaller. Check the pressure; if it is adequate, carbon is plugging the fuel passages, the needle valve, and/or the nipple orifice. Use a screwdriver or a wrench to tap the body of the burner while it is lit, turning the control knob backward and forward. This may well dislodge the carbon, generating a shower of sparks. If the burner has a built-in cleaning needle (or pricker), push it *gently* into the orifice a couple of times. Do not force it—cleaning needles tend to ex-

pand, jam up, and break off in hot burners. In general, use the cleaning needle only on a cold burner. (Note that carbon builds up more quickly when burners run on a low light—run the burners as hot as possible.)

At the first opportunity, dump your fuel and refill tanks with a clean, clear replacement.

Eventually carbon in the fuel passages will plug a burner completely and no amount of normal stripping down and cleaning will clear it out. Since carbon is just about chemically inert, no solvent can remove it; the burners must be junked (but see "Salvaging a Carbon-Seized Burner" in this chapter).

The flame is always too small. Check the tank pressure, the fuel flow, and the burner for carbon formation. If the control knob only turns through 90 degrees, the cleaning needle (pricker) is incorrectly installed (see "Overhaul" section).

The flame surges. The burner is too far from the tank and pressure surges are occurring in the fuel line. Fit a surge restrictor in the base of the burner. Note: Some stoves, such as Shipmates, have a built-in pulsation dampener. This is nothing more than a cushion of air trapped in the stove's fuel manifold. It acts like an accumulator tank on a water system (see Chapter 12) and, just like an accumulator tank, the manifold can lose its air cushion. To replace it: If the fuel tank is above the stove, maintain tank pressure and use the oven until the tank runs out of fuel; if the fuel tank is below the stove, shut off all burners, release the pressure on the tank, and open the oven burner. The fuel will siphon back to the tank and restore the air cushion.

A small flame burns around the control knob. The packing on the handle stem is leaking. Tighten the packing nut. If this fails, replace the packing (see "Overhaul" section).

Burner leaks fuel when not in use. If the knob turns 180 degrees or more, the cleaning needle is incorrectly installed (see "Burner Reassembly"). Otherwise the knob is in the clean position (needle up) rather than closed, or the needle valve is not seated properly and needs replacing (see "Overhaul" section). Never attempt to stop a leak by forcing the control knob—you will only damage the valve or its seat. (This may be why it is leaking in the first place.)

Overhaul

Kerosene and diesel burners are basically the same; alcohol ones are very similar. Before working on any burner, release all tank pressure. If the burner is above the tank, open the burner control knob and allow the fuel line to bleed back into the tank. If the burner is below the fuel tank, close the tank outlet valve (if fitted) or drain the tank, and then break the fuel line loose at the burner and drain it.

Burner removal and replacement. Most burners are factory installed with a high-temperature, thread-sealing compound— the burners can prove quite difficult to undo and even harder to seal up again when put back. Since very few problems require burner removal to solve, *only remove a burner when absolutely necessary.* If a burner must be removed, place a wrench on the flat at the burner base; never apply force to the burner top.

When refitting burners it helps to have a supply of soft —or *annealed*—copper washers, or asbestos washers (copper is better). These can be obtained from Force 10 in Canada, to name just one source. Most diesel engine fuel-injection shops also will have a selection of soft copper washers, since they are used for many sealing applications on fuel-injection systems.

Finally, existing copper washers that have hardened can be annealed by being heated to a cherry red (with a propane torch or another burner) and dropped into cold water. (Note: Some readers will object, since annealing generally is done by heating and cooling *slowly.* Copper has unique properties and requires rapid cooling to anneal properly.)

If the burner has a priming cup, fit a washer on it and then one on the adaptor for the incoming fuel line.

Burner disassembly. Remove the burner's outer and inner steel caps—they pull off. The outer cap may have a retaining wire, which must be removed before the cap can be pulled off. The cap may need to be twisted around until two small retaining tags on the burner body line up with flat spots on the rim of the cap before it can be removed.

Unscrew the nipple. This requires a special wrench (see Figure 14-8). A piece of masking tape stuck in the end of the wrench will grip the nipple and make it easier to lift out.

Open the control knob. This raises the cleaning needle into the nipple opening. Using a pencil with an eraser on its end, push the eraser down onto the cleaning needle. Continue to open the control knob, lifting gently on the pencil, until the cleaning needle comes free.

Take out the spring clip that holds the control knob stem and remove the control knob. Undo the packing nut from the valve stem. Replace the control knob and continue undoing the valve until the valve threads disengage from the burner body. Pull the valve out (if the packing is tight, it may need a pretty good pull). The packing will come with the valve.

Clean all parts and inspect the tapered end of the valve for any "step." This is where it seats in the burner body. If the burner has been leaking when turned off, damage to the valve face or seat is a likely cause. Valve faces and seats are not repairable; when these are damaged, the entire burner must be replaced.

Filter. Kerosene and diesel burners do not incorporate filters, but most alcohol burners do. The filter is likely to be at the base of the burner on the incoming fuel line. Quite possibly another filter is up inside the body of the burner.

Some filters can be pulled out with tweezers or needle-nose pliers. Others are composed of a sintered bronze filter that is

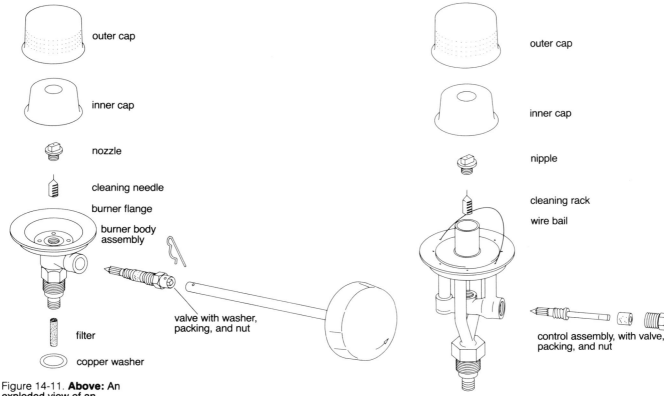

outer cap

inner cap

nozzle

cleaning needle

burner flange

burner body assembly

valve with washer, packing, and nut

filter

copper washer

outer cap

inner cap

nipple

cleaning rack

wire bail

control assembly, with valve, packing, and nut

expanded copper washer

aluminum orifice plate

burner fitting

Figure 14-11. **Above:** An exploded view of an alcohol burner.

Figure 14-12. **Right:** An exploded view of a kerosene burner.

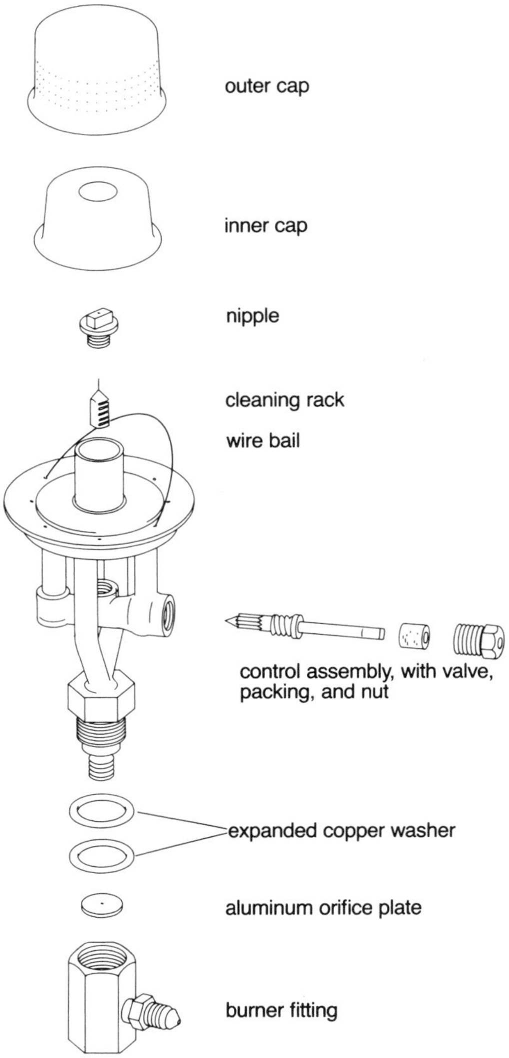

wrapped in a screen and jammed in the burner. These may prove impossible to pull out. The filter will have to be drilled out with great care—it will be soft. The drill bit is liable to pass straight through the filter and damage the burner. It is best to drill a little and have another go at tugging and pulling out the rest of the filter. Select a drill bit slightly smaller than the filter so as not to damage any threads in the burner.

Burner reassembly. All stove manufacturers use burners made by Optimus (Sweden) or Hippolyter (Portugal). Quality is about the same, and burners are broadly interchangeable. However, the gearing on the valve spindles and cleaning needle (pricker) units is different, and the nipples (nozzles) and cleaning needles may be different. So, when mixing parts, keep the valve spindles, cleaning needle units, and nozzles as matched sets. When replacing these parts, stay with the same manufacturer.

Thoroughly clean out all passages, using compressed air if available. Install any filters; sintered bronze filters are wrapped in braid to make a tight fit. Screw a new valve spindle in until it bottoms out in the burner. Push in the valve stem packing,

washers, and packing gland nut. Put the control knob back on the valve stem and replace the spring clip. Tighten the packing nut while rotating the control knob backward and forward until the packing begins to bind on the valve stem. Screw the control knob back in until it is closed.

Look through the hole in the top of the burner and locate the valve spindle gear on one side. Skewer a cleaning needle with the eraser on a pencil and lower it into the burner, its teeth facing the valve spindle gear teeth, until the cleaning needle bottoms out on the gear. Press lightly down on the pencil while slowly undoing the control knob. The valve spindle gear teeth will be felt to bounce on the cleaning needle gear teeth: count four distinct "clicks." (Kenyon stoves have five clicks.)

Slowly screw the control knob back in. It will draw the cleaning needle down into the burner. If it jams, start again. Close the valve all the way and screw the nipple back on with the special wrench.

Open the valve all the way, noting how much the control knob rotates from fully closed to fully open. If it rotates only 90 degrees, the cleaning needle is not down far enough into the burner—start again. If the knob rotates more than 135 degrees (180 degrees on Kenyon stoves), the cleaning needle is in too far and liable to bottom out before the valve closes, causing the burner to leak when turned off—start again.

Diesel "Drip-Pot" Stoves

A valve allows a metered amount of fuel into an open combustion chamber, where it is ignited. Air is provided by natural draft or a fan. The burning fuel heats the combustion chamber until incoming fuel is vaporized. At this point the stove functions similarly to a kerosene or alcohol stove, but without the pressurized tank.

The heart of this kind of burner is the fuel-metering valve—a simple device set up in line with and level with the combustion chamber. The fuel level in the valve determines the (unlit) fuel level in the burner (Figure 14-13).

Because incoming fuel vaporizes on entry into the combustion chamber, the fuel level in the burner is lower than that in the valve. A knob regulates the valve level, and therefore the rate of flow (and heat output of the burner). Raising the valve level increases the differential with the combustion chamber and speeds up the flow rate.

In a boat *the combustion chamber and valve must be in line fore and aft;* if not, every time the boat heels the valve will either be higher than the combustion chamber, causing flooding, or lower, causing fuel starvation.

Valves are designed to operate with a simple gravity feed from a tank. A fuel pump can be used instead, but its output pressure must be low (less than 3.5 psi on Dickenson stoves and heaters) or it will overwhelm the valve and cause flooding.

Given sufficient draft, drip-pot stoves burn cleanly (no black smoke or soot). The stack (also called flue or chimney) must be

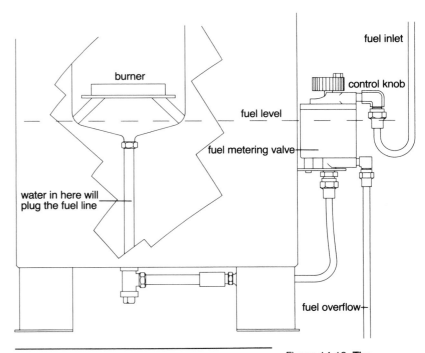

large enough, long enough, and straight up—any bends can cause problems.

One problem I have experienced is water finding its way down a chimney into the combustion chamber. Since water is heavier than diesel, even a few drops sitting in the fuel inlet will act as a plug and prevent diesel entering the chamber—the stove will not light. The water can be soaked up with pieces of tissue paper or sucked out with a vacuum cleaner.

Figure 14-13. **The operation of a diesel "drip-pot" burner.**

Water Heaters and Electric Stoves

If a stove or heater fails to work, first check the fuses, breakers, terminals, and the voltage at the appliance (see Chapter 3). If these are OK, *and only if it can be done safely* (the procedure exposes live terminals; 115 volts is lethal), turn on the appliance and check for voltage at the heating element terminals. If voltage is present, the element is almost certainly burned up; if voltage is not present, the switches, thermostats, and/or wiring are faulty. The following tests also can be made.

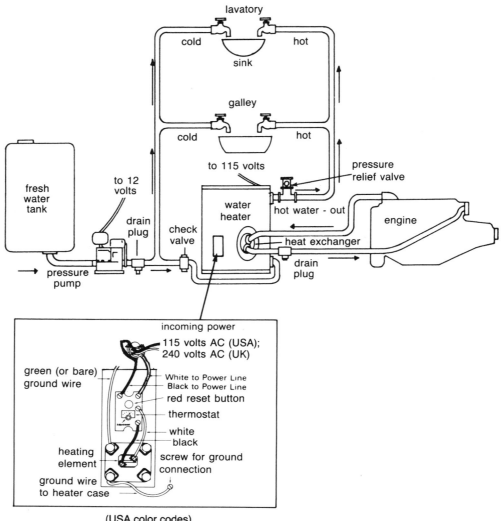

Figure 14-14. **Typical onboard water heater installation.** Water is heated both by the electric water heater and by engine cooling water via a heat exchanger.

(USA color codes)

1. Turn off the power and disconnect the appliance. Set an ohmmeter on the R × 100 scale and check the resistance from each heating element terminal to the equipment case. *Any continuity shows a dangerous short in the element or its wiring.*

2. Now disconnect the heating element: Stove burners simply unplug; water heater elements have two wires; other elements, such as electric toasters, can be broken loose at one end. Test with an ohmmeter (R × 1) across both element terminals. Resistances are typically low (around 12 ohms per kW on 115-volt systems; 50 ohms per kW on 230-volt systems). *An open circuit indicates a burned-out element.*

Troubleshooting Water Heaters

Thermostat testing. Almost all marine heaters have a single element. Check for voltage across the power leads coming into the thermostat (generally at the top). If present, turn the thermostat on "HIGH," press any reset button, and check for voltage at the heating element. If there is none, replace the thermostat. (These tests should be done when the unit is cold; when it is hot, the thermostat may have opened the circuit and cause you to think it has burned up.)

Element burnout. The number one cause is turning on the heater when the water tank is empty. The element will burn out in minutes. *Anytime the heater has been drained, it must be refilled completely before it can be turned on.*

To replace an element, drain the tank and unscrew the burned-out one. Put in a new gasket and then screw in the new element. Check for leaks before replacing covers.

Miscellaneous notes.

The safety valve (relief valve) vents water. Check the thermostat setting—it may be too high. Try reducing it. If the valve still vents, turn off the heater and let it cool. Still venting when cooled? The valve is defective. If the venting stops after the unit has cooled, the thermostat is probably not cutting off.

If the water heater has a heat exchanger and the relief valve (safety valve) vents only when the engine is running, the operating temperature of the engine may be too high for the water heater. (This is known to happen in some freshwater-cooled engines.) Take the water supply to the heat exchanger from a cooler part of the engine cooling circuit.

Constantly dripping relief valve. Trash is probably in the valve seat. Take the valve off and clean it.

On-demand water heater cycles on and off with the water pump. The water system ac-cumulator tank has become waterlogged (see Chapter 12). Restore its air charge.

On-demand heater won't kick on. The flow rate is probably inadequate, or the flow valve on the water heater is clogged. Check for kinked lines and pump problems to correct the flow rate. If the valve is clogged, clean it.

Rusty water. "Glass-lined" water heaters are, in fact, made of porcelain-coated steel. All-stainless heaters are preferred in marine use since in time the porcelain cracks and then the steel rusts. When this happens it is time to replace the heater. Before condemning an old water heater, make sure that it is really the source of the rust. Break loose a connection on the supply side of the heater; if the water here is rusty, the heater is not the culprit. Also consider whether the boat has been through any unusual turbulence lately—the "rust" may be nothing more than sediment stirred up from the bottom of the heater's tank.

Freezing. Freezing destroys any water heater; the tank bursts. Be sure to drain the tank when winterizing. Alternately, add *propylene* glycol antifreeze (which is nontoxic), not ethylene glycol (automotive antifreeze) which is toxic.

Testing Lights

Incandescent Lights

All incandescent lights are resistive loads—that is to say the circuit includes a section of high-resistance wire. As current flows through this wire it heats up and gives off light.

Testing such circuits is straightforward (see Chapter 3). Turn off all power. An ohmmeter set to the R × 100 scale and connected across the light bulb terminals will register a small resistance. If it reads "INFINITY," there is an open circuit—in other words, the bulb is burned up.

Fluorescent Lights

Fluorescents incorporate a transformer (also known as a *ballast*) and a starter—a

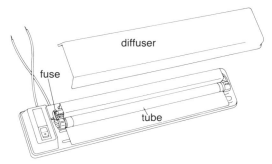

Figure 14-15. **A typical fluorescent light fixture.**

cylinder that plugs into a fixture inside the lamp base. The exception to the rule is 12-volt fluorescents, which do not have starters. If a fluorescent lamp flickers on and off, or will not come on:

Kerosene and "White Gas" Lanterns

Principles of lantern burners are the same as for other pressurized burners. The vapor is burned inside a knit sock or bag called a *mantle,* which becomes white hot, giving off light. Mantles are extremely delicate—the slightest touch will cause them to fall apart.

Mantle replacement is straightforward. Remove all traces of the old mantle, including the asbestos string that was used to tie it on. The new mantle can be handled until first lit. Slide the open end over the ceramic tube in the lantern and tie it on with its asbestos string. Arrange the mantle uniformly around the tube and make sure it is hanging evenly with no major creases (**A**).

Set the mantle on fire (**B**). It will smolder slowly, shrinking and giving off unpleasant fumes as a coating on it burns off (**C**). When all the coating is burned off, the mantle will assume its finished size and shape, and the lantern is ready to use.

After lighting (**D**), a mantle is extremely fragile. Any sudden knocks—even the slightest touch—will cause it to disintegrate (**E**). Although a mantle with just a hole in its side will still give off light, it should not be lit. A hot jet of flame will shoot out of the hole, quite likely cracking the lantern glass.

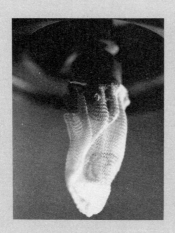

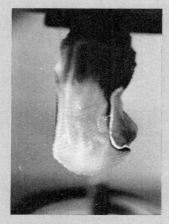

Figure 14-16A-E. Replacing a mantle on kerosene and white gas lanterns.

1. Check the power supply and voltage drop at the appliance as always.
2. Switch off the unit, remove the tubes, clean all contacts and pins (with a clean rag or 400-to 600-grit wet-or-dry sandpaper) on the light fixture and tubes, replace the tubes and try again. Tubes are removed by twisting through 90 degrees and pulling down gently.
3. Still no light? Try a new tube. If the unit has more than one tube, replace all tubes.
4. Still no light? Try a new starter if the unit incorporates one.
5. Still no light? Replace the ballast. The new one will have a wiring diagram with it, or one will be glued to the lamp base.

Fluorescent lights wear out: The more frequently they are turned on and off, the more quickly they wear out. This is more of a determining factor than the amount of time they remain on. Single-tube fluorescents are likely to cause more radio interference than double-tube units, but all can cause problems (see Chapter 7, "Interference").

Quartz Halogen Lights

Most navigation lights on new boats now use quartz halogen lights since they provide more light for less amp draw. These bulbs are extremely delicate and must be handled with care (especially at $10 to $15 a lamp!). *Do not touch the bulb*—always grip it in a piece of paper. The bulbs are simply pulled out of their sockets or pushed in—no twisting needed. Each quartz halogen bulb has two wires that stick straight out; be sure the wires are straight before fitting a new bulb. At the base of the bulb is a small indentation that will mate up with a spring clip in the fixture to hold the bulb in place.

CHAPTER 15

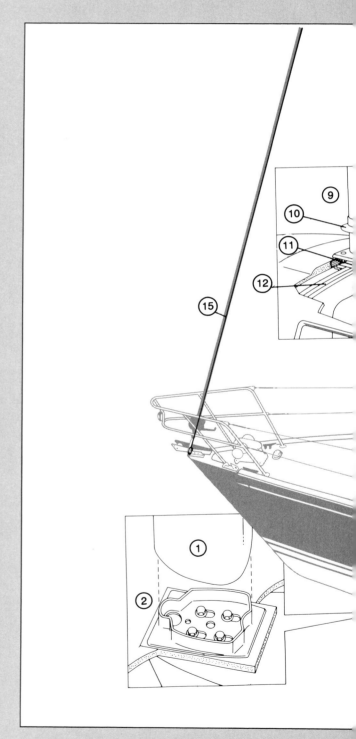

Figure 15-1. **Keeping masts aloft is a product of proper design, installation, maintenance, and tuning.**

   (1) keel-stepped mast
   (2) mast step
   (3) chainplate
   (4) backstay
   (5) boom
   (6) spreader
   (7) upper shroud
   (8) lower shroud
   (9) deck-stepped mast
(10) boot
(11) backing plate
(12) bulkhead
(13) babystay
(14) turnbuckle
(15) forestay

Spars and Standing Rigging

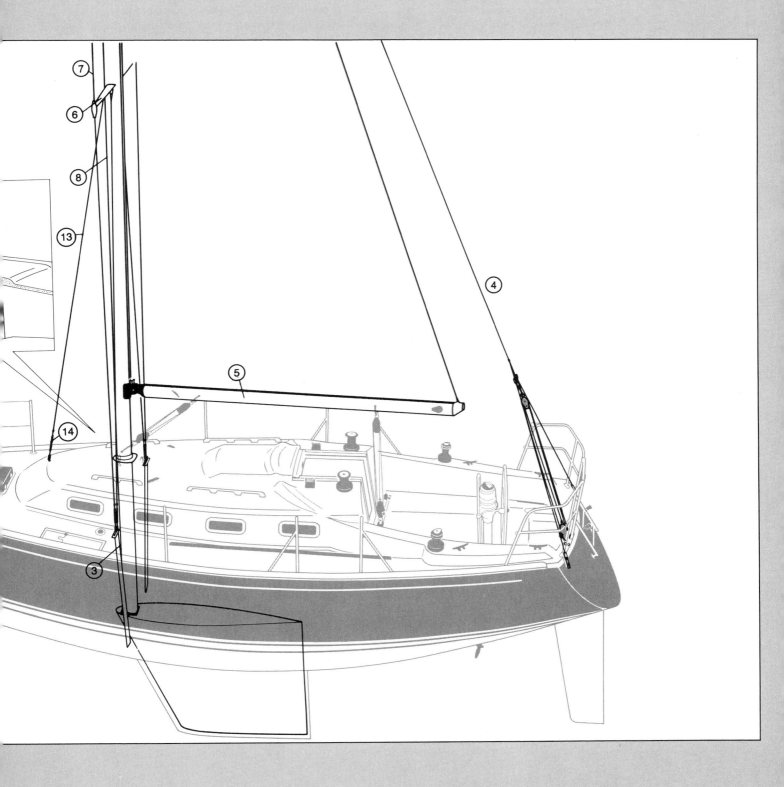

Spars

Wooden Spars and Spreaders

Wooden spars, especially when varnished, are a high-maintenance item. All masts, booms, and spreaders need regular close inspection for telltale signs of delamination and rot, and will need repainting or revarnishing at least every few years, probably every year if varnished and kept in the tropics.

Construction. In the days when labor was cheap, very fine round and oval spars were constructed. The procedure was to laminate a hexagon or octagon, and then round out the corners. Nowadays wooden spars are almost invariably a box section, which is much less labor intensive and far easier to clamp up. The occasional mast will incorporate a double-box section, with the outer box laminated to the inner one (Figure 15-2).

Since no planks will be long enough to run the complete length of a mast side, several planks must be joined together. The usual joint is a simple *scarf*, in which a taper is cut in both boards and the two glued together (Figure 15-3A). The taper should have a "slope" (ratio) of at least 1:8, i.e., with a board one inch (25 mm) thick the taper should extend over a length of eight inches (20 cm). The feather edge of the taper is weak and susceptible to damage until it is glued up; sometimes it is squared off (Figure 15-3A), but this is a more difficult and time-consuming joint to execute properly and is not often done. In the finished box spar, the scarf joints in the four sides must be staggered up and down the length of the spar so that no two are in

close proximity. The exterior tapers should be pointing down so that water cannot work into the joint.

Some spars are hollow from top to bottom, with just a blocking piece at the head to keep water out of the masthead fittings. Such a spar tends to distribute loads evenly over its whole length. Many spars include additional internal reinforcement (blocking) at the spreader-attachment points and the base (Figure 15-3B). In any event, such blocking should always be tapered at top and bottom to eliminate "hard" spots that would tend to concentrate stresses. The

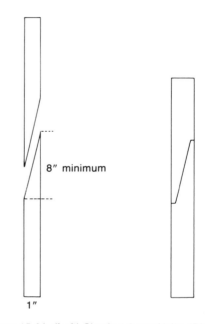

Figure 15-3A. **(Left)** Simple 1:8 scarf joint. **(Right)** Squared-off scarf joint.

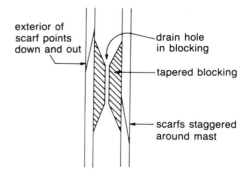

Figure 15-3B. **Details of proper wooden mast construction.**

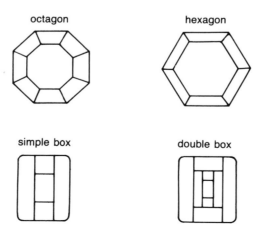

Figure 15-2. **Wooden mast construction.**

blocking also must provide a free passage for water to drain out.

Plastic resin, resorcinol, and epoxy glues are all used. To be effective, the first two require very close fits in all the joints—they have no gap-filling properties. Epoxies are more tolerant. Resorcinol leaves an unsightly dark purple glue line at joints. In the event of having to make repairs, a suitable epoxy (e.g., WEST System; System Three; or SP) is probably the best bet.

All wood spars should be treated internally with fungicide. While external rot can normally be found and repaired before a failure occurs, internal rot is an undetectable time bomb waiting to bring the rig down. If in doubt about your spar, the next time it is unstepped pour a gallon of rot-proofing agent (e.g., Cuprinol) into it, and slosh it gently from end to end, rotating the spar periodically, until the wood is thoroughly saturated.

Paint or varnish. Varnished spars on a traditional boat look beautiful, but they do require an enormous amount of work, especially in hotter climates. Even the most expensive varnishes with ultraviolet blockers will hold up no more than two years in the tropics, normally only one. (We just scrape by for two years on our spars and we apply 15 coats of varnish!) The topsides of spreaders will *never* go more than a year, and are frequently cracking and peeling within a few months. This admits moisture, which then is trapped by the intact varnish on the undersides and inboard ends of the spreaders; thus rot rapidly develops. In my opinion, this makes a strong case for painting, rather than varnishing, the upper spreader surfaces.

Aside from looks, varnish does have one other major advantage—any water that penetrates the varnish is immediately apparent as a dark stain in the wood below. Failures with painted surfaces are far less obvious—the paint generally has to blister or the wood become spongy (in which case rot is well advanced) before problems are noticed. Painted spars will, however, hold up for as long as five years between coats, especially with many of the newer paints.

Danger areas.

Fasteners. Any fastener, even when properly bedded but especially when improperly bedded, is a potential source of water ingress and thus rot. The loads that

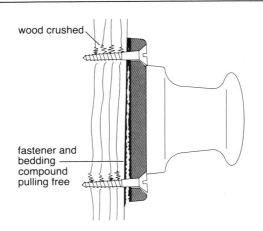

Figure 15-4. Fasteners subjected to excessive loads, such as those holding this halyard winch, can crush the wood surrounding them, allowing fasteners to loosen further and water to penetrate.

wood crushed

fastener and bedding compound pulling free

modern rigs impose on fittings, combined with undersized or insufficient fasteners, frequently will cause the fasteners to crush surrounding woodwork. The fastener loosens, bedding compounds pull free, and water wicks in (Figure 15-4). Loose hardware is a sure sign of trouble, but the wood surrounding even securely fastened hardware should be inspected closely, at least annually, for signs of deterioration.

Where problems are being experienced with excessive loads on the wood, the Gougeon Brothers (manufacturers of WEST System epoxies) have shown that an effective answer is to drill an oversized hole, fill this with epoxy, and set the fastener in this epoxy plug. The epoxy penetrates and bonds to the surrounding wood and, with a considerably larger surface area than the original fastener, dissipates the loads on the fastener over a much greater area.

Several years ago, after ripping a couple of cleats off our mast and an outhaul track off a boom, we rebedded all the hardware using the Gougeon Brothers' techniques. Since then the only problem came when I wanted to move a couple of cleats—I had to cut them off with an angle grinder! Perhaps some grease on the threads would make it possible to back out the fasteners later.

The specific procedure is as follows (see Figure 15-5):

1. Drill a pilot hole to the depth of the fastener.
2. Drill the oversized hole to a little *less* than the depth of the fastener.
3. Fill the hole with epoxy and top up as the wood soaks it up. On vertical surfaces, first wet out the hole (a pipe cleaner works well) and then thicken

Figure 15-5. For longest life, fasteners subjected to high loads should be bedded in epoxy. Detailed instructions are in the text.

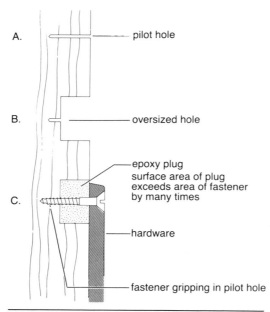

A. — pilot hole

B. — oversized hole

— epoxy plug
surface area of plug exceeds area of fastener by many times

C. — hardware

— fastener gripping in pilot hole

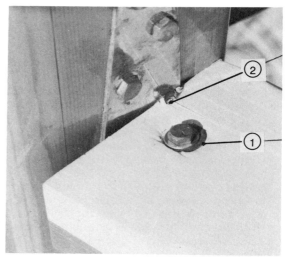

the epoxy with microballoons or talc—as much as is needed to stop the glue draining out. In a pinch, talcum powder works well as a thickening agent.

4. Clean the fastener (acetone works well) and install it when the epoxy begins to gel. The section of fastener that runs down into the pilot hole (at the bottom of the oversized hole) should provide just enough grip to snug up the fastener until the glue sets.

Interestingly enough, the Gougeon Brothers also have shown convincingly that on most applications a stainless steel machine screw makes a much stronger fastener than either a regular wood screw or a self-tapping screw. Their book, *The Gougeon Brothers on Boat Construction,* is a gold mine of useful information for anyone with extensive woodwork in his or her boat.

Exit holes: *Any* exit holes for electric cables or halyards are likely to let in water sooner or later. The worst case is where a cable runs down into a mast, providing a perfect path for water to trickle in. All cables should have drip loops where they exit the mast, and the exit holes should be angled downward (Figure 15-8).

Base of spreaders: As noted previously, the upper faces of wooden spreaders are notorious for letting in water, which drains down into the spreader bases (due to the angle of the spreaders) and becomes trapped. Another common source of

Figure 15-6. How *not* to install a spreader. These are top and bottom views of a spreader installation on a *brand new mast.* (1) No upper spreader plate. The wood is crushed already, and is sure to soak up water and rot. Any up-or-down loading on the spreader will bend the mounting bolt and crush the wood further. (2) The single bolt has allowed the spreader to rotate and crush its inner face. Note the split in the grain, already extending up the spreader. (3) As the bolt works against the upper spreader face, it will embed itself and loosen. The lock washer will exert no tension. (4) The nylon locking ring of the Nyloc nut engages no threads and therefore will not lock. This spreader is likely to fail before long, bringing the mast down with it.

spreader problems: the holes through the spreaders for mounting pins. As often as not the spreader hardware consists of a stainless steel plate fastened on the top and bottom sides with two clevis pins passing through both the plates and the spreader. Water can run down the pins and into the spreader.

This problem with spreader mounting holes is easily cured in one of two ways: (1) Remove one of the plates, drill oversized holes in the spreader, fill with epoxy, and allow to set. Then replace the plate and drill through the epoxy plug for the clevis pins (Figure 15-7 top). (2) Design the spreader-mounting bracket so that the wood does not protrude into the area of the clevis pins (Figure 15-7 bottom).

Base of the mast: With both deck-stepped and keel-stepped masts, the heel fitting is a notorious source of dampness and rot. It must be designed to allow any water running down either inside or outside the spar to drain away and also to provide a free flow of air around the heel. The heel fitting needs regular close inspection.

Mast partners: On keel-stepped masts, mast partners can be the source of problems for similar reasons as above—dampness and poor air circulation.

Masthead: Problems can develop on uncapped masts, or masts with improperly sealed head boxes. On many traditional rigs the stays and cap shrouds are looped around the masthead and supported by blocks of wood on the mast side (Figure 15-8A). The masthead itself is bare. The end grain *must* be properly capped, a function traditionally served by sheet copper or a wooden disc. Even if the rest of the spar is varnished, paint the top few feet for added protection—it will look perfectly shipshape.

Other spars have masthead boxes incorporating halyard sheaves and attachment points for stays and shrouds (Figures 15-8B and 9). Older designs tend to be let into and attached to the sides of the spar, leaving exposed woodwork. Newer spars sometimes have an all-purpose head box, which simply drops over the top of the mast. In the latter case, the head box must be sealed (i.e., welded shut with a plate) below the sheaves so that no water can ever make its way down into the spar. Electric cables that are run internally in the mast can exit the spar below the head box and run up its outside rather than upset its watertight integrity. For maintenance and overhaul of head boxes, see the relevant section later in this chapter.

Sprung seams: Over time the constant flexing of a mast as it works may weaken and eventually crack some of the glue

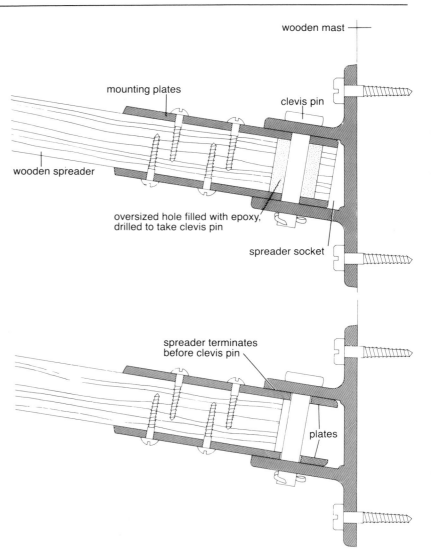

Figure 15-7. Two superior approaches to spreader base fittings. Contrast these with the example shown in Figure 15-6. (**Top**) A clevis pin mounted through an epoxy plug. (**Bottom**) Top and bottom spreader plates extended past wooden spreader.

lines. This is more likely if the mast is improperly tuned (excessive mast bend; slack rigging—see section later in this chapter). I even know of one case where a direct lightning strike opened up seams.

Bowsprits: These are prone to rotting in three distinct areas:

1. At the tip where the "cranse iron" (the bobstay and headstay hardware) attaches;

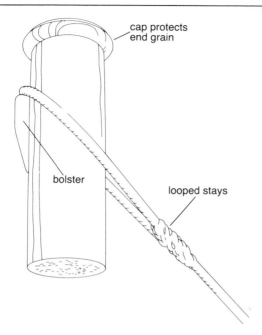

Figure 15-8A. **Traditional masthead attachments.**

cap protects
end grain

bolster

looped stays

Figure 15-8B. **Wooden spar with head box.**

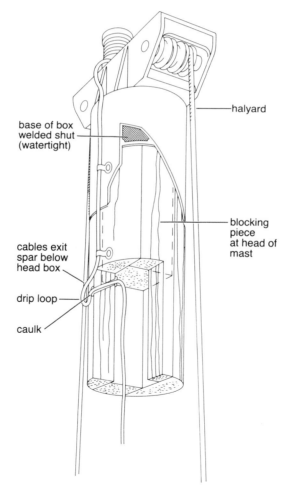

halyard

base of box
welded shut
(watertight)

cables exit
spar below
head box

drip loop

caulk

blocking
piece
at head of
mast

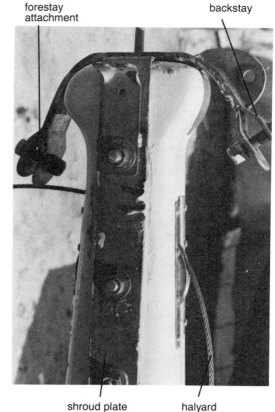

forestay
attachment

backstay

shroud plate   halyard

Figure 15-9. **Wooden spar with external masthead hardware.**

2. At the bow of the boat where there is generally another collar of sorts;
3. At the butt block or bitts.

It really is essential to remove all the hardware periodically (every few years) and closely inspect the wood beneath. The loss of a bowsprit endangers the whole rig, and it is not worth taking chances.

Repairs. One of the principal advantages of wooden spars is that they can be repaired, generally being returned to an as-good-as-new condition.

Anytime the protective paint or varnish layer is damaged, it should be patched up as soon as possible (as long as the underlying wood is dry). Lin and Larry Pardey, widely published cruising sailors, carry a finger-nail polish jar (the kind with the brush attached to the underside of the lid) filled with varnish. Whenever they have a minor scratch, they can paint over it immediately, without the fuss of digging out varnish cans, brushes, and brush cleaner.

Since the brush is kept in the jar, it doesn't need cleaning. An excellent idea.

Small areas of damage to spars are treated by chiseling out the affected area and cutting an insert to fit. Preferably the insert, or Dutchman, should be made of the same kind of wood with the grain running in the same direction.

Large areas of rot or damage must be cut back to clean wood. Fresh planks then are fitted in. As often as not the hardest part of a major repair is finding an adequate bench to support the spar and enough clamps to fit the new pieces (which should be clamped at least every 12 inches).

The important steps to remember are to:

1. Keep the scarf-joint ratios at or above 8:1;
2. Stagger the joints around the spar;
3. Have the outsides of joints pointing down;
4. Treat interior surfaces with an anti-rot solution;
5. Taper all internal blocking;
6. Find out what caused the problem in the first place and fix it!

Aluminum Spars and Spreaders

(In the following sections on aluminum spars, I am greatly indebted to David Potter of Kemp Spars and his book, *The Care of Alloy Spars and Rigging*, published by Grafton Books under the Adlard Coles imprint.) When set up right, modern aluminum spars are long-lived and almost maintenance-free. However, the failure to carry out the little maintenance required, or to spot and rectify danger signals on just one fixture, can result in the loss of a whole rig, potentially threatening both boat and crew.

Construction. Aluminum spars are *extruded*—that is to say molten aluminum is pushed through a mold, cooling and gelling as it goes. The interior parts of the mold are held in place by metal rods attached to the exterior parts of the mold. The aluminum has to flow around these retaining rods and reform on the other side.

The extrusion is tempered, or hardened, in the process. (Tempering of metals, with the exception of copper, which behaves in reverse of most metals, is done by raising the metal to a high heat and then cooling it rapidly.) The upper section of most masts then is progressively tapered. This is done by cutting a section out of the extrusion, bringing the halves together, and welding them back up. However, the welding process reheats the metal around the weld and then allows it to cool relatively slowly. This effectively undoes the tempering in the area of the weld, softening the metal. (This process is known as annealing—once again copper works in reverse, being hardened by heating and slow cooling.) Quality spars are tempered *after* the tapering.

Some masts have various fixtures welded in place, such as the head box, spreader sockets, winch bases, and halyard exit boxes. This is not really a good idea because welding makes the mast soft in these areas. The mast is now *anodized* or painted.

Anodizing or painting. Aluminum is notoriously hard to coat. The surface oxidizes very rapidly (which gives it that typical grey appearance of untreated metal) and surface coatings will not adhere to the oxidized metal.

Once the initial oxidation has occurred the surface becomes relatively stable. Apart from its unsightliness and the fact that it leaves grey deposits on sails and halyards, untreated aluminum works fine for spars (many European aluminum boatbuilders leave their hulls bare). Surface coatings are therefore largely cosmetic.

Anodizing electrochemically builds up a hard protective coating both *within* the surface metal of the aluminum and on it (as opposed to paint, which only sits on the surface). When anodizing, the *inside* of the mast also is treated, though not to the same extent as the outside. Should an anodized surface become scratched or damaged it cannot be reanodized—the best thing to do is to clean the bare metal and then polish it with a good-quality, liquid-silicone polish (for cars or boats).

In order to get paint to key into aluminum, the surface first must be cleaned and microscopically roughened to improve the adhesion of the paint. This can be done with sanders but generally is done by treating with phosphoric acid, which eats into—etches—the surface of the metal, removing oxidation in the process. This acid is washed off and the bare metal immediately treated with a zinc chromate primer, which inhibits fresh oxidation. The paint is applied as soon after as possible to seal the surface—generally with primer of two-part epoxy followed by one of the new two-part linear polyurethane top coats (e.g., Awlgrip; Imron; Interthane Plus).

Damaged painted areas can be restored by the owner using the same steps. Various companies (e.g., the Gougeon Brothers) market aluminum "pre-bonding" kits with the necessary acid for etching, zinc chromate primer, and instructions for use. Some of the linear polyurethanes also are available for application by brush. (Observe all safety warnings—these paints are hazardous!) The resulting touch-up job will not match an original sprayed finish, but can come close.

In any event, painted masts will need repainting sooner or later, whereas anodizing generally lasts for the life of the spar. Another advantage to anodizing is that it will show up stress areas (the anodizing takes on a crazed pattern or goes dull white) more clearly than painted masts (Figure 15-11).

Danger areas. Welds: As stated, during the extrusion process aluminum spars are hardened. Any welding causes localized softening (annealing) of the extrusion. Vertical welds up and down a spar (e.g., for tapering) present no great problems, but any welds *around* the spar produce a weak section prone to buckling. Notable in this respect are welded spreader sockets,

Figure 15-11. **Stress patterns show up clearly on an anodized aluminum mast.**

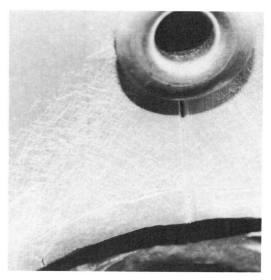

especially where the sockets wrap a good way around the spar.

Any clustering of welded fittings, winch bases, or the like around one area of the mast will produce a weak section. Welding shroud tangs can soften the tangs: Flexing of the shrouds will lead to fatigue and failure. Excessive heat when welding in head boxes will sometimes soften the metal where the forestay and backstay toggles attach, and thus lead to failure.

All welded fixtures should be inspected regularly and carefully for any signs of cracks around the welds or deformation of the fixture or mast wall.

Hardware and fasteners: Aluminum is fairly well down the list in the table of noble metals (see Chapter 4). Most hardware and fasteners are well up (e.g., bronze and stainless steel). Add a little salt water and you have excellent conditions for galvanic interaction.

Figure 15-12. **Dissimilar metals used to mount hardware can cause galvanic corrosion problems on aluminum masts. Grease fasteners well, and regrease annually.**

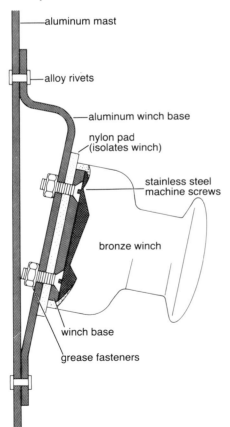

aluminum mast

alloy rivets

aluminum winch base

nylon pad (isolates winch)

stainless steel machine screws

bronze winch

winch base

grease fasteners

Larger items of hardware *must* be insulated from the spar with a nylon or similarly electrically inert pad (Figure 15-12). Where this is impractical, a zinc chromate paste between the hardware and mast wall will help protect the aluminum, serving in the same manner as a sacrificial zinc anode.

Fasteners present special problems. Alloy rivets are compatible with aluminum but will be rapidly eaten away if in contact with more noble metals. They work well for fastening aluminum spreader brackets, winch bases, exit boxes, and so on, but cannot be used on stainless or bronze hardware. These items generally are attached with Monel rivets or stainless steel self-tapping and machine screws.

Stainless steel fasteners should be greased to slow corrosion, but essentially nothing will stop it. Sooner or later oxidized aluminum will build up around the fastener and freeze it in place—attempts to remove it will likely just shear off the head. Since aluminum oxide has a greater volume than the original aluminum, sometimes enough pressure is generated to break fasteners without any outside help!

If it is ever likely that the fittings held in place with stainless steel fasteners will need to be removed (e.g., boom ends with internal lines and fittings), the fasteners should be pulled annually and regreased to prevent them from becoming locked in place. (Although rarely done, corrosion on through-bolts can be slowed to an absolute minimum by placing the fasteners in a nylon sleeve and using nylon washers under the nuts. The problem is that under high loads the nylon is likely to collapse, which means insulating fasteners in this fashion has limited applicability.)

Spreaders and spreader sockets: Spreaders are either round tubes or have an airfoil ("streamlined") cross-section. The former are designed for compression loads only and must not be forced backward and forward, or up and down. The latter will take some fore-and-aft loading and are used where bends are induced in the mast to improve sailing performance, but once again they will take very little up-and-down loading.

In order to avoid up-and-down loads, *spreaders must be set up to bisect the angle of the shroud they support,* and then the spreader ends must be *locked in this position.* On double-spreader rigs where two shrouds pass over the lower spreader, that spreader

Figure 15-13. **Aluminum mast repairs.** This boat fell over in the yard, crushing the mast at the spreaders. The ruined section of mast was cut out and a new section spliced in.

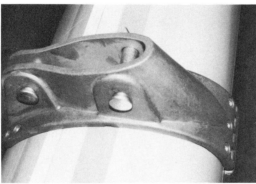

splice   new section   splice

must be set up to bisect the angle formed by the *lower* shroud. It is amazing how many boats violate this rule, risking a collapsed spreader and the loss of the whole rig. If the spreader tips have no locking devices, cable clamps can be placed around the shrouds above and below the spreader.

Some spreaders (normally tubular ones) are "flexibly" mounted with a limited swing fore and aft to relieve stresses created by flexing masts and rigging. Most spreaders, however—particularly airfoil-section spreaders—are rigidly mounted. Unfair loads can be generated by excessive mast bend, the pumping action of slack

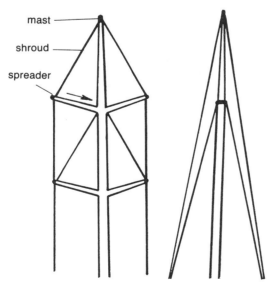

Figure 15-14. **This excellent type of spreader socket distributes the spreader's loads over a substantial area of the mast.**

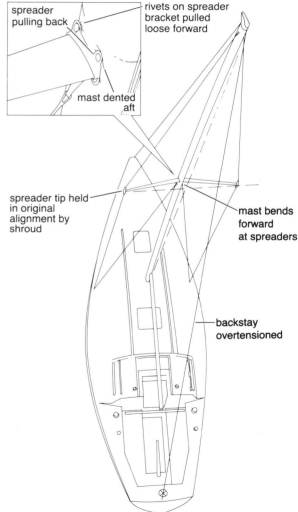

spreader pulling back

rivets on spreader bracket pulled loose forward

mast dented aft

spreader tip held in original alignment by shroud

mast bends forward at spreaders

backstay overtensioned

Figure 15-16. **Effect of excessive mast bend on spreaders.**

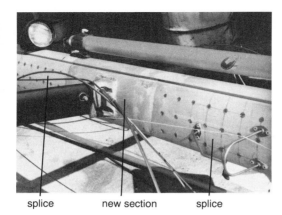

mast

shroud

spreader

Figure 15-15. (**Left**) Correct spreader installation. All loads are compression loads transmitted directly to the mast. (**Right**) No spreaders. This configuration gives very little support to the masthead because of the narrow angles between shrouds and mast. The taller the mast, the narrower the angles.

lee-side rigging, or allowing a mainsail to bear against the spreaders when running downwind.

The most excessive fore-and-aft loads generally arise as a result of cranking down on a backstay adjuster, causing the mast to flex forward at the spreaders. The spreader sockets try to pull free of the mast wall on the forward edge and to compress the mast on the aft edge. Look for cracked welds or loose rivets on the front face, and dented mast walls to the rear. Any damage is going to require a specialist's attention.

Semiflexible tubular spreaders frequently bear on a hardened rubber pad in the base of the spreader socket. If excessive play is evident, check this pad and replace it if it is damaged or perished.

Cutouts: Aluminum spars inevitably have a number of holes cut into them for various fittings (e.g., exit boxes) and access hatches. These must never be concentrated in any one area or severe weakening of the spar will result. All cutouts should have rounded corners to reduce stress concentration. If cracks start to radiate out from corners, they can be halted temporarily by drilling a small hole (up to ¼ inch or 6 mm) at the point of the farthest extension of the crack (Figure 15-17). Keep loads on the rig down.

Mast heels: Mast heels are particularly susceptible to corrosion. Keel-stepped masts are down in the (generally damp) bilges, while deck-stepped masts are subject to constant saltwater spray. The mast step needs to be kept drained and ventilated. Periodically washing off salt will slow down corrosion. Stainless fasteners should be pulled and greased annually.

Maintenance and overhaul. *Masthead boxes:* Modern masthead boxes integrate halyard and topping-lift sheaves, masthead electrical equipment mounts, cap shroud tangs, and forestay and backstay attachment points into one neat and seaworthy package.

On aluminum spars the head box is open at its base to allow electric cables, halyards, and topping lifts to be run inside the mast. On wooden spars the box should be sealed below the sheaves to keep water out of the mast.

Head boxes are either welded in place or bolted. The latter have the significant

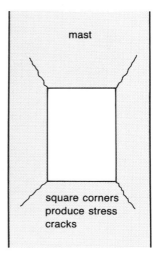

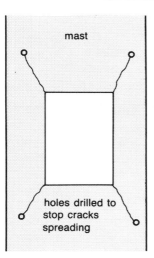

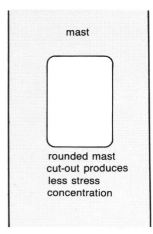

Figure 15-17. **Mast cutouts. To prevent severe weakening of the mast, these should be well staggered.**

advantage that the whole box is fairly easily removed for overhauling sheaves (see Figure 15-18).

If halyards become recalcitrant, it is important to go aloft and find out why as soon as possible. Salt crystals will plug masthead sheaves just as they will freeze up deck-level blocks. Attempts to free a sheave by dragging a halyard over it will only score the sheave and abrade the halyard. Slack off all the halyards. Once aloft, check all the sheaves for free movement. Flex the sheaves up and down; there should be no binding nor any undue play.

Removal of sheaves: This is straightforward enough, but there is always the risk of dropping parts down inside the mast. The first step therefore, is to tape a piece of line to each sheave, turn the sheave until the line can be pulled out the

head box assembly

head box installed

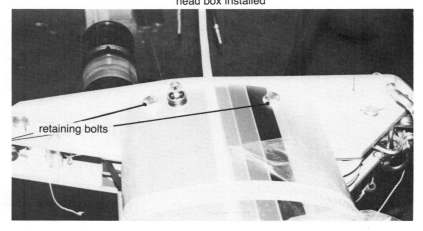

retaining bolts

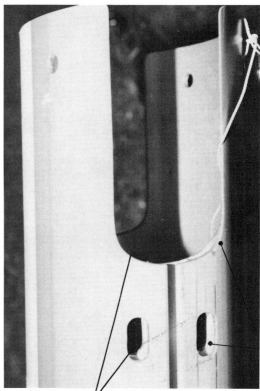

note well rounded cut-outs

Figure 15-18. **Removable head box, which fits into the U-shaped cutout in the mast.**

other side, and then tie the sheave off securely. The sheave pins are held in place by small plates screwed to the box on either side or by cotter pins (split pins). These plates or cotter pins are removed and the sheave pin driven out, using a punch and hammer if necessary. The sheaves then can be withdrawn with the lines already tied around them. Clean and inspect the sheaves and pins. Before replacing, lubricate with a light machine oil or penetrating oil (WD-40, etc.).

Replacing halyards: It is important to maintain a free fall inside the mast and not to tangle with other lines. First set up all other halyards tightly to hold them in their normal alignment; next attach a short length of light chain as a weight to a messenger line and feed it over the appropriate sheave at the masthead. Feed the messenger line down into the mast, and retrieve the chain at the base through the appropriate exit hole using a piece of bent

coat hanger. Tie the messenger line to the halyard and use it to pull the halyard up through the mast. The same technique is used for running electric cables inside the internal conduit. Note: When not in use halyards should be secured so that they don't slap on the mast continually. Apart from the irritation of the noise, sooner or later this action will wear through anodizing or paint.

Spinnaker halyards: These are generally led through blocks suspended at the masthead. The blocks swivel to accommodate changing spinnaker positions but at the same time provide a constantly fair lead for the halyards to the masthead sheaves, thus eliminating undue friction.

However, on some excessively windage-conscious boats (e.g., racing boats), the suspended blocks are dispensed with and the spinnaker halyards run straight off the masthead sheaves. Fairing pads are fixed around the box exit and, whenever the pull of the spinnaker halyard is off to one side, it drags over these pads. This leads to wear of the pads and halyards, and considerable friction when raising and lowering the spinnaker. If this kind of rig is used, the fairing pads and halyards will need regular inspection.

Sail track and slides: Only nylon sail slides should be used on aluminum spars, since metal will score the track and generate galvanic corrosion. Periodically flush salt crystals out of the slides and track, which then can be lubricated with silicone car or boat polish (not grease). Masts with a luff groove (as opposed to a track) will accept either special sail slides or a bolt-rope.

If the sail slides are correctly matched to the track or groove and everything is clean and polished, but the sail tends to jam, the problem most likely lies in the method of attaching the slides to the sail, rather than in the mast and slides (Figure 15-20).

End of season: When a mast is unstepped at the end of the sailing season, it and all its rigging should be washed free of salt crystals and the inside of the mast hosed out. Pay particular attention to hard-to-reach areas and the mast heel. Do not use detergents, since some can cause corrosion. (If detergents *are* used, be sure to rinse well.)

Check all moving parts for free operation or undue wear and lubricate lightly with a penetrating oil such as WD-40. Remove and grease any stainless steel fasteners that must not be allowed to freeze up.

Figure 15-19. Removable head box. To remove sheaves pull out the cotter key (split pin) and knock out the clevis pin. Be sure to tie a lanyard around the sheaves to prevent their falling into the mast. The owner of this mast got tangled up in a drawbridge as it was opening and was picked up by the masthead, which tore the head box from the mast. This is not a recommended method for removing a head box.

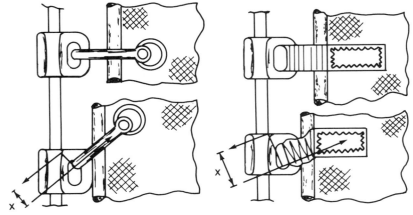

Figure 15-20. **Attaching slides to the sail.** Use a round shackle (left) that can move freely in the slide. Keep the distance marked X small; this will allow the slide to run freely. At right, the slide is attached by a fabric band; distance X is too great and the slide will jam.

Going Aloft

Having been at a masthead for several hours at a time on more than one occasion, let me tell you that comfort (or, at the least, minimizing discomfort) is a prime consideration. I would advise sailboat owners to get one of those deep-sided canvas bosun's chairs with lots of pockets all the way around. Just one point: The pockets tend to sag and do not retain tools securely—it is worth putting a little piece of Velcro tape on the larger ones to close them off.

Safety

- Do *not* hook a bosun's chair to a snap shackle on the halyard. Use a screw shackle or a bowline.
- Do *not* use a wire halyard with a rope tail. If this must be done, first check the rope-to-wire splice *very closely.*
- Do *not* use a winch directly below the mast to go aloft—any tool dropped will land on the winch operator who (if still conscious) will probably let go of the rope tail, and down you will come. Rig a block and take the line to a cockpit winch.
- Do *not* use electric winches—it is all too easy for the winch operator to run the bosun's chair up into the head box and tear the halyard loose from the bosun's chair.
- *Do* set up another external halyard or taut line so that you have something to hang onto and help pull yourself up. In the event of a riding turn on the winch (which can create quite a dangerous situation as it is unwrapped), you can take the weight off the hoisting line.
- *Do* place a safety line or strap around the mast as you go aloft. Should the hoisting line fail or come loose, the safety strap will hold you. It will have to be undone and reset at each spreader.
- *Do* tie off once up. This is a most basic safety precaution. It also frees up both hands for working. A good strong belt will be more comfortable than a piece of line. Have the winch operator *cleat off the hoisting line* even if using a self-tailing winch.

The most difficult work aloft is repairing things *on top of* the mast—for example, masthead lights. The bosun's chair most likely will not get you high enough. I take up a couple of short lengths of line and hang "stirrups" from the masthead, one higher than the other, such that the lower one puts my chest

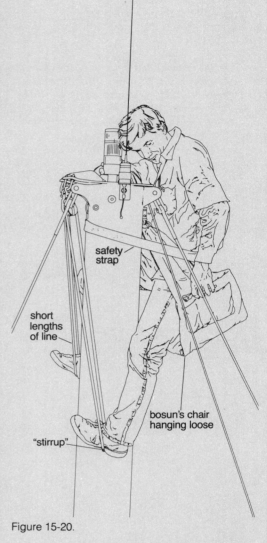

safety strap

short lengths of line

"stirrup"

bosun's chair hanging loose

Figure 15-20.

at masthead level (with a straight leg), and the other (about a foot higher) allows me to push myself up a little more if necessary (see Figure 15-20). I stay in the bosun's chair so that if I slip it will hold me, and strap myself off as high as possible. It's still a pretty nerve-wracking business. Do you have any better method?

Table 15-1. Spar Maintenance Checklist.

| Item or Aspect | Spar Material | |
	Wood	Aluminum
Finish	Check for bare spots, blistering, peeling, cracking, and delaminating. Remove and replace all rotted areas. Refinish.	If spars are anodized, clean and polish any bare spots. If spars are painted, clean, acid-etch, and repaint bare spots.
Fasteners	Check for separation of wood and fastener, water ingress, and rot. Repair and rebed as necessary.	Check for stress patterns, looseness, cracks, and corrosion. Remove any fasteners that must come out periodically; clean, grease, and replace.
Spreaders	Pay particular attention to spreader tops and the attachment points to the mast.	Check spreader sockets for cracks (especially if welded), mast deformation, and loose rivets. Check any rubber pads in semiflexible spreader sockets.
Spreader angles	Make sure all spreaders bisect their shrouds.	Same as for wooden spars.
Heel fitting	Check for water and rot.	Check for corrosion.
Masthead	Check sheaves for free-spinning and wear; where sheaves are set in the mast, check for water ingress into the masthead.	Check sheaves for free-spinning and wear.
Mast track	Check all mast track for loose fasteners and misaligned joints.	Same as for wooden spars.
Storage	Wash off all salt, dry, and store in a cool, dry place with adequate support.	Same as for wooden spars. Keep all rigging out of contact with the spars.

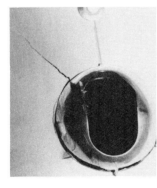

Note the bulging.

Figure 15-21. Check for these typical trouble spots around the shroud socket area of a mast wall: (**Left**) Mast wall distorted by T-ball shroud socket; (**Right**) mast wall cracked by shroud socket.

Inspect all welds and fasteners for cracks and movement, particularly spreader sockets. Check the mast wall around the spreader sockets and shroud tangs for distortion. Inspect the forestay-and backstay-mounting holes in the head box for signs of elongation.

Before storing a mast, *dry it well.* It is excellent practice to apply a coat of silicone boat or car wax polish. Support the mast evenly at several points along its length so that no section is sagging. *Never* store stainless steel rigging against aluminum spars, since corrosion is likely.

Downwind: Whisker and Spinnaker Poles

All poles used for winging out sheets and sails are designed for *compression loading only*—that is to say, the poles must be set up so that all loads are transmitted directly along the length of the pole to the heel fitting (generally mounted on the mast). In this respect poles are very like spreaders—flexing loads (such as wrapping the pole around a shroud) are likely to cause a pole to buckle.

So far as possible a pole must be set up at right angles to the mast. The more a pole deviates from a right angle, the more likely it is to be driven up or down the mast, suffering damage in the process.

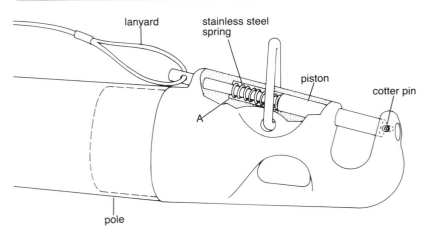

lanyard · stainless steel spring · piston · cotter pin · A · pole

Figure 15-23. **Typical arrangement of pole end fittings.** Salt deposits in the cylinder that inhibit the free operation of the piston can be removed by judicious applications of hot water and vinegar.

There are dozens of different end fittings for poles. Almost all include an anodized aluminum casting together with some form of spring-loaded pin (a piston). Poles are subject to a lot of saltwater spray. Galvanic interaction between the stainless steel spring and piston and the aluminum housing is common, more so on poles that are rarely used. Since the pistons are a close fit in the housings, they frequently freeze up.

Telescoping poles and end fittings need frequent flushing with fresh water. Where excessive salt builds up, white vinegar will dissolve it. Avoid using detergents; some attack anodized aluminum.

Even if not used, poles frequently should be "exercised." Lack of use is the biggest problem in the life of poles and

end fittings. End fittings can be greased lightly with Teflon-based grease to inhibit corrosion.

Where an end fitting does freeze up, it generally can be easily restored to service, usually as shown in Figure 15-23.

The spring-loaded piston is held in place by the cotter pin. If this is removed, the piston and spring can be slid out of their cylinder (it will be necessary to remove the lanyard). If the piston is frozen up, hot water and vinegar will remove most deposits; then it can be knocked out with a punch, hitting it at the end where the lanyard attaches. Be sure to get a good sized punch and hit it squarely—if the top of the piston gets burred, it is not going to pass through the narrow part of the cylinder bore. In serious cases of corrosion, the spring and cylinder bore will be completely plugged with aluminum oxide, and quite a bit of force will be needed to free things up.

After repeated freeze-ups, several years ago we drilled out our cylinders by running in an oversized drill from the cotter-pin end (we opened the cylinders up by an extra 1/32 inch). We have never had a problem since. (Note: This will destroy any anodizing, but since it was completely corroded anyway we weren't worried.) *It is absolutely vital to drill no farther than point "A"* in Figure 15-23—if the drill goes all the way through, the piston spring will have nothing to seat on and the fitting will be ruined.

Standing Rigging

Wire Rope

Aside from the use of stainless steel rod rigging on racing boats, almost all rigging is done with stainless steel wire rope. First, the terminology. The basic unit of construction is a *wire*. A straight length of wire is used as a *center wire,* and then a number of other wires are *laid up* around the center wire to form a *strand*. One strand is used as a *core cable* and other strands, or individual wires, are laid up around this core to form the finished cable, known as *wire rope* (see Figure 15-24).

When forming strands and cables, the individual wires or strands are *not* bent

around their center wires or cores: All of the individual wires are manufactured with the required bends already built in so that they naturally take up the right position without stressing—this is known as pre-forming. Depending on the direction in which the wires or strands are laid up in relation to their center wire or core, they are *right lay* or *left lay.* Under a load, a cable laid up in only one direction tends to unravel and stretch, therefore the outer layers of wire rope are laid up in a direction opposite to that of the inner layers—any tendencies to unravel or stretch cancel out.

The fewer the wires and strands in the construction of a cable, the greater its strength and the less its stretch, the ultimate being a "cable" of only one solid strand—i.e., rod rigging. However, the fewer the wires and strands, the less the flexibility and therefore the greater the tendency for it to fatigue and fail. To be on the safe side, rod rigging should be changed every two years.

Almost all standing rigging uses 1 × 19 wire rope. This consists of an inner strand (the core), which has six pre-formed wires laid up around one straight center wire (giving a total of seven wires). Twelve more individual pre-formed wires are laid up around this core. The designation "1 × 19" refers to the fact that there is one strand (the core) and a total of 19 individual wires (Figure 15-25).

Where greater flexibility is required, 7 × 7 and 7 × 19 cable is used. A 7 × 7 cable has 7 strands with 7 wires each (the strands are the same as the core in 1 × 19 wire rope); 7 × 19 wire has 7 strands with 19 wires each (each strand is the same as 1 × 19 wire rope). The 7 × 19 wire—the most flexible—is commonly used for steering cables and halyards.

Wire rope is rated at a breaking strength, which is just that—the load under which it breaks. Industrial practice, where lives are frequently at stake, is to establish a safe working load of 20 percent to 25 percent of the breaking strength. In marine use a safe working load of up to 50 percent of the breaking strength is frequently used (it cuts cost as well as weight aloft). The argument is that the rigging is always in column (i.e., straight) and the rope less likely to fatigue. This takes no account of the constant flexing that can rapidly build up a very high number of fatigue cycles. When rigging or re-rigging a boat it is far better to use the safer industrial practice—establish a safe working load of no more than 25 percent of breaking strength (Table 15-2).

Making End Connections (Terminals)

Eye terminals using thimbles. At one time, when galvanized wire rope was the norm, almost all rigging was formed into an eye around a thimble and then spliced back into itself. Today wire splices have been almost completely superseded by cable clamps and Nicopress (Talurit) sleeves.

Cable clamps (otherwise known as Crosby or Bulldog clamps) have a U-bolt

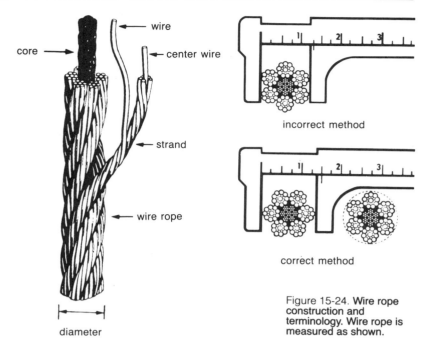

incorrect method

correct method

Figure 15-24. **Wire rope construction and terminology. Wire rope is measured as shown.**

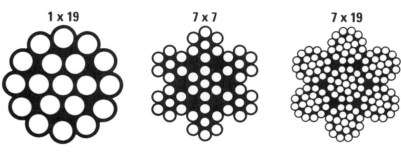

1 x 19   **7 x 7**   **7 x 19**

Figure 15-25. **Strand arrangement of the most commonly seen types of wire rope.**

and a "saddle." The saddle is scored with grooves to match the lay of the external wires in the rope it goes around. When using cable clamps, *the saddle always goes over the standing (loaded) part of the cable* and the U-bolt over the bitter end, since the U-bolt tends to crush and weaken the rope.

Two, and preferably three, clamps should be used, spaced two to three inches (50 to 75 mm) apart and snugged tight. Galvanized cable clamps in sizes below ⅜ inch (10 mm) have a tendency to shear off when tightened; stainless clamps are much stronger.

Nicopress (Talurit) fittings consist of a copper sleeve that is slid up the cable. The bitter end is wrapped around a thimble

Table 15-2. Breaking Loads for Stainless Steel Wire Rope.[1]

Nominal Diameter (strand size)		1 × 19 Minimum Breaking Load		7 × 7 Minimum Breaking Load		7 × 19 Minimum Breaking Load	
MM	Inches	Pounds	Kilograms	Pounds	Kilograms	Pounds	Kilograms
2	—	704	320	532	242	—	—
2.5	—	1,100	500	—	—	—	—
3	1/8	1,584	720	1,199	545	1,122	510
4	5/32	2,816	1,280	2,130	968	2,134	970
4.76	3/16	3,960	1,800	—	—	2,827	1,285
5	—	4,400	2,000	3,322	1,510	3,124	1,420
5.56	7/32	5,295	2,470	—	—	3,857	1,753
6	—	6,336	2,880	4,796	2,180	4,488	2,040
6.35	1/4	7,084	3,220	—	—	5,031	2,287
7	9/32	7,810	3,550	6,534	2,970	6,116	2,780
8	5/16	10,208	4,640	8,514	3,870	7,986	3,630
9	—	12,914	5,870	—	—	—	—
9.53	3/8	14,476	6,580	—	—	11,330	5,150
10	—	15,950	7,250	13,310	6,050	12,474	5,670
11	7/16	19,294	8,770	—	—	—	—
12	—	22,880	10,400	19,162	8,710	17,952	8,160
12.7	1/2	25,630	11,650	—	—	20,123	9,147
14	9/16	31,196	14,180	26,180	11,900	24,420	11,100
16	5/8	40,832	18,560	—	—	—	—
19	3/4	47,564	21,620	—	—	—	—
22	7/8	63,954	29,070	—	—	—	—
26	1	89,320	40,600	—	—	—	—

1. The loads given are based on Norseman figures. Each company gives slightly different figures.

Figure 15-26. Although rigging eyes spliced in wire rope around thimbles are seldom seen these days, eyes retained by cable clamps or Nicopress (Talurit) sleeves are a common sight. They are just as secure as a splice, and far easier to make. Be sure to use the proper size thimble and the proper tool for crimping the sleeve, such as the portable Nicopress tool shown here. If using cable clamps, be sure the saddle rests on the *standing* part of the wire rope.

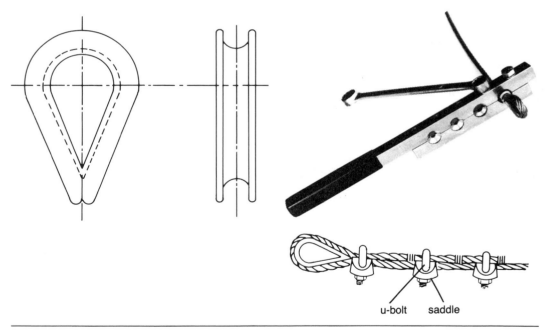

u-bolt   saddle

and fed back through the eye alongside the standing part. The sleeve is crimped (swaged) with a special tool. The finished eye splice is both strong and neat, but inevitably some deformation of the wire occurs, reducing its strength. A Nicopress kit (the swaging tool and a collection of differently sized thimbles and sleeves) is highly recommended for inclusion in any emergency rigging kit.

All wire terminals using thimbles suffer from a number of problems:

1. Unless impractically large thimbles are used, 1 × 19 wire, especially in sizes over 1/4 inch or 6 mm, cannot be

wrapped around a thimble without deforming its lay (and therefore weakening it). Both 7 × 7 and 7 × 19 wire are more tolerant, and for this reason thimbles and cable clamps are used extensively as wire terminals in steering systems.

2. Almost all thimbles are relatively lightweight and open at the base. Under a load the thimbles tend to pinch, slacking the fit of the cable, or even collapse. It is preferable to use thimbles with the base welded shut or, best of all, thimbles machined from solid metal (hard to find and expensive—Edson International manufactures one or two sizes).

3. Cosmetically speaking, cables terminated in thimbles are nowhere near as attractive as most other terminations.

Swages. Swaged terminals are manufactured to make a close fit over the end of the wire rope for which they are designed. The section of the terminal around the rope is then passed through a set of rollers and subjected to enormous pressure. The metal of the terminal is squeezed down into the lay of the cable and effectively "cold welded" to the cable.

With the right equipment and skilled operators, swaging produces fast, neat, low-profile bonds exceeding the breaking strength of the wire rope, and is therefore popular with boat manufacturers and riggers alike. However, it must be done right.

All swaging tends to work-harden the metal involved. The use of incorrect swaging pressures and/or the repeated rolling of fittings will make the terminal brittle and prone to develop hairline cracks. It is not uncommon for improperly swaged fittings to fail within two years.

Unfortunately it is generally not possible to tell with a visual inspection whether swaging has been done correctly (unless a terminal is obviously banana-shaped, in which case it should be immediately discarded). If you are having any swaging done, take it to a reputable rigging loft rather than the unskilled worker on a hand-operated machine in the corner of a local boatyard's workshop.

Compression fittings. There are a number of compression-type fittings on the market, the best known being those made by Norseman, Sta-Lok, and Castlok (Figure 15-29). They all work on the same principle. A belled sleeve, tapered and

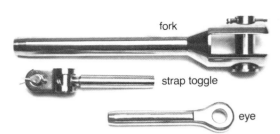

Figure 15-27. **Swaged terminals look so nice when new, but unless done by skilled professionals, they have a relatively high rate of failure.**

Figure 15-28. **Even professionally done swages are hard to check for hidden flaws. Corrosion in the socket is a particular problem. The swages on the left are banana shaped and cracked.**

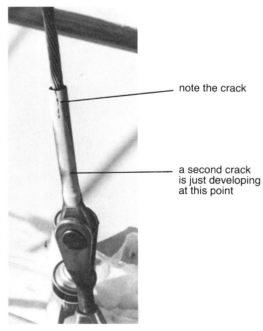

note the crack

a second crack is just developing at this point

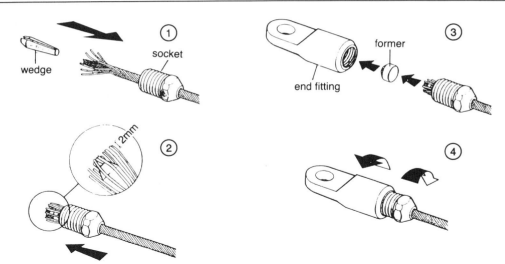

Figure 15-29A. Alternatives to swaged terminals, such as the Sta-lok, Norseman, or Castlok rigging terminals, are fully as secure as swages, and can be installed relatively easily by the boat owner—even at sea. Sta-lok terminals are designed for use with preformed 1 × 19, 7 × 7, and 7 × 19 wire rope. The 1 × 19 wedge is plain, but the wedge for 7 × 7 and 7 × 19 rope has a castellated ring with six gates to take the strands. These are not interchangeable. (1) Cut the cable cleanly. (There should be no protruding wires.) Slip the *socket* over the end of the cable, and unlay the outer wires or strands to expose a section of the center core equal in length to the *wedge.* (2) Slip the wedge over the center core of the cable (narrow end first), leaving about 3/32 inch (2mm) of core and outer wires protruding beyond the wide end of the wedge. Re-lay the outer wires or strands around the wedge, taking care to retain the wedge in its correct position. Carefully pull the *socket* into position over the wedge to prevent the wires or strands from

unlaying. Check the assembly to ensure that the outer wires are spaced evenly around the top of the wedge, and that none of the wires have slipped into its slot. Each of the six outer strands of 7-strand ropes should lie in the "gates" provided (not illustrated). (3) Insert the *former* into the threaded hole in the end fitting. Screw the *end fitting* onto the already assembled unit and tighten with a wrench. Too much force can damage the threads; use no more than can be applied with one hand. (4) To waterproof the fitting, unscrew the two parts and insert a raisin-size blob of silicone caulking on the former, inside the bottom of the end fitting. Apply two or three drops of Loctite on the male thread of the socket; screw both parts together again, and tighten. The end fitting may be unscrewed whenever required for inspection or rewiring. When rewiring, cut off and discard the end of the cable and the old wedge. Always use a new wedge when rewiring. The remainder of the terminal parts may be reused a number of times if undamaged.

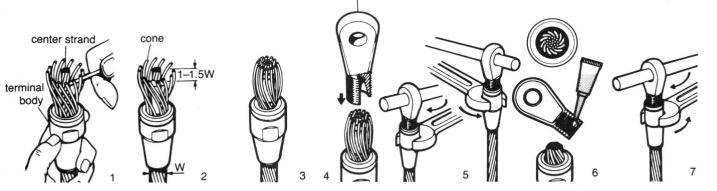

Figure 15-29B. To assemble Norseman terminal fittings: (1) Slide the terminal body over the wire rope, and unlay the outer strands from the center strands. (2) Slide the cone down over the center strand, leaving exposed a length equal to 1.5 times the full diameter of the rope. (3) Relay the outer wires or strands, spaced evenly around the cone. (4) Fit all the protruding wires into the blind recess of the terminal end fitting (eye, fork, stud, etc.), and start threading the body and end fitting together. (5) Complete the assembly, turning the appropriate component in the direction of the lay of the rope, as shown in the

sketch. Tighten until the resistance indicates that the cone is being compressed into the body of the terminal. *Do not overtighten;* you may damage the threads. (6) Unscrew the fitting to inspect and ensure that the wires are evenly spaced and closed neatly over the cone. Apply a thread-locking adhesive, such as Loctite, to the threads. (7) Insert a blob of marine sealant, such as 3M 5200, into the end fitting's blind hole and retighten the assembly. Repeat if necessary until the sealant oozes from the body end. Wipe clean.

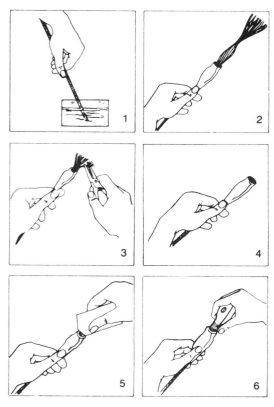

Figure 15-29C. To install Castlok fittings: (1) Thoroughly degrease the end of the cable with a solvent such as acetone. (2) Push the cable through the narrow end of the sleeve and expose 2 to 3 inches of wire beyond the end. Unlay the strands for approximately ¾ turn. (3) Retract the cable *partially* into the sleeve, leaving the end of the cable just exposed. Unlay all the wires in the center strand (1 × 19 wire rope) or in each strand (7 × 7 and 7 × 19 wire rope). (4) Retract the cable back into the sleeve until the end is at the bottom of the threads. (5) Read the manufacturer's instructions on the preparation and use of resin thoroughly. Inject the resin into the threaded opening until the sleeve is filled to the top of the threads. (6) Screw the stud into the sleeve to the end of the threads. This forces the resin into and around the cable and seals the juncture of wire and sleeve, as well as locking the threads of the stud into place. Allow the assembly to cure for 24 hours before using.

the bond is stronger than the cable itself. In the case of Castlok fittings, epoxy glue is used in place of a metal cone. The glue sets up, forming a solid, incompressible plug, which serves much the same function as the cone (which is why I have included these terminals here).

This type of fitting (particularly Castlok) causes less deformation of, and places less stress on, the wire rope than any other. Corrosion resistance is also unequalled—in the case of Norseman and Sta-Lok fittings, silicone rubber placed in the terminal prevents moisture from entering; with Castlok, glue completely fills the terminal and squeezes out and up the lay of the rope, where it emerges from the sleeve. All three can be relatively easily fitted in the field with basic tools, and all three are reusable (although melting the glue out of an old Castlok fitting requires careful use of a propane torch).

Fitting Rigging to a Boat

All boats use *chainplates* to fasten stays and shrouds to the boat (stays run in a fore-and-aft direction, shrouds atwartships). Chainplates are nothing more than heavy metal straps securely fastened to the hull, with a hole in the top through which a *clevis pin* passes. Unfortunately there is no international standardization of pin sizes, which often makes matching of chainplates, clevis pins, and end fittings a matter of trial and error.

Next come *turnbuckles* (rigging screws) to tension the rig. A turnbuckle is a hollow sleeve, threaded at both ends but with one thread being right-handed (normal) and the other left-handed (reverse thread). The right-handed thread should be uppermost. A threaded stud goes in each end, one right-handed, one left-handed. Turning the turnbuckle one way pulls both studs in, tightening the rig; turning it the other way pushes both studs out, loosening the rig.

Various means are used to make the connections from chainplates to turnbuckles and turnbuckles to wire rope. The most common are solid toggles, strap toggles, forks, eyes, and straight-threaded terminals (see Figure 15-30). However the connections are made, the lower ends of all stays and shrouds must be free to flex in all directions. This movement generally is provided by a strap toggle.

threaded toward its lower end, is slid up the cable. The outer wires or strands of the cable are unlaid and a tapered wedge or cone is slid up over the core. The outer wires or strands are then reformed around the wedge or cone, the sleeve is slid down over the top, and the terminal itself screwed into the sleeve. The individual wires or strands of the cable are sandwiched between the sleeve and the wedge or cone, and held firmly. In all instances

Figure 15-30A. Turnbuckles come with a variety of end fittings to tailor them to different situations aboard.

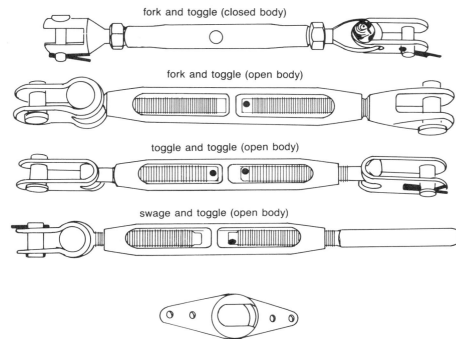

fork and toggle (closed body)

fork and toggle (open body)

toggle and toggle (open body)

swage and toggle (open body)

Figure 15-30B. The ball-and-socket shroud terminal, increasingly popular on aluminum masts, allows a certain amount of flexing in all directions.

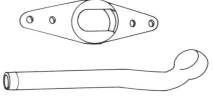

Figure 15-31. Stays are subject to considerable flexing and therefore must have toggles—top and bottom—to prevent early rigging failure. (**Left**) Toggles allow flexing in either direction. (**Right**) Use of a shackle as a temporary toggle. The shackle pin has been lashed correctly with seizing wire.

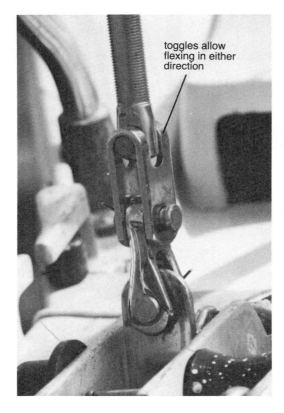

toggles allow flexing in either direction

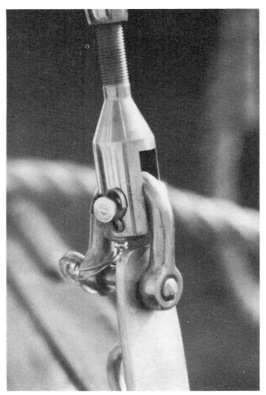

Table 15-3. Rigging Checklist.

Part or Aspect	Procedure
Cable terminals	Check all clevis pins, toggles, forks and eyes for elongation, wear, and spreading of toggles or forks. Check all cables at terminal exits for signs of stranding.
Cable clamps	Make sure cables are wrapped tightly around thimbles. Check thimbles for distortion. Make sure that clamps are tight.
Swages	Discard any banana-shaped swages and swages with signs of cracking or repeated rolling.
Turnbuckles	Undo all turnbuckles; clean, regrease, and reinstall.
Ball-and-socket shroud terminals	Check the socket and mast for any signs of deformation.
Shroud tangs	Remove the mounting bolt and check for crevice corrosion.
Alignment	Check all chainplates and rigging terminals for alignment. Pay particular attention to the correct placement of toggles and to even loading on fork terminals.

Where the upper ends of shrouds attach to a mast, by far the most common practice is to terminate the wire rope with an eye fitting, which slips between two metal plates (tangs) fastened to the mast. A clevis pin passes through the tangs and the eye and is secured with a *cotter pin* (split pin). This allows fore-and-aft flexing but no athwartships play.

A second method of attaching shrouds, becoming increasingly popular on aluminum masts, is to fasten a slotted ball socket inside the mast wall. The shroud is terminated in a swaged-on T terminal (see Figure 15-30B). With the shroud slack, the T is held sideways, slipped into the slot, and then turned back to its proper position; the shroud is then tensioned. The curved face of the T-end rests in the ball socket and is free to flex a limited amount in all directions.

Stays, especially headstays, are subjected to considerable flexing in all directions and *must have a toggle at the head as well as the foot.* A typical arrangement is to run a clevis pin between two plates welded to the head box. A strap toggle is hung from the clevis pin (see Figure 15-32). Where

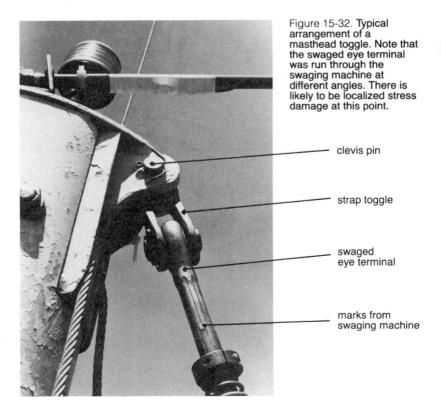

Figure 15-32. **Typical arrangement of a masthead toggle.** Note that the swaged eye terminal was run through the swaging machine at different angles. There is likely to be localized stress damage at this point.

clevis pin

strap toggle

swaged eye terminal

marks from swaging machine

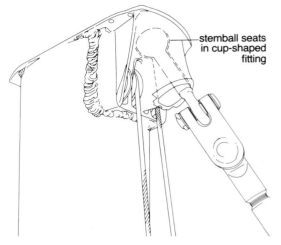

Figure 15-33. Stemball fittings, as fitted to Isomat spars, act much like a toggle.

stemball seats in cup-shaped fitting

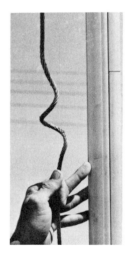

Figure 15-34. **Top**: Stranded wire rope. **Middle**: Fractured strands sticking out. Remember: "There is no acceptable number of broken wires in a rope." **Bottom**: This deformed wire rope is the result of halyard wrap on a roller-reefing unit (see Chapter 16).

the head box has a single, central mounting plate, a slotted strap toggle fits up either side of the plate. Otherwise the installation is the same.

A French company, Isomat, is making a big dent in the spar market, both in Europe and the USA. Many Isomat spars have what is called a *stemball* fitting as the upper (swaged) terminal on the forestay (see Figure 15-33). This acts as a toggle, allowing limited flexibility in all directions.

Stemballs are fine with hanked-on sails, but they are not adequate to handle the additional flexing imposed by roller-reefing headsails. Where a roller reefer is fitted, the stemball will need adapting so that it is fully toggled.

If a backstay is used as an antenna (aerial) for an SSB (single sideband) or Ham radio, insulators are fitted at the top and bottom of the stay. These come with both swaged and compression-type wire rope terminals. Many rigs also incorporate a backstay tension adjuster, which may be an arrangement of blocks with a tackle, an oversize turnbuckle with handles attached to the barrel, or a hydraulically operated cylinder.

Inspection and Maintenance

Rigging is designed for direct in-line loading only. Any flexing fatigues the wire rope. Without toggles the stress is concentrated at the exit points from the wire rope terminals; with toggles it is distributed through the cable as a whole. *The use of toggles is essential* to reduce stress, but eventually the "fatigue cycles" still will build up to the point at which the rigging fails.

Given the inevitability of failure, how soon should properly installed and maintained rigging be routinely replaced? Norseman recommends: after once around the world in the Whitbread race; after three heavy races such as the Transatlantic or Round Britain; after five to eight years of seasonal ocean racing; after 10 years around the buoys: and after possibly 12 to 15 years of summer cruising. In the meantime, rigging should be given a close annual inspection for any of the following danger signs:

"Stranded" wire rope. Wire rope rarely breaks without some warning. Usually before total failure, one or two individual wires fracture and stick out, forming nasty "fish hooks." The most likely places are right where the rope enters terminal fittings (Figure 15-34). *There is no acceptable number of broken wires in a rope.* Even if only *one* has failed, the cable has been severely overstressed and needs immediate replacement.

Deformed wire rope. When a wire rope is dragged through too sharp a turn (e.g., on undersized sheaves; spinnaker halyards dragging around masthead fairing pads; or roller-reefing halyards wrapping around the forestay), the rope will be permanently deformed (it generally forms a spiral when not under tension). *It cannot be straightened again;* this would merely compound the problem by putting the rope through more severe stresses. It will fail sooner rather than later and needs replacing.

Stress points on hardware.

1. Chainplates must be lined up exactly with the shroud or stay that they support.
2. If tangs or chainplates incorporate any bends or welds (most do), the bends and welds are the most likely points of failure. At the first sign of cracks or pinholes they should be replaced. A magnifying glass helps in inspection, but better yet is annual use of one of the proprietary crack-detection sets on the market (Spotcheck; Magnaflux; etc.).
3. Swages are especially prone to cracking down the body of the swage. *No cracks are acceptable!* If a swage is at all curved (banana-shaped), it also needs replacing—it has been improperly fitted and may fail without warning.
4. T-Terminals on shrouds will develop small cracks on the inside of the radius as they fatigue. The mast-reinforcement plates may develop elongated slots or loose rivets, or distort the mast wall.

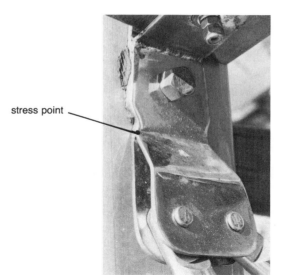

Figure 15-35. **Stress points on hardware.**

stress point

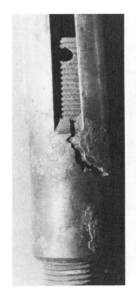

chain plate   stress point

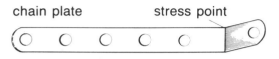

mast tang

stress point

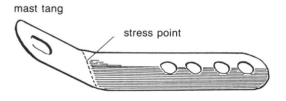

5. Thimbles will start to collapse (elongate), work loose in their cable eyes, and wear through at the point of pressure on the thimble. Cable clamps need retightening periodically.

6. If any fork terminal is unevenly stressed, sooner or later the loaded side is likely to crack and break off. Eye terminals are inherently stronger and alignment is not so critical.

7. Turnbuckles of *all*-stainless steel construction have a bad habit of galling, a process of cold-welding that destroys the threads and makes it impossible to screw or unscrew them. Almost always the cause is dirt in the threads. If at any time a turnbuckle (or any other threaded fitting for that matter) becomes hard to turn, *don't force it.* Spray it with penetrating oil, give the threads time to cool down (a surprising amount of heat is generated), screw it back the other way, lubricate again, and then keep working it backward and forward and hope it frees up. Bronze and stainless turnbuckles with bronze thread inserts or bronze studs are far less prone to galling than all-stainless steel ones.

8. Every clevis pin should be withdrawn annually and inspected for wear on the pin itself and for elongation of the holes or cracks around the holes through which it passes. Stainless steel will tolerate a certain amount of elongation without serious loss of strength, but *aluminum will not.* If the mounting holes in aluminum brackets are stretching, the bracket is being overloaded and failure is not far off.

9. Clevis pins, eyes, and strap toggles must be closely matched with only small clearances. Overly-long clevis pins will allow toggles to spread and the pins to bend; undersized eyes will allow the clevis pin to bend. In both cases the pin is likely to fail.

10. Cotter pins (split pins) need to be opened out 20 to 30 degrees and should be taped to avoid snagging sheets and other lines.

11. Many shroud tangs (and some other items of hardware) are held with a bolt through the mast. These bolts can suffer from hidden crevice corrosion and should be withdrawn and inspected annually. When replacing, be sure to securely lock the retaining nut either with a cotter pin or by peening over the threads on the end of the bolt. (If a Nyloc nut is used—one with a nylon insert that stops it from working loose—replace the nut.)

Corrosion. Stainless steel is corrosion-resistant so long as it has a free flow of air (oxygen) over its surface. Remove this oxygen and add a little stagnant water and it

Figure 15-36. **To prevent clevis pin failure, ensure that strap toggles match their eye fittings. The clevis pin on the left fits correctly; the one on the right has excessive clearance, and will bind and ultimately fail under load.**

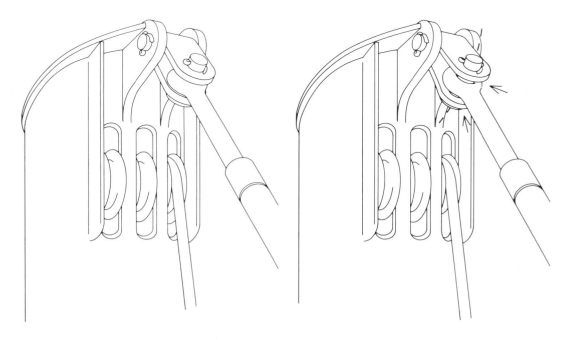

can corrode quite rapidly. *These are exactly the conditions found in many lower wire terminals and closed-body turnbuckles, and around some clevis pins* (particularly those passing through wooden spreaders). Crevice and pinhole corrosion in these fittings is often virtually undetectable and can lead to a serious rigging failure without warning.

Wherever possible all lower terminals should be filled with something to keep water out. Sta-Loks and Norsemans are made up with silicone rubber; Castloks are automatically filled with glue. Swages present a special problem and are notorious for sudden failure in the tropics. When new, and before their first soaking in salt water, lower swage terminals can be heated *gently* until beeswax can be melted down into the lay of the cable to fill any air spaces.

All turnbuckles and any other fittings with threaded studs should have any rigging tape removed, be completely undone, and have the body and threads checked for corrosion once a year. After a thorough cleaning they should be lightly greased before reassembly; preferably with a Teflon-based grease.

Annual maintenance. In addition to the above recommendations, the rigging should be washed of all dirt and salt before the winter lay-up. Boots or tapes on spreader tips should be removed for cleaning and inspection. If the rigging is left attached to aluminum spars, make sure the stainless wire is not resting on the aluminum; corrosion would be the likely result.

Tuning a Rig

Static tuning. Before stepping a mast it is useful to measure the *exact* length of the cap shrouds (the two shrouds coming from the masthead down to chainplates in line with each side of the mast). Next, check the chainplates to see that they are the same distance out from the base of the mast and the same height above the deck. Finally, measure from the centerline of the mast aperture in the deck, or the deck plate if deck-stepped, to each chainplate to make sure the mast is centered in the boat. The two measurements should be within an inch of each other.

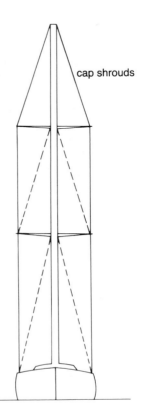

cap shrouds

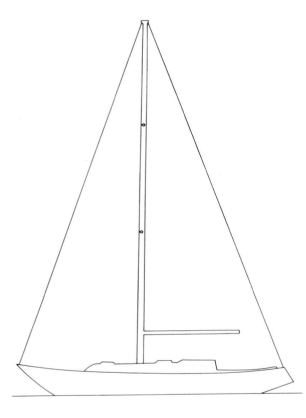

Figure 15-37A. Static rig tensioning. **(Left)** Center the mast athwartships with the cap (upper) shrouds and set up tight. **(Right)** Set the *rake* with the forestay and backstay(s) and set up tight.

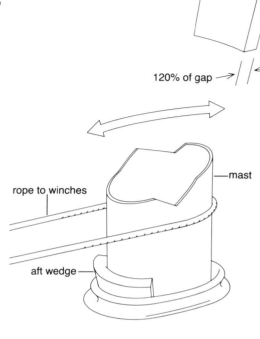

Figure 15-37B. For keel-stepped masts, set the fore-and-aft wedges in place. Compress the first pad by running a line passed around the mast to the sheet winches, then slip in the second pad.

30% to 35% of mast circumference

120% of gap

mast

rope to winches

aft wedge

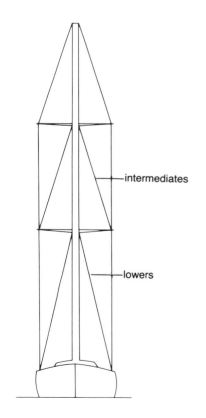

Figure 15-37C. Pull the mast into a straight column athwartships using first the intermediates, then the lower shrouds. Use little more than hand tension.

intermediates

lowers

The masthead is centered before any other tuning is done. Given equal-length cap shrouds and equally spaced chainplates, if the cap-shroud turnbuckles are set to the same length and tensioned equally when the mast is first stepped, the masthead must be centered in the boat athwartships. Another method of checking this is to tie off a halyard so that its free end just reaches the top of one of the cap shroud chainplates. When moved across to the other side of the boat, it should just touch the other chainplate.

The fore-and-aft masthead alignment is set up by adjusting the forestay and backstay. (If the rig has twin backstays, these too should be measured before stepping the mast so that they can be adjusted equally.) Most masts are set up vertically, but some are raked aft a degree or two. None are raked forward. If the boat is sitting level in the water, a weighted line hung from the masthead (or set out far enough to compensate for taper) will act as a plumb bob, but generally the fore-and-aft angle can be eyeballed from dockside with more than enough precision.

In a modern boat, where the rig is set up relatively tightly, the cap shrouds are tensioned to around 15 percent of their breaking strain, or 10 percent of the boat's displacement. Because they are the longest shrouds, and therefore subject to the most stretch, they are set up tighter than intermediate (if fitted) and lower shrouds. A backstay is tensioned to around 20 percent of its breaking strain (which in turn tensions the forestay). There are a number of relatively cheap ($20) tension gauges on the market; they are a useful investment. Always take up on the cap-shroud turnbuckles an equal amount to keep the masthead centered athwartships.

With keel-stepped masts, wedges (chocking) are now installed at the partners (the reinforcement around the hole in the deck). Wood can be used on wood spars, but hard rubber is always used on aluminum—one pad in front and one to the rear. The total thickness of the pads should be 120 percent to 125 percent of the total gap between the mast and partners. The total length of the pads should add up to 30 to 40 percent of the total circumference of the mast. No pads are placed at the mast sides. The pads will be easier to slip in if soaked in dishwashing liquid.

The most inaccessible pad is slipped in first. A line is tied around the mast and led

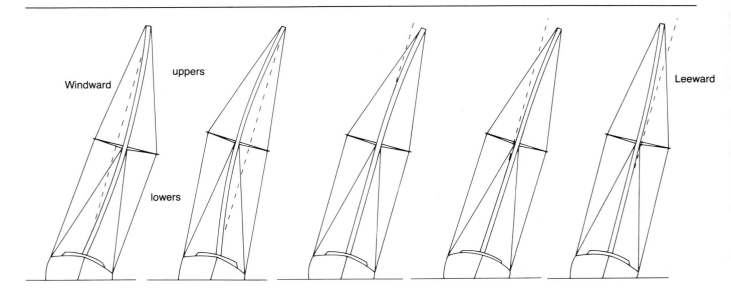

Figure 15-38. Tuning under sail. **Far left:** Windward lowers too loose. Masthead correctly positioned, but spreaders out of column. **Left of center:** Windward lowers too tight. Masthead correctly positioned, but spreaders out of column. **Center:** Cap shrouds slack. Spreaders in column but masthead sagging off. **Right of center:** Both cap shrouds and lowers slack. Mast sags off along its whole length. **Far right:** Both cap shrouds and lowers tight. Mast dragged up to windward along its entire length.

through suitable blocks to a cockpit winch so that the mast can be pulled forward or backward to compress the first pad and allow the second one to be forced in (Figure 15-37B). The pads should be held to the mast with a large hose clamp (Jubilee clip) so that they do not work their way out when the boat is sailing.

Now sight up the mast track or luff groove and pull the mast into a straight column athwartships using first the intermediate (if fitted) shrouds and then the lower shrouds. Intermediate shrouds are set up a little less tightly than upper shrouds; lowers, just a little more than hand-tight. Where a rig has an inner forestay and/or double lower shrouds, it is preferable to induce a slight forward bow in the mast at this time. This helps to flatten the mainsail—in any case, when under sail the headsail tension on the forestay will tend to pull the masthead forward and so bring the mast back into a straight line.

Tuning under sail. It is time to go sailing. With the boat hard on the wind (force 4 to 6), the lee-side rigging should not be slack (although it will lose *some* of its tension). If necessary, take up some more on the turnbuckles, but be sure to do this equally on both sides. The cap shrouds should need very little, if any, additional tensioning. Once they have been set up at the dock, final tuning should really be done using the lower shrouds to alter mast shape.

It is desirable that, when sighting up the sail track, the mast should always remain straight in an athwartships direction. In strong winds the masthead almost always will sag off a little bit to leeward. If the masthead is curving up to *windward,* the windward lower shrouds are too slack; if it is sagging off excessively to *leeward,* the windward lower shrouds are probably too tight.

Under moderate sailing loads, the forward bend induced in the mast at dockside will tend to straighten out. Any tendency for the masthead to curve forward must be counteracted by tightening the backstay(s). It is almost impossible to overtighten backstays using just a spike or screwdriver through the turnbuckle—the tension achieved will never even come close to that produced by a hydraulic backstay adjuster.

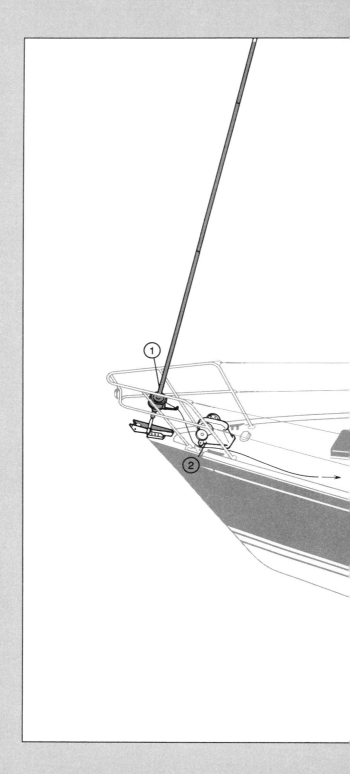

CHAPTER 16

Figure 16-1. **These are other high-repair-cost items that can remain virtually trouble free through the application of proper maintenance procedures.**

(1) roller furling jib
(2) anchor windlass
(3) boom vang
(4) turning block
(5) line stopper
(6) backstay adjuster
(7) winch
(8) mainsheet
(9) topping lift
(10) genoa track

Running Rigging, Deck Hardware, and Roller Reefing

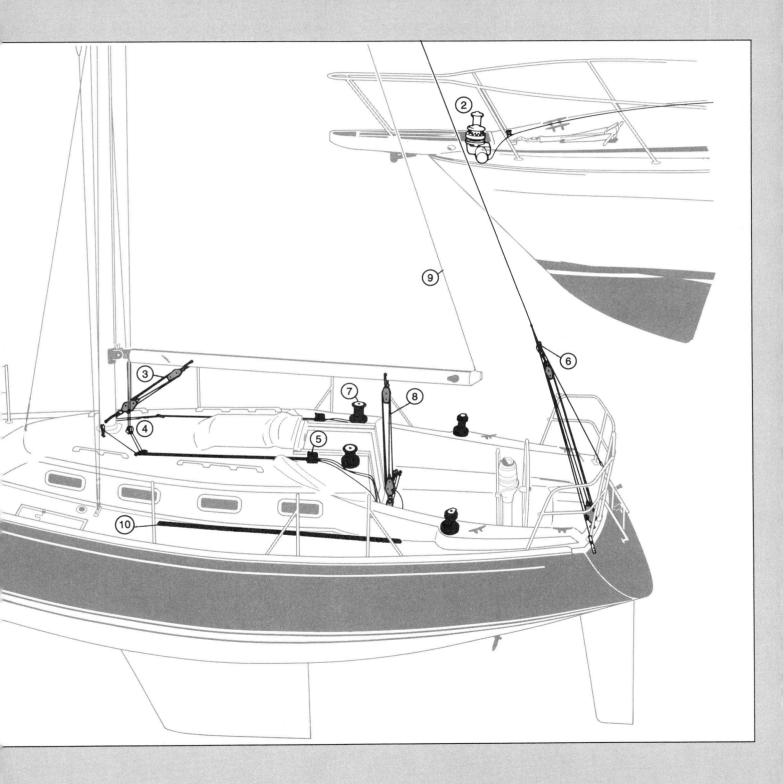

Blocks

Terminology and Loading Factors

First, some nomenclature. The basic unit of running rigging is a *block*. The wire or rope is led around a *sheave*. This sheave turns on either a *bushing* (sleeve) or a *bearing*. Bearings consist of either a number of balls set in a machined groove (a *race*) or else *rollers* (pins set on end around a central shaft). On either side of the sheave is a *cheek plate* (side plate or shell). The cheek plates are reinforced by straps through which pass the central bearing shaft, fasteners to hold the block together, and the fastening for the block head assembly— the means by which it is attached to the boat (Figure 16-2).

Sheaves may be either plastic or aluminum; bushings may be bronze or plastic; ball bearings are generally plastic. (Note, I am using the term "plastic" to cover some widely varying materials.) Rollers are usually bronze or stainless steel. Cheek plates may be plastic, aluminum, or stainless steel. Straps are always stainless steel except in a few expensive racing blocks where titanium is used.

Blocks are designed to take a direct pull on the sheave with only minimal sideways loading. A variety of head fittings is available to ensure the correct alignment of block and line (straight shackles,"upset" shackles, swiveling heads, spring-loaded bases, etc.). Blocks are rated at their "safe working load," which is generally 50 percent of the breaking strength of the hardware.

Loads on blocks are directly related to the angle through which a line is turned. For example, a block that does not turn a line at all is subjected to no load, while one

Figure 16-3. **Block Loading Factors.** The load on a block depends on the tension of the line passing through the block and the turning angle involved.

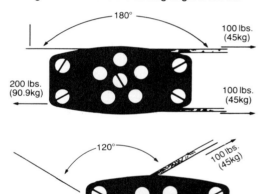

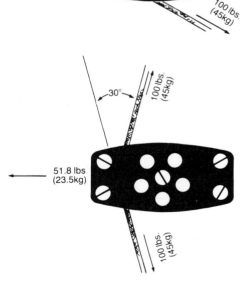

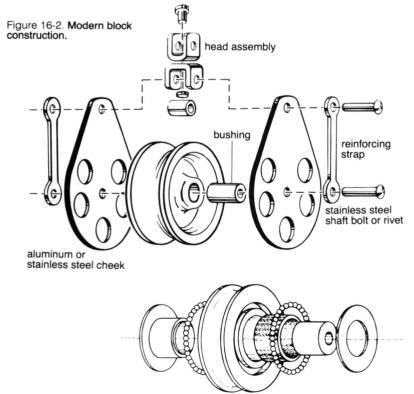

Figure 16-2. **Modern block construction.**

head assembly

bushing

reinforcing strap

stainless steel shaft bolt or rivet

aluminum or stainless steel cheek

that turns a line through 180 degrees is subjected to a load of *double* the pull on the line. Figure 16-3 illustrates block loading factors.

Problems With Blocks

Overloading. If blocks are subjected to greater loads than they are designed for, or more than minimal sideways loading through improper alignment, the sheaves, bushings, and/or bearings will deform and friction will build up rapidly. Even correctly rated blocks may start to deform if left permanently loaded (when not sailing all blocks should be left in an unloaded state so far as is possible). Sometimes deformed plastic bearings and sheaves will recover their proper shape after a period of rest, but frequently damage is permanent. In cases of extreme overloading, blocks will "explode" (disintegrate) without warning, creating a serious safety hazard.

Improper sheaves. Three factors are important in sheave selection—the overall diameter of the sheave; the shape of its groove; and the material from which it is constructed.

Diameter. Pulling any wire or rope around a sheave deforms the lay of the line or wire. The tighter the curve, the greater the distortion.

Groove shape. The groove in a sheave must match the shape of the line or wire passing over it if it is to provide maximum support and minimum distortion. A groove suitable for 1/2-inch (13-mm) Dacron line will provide poor support for 1/4-inch (6-mm) 7 × 19 stainless steel wire rope. Even different kinds of line use different groove shapes—Kevlar likes a flatter groove than Dacron. Grooves for wire rope are frequently scored to match the lay of the outer strands of the rope.

Materials. Sheaves for synthetic line are generally plastic while those for wire rope are almost always aluminum in order to withstand the greater abrasion. Wire would soon tear up plastic sheaves.

Salt and dirt. Every time a block gets wet and dries out salt crystals are left behind. In time the accumulation of salt in the bearings increases friction. This in turn increases wear on the moving parts, or else the block freezes up completely—especially common with infrequently used blocks.

Corrosion. Almost all blocks incorporate two or more galvanically incompatible metals, so sooner or later corrosion is inevitable. Aluminum sheaves and cheek plates, being the least noble metal involved, get eaten away. Stainless steel shafts suffer from crevice corrosion. The buildup of aluminum oxides in a block, together with salt and dirt, helps to freeze it up. It should be noted that aluminum cheek plates are primarily a weight-saving measure aimed at racing boats. Since the blocks will be replaced every few seasons, corrosion will be minimal. These blocks have also been widely used by manufacturers of cruising boats, but in this case, blocks need to hold up for many years; corrosion frequently becomes a problem. Cruising sailors should specify blocks with stainless steel or plastic cheek plates.

Maintenance

Cleaning. All blocks need flushing with fresh water several times a season to wash out salt crystals, dirt, and any by-products of corrosion. Particularly stubborn deposits will generally succumb to hot water. If not, use plain white (clear) vinegar, but rinse after flushing. Detergents generally should not be used on anodized aluminum, since some contain chemicals that will attack anodizing. Stains on stainless steel can be removed with copper scouring pads or a bronze wire brush (not steel wire wool, since tiny flecks of steel left behind will rust and leave more stains).

Sheaves should be spun to ensure free turning without excessive play. No lubrication is needed, but a shot of WD–40 or some silicone spray will do no harm.

Disassembly. Smaller, cheaper blocks are riveted together and cannot be dis-

Figure 16-4. Block sheaves are available for use with different types of rope or wire. Use of the incorrect sheave can lead to early failure of the rope.

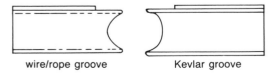

wire/rope groove   Kevlar groove

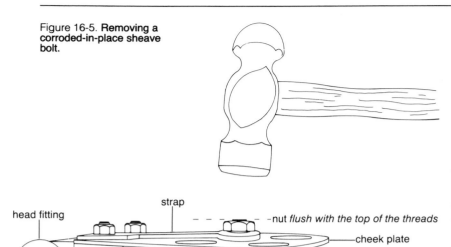

Figure 16-5. **Removing a corroded-in-place sheave bolt.**

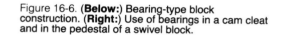

head fitting

strap

nut *flush with the top of the threads*

cheek plate

sheave

bolt frozen
in place

block of wood

assembled. If cleaning and lubrication does not return a block to service it will have to be discarded. Larger and more expensive blocks are bolted together, and thus can be disassembled when necessary.

Frequently, through-bolts become corroded in place. Remove the nuts, flush with hot water and white vinegar, and spray with penetrating fluid. Grip the bolt head and try working it backward and forward to free it up. If this fails, put the nut back on and screw it down until just flush with the top of the threads on the bolt, support the block on the other side, and hit the nut smartly with a hammer (Figure 16-5). This should jar things loose. Then go back to twisting the bolt back and forth.

Sheaves that ride on bearings (as opposed to bushings) generally have a retaining plate to hold the balls or rollers in place. The bearings come out complete with the sheave, and are then accessible by removing the retaining plates. Inspect the bearing races for any indentations and the balls for flat spots. In either case, replace.

Figure 16-6. **(Below:)** Bearing-type block construction. **(Right:)** Use of bearings in a cam cleat and in the pedestal of a swivel block.

cam cleat

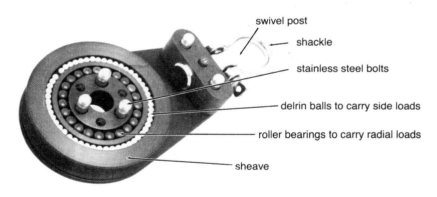

swivel post

shackle

stainless steel bolts

delrin balls to carry side loads

roller bearings to carry radial loads

sheave

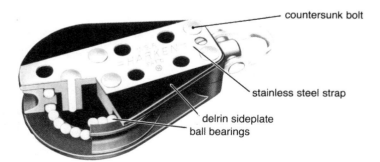

countersunk bolt

stainless steel strap

delrin sideplate
ball bearings

Winches

Winches may be operated with a handle inserted in the top (top-acting) or bottom (bottom-acting). In the case of larger winches on racing boats, they may be set up with handles on both sides ("coffee grinders"). Most are designed so that the drum turns in only one direction and locks in the other. The exception is halyard winches, which have a brake. When the brake is released the drum is free to rotate in reverse.

Regardless of individual differences the operating principles remain the same. There is a high degree of similarity among different types of winches and also among similar winches from one manufacturer to another. The following focuses on top-acting winches, since these constitute the overwhelming majority.

All winches incorporate dissimilar metals, notably bronze, stainless steel, and, in many cases, aluminum. All are subject to saltwater spray to a greater or lesser extent, leading to the accumulation of salt crystals inside the winch over time. Here we have all the ingredients for galvanic interaction, especially between aluminum parts and stainless steel and bronze gears, shafts, and fasteners.

Almost all winches are lightly greased internally. In some environments there is quite a bit of dust and sand in the atmosphere. In any event, given time the grease will clog with dirt and salt, reducing its lubricating properties. The winch will stiffen up (this is most easily felt by rotating the drum backward by hand with no load on it—it should be free spinning) and wear will accelerate.

For these reasons winches need regular cleaning—Lewmar recommends a monthly hosing down and light oiling and greasing; a partial stripdown two or three times a season; and a complete stripdown once a year. With this kind of attention most winches will operate troublefree for many years.

stainless steel   aluminum
fastener   self-tailer

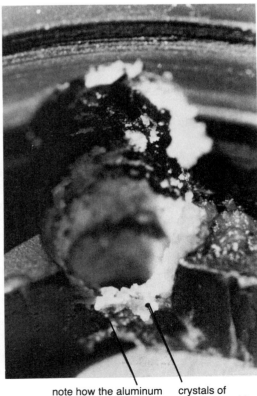

note how the aluminum   crystals of
is eaten away   aluminum oxide
                         and salt

Figure 16-7. Galvanic corrosion around a stainless steel fastener in an aluminum self-tailing mechanism.

Given the ease and speed with which a winch can be serviced, it is a shame that so many boat owners go from one year to the next without paying the slightest attention to their winches. If servicing is left until a noticeable problem has developed (extreme stiffness; drum freewheels in both directions; etc.), the winch is likely to have suffered unnecessary and permanent damage.

How They Work

If I take a winch drum and fit a handle in line with its outer edge, any turning force I exert on this handle will be the same as the pull of the winch (assuming no friction losses, etc.). If I now lengthen my winch handle until it is twice as long as the distance from the outer edge of the drum to its pivot point, the same force on the handle will produce double the pull at the winch (see Figure 16-8). The trade-off is that the handle is now moving through twice the distance that it was before: If I keep turning at the same speed as before, I only pull in half as much line in the same time—in effect, I have a two-to-one (2:1) gear ratio.

This relationship between the distance of the winch handle and drum from the pivot point of the drum is what imparts power to small, simple winches. The actual mechanism is as follows:

The winch handle turns a shaft (*spindle*) with a gear on it. The body of the winch (the drum) contains hinged, spring-loaded metal pieces, called *pawls,* which bear against this gear. When the spindle is turned in one direction the pawls engage the spindle gear, locking the drum to the spindle so that drum and spindle turn as one. When the spindle is turned in the

other direction the pawls hinge inward against their springs and disengage the spindle gear, allowing the drum to remain stationary (this is known as *ratcheting* or freewheeling).

At this point we have the ability to turn the drum, but when we let go of the winch handle there is nothing to stop the drum from spinning in reverse when under a load. Another set of spring-loaded pawls in the drum, operating in the opposite direction to the first set, engages a second gear on the winch mounting plate (winch base). This gear is forever locked in one place. Cranking on the winch handle turns the drum, which ratchets around the base-plate gear. When the winch handle is released the second set of pawls engages the

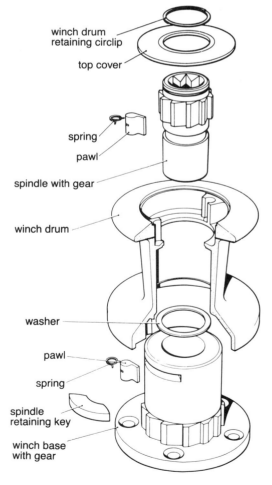

Figure 16-9. **Single speed, direct drive, top-acting winch.**

winch drum retaining circlip

top cover

spring

pawl

spindle with gear

winch drum

washer

pawl

spring

spindle retaining key

winch base with gear

Figure 16-8. **Winches: How they work.** The line pull of the winch equals four times the turning force on the handle.

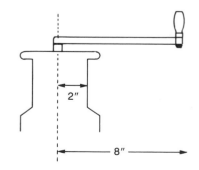

2"

8"

baseplate gear and prevents the drum from spinning in reverse.

What I have just described is a single-speed, direct-drive, top-acting winch: single-speed because there is always the same gear ratio between the spindle (i.e., winch handle) and drum; direct-drive because the spindle directly engages the drum; and top-acting because the winch handle is inserted in the top.

A reel halyard winch is essentially the same, with the exception that the baseplate gear is itself free to rotate but has a brake band around it, which is fastened to the baseplate (Figure 16-10A). When the brake band is tightened, it locks the baseplate gear to the baseplate and the winch operates as above. When the brake band is loosened, the baseplate gear is free to rotate and the drum unwinds. But note that as it unwinds, the drum pawls engaging the spindle gear will lock the drum and spindle together and spin the spindle with the drum. Thus, if the winch handle is left in the winch it too will spin, and herein lies the cause of many a broken finger and wrist. *Never release the brake on a halyard winch with the handle in place.* (Note that the same situation arises with a regular winch if the pawls engaging the baseplate gear fail for any reason—*never leave handles in winches!*)

When the winch handle is turned on a single-speed winch it engages the drum in only one direction and freewheels (ratchets) in the other. On a two-speed winch the

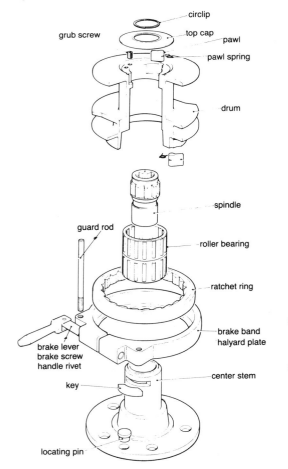

Figure 16-10A. **Reel-type halyard winch.**

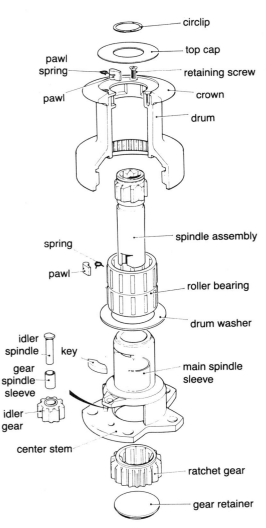

Figure 16-10B. **Two speed winch.**

handle also engages the drum in the second direction, but at a different gear ratio (i.e., given the same winch handle speed, the drum turns at a different speed). This is achieved as follows:

There is the usual single-speed gear machined onto the spindle. The spindle also fits inside a second gear. Pawls on the spindle ratchet inside this second gear when the winch handle is cranked in the first (single-speed) direction. The pawls engage the inside of this second gear when the winch handle is turned in reverse (the single-speed gear itself ratcheting at this point). The spindle and second gear are now turning in reverse. Obviously, to be of any use the drum itself must continue to turn in the single-speed direction; otherwise it would just oscillate backward and forward as the handle was cranked backward and forward. An "idler gear" is fitted between the second spindle gear and the drum; this converts the backward spindle movement into forward drum movement (Figure 16-10B).

With this arrangement, although it is a little hard to visualize, any load on the drum (e.g., line pull) tries to turn the spindle in one direction via the first (single-speed) gear, and in the opposite direction via the second gear. Since the spindle cannot rotate in two directions at once, the winch is effectively locked in place by these counterposed forces. When the drum is spun the other way (freewheeled) both gears ratchet, allowing it to turn.

In order to make a winch more powerful, the gear ratio between the handle and drum must be increased. This could be done by increasing the length of the winch handle, but this is clearly impractical. Instead, what is done is to fit more gears into the winch and play with the relative gear sizes. The net result is that a large three-speed winch can look quite complicated, but in reality the principles remain the same as for the simpler winches.

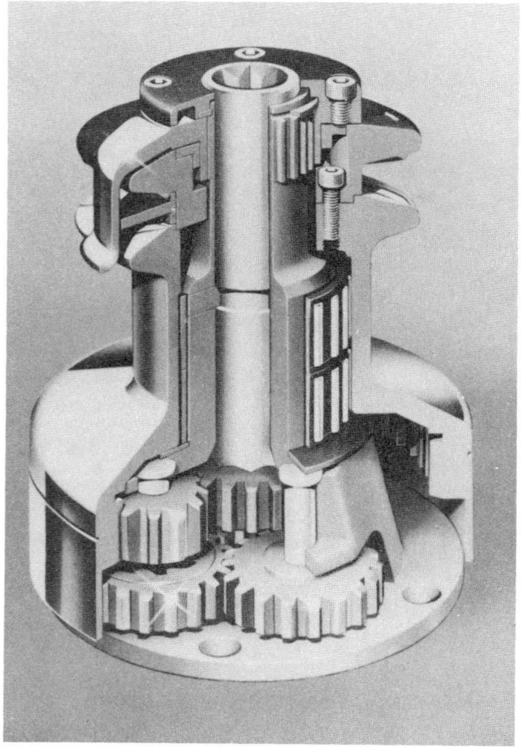

Overhaul

Winch manufacturers have done an outstanding job of making winches fast and easy to strip down. There is really no excuse for not keeping up with routine maintenance. However, the pawls and pawl springs, in particular, are very small, easily lost, and absolutely indispensable to winch operation. Before dismantling, clear the area around a winch and plug any nearby drains—sometimes the pawls and springs hang up and fly out at unexpected moments. Even better, keep spares on board in case any do get lost or broken.

The top of the winch must first be removed (Figure 16-12A). On some the whole top unscrews; others are variously retained with machine screws, socket head screws, or spring clips, often called *circlips* (Figure 16-12B). Beneath the top cover may be a couple of collets fitted into slots in the spindle (Figure 16-12C). Removal should be self-evident. If the winch has a self-tailing mechanism this comes off next. First note the position of the stripper arm in relation to the boat so that it can be put back in the same place. The winch drum now can be lifted off (Figure 16-12E)—this is where care must be taken to watch out for loose pawls, especially any fitted in the base of the drum.

On all but the largest winches all of the bearings and gears are now accessible. The bearings should be retained in a "cage" and may be inside the drum or on the center stem. With the bearings removed, somewhere in the center stem will be a key or collets, which must be gently pried out to release the spindle.

Figure 16-11. Larger winches, with higher gear ratios to handle higher loads, are more complex than simple winches.

Figure 16-12. **Step-by-step winch disassembly for cleaning and maintenance.** Remove screws (**A**) or circlip (**B**). If the winch is self-tailing, pull out retaining collets (**C**). On a halyard winch the halyard must be released from the drum, accomplished here by undoing the two "grub" (allen) screws (**D**). Lift off the drum and bearings (**E**), and oil the top drum pawls (**F**). *(Note: Sequence continues on next page.)*

Winches 447

Figure 16-12 (*cont.*)
Remove the spindle. For clarity, the spindle shown here has been removed already. The plastic key, which fits into a groove in the spindle and is itself retained by the bearings fitted around the winch stem, holds the spindle in place (**G**). You can pry loose a spindle, or gear shaft (**H**). Finally, remove the gears (**I**).

groove in spindle

winch stem

key

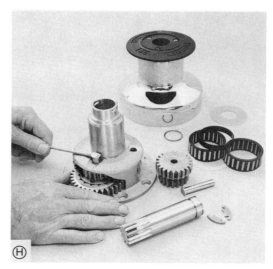

If any corrosion is present, the spindle itself may be a little hard to remove. A good spraying with penetrating oil will help, and a winch handle can be locked in place and used to work the spindle out (Figures 16–12F and G). Any gears will be retained by shafts (also called spindles) that simply lift out (Figures 16–12H and I). Larger winches have replaceable sleeves around the gear shafts, or the gears themselves ride on small roller bearings.

Gear shafts, sleeves and/or bearings should all go back in the same place. It is best to lay everything out on a clean work surface, with the various parts the right way up and in the correct relationship to each other.

Thoroughly clean everything in kerosene (paraffin) and dry with a lint-free rag. Inspect the gears for worn, chipped, or "stepped" teeth; the stainless steel shafts for crevice corrosion; the bearings for corrosion or flat spots; the center stem and inside of the drum for corrosion; above all the pawls for any signs of wear or chipping; and the pawl springs for corrosion and loss of tension. Anodized aluminum self-tailing mechanisms retained by stainless steel fasteners are especially susceptible to corrosion around the fasteners. A little Never Seize or the like on the fastener threads will help to keep this at bay.

Reassembly is the reverse of disassembly. Pay special attention to those all-important pawls and springs, which should be lightly oiled (3-In-One Oil; Marvel Mystery Oil). Make sure that ratchet gears are right side up and the parts properly seated. *Do not grease* the pawls—the grease is likely to attract dirt and salt until eventually the pawls bind in their housings and fail to operate. Gears and bearings should be *lightly* greased, however, with a Teflon-based marine grease (Lubriplate, Marine Lube A, etc.).

No oil or grease should ever be applied to the brake band or mechanism on any halyard winch—this can create a serious safety hazard.

Note that gear shafts fit into holes in the base plate. During cleaning operations particles of dirt are liable to fall into these holes. They must be scrupulously cleaned out or the shafts will not seat properly. The shafts themselves have odd-shaped heads fitting into machined recesses and *must be properly seated*. The spindle key fits into a machined groove in the spindle. If it won't go in, *don't force it* (in fact, *nothing* on a winch needs forcing). Raise or lower the spindle a fraction until the key is an easy fit.

Refitting a self-tailing mechanism: If it has a separate stripper ring make sure that this is placed under the stripper arm (it fits in a slot) and put the stripper arm back in the necessary relationship to the boat to make the sheet fall in the correct place (Figure 16-13F). Any fasteners just need to be pinched up—don't overtighten, especially where plastic housings are involved.

Figure 16-13A. **Maintenance and reassembly procedures. A large 3-speed winch disassembled. You'd better keep all the parts organized and the right way up!**

Figure 16-13B. **Oil the pawls.**

Figure 16-13C. **Lightly grease the spindles and bearings.**

Figure 16-13D,E. **Where there is a choice, make sure that ratchet gears are the right way up. Those shown at left are wrong; pawls are not seating properly. Those shown at right are correct, with pawls seated fully.**

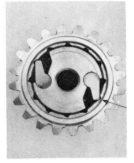 

Figure 16-13F. **Reassembling a self-tailing mechanism. Note the stripper arm being lined up to fit under the feeder arm.**

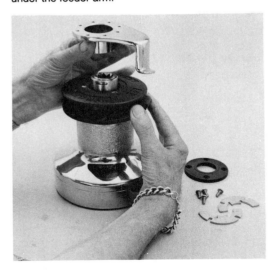

Winches   449

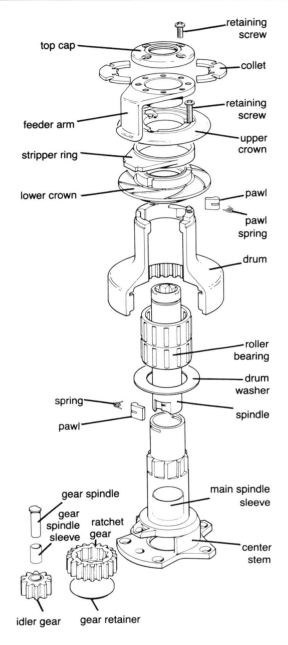

Figure 16-14. **Self-tailing winch.**

Labels (top to bottom, left and right):
top cap — retaining screw — collet — feeder arm — retaining screw — upper crown — stripper ring — lower crown — pawl — pawl spring — drum — roller bearing — drum washer — spring — spindle — pawl — gear spindle — main spindle sleeve — gear spindle sleeve — ratchet gear — center stem — idler gear — gear retainer

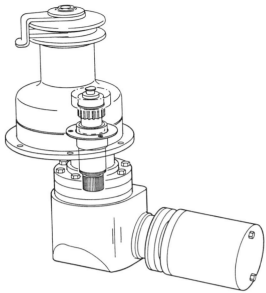

Figure 16-15. **Electric-powered winch.** The winch is essentially the same as a manual winch with the exception of some minor modifications to take the motor drive.

Powered Winches

Powered winches are becoming more popular. Until recently almost all had electric motors, but now there is a trend toward some very sophisticated hydraulic systems (e.g., Lewmar's Commander system). In any event, the winch end of things is just the same as a manual winch, except for some minor modifications to the spindle to allow a motor to be geared in from below.

The motor end of powered winches is the same as for powered windlasses—see the relevant sections later in this chapter. Some two-and three-speed winches are also being powered; here sensitive electronic equipment, linked into a central microprocessor, senses the load on a winch and reverses the motor at a certain trip point. This has the same effect as reversing the direction of cranking on a winch handle—i.e., it engages another gear. At higher loads an electromagnet is tripped to engage a third gear (where fitted).

If a two-speed winch only operates at one speed, try reversing the power leads *from* the control unit *to* the motor (*not* the power leads *to* the control unit—you would probably wreck it).

Faced with a motor failure, run all the usual voltage tests (see "Electric Windlasses" in this chapter) and jump the motor directly from the battery to make sure it really is at fault. Check the brushes, brush springs, and commutator; run the motor tests outlined in Chapter 6.

Anchor Windlasses

Anchor windlasses may be horizontal or vertical. In the former the drum (for rope) and *wildcat* (gypsy, for chain) stick out the sides; in the latter they are set one on top of the other. Windlasses are both manually operated and powered, the majority of the latter having electric motors, but some being hydraulically driven.

Maintenance

Windlasses are generally low-maintenance, trouble-free items. The most essential part of preventive maintenance is to keep the windlass covered when not in use, and occasionally wash down the exterior surfaces with fresh water. Open-gear (non-lubricated) windlasses should be flushed out at the same time.

Most windlasses run in an oil or grease bath. Infrequent use causes the lubricant to settle out. Aside from maintaining oil levels, the windlass should be periodically cranked to distribute lubricant around the gears. Most gears, sprockets, and chains are steel—a failure to turn the windlass over from time to time will lead to rusting and seizure. A sample should be taken annually from the base of the gearbox to check for salt water or emulsification. In either case the gearbox should be flushed and fresh lubricant added. (To clean out a grease-filled box the windlass must be unbolted and the baseplate removed—see below.) Sometimes special greases are used that coat and adhere to the internal parts better than a normal grease. Refer to the manual.

Clutch cones and brake linings need annual lubrication; the manual will specify the type of lubricant. The clutch nut is undone and the wildcat slipped off to gain access to the clutch or brake pad. Where the windlass has a plated steel shaft be sure to remove the rope drum annually and grease the shaft or the two will seize up and be *impossible* to separate.

Problems Common To All Windlasses

Corrosion. Anchor windlasses occupy one of the most exposed positions on any boat, subject to constant saltwater drenchings. Since most incorporate dissimilar metals (notably aluminum, bronze, steel, and stainless steel), there is an obvious potential for galvanic interaction. Windlasses should therefore be periodically washed down with fresh water, and *should be kept covered*. However, in practice most external corrosion problems tend to be cosmetic or peripheral to the main functioning of the windlass (e.g., blistered paintwork on aluminum windlasses; oxidizing of aluminum housings and baseplates around stainless steel fasteners). These problems can be irritating and make disassembly and overhaul difficult, but rarely interfere with the basic functioning of the windlass.

Far more damaging is internal corrosion, which leads to seizure. As noted, many gears, sprockets, chains, and even shafts are steel or plated steel *and will rust if not lubricated*. It is essential to turn windlasses over regularly, to maintain oil and grease levels, and to ensure that no water enters the windlass case. Corrosion from condensation alone can seize up an unused windlass. Windlasses in anchor wells, even though closed off and protected, are actually more prone to corrosion than those on foredecks—the anchor well produces a wonderfully warm and humid atmosphere!

In time the galvanizing will strip off anchor chains. In certain instances this can happen quite rapidly, such as on a boat anchored on top of a steel wreck. Galvanic interaction can strip the zinc off the anchor chain in a matter of days! The chain should be turned end for end each year, and regalvanized when it starts to rust. Turning the chain also ensures that all connections and links (shackles, swivels, chain-to-rope splices, and the fastening on the bitter end) get undone and inspected at least once a year. Be sure to properly seize all shackles with stainless steel wire after doing them back up.

Snubbing loads. The majority of operating problems arise from overloading a windlass through excessive snubbing loads. When an anchored boat is lying to all-chain rode (anchor line) in choppy seas, the foredeck can pitch up and down through many feet, gaining considerable momentum in the process. If the anchor is well buried, as it should be, the anchor windlass is subjected to repeated shock loading when the bow comes up. We first used our Simpson Lawrence SL555 wind-

Figure 16-16. Windlass shaft sheared by snubbing loads.

lass in winds over 40 knots in a shallow lake with a nasty chop: We sheared the main windlass shaft cleanly in half!

Anchor windlasses just are not designed to handle heavy snubbing loads, although from time to time some are inevitable and even necessary, particularly when breaking out a deeply buried anchor. In general, though, the windlass always should be protected against shock loads. This is done as follows:

1. Drop the anchor, pay out adequate scope (at least 4:1 on chain) and set the anchor (make sure it is dug in).
2. Attach a length of *nylon* line (the snubbing line) to the anchor chain at the bow roller, leave a few feet to dangle, and firmly cleat off the other end to a samson post or equivalent (Figure 16-17).
3. Pay out some more chain until the snubbing line is taking all the anchoring loads, and then feed out a foot or two more and lock off the windlass.

It is important to use nylon rope for a snubbing line, since it will stretch and act as a shock absorber. Three-strand nylon is better in this respect than plaited (braided) types. The size of the line will depend on the boat's weight and the sea conditions—too heavy a line will not stretch; too light will break. Three-eighths inch works well on most boats to around 25,000 pounds; ½ inch up to 40,000 pounds; ⅝ inch there-

after. Only a few feet is required—certainly no more than 15 feet need be let out in most conditions. The amount of chain left dangling (note loop in Figure 16-17) should be about one-quarter the length of the snubbing line. In a strong blow the line will stretch tight, allowing the chain and windlass to take some of the load. Nylon will tolerate repeated stretching to 125 percent of its original length without failure.

Many people use chain hooks to attach the snubbing line to the chain. Having lost several I now use two half-hitches and have never had a snubber either slip or prove too difficult to undo. The key is to make the second hitch *below* the standing part (note in Figure 16-17). If the second hitch is made above the standing part, the lower half of the knot will roll over the top half and jam under load.

Jumping chain. Sometimes chain will jump off a wildcat. This can be the result of an improper match between chain and wildcat (every different chain size and type—proof-coil, BBB, and high test—needs its own wildcat), but can also arise through improper chain leads and twisted chains.

One of the big difficulties is that there is no international standard for chain sizes. Even within individual countries, chain manufacture still tends to be a small shop operation, and variations in chain of nominally the same size are common. The only

Table 16-1. Approximate Chain Dimensions.[1]

Type of Chain	Trade Size in Inches	Size Material in Inches	Working Load Limit Pounds	Nominal Inside Length in Inches	Nominal Inside Width in Inches	Maximum Length 100 Links in Inches	Links per Foot	Weight per 100 Feet Pounds
Proof Coil Chain	5/16	11/32	1,900	1.10	0.50	114	11	106
	3/8	13/32	2,650	1.23	0.62	128	9¾	155
	7/16	15/32	3,500	1.37	0.75	142	8¾	217
	1/2	17/32	4,500	1.54	0.79	156	7¾	270
High-Test Chain	5/16	11/32	3,900	1.01	0.48	105	12¼	110
	3/8	13/32	5,400	1.15	0.58	121	10½	160
	7/16	15/32	7,200	1.29	0.67	134	9⅛	216
	1/2	17/32	9,200	1.43	0.76	148	8½	280
BBB Coil Chain	5/16	11/32	1,950	1.00	0.50	104	12	120
	3/8	13/32	2,750	1.09	0.62	113	11	173
	7/16	15/32	3,625	1.21	0.68	126	9¾	232
	1/2	17/32	4,750	1.34	0.75	139	9	307

1. Working load must not be exceeded. European chain is measured in millimeters, but there are differences in measurements from one country to another.

sure way to match the chain and wildcat is to take the wildcat to the chain. Better still, order chain from the windlass manufacturer at the time you purchase the windlass.

It is USA practice to make chain 1/32 inch larger than its nominal size (trade size), so 5/16-inch chain is in fact 11/32 inch, and 3/8-inch chain is 13/32 inch! This makes USA chain heavier and more costly than in the UK and other areas where the trade size is the same as nominal.

Europe is beginning to standardize around International Standard ISO 4565, "Small Craft Anchor Chains," but this is gaining no following in the USA (probably because all dimensions are given in millimeters).

On a horizontal windlass the wildcat must be at least as high as the bow roller so that the chain feeds *at least horizontally and preferably up to* the wildcat (Figure 16-18). This ensures proper engagement of the chain and wildcat. On the other side of the wildcat, the chain ideally should have a free fall of a foot or two so that its weight maintains a little pull on the wildcat. With vertical windlasses it is sometimes necessary to have someone tail the chain from below (i.e., maintain pressure on it). If this is not done, the chain can get jammed between the stripper and the deck opening.

If a boat swings around its anchor repeatedly the chain can twist up. When the anchor is weighed, the chain has a tendency to sit on the surface of the wildcat

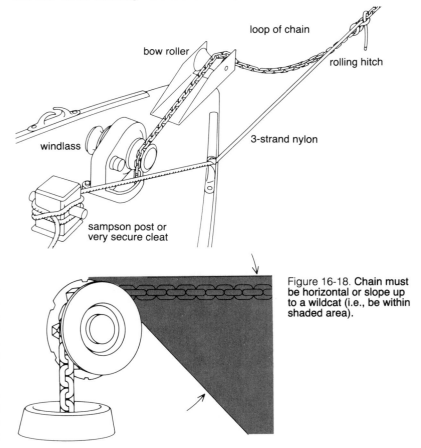

Figure 16-17. Relieve the load on winches with a snubbing line. On boats with bowsprits and bobstays, lead the snubbing line through a bulwark chock. The boat will lie slightly off the wind and the bobstay will not "saw" on the snubbing line and anchor chain.

Figure 16-18. Chain must be horizontal or slope up to a wildcat (i.e., be within shaded area).

rather than seat in it. The chain can then skip back out. Swivels fitted between the chain and anchor will help to eliminate the twist in the chain, but having looked at a few and used one or two I suspect that most swivels form *the* weak link in an anchor system. It is a rare occasion indeed when twisted chain is anything more than a minor irritation, and I prefer to live with this.

Windlass failures. Wearing of bushings, shafts, and gears will eventually cause gears and ratchets to slip; pawls may break or stick in their housings. Excessive loads can cause shafts to shear and teeth to strip off. Windlasses are potentially quite dangerous—many a finger has been lost through improper use or sudden failure. The first sign of trouble is the time to strip the windlass down and check it out. If the windlass has been well lubricated this is a simple and straightforward procedure, but where corrosion has been allowed to set in it may prove just about impossible.

Horizontal Manual Windlasses.

How they work. Before delving into a windlass, it helps to understand how it works. The engineering problem that has to be overcome is how to convert back-and-forth (reciprocal) motion of the operating lever into a constant rotation at the main shaft. Two approaches are followed, which I intend to call "spur gearing" and "ratchet gearing."

Spur gearing: A gear (the crank gear) is keyed to the same shaft that the crank handle turns backward and forward. Two smaller gears (spur gears) are placed in contact with the crank gear. These spur gears have oversized bore holes that allow them to flop back out of contact with the crank gear. A spring between the two spur gears holds them up against the crank gear. One spur gear also contacts a gear (the drive gear) keyed to the output shaft; the other spur gear contacts an idler gear, which in turn is permanently engaged with the drive gear.

When the crank handle is moved in one direction (clockwise in Figure 16-19A through 16–19D), the crank gear traps the lower spur gear between itself and the drive gear, turning the drive gear. The drive gear not only turns the main shaft and wildcat, but at the same time turns the idler gear. The second (upper) spur gear

finds itself between the idler gear and the crank gear, which are turning in opposite directions. It is bounced out of the way against the spring pressure.

When the crank handle is moved in the other direction the crank gear turns counterclockwise (anticlockwise) and traps the upper spur gear between itself and the idler gear. This turns the idler gear, which reverses the direction of rotation and so imparts the same rotation as before to the drive gear and output shaft. The lower spur gear finds itself between the drive gear and crank gear, which are moving in opposite directions. It is bounced out of the way against the spring pressure.

When the wildcat (gypsy) is under a load, both spur gears are forced down into contact with the crank gear, but in *opposite* directions of rotation. The counterposed forces lock the windlass up and prevent the wildcat from letting out chain. Some means is needed to release the wildcat in order to drop the anchor.

The wildcat is not itself keyed to the drive shaft. It is either tapered on its inner face and sits on a tapered friction pad (a *cone clutch*), the latter being locked to the shaft; or the wildcat is trapped between a flange on the drive shaft and a friction (brake) pad or lining. In both cases a handwheel or clutch nut, threaded to the end of the main shaft, can be tightened to trap the wildcat and lock it to the shaft, or loosened to let the wildcat freewheel. Tension on the handwheel or clutch nut acts as a brake to control the rate of release of chain.

A second (low) speed is easily added to this windlass by placing another small (low speed) crank gear in contact with the primary (high speed) crank gear. When the operating lever is used to crank the low-speed gear backward and forward this gear turns the high-speed gear, but at a greatly reduced rate. From there on everything is the same as above.

Ratchet gearing (see Figure 16-21). The crank handle rotates around the output (wildcat) shaft with a gear on either side. One gear (the direct-drive gear) is keyed to the output shaft; the other (the counter-drive gear) floats (i.e., is free to rotate around the shaft). On either side of the crank handle assembly are pawls, which are counterposed (i.e., face in opposite directions) to one another.

When the crank handle is moved one way, one pawl engages the direct-drive gear, turning it and therefore the output

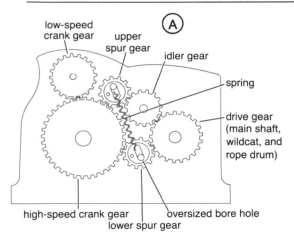

low-speed crank gear
upper spur gear
idler gear
spring
drive gear (main shaft, wildcat, and rope drum)
high-speed crank gear
lower spur gear
oversized bore hole

Figure 16-19A,B,C. **The operation of a spur-geared manual horizontal anchor windlass. Pulling back and pushing forward on the winch handle both rotate the wildcat and rope drum in the same direction (B). A load on the wildcat forces both spur gears against the crank gear, locking the windlass (C).**

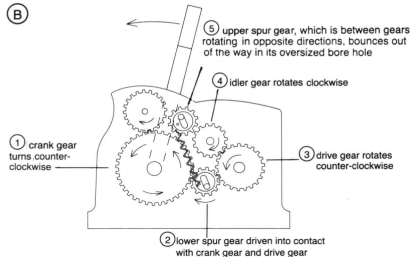

(B)

(5) upper spur gear, which is between gears rotating in opposite directions, bounces out of the way in its oversized bore hole

(4) idler gear rotates clockwise

(1) crank gear turns counter-clockwise

(3) drive gear rotates counter-clockwise

(2) lower spur gear driven into contact with crank gear and drive gear

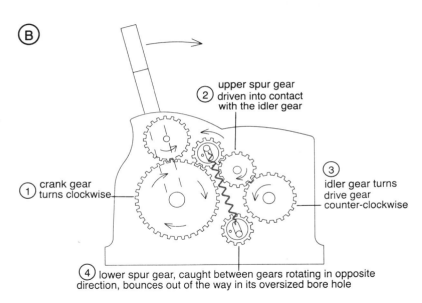

(B)

(2) upper spur gear driven into contact with the idler gear

(1) crank gear turns clockwise

(3) idler gear turns drive gear counter-clockwise

(4) lower spur gear, caught between gears rotating in opposite direction, bounces out of the way in its oversized bore hole

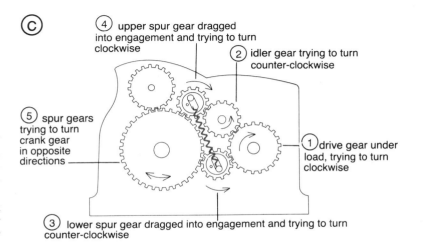

(C)

(4) upper spur gear dragged into engagement and trying to turn clockwise

(2) idler gear trying to turn counter-clockwise

(5) spur gears trying to turn crank gear in opposite directions

(1) drive gear under load, trying to turn clockwise

(3) lower spur gear dragged into engagement and trying to turn counter-clockwise

shaft. The other pawl bounces over the counter-drive gear. When the handle reverses, the direct-drive pawl bounces free while the counter-drive pawl engages and turns the counter-drive gear.

The counter-drive gear meshes with an intermediate gear. This in turn meshes with a second intermediate gear, which also engages the direct-drive gear. When the counter-drive gear turns one way, the direct-drive gear turns the other way (i.e., the same way as before).

When a load is applied to the wildcat, and through it to the direct-drive gear, the reverse rotation brings *both* direct-drive and counter-drive gears up against their pawls but from opposite directions. The counterposed forces effectively lock up the windlass. The wildcat can only be released via a cone clutch or brake, just as with a spur gear-type winch.

A variation on the same theme keys the crank handle to an auxiliary shaft with two different sized gears on it. Both gears are mounted on roller clutches such that they freewheel (ratchet) in one direction and grip in the other. The clutches are installed in opposite directions (i.e., one locks one way, the other the opposite way). The larger gear directly engages an output gear on the main shaft; the smaller gear engages the output gear via an idler gear

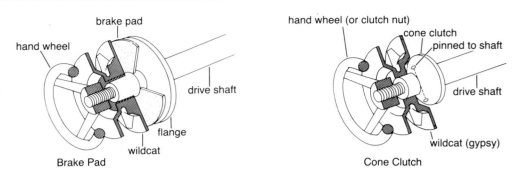

Figure 16-19D. **Chain is veered by loosening the wildcat's cone clutch or brake pad. Tighten the hand wheel or clutch nut when you have sufficient scope. Careful; this is a good place to lose a finger!**

brake pad

hand wheel

drive shaft

flange

wildcat

Brake Pad

hand wheel (or clutch nut)

cone clutch

pinned to shaft

drive shaft

wildcat (gypsy)

Cone Clutch

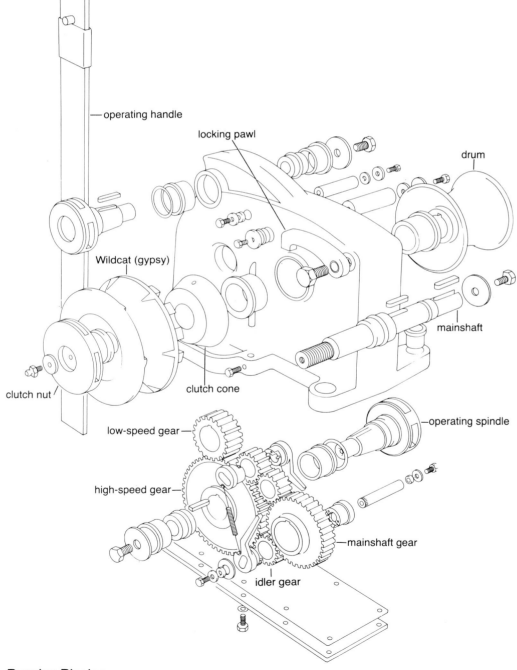

operating handle

locking pawl

drum

Figure 16-20. **The spur-geared manual windlass revealed: the popular SL555 from Simpson Lawrence.**

Wildcat (gypsy)

mainshaft

clutch nut

clutch cone

operating spindle

low-speed gear

high-speed gear

mainshaft gear

idler gear

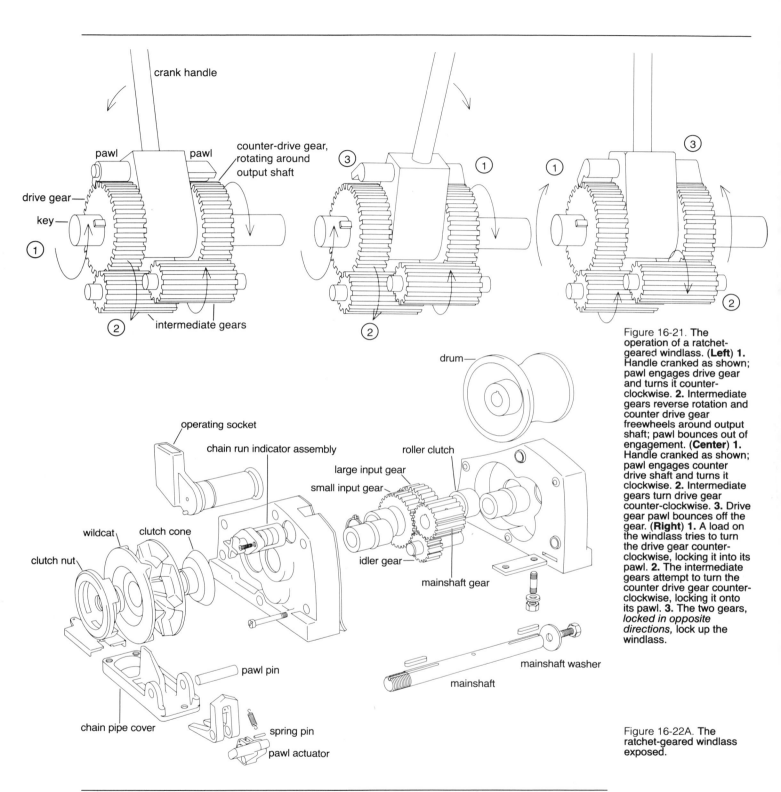

crank handle

pawl · pawl

counter-drive gear, rotating around output shaft

drive gear—

key—

intermediate gears

drum—

operating socket

chain run indicator assembly

roller clutch

large input gear

small input gear

wildcat · clutch cone

clutch nut

idler gear

mainshaft gear

pawl pin

chain pipe cover

spring pin

pawl actuator

mainshaft washer

mainshaft

Figure 16-21. The operation of a ratchet-geared windlass. (**Left**) **1.** Handle cranked as shown; pawl engages drive gear and turns it counter-clockwise. **2.** Intermediate gears reverse rotation and counter drive gear freewheels around output shaft; pawl bounces out of engagement. (**Center**) **1.** Handle cranked as shown; pawl engages counter drive shaft and turns it clockwise. **2.** Intermediate gears turn drive gear counter-clockwise. **3.** Drive gear pawl bounces off the gear. (**Right**) **1.** A load on the windlass tries to turn the drive gear counter-clockwise, locking it into its pawl. **2.** The intermediate gears attempt to turn the counter drive gear counter-clockwise, locking it onto its pawl. **3.** The two gears, *locked in opposite directions*, lock up the windlass.

Figure 16-22A. The ratchet-geared windlass exposed.

(on an idler shaft). Operation is then as above (Figure 16-21).

Yet another variation on the same theme is the popular small Simpson Lawrence Hyspeed (510) windlass, which has two bicycle sprockets mounted on the main shaft on opposing ratchets (Figure 16-22B). The operating lever drives two chains backward and forward, turning the sprockets. One chain drives its sprocket directly; the other chain is fed around rollers to reverse the direction of drive. When the handle is

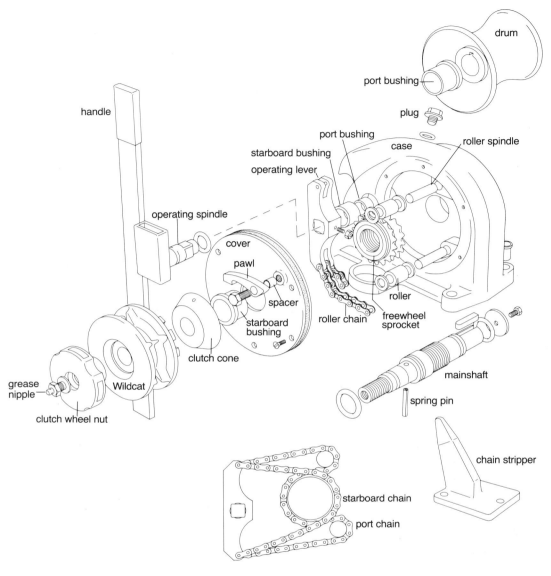

Figure 16-22B. **Chain-drive ratchet-geared windlass.**

cranked one way, one sprocket turns the shaft while the other freewheels; cranking the other way engages the second sprocket while the first freewheels.

Dismantling and repair. While the windlass is still securely fastened to the foredeck remove the clutch nut or handwheel, and the rope drum retaining bolt. Pull off the drum and wildcat.

Wildcats will jam on clutch cones when ungreased and unused—loosen the clutch nut and then lever the wildcat free. Plated steel shafts will corrode to rope drums and may not come free, even with a 10-ton press! In this case the output shaft must be hacksawed through, obviously necessitating subsequent replacement.

Now remove the windlass from the foredeck (generally four bolts). Some windlasses use no lubrication and have an open base. Others are filled with oil or grease and have a plate that must be removed.

With the base open tap out the main shaft—in some cases it may come out either side of the windlass, but if the holes in the sides of the windlass casing differ in size, it will have to come out the side with the largest hole. The drive gear or sprockets, and any other gears and parts mounted on the shaft, will all come loose and can be retrieved through the base of the windlass. Watch out for keys locking gears to shafts—they are easily lost and hard to replace.

Any other gears are removed the same way. The various shafts will have retaining screws, seals, and/or plates; once these are undone the shaft is knocked out and the gear falls into the windlass.

Inspect the gears for broken or chipped teeth, or "steps" in the teeth; inspect the shafts for ridges; slide the gears back on their shafts and check for play; slip the shafts into the windlass housing and also check for play. Most shafts fit into removable bushings. If these need replacing, they generally can be knocked out with a suitably sized *drift;* a socket with an outside diameter a little less than the diameter of the bushing works well. The important thing is to exert an even pressure over the whole bushing.

Fitting new bushings will be greatly facilitated if boiling water is poured over the housing to expand it. But first, warm the *entire* housing to avoid any sudden localized heating, which could cause castings to crack. Knock the new bushing in using a piece of hardwood as a drift.

Windlasses frequently use only a small portion of their gears (e.g., the main crank gear on spur gear windlasses generally only moves back and forth through 90 degrees), and loads are concentrated on only one side of shafts and bushings. Faced with certain breakdowns and no spare parts, it may be possible to get by temporarily by turning bushings and gears through 90 or 180 degrees and reassembling.

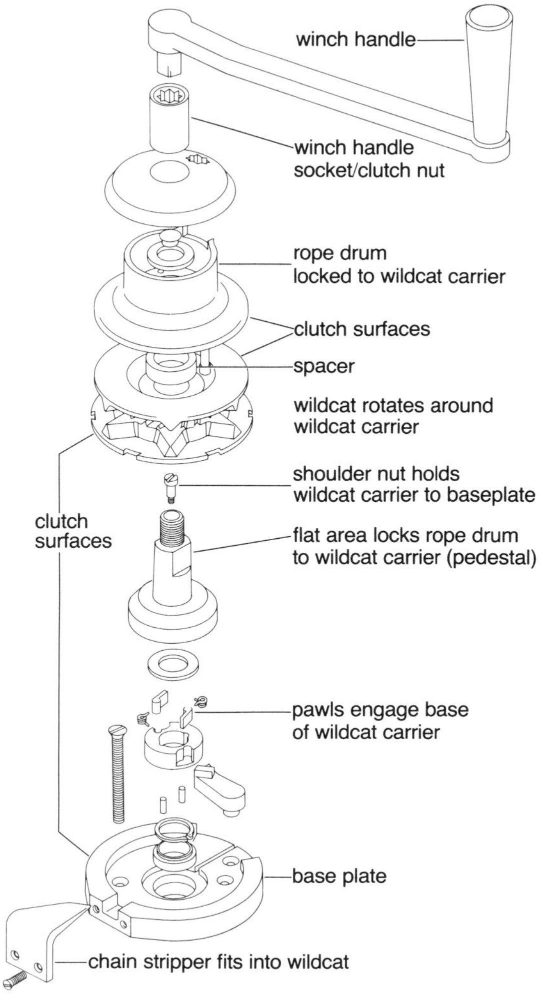

Figure 16-23. **Vertical manual windlasses are gearless, the length of the winch handle providing the only leverage. Cranking in tightens the clutch nut, trapping the wildcat between the clutch friction surfaces. Continued cranking rotates the drum, ratcheting in the anchor rode. The pawls prevent it from unwinding. Reversing the winch handle's direction loosens the clutch nut, and allows chain or warp to veer out. Note: The clutch surfaces are metal-to-metal. Trapped particles of dirt will lead to scoring. To compensate, some units have renewable friction pads.**

Vertical Manual Windlasses

A vertical manual windlass has a winch handle socket in the top of its drum. A winch handle is used to turn the drum and wildcat, winching in the anchor. Ratchets on the windlass pedestal engage the drum to keep it from unwinding. Between the drum and wildcat is a friction pad or surface. Turning the winch handle in reverse unscrews a clutch nut, allowing the wildcat to freewheel and let out chain.

Unscrewing the clutch nut completely allows the drum and wildcat to be lifted off, exposing any clutch cones (friction pads) if fitted, as well as pawls and springs. Inspect the clutch cones (or friction surfaces between the drum, wildcat, and winch base if no clutch cones are fitted) for

excessive wear or scoring. Pay particular attention to the pawls and pawl springs (see the relevant sections on winches earlier in this chapter).

Electric Windlasses

How they work. A large electric motor (usually a modified starter motor) drives the windlass through a reduction gearbox. Two types of gearing are normally used: offset (spur) gears (Figure 16-24); and worm gears (Figure 16-25); motors are reversible by switching the power leads, although in most installations the motor is only used for hauling in the anchor. The anchor is generally let out as in manual installations (i.e., by loosening the clutch nut). In all cases the wildcat and drum are

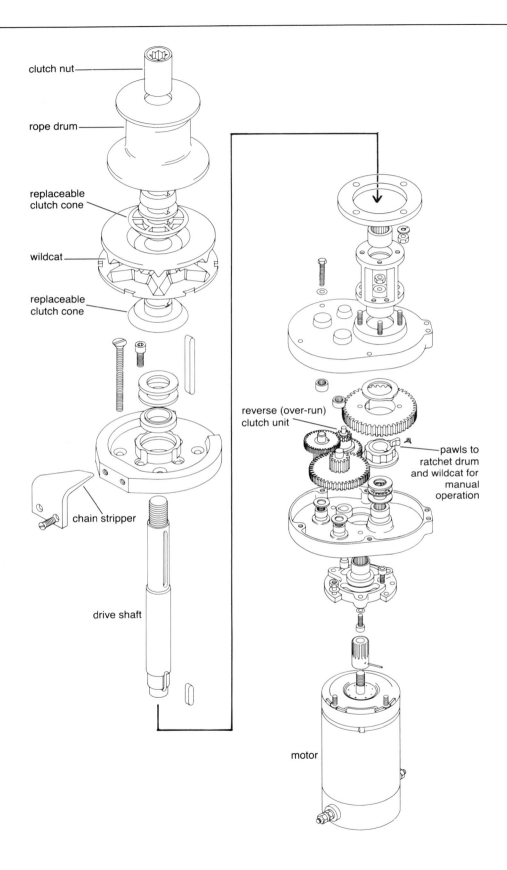

Figure 16-24. **Electric windlass with offset gearing.**

clutch nut

rope drum

replaceable clutch cone

wildcat

replaceable clutch cone

chain stripper

drive shaft

reverse (over-run) clutch unit

pawls to ratchet drum and wildcat for manual operation

motor

Table 16-2. Windlass Current Draw Vs. Load.[1]

Load (pounds)	Current Draw (amps)	Speed of Recovery (meters/minute)
500	110	8.6
1,000	170	7.2
1,500	230	5.8
2,000	290	4.3
2,500	350	2.9
3,000	410	1.5

1. These data are based on a Lewmar 2000 (12-volt), which takes a working load of 1,000 pounds and a maximum load of 2,000 pounds.

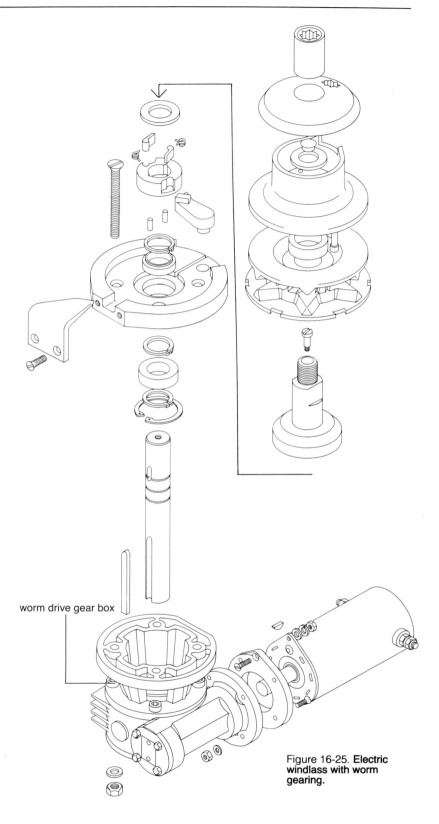

ratcheted so that they can be operated manually in the event of windlass failure, independent of the motor and gearing. However, manual operation is direct-drive (no gearing) and therefore provides very little power.

Offset (spur) gears. Offset gears are far more efficient than worm gears, which typically absorb up to 45 percent of motor output, dissipating it as heat. Because of the efficiency of offset gearing, when a load is placed on the windlass the gears can spin the motor in reverse, allowing the windlass to let out chain or line. This type of electric windlass has to incorporate a braking device; typically a clutch locks the gears when the windlass is not in use, but is electrically released via a solenoid as soon as the motor is energized.

Worm gears. Worm gears provide a tremendous amount of resistance to being driven backward by a load on the windlass. No separate clutch/brake is needed. However, they are, as noted, very inefficient. The main rationale for their use is that they tend to be cheaper, and they enable a more compact installation to be made (the motor is horizontal rather than vertical), which interferes less with headroom in the boat.

Lewmar employs a very fine-toothed modified worm gear (called a *spiroid gear*) in its powered winches and windlasses (Figure 16-26).

Problems with electric windlasses.

Water leaks. Most motors are installed below decks beneath the windlass. Snub-

worm drive gear box

Figure 16-25. **Electric windlass with worm gearing.**

bing loads on the windlass, and inadequate decks, will lead to flexing, and this will open up deck seals. *Any* failure of the deck seal will allow water down below.

At best, this water is liable to drip on wiring and terminals, leading to corrosion and voltage drop. At worst it will penetrate motor seals and destroy motors.

Chain damage. If the motor and its wiring are not fully protected in the chain locker, the chain may damage either or both when swinging around in a seaway.

Voltage drop. Windlasses at full (stalling) load pull tremendous amperages (anywhere from 200 to 500 amps on mid-sized boats). Generally batteries are situated at some distance. Supply cables have to be selected to handle these loads with a *maximum* 10-percent voltage drop *at full load*— refer to the tables in Chapter 3. Remember to count the distance to *and* from the windlass. Undersized cables are a common problem.

Next, check the state of the battery and battery capacity. Undersized and poorly charged batteries also will create voltage drop, and this in turn will lead to overheated motors and potential burnout. Circuit breakers, too, are frequently undersized, designed to handle normal operating loads and not stalling loads. They then are inadequate for the odd occasion when you need to break out a really stubborn anchor.

Stalling and thermal cutouts. Windlass motors are designed only for intermittent use (sometimes as little as a couple of minutes at a time). If used under heavy loads, or with high voltage drops, they will soon heat up. Most have thermal overload trips and will cut out. Once tripped they are likely to take a long time to cool down. If a motor stalls, *stop using it and let it cool a*

Figure 16-26. Electric windlass unit with spiroid gearbox.

Figure 16-27. Proper windlass installation. The unprotected windlass motor **(left)** is subjected to salt corrosion, and can be shorted out by the chain. Enclosing the motor **(center)** solves both of these problems. The best solution is to mount the windlass assembly outside the chain locker.

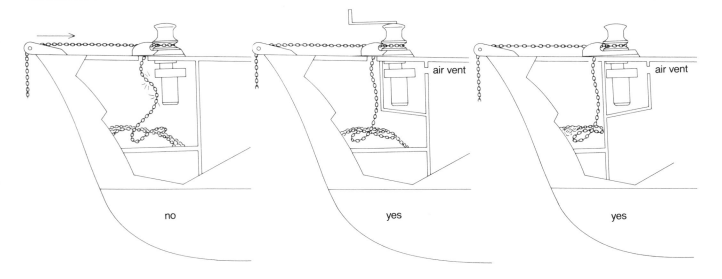

no   yes   yes

Table 16-3. Approximate Sizes of Electric Cable.[1]

| Distance from Battery to Windlass | | | | | Cable Size | |
| 12 Volt | | 24 Volt | | | | Approximate |
Meters	Feet	Meters	Feet	MM²	AWG	
N.A.	N.A.	3.50	11.5	25	3	
2.85	9.5	4.75	15.5	35	2	
4.10	13.5	6.80	22.0	50	1/0 (0)	
5.45	18.0	9.05	30.0	70	2/0 (00)	
6.75	22.0	11.20	37.0	95	3/0 (000)	
7.65	25.0	12.70	42.0	120	4/0 (0000)	
9.85	31.5	16.30	53.5	150	5/0 (00000)	
11.10	36.5	18.40	60.5	185	7/0 (0000000)	
					9/0	
12.75	42.0	21.10	69.0	240	(000000000)	
300-amp circuit breaker needed		200-amp circuit breaker needed				

1. Sizes given are for an electric windlass with a maximum 2,000-pound line pull; 290 amps at 12 volts, 175 amps at 24 volts. The total cable run is two times the distances given. Voltage drop at maximum load should not exceed 2 volts.

while. If it trips repeatedly on thermal overload, it is too small or incorrectly installed (inadequate wiring, etc.).

Remote switches. Most electric winches use remote switches that operate a solenoid to close the main contactors to the motor (just as in a starter-motor circuit, see Chapter 6). Where the winch has a power-down, as well as up, function, two switches are used—the second reversing the power supply to the motor (see Figure 16-28A and B). *Never operate both switches at the same time;* this will create a dead short.

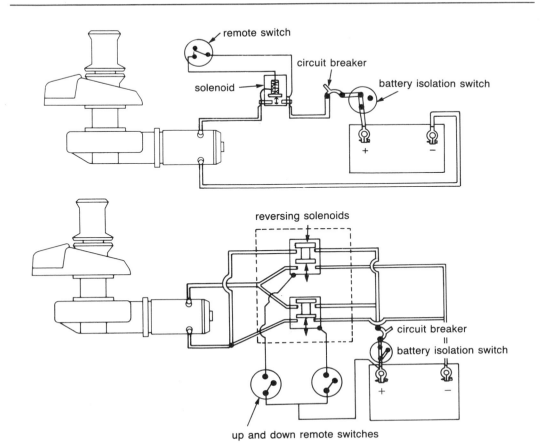

Figure 16-28A. **Wiring diagram for a non-reversing electric windlass.**

Figure 16-28B. **Wiring diagram for a reversing-type electric windlass.** Note: Operating both switches simultaneously will cause a dead short to the battery.

Refer to the section in Chapter 6 on starter motors for various steps for testing switches and solenoids.

Lewmar uses *air bellows* in place of switches. A small air chamber with a diaphragm is connected, via PVC tubing, to another chamber and diaphragm attached to the solenoid switch. Depressing the first diaphragm causes air pressure to move the second diaphragm, which operates the switch. There are no external switches on deck likely to get wet and corrode.

If the air bellows fail, jump out the solenoid to see if the bellows circuit is at fault. If the motor now runs, check for air leaks on the PVC tubing connections, collapsed or damaged tubing, or holes in the diaphragms.

Another situation can arise with long tubing runs in hot areas (e.g., engine rooms, or under teak decks, which soak up the sun). The air in the tube can expand enough to trip the switch and set the motor off! Bleed off some air pressure and see about shortening, or rerouting, the tubing.

Motor failures. Before writing off a motor, check the brushes, brush springs, and commutator and run the various tests outlined in Chapter 6.

Dismantling and repair. The top (above decks) end is similar to a winch and generally simplicity itself to take apart. Motor removal is also very straightforward—the removal of two or three bolts should allow it to be pulled out.

Gearboxes must be tackled carefully with close attention to where, *and what way around,* everything goes. Note in particular that Lewmar's spiroid gearboxes are built to close tolerances. *Extreme precision* is required on reassembly to ensure correct meshing of the gears. It is best not to delve into gearboxes unless absolutely necessary.

Hydraulic Windlasses

How they work. A separate pump supplies hydraulic oil at high pressure (typically up to 2,000 psi) to a hydraulic motor on the base of the windlass. Reversing oil flow reverses winch operation. Cutting off oil flow locks the winch. As with all other windlasses, a manual clutch/wildcat release for letting out chain is provided, and the wildcat is ratcheted for manual operation in the event of motor failure. Oil pressure can be supplied by either an engine-driven

pump or an electric pump (e.g., Lewmar Commander systems).

Problems with hydraulic windlasses.

Leaks. Leaks, as ever, are the bane of any hydraulic system. Leaks lead to air in the system, and then pumps can become air-bound. If the hydraulic pump is working but the windlass fails to work, check the oil level in the system; top up and purge (bleed) as necessary; find out where lost oil is going.

Dirt and moisture. The next most common causes of hydraulic problems—hydraulic systems must be *scrupulously* clean. Pumps and motors are built to *very close* tolerances. Valves will not seat with even a speck of dirt on them. Pistons and cylinders will score. When installing hydraulic hoses, be very careful not to get sawdust in them as they are pushed through holes in bulkheads, and watch out for dirt in quick-fit connectors. All units should have a filter on the return line to the hydraulic tank.

Moisture can arise from condensation in hydraulic oil tanks; periodically drain a sample of oil from the base of the tank and check for contamination. If not removed, moisture will cause rust on all kinds of sensitive parts and lead to expensive damage.

Undersized hydraulic lines. Hydraulic lines that are too small for the system they are serving create pressure drops, overheated pumps, and loss of performance (just as undersized wiring causes voltage drop and overheated motors). Anchor windlasses, in particular, are frequently at the end of long hose runs, so make sure the hoses are adequate; keep bends to a minimum; and avoid tight radiuses. Hydraulic plumbing is covered in more detail in Chapter 13, on steering systems.

Electrical problems. Most hydraulic systems are operated via electric solenoid valves, remote switches, etc. These are, in actual fact, the most likely source of problems—see all the relevant sections on electric windlasses.

Dismantling and repair. As with an electric windlass, the top (above decks) end is similar to a winch, and generally simple to take apart. Below decks will be the motor and a reduction gearbox. Hydraulic motors and gearboxes are built to close tolerances and should be left alone (the more

hydraulic motor

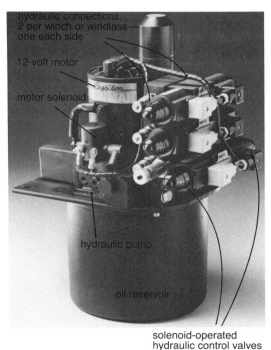

hydraulic connections,
2 per winch or windlass—
one each side

12-volt motor

motor solenoid

hydraulic pump

oil reservoir

solenoid-operated
hydraulic control valves
direct the oil flow

Figure 16-29. **Hydraulic windlass** *(far left)*, **and an electric-powered hydraulic powerpack** *(left)*. Solenoid-operated hydraulic control valves (upper right on the powerpack) direct oil to the winch through the connectors (two per winch; one each side).

so as spare parts are most unlikely to be on board). About the only thing that might be done is to unbolt the motor to see if it is spinning when the windlass is turned on. If not, the problem lies in the pump, plumbing, or electrical circuits, and not the motor itself. While the motor is out, try to operate the windlass manually, just to make sure it is not frozen up.

Roller Reefing and Furling

Almost all new sailboats are now fitted with *roller-reefing* headsails, and a good many with roller-reefing mains and mizzens. A high proportion of older boats are being retrofitted with roller-reefing headsails. The market is huge and everybody wants a piece of the action.

There are a number of potential mechanical problems with roller reefers; when used hard, most seem to succumb sooner or later, regardless of make. Headsail damage is also more common with roller reefers than with conventional hanked-on sails: roller-reefing headsail repairs are a meal ticket for some sailmakers around the cruising circuit. The following sections look at various roller-reefing failures, their causes, and means to reduce their probability.

How They Work

There are two principal types of roller reefing. The first, more properly called *roller furling*, takes a headsail with a wire luff. A swivel drum is attached to the tack of the sail with the drum shaft fixed to the deck. The sail is tensioned as normal with the halyard. When the drum is turned (by means of a furling line) the sail is rolled up around its own luff wire (Figure 16-30).

This is strictly a *furling* rig to be used when the sail is luffing (i.e., not filled with wind). Attempts to furl or reef a sail under load will twist the luff wire and sail (the tack of the sail will wrap up before its head). This is the major problem with these rigs, which can be avoided by use only under the proper conditions, as stated.

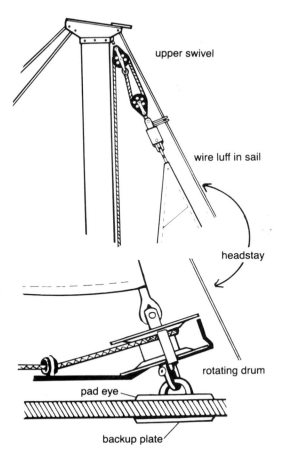

Figure 16-30. **Roller-furling headsails.** Note that the headstay is independent of the furling mechanism.

upper swivel

wire luff in sail

headstay

rotating drum

pad eye

backup plate

The principal advantage of this rig is that it is completely independent of the headstay and so forms no part of the standing rigging—failure does not jeopardize the mast. Sails also can be dropped and changed as easily as regular hanked-on headsails.

The second type of rig employs a "foil"—an aluminum extrusion into which the luff tape of a sail slides. This foil is fitted around the headstay. (On a few units, the foil *is* the headstay.) An upper swivel fits around the foil and attaches to the halyard and the head of the sail; a lower drum grips the foil. When the drum is turned the foil rotates and wraps the sail around itself. Since the foil is rigid and grips the sail along its whole length (more or less), the sail is rolled up evenly (there is no twist between the tack and the head). For this reason (and this is their principal advantage) these rigs can be used for reefing and are commonly know as roller "reefers."

The principal disadvantage of a roller reefer is that it is incorporated in the standing rigging. Failure can, in certain instances, lead to the loss of the headstay and so jeopardize the mast. Aside from this, the roller reefer cannot be put up and

Figure 16-31. **Roller-reefing headsail.** The headstay passes through the luff foil, making the furling unit part of the standing rigging.

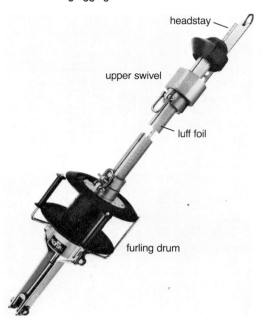

headstay

upper swivel

luff foil

furling drum

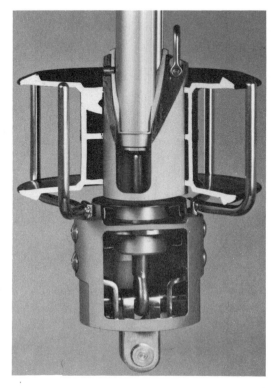

taken down without disconnecting the headstay. This means that many problems (for example, with a foil section) are just about irreparable at sea and may render the headsail unusable. Unless an auxiliary headstay is fitted (few are) and standby hanked-on headsails kept on board (this too is rare), the boat is left without its principal sail.

A secondary problem is the difficulty of making sail changes, for example shortening sail in a blow. A conventional sail can be dropped and gasketed (tied off to make it manageable) and then unhanked. A roller reefer has to be pulled out of its luff groove in the foil. In order to do this the whole sail must be unfurled and the sheets eased. In any kind of a wind, the sail left in the foil will be flogging around while the loose sail will be building up on the foredeck and trying to take off.

Thus taking down roller-reefing headsails can be tough—but setting the new sail is even worse. It has to be fed into the luff groove just right, and eased on up with the halyard. The portion of sail set will be banging around; the sail still to be set will be billowing all over the deck. No matter what claims are made for various "prefeeders," headsail changes on roller reefers are no fun, especially for the shorthanded!

Problems And Answers

The following focuses on roller reefers, but the section on bearings and swivels is applicable to roller furlers.

Headstay failure. Headstay failure is not common, but it is more common than on rigs without roller reefers. Since it is potentially so catastrophic, it deserves special attention.

A hanked-on headsail has its tack attached at the deck. A roller-reefed sail is tacked to the top of the furling drum. With a hanked-on sail, sideways loading (which generates headsail sag) is spread uniformly from the tack up through the stay; on a roller reefer there is a concentration of stress at the drum. *Whatever method is used to mount the drum, it must be properly toggled.* Many are not. If the drum is fastened to the stemhead with metal straps, a toggle needs to be placed between the straps and the stemhead (Figure 16-32).

 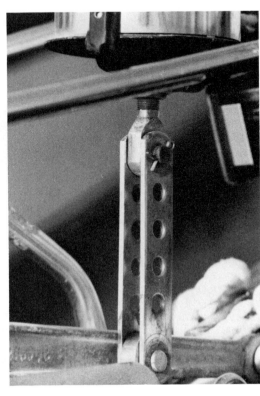

Figure 16-32A,B. **Heading off problems with roller-reefing installations. The arrangement shown far left allows only sideways flexing, while that shown at left permits only fore-and-aft flexing.**

Figure 16-32C. Correctly installed headstay and roller-reefing gear. The toggles allow flexing in either direction.

Figure 16-32D. Headsail roller-furling gear. This headstay has no toggle, but this is permissible because headsail sag affects only the headsail luff wire and mounting, which is adequately toggled.

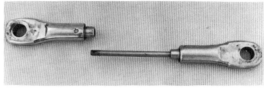

Figure 16-33. This piece was used to raise an expensive roller reefing rig off the foredeck. As the rig was unwound and rewound, the rod twisted until it failed (after only a few months' use). The rig (sail, foil, and furling drum) came loose and flailed around, endangering life and limb.

Figure 16-34. Roller-reefing swivel unit. This is no way to treat a roller-reefing unit! Sand is certain to enter into the bearings, causing them to seize.

Many roller-reefing drums are fastened to a turnbuckle (rigging screw) rather than the stemhead. Harken, a leading manufacturer, has a specially designed turnbuckle with a beefed-up lower stud to carry the extra side loading, but so far as I know it is the only one.

Fastening the drum to a turnbuckle (rather than the stemhead) has a couple of potential disadvantages. If the bearings become stiff, or when reefing and unfurling under a load, the sail can generate fairly high twisting (torsional) loads on the turnbuckle. These can undo the lower turnbuckle stud, or occasionally lead to a complete failure of the lower portion of the turnbuckle or its mounting hardware. Alternatively, the torsional stresses can *unlay the headstay*, leading to wire fatigue and failure. This is very hard to detect since the stay is completely covered by drum and foil.

If the turnbuckle or stay fails, since the drum is not independently fastened to the deck in any way, the whole headstay, foil, sail, and drum assembly will break loose and start flogging around. The masthead is left with no support and the mast is in

imminent danger of collapse. In order to get things back under control, the sail must be taken down, but to do this it must be taken out of its groove, and to do this *it must be completely unfurled*—compounding problems!

A variation on this disaster sometimes occurs when a turnbuckle-mounted drum is raised off the deck with a distance piece of some sort. Such distance pieces must be designed to withstand high torsional loads—rod rigging and wire rope are out of the question. Heavy metal straps should be used, properly toggled.

Not only must a drum be properly mounted and toggled, it is also vital to *fully toggle the headstay at the masthead*. A hanked-on headsail is dropped when not in use; a roller-reefing headsail stays on the headstay. The combined weight of the foil, sail, and swivels is considerable. Anytime the boat is pounding or rolling (e.g., motoring into a head sea), the whole shooting match flexes all over the place. (Try placing your hand well up your rolled up sail and see just how much you can bounce it around, no matter how tightly the rig is set up.) The headstay is subjected to severe additional flexing on top of normal sideways loading. *Masthead toggles are essential* (see page 431).

More and more boats have Isomat spars. These have a stemball fitting on the forestay at the masthead (see Figure 16-35). *The stemball will not provide adequate toggle action for a roller-reefing headsail.* An adaptor and toggle should be set in place as shown in the illustration.

Bearings. Swivel and drum bearings are variously made of carbon steel, stainless steel, plastic, or a combination of stainless steel and plastic. The multiplicity of bearing types (and advertisers' claims that they have developed the perfect bearing!) is a reflection of the problems experienced in finding bearings that will hold up in roller reefing applications.

The loads on bearings can be high, especially if attempts are made to reef or furl a sail under tension, using a cockpit winch on the furling line (something which most manufacturers say should *not* be done, but which unfortunately is done routinely by many sailors, often with destructive results). These loads are not spread uniformly around a bearing since the tack and head of the sail, and the halyard, must all be attached off-center to clear the foil and headstay (see Figure 16-36). This generates point loading—pressure is concentrated on only a small area of the bearings and bearing housings (races). This problem does not arise with roller *furling* rigs since there is no foil or headstay to contend with and all attachments are made to the center of the various swivels.

Furlex has tried to solve some of these problems by incorporating a patented "lash compensator" in its swivels. The lash compensator cancels out the off-center pull of the sail and halyard and reduces point loading. It certainly looks like a good idea, and they claim their swivels are free-turning under high loads, but the idea is too new to evaluate (at least in the USA).

The only bearings hard enough to consistently withstand abuse and unfair point loading are those made of carbon steel, which is several times harder than stainless steel and many times harder than plastic. But any kind of steel, of course, is terribly susceptible to rust in a salt atmosphere. Carbon steel bearings (Schaefer roller furling rigs; ProFurl) must be greased for life (special greases are used) and *sealed*. The bearing seal is probably the most important part of the unit over the long run!

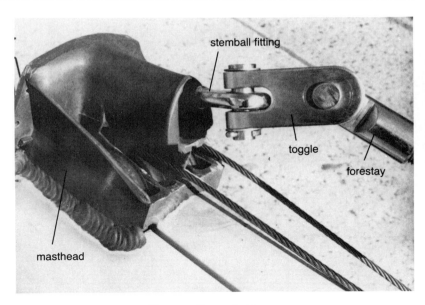

Figure 16-35. Isomat spar with stemball-mounted (see Figure 15-33) stay modified to include a toggle to protect against flexing caused by a roller-reefing rig. Note that the head box is welded in place, leaving the sheave pins inaccessible and no way to remove the sheaves—a poor bit of design.

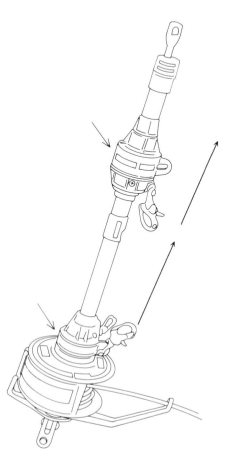

Figure 16-36A. **Off-center point loading places high demands on the bearings of roller-reefing systems. See Figure 16-36B for a proposed solution.**

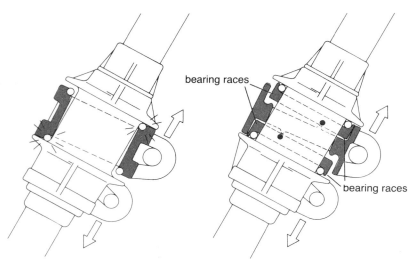

Figure 16-36B. The lash compensator from Furlex seeks to solve the problem in Figure 16-36A. The off-center load is concentrated at the two points marked, which are so placed that the bearing races spread the pressure evenly over the balls.

Because of problems with grease seals, most roller reefers use stainless steel bearings (e.g., Merriman/Facnor; Furlex). Stainless steel bearings have balls made of 316 stainless steel running in races of 304 stainless steel. The bearings are almost always open so that they can be periodically flushed clean with fresh water. This should be done "every three to four weeks. Ideally you should wash the unit after every sail to remove salt" (Hood Seafurl owner's manual). After washing, bearings should be lightly sprayed with WD–40 or some other penetrating oil.

Very few owners flush the bearings more than once a season, and certainly no cruising sailor is going to pour a bucket of precious fresh water down the roller reefer after every sail! So inevitably, salt and dirt accumulate in the majority of units.

For manufacturing reasons, different types of stainless steel are used in the balls and races. In the presence of salt, corrosion between the two can occur. Even more likely is galvanic interaction where the stainless races fit into their aluminum housings.

Another problem is that stainless steel is hard, but not that hard. If the rig is left heavily loaded in one position for long periods of time, the balls can deform and the races indent, especially if corrosion occurs at the point of contact between the balls and races. The bearing begins to run roughly, friction builds up, and all kinds of other problems develop.

Stainless steel running on stainless steel has a nasty habit of *galling*, also called *cold-welding*—a process in which molecules on the surface of one part transfer to the surface of the other. This tendency is exacerbated by anything increasing friction, such as rough bearings or salt. The bearing is then rendered useless. To inhibit galling the bearings are usually impregnated with special greases when manufactured, and must be kept clean (flushed out). After time the grease is worn and washed away and needs renewing. See the section on maintenance later in this chapter.

By alternating stainless and plastic ball bearings (the races are still stainless) the chances of galling are significantly reduced, though not eliminated, and friction is lessened. Hood and Plastimo, among others, have used this approach. However, the plastic, being softer, carries very little of the bearing load, thus effectively reducing the loadbearing portion of the bearings.

Finally, *all*-plastic balls are sometimes used, notably by Harken. The balls run in an inner race of nickel-plated silicon bronze and an outer race of specially coated and hardened aluminum. In order to compensate for loss of hardness the bearings are increased in size and number and must be carefully engineered to spread the loads; otherwise ball deformation is inevitable. For this reason Harken bearings are much more widely spaced than those on a ProFurl unit. This helps to spread the load.

Once friction begins to develop in any bearing, the drum-mounting shaft and halyard swivel tend to turn with the foil during furling and unfurling operations, exerting torsional stresses on the drum-mounting hardware and pulling the halyard around the forestay. (Halyard wrap is probably *the* most common problem with roller reefers and is dealt with in more detail below.) The greater the bearing friction, the more the torsional stresses. Sooner or later something will give—the drum mount or turnbuckle, the halyard, or the headstay.

If a roller reefer is becoming hard to operate, it should *never* be forced. The use of cockpit winches, and worse still electric winches (since these give no feel for what is going on), is a strict no-no! Go forward and find out what the problem is before you break something expensive.

Because of potential bearing problems, almost all manufacturers recommend slacking the halyard before reefing or unfurling, as well as easing the sheets and allowing the sail to luff, though not to flog. These measures lessen friction and point loading on the bearings. However, most halyard winches and halyard cleats are mounted on the mainmast. One of the principal reasons for having a roller reefer in the first place is to avoid having to go forward when the wind begins to pipe up and it is time to shorten sail. In practice, very few sailors slacken the halyard from one month to the next, let alone every time they use the reefing gear. No wonder there are so many bearing and related problems!

It also should be noted that if a backstay is tensioned *after* the halyard has been tensioned, as the masthead moves aft the halyard is tensioned further, frequently putting excessive loads on roller reefing bearings. *First* tension a backstay; only then tension a halyard.

Extrusions and extrusion bearings. The aluminum extrusions used for foils vary greatly in strength, shape, and the means used to join individual sections together. All are critical to a smoothly operating, long-lived roller reefer.

The reefing drum turns the lower end of the extrusion only. If a sail is furled under a load (it is not supposed to be with most units, but frequently is), the extrusion is subjected to strong torsional (twisting) forces. *Many lightweight extrusions cannot handle these stresses*—the extrusion buckles and/or the joints deform.

Foil extrusions come in numerous shapes (Figure 16-37). A round extrusion requires a uniform pressure to furl or unfurl the sail even when the sail is loaded and the extrusion sags off to leeward. It will turn smoothly and wrap tightly. In contrast, oval-shaped extrusions may work well at the dock, but under a load and the inevitable headstay sag, they tend to rotate unevenly and jerkily, increasing stresses on the extrusion and its joints. Inadequate headstay tension will exacerbate this situation.

Most joints are made with extruded sections (splice pieces; sleeves), which make a close fit inside the sections of foil being connected. Inside the splice a plastic bearing will be fitted around the headstay. This centers the foil on the headstay and re-

Figure 16-37. Roller-reefing extrusions. *Above left:* A round extrusion turns smoothly and wraps tightly, but creates more windage. *Above right:* More streamlined extrusion with twin luff grooves. *Right:* A streamlined oval extrusion with twin luff grooves—preferred for racing.

duces friction during furling and unfurling operations.

The foil sections and splice pieces are variously held together with pins, set screws, spring-loaded buttons, pieces of wire, silicone caulking, and glue. In time, torsional stresses loosen all but the best joints. Loose joints lead to luff groove misalignment, and then the sail starts to hang up in the joints. Luff tapes jam, making it impossible to take sails up and down, and sails get torn. There is no solution to this problem short of new foils and connections. (Harken has pointed out to me that they have experienced joint failures where installers have failed to use the Loctite glue provided for their foil joints, or applied the glue in the wrong conditions—too cool, too wet—leading to joint failures. In these instances the joints can frequently be repaired without the need for new foil sections and connectors. See their troubleshooting literature for the correct procedure.)

One or two units incorporate full-length PVC inserts around the headstay, which act as a bearing and keep the stainless steel stay insulated from the aluminum foil. However, other manufacturers claim that when the headstay and foil sag under a load, this setup increases friction unacceptably. In any event PVC absorbs chlorine, which attacks stainless steel.

Instead of a full-length headstay liner, most units have bearing inserts that are placed around the headstay at each joint in

Figure 16-38. **Extrusion joints.**

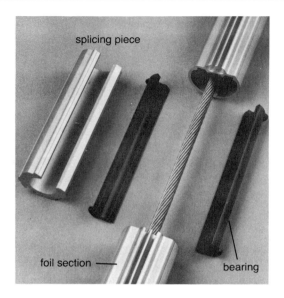

splicing piece

foil section

bearing

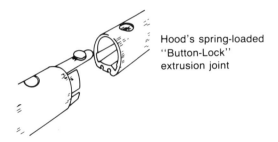

Hood's spring-loaded "Button-Lock" extrusion joint

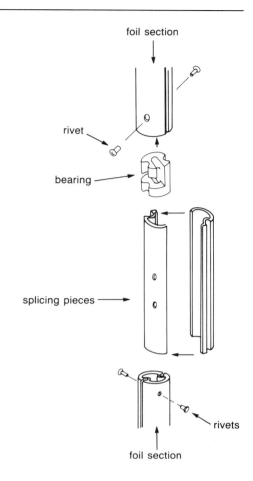

foil section

rivet

bearing

splicing pieces

rivets

foil section

---

the foil. The idea is to use only as many inserts as are strictly necessary to keep the foil centered on the headstay (and out of contact with the stay itself) even under conditions of maximum headstay and foil sag. This reduces friction to a minimum while keeping the foil and stay apart.

Halyard wrap. Halyard wrap occurs when the upper half of the halyard swivel turns with the lower half, foil and sail, wrapping the halyard around the forestay. Wire halyards become permanently deformed and rope halyards can be seriously abraded and weakened. The foil may be damaged if the swivel is well down it (which it shouldn't be—see below). If excessive pressure is applied (e.g., winching in the furling line) the headstay itself or its end terminal and hardware may be damaged, endangering the mast. In extreme cases, if the furling line is put on a winch, the halyard can saw through the foil, grab the headstay, and twist it until it parts.

By far the most common cause of halyard wrap is improper installation in the first place, even by "factory authorized" rigging lofts. There are three common, and interrelated, faults:

1. The angle the halyard makes with the headstay is too small;
2. The swivel is too low; or
3. The swivel is too high.

When a sail is hoisted, the halyard should angle away from the headstay by 10 to 30 degrees (Figure 16-39A and B). If the halyard runs parallel to—or worse still angles into—the headstay, there is very little to stop it wrapping around the stay; the slightest friction in the upper swivel (such as is almost sure to develop over time) will cause halyard wrap. If necessary, the halyard must be led through a fairlead fastened to the front of the mast to provide the correct lead angle (Figure 16-39C).

Running Rigging, Deck Hardware, and Roller Reefing

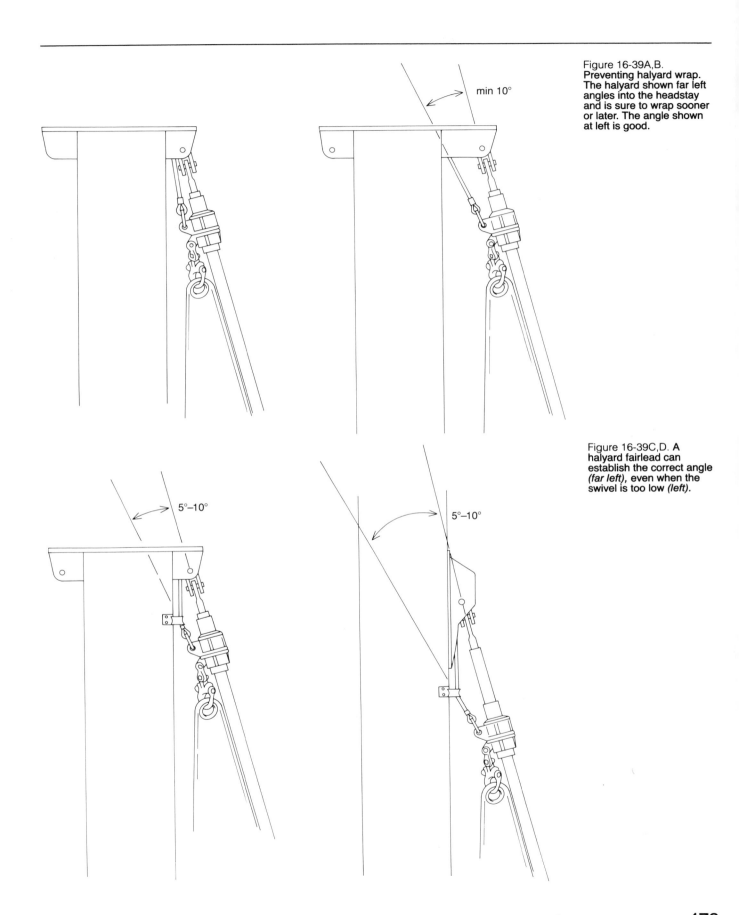

Figure 16-39A,B. Preventing halyard wrap. The halyard shown far left angles into the headstay and is sure to wrap sooner or later. The angle shown at left is good.

Figure 16-39C,D. A halyard fairlead can establish the correct angle *(far left)*, even when the swivel is too low *(left)*.

min 10°

5°–10°

5°–10°

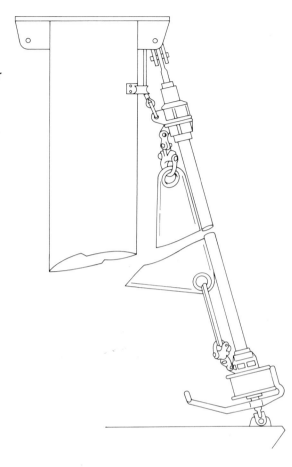

Figure 16-39E. A superior solution to the low swivel and fairlead is to add a pendant to the tack. . .

Figure 16-39F. . . . or the head of the sail.

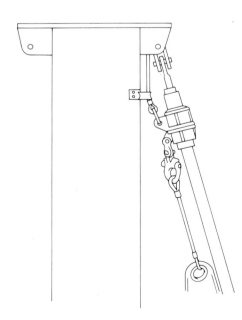

The lower the swivel on the foil, the longer the exposed length of halyard, the smaller the halyard angle, and the greater the chance of halyard wrap. When a sail is hoisted and winched up to its maximum halyard tension, the swivel should be almost at the top of the foil. If not, *a pendant must be fitted to either the head or the tack of the sail to allow the swivel to come up this far* (Figure 16-39D through F). If you intend to use more than one sail on the same roller reefer, you *must supply each sail with a pendant such that the upper swivel always hoists to the same position.*

However, it is equally important that no pendant allow the swivel to come even partially off the top of the foil. If this happens the off-center loads on the swivel will cause it to cock to one side, jamming on and damaging the foil.

Most swivels slide up and down the foil on nylon pads (inserts or bushings). In time the off-center loads on the swivel cause these pads to wear down on opposite sides at the top and bottom (this problem is most likely with oval foils). The swivel cocks a little to one side (Figure 16-39G). In some cases, as the foil turns in reefing and unreefing operations, it catches on the upper (halyard) half of the swivel, dragging it around with it and wrapping the halyard around the headstay. New pads are needed, but as a temporary expedient on oval foils with two luff grooves set 180 degrees apart, hoisting the sail in the other groove will throw the loads on the unworn part of the pads and return the swivel to service.

One or two units incorporate specific anti-wrap devices (e.g., Facnor/Merriman; ProFurl)—generally a *deflector ring* fitted around the headstay above the foil to hold halyards off the headstay. The ProFurl unit has a solid metal strap between the top of the upper swivel and the halyard. If the swivel turns, this strap comes up against a protrusion on the deflector ring (which Profurl calls Multitop) and the swivel then turns no farther, thus providing a positive lock against halyard wrap. Harken has a mast-mounted sheave performing the same function as the fairlead in Figure 16-39C, but with less friction.

Riding turns on the furling drum. Another common problem. The causes are just the same as for riding turns on winches—inadequate tension and incorrect sheet lead angles. If the furling drum does not include an integral sheet lead, a suit-

Running Rigging, Deck Hardware, and Roller Reefing

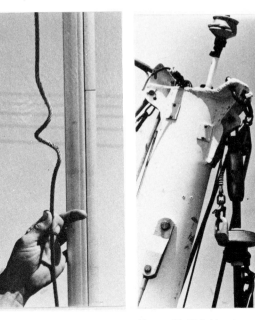

Figure 16-39G. The off-center loading of this rig wore the nylon bushing in the halyard swivel, causing it to hang up on the extrusion at the point shown. Note the excessively large clearance worn into the opposite side.

Figure 16-39H,I. The halyard then wrapped around and ultimately destroyed the extrusion *(left)*. Note that the swivel was mounted too low; it should have come almost to the top of the extrusion. *Right:* This is what happened to the halyard!

Figure 16-39J. **Here's** another rig with an incorrect halyard lead angle. Take a look around the anchorage; you'll see dozens!

able pad eye or block must be set up on deck to ensure that the furling line runs onto the drum *at an angle of 90 degrees to the headstay* (Figure 16-41). During furling and unfurling operations always maintain a moderate tension on the furling line to keep it from jumping around on the drum.

Sail damage. Headsail damage is more prevalent with roller reefers than with hanked-on headsails. Generally the genoa is set up as the primary (and frequently the only) sail for the roller reefer. When the wind pipes up, there is either no smaller sail to set or, rather than set it, the genoa is steadily reefed down. Sooner or later the sail encounters wind strengths for which it is not designed and blows out. Correct sail design will help to alleviate stresses (generally radial or vertical panels), as will the use of heavier sailcloth in the panels closest to the leech—those still operational when the sail is reefed.

When reefing down, if the halyard and sheets are eased too far the sail rolls up loosely. In a gale of wind the poorly furled head of the sail will flog around and eventually tear up. Furling a sail tightly is essential if leaving a boat for any length of

Figure 16-39K. This wire halyard wrapped around the forestay, which sawed through it: Down came the sail. The disappointed owner (this was the second offense) complained that it had spoiled his day's sailing. He should look on the bright side. The halyard could just as easily sawed through his forestay: Down comes the mast. For a look at what caused his problem, see Figure 16-39A.

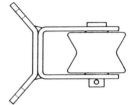

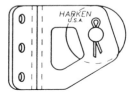

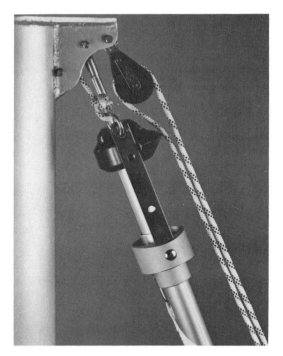

Figure 16-40A–D. Halyard anti-wrap devices. *Left:* Harken's mast-mounted sheave acts as a fairlead, but has less friction. *Center:* Two views of ProFurl's "Multitop," which uses a halyard deflecting ring to prevent halyard wrap. *Right:* Facnor/Merriman's halyard deflector ring.

Figure 16-41. To prevent riding turns on the drum, the furling line must enter the drum at right angles to the headstay. Moving the forward lead block fore-and-aft centers the line vertically in the opening.

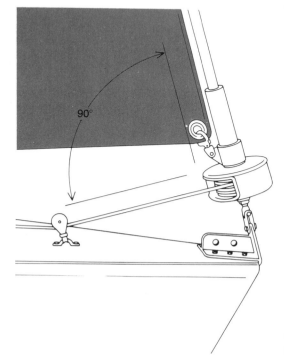

90°

time. Once the sail is furled, continue turning it a few more times to wrap the sheets around it.

Since the sails are exposed to the sun's ultraviolet rays, they must be adequately protected against degradation of the sail-cloth. All too often one sees roller reefing sails with torn and tattered UV covers—slowly and steadily sunlight will be literally eating up the outer wrap of the sail. The next time it is put to a test, it is likely to fail; once a tear starts, it is going to run clear across the sail.

Finally, as previously mentioned, tor-sional stresses on the foil will loosen and deform joints and create misalignment in the luff groove. The luff tape of the sail hangs up and the sail is likely to tear when being hoisted or taken down.

Powered headsail reefers. Some larger rigs are driven by electric and hydraulic motors. Older hydraulic units tend to have a direct drive from the hydraulic motor, and rely on the motor check valves to

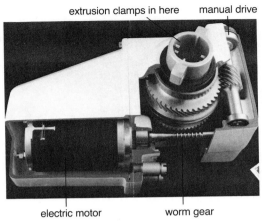

extrusion clamps in here   manual drive

electric motor   worm gear

Figure 16-42. **Worm gearing on an electrically powered headsail reefer.**

maintain oil pressure and keep the sail in position. Any pump, check valve, or seal leaks result in creep and in the sail slowly unwinding.

Some units also have adapted industrial hydraulic equipment with *steel* interiors. Water in the hydraulic oil (such as from condensation in oil reservoirs) leads to rusting of sensitive parts and thus all kinds of problems. For other problem areas and troubleshooting see the earlier sections of this chapter on hydraulic windlasses.

Newer hydraulic drive units use worm gearing (which acts as an effective brake against the sail unwinding) and all-stainless steel construction. Electrically driven units are very similar (on the motor and control side) to electrically powered windlasses—refer to the relevant section for troubleshooting.

Maintenance

Some roller reefers are advertised as "maintenance free." It would be a foolish owner who took this too literally! All roller reefers incorporate dissimilar metals in the drum assemblies, foil joints, and upper swivels. The drum assemblies in particular are subjected to a great deal of saltwater spray and therefore are prone to galvanic corrosion. At the very least this unit needs a thorough flushing with fresh water several times a season and before a winter lay-up.

If the drum and swivel have open bearings, they should be rotated while being flushed. This helps to get all the salt and dirt washed out. Plastic and stainless steel bearings will benefit from a good shot of WD-40. At the end of the season, after stainless steel bearings have been thoroughly washed out, pump in a little Teflon-based waterproof grease and spin the units to spread the grease around the balls and races.

Before winter lay-up wash the foil. No detergents should be used on anodized aluminum, since some detergents contain corrosive substances. If detergents are used, be sure to rinse well. After washing, liberally coat all aluminum surfaces with a silicone car or boat polish.

Summary: DOs and DON'Ts

- Do install the unit properly with:

1. The halyard swivel at the top of the foil as close to the masthead sheave as possible.
2. The halyard angled away from the swivel by at least 10 degrees.
3. All the sails to be used fitted with suitable pendants to ensure that the swivel is hoisted to the same height with each one.

- Do keep the headstay tight to avoid foil sag.
- Do slack off the halyard, ease the sheets, and luff up when reefing.
- Do retain *moderate* tension on sheets and furling line at all times to avoid loose wraps and riding turns on the furling drum.
- Do flush stainless and plastic bearings at regular intervals with fresh water.
- Do slack the halyard at all times when the sail is furled to avoid prolonged point loading on the bearings.
- Do install adequate toggles at both ends of the headstay and on the drum mount (where appropriate).
- Do check the lower turnbuckle terminal on turnbuckle-mounted units to make sure that it is not backing off.
- Don't try to reef the sail against full sheet tension.
- Don't reef with a highly tensioned halyard.
- Don't tension the backstay after tensioning the halyard.

- Don't leave the halyard tensioned when the sail is not in use.
- Don't force the furling line. If it jams, or there is unusual resistance, *find out why:* check for halyard wrap, a riding turn on the furling drum, or rough bearings.
- Don't let the sail flog when reefing—uneven tension on the furling line is likely to cause a riding turn.
- Don't force a sail up or down its luff groove.
- Don't use reefed sails in wind conditions stronger than the sailcloth is designed to tolerate.

In-Mast And Behind-The-Mast Reefing

How they work. The success of roller reefing headsails has resulted in the adaptation of the same hardware to furling and reefing applications for mainsails and mizzens. In almost all instances, existing headsail reefing equipment with minor modifications or no modifications is either installed inside a specially built mast (Hood's Stoway; Metalmast Marine's Reef Away; Kemp's Furlin) or just behind the mast.

Exactly the same principles apply as for headsail reefing. The sail feeds into a slot in a foil. The head of the sail is attached to a swivel, which fits around the foil, and is hoisted by the sail halyard; the tack of the sail attaches to a furling drum or some other fitting attached to the foil. The foil is rotated to wind up the sail.

Now for some minor variations. The foil on a behind-the-mast reefer must be set up on the equivalent of a substitute headstay, and this stay must be kept well tensioned to prevent sail sag. Generally a rod is fitted between a bracket at the masthead and a fixed gooseneck, then tensioned by tightening a nut on the underside of the gooseneck mount. The foil rotates around the rod.

In-mast reefers, which have a narrow slot in the mast, are not subject to sail sag—the slot in the mast provides support along the length of the sail. So long as the *sail* is tensioned (via its halyard), there is no need for any tension on the foil or any rod around which it rotates. In fact, there is not even a need for the rod at all—the foil can simply be set up in bearings attached to the inside of the mast (e.g.,

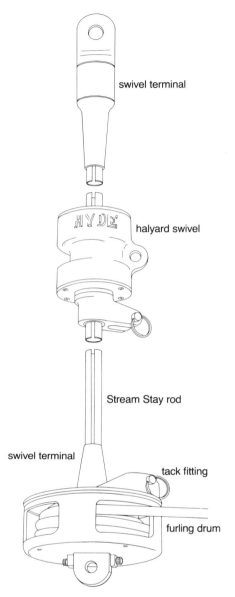

Figure 16-43A. The Hyde "Stream Stay"—a popular option for retrofitted behind-the-mast roller reefing that also serves as a roller-reefing headsail unit. The Stream Stay has a solid aluminum extrusion, mounted on its own swivels, that replaces the existing headstay or behind-the-mast stay.

Figure 16-43B. MetalMast Marine's "Reefaway"—a hybrid with all the features of behind-the-mast reefing, but placed inside a separate, open-backed mast extrusion. The Hyde "Stream Stay" also may be mounted in this fashion.

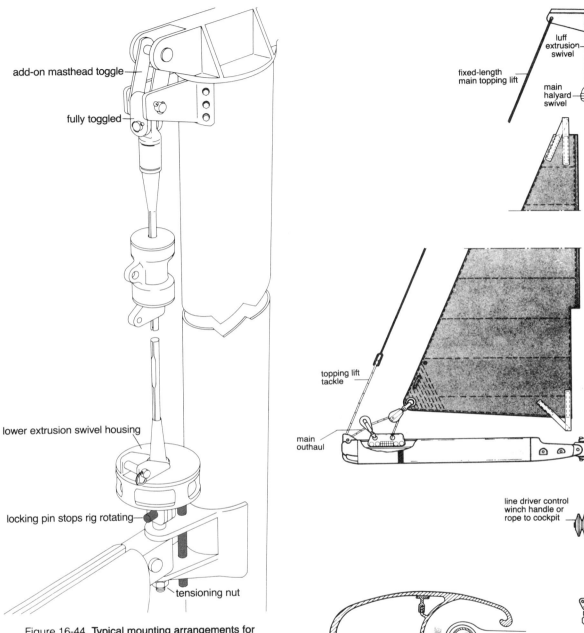

add-on masthead toggle

fully toggled

lower extrusion swivel housing

locking pin stops rig rotating

tensioning nut

Figure 16-44. **Typical mounting arrangements for behind-the-mast reefing. At the masthead. . . and at the tack.**

luff extrusion swivel

fixed-length main topping lift

main halyard swivel

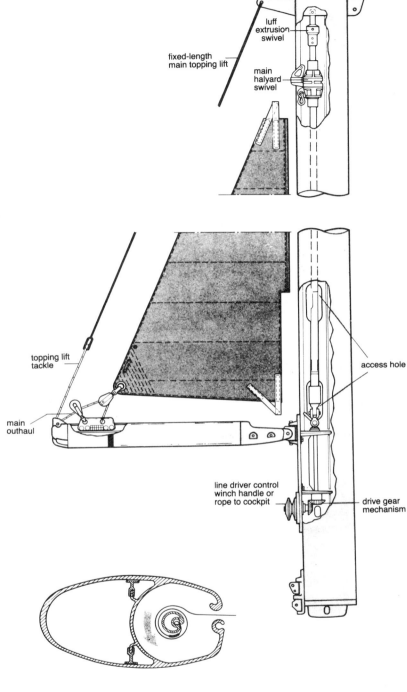

topping lift tackle

main outhaul

access hole

line driver control winch handle or rope to cockpit

drive gear mechanism

Foil section, designed so the sail will lead on easily and roll up smoothly.

Figure 16-45. **In-mast reefing arrangement.**

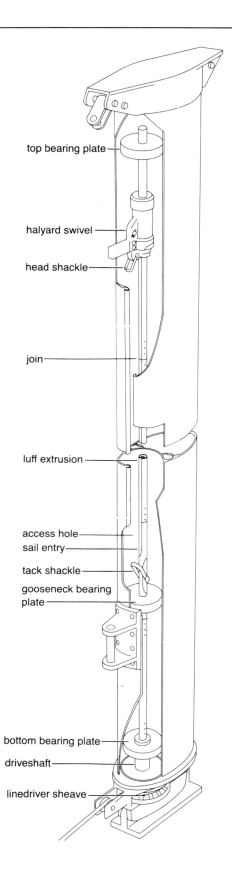

Figure 16-46. **In-mast reefing with an untensioned luff rod. The linedriver can be fitted as shown only on a deck-stepped mast.**

top bearing plate

halyard swivel

head shackle

join

luff extrusion

access hole
sail entry

tack shackle

gooseneck bearing plate

bottom bearing plate

driveshaft

linedriver sheave

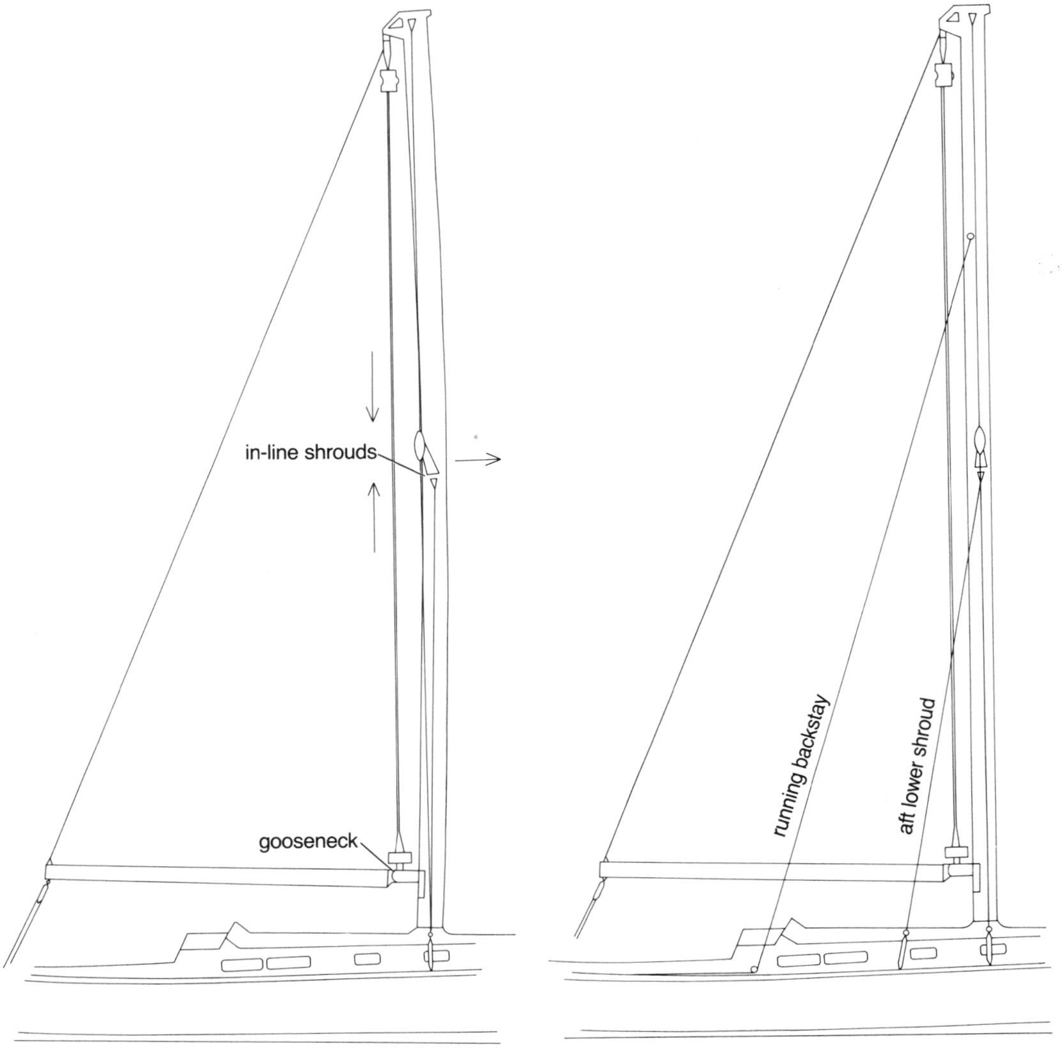

Figure 16-47. **Behind-the-mast reefers impose severe strains on the mast, which must receive additional support (right).**

in-line shrouds

gooseneck

running backstay

aft lower shroud

Kemp's Reefin). However, where most slots are wider inadequate rod or foil tension *can* allow the foil to sag into the slot and jam.

Foils may be turned by a conventional furling drum, a line driver, a motor, or by cranking with a winch handle (in the event of motor failure). A line driver resembles the jaws on a self-tailing winch. An "endless" line (i.e., one big loop) feeds through the jaws, around various blocks, and back to a similar unit in the cockpit. A winch handle is used to turn the cockpit driver, cranking the sail in or out. Line drivers either are installed directly on a foil, or set

in the aft face of the mast, turning the foil via a set of bevel gears.

Problems and answers. Much of the information in the section on roller-reefing is applicable, especially that relating to bearings, foil extrusions, halyard wrap, and maintenance. In addition, certain other points need noting.

Mast bend. In-mast reefers cannot accommodate mast bend—the foil extrusion and sail will hang up on the mast. Behind-the-mast reefers will suffer from changing rod tension with changes in mast shape.

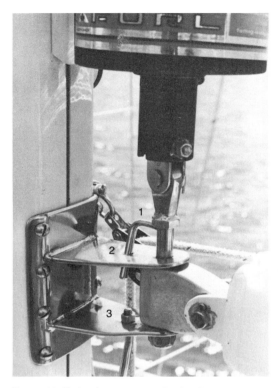

Figure 16-48. Inadequate mounting hardware on behind-the-mast reefing. This is a brand new boat, but already the pin (1) is bending. Soon its weld will break and the whole rig will unwind uncontrollably. The two gooseneck retaining plates (2 and 3) are also flexing upward. In time these welds will crack and the whole boom and sail assembly will come adrift.

Because the actual mounting is generally a customized affair, you are very much in the hands of the rigger. Be sure to use someone with experience with your specific gear.

Figure 16-49. Excessive in-mast rod tension will distort the mounting bracket, potentially throwing out bearing alignment and gear engagement.

bearing

luff rod

bevel gears

line driver on face of mast

mounting bracket slots into the outer wall of the mast

Note that *behind-the-mast reefers should be fully toggled at top and bottom to accommodate sail sag* (see the section on headsail reefing). Retrofitted behind-the-mast reefers impose severe bending stresses on masts (rather like the string on a bow). *Aft* lower shrouds are an absolute necessity to keep the mast in column (straight)—*in-line* shrouds will not work. Running backstays may be needed to keep the mast from "pumping" in heavy seas. Some masts still may not be able to take the added strain. In-mast reefing does not suffer from the same problems since the mast loading is all in direct compression.

Tension. Moderate tension must be maintained at all times on the clew of the sail when reefing and unfurling. If this is not done, the sail will wrap and unwrap loosely, jamming up inside the mast or mast slot. Some first-generation units jammed up so badly that the sails had to be cut out! This has been largely eliminated by improving the ratio of foil sizes to slots. Nevertheless it still may prove impossible to wind up a jammed sail and start again. The tack of the sail sometimes has to be disconnected, the halyard slacked, and the whole sail pulled down and reset.

In-mast rod tension. Where an *in-mast* foil is mounted on a rod, excessive tension on the rod will merely distort mounting brackets, damage bearings, and wear out bevel gears, etc. In certain cases (e.g., where a line driver is mounted on the face of a mast), it may drag the foil-mounted bevel gear out of contact with the line-driver bevel gear, leading to gear damage and/or a complete loss of furling capability. As mentioned previously, tensioning *in-mast* mounting rods will do nothing to improve sail shape or performance.

Motor failures. See the relevant sections on powered windlasses—motor installations are very similar (both electric and hydraulic).

Fluting. Any time a boat with a slotted mast is berthed, the sail is rolled up, and the wind moves aft of the beam, the wind will make a moaning noise as it blows across the slot (just like blowing across the top of a bottle). This is easily stopped by hoisting a strip of sailcloth (an anti-vibration strip or "flute stopper") up the slot. The problem does not occur at anchor since the boat will stay head to wind.

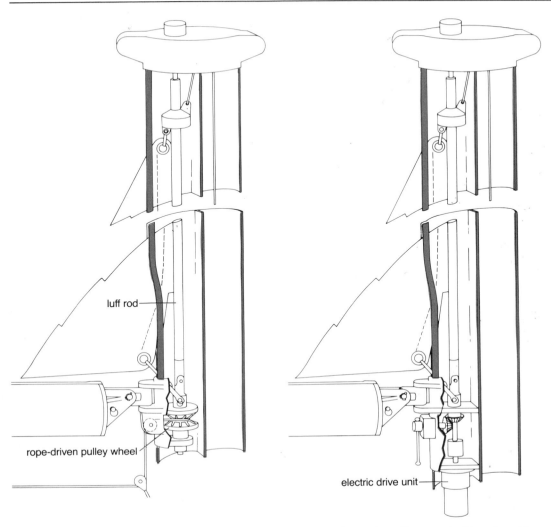

luff rod

rope-driven pulley wheel

electric drive unit

Figure 16-50. **In-mast reefing drive options.** Standard small mast gooseneck features rope-driven pulley wheel set at right angles to the luff rod, with furling lines led aft (**left**).

Electric-drive unit positions an electric motor and reduction gear and clutch under the bevel gears that drive the luff rod. Most manufacturers also produce hydraulic-drive units.

Glossary

Accumulator—an air-filled tank used to smooth out pressure in a freshwater system; also a tank used in a refrigeration system to trap liquid refrigerant that might otherwise damage the compressor.

Aerial—see *antenna.*

Alligator clip—a spring-loaded metal clip with serrated jaws used for hooking test lines into electrical circuits.

Alignment—the bringing together of two coupling halves in near-perfect horizontal and vertical agreement.

Alkaline—the electrolyte in Ni-Cad batteries, diluted potassium hydroxide.

Alternating current (AC)—an electrical current reversing its direction at regular intervals. Each repetition of these changes is a cycle and the number of cycles that take place in one second is the frequency.

Alternator—a machine for generating electricity by spinning a magnet inside a series of coils. The resulting power output is alternating current. In DC systems this output is rectified via silicon diodes.

Ambient conditions—the surrounding temperature or pressure, or both.

Ammeter—an instrument for measuring current flow.

Ampere (amp)—a measure of the rate of electric current flow.

Ampere-hour (Ah)—a measure of the amount of electricity stored in a battery.

Annealing—a process of softening metals.

Anode—the positive terminal of a battery or cell.

Antenna (aerial)—a conductor that radiates or collects radio waves.

Antenna gain—the measure of the effectiveness of an antenna.

Antifreeze—a chemical that lowers the freezing point of water.

Antisiphon valve—a valve that admits air to a line and prevents siphonic action.

Aqualift—an engine exhaust and silencing system in which cooling water is injected into the exhaust and carried out by the exhaust gases.

Armature—the rotating windings in a generator (AC or DC).

Atmospheric pressure—the pressure of the air at the surface of the earth, conventionally taken to be 14.7 psi.

Atomizer—see *injector.*

Automotive battery—see *battery.*

Autopilot—a power-driven device for steering a boat on a preset compass course.

Auxiliary coil—an additional set of windings in the stator of some AC alternators, used to power a voltage-regulation or battery-charging circuit.

AVO meter—see *multimeter.*

Babbitt—a soft white metal alloy frequently used to line replaceable shell-type engine bearings; also used in the traversing nut on worm steering.

Back pressure—a buildup of pressure in an exhaust system.

Backstay—a wire rope giving aft support to the mast.

Ball valve—either a valve with a spring-loaded ball or one with a ball rotating in a spherical seat.

Battery—*Automotive:* a lead-acid battery with many thin plates and low-density active material.
Deep-cycle: a lead-acid battery with thicker, stronger plates and high-density active material.
Wet-type: a conventional lead-acid battery with liquid electrolyte.
No-maintenance: either a sealed, conventional wet battery with excess electrolyte or a sealed gel-type battery.
Gel-type: a thin-plate lead-acid battery in which electrolyte is trapped in a gel.
Nickel-cadmium (Ni-Cad): a battery using an alkaline electrolyte, dilute potassium hydroxide.

Battery isolation switch—a switch installed next to the battery and carrying full battery output, used to isolate the battery from all circuits.

Battery sensed—a voltage regulator that senses system voltage at the battery (as opposed to at the alternator).

Bearing—a device for supporting a rotating shaft with minimum friction. It may take the form of a metal sleeve (a bushing), a set of ball bearings (a roller bearing), or a set of pins around the shaft (a needle bearing).

Bearing race—the outer cage within which a set of balls rotates in a roller bearing.

Bearing tube—see *rudder tube.*

Behind-the-mast reefing—an adaptation of headsail reefing systems to main and mizzen masts.

Bendix—the drive gear (pinion) arrangement on a starter motor.

Bevel gear—a means of transmitting drive through a 90-degree angle.

Binnacle—a housing for a compass.

Bleeding—the process of purging air from a fuel or hydraulic system.

Block—the general term for a rigging pulley.

Blocking diode—a diode used to permit charging of more than one battery from one power source without paralleling the battery outputs.

Blow-by—the escape of gases past piston rings or closed valves.

Bobstay—a stay from the tip of the bowsprit to the waterline.

Bonding—the process of electrically tying together all major fixed metal items on a boat.

Bosun's chair (a corruption of boatswain's chair)—a canvas seat used for hoisting someone up a mast.

Bottle screw—see *turnbuckle*.

Bowsprit—a horizontal spar projecting forward from the bow of some boats.

Bridge rectifier—an arrangement of diodes for converting alternating current (AC) to direct current (DC).

Brush—a carbon or carbon composite spring-loaded rod used to conduct current to or from commutators or slip rings.

Btu (British thermal unit)—a unit used to measure quantities of heat.

Bulldog clamp—see *cable clamp*.

Bushing—see *bearings*.

Buss bar (busbar)—a heavy copper strap used in breaker boxes and circuit panel boxes for carrying high currents and making multiple connections.

Butane—see *LPG*.

Cable clamp—a U-shaped bolt with a saddle used to join or to make loops in wire rope.

Cam—an elliptical protrusion on a shaft.

Cam cleat—a cleat with two spring-loaded, toothed jaws that trap and hold a line.

Capacitor—a device for storing electric energy. A capacitor blocks the flow of DC but lets AC through (analogous to a flexible membrane that will oscillate but not allow flow through it).

Cap shroud—see *shroud*.

Carbon/ceramic seal—a type of seal found on some pump shafts. A spring-loaded carbon ring, sealed to the shaft, bears against a ceramic seat, sealed to the pump housing.

Cathode—the negative terminal of a cell or battery.

Caulking—various semiflexible compounds used to seal seams. Sometimes applied with less precision to sealing and bedding compounds.

Cell—a single unit that makes electricity through chemical energy. A group of cells makes a battery.

Centrifugal action—the process of imparting velocity to a liquid through a spinning impeller that drives the liquid from the center of a pump housing to its periphery.

Chainplates—the metal straps bolted to a hull to which the standing rigging attaches.

Check valve—an electrical or mechanical valve that allows flow in only one direction.

Cheek plates—the plates that enclose the sheave on a block.

Choke—a coil so designed that it filters out unwanted radio frequencies (noise).

Circlip—see *snap ring*.

Circuit—the path of electric current.
A *closed circuit* has a complete path.
An *open circuit* has a broken or disconnected path.
A *short circuit* has an unintentional direct path bypassing the equipment (appliance, resistance) in the circuit.

Circuit breaker—a load-sensitive switch which trips (opens a circuit) if a threshold-exceeding current flows through it.

Clevis pin—a metal pin with a flattened head at one end and a hole for a cotter pin (split pin) at the other. It is used to fasten rigging together.

Clew—the lower, aft corner of a sail.

Clutch—a device used to couple and uncouple a power source from a piece of equipment. It may be manually, hydraulically, or electromagnetically operated.
A *cone clutch* forces a tapered seat onto a tapered friction pad.
A *brake-band clutch* tightens a friction band around a smooth face on a gear.
A *disc clutch* holds alternating metal and friction plates together.

CNG—compressed natural gas.

Coaxial cable—a cable enclosed in an insulating sleeve (or dielectric), then a metal braided sleeve, and finally another insulating sleeve.

Cold-cranking amps—the number of amps a battery at 0°F (-17.8°C) can deliver for 30 seconds and maintain a voltage of 1.2 volts per cell or more.

Cold plate—a refrigerator or freezer tank containing an evaporator coil and a solution with a freezing point below that of water.

Collet—a metal chip designed to hold winch spindles and engine valves in place.

Common ground point—a central stud, normally connected to the earth's ground via a through-hull fitting, to which are attached AC and DC grounding circuits (except with some isolation transformers), any bonding circuit, and various radio and lightning grounds.

Commutator—the copper segments that are arranged around the end of an armature and on which the brushes ride.

Compression ratio—the volume of a combustion chamber with the piston at the top of its stroke as a proportion of the total volume of the cylinder with the piston at the bottom of its stroke.

Compressor—a device used to compress refrigeration gases.
A reciprocal compressor has two pistons attached to a rotating crankshaft as in a conventional engine.
A swash-plate ("wobble plate") compressor has five or six pistons attached to a plate that oscillates, driven by a rotating cam.

Condenser—a unit designed to remove sufficient heat from a compressed refrigeration gas to make the gas condense into a liquid.

Conditioning—see *equalization* (of battery).

Conductance—a measure of the ability to conduct electricity.

Conduit—a pipe in which electric cables are run; also a reinforced sheathing used with steering and engine control cables.

Cone clutch—see *clutch*.

Constant-current voltage regulation—see *voltage regulation*.

Continuity—a complete path or circuit through which current can flow.

Corrosion—a process that leads to the destruction of two metals.
Galvanic corrosion arises when two dissimilar, electrically connected metals are immersed in an electrolyte (e.g., salt water). A current is generated, leading to a transfer of electrons from one metal (the anode or "less noble") to the other (the cathode or "more noble"). As a result the anode corrodes.
Pinhole and crevice corrosion are the results of galvanic corrosion occurring in just one piece of metal due to minute differences in the microscopic structure of the metal.
Stray-current corrosion is the result of external current leakage through metal fittings in contact with an electrolyte, such as salt water. Where the current leaves a fitting (the anode), massive corrosion can occur. The term *electrolysis* refers to the passage of electricity through the electrolyte.

Cotter pin—a pin with two legs. With legs together the pin is placed through the hole in a clevis pin. The legs are then opened (separated) outward to prevent the cotter pin from backing out of the hole. The cotter pin, in turn, prevents the load-bearing clevis pin from backing out of *its* retaining hole.

Creep—the slow seepage of hydraulic fluid down the sides of a piston or ram, or through check valves, leading to gradual movement of the rudder or steering wheel.

Crimp-on terminal—a fork, spade, or ring terminal fitted to electric cables with a crimp-on tool.

Crosby clamp—see *cable clamp*.

Cup washer—a dished leather or neoprene washer fitted to the rod end in some piston-style pumps.

Current—the rate of flow of electricity (measured in amps).

Cutless bearing—a ribbed rubber sleeve in a metal tube, used to support a propeller shaft.

CVJ (constant velocity joint)—a type of propeller shaft coupling that permits considerable engine misalignment.

Cycles—see *alternating current*.

Deep-cycle battery—see *battery*.

Diaphragm—a reinforced rubber membrane that moves in and out in certain pumps.

Dielectric—an insulating material. See *coaxial cable*.

Diffusion—the process by which the acid in a battery electrolyte permeates the active material in the plates.

Diode—an electronic check valve.

Direct current (DC)—an electric current that flows in one direction only.

Disc-drive steering—see *radial-drive steering*.

Double-pole switch—a switch that makes or breaks two separate connections at the same time.

Dowel—a round metal or wooden pin.

Drier—a cylinder containing hygroscopic (water-absorbing) material used to remove moisture from refrigeration circuits.

Drift—any suitably sized round metal bar used to knock out bushings, clevis pins, and the like.

Drip loop—a deliberately induced low spot in a run of electrical cable designed to keep moisture out of terminal boxes, etc.

Drive ratio—the ratio between the radius of a driven pulley and the radius of the driving pulley.

Duckbill valve—a hemispherical rubber valve with a slit in it and with protruding rubber lips. Internal pressure forces the lips apart; external pressure closes the lips, sealing the valve.

Dynamo—see *generator*.

Earth—the reference point ("ground potential") for AC circuits.

Earth leak—see *ground fault*.

Electric motor—a device for converting electromagnetic force into rotary motion.
Universal motors operate on both AC and DC. *Permanent-magnet motors* also run on both currents.
Induction motors operate on AC only.

Electrolysis—see *corrosion*.

Electrolyte—the solution in a battery; a liquid conductor of electricity.

Electrolytic corrosion—corrosion arising as a result of electrolysis.

Electromagnet—a magnetic force induced by passing a direct current through a coil wrapped around an iron core (shoe).

Electromagnetic clutch—a cone clutch in which the driving and driven halves are pulled together by an electromagnet.

Electron—the smallest charge of negative electricity.

Equalization—the process of driving a liquid electrolyte (wet) lead-acid battery up to its highest natural voltage in order to reconvert sulfated plate material back into active material.

Eutectic—a particular level of a salt solution at which the whole solution freezes at one specific temperature (as opposed to progressively freezing through a process of ice crystalizing out as temperatures lower).

Evaporator—the unit in which liquid refrigerant converts back into a gas, absorbing latent heat in the process.

Excitation—the initial magnetism induced in a field winding in order to initiate alternator or generator output.

Excitation windings—a separate set of coils built into the stator on brushless AC alternators, and used to induce field current in the rotor.

Expansion valve—a valve with a minute, adjustable orifice used to separate the high-and low-pressure sides of a refrigeration system, and through which the liquid refrigerant sprays into the evaporator.

Extrusion—a complex metal (normally aluminum) shape produced in continuous lengths.

Fail-safe diode—a diode set to block current flow at normal voltages but to open with abnormally high voltage. Used to protect alternator diodes against accidental open-circuiting.

Fast fuse—used to protect alternator diodes against accidental reverse polarity.

Feed pump—see *lift pump.*

Feeler gauge—thin strips of metal machined to precise thicknesses and used for measuring small gaps.

Fid—a softwood plug to hammer up and block off a through-hull fitting or hull opening below the waterline in the event of a failure of the through hull.

Field windings—electromagnetic coils used to create magnetic fields in alternators, generators, and electric motors.

Filament—a very fine piece of high-resistance wire that glows red (or white) hot when a current is passed through it.

Filter—an electrical device for screening out unwanted interference; also a device for screening out impurities in fuel, air, or water.

Filter/drier—see *drier.*

Flap valve—a simple rubber flap, sometimes weighted. Fluid pressure opens it in one direction and closes it in the other.

Flashing the field—the use of an external DC source to supply momentary excitation to alternator or generator field coils.

Flax—a natural fiber used in packing.

Flexible impeller pump—a pump with a rubber impeller and a cam on one side of the pump chamber. As the impeller passes the cam, its vanes are squeezed down, expelling fluids trapped between them. The vanes then spring back, sucking in more fluid.

Float charge—the current required to maintain a battery at full charge without overcharging.

Forestay—a wire rope giving forward support to a mast.

Frequency—see *alternating current.*

Fuse—a protective device designed to break a circuit by melting if the current goes above a certain level.

Galvanic corrosion—see *corrosion.*

Gain—see *antenna gain.*

Galling—a process of "cold-welding" that can completely seize up stainless steel fasteners, particularly when their threads are dirty or damaged.

Gasket—a piece of material placed between two parts to seal them against leaks.

Gassing—a process in which battery electrolyte breaks down, giving off hydrogen and oxygen.

Gate valve—a valve in which a flat metal plate (gate) screws down to block off flow.

Gauge set—a pair of gauges mounted on a manifold, which can be connected to a refrigeration unit to measure high and low pressures, and to vacuum down and charge the unit.

Gear ratio—the relative size of two gears. If the gears are in contact, their relative speed of rotation will be given by the gear ratio. Example: If the gear ratio is 8:1, the smaller gear will rotate eight times faster than the larger gear.

Generator (commonly known as a *dynamo* **in the UK)**—a machine for generating electricity by spinning a series of coils inside a magnet. The resulting power output is alternating current. In DC systems, this output is rectified via a commutator and brushes.

GFI (ground fault interrupter)—a safety device that breaks a circuit anytime a short to ground occurs; also known as a *residual current circuit breaker.*

Glow plug—a heating element installed in diesel engine precombustion chambers to aid in cold-starting.

Gooseneck—a swivel fitting that holds a boom to a mast.

Governor—a device for maintaining an engine or electric motor at a constant speed, regardless of load.

Graphite tape—used in stuffing boxes.

Grid—a lead alloy framework that supports the active material of a battery plate and conducts current.

Ground—a connection between an electric circuit and the earth, or some conducting body serving in place of the earth.

Grounded conductor—a normally current-carrying AC conductor maintained at earth's potential (i.e., the neutral wire).

Grounding conductor—a normally non-current-carrying AC conductor maintained at the earth's potential (i.e., the ground wire).

Ground fault—a current leak to ground bypassing proper circuits.

Ground point—see *common ground point*.

Gudgeon—one-half of a rudder hinge, the other half being the pintle.

Gypsy—a wheel on a windlass notched for chain.

Halyard—a wire rope or synthetic rope used to raise a sail.

Halyard wrap—the twisting of a headsail halyard around the forestay.

Head—a marine toilet.

Head box—the assembly of sheaves and wire rope attachments at the top of a mast.

Header tank—a small tank set above an engine on heat-exchanger-cooled systems. The header tank serves as an expansion chamber, coolant reservoir, and pressure regulator (via a pressure cap).

Heat exchanger—a vessel containing a number of small tubes through which cooling water is passed, while raw water is circulated around the outside of the tubes to carry off heat from the cooling water.

Heat-shrink tape and tubing—insulating tape that shrinks and melts when heated to form an effective seal. Also known as *self-amalgamating tape*.

Heat sink—a mounting for an electronic component designed to dissipate heat to the atmosphere.

Hemp—see *flax*.

Hertz (Hz)—the unit of frequency of an alternating current. One hertz equals one cycle per second.

Hold-over plate—see *cold plate*.

Hose adaptor—a standard plumbing fitting on one end with a suitable hose connection on the other.

Hose barb—a tapered and ridged fitting that slides up inside of a hose.

Hose clamp—an adjustable stainless steel band for clamping hoses. Also known as a *Jubilee clip* in the UK.

Hunting—a rhythmical cycling up and down in speed of a governed engine.

Hydraulic steering—steering using a manual hydraulic pump driven by the steering wheel, and operating a hydraulic piston (ram), which turns the rudder via a tiller arm.

Hydrometer—a float-type instrument used to determine the state of charge of a battery by measuring the specific gravity of the electrolyte (i.e., the amount of sulfuric acid in the electrolyte).

Impedance—a kind of alternating current resistance; the ratio of voltage to current.

Impeller—the rotating fitting that imparts motion to a fluid in a rotating pump.

Impressed current cathodic protection—a means of protecting underwater hardware by pushing controlled amounts of current into the water.

Incandescent light—a light with filaments.

Inches of mercury—a scale for measuring small pressure changes, particularly those below atmospheric pressure (vacuums).

Inductance—a property of a conductor or coil that determines how much voltage will be induced in it by a change of current in it.

Induction motor—an AC motor in which the stator coils generate a rotating magnetic field that drags the rotor around.

In-mast reefing—roller reefing for mains and mizzens installed inside specially extruded masts.

Injection pump—a pump designed to meter out precisely controlled amounts of diesel fuel and then raise it to injection pressures at precisely controlled moments in an engine cycle.

Injector—a device for atomizing diesel fuel and spraying it into a cylinder.

Injector nut—the nut that holds a fuel line to an injector.

Insulated return—a circuit in which both the outgoing and returning conductors are insulated.

Insulation—a material with extremely high electrical or thermal resistance.

Interference—undesired radio wavelengths.

Inverter—a device for changing DC to AC.

Ion—a charged molecule.

Isolation transformer—a transformer that transfers power from one winding to another magnetically and without any direct connection.

Isolator—a device that blocks small alternating currents but closes a circuit when faced with higher voltages.

Joker valve—see *duckbill valve*.

Jubilee clip—see *hose clamp*.

Kilo—1,000, as in kilowatt or kilohertz.

Latent heat—heat absorbed or given up during changes of state with no change of temperature.

Life cycles—the number of times a battery can be pulled down to a certain level of discharge and then recharged before the battery fails.

Lift pump—a low-pressure pump in a fuel-injection system supplying fuel from the tank to the injection pump.

Line driver—a winch with a set of jaws that grips an endless line (a continuous loop).

Liquid slugging—liquid refrigerant entering a compressor due to excess refrigerant being fed into the evaporator.

Live—a circuit energized with electricity.

Loading coil—a coil placed in series with an antenna and used to tune it.

Load testing—the use of a high load for a short period of time to test a battery and check its ability to perform under actual engine starting conditions.

Lower shroud—see *shroud*.

LPG (liquefied petroleum gas)—petroleum gases, principally propane and butane, that liquefy at relatively low pressures (below 200 psi).

Macerator—a specially designed impeller for breaking up solids prior to pumping.

Machine screw—a countersunk, slotted screw with machined threads such as are found on bolts.

Machine sensed—a voltage regulator that senses system voltage at the alternator as opposed to at the battery.

Manifold—a pipe assembly, attached to an engine, that conducts air into the engine or conducts exhaust gases out of it; any pipe assembly with more than one fitting screwed into it, for example, a gauge set manifold.

Manometer—a U-shaped, water-filled tube used for measuring very low pressures (commonly from 0 to 1 psi).

Mega—1,000,000, as in megawatt and megahertz.

Microfarad (MFD or µF)—one-millionth of a farad; a measure of capacity.

Milliamp (millivolt)—one-thousandth of an amp (volt).

Mole wrench—Vise-Grips.

MOV (metal oxide varistor)—one kind of transient voltage suppressor. MOVs have an open circuit until hit by a high voltage (a voltage spike or surge) and then conduct to ground in order to short out the spike (surge).

Multimeter—an essential tool for circuit testing. Also known as a VOM (volt-ohm meter) or an AVO (amps-volts-ohms meter).

Needle bearing—see *bearings*.

Noble metal—a metal high on the galvanic table. Noble metals are likely to form a cathode in any cases of galvanic corrosion and therefore are unlikely to corrode.

Noise—a general expression for electrical interference.

Offset gear—an arrangement of gears in which one gear engages another on the same plane (i.e., the gears are in line with one another).

Ohm—the standard unit of measurement of resistance.

Ohmmeter—an instrument for measuring resistance. Usually incorporated as one "channel" of a multimeter.

Open circuit—see *circuit*.

Open-circuit voltage—the voltage of a rested battery that is not receiving or delivering power.

Orifice—a very fine opening in a nozzle.

Outhaul—a device for tensioning the foot of a main or mizzen sail.

Overcharging—forcing excessive current into a battery. The battery will heat up and start to gas.

Packing—square, grease-impregnated, natural fiber rope, usually hemp (flax), used to seal stuffing boxes. Sometimes graphite tape is substituted.

Packing gland—see *stuffing box*.

Parallel connection—connecting battery positive terminals together, and negative terminals together, to increase system capacity without increasing voltage.

Pawl—a spring-loaded metal piece used in winch ratchets.

Pedestal—the column on which a steering wheel and various engine controls are mounted; generally topped with a binnacle and compass.

Pilot light—a constantly burning small flame used to ignite main burners on a gas appliance.

Pinion—a small gear designed to mesh with a large gear (for example, a starter motor drive gear).

Pintle—one-half of a rudder hinge, the other half being a *gudgeon*.

Pitch—the total distance a propeller would travel in one revolution, as determined by the amount of deflection of its blades, if there were no losses as it turned.

Planetary gears—an arrangement of small gears around a central drive gear, with a large ring gear around the outside of the small gears.

Points—the metal pieces that make and break the circuit in various switching devices, such as pressure switches, solenoids, circuit breakers, ordinary switches, etc.

Point loading—uneven loading on a bearing, which throws all the pressure on one part of the bearing instead of distributing it evenly over the whole bearing.

Polarity—the distinction between positive and negative conductors in a DC system; the opposite magnetic poles in an alternator, a generator, or an electric motor.

Polarity indicating light—a test light on AC circuits that allows one to check that the neutral wire is the grounded conductor and not the hot wire.

Polysulfide adhesive sealant—used for bedding hardware, trim, and teak decks. Sometimes loosely called *caulking*.

Polyurethane adhesive—used for bedding hardware and trim, bonding hull-to-deck joints, etc. Sometimes loosely called *caulking*.

Potentiometer—a variable resistance used for adjusting some voltage regulators.

Primary winding—the incoming side of a transformer.

Propane—see *LPG*.

PSI (pounds per square inch)—Pressure measurement. Psia (pounds per square inch absolute) measures actual pressure with no allowance for atmospheric pressure. Psig (pounds per square inch gauge) measures pressure with the gauge set to zero (0) at atmospheric pressure (14.7 psia). In other words psig = psia−14.7. Unless otherwise stated, psi always refers to psig.

Pulley—a drive wheel grooved to accept a V-belt.

Purging—the process of removing all air from a refrigeration gauge set before connecting to a refrigeration system. Also, bleeding a diesel engine fuel system.

Pyrometer—a gauge for measuring exhaust temperatures.

Quadrant—a type of rudderhead fitting to which the steering cables are attached.

Quartz halogen—a special type of bulb element that gives off more light per watt consumed than conventional incandescent filaments.

Race—the inner and outer cases on a bearing between which the balls are trapped.

Rack-and-pinion steering—traditionally a geared quadrant attached to the rudderpost is driven by a small pinion on the steering wheel drive shaft. A more modern version has the steering wheel driving a beveled gear in the pedestal with the output transmitted by solid rods to a tiller arm attached to the rudderpost.

Radial-drive steering—a large pulley wheel attached to the rudderpost is turned via cables driven by the steering wheel.

Ratchet—a gear so designed that spring-loaded pawls lock it in one direction but allow it to rotate, or ratchet, in the other.

Raw water—the seawater side of cooling systems.

Reciprocal—up and down motion.

Rectifier—see *diode*. A bridge rectifier is an arrangement of diodes to convert AC to DC.

Refrigerant—the gas used in refrigeration and air-conditioning systems (either R–12 or R–22 in boat use; sometimes referred to as Freon–12 and Freon–22, which are trade names of the DuPont Company).

Relay—an electromechanical switch activated by a small current in its coil.

Reserve capacity—the time in minutes that a battery will deliver 25 amps before dying.

Residual magnetism—magnetism remaining in field winding shoes after all current has been cut off to the field windings.

Resistance—the opposition an appliance or wire offers to the flow of electric current, measured in ohms.

Reverse polarity—connecting a battery backwards, i.e., connecting the positive terminal to the negative cable and the negative terminal to the positive cable.

RFD (receiver/filter/drier)—see *drier*.

Rheostat—a variable resistance.

Riding turn—the result of one turn on a winch "riding" up over another, effectively locking it up.

Rigging screw—see *turnbuckle*.

Ripple—undesired alternating current superimposed on a direct current power supply.

Roller bearings—see *bearings*.

Roller chain—bicycle-type chain, generally made of stainless steel, used primarily in steering systems, but also in some windlasses.

Roller furling—furling a sail by rolling it around its own luff wire. The sail can only be used fully unfurled. This is not a reefing system.

Roller reefing—furling a sail by rolling it around a solid luff extrusion. Sails can be used partially furled (i.e., reefed).

Rosin-core solder—a type of solder for electrical work with rosin-type flux set in a hollow tube.

Rotary seal—a carbon/ceramic-type seal used in place of a stuffing box on a propeller shaft.

RotoLock valves—a type of valve found on refrigeration compressors.

Rotor—the name given to the rotating field winding arrangement in an alternator.

Rudderpost, pipe, or stock—the metal post around which a rudder is constructed and to which a tiller arm or quadrant is attached.

Rudderstops—solid stops that limit the turning radius of a rudder. They must always stop the rudder before the limits of the steering system are reached.

Rudder tube—the hollow tube in which rudderpost bearings are set. It frequently terminates in a stuffing box.

Running backstays—intermediate backstays set up on quick release levers.

Running rigging—rigging used to hoist and control sails.

Sacrificial anodes—anodes of a less noble metal (generally zinc) electrically connected to underwater hardware and designed to corrode, thereby protecting the rest of the hardware.

Samson post—a strong post in the foredeck.

Screening—the placing of electronic equipment in grounded metal boxes to reduce interference.

Secondary winding—the output winding of a transformer.

Self-amalgamating tape—see *heat-shrink tape*.

Self-discharge—the gradual loss of capacity of a battery when standing idle.

Self-limiting—a built-in feature of some stator windings that limits alternator output to a certain maximum irrespective of speed.

Self-steering—an apparatus that holds a sailboat on a set course in relation to the wind.

Separators—the material used to divide one battery plate from another.

Series connection—a circuit with only one path for the current to flow. Batteries or appliances are connected one after another; in the case of batteries, negative to positive. Batteries in series deliver greater voltage but no greater capacity than a single battery.

Series-wound motors—a DC motor in which the field winding is connected in series with the armature. If unloaded, series-wound motors run away and can self-destruct.

Servopendulum—the principle underlying many self-steering devices.

Shaft lock—a device to stop a freewheeling propeller shaft.

Sheave—the pulley within a block.

Shielding—the placing of electric cables within grounded, braid-covered sheaths (or copper tubing) in order to reduce interference.

Shim—a specially cut piece of shim stock used as a spacer in specific applications, generally engine alignment.

Shim stock—very thin, accurately machined pieces of metal.

Short circuit—see *circuit*.

Shroud—wire rope supporting a mast in an athwartships direction. Cap shrouds (upper shrouds) run to the masthead; intermediate shrouds to the upper spreaders (if fitted), and lower shrouds to the lower spreaders.

Shunt—a special low-resistance connection in a circuit enabling an ammeter to be connected in parallel with the circuit.

Shunt-wound motors—the field windings and armature are connected in parallel.

Silicone sealant—useful as bedding under through-fastened hardware, and for some wiring applications. May be used as a gasket or waterproof sealant over wiring connections. Sometimes loosely referred to as *caulking*.

Sine wave—the wave made by alternating current when voltage is charted against time.

Siphon—the ability of a liquid to flow through a hose if one end is lower than the liquid level, even if the hose is looped above the liquid level.

Siphon break—see *antisiphon valve*.

Slinger—a washer on an electric pump shaft designed to deflect any leakage past the shaft seals away from the motor.

Slip rings—insulated metal disks on a rotor or armature shaft through which current is fed, via brushes, to or from armature or rotor windings.

Slow blow fuse—a fuse with delayed action for use with motors with high starting loads.

Skeg—a small keel aft used to support a rudder.

Snap ring—a spring-tensioned ring that fits into a groove on the inside of a hollow shaft, or around the outside of a shaft.

Snap ring pliers—special pliers for installing and removing snap rings.

Snubber—see *fail-safe diode*.

SNR (signal-to-noise ratio)—the ratio of the desired signal to the background noise.

Solenoid—a powerful relay.

Spade rudder—a rudder with no support beneath the hull.

Spanner—a wrench.

Specific gravity—a measure of the density of the electrolyte in a battery, i.e., the strength of the acid and therefore the battery's state of charge.

Spike—a sudden high-voltage peak superimposed on a DC system.

Spindle—a shaft in a winch.

Spiroid gear—a particular type of worm gear.

Split charging—charging two or more batteries independently from one charging source.

Split pin—see *cotter pin*.

Spreader—a strut on a mast to improve the angle of shrouds and stiffen the mast panels.

Spreader socket—the means of attaching a spreader to a mast.

Spur gears—a variation of offset gears.

Standing rigging—permanently attached rigging supporting a mast.

Standpipe—a variation of an Aqualift exhaust.

Stator—the stationary armature on an alternator within which the rotor spins.

Stays—devices to provide fore-and-aft support for a mast.

Stray-current corrosion—see *corrosion*.

Stuffing box—a device for making a watertight seal around a propeller shaft at the point where it exits the boat.

Sulfation—the normal chemical transformation of battery plates when a battery discharges. If a battery is left in a discharged state, the sulfates crystalize and harden, causing a permanent loss of capacity.

Sun gears—see *planetary gears*.

Supercharger—a blower mechanically driven by an engine and used to pressurize the inlet air.

Superheat—an adjustment of an expansion valve in a refrigeration system designed to produce maximum efficiency while providing a margin of safety against liquid slugging at the compressor.

Suppressor—a resistor put in series with a spark plug lead to reduce ignition-radiated interference.

Surge—see *spike*.

Surge protector—see *fail-safe diode*.

Swage (swedge)—a wire rope terminal in which the terminal is cold-welded to the rope by extreme pressure.

Swash plate—see *compressor*.

Tack—the lower forward corner of a sail.

Tailpiece—a hose adaptor that screws onto a through hull or seacock.

Tang—a fitting on a mast to which rigging attaches.

Thermistor—a resistor that changes in value with changes in the temperature.

Thermocouple—a device containing two dissimilar metals, which generates a very small voltage when heated. It is used to open a solenoid on gas appliances; if the flame fails, the solenoid closes.

Thermostat—a heat-sensitive device used to control the flow of coolant through an engine; or a heat-sensitive switch used to turn a water heating element off and on.

Thickness gauge—see *feeler gauge*.

Thimble—a grooved metal fitting around which loops in wire rope are formed.

Tinning—the process of getting solder to adhere to a soldering iron, wire end, or fitting.

Tiller arm—a short lever arm bolted to a rudderpost.

Toggle—a swivel joint used in rigging.

Topping lift—a line used to hold a boom off the deck.

Transformer—an AC device consisting of two or more coils used to magnetically couple one circuit to another. Depending on how the coils are wound, it can be used to lower or raise voltage. See also *isolation transformer*.

Transient voltage suppressor—see *fail-safe diode*.

Traversing nut—the nut that rides up and down the worm gear in worm steering.

Trickle charge—a continuous low current charge.

Trim tab—a small rudder hinged to the trailing edge of a main or auxiliary rudder.

Turbocharger—a blower driven by engine exhaust gas and used to pressurize the inlet air.

Turnbuckle—an adjustable fitting used to tension standing rigging.

Two-pole switch (or breaker)—see *double-pole switch*.

Ty-wraps—plastic cable ties used for bundling up cables and/or fastening them to a hull side.

Undercharging—the failure to bring a battery to full charge. This leads to sulfation and a permanent loss of capacity. See *sulfation*.

Upper shroud—see *shroud*.

Vacuum—pressure below atmospheric pressure.

Vacuum pump—a pump to suck a refrigeration system into an almost complete vacuum.

Valve—a device to allow gases in and out of a cylinder at precise moments, or a means of controlling the flow of liquids, such as a ball valve, a gate valve, etc.

Valve clearance—the gap between a valve stem and its rocker arm when the valve is fully closed.

Valve cover—the housing of an engine bolted over the valve mechanism.

Vane pumps—pumps with hard plastic blades (vanes) slotted into a central rotating hub.

Variable pitch propeller—one in which the pitch of the blades is adjustable.

Varistor—a resistor that changes in value with changes in voltage.

Vented loop—see *antisiphon valve*.

Vise-Grips—Mole wrench.

Volt—a unit of measurement of the "pressure" in an electrical system.

Voltage drop—the loss in "pressure" in wiring, switches, and connections due to unwanted resistance.

Voltage regulation—the process of controlling the output of an alternator or a generator. The output is normally matched to the battery's state of charge, tapering down as the battery comes up to full charge; this is constant-potential regulation. Alternatively, output can be maintained at a certain level irrespective of state of charge; this is constant-current regulation.

VOM (volt-ohm meter)—see *multimeter*.

Water generator—a generator (or alternator) driven by a towed impeller.

Watt—a unit of electrical power.

Wavelength—the distance between successive crests of a wave (radio, sound, or water).

Wear plate—a replaceable plate found in some pumps.

Wildcat—see *gypsy*.

Wind generator—a generator (or alternator) driven by the wind.

Windings—coils in a motor or transformer.

Worm gear—a particular type of high-reduction gear used to redirect a drive force or torque through a 90-degree angle.

Worm steering—the application of worm gearing to a steering unit.

Wrench—spanner.

Yaw—the characteristic of a boat, particularly a sailboat running downwind, to wander rhythmically either side of a course line.

Zone of security—the protected area beneath a lightning rod.

Appendix A: Checklist of Winterizing Procedures

It is far better to perform most routine maintenance at the end of the season when laying up rather than when recommissioning for the next season. Engines, in particular, will benefit from clean oil. Problem areas will be identified with plenty of time to fix them.

Note: Whenever using antifreeze, *remember that ethylene glycol (automotive antifreeze) is poisonous,* so do not put it in freshwater systems.

Use *propylene glycol,* which is nontoxic.

Laying-Up

Engine and Gear Train

- Change the engine and transmission oil at the beginning of the winter. The old oil will contain all kinds of harmful acids and contaminants, which you don't want to work on the engine and transmission all winter long.
- Change the antifreeze on freshwater-cooled engines. The antifreeze itself does not wear out, but it has various corrosion-fighting additives that do.
- Drain the raw-water system, taking particular care to empty all low spots. Remove rubber pump impellers, lightly grease with petroleum jelly, and replace. Leave the pump cover screws loose so that the impellers won't stick in the pump housings. Run the engine for *a few seconds* to drive any remaining water out of the exhaust. Wash salt crystals out of any vented loops.
- Check the primary fuel filter and fuel tank for water and sediment; clean as necessary. Keeping the tank full will cut down on condensation.
- Squirt some oil into the inlet manifold and turn the engine over a few times (without starting) to spread the oil over the cylinder walls.
- Grease all grease points.
- Remove the inner wires of all engine control cables from their outer sheaths; clean, inspect, grease, and replace. Check the sheathing as outlined in Chapter 9.
- Seal all openings into the engine (e.g., air inlet, exhaust) and the fuel tank vent. *Put a conspicuous notice somewhere that you have done this so that you remember to unseal everything at the start of the next season.*
- Inspect all flexible feet and couplings for signs of softening (generally from oil and fuel leaks) and replace as necessary.
- Inspect all hoses for signs of softening, cracking, and/or bulging, especially hoses on the hot side of the cooling and exhaust systems.
- Check the propeller shaft coupling set screws or through-bolt.

- If hauling out: check for propeller blade misalignment; flex the propeller and propeller shaft to check for Cutless bearing wear; tighten any strut mounting bolts; inspect a stainless steel propeller shaft for any signs of crevice corrosion and remove the propeller nut and check under it.

Batteries
Bring to a full charge. Equalize deep-cycle batteries. Top up. Clean the battery tops. Unless the batteries are being properly float-charged (via a solar panel or battery charger with *float* regulation) remove from the boat and store in a cool dry place. Bring to a full charge once a month.

Generators and Electric Motors
Clean and spray with a moisture-dispelling aerosol such as WD-40. Brush springs, in particular, will benefit from a shot of spray. Where generators have grease or oil fittings, give one shot or put in a drop. Pay particular attention to starter motor pinions.

Electrical Circuits
Clean corrosion off all terminals and connections and protect with petroleum jelly or a shot of WD-40 or other moisture-dispelling aerosol. Pay particular attention to all external outlets, especially the AC shorepower socket. Open up all coaxial connections if there is any possibility of water ingress; clean, repair as necessary, and reseal.

Electronic Equipment
Remove to a warm, dry place.

Refrigeration and Air-Conditioning Units
Drain any condenser raw-water circuits. If loops in the circuits make this impossible, pump 30- to 50-percent antifreeze solution through the unit. Spray a compressor clutch (WD-40).

Toilets
Drain and/or pump a 30- to 50-percent antifreeze solution through the system. (Note: Specialized holding tanks, such as Raritan's ElectroSan, must be winterized according to the manufacturer's instructions.) Break loose the discharge hose and check for calcification. Wash out all vented loops.

Pumps
Drain and/or pump through a 30- to 50-percent antifreeze solution. Remove flexible impellers, lightly grease (a Teflon-based grease) and put back. Leave pump covers loose; only tighten down when recommissioning. Inspect all vanes, impellers, etc. for wear, and check for shaft seal leaks. If wintering in the water, check the bilge-pump float switch, wiring, switch, and the state of charge of the battery.

Freshwater Systems

Pump out the tanks and drain the system. Clean the tanks. If antifreeze is used in any pumps, make sure it is *propylene glycol.* Lightly oil connecting rod bearings (if fitted) on freshwater pumps.

Stuffing boxes

If hauling out, repack. If wintering in the water, tighten down to stop any drip. *Be sure to loosen before reusing the propeller or the shaft will overheat* (post a note in a prominent place).

Seacocks

If hauling out, pull and grease all seacock plugs where this is possible. Dismantle and grease gate valves. If wintering in the water, close all seacocks (except cockpit drains) and make a close inspection of cockpit drain hoses and clamps.

Hydraulic Systems

Drain a little oil and check for water or contaminants. Top up as necessary. Check all seals and hoses for signs of leaks, and hoses for damage (see the section on cable sheaths in Chapter 9).

Water heaters

Drain out all water. Leave a conspicuous notice somewhere so that you will be sure to refill before turning electric element heaters back on.

Stoves

Drain a little fuel from kerosene and/or alcohol tanks and check for any water or contaminants. Close LPG or CNG gas valves *at the cylinder.* It is a good idea to renew filaments on filament-type igniters at least every two years.

Steering

Lightly oil cables, and oil or grease sheave and pedestal bearings as called for. Pay particular attention to the worm gear (if fitted) and other steel parts which might seize up. Remove cables from conduits; clean, inspect, grease, and replace. Check all sheave mountings, bracing, and rudder stops. Check the rudderhead and tension the cables. With pedestal-type rack-and-pinion steering, remove the top plate and input socket screws; clean, grease, and replace.

Running Rigging

Wash all blocks. Disassemble and clean where possible. Use hot water and vinegar on stubborn salt deposits. Lubricate and reassemble. Wash all synthetic lines in a warm detergent solution. Adding a little bleach will do no harm.

Spars and Standing Rigging

- *Wooden spars and spreaders:* Wash and inspect closely for any signs of rot (e.g., softening or discoloration), especially on spreaders and around fasteners and exit holes. Seal bare spots even if you are not varnishing or painting at this time.

- *Aluminum spars:* Wash and inspect for signs of corrosion, distortion of mast walls (especially around spreader sockets), crazing of anodizing, and hairline cracks (especially around welds and cutouts). Remove and grease any fasteners that must be prevented from freezing up. Wax the spar before storing.

- *All spars:* Withdraw mast tang bolts and check for crevice corrosion. Remove boots or covers from spreader tips. Remove head box sheaves and inspect shafts and sheaves. Lubricate and replace. Remove turnbuckle boots, tape, etc. Undo all turnbuckles; clean, inspect and grease. Pay close attention to clevis pins; when replacing, tape over the ends of split pins (cotter pins). Inspect swages for hairline cracks. Wash all rigging. Do not store stainless steel rigging against aluminum spars.

Winches, Windlasses, and Deck Hardware

Strip down, clean, grease, and oil all winches. Pay particular attention to pawls and pawl springs. Check the lubricant in windlasses for water and change as necessary. Crank windlasses over to spread lubricant around the internal parts. Remove the rope drum and wildcat (gypsy) and grease clutches and shafts. Check fasteners on all deck hardware; check carefully for flaws in the bedding (caulking) that might cause deck leaks.

Roller-Reefing Gear

Thoroughly flush all open bearings with warm, fresh water. Regrease or lubricate as called for by the manufacturer, spinning the bearings to spread the lubricant around. Wash extrusions and apply wax. Pay close attention to all joints. Do not leave the sail up. It should be stowed for the winter.

Sacrificial Anodes

Inspect and change all zincs as necessary (hull, rudder, propeller shaft, engine cooling system, refrigeration condenser, etc.).

Recommissioning

1. Check the lay-up list and complete those jobs that weren't done.
2. *Observe and obey all conspicuous notes,* and envision areas that should have such notes but do not (plugged off engine air inlets and exhausts; overtightened packing nut; empty hot water tank; etc).
3. Check all hoses and through-hull connections (hose clamps).
4. Check the refrigerant charge on refrigeration systems—engine-driven compressor seals are especially prone to drying out and leaking during long periods of shutdown.

5. "Exercise" (i.e., switch on and off a few times) all switches—this helps to clean surface corrosion off terminals. Open and close seacocks; spin blocks and windlasses. Turn the steering wheel from side to side and check for any stiff spots or binding. Spin the drum and halyard swivels on roller reefers.

6. Tighten down all flexible impeller pump covers; prime centrifugal pumps.
7. Once in the water, allow the hull to stabilize (this takes a few days on wooden hulls) and then check the engine alignment.

Appendix B: Freeing Frozen Parts and Fasteners

Problems with frozen fasteners are inevitable on boats. One or more of the following techniques may free things up.

Lubrication

- Clean everything with a wire brush (preferably one with brass bristles), douse liberally with penetrating oil, and wait. Find something else to do for an hour or two, overnight if possible, before having another go. Be patient.
- Clevis pins: After lubricating and waiting, grip the large end of the pin with Vise-Grips (Mole wrench) and turn the pin in its socket to free it. If the pin is the type with a cotter pin (also known as a cotter key or split pin) in both ends, remove one of the cotter pins, grip the clevis pin, and turn. Since the Vise-Grips will probably mar the surface of the pin, it should be knocked out from the other end.

Shock Treatment

An impact wrench is a handy tool to have around. These take a variety of end fittings (screwdriver bits; sockets) to match different fasteners. The wrench is hit hard with a hammer and hopefully jars the fastener loose. If an impact wrench is not available or does not work, other forms of shock must be applied with an acute sense of the breaking point of the fastener and adjacent engine castings, etc. Unfortunately this is generally only acquired after a lifetime of breaking things! Depending on the problem, shock treatment may take different forms:

- A bolt stuck in an engine block: Put a sizable punch squarely on the head of the bolt and give it a good knock into the block. Now try undoing it.
- A pulley on a tapered shaft, a propeller, or an outboard motor flywheel: Back out the retaining nut *until its face is flush with the end of the shaft* (this is important to avoid damage to the threads on the nut or shaft). Put pressure behind the pulley, propeller, or flywheel as if trying to pull it off, and hit the end of the retaining nut or shaft smartly. The shock will frequently break things loose without the need for a specialized puller.

- A large nut with limited room around it, or one on a shaft that wants to turn (for example, a crankshaft pulley nut): Put a short-handled wrench on the nut, hold the wrench to prevent it from jumping off, and hit it hard.
- If all else fails, use a cold chisel to cut a slot in the side of the offending nut or the head of the bolt, place a punch in the slot at a tangential angle to the nut or bolt, and hit it smartly.

Leverage

- Screws: With a square-bladed screwdriver, put a crescent (adjustable) wrench on the blade, bear down hard on the screw, and turn the screwdriver with the wrench. If the screwdriver has a round blade, clamp a pair of Vise-Grips to the base of the handle and do the same thing.
- Nuts and bolts: If using wrenches with one box end and one open end, put the box end of the appropriate wrench on the fastener and hook the box end of the next size up into the free open end of the wrench to double the length of the handle and thus the leverage.
- Cheater pipe: Slip a length of pipe over the handle of the wrench to increase its leverage.

Heat

Heat expands metal, but for this treatment to be effective, frozen fasteners must frequently be raised to cherry-red temperatures. These temperatures will upset tempering in hardened steel, while uneven heating of surrounding castings may cause them to crack. Heat must be applied with circumspection.

Heat applied to a frozen nut will expand it outward, and it can then be broken loose. But equally, heat applied to the bolt will expand it within the nut, generating all kinds of pressure that helps to break the grip of rust, etc. When the fixture cools it will frequently come apart quite easily.

Broken Fasteners

- Rounded-off heads: Sometimes there is not enough head left on a fastener to grip with Vise-Grips or pipe (Stillson) wrenches, but there is enough to accept a slot made by a hacksaw. A screwdriver can then be inserted and turned as above.
- If a head breaks off it is often possible to remove whatever it was holding, thus exposing part of the shaft of the fastener, which can be lubricated, gripped with Vise-Grips, and backed out.
- Drilling out: It is very important to drill down the center of a broken fastener. Use a center punch and take some time putting an accurate "dimple" at this point before attempting to drill. Next use a small drill to make a pilot hole to the desired depth. If Ezy-Outs or "screw extractors" (hardened, tapered steel screws with reversed threads, available from tool supply houses) are on hand, drill the correctly sized hole for the appropriate Ezy-Out and try extracting the stud. Otherwise drill out the stud *up to the insides of its threads but no farther,* or irreparable damage will be done to the threads in the casting. The remaining bits of fastener thread in the casting can be picked out with judicious use of a small screwdriver or some pointed instrument. If a tap is available to clean up the threads, so much the better.
- Pipe fittings: If a hacksaw blade can be gotten inside the relevant fittings (which can often be done using duct tape to make a handle on the blade), cut a slit in the fitting along its length, and then place a punch on the outside alongside the cut, hit it, and collapse it inward. Do the same on the other side of the cut. The fitting should now come out easily.

Miscellaneous

- Stainless steel: Stainless-to-stainless fasteners (for example, many turnbuckles) have a bad habit of "galling" when being done up or undone, especially if there is any dirt in the threads to cause friction. Galling (otherwise known as "cold welding") is a process in which molecules on the surface of one part of the fastener transfer to the other part. Everything seizes up for good. Galled stainless fastenings cannot be salvaged—they almost always end up shearing off. When doing up or undoing a stainless fastener, if any sudden or unusual friction develops stop immediately, let it cool off, lubricate thoroughly, work the fastener backward and forward to spread the lubrication around, go back the other way, clean the threads, and start again.
- Aluminum: Aluminum oxidizes to form a dense white powder. Aluminum oxide is more voluminous than the original aluminum and so generates a lot of pressure around any fasteners passing through aluminum fixtures—sometimes enough pressure to shear off the heads of fasteners. Once oxidation around a stainless or bronze fastener has reached a certain point it is virtually impossible to remove the fastener without breaking it.
- Damaged threads: If all else fails, and a fastener has to be drilled out, the threads in the casting may be damaged. There are two options.

  1. To drill and tap for the next larger fastener.
  2. To install a Heli-Coil insert. A Heli-Coil is a new thread. An oversized hole is drilled and tapped with a special tap, and the Heli-Coil insert (the new thread) is screwed into the hole with a special tool. You end up with the original sized hole and threads. Any good machine shop will have the relevant tools and inserts.

Appendix C: Tools and Spare Parts

The following tool and spare parts list may cause some people to accuse me of letting my imagination run wild. Let me assure you we have all of this and more (including oxyacetylene, rolls of copper tubing, and a complete variable pitch propeller unit) on board, and have used almost everything at one time or another on our boat or someone else's. (Note: When ordering spares, always include the model number *and the serial number* of the equipment the spares are for, in case there have been changes within a model range.)

Mechanic's Toolbox

Screwdrivers—Phillips head and slotted—a selection. Especially useful is a short-handled version of each for awkward corners.

Open end/box end wrench (spanner) set—¼″ to 1″ (or metric equivalent, *or both* if you have a mixture of American and metric nuts and bolts)

⅜″ drive socket set, ¼″ to 1″ (or metric, as above). The ⅜″ is much easier to handle in tight spaces than a ½″ drive, but with the larger sized sockets (over ¾″) will get severely stressed, so buy only top-quality ratchets and extensions.

6″ and 10″ crescent (adjustable) wrench

6″ and 10″ Vise-Grips (Mole wrench)

12″ and 18″ pipe wrench—preferably aluminum, which is much lighter and won't rust nearly as badly (although aluminum wrenches still have steel jaws)

Side-cutting needlenose pliers

Ball peen hammer

Set of Allen wrenches (keys)

Set of feeler (thickness) gauges—inches or metric, as appropriate

Aligning punches—these taper to a reasonably fine head

Straight punches—for knocking out recalcitrant clevis pins, etc.

Cold chisels

Files—flat, half round, and round

Scrapers—for removing old gaskets

Brass bristle wire brush—steel bristles leave flecks of rust

Emery cloth

Fine and medium grinding paste

Hacksaw and blades—buy one in which the end fittings are captured, i.e., cannot fall out when the blade breaks, or they are sure to get lost

Snap ring (circlip) pliers—both inside (internal) and outside (external)

Pulley puller—very useful on occasion

Set of taps and dies—American, metric, or both

Propane torch

Small vise—if it can be accommodated (some very neat ones clip into a standard winch socket)

Engine and Mechanical Supplies

Engine and gearbox oil

Oil filter (and sealing rings) and an oil filter wrench

Fuel filters and a fuel filter wrench (where needed)

Filter funnel for taking on fuel

Grease gun

Greases (Teflon, water pump)

Oil squirt can

Silicone spray

WD-40

Valve cover gasket

Injector sealing washers (if fitted)

Injector

Set of injector lines (injection pump to injectors)

Lift pump (feed pump) diaphragm

Pump overhaul kits for all cooling water pumps (impellers/diaphragms; seals; and bearings)

Gasket cement

Thermostat

Hoses (including oil cooler hoses)

O-ring kit (an assortment)

All belts

Packing (or graphite tape)

Wrench (spanner) for packing nut

Packing removal tool

¼″, ⁵⁄₁₆″, ⅜″ and ½″ stainless steel threaded rod

Stainless steel nuts and lock washers for the above

Length of ¼″ and ⅜″ keystock

Flare tubing kit (if there is any flared copper tubing on board)

Tubing cutters

Electrical Tool Kit

Different sizes of multistrand copper cable

Wire strippers/crimpers

Appropriate crimp-on terminals

Heat-shrink (self-amalgamating) tape and tubing

Electrician's putty

Insulating (electrician's) tape

Soldering iron, solder, and flux (rosin type)

Spare coaxial end fittings and connectors

Hydrometer for battery testing

Battery terminal puller

Multimeter (VOM)

Test light(s)

Amprobe for measuring AC amps (if the boat has a lot of AC equipment)

Ground fault tester for checking dockside power

Insulated magnet wire and ferrite rod for making noise suppression chokes, and one or two 1.0 μF, 200-volt capacitors

Flashlight batteries

Fuses

Petroleum jelly—for greasing terminals

Woodworking Tool Kit (choose to suit)

Crosscut saw

Chisels

Wood bits (drill bits)

Plug cutters

Set square

Framing square

Bar clamps

Doweling

Epoxy glue and thickeners

Plastic resin glue (e.g., Weldwood)

Tenon (back) saw

Mallet

Countersink

Tape measure

Bevel square

C clamps
Plane
Sandpaper—wet-or-dry, #180 grit to #400

Power Tools (where appropriate)

Electric drill—½″ chuck
Set of drill bits—1/16″ to ½″
Set of hole saws—very useful, buy good quality
Jig saw
Circular saw
Palm (block) sander
Router and bits

General Supplies

Paint, varnish, and brushes
Paint scrapers
Thinners
Acetone
Fiberglass cloth, matt, and disposable brushes
Fasteners—bronze threaded nails; bronze or stainless steel screws; stainless steel nuts and bolts
Duct tape
Masking tape
Teflon tape—very useful
Bedding (caulking)—polyurethane adhesive such as 3M 5200; polysulfide adhesive sealant such as Boatlife or Thiokol; silicone sealant
Old inner tube—when cut up in strips and wrapped tightly around ruptured hoses, it seals very effectively
Selection of *all stainless steel* hose clamps (jubilee clips)—be sure to check the screws, which are frequently only nickel plated.
Copper pipe and fittings—where appropriate
PVC pipe, fittings, and glue—check the glue annually and replace as necessary, it may dry out
Sail repair kit
Selection of hoses and hose adaptors (hose barbs, etc.)
Antifreeze—ethylene glycol for general use; *propylene glycol for freshwater systems*

Rigging Kit

Length of cable as long as the longest stay on the boat—preferably 7 × 19, which is more flexible than 1 × 19 and can be used in steering repairs
End fittings for the above—StaLok, Norseman or Castlok. If using 7 × 19 wire be sure to get the correct inserts if they differ from those used on 1 × 19 wire.
Turnbuckles, toggles, forks, and eyes—StaLok, Norseman, or Castlok
Bolt cutters
Nicopress (Talurit) kit

Cable clamps (Crosby clamps; bulldog clamps)—matched to cable sizes
Thimbles—matched to cable sizes
Shackles
Seizing wire
Complete chain and wire rope assembly for wheel steering
Selection of clevis pins and cotter pins (split pins)
One or two spare blocks

Specific Supplies

Pump overhaul kit—impeller/diaphragm/vanes/cup washers; seals; bearings; and any valves for every pump on board
Spare DC motors for electric pumps, especially vital ones (e.g., an electric toilet or refrigeration condenser pump)
Brushes for universal or permanent magnet motors
Freshwater pump overhaul kit and pressure switch
Manual toilet overhaul kit—valves, piston cup washers or O-rings, piston rod seal (get extra spares)
Baby (mineral) oil
Muriatic acid
Winch pawls and springs
Generator brushes and capacitors
AC electric motor capacitors
Wind generator vanes (blades) and brushes—where appropriate
Self-steering wind vanes
Autopilot belts—where appropriate
Hydraulic oil if there are any hydraulic systems on board
Electric water heater element and thermostat
Gas stove and appliance thermocouples and/or optical sensors
Burner and pressure tank repair kit—kerosene or alcohol stove nipple (orifice) wrench, 10mm wrench (spanner) for the valve stem packing, an eraser-tipped pencil (for removing cleaning needles) and cup washers for the fuel tank pump
Spare burners and burner parts (valve stems, cleaning needles and nipples); sealing washers
Mantles for pressurized kerosene (white gas) lanterns, or gas lanterns
Refrigeration supplies:
    Refrigerent—R-12 and/or R-22
    Rotolock valve wrench
    Gauge set
    Leak detection kit—to fit the propane torch in the mechanic's tool kit
    Refrigeration oil
    Receiver/filter/drier (or filters and sight glass if the unit has individual components)
    Compressor head set (valve plate and gaskets)

Compressor clutch coil
Special tools for removing the compressor pulley
Condenser water pump overhaul kit
Expansion valve
Vacuum pump—optional for the really serious!
Sacrificial zinc anodes
Multifunction 'key' for undoing fuel and water fill caps, and deck plates—very useful little item
Softwood fids—to fit all seacocks and hull openings below the waterline

One or two plywood blanks—to fit portholes, with some means of quickly securing them, in case a porthole gets stove in
Hydraulic systems:
Length of hydraulic hose as long as the longest hose run on the boat
Sufficient fittings to be able to use hose length to replace any hose run
Hydraulic oil—a good reserve supply
Spare filter

Appendix D: Useful Tables

Table D-1. Fraction, Decimal, and Metric Equivalents

Fractions	Decimal In.	Metric mm.	Fractions	Decimal In.	Metric mm.
1/64	.015625	.397	33/64	.515625	13.097
1/32	.03125	.794	17/32	.53125	13.494
3/64	.046875	1.191	35/64	.546875	13.891
1/16	.0625	1.588	9/16	.5625	14.288
5/64	.078125	1.984	37/64	.578125	14.684
3/32	.09375	2.381	19/32	.59375	15.081
7/64	.109375	2.778	39/64	.609375	15.478
1/8	.125	3.175	5/8	.625	15.875
9/64	.140625	3.572	41/64	.640625	16.272
5/32	.15625	3.969	21/32	.65625	16.669
11/64	.171875	4.366	43/64	.671875	17.066
3/16	.1875	4.763	11/16	.6875	17.463
13/64	.203125	5.159	45/64	.703125	17.859
7/32	.21875	5.556	23/32	.71875	18.256
15/64	.234375	5.953	47/64	.734375	18.653
1/4	.250	6.35	3/4	.750	19.05
17/64	.265625	6.747	49/64	.765625	19.447
9/32	.28125	7.144	25/32	.78125	19.844
19/64	.296875	7.54	51/64	.796875	20.241
5/16	.3125	7.938	13/16	.8125	20.638
21/64	.328125	8.334	53/64	.828125	21.034
11/32	.34375	8.731	27/32	.84375	21.431
23/64	.359375	9.128	55/64	.859375	21.828
3/8	.375	9.525	7/8	.875	22.225
25/64	.390625	9.922	57/64	.890625	22.622
13/32	.40625	10.319	29/32	.90625	23.019
27/64	.421875	10.716	59/64	.921875	23.416
7/16	.4375	11.113	15/16	.9375	23.813
29/64	.453125	11.509	61/64	.953125	24.209
15/32	.46875	11.906	31/32	.96875	24.606
31/64	.484375	12.303	63/64	.984375	25.003
1/2	.500	12.7	1	1.00	25.4

Table D-2. Inches to Millimeters Conversion Table

Inches	Millimeters	Inches	Millimeters	Inches	Millimeters
0.001	0.0254	0.010	0.2540	0.019	0.4826
0.002	0.0508	0.011	0.2794	0.020	0.5080
0.003	0.0762	0.012	0.3048	0.021	0.5334
0.004	0.1016	0.013	0.3302	0.022	0.5588
0.005	0.1270	0.014	0.3556	0.023	0.5842
0.006	0.1524	0.015	0.3810	0.024	0.6096
0.007	0.1778	0.016	0.4064	0.025	0.6350
0.008	0.2032	0.017	0.4318		
0.009	0.2286	0.018	0.4572		

Table D-3. Torque Conversion Table, Pound Feet to Newton Meters

Pound-Feet (lb.-ft.)	Newton Metres (Nm)	Newton Metres (Nm)	Pound-Feet (lb.-ft.)
1	1.356	1	0.7376
2	2.7	2	1.5
3	4.0	3	2.2
4	5.4	4	3.0
5	6.8	5	3.7
6	8.1	6	4.4
7	9.5	7	5.2
8	10.8	8	5.9
9	12.2	9	6.6
10	13.6	10	7.4
15	20.3	15	11.1
20	27.1	20	14.8
25	33.9	25	18.4
30	40.7	30	22.1
35	47.5	35	25.8
40	54.2	40	29.5
45	61.0	50	36.9
50	67.8	60	44.3
55	74.6	70	51.6
60	81.4	80	59.0
65	88.1	90	66.4
70	94.9	100	73.8
75	101.7	110	81.1
80	108.5	120	88.5
90	122.0	130	95.9
100	135.6	140	103.3
110	149.1	150	110.6
120	162.7	160	118.0
130	176.3	170	125.4
140	189.8	180	132.8
150	203.4	190	140.1
160	216.9	200	147.5
170	230.5	225	166.0
180	244.0	250	184.4

Table D-4. Feet to Meters Conversion Table

Feet – metres 1 foot = 0.3048 m			
ft.	**met.**	**ft.**	**met.**
1	0,305	31	9,449
2	**0,610**	**32**	**9,754**
3	0,914	33	10,058
4	**1,219**	**34**	**10,363**
5	1,524	35	10,668
6	**1,829**	**36**	**10,973**
7	2,134	37	11,278
8	**2,438**	**38**	**11,582**
9	2,743	39	11,887
10	**3,048**	**40**	**12,192**
11	3,353	41	12,497
12	**3,658**	**42**	**12,802**
13	3,962	43	13,106
14	**4,267**	**44**	**13,441**
15	4,572	45	13,716
16	**4,877**	**46**	**14,021**
17	5,182	47	14,326
18	**5,486**	**48**	**14,630**
19	5,791	49	14,935
20	**6,096**	**50**	**15,240**
21	6,401	51	15,545
22	**6,706**	**52**	**15,850**
23	7,010	53	16,154
24	**7,315**	**54**	**16,459**
25	7,620	55	16,764
26	**7,925**	**56**	**17,069**
27	8,230	57	17,374
28	**8,534**	**58**	**17,678**
29	8,839	59	17,983
30	**9,144**	**60**	**18,288**

Table D-5. Meters to Feet Conversion Table

Metres – Feet 1 metre = 3.2808 feet	
met.	**feet**
1	3,28
2	**6,56**
3	9,84
4	**13,12**
5	16,40
6	**19,69**
7	22,97
8	**26,25**
9	29,53
10	**32,81**
11	36,09
12	**39,37**
13	42,65
14	**45,93**
15	49,21
16	**52,49**
17	55,77
18	**59,06**
19	62,34
20	**65,62**

Table D-6. Inches to Centimeters Conversion Table

Inches – centimetres 1 inch = 2.54 cm	
inches	**cm**
1	2,54
2	**5,08**
3	7,62
4	**10,16**
5	12,70
6	**15,24**
7	17,78
8	**20,32**
9	22,86
10	**25,40**
11	27,94
12	**30,48**

Table D-7. Degrees Fahrenheit to Degrees Celsius/Centigrade Conversion Table

°F	°C	°F	°C	°F	°C	°F	°C	°F	°C	°F	°C	°F	°C	°F	°C
-454	-270	-31	-35	19.4	-7	70	21.1	120.2	49	171	77.2	225	107.2	660	348.9
-450	-268	-30	-34.4	20	-6.7	71	21.7	121	49.4	172	77.8	230	110	662	350
-440	-262	-29.2	-34	21	-6.1	71.6	22	122	50	172.4	78	235	112.8	670	354.4
-436	-260	-29	-33.9	21.2	-6	72	22.2	123	50.6	173	78.3	239	115	680	360
-430	-257	-28	-33.3	22	-5.6	73	22.8	123.8	51	174	78.9	240	115.6	690	365.6
-420	-251	-27.4	-33	23	-5	73.4	23	124	51.1	174.2	79	245	118.3	698	370
-418	-250	-27	-32.8	24	-4.4	74	23.3	125	51.7	175	79.4	248	120	700	371.1
-410	-246	-26	-32.2	24.8	-4	75	23.9	125.6	52	176	80	250	121.1	710	377
-400	-240	-25.6	-32	25	-3.9	75.2	24	126	52.2	177	80.6	255	123.9	716	380
-390	-234	-25	-31.7	26	-3.3	76	24.4	127	52.8	177.8	81	257	125	720	382
-382	-230	-24	-31.1	26.6	-3	77	25	127.4	53	178	81.1	260	126.7	730	388
-380	-229	-23.8	-31	27	-2.8	78	25.6	128	53.3	179	81.7	265	129.4	734	390
-370	-223	-23	-30.6	28	-2.2	78.8	26	129	53.9	179.6	82	266	130	740	393
-364	-220	-22	-30	28.4	-2	79	26.1	129.2	54	180	82.2	270	132.2	750	399
-360	-218	-21	-29.4	29	-1.7	80	26.7	130	54.4	181	82.8	275	135	752	400
-350	-212	-20.2	-29	30	-1.1	80.6	27	131	55	181.4	83	280	137.8	760	404
-346	-210	-20	-28.9	30.2	-1	81	27.2	132	55.6	182	83.3	284	140	770	410
-340	-207	-19	-28.3	31	-0.6	82	27.8	132.8	56	183	83.9	285	140.6	780	416
-330	-201	-18.4	-28	32	0	82.4	28	133	56.1	183.2	84	290	143.3	788	420
-328	-200	-18	-27.8	33	0.6	83	28.3	134	56.7	184	84.4	293	145	790	421
-320	-196	-17	-27.2	33.8	1	84	28.9	134.6	57	185	85	295	146.1	800	427
-310	-190	-16.6	-27	34	1.1	84.2	29	135	57.2	186	85.6	300	148.9	806	430
-300	-184	-16	-26.7	35	1.7	85	29.4	136	57.8	186.8	86	302	150	810	432
-292	-180	-15	-26.1	35.6	2	86	30	136.4	58	187	86.1	310	154.4	820	438
-290	-179	-14.8	-26	36	2.2	87	30.6	137	58.3	188	86.7	320	160	824	440
-280	-173	-14	-25.6	37	2.8	87.8	31	138	58.9	188.6	87	330	165.6	830	443
-274	-170	-13	-25	37.4	3	88	31.1	138.2	59	189	87.2	338	170	840	449
-270	-168	-12	-24.4	38	3.3	89	31.7	139	59.4	190	87.8	340	171.1	842	450
-260	-162	-11.2	-24	39	3.9	89.6	32	140	60	190.4	88	350	176.7	850	454
-256	-160	-11	-23.9	39.2	4	90	32.2	141	60.6	191	88.3	356	180	860	460
-250	-157	-10	-23.3	40	4.4	91	32.8	141.8	61	192	88.9	360	182.2	870	465
-240	-151	-9.4	-23	41	5	91.4	33	142	61.1	192.2	89	370	187.8	878	470
-238	-150	-9	-22.8	42	5.5	92	33.3	143	61.7	193	89.4	374	190	880	471
-230	-146	-8	-22.2	42.8	6	93	33.9	143.6	62	194	90	380	193.3	890	477
-220	-140	-7.6	-22	43	6.1	93.2	34	144	62.2	195	90.6	390	198.9	896	480
-210	-134	-7	-21.7	44	6.7	94	34.4	145	62.8	195.8	91	392	200	900	482
-202	-130	-6	-21.1	44.6	7	95	35	145.4	63	196	91.1	400	204.4	910	488
-200	-129	-5.8	-21	45	7.2	96	35.6	146	63.3	197	91.7	410	210	914	490
-190	-123	-5	-20.6	46	7.8	96.8	36	147	63.9	197.6	92	420	215.6	920	493
-184	-120	-4	-20	46.4	8	97	36.1	147.2	64	198	92.2	428	220	930	499
-180	-118	-3	-19.4	47	8.3	98	36.7	148	64.4	199	92.8	430	221.1	932	500
-170	-112	-2.2	-19	48	8.9	98.6	37	149	65	199.4	93	440	226.7	940	504
-166	-110	-2	-18.9	48.2	9	99	37.2	150	65.6	200	93.3	446	230	950	510
-160	-107	-1	-18.3	49	9.4	100	37.8	150.8	66	201	93.9	450	232.2	960	516
-150	-101	-0.4	-18	50	10	100.4	38	151	66.1	201.2	94	460	237.8	968	520
-148	-100	0	-17.8	51	10.6	101	38.3	152	66.7	202	94.4	464	240	970	521
-140	-96	1	-17.2	51.8	11	102	38.9	152.6	67	203	95	470	243.3	980	527
-130	-90	1.4	-17	52	11.1	102.2	39	153	67.2	204	95.6	480	248.9	986	530
-120	-84	2	-16.7	53	11.7	103	39.4	154	67.8	204.8	96	482	250	990	532
-112	-80	3	-16.1	53.6	12	104	40	154.4	68	205	96.1	490	254.4	1000	538
-110	-79	3.2	-16	54	12.2	105	40.6	155	68.3	206	96.7	500	260	1004	540
-100	-73.3	4	-15.6	55	12.8	105.8	41	156	68.9	206.6	97	510	265.6	1022	550
-94	-70	5	-15	55.4	13	106	41.1	156.2	69	207	97.2	518	270	1050	566
-90	-67.8	6	-14.4	56	13.3	107	41.7	157	69.4	208	97.8	520	271.1	1100	593
-80	-62.2	6.8	-14	57	13.9	107.6	42	158	70	208.4	98	530	276.7	1112	600
-76	-60	7	-13.9	57.2	14	108	42.2	159	70.6	209	98.3	536	280	1150	621
-70	-56.7	8	-13.3	58	14.4	109	42.8	159.8	71	210	98.9	540	282.2	1200	649
-60	-51.1	8.6	-13	59	15	109.4	43	160	71.1	210.2	99	550	287.8	1202	650
-58	-50	9	-12.8	60	15.6	110	43.3	161	71.7	211	99.4	554	290	1250	677
-50	-45.6	10	-12.2	60.8	16	111	43.9	161.6	72	212	100	560	293.3	1292	700
-40	-40	10.4	-12	61	16.1	111.2	44	162	72.2	213	100.6	570	298.9	1300	704
-39	-39.4	11	-11.7	62	16.7	112	44.4	163	72.8	213.8	101	572	300	1350	732
-38.2	-39	12	-11.1	62.6	17	113	45	163.4	73	214	101.1	580	304.4	1382	750
-38	-38.9	12.2	-11	63	17.2	114	45.6	164	73.3	215	101.7	590	310	1400	760
-37	-38.3	13	-10.6	64	17.8	114.8	46	165	73.9	215.6	102	600	315.6	1450	788
-36.4	-38	14	-10	64.4	18	115	46.1	165.2	74	216	102.2	608	320	1472	800
-36	-37.8	15	-9.4	65	18.3	116	46.7	166	74.4	217	102.8	610	321.0	1500	816
-35	-37.2	15.8	-9	66	18.9	116.6	47	167	75	217.4	103	620	326.7		
-34.6	-37	16	-8.9	66.2	19	117	47.2	168	75.6	218	103.3	626	330		
-34	-36.7	17	-8.3	67	19.4	118	47.8	168.8	76	219	103.9	630	332.2		
-33	-36.1	17.6	-8	68	20	118.4	48	169	76.1	219.2	104	640	337.8		
-32.8	-36	18	-7.8	69	20.6	119	48.3	170	76.7	220	104.4	644	340		
-32	-35.6	19	-7.2	69.8	21	120	48.9	170.6	77	221	105	650	343.3		

Table D-8. Nautical Miles to Kilometers Conversion Table

1 Nautical Mile = 1.8520 Kilometres
(identical conversion for Knots — Kilometres/hour)

nm	0	1	2	3	4	5	6	7	8	9	nm
0	0	1,85	3,70	5,56	7,41	9,26	11,11	12,96	14,82	16,67	0
10	18,52	20,37	22,22	24,08	25,93	27,78	29,63	31,48	33,34	35,19	10
20	37,04	38,89	40,74	42,60	44,45	46,30	48,15	50,00	51,86	53,71	20
30	55,56	57,41	59,26	61,12	62,97	64,82	66,67	68,52	70,38	72,23	30
40	74,08	75,93	77,78	79,64	81,49	83,34	85,19	87,04	88,90	90,75	40
50	92,60	94,45	96,30	98,16	100,01	101,86	103,71	105,56	107,42	109,27	50
60	111,12	112,97	114,82	116,68	118,53	120,38	122,23	124,08	125,94	127,79	60
70	129,64	131,49	133,34	135,20	137,05	138,90	140,75	142,60	144,46	146,31	70
80	148,16	150,01	151,86	153,72	155,57	157,42	159,27	161,12	162,98	164,83	80
90	166,68	168,53	170,38	172,24	174,09	175,94	177,79	179,64	181,50	183,35	90
100	185,20	187,05	188,90	190,76	192,61	194,46	196,31	198,16	200,02	201,87	100

Kilometres — Nautical Miles
1 Kilometre = 0.5400 Nautical Miles
(identical conversion for Kilometres/hour into Knots)

km	0	1	2	3	4	5	6	7	8	9	km
0	0	0,54	1,08	1,62	2,16	2,70	3,24	3,78	4,32	4,86	0
10	5,40	5,94	6,48	7,02	7,56	8,10	8,64	9,18	9,72	10,26	10
20	10,80	11,34	11,88	12,42	12,96	13,50	14,04	14,58	15,12	15,66	20
30	16,20	16,74	17,28	17,82	18,36	18,90	19,44	19,98	20,52	21,06	30
40	21,60	22,14	22,68	23,22	23,76	24,30	24,84	25,38	25,92	26,46	40
50	27,00	27,54	28,08	28,62	29,16	29,70	30,24	30,78	31,32	31,86	50
60	32,40	32,94	33,48	34,02	34,56	35,10	35,64	36,18	36,72	37,26	60
70	37,80	38,34	38,88	39,42	39,96	40,50	41,04	41,58	42,12	42,66	70
80	43,20	43,74	44,28	44,82	45,36	45,90	46,44	46,98	47,52	48,06	80
90	48,60	49,14	49,68	50,22	50,76	51,30	51,84	52,38	52,92	53,46	90
100	54,00	54,54	55,08	55,62	56,16	56,70	57,24	57,78	58,32	58,86	100

This is how it works!
Example 43 nm = ?? km
Go down the first column until you come to 40, then move across to 3.
The result is where the two rows meet (79.64 km)
For values of over 100, the decimal point should be adjusted.
Conversely: 43 km = ?? nm
43 km = 23.22 nm

Table D-9. Kilowatts to Horsepower
Conversion Table

Kilowatts (kW) into Horsepower (HP)
1 kW = 1.3596 HP

kW	0	1	2	3	4	5	6	7	8	9	kW
0	0	1,3596	2,72	4,08	5,44	6,80	8,16	9,52	10,88	12,24	0
10	13,60	14,96	16,32	17,67	19,03	20,39	21,75	23,11	24,47	25,83	10
20	27,19	28,55	29,91	31,27	32,63	33,99	35,35	36,71	38,07	39,43	20
30	40,79	42,15	43,51	44,87	46,23	47,59	48,95	50,31	51,66	53,02	30
40	54,38	55,74	57,10	58,46	59,82	61,18	62,54	63,90	65,26	66,62	40
50	67,98	69,34	70,70	72,06	73,42	74,78	76,14	77,50	78,86	80,22	50
60	81,58	82,94	84,30	85,65	87,01	88,37	89,73	91,09	92,45	93,81	60
70	95,17	96,53	97,89	99,25	100,61	101,97	103,33	104,69	106,05	107,41	70
80	108,77	110,13	111,49	112,85	114,21	115,57	116,93	118,29	119,64	121,00	80
90	122,36	123,72	125,08	126,44	127,80	129,16	130,52	131,88	133,24	134,60	90
100	135,96	137,32	138,68	140,04	141,40	142,76	144,12	145,48	146,84	148,20	100

Horsepower (HP) into Kilowatts
1 HP = 0.7355 kW

HP	0	1	2	3	4	5	6	7	8	9	HP
0	0	0,7355	1,47	2,21	2,94	3,68	4,41	5,15	5,88	6,62	0
10	7,36	8,09	8,83	9,56	10,30	11,03	11,77	12,50	13,24	13,97	10
20	14,71	15,45	16,18	16,92	17,65	18,39	19,12	19,86	20,59	21,33	20
30	22,07	22,80	23,54	24,27	25,01	25,74	26,48	27,21	27,95	28,68	30
40	29,42	30,16	30,89	31,63	32,36	33,10	33,83	34,57	35,30	36,04	40
50	36,78	37,51	38,25	38,98	39,72	40,45	41,19	41,92	42,66	43,39	50
60	44,13	44,87	45,60	46,34	47,07	47,81	48,54	49,28	50,01	50,75	60
70	51,49	52,22	52,96	53,69	54,43	55,16	55,90	56,63	57,37	58,10	70
80	58,84	59,58	60,31	61,05	61,78	62,52	63,25	63,99	64,72	65,46	80
90	66,20	66,93	67,67	68,40	69,14	69,87	70,61	71,34	72,08	72,81	90
100	73,55	74,29	75,02	75,76	76,49	77,23	77,96	78,70	79,43	80,17	100

This table is very simple to use. Read off the tens in the vertical scale and the units in the horizontal scale. The answer is where the two lines meet.

Example (above): convert 63 kW into HP. Go down the first column until you find 60 and the across until you come to 3. The result is where the two rows join.
63 kW = 85.65 HP.
For values of over 100, the decimal point should be adjusted.

Example (below): Convert 65 HP into kW. Go down the first column until you find 60 and then across until you come to 3. The result is where the two rows join.
63 HP = 46.34 kW.
For values of over 100, the decimal point should be adjusted.

Table D-10. Pounds per Square Inch to Kilograms per Square Centimeter Conversion Table

lb. per sq. inch	0 kg per sq. cm	1 kg per sq. cm	2 kg per sq. cm	3 kg per sq. cm	4 kg per sq. cm	5 kg per sq. cm	6 kg per sq. cm	7 kg per sq. cm	8 kg per sq. cm	9 kg per sq. cm
0	..	0.0703	0.1406	0.2109	0.2812	0.3515	0.4218	0.4922	0.5625	0.6328
10	0.7031	0.7734	0.8437	0.9140	0.9843	1.0546	1.1249	1.1952	1.2655	1.3358
20	1.4061	1.4765	1.5468	1.6171	1.6874	1.7577	1.8280	1.8983	1.9686	2.0389
30	2.1092	2.1795	2.2498	2.3201	2.3904	2.4607	2.5311	2.6014	2.6717	2.7420
40	2.8123	2.8826	2.9529	3.0232	3.0935	3.1638	3.2341	3.3044	3.3747	3.4450
50	3.5154	3.5857	3.6560	3.7263	3.7966	3.8669	3.9372	4.0075	4.0778	4.1481
60	4.2184	4.2887	4.3590	4.4293	4.4997	4.5700	4.6403	4.7106	4.7809	4.8512
70	4.9215	4.9918	5.0621	5.1324	5.2027	5.2730	5.3433	5.4136	5.4839	5.5543
80	5.6246	5.6949	5.7652	5.8355	5.9058	5.9761	6.0464	6.1167	6.1870	6.2573
90	6.3276	6.3980	6.4682	6.5386	6.6089	6.6792	6.7495	6.8198	6.8901	6.9604
100	7.0307	7.1010	7.1713	7.2416	7.3120	7.3822	7.4525	7.5228	7.5932	7.6635

kg per sq. cm	0 lb. per sq. in.	1 lb. per sq. in.	2 lb. per sq. in.	3 lb. per sq. in.	4 lb. per sq. in.	5 lb. per sq. in.	6 lb. per sq. in.	7 lb. per sq. in.	8 lb. per sq. in.	9 lb. per sq. in.
0	..	14.22	28.45	42.67	56.89	71.12	85.34	99.56	113.79	128.01
10	142.23	156.46	170.68	184.90	199.13	213.35	227.57	241.80	256.02	270.24
20	284.47	298.69	312.91	327.14	341.36	355.58	369.81	384.03	398.25	412.48
30	426.70	440.92	455.15	469.37	483.59	497.82	512.04	526.26	540.49	554.71
40	568.93	583.16	597.38	611.60	625.83	640.05	654.27	668.50	682.72	696.94
50	711.17	725.39	739.61	753.84	768.06	782.28	796.51	810.73	824.95	839.18
60	853.40	867.62	881.85	896.07	910.29	924.52	938.74	952.96	967.19	981.41
70	995.63	1009.9	1024.1	1038.3	1052.5	1066.8	1081.0	1095.2	1109.4	1123.6
80	1137.9	1152.1	1166.3	1180.5	1194.8	1209.0	1223.2	1237.4	1251.7	1265.9
90	1280.1	1294.3	1308.6	1322.8	1337.0	1351.2	1365.4	1379.7	1393.9	1408.1
100	1422.3	1436.6	1450.8	1465.0	1479.2	1493.4	1507.7	1521.9	1536.1	1550.3

Table D-11. Pound Feet to Kilogram Meters Conversion Table

lb./ft.	0 kg metre	1 kg metre	2 kg metre	3 kg metre	4 kg metre	5 kg metre	6 kg metre	7 kg metre	8 kg metre	9 kg metre
0	..	0.138	0.277	0.415	0.553	0.691	0.830	0.968	1.106	1.244
10	1.383	1.521	1.659	1.797	1.936	2.074	2.212	2.350	2.489	2.627
20	2.765	2.903	3.041	3.180	3.318	3.456	3.595	3.733	3.871	4.009
30	4.148	4.286	4.424	4.562	4.701	4.839	4.977	5.115	5.254	5.392
40	5.530	5.669	5.807	5.945	6.083	6.222	6.360	6.498	6.636	6.775
50	6.913	7.051	7.189	7.328	7.466	7.604	7.742	7.881	8.019	8.157
60	8.295	8.434	8.572	8.710	8.848	8.987	9.125	9.263	9.401	9.540
70	9.678	9.816	9.954	10.093	10.231	10.369	10.507	10.646	10.784	10.922
80	11.060	11.199	11.337	11.475	11.613	11.752	11.890	12.028	12.166	12.305
90	12.443	12.581	12.719	12.858	12.996	13.134	13.272	13.411	13.549	13.687
100	13.826	13.964	14.102	14.240	14.379	14.517	14.655	14.793	14.932	15.070

kg/m	0 lb. ft.	1 lb. ft.	2 lb. ft.	3 lb. ft.	4 lb. ft.	5 lb. ft.	6 lb. ft.	7 lb. ft.	8 lb. ft.	9 lb. ft.
0	..	7.23	14.47	21.70	28.93	36.17	43.40	50.63	57.87	65.10
10	72.33	79.56	86.80	94.03	101.26	108.50	115.73	122.96	130.20	137.43
20	144.66	151.89	159.13	166.36	173.59	180.83	188.06	195.29	202.52	209.76
30	216.99	224.22	231.46	238.69	245.92	253.16	260.39	267.62	274.86	282.09
40	289.32	296.55	303.79	311.02	318.25	325.49	332.72	339.95	347.19	354.42
50	361.65	368.88	376.12	383.35	390.58	397.82	405.05	412.28	419.52	426.75
60	433.98	441.21	448.45	455.68	462.91	470.15	477.38	484.61	491.85	499.08
70	506.31	513.54	520.78	528.01	535.24	542.48	549.71	556.94	564.18	571.41
80	578.64	585.87	593.11	600.34	607.57	614.81	622.04	629.27	636.51	643.74
90	650.97	658.23	665.44	672.67	679.90	687.14	694.37	701.60	708.84	716.07
100	723.30	730.53	737.77	745.00	752.23	759.47	766.70	773.93	781.17	788.40

Table D-12. Coated Abrasive Grit Sizes

Grade	Garnet, Aluminum Oxide, or Silicon Carbide		Emery Cloth	Flint
Very fine	600, 500			
	400	10/0		
	360			
	320	9/0		
	280	8/0		
	240	7/0		
	220	6/0		Extra fine
Fine	180	5/0	3/0	
	150	4/0	2/0	
	120	3/0		Fine
Medium			0	
	100	2/0		
			1/2	
	80	0	1	Medium
			1 1/2	
	60	1/2		
Coarse			2	
	50	1		Coarse
			2 1/2	
	40	1 1/2		
	36	2		
Very coarse			3	Extra coarse
	30	2 1/2		
	24	3		
	20	3 1/2		
	16	4		
	12	4 1/2		

Table D-13. Comparative Sheet Metal Thicknesses

Gauge No.	Uncoated Steel and Stainless Steel*	Aluminum, Brass, and Copper
28	0.015″ (1/64″)	0.012″
26	0.018″	0.016″ (1/64″)
24	0.024″	0.020″
22	0.030″	0.025″
20	0.036″ (1/32″)	0.032″ (1/32″)
18	0.048″ (3/64″)	0.040″
16	0.060″ (1/16″)	0.051″
14	0.075″ (5/64″)	0.064″ (1/16″)
12	0.105″ (7/64″)	0.081″ (5/64″)

*Galvanized steel is slightly thicker than uncoated or stainless steel.

Table D-14. Equivalencies

Square Measure Equivalents

1 square yard = 0.836 square meter
1 square foot = 0.0929 square meter = 929 square centimeters
1 square inch = 6.452 square centimeters = 645.2 square millimeters

1 square meter = 10.764 square feet = 1.196 square yards
1 square centimeter = 0.155 square inch
1 square millimeter = 0.00155 square inch

Cubic Measure Equivalents

1 cubic inch = 16.38706 cubic centimeters
100 cubic inches = 1.64 liters
1 Imperial gallon = 4.546 liters
1 Imperial quart = 1.136 liters
1 US gallon = 3.785 liters
1 US quart = 0.946 liter

1 cubic centimeter = 0.061 cubic inch
1 liter (cubic decimeter) = 0.0353 cubic foot = 61.023 cubic inches
1 liter = 0.2642 US gallon = 1.0567 US quarts = 0.2200 Imperial gallon

Weight Equivalents

1 Imperial ton (UK) = 2240 pounds (long ton)
1 short ton (USA) = 2000 pounds
1 ton (of 2000 pounds) = 0.9072 metric ton
1 ton (of 2240 pounds) = 1.016 metric tons = 1016 kilograms
1 pound = 0.4536 kilogram = 453.6 grams

1 metric ton = 2204.6 pounds
1 kilogram = 2.2046 pounds

Miscellaneous Equivalents

1 Imperial gallon (UK) = 1.2 gallons (US)
1 h.p. = 2,544 Btus
1 kw = 3,413 Btus

Appendix E: Electrical Symbols

The following is a compilation of common electrical symbols.

Lines crossing without connection

Lines crossing with connections

Instrument case, nonconductive or ungrounded

Instrument case, grounded

AC plug connection

AC receptacle

Resistance

Incandescent light bulb

Coil (winding)

Transformer, isolating (with or without the two bars)

Transformer, non-isolating

Circuit breaker

Switch

Fuse

Diode

Capacitor

Variable resistor

Thermistor-varistor

Illustration and Photo Credits

ABI, Table 16–1

ABYC, Tables 3–1, 3–2, 4–1, 4–5

AC Delco, Figures 2–14, 2–15A, 2–18, 2–22

AC Spark Plug Division, GM Corporation, Figure 8–23

Alco Controls, Figure 10–32

Allison Transmission, Figure 9–10

Allcraft Corporation, Figures 8–37, 14–14

Ampair, Figures 5–11, 5–12B, 5–12C, 5–12P

Aquadrive, Figures 9–19, 9–20

ARCO Solar, Figures 5–16, 5–17

Autohelm, Figures 13–24B, 13–24C, 13–26

Battery Council International, Figures 1–2, 1–5B, 1–9, 2–3A, 2–3B, 2–4A, 2–4B, 2–4C; Table 2–1

Blake and Sons, Figures 11–8A, 11–14A, 12–32

Borg Warner, Figures 9–3A, 9–3B

Brookes and Gatehouse, Figure 13–24D

Castlok Marine, Figure 15–29C

Caterpillar Inc., Figures 8–8, 8–18A, 8–24, 8–25, 8–28, 9–18A, 9–18B, 9–18C

Climate Control Company, Figure 10–20

CPT, Figure 13–24A

Deep Sea Seals, Figure 9–24

Delco Remy, Figure 1–10

Detroit Diesel Corporation, Figures 6–17D, 6–18A, 6–18B, 8–4, 8–18C, 8–18D, 9–5

Dole Refrigeration Company, Figure 10–9

Edson International, Figures 13–3F, 13–4B, 13–4E, 13–10A, 13–12A, 13–17C

Force 10, Figure 14–8

Forespar, Figure 11–2B

Four Seasons, Figure 10–5

French, John, from *Electrics and Electronics for Small Craft*, Beekman Publishers, Figures 7–11A, 7–11B (adapted)

Frigoboat, Figures 10–7, 10–11, 10–12A, 10–13A

Furlex, Figure 16–37

Garrett Automotive Products Co., Figure 8–42

Gibb, Figures 15–27, 15–30A, 15–30B

Groco, Figures 11–14B, 12–21, 12–22A

Grunert, Figure 10–12B

Halyard Marine, Figures 9–24, 9–25

Harken, Figures 3–7A, 16–4, 16–6, 16–40A, 16–41

Hart Systems Inc., Figure 8–53

Heart Interface, Figures 1–5A, 5–7, 5–8A, 5–8B, 5–9

Holset Engineering Co. Ltd., Figure 8–43

Hood, Figures 16–38, 16–50

Hurth, Figures 9–6A, 9–6B, 9–6C, 9–7

Hydrovane, Figure 13–21B

ITT/Jabsco, Figures 8–32, 11–4A, 11–9B, 11–10, 12–2, 12–5, 12–9, 12–10, 12–15, 12–18, 12–19, 12–20, 12–22B, 12–24B, 12–25, 12–26; Table 12–1 (adapted)

Kemp Spars, Figures 16–45, 16–46, 16–49

Kenyon Marine, Figures 14–7, 14–9, 14–11A

Kohler Generators, Figures 6–8A, 6–8B, 8–40; Tables 5–1, 5–2

Lewmar, Figures 13–14, 16–9, 16–10A, 16–10B, 16–11, 16–12, 16–13, 16–14, 16–15, 16–26, 16–29; Tables 16–2, 16–3

Loos and Co., Figures 15–24, 15–26, 15–29C

Lucas/CAV Ltd., Figures 2–5, 2–6B, 2–7. 2–8A, 2–8B, 2–13, 8–2, 8–5, 8–6, 8–7, 8–9, 8–11A, 8–11B, 8–12, 8–15A, 8–15B, 8–18B

Lucas Marine, Figures 7–8, 7–10, 7–11C

Lunaire Marine, Figures 10–8, 10–10A, 10–10B

Marine Vane Gears, Ltd., Figures 13–19B, 13–21A

Max Prop, Figures 9–31, 9–32

MDC, Figures 5–5A, 5–5B

Merriman Yacht Specialties, Inc., Figures 13–4C, 13–5B, 13–12, 13–17B, 16–40D

Metal Mast Marine, Figure 16–43B

Miller, Conrad, from *Your Boat's Electrical System 1981–1982*, page 262, Hearst Books: New York, Table 6–2 (adapted), Figure 2–3C

Munster Simms, Figures 12–6, 12–29A, 12–29B, 12–30, 12–31, 12–33A, 12–33B

NMEA Guide to Marine Electronics, Figures 7–3B (adapted), 7–5A, 7–5B, 7–7

Norseman, Figures 15–25, 15–26, 15–27, 15–29B, 15–30A, 15–30B; Table 15–2

Ocean Navigator, Figures 7–2 (adapted), 10–19

Perkins Engines Ltd., Figures 8–14, 8–16, 8–17B, 8–17C, 8–17D, 8–17E, 8–44

Potter, David, from *The Care of Alloy Spars and Rigging*, page 81, Adlard Coles, Ltd., Figure 15–20

ProFurl, photos by D. Regnier, Figures 16–31 16–37, 16–38, 16–40B, 16–40C, 16–42

Racor, Figures 8–10A, 8–10B

Raritan Engineering, Figures 5–5B, 5–5C, 11–5, 11–6D, 11–7B, 11–7C, 11–9A, 11–11A, 11–11B, 11–13, 14–14

Rolls and Rae Engineering, Figures 1–3B, 1–4B, 1–4C, 1–6D

Rutland Windcharger, Figure 5–13

RVG, Figure 13–19A

SAE, Table 3–5

Sailomat, Inc., Figure 13–20

Sanden International, Figures 10–21, 10–24, 10–25A through 10–25M, 10–26A through 10–26R, 10–27

S&F Tool Co., Figure 15–26

Schaefer Marine Products, Figures 16–2, 16–3, 16–30

SeaLand Technology Inc., Figures 11–6A, 11–12A, 11–12B

Shaft Lok, Inc., Figures 9–33, 9–34

Shipmate Stove Division, Figure 14–4

Simpson Lawrence, Figures 9–26, 11–2A, 11–6C, 16–20, 16–22A, 16–22B, 16–24, 16–25, 16–27

Smead, David and Ishihara, Ruth, from *Living on Twelve Volts with Ample Power*, Rides Publishing Company, Figure 5–19

Southwire, Table 3–4

SpaCreek Inc., Figure 2–24

Sta-Lok, Figure 15–29A

Stream Stay, Figures 16–43A, 16–44

Surrette Battery Co., Figures 1–3A, 1–5C
Universal Enterprises, Figures 3–16, 3–17
Vaitses, Alan H., from *What Shape Is She In?*, International Marine Publishing Company, Figure 8–37
VDO Marine, Figures 8–46, 8–47B, 8–49, 8–50, 8–51E, 8–52
Wagner Marine, Figures 13–13B, 13–28
Westerbeke, Figures 2–32, 6–2, 6–3, 6–4A, 6–4B, 6–6, 6–9A, 6–9B, 6–9C, 6–9D, 6–10; Table 6–1
Whitlock Marine, Figures 13–3C, 13–3D, 13–3E, 13–4A, 13–4D, 13–5A, 13–8, 13–9B, 13–10A, 13–10C, 13–12B, 13–15, 13–17A
Wilcox Crittenden, Figure 9–23

Line art by Jim Sollers: Figures 1–1, 2–1, 2–16D, 2–19, 2–36, 3–1, 3–2, 3–3, 3–4, 3–5, 3–19, 3–27B, 3–27C, 3–29, 3–31, 4–1, 4–2A, 4–4, 4–7, 4–9, 4–10, 5–1, 5–12A, 5–13, 5–20, 6–1, 6–2, 6–11, 6–12, 6–15, 7–1, 7–5, 7–8, 7–9, 8–1, 8–20, 8–36, 8–45, 8–54, 9–1, 9–2, 9–8, 9–9, 9–11, 9–13, 9–14, 9–15, 9–17, 9–22, 9–27, 9–28, 9–30, 9–35, 10–1, 10–35, 11–1, 11–3, 11–4, 11–14, 11–15, 12–1, 12–3, 12–4, 12–11, 12–12, 12–13, 12–14, 12–16, 12–17, 12–24, 12–27, 12–28, 13–1, 13–2A, 13–2E, 13–7, 13–9A, 13–13, 13–14, 13–17C, 13–18, 13–19A, 13–23, 13–27, 14–1, 14–2, 14–6, 14–10, 14–11, 14–12, 14–13, 14–14, 15–1, 15–4, 15–5, 15–7, 15–8, 15–12, 15–16, 15–20, 15–21, 15–22, 15–33, 15–36, 15–37, 15–38, 16–1, 16–5, 16–17, 16–18, 16–19, 16–20, 16–21, 16–22, 16–23, 16–24, 16–25, 16–27, 16–36, 16–39, 16–41, 16–43, 16–44, 16–46, 16–47, 16–50.

Jim Sollers gratefully acknowledges the following for their assistance in providing references for his illustrations: Frederick H. Hannasch, Richard Bertram & Co., Yachts (brokers), Miami, FL; Richard D. Holtz, technical literature publisher, Glen Kreider, director of design engineering, Norman Welsh, manager of electrical design engineering, and Jill Shave, manager of marketing services, Bertram Yacht (manufacturer), Miami, FL; Alan Miller marketing manager, C&C Yachts, Niagara-on-the-Lake, Ontario, Canada; David L. Jackson, news service coordinator, Engine Division, Caterpillar Inc., Mossville, IL; Will Keene, vp sales, Edson International, New Bedford, MA; Kevin Porter, Gowan Inc. (Kohler Generator sales), Portland, ME; Louise E. Falt, Kennebec Marine Co. (Dickinson Stove sales), Portland, ME; Mike Bingen, manager of marketing and sales, Engine Group, Medalist Industries (Universal Diesel), Oshkosh, WI; Chuck Ballenger, training, and Jackie Gilbert, customer service, Detroit Diesel (Perkins Diesel), Detroit, MI; Dick McElman, owner, Scandia Yacht Sales (Tartan dealer), Woolwich, ME; Tim Jackett, chief engineer, Tartan Marine, Grand River, OH; Jerry Gibbs, technical representative, and John Oberg and Rachel Biele, advertising, Volvo Penta, Rockleigh, NJ.

Special thanks to the sales staff at Chase Leavitt & Co., Shipchandlers, Portland, ME, for their invaluable help as they patiently explained and demonstrated a wide variety of marine hardware: Michael Arpin, Stephen S. Billings, Louis A. Deering, Matt Ellis, and Salli Hancock.

Additional thanks to Dana DeVos, Bob Cott, and Raissa Marking, who modeled the hands and figures in various drawings.

In addition to these credits, many photos and tables are the author's own; otherwise uncredited illustrations are the work of the TAB Books, Inc. Art Department.

Index